The
PORTABLE
MBA
DESK
REFERENCE

SECOND EDITION

The Portable MBA Series

The

PORTABLE
MBA
DESK
REFERENCE

SECOND EDITION

AN ESSENTIAL BUSINESS
COMPANION

Nitin Nohria, Harvard Business School
Editorial Director

JOHN WILEY & SONS, INC.

New York • Chichester • Weinheim • Brisbane • Singapore • Toronto

Copyright © 1998 by Wordworks, Inc. All rights reserved.

Published by John Wiley & Sons, Inc.
Published simultaneously in Canada.

This publication is designed to provide accurate and authoritative information in regard to the subject matter covered. It is sold with the understanding that the publisher is not engaged in rendering professional services. If professional advice or other expert assistance is required, the services of a competent professional person should be sought.

Library of Congress Cataloging-in-Publication Data:
The portable MBA desk reference : an essential business companion /
    Nitin Nohria, editorial director.—2nd ed.
        p.   cm.—(The Portable MBA series)
    Includes bibliographical references and index.
    ISBN 0-471-24530-5 (cloth : alk. paper)
    1. Industrial management—Handbooks, manuals, etc.   2. Business—
Handbooks, manuals, etc.   3. Business information services—United
States—Handbooks, manuals, etc.   I. Nohria, Nitin, 1962–   .   II. Series.
HD38.15.P67   1998
650—dc21   98-3767
                                                                             CIP

Printed in the United States of America.

10 9 8 7 6 5 4 3 2 1

Acknowledgments

Special thanks to the following experts who graciously lent their time and knowledge in helping to prepare this second edition of *The Portable MBA Desk Reference:* Allan R. Cohen, Academic Vice President, Babson College, editor of *The Portable MBA in Management* and coauthor of *Managing for Excellence* and *Influence Without Authority;* Leonard Fuld, President and founder, Fuld & Company, author of *The New Competitor Intelligence;* John S. Gordon, Founder and Principal Management Consultant, Smart Decisions, Inc., author of six books including *Profitable Exporting* and *U.S.-EC Trade Resources;* Herman Holtz, author of *How to Succeed as an Independent Consultant;* John Leslie Livingstone, independent consultant, Adjunct Professor of Accounting at Babson College, former partner, Coopers & Lybrand, and editor of *The Portable MBA in Finance and Accounting;* John J. McAuley, Vice President–Economist, Wilkinson Boyd Capital Markets, Inc.; Richard G. Newman, D.B.A., Professor of Management Sciences (ret.), coauthor of *The Capital Equipment Buying Handbook* (forthcoming) and *Supplier Price Analysis;* and Charles Schewe, Professor of Marketing, University of Massachusetts, Amherst, and coauthor of *The Portable MBA in Marketing.*

Thanks are due, also, to the following esteemed experts, both from academe and professional practice, who contributed to the first edition of *The Portable MBA Desk Reference:* Edward I. Altman, Tony Antin, Alvin Arnold, William Bygrave, Joan Canning, Karmen N. T. Crowther, David J. Curry, Jeff Davidson, Don Debelak, Christopher Engholm, Liam Fahey, Michael Fetters, Richard Freierman, Robert Gaston, David Gumpert, Alexander Hiam, Craig Hickman, Richard Mandel, John J. McAuley, Stephen T. McClellan, Darien McWhirter, Patrick D. O'Hara, Charles A. Peck, Lee Tom Perry, Eric Press, Robert L. Purvin, Jr., Judith Walthrop, Lawrence Tuller, and Philip K. Y. Young.

Lastly, this book would not have been possible without Helen Rees and Donna Carpenter at Wordworks and their dedicated editorial staff; and, at Wiley, Henning Gutmann; Jennifer Amadril—for yeoman work in tracking down key facts and coordinating the many facets of a complex project; and Linda Witzling, for production expertise, flexibility, and patience.

Nitin Nohria
Boston, Massachusetts
June 1998

Contents

❧ *Appendixes*   *577*

Introduction: How to Use *The Portable MBA Desk Reference, Second Edition*

It's not enough to be an accountant and just know accounting. Or to be a marketer and just know marketing. Or, for that matter, to be a manager and just know management. In today's business environment, as companies downsize, reorganize, grow, and cope with rapidly changing technology and information sources, executives, managers, entrepreneurs, and even students are expected to become de facto experts in all areas of business. Production managers have to know about marketing, financial planners have to know about corporate strategy, and accountants have to know about both monetary and human costs. The key to this knowledge is information. That information is here, in the second edition of *The Portable MBA Desk Reference.*

For information to have value, it has to be accessible. If you can't find something immediately, the information might just as well not exist. Ease and speed of access are the two characteristics that make *The Portable MBA Desk Reference the* standard business reference for practitioners and students of business. *The Portable MBA Desk Reference* is unique, both in the nature of the information that it contains and in the way its contents are organized to provide users with easy access to the data they seek.

Part One: A-to-Z Reference of Essential Business Topics

The first section of the *Desk Reference,* "A-to-Z Reference of Essential Business Topics," is an alphabetical listing of hundreds of phrases, rules, principles, theories, laws, trends, formulas, and strategies related to the practice of business. These listings are drawn from eight major business disciplines: accounting, economics, finance, international business, management, manufacturing, marketing, and strategy. Entries include a wide-ranging collection of topics such as "double declining balance depreciation," "cost of capital," "total quality management," "just-in-time," and "conjoint analysis." The "A-to-Z Reference" goes beyond the simple definitions that might be found in a more conventional business reference. Each entry begins with a concise definition, then goes on to include a description, discussion, or practical example of the topic at hand.

There is a strong emphasis on the business impact of the topics included in the "A-to-Z Reference" section. It is not enough to simply understand the definition of concepts such as "last in, first out (LIFO)" or "return on investment (ROI)." You need to know how they affect a business, the decisions made by its managers and employees, and its bottom line. The "A-to-Z Reference," with its clear examples and comprehensive discussions, explains all aspects of these important subjects.

To give you an idea of the range of material covered in Part One, here are a few additional examples:

- News reports frequently refer to "leading economic indicators." The entry for *leading, coincident, and lagging indexes* explains what these indicators are, describes the government agencies that issue them, and explains the components of each.

- You've heard of S corporations and their potential tax advantages. The *S corporation* entry explains precisely what an S corporation is and how a small business can qualify for S status.

- Business is rife with not only buzzwords but buzz phrases. What exactly are *benchmarking, activity-based costing,* and *debt/equity swaps?* Part One provides a convenient way to find out.

- There are innumerable tools of financial analysis to help manage a business more efficiently. In Part One, the most important ones are explained with detailed, worked-out examples.

For additional explanation and elaboration, each entry in Part One, where appropriate, includes cross-references to other topics covered within this section.

Part Two: Sources of Business Information

Sometimes, it's easy enough to know the basics about a topic, such as "business plans," "market research," or "new-product development." But sometimes you need much more information—for example, when you have to actually write a business plan, conduct market research, or develop a new product. When you do, you'll want to consult "Sources of Business Information," the second section of the *Desk Reference.*

The "Sources of Business Information" section is designed to give you the quickest and easiest route to the information you need. Increasingly, such information can be found on the World Wide Web, and the second edition of the *Desk Reference* has been updated to provide Internet addresses wherever applicable. It lists and describes (alphabetically by title) hundreds of books, databases, online services, periodicals, professional groups, government agencies, and research groups that offer current, detailed, and practical information on almost any business issue. Individual listings are organized under 48 broad headings, each focusing on a specific business topic such as economic data, accounting, the job market, and so on. Each listing offers a brief description of the source, name of author(s), publisher's name, and date/frequency of publication, as well as information via electronic access.

The uses to which you can put the "Sources of Business Information" section are many and varied:

- If you have to do a strategic marketing plan that analyzes the demographics for a new product line, look through the "Demographics, Marketing Data, and Market Research" section for a description of the sources that will provide you with the information you need.

- That same strategic plan also needs your assessment of how the long- and short-term economic picture affects your product line. Go to the "Economic Data, Trends, and Projections" section to find the best sources for that information.

- Perhaps you want to begin exporting your product line internationally. The "Exporting and Importing" section shows where to get information on how to do this and also provides a breakdown of some of the many resources offered by the U.S. Department of Commerce.

- Finally, say you want to sell your product by direct mail. The "Direct Marketing" section shows where to get the right prospect lists to make your campaign work.

A "Directory of Publishers, Vendors, and Databases" at the end of Part Two provides addresses and phone and fax numbers to enable users of the *Desk Reference* to locate and request information from the various sources easily.

Appendixes

The Appendixes present a compendium of useful business facts, figures, and lists. Some can help you pinpoint opportunities such as the list of *Inc.* magazine's 500 fastest-growing private companies. And some will help you in your quest for more information. Say you want to export your new product line of personal computers to Poland. The Appendixes include two lists to help you out. "Industry Specialists of the International Trade Administration of the Department of Commerce" tells you who can provide you with specific information about exporting your product and how to reach them. "Country Desk Specialists" (also from the International Trade Administration) will provide you with information on just about every country of the world, from Afghanistan to Zimbabwe.

In short, you can consult *The Portable MBA Desk Reference* on nearly any subject and feel confident that either the information you need will be there, or the *Desk Reference* will tell you exactly where to go get it. We believe it will become one of your most frequently used business tools.

Part I
An A-to-Z Reference of Essential Business Topics

Part II
Sources of Business Information

Appendixes

An A-to-Z Reference of Essential Business Topics

How to Use
the A-to-Z Reference

The A-to-Z Reference of Essential Business Topics provides a concise, comprehensive, and convenient source of business information. Entries are included on the basis of their practical application to business. Any phrase, rule, principle, theory, formula, law, or strategy likely to affect or influence a businessperson's professional life or be useful to him or her is listed and explained here.

The A-to-Z Reference covers eight major business disciplines: accounting, economics, finance, international business, management, manufacturing, marketing, and strategy. Entries are arranged alphabetically, and cross-referenced terms are printed in **boldface italics.** Cross references include the standard *see* and *see also* as well as *compare to,* an innovative feature that allows consideration of similar topics in order to see how they might differ from, relate to, or interact with one another.

Entries in the A-to-Z Reference section were chosen with an eye toward considering their strategic impact on a business and its operations. In addition to providing a straightforward definition, many entries go on to discuss practical examples and possible uses for the topics covered. A number of entries were also chosen based on their value as reminders of useful ratios and formulas, such as *current ratio, return on assets,* and *inventory turnover.*

Together, the entries in the A-to-Z Reference section combine to form a complete, accurate, and practical resource that can be used in any business situation.

The entries in Part I are arranged alphabetically; following is a list of the entries arranged by business topic.

Entries Arranged by Business Topic

Accounting and Finance

absorption costing
accelerated cost recovery system (ACRS)
accelerated depreciation
accounting change
accounting equation
accounting period
accounting rate of return (ARR)
accounts payable
accounts receivable
accounts receivable turnover
accrual accounting
accrued expense
accumulated benefit obligation (ABO)
acid test ratio
acquisition
activity-based costing (ABC)
activity-based management (ABM)
additional paid-in capital
adverse opinion
affiliated company

allowance for bad debts
alpha
American Depository Receipts (ADRs)
American Institute of Certified Public
    Accountants (AICPA)
American Stock Exchange (AMEX)
amortization
annual percentage rate (APR)
annual report
annuity
antitrust legislation
arbitrage
arbitrage pricing theory (APT)
arithmetic return
arm's-length transaction
asset
asset turnover
asset value business valuation method
audit
audit opinion
Auditing Standards Board (ASB)
average cost method
backorder
balance sheet
balloon
Bank for International Settlements (BIS)
banker's acceptance (BA)
bankruptcy
barrier to entry
barrier to exit
Barron's Confidence Index
basis points
bear hug
bearer bond
bellwether
benchmarking
best effort
best execution
beta
Big Six
blank check offerings
blind pool offerings
blue chip
bond
bond buyback
bond valuation
bond yield

book value
book value per share
bookkeeping
borrowing base
Bourse
breakeven analysis
business combination
buyback
call
call feature
capital
capital asset
capital asset pricing model (CAPM)
capital flight
capital gains
capital lease
capital market theory
capital markets
capital stock
capital structure
capitalization
carrying costs
cash basis accounting
cash dividend
cash equivalent
cash flow
cash flow statement
cash-to-current-liabilities ratio
central bank
certified public accountant (CPA)
change in accounting estimate
change in accounting principle
Chapter 7
Chapter 9
Chapter 11
chart of accounts
Chicago School
COMEX
comfort letter
commercial paper
commission
commodity
common stock
common stock equivalent
common stock valuation
complex capital structure
compound interest

financial futures
financial highlights
financial public relations
financial statement
finished goods inventory
first-in, first-out (FIFO)
fiscal policy
fiscal year
fixed asset
fixed costs
float
forced conversion
forecast error
forecasting
foreign currency translation
foreign direct investment (FDI)
foreign exchange
Foreign Sales Corporation
forward contract
forward integration
forward scheduling
full-cost method
functional currency
funded pension plan
funds provided from operations
future value
future value of an annuity
general and administrative expenses
generally accepted accounting principles
   (GAAP)
going private
going public
goodwill
gross profit
hard currency
holding period return
income from continuing operations
income statement
incremental cost
indexing
indirect cost
indirect method
inflation
inflation accounting
initial public offering (IPO)
intangible asset
interest expense

interest rate
internal rate of return
inventory
inventory turnover
investment
journal entry
junk bonds
Keogh plan
last-in, first-out (LIFO)
latent market
leasehold improvement
leverage
leveraged buyout (LBO)
leveraging
liability
LIFO liquidation
LIFO reserve
limited partnership
liquidity
list broker
load
load profile
loading
London Interbank Offered Rate
   (LIBOR)
long bond
long-term asset
long-term liability
lower of cost or market
marginal cost
marginal revenue
marginal revenue = marginal cost rule
market
market aggregation
market capitalization rate
market life cycle
market risk
market risk premium
market saturation
market segmentation
market share
market value
markup
matching concept
materiality
maturity date
medium-term notes

shelf registration
short-term debt
simple capital structure
simple interest
sinking fund
spin-off
spot
spreadsheet
statement of cash flows
statement of shareholders' equity
Statements of Financial Accounting Concepts (SFAC)
Statements of Financial Accounting Standards (SFAS)
stock dividend
stock index
stock split
stockholders' equity
straight-line depreciation
subordinated debt
subsidiary company
successful efforts method
sum-of-the-year's-digits (SYD) method
sunk costs
10-K
10-Q
tangible asset
tax haven
tender offer
trade credit (domestic)
trade credit (international)
trade deficit
trade finance
transaction
transaction, monetary
transfer price
treasury stock
turnover ratio
underwriting
unearned revenue
unfunded
units of production method
unqualified opinion
useful life
Value Line Investment Survey
value-added tax (VAT)
variable, dependent

variable, independent
variable cost
variable costing
variable rate bonds
venture capital
warrants
working capital
work-in-process inventory
write-down
write-off
yield to maturity
zero-coupon security

Economics

balance of trade
Bretton Woods Agreement
budget deficit and debt
business cycle
capital stock
cartel
caveat emptor
caveat venditor
central bank
certainty equivalents
Clayton Act of 1914
Consumer Credit Protection Act
Consumer Goods Pricing Act of 1972
Consumer Product Safety Act of 1972
control limit
cost-benefit analysis
demand
discount rate
exchange rates
externality
Federal Reserve
fiscal policy
foreign exchange
forward contract
gross domestic product (GDP)
hard currency
housing starts and residential construction
industrial goods
industrial policy
Inter-American Development Bank
interest rates
International Monetary Fund (IMF)

investment
kaizen
Keynesian economics
labor force
leading, coincident, and lagging indexes
(LCLg)
marginal cost
monetarism
monetary aggregates
monetary policy
money center banks
opportunity cost
outputs
perfect competition
personal consumption expenditures
predatory pricing
price controls
prime rate
production function
productivity
saving
shortage
shutdown situation
soft currency
spending multiplier
supply
surplus
trade deficit
unemployment rate
value-added tax (VAT)

International Business

balance of payments
balance of trade
Bank for International Settlements (BIS)
Berne Convention (for the Protection of
Literary and Artistic Works) of 1886
capital flight
cartel
central bank
countertrade
debt/equity swap
development banks
dumping
Edge Act
eurobond
eurocurrency

eurodollar
European Community (EC)
European Union (EU)
exchange rates
Eximbank's City-State Agency Coopera-
tion Program
Export/Import Bank (Eximbank)
Foreign Credit Insurance Association
(FCIA)
foreign currency translation
foreign direct investment (FDI)
foreign exchange
Foreign Sales Corporation (FSC)
forward contract
General Agreement on Tariffs and Trade
(GATT)
global marketing
industrial policy
industrial production
International Monetary Fund (IMF)
International Monetary Market (IMM)
keiretsu
letter of credit (L/C)
London Interbank Offered Rate
(LIBOR)
North American Free Trade Agreement
(NAFTA)
offshore financial center
Organization for Economic Cooperation
and Development (OECD)
Organization of Petroleum Exporting
Countries (OPEC)
parallel trade
regional banks
Section 936
tax haven
trade credit (international)
trade deficit
trade finance
venture capital

Management

affirmative action (AA)
American Management Association
(AMA)
Americans with Disabilities Act
annual report

attribution theory
baby boomers
benchmarking
bona fide occupational qualifications
   (BFOQs)
business process reengineering
Chapter 7
Chapter 11
chief (or corporate) executive officer
   (CEO)
chief financial officer (CFO)
chief operating officer (COO)
Child Protection Act of 1966
compressed work week
comptroller
concurrent engineering
conjoint analysis
conservatism
controller
coproduction
copyright
corporate communication
corporate culture
corporation
cost center
cost leadership
cost-benefit analysis
cost-plus pricing
cybernetics
cyberspace
decentralization
decision making
decision support system
decision tree
defined benefit pension plan
defined contribution pension plan
Delphi analysis
disclaimer
disclosure
diversification
downsizing
economies of scale
economies of scope
electronic data interchange (EDI)
e-mail
employee discharge
employee stock ownership plan (ESOP)

empowerment
ERG theory
expectancy theory
experience curve
expert system
externality
401(k)
flowchart
franchise
functional organizational design
group
group cohesion
group norms
idle time
incentive plans
incremental cost
indirect cost
informal organizational structure
innovation
intellectual property
job description
job enrichment
job process system
joint venture (JV)
Keogh plan
leadership
learning curve
leveraged buyout (LBO)
limited partnership
management by objective (MBO)
management control systems
management information system (MIS)
Maslow's hierarchy of needs
matrix structure
merger
mission statement
Myers-Briggs Type Indicator (MBTI)
new-product development
organizational environment
outsourcing
pay for performance
pension fund
pension plan
power
privately held company
profit center
publicly held company

quality circle
quality of work life (QWL)
regression analysis
research validity, external
research validity, internal
response time
reward systems
S corporation (subchapter S corporation)
scientific management
self-managed work teams
sexual harassment
span of control
spin-off
stock split
stockout
synergy
team building
technology transfer
total quality management (TQM)
transformation process

Manufacturing

ABC classification system
acceptable quality level (AQL)
acceptance sampling
age discrimination
aggregate plan
artificial intelligence (AI)
automated storage and retrieval system
    (AS/RS)
automatic guided vehicle system (AGVS)
autonomation
backlog
backward scheduling
balance delay
bandwidth
bar code
baud
beginning inventory
benchmarking
bill of lading
bill of material (BOM)
blanket purchase order
bottleneck
break-even analysis
buffer stock
business process reengineering

capacity
cellular production
chase demand
computer numerical control
computer-aided design (CAD)
computer-aided engineering (CAE)
computer-aided manufacturing (CAM)
computer-integrated manufacturing
    (CIM)
concurrent engineering
conglomerate
continuous improvement
control chart
critical path method (CPM)
critical ratio analysis
cycle
cycle counting
cyclical inventory
decoupling inventory
design capacity
design for manufacturability
direct numerical control (DNC)
dispatching
economic order quantity (EOQ)
economies of scale
effective capacity
efficiency
engineering change order (ECO)
expediting
Fair Package and Labeling Act of 1966
finite loading
fixed interval reorder system
flexible manufacturing system (FMS)
flighting
flow process
flow shop
forward scheduling
Gantt chart
group technology
infinite loading
inputs
intermittent production
inventory forms
inventory functions
inventory turnover
job process system
Johnson's rule for dual workstations

just-in-time (JIT)
kanban
layout
lead time
learning curve
level production
line balancing
loading
longitudinal panel
lot tolerance percentage defective
   (LTPD)
make-to-order (custom-made)
make-to-stock
manufacturing margin
manufacturing resource planning
   (MRPII)
marginal cost
master production schedule (MPS)
materials requirements planning (MRP)
mechanization
methods-time measurement (MTM)
modularity
multiple sourcing
newsboy problem
numerical control (NC)
operations
paced line
Pareto chart
Pareto efficiency
participative design
periodic inventory review system
planning horizon
plant within a plant (PWP)
process control
production plan
Program Evaluation and Review Technique (PERT)
prototype
purchasing
quality circle
queue time
rate card
remanufacturing
response time
rough-cut capacity planning
runout method
safety stock

sampling
segmentation
sequencing
setup costs
shop floor control
single-sourcing
Six Sigma
slack
spoilage
standard cost
throughput time
time study
two-bin system
type I error
type II error

Marketing

ad response
advertising
advertising agency
advertising allowance
Advertising Council Inc. (ACI)
advertising frequency
afternoon drive time
alternate weeks (A/W)
American Academy of Advertising (AAA)
American Advertising Federation (AAF)
American Association of Advertising
   Agencies (AAAA)
American Marketing Association (AMA)
area of dominant influence (ADI)
attractiveness test
automatic merchandising
available market
bandwagon effect
behavioral response
behavioral segmentation
bleed ad
body copy
brand
brand awareness
brand equity
brand extension
brand management
brand mark
brand name
brand-switching matrix

point-of-purchase (POP) advertising
potential market
preference segmentation
press release
pretesting
price elasticity of demand
primary data
private label
product attributes
product concept
product life cycle
product maturity
product mix
product positioning
psychographic segmentation
public relations (PR)
public-service advertisement (PSA)
pull strategy
purchasing, high and low involvement
push strategy
quantity discount
reach
rebate
reference group
regression analysis
relationship marketing
repeat rate
research validity, external
research validity, internal
reseller market
response rate
response time
retailer
rollout market entry
sales promotions
sales representative
sales response function
sampling frame
secondary data
served market
share of voice
skimming
societal marketing
stockout
storyboard
straight rebuy
target market

target return pricing
telemarketing
television rating
television share
test market
trademark
transit advertising
undifferentiated marketing
utilization
variable pricing
vertical marketing system (VMS)
volume segmentation
wholesaler
word-of-mouth advertising

Strategy

backward integration
barrier to entry
barrier to exit
better-off test
business strategy
cash cow
competitive advantage
competitor analysis
coproduction
core competence
corporate strategy
cost-of-entry test
cost-plus pricing
decentralization
Delphi analysis
diversification
externality
first mover
five forces model
focus strategy
forward integration
fragmented industry
generic competitive strategies
growth/market share matrix
harvesting
horizontal integration
industry attractiveness test
joint venture (JV)
management's discussion and analysis of
    operations (MD&A)
mission statement

organizational environment
partnership
Profit Impact of Market Strategies
    (PIMS)
seven-S framework
strategic business unit (SBU)
strategic planning

supplier credit
supplier power
SWOT analysis
synergy
technology transfer
value chain
vertical integration

AAA (1) The highest rating for a **bond** as determined by the Standard and Poor's Corporation.

See also **bond.**

AAA (2) *See* **American Academy of Advertising**

Aaa The highest **bond** rating issued by Moody's Investors Service.
See also **bond.**

AAAA *See* **American Association of Advertising Agencies**

AAF *See* **American Advertising Federation**

ABC *See* **activity-based costing**

ABC analysis *See* **ABC classification system**

ABC classification system A management technique, prevalent in **inventory** control, in which analysts separate items into three groups based on cost, volume, and added value.

Also called *ABC analysis* or *distribution by value,* this technique takes into account the observation that most companies have in their inventories high-, medium-, and low-value items. Although the percentages are estimates and will vary from company to company, the ABC classification system breaks down the inventory as follows:

A, *high-value items:* The 10 to 15 percent of the items that constitute 50 to 70 percent of the total value of the inventory.

B, *medium-value items:* The 20 to 25 percent of the items that make up 15 to 20 percent of the total value of the inventory.

C, *low-value items:* The 60 to 70 percent of the items that account for only 10 to 35 percent of the total value of the inventory.

Typically, inventory managers first identify the A items and keep close tabs on them since they constitute the lion's share of the total value. Next, they identify the C items, those that occupy the lowest percentage of total value. Whatever is left over falls into the B category. Performing a **cost-benefit analysis** on the inventory, managers discover that they can spend more money and time monitoring the A items—say, once a week—whereas C items might require inventorying only once a quarter.

Although companies always need to keep some items on hand and thus can still profit from the ABC classification system, those that subscribe to *just-in-time* (*JIT*) inventory find that they have less money tied up in reserve stocks.

ABO   *See accumulated benefit obligation*

absorption costing   An accounting method that does not distinguish between *direct costs* and *variable costs* in calculating the cost of manufactured goods.

Under the method of variable costing, which managers use primarily for internal purposes such as monitoring production and setting prices, the cost of manufacturing goods does not include fixed factory costs. The company has to heat the factory, for instance, whether it produces one item or ten thousand; accordingly, this cost is listed as an expense.

In contrast, absorption costing is required under *generally accepted accounting principles* (*GAAP*), whenever an accounting is made for external purposes such as *annual reports* to shareholders. Rather than treating fixed factory costs as expenses, absorption costing considers these as part of the cost of manufacturing the goods. Likewise, nonmanufacturing costs such as selling and general administrative expenses are absorbed into the selling price of the products or services.

The income from these operations can vary markedly, depending on which accounting system is used and whether all the goods are sold. If a company sells every unit it manufactures, the income as computed by absorption costing will be the same as that computed by variable costing. If, however, the number of units produced exceeds the number actually sold, income figured by absorption costing will be greater than that figured by variable costing. Conversely, if the number of units sold is less than the number produced, the income reported by absorption costing will be less than that reported by variable costing.

EXAMPLE: XYZ Corporation makes 80 units and seeks to sell them for $100 each. It costs $40 to make each unit, and the company incurs $20 per unit in fixed factory costs. The following table presents a comparison of the two accounting systems, absorption and variable costing:

	Variable costing unit cost = $40: $40 variable		Absorption costing unit cost = $60: $40 variable + $20 fixed	
Sales (80 units @ $100)		$8,000		$8,000
Cost of good sold:				
Beginning inventory	$ 0		$ 0	
Cost of producing goods (100 units)	4,000		6,000	
Available for sale	4,000		6,000	
Ending inventory (unsold goods = 20 units)	800		1,200	
Cost of goods sold	3,200		4,800	
Gross margin		4,800		3,200

	Variable costing unit cost = $40: $40 variable		Absorption costing unit cost = $60: $40 variable + $20 fixed
Less: Production overhead			
(100 units @ $200 fixed costs)	2,000		0
Selling and administrative costs	2,800		2,800
Total costs		4,800	2,800
Income before taxes		$ 0	$ 400

The primary difference between the two accounting systems is evident in the highlighted portion of the table showing the cost of producing 100 units. Absorption costing includes the *fixed costs* of $20 per unit, or $2,000, whereas variable costing refers to this amount as production *overhead.*

Managers should take care to distinguish the two accounting methods and to use variable costing when they want to monitor a product's cost and pricing (Fess and Warren 1993, 921–924).

accelerated cost recovery system (ACRS)   For federal income tax purposes, an accounting method that allows companies or individuals to take higher *depreciation* rates for certain *assets* in the initial years of the assets' life.

Prior to 1980, taxpayers had to use the straight-line method to calculate depreciation. If, at the beginning of its *fiscal year,* a company purchased a $21,000 truck, it could depreciate the vehicle over five years and recover $4,000 per year (assuming that, at the end of the period, the company could sell the truck for $1,000). This depreciation method, however, discouraged many from investing in new products because they had to wait so long to recover their expenses.

To encourage companies to invest in new assets and thus to improve production, the U.S. Congress enacted the Economic Recovery and Tax Act of 1981, which covered items purchased for business purposes after 1980. That legislation contained the so-called 3-5-10 rule, which allowed a company (or individual) to deduct a higher percentage of an asset's cost in the early years of its *useful life,* defined as 3, 5, or 10 years. In 1986, Congress emended this legislation under the *modified Accelerated Cost Recovery System* (*MACRS*), expanding to eight the number of classes of an item's useful life: 3, 5, 7, 10, 15, 20, 27.5, and 31.5 years. Property such as automobiles and light-duty trucks falls into the 5-year category, whereas most other business equipment is classified as 7-year property. The two highest classes, reserved for real estate, use the *straight-line depreciation* method.

EXAMPLE: A company buys a new piece of equipment that falls under the three-year property class and costs $6,000. If it uses the straight-line (half-year) convention, the company can deduct only $1,000 in the first and fourth years of the asset's life ($6,000/3 = $2,000; $2,000/2 = $1,000). The following table shows the deductions permissible under the straight-line or half-year convention and under the standard ACRS method:

Year	Straight-line (half-year) depreciation	Cost	×	ACRS percentage	=	ACRS deduction
1	$1,000	$6,000	×	33.3%	=	$1,998
2	2,000	6,000	×	44.5%	=	2,670
3	2,000	6,000	×	14.8%	=	888
4	1,000	6,000	×	7.4%	=	444
	$6,000			100.0%		$6,000

*See also **accelerated depreciation; double declining balance depreciation; modified accelerated cost recovery system (MACRS).***

accelerated depreciation An accounting method that recognizes higher amounts of *depreciation* in the early years of a *fixed asset*'s useful life and lower amounts in the later years.

Some office equipment—a computer, say—is more efficient and productive in the years immediately following its purchase. As it gets older, it requires more maintenance and becomes increasingly inefficient or obsolete. Because the benefits many assets provide decline over time, proponents of accelerated depreciation reason that the greatest portion of the deductions should come in the early years of the asset's *useful life.* In the case of personal computers, that useful life may be no more than 18 months or two years. The Internal Revenue Service (IRS), however, assigns a useful life of five years to computers. Enterprises can receive a tax benefit by writing off larger depreciation charges in the first years, but for their financial reporting they can choose the depreciation method that best suits them.

*See also **amortization; double-declining balance depreciation; sum-of-the-years'-digits (SYD) method.***

acceptable quality level (AQL) A measure of quality control by which a company's managers specify that they will accept a certain percentage of defective goods or materials rather than rejecting the entire lot.

If managers allow an AQL of 0.5 percent, they will accept a shipment of 1,000 items so long as no more than 5 are defective. Because incoming shipments can be very large, it is too expensive and time-consuming to examine every item. An established AQL guides inspectors in examining a random sample of the shipment and accepting or rejecting the whole on the basis of the outcome; however, the validity of their decision rests primarily on the sufficiency and representativeness of the sample they choose.

*See also **type I** and **type II errors.***

acceptance sampling A technique whereby a small sample of an incoming lot is taken. If a predetermined number of defects, known as *c,* the acceptance number, or fewer are found defective, the entire lot is accepted. The concept is that defects are randomly scattered in the lot. Acceptance sampling depends on four parameters: the α risk, the probability of rejecting a good lot; the β risk, the probability of accepting a bad lot; the AQL, the long-run average *acceptable quality level* (*AQL*) or the average percentage the buyer is willing to accept as defective and still accept the lot; and the LTPD, the lot tolerance percent defective, which is the maximum percentage defective a buyer is willing to accept in a single lot. By using a cumulative binomial probability table (Thorndyke chart), the buyer is able to determine both sample size and acceptance number. Thus, after proper use of the probability distribution, if the values for the four variables show a sample size $n = 100$ and $c = 3$, the incoming inspection will randomly sample 100 units. If 3 or more are found defective, the entire lot is deemed defective and returned to the supplier for 100 percent inspection or any other form of corrective action.

accounting change   A modification in any of three areas: (1) an accounting principle, such as an organization's *fiscal year* or *accrued expenses;* (2) an accounting estimate, such as an asset's *useful life;* or (3) a reporting entity, such as a shift from a sole proprietorship to a *partnership* or *corporation.*

   Accounting changes require appropriate notification to stakeholders and agencies such as the *Financial Accounting Standards Board* (*FASB*), the Internal Revenue Service (IRS), and the *Securities and Exchange Commission* (*SEC*).

accounting equation   The formula that expresses the dual nature of accounting:

$$\text{Assets} = \text{liabilities} + \text{owner's equity}$$

   The accounting equation observes that every business *transaction* has two effects on an organization's or an individual's accounts: When a company makes a sale of $100, for example, it receives $100 in cash and gives up $100 worth of its products or services.

EXAMPLE: Jones and Roberts are starting a new business and open a bank account with $50,000 of their own money. Their business now has an *asset,* $50,000 in cash, which is called the *first aspect.* As owners, Jones and Roberts have a claim (the *second aspect*) against this amount. In other words,

$$\text{Assets (cash)} = \text{owners' equity}$$
$$\$50,000 = \$50,000$$

   If the new company now borrows $25,000 from the bank, its accounting records will change in two respects: (1) Cash will increase to $75,000, and (2) the company will incur a *liability* of $25,000. Expressed as a T-account, the *balance sheet* looks like this:

Assets		Liabilities + owners' equity	
Cash	$75,000	Loan	$25,000
		Owners' equity	50,000
Total assets	75,000	Total liabilities and owner's equity	75,000

   See also **bookkeeping.**

accounting period   The time covered by an individual's or an organization's *financial statements.*

   Accounting periods typically run for 12 consecutive months, the *fiscal year,* divided into four quarters. The fiscal year can correspond to the calendar year (January 1 to December 31), or it can be any period of 12 consecutive months that a company desires. The most frequently used is July 1 to June 30, although agricultural businesses often select a period of consecutive months more convenient to their concerns. The Campbell Soup Company, for example, begins its accounting period in August.

Selecting an accounting period represents an important managerial decision, particularly in seasonal industries. A toy retailer, whose sales occur primarily in late December, should not set December 31 as the end of the accounting period: The huge returns that come in January will distort the picture of the retailer's *revenue.* As Toys "Я" Us has done, choosing January 31 as its fiscal year-end date is obviously a more sagacious option.

accounting rate of return (ARR)   In corporate finance, a measure of an *investment*'s potential profitability as calculated by the following equation:

$$ARR = \frac{\text{expected net income}}{\text{average investment}}$$

Managers apply this measure of profitability to *assets* large and small, an entire plant or a machine to go in it. Also called *simple* or *average* rate of return, the ARR requires managers to estimate the *useful life* of the asset and to use one of several *depreciation* methods in order to calculate the average investment represented by the asset.

As an illustration, assume that a publishing company wishes to purchase a printing press for $500,000 and estimates that its useful life will be nine years, after which the press can be sold for $5,000. The purchasing manager also estimates that the new press will generate income of $360,000 during this period, or $40,000 per year. Using a *straight-line depreciation,* the manager calculates that the press will decline in value $5,000 each year during this period:

$$\frac{\text{Cost} - \text{salvage value}}{\text{Asset's useful life}} = \frac{\$500,000 - \$5,000}{9}$$

Average investment = $50,000

Accordingly, the accounting rate of return is:

$$ARR = \frac{\$40,000 - 5,000}{\$50,000} = 0.7 \text{ or } 70\%$$

In this example, the press has a particularly high rate of return and thus represents an excellent purchase, assuming the projections of income hold true. If managers have a choice between two (or more) presses, they can use the accounting rate of return to evaluate the potential profitability of each machine, choosing the one that gives the higher ARR (Brigham and Gapenski 1994, 391–392; Fess and Warren 1993, 1057).

accounts payable   The amount a company or individual owes for products and services purchased on *credit.*

On the *balance sheet,* accounts payable are *current liabilities.*

accounts receivable   The amount owed to a company or an individual for products and services purchased on *credit.*

On the *balance sheet,* accounts receivable represent *current assets.*

accounts receivable turnover   The ratio of sales to the average *accounts receivable* for a given period:

$$\text{Accounts receivable turnover} = \frac{\text{sales}}{\text{average accounts receivable}}$$

This turnover rate provides a measure of the company's success in collecting what it is owed. The lower the turnover rate, the longer that company holds its receivables. And as a general rule, the longer an account receivable is held, the less likely it is to be collected.

To calculate the turnover rate, specify the time period and divide sales by the average accounts receivable during that period.

EXAMPLE: A company racks up sales of $200,000 during its *fiscal year*. At the beginning of that period, its accounts receivable add up to $50,000; at year's end, there is $30,000 still outstanding. Its average is simply the sum of these two amounts divided by 2:

$$\text{Average accounts receivable} = \frac{\$50,000 + 30,000}{2} = \$40,000$$

The company's turnover rate, therefore, is:

$$\frac{\$200,000}{\$40,000} = 5 \text{ times}$$

This ratio indicates that the company collected five times its average amount of accounts receivable during its fiscal year; put another way, the company requires an average of 2.4 months (12 months divided by 5) to collect an account receivable.

accrual accounting   The accounting method that recognizes *revenue* when it is earned and expenses when they are incurred, regardless of when the company or an individual (a sole proprietor) actually receives or disburses cash for products and services sold or bought.

There are two bases for reporting revenues and expenses: *cash* or *accrual.* For tax purposes, most individuals and some small businesses or firms use the cash basis. According to *generally accepted accounting principles* (**GAAP**), however, the accrual method is the only one permitted for **corporations.** Anytime a company or individual makes a sale on *credit,* it recognizes revenue, even though it may not yet have received payment. Conversely, any *accounts payable* (e.g., salaries) at the end of an *accounting period* are listed as expenses.

accrued expense   Any expense incurred, but not yet paid at the end of an *accounting period.*

Also called *accrued liabilities,* these expenses do not necessarily represent delinquencies in payment. A company that purchases $5,000 worth of office supplies on *credit* on December 29 will show that amount as an accrued expense on its *balance sheet* for its *fiscal year* ending on December 31.

accumulated benefit obligation (ABO)   The *present value* of the amount a company would owe its *pension plan* if all its eligible employees retired today.

The *Financial Accounting Standards Board* (**FASB**) issued its Statement #87, "Employers' Accounting for Pensions," in 1985, stipulating that a company had to report on its **balance sheet** the present value of accrued pensions. Any deficit must be counted as a **liability** (Brealey and Myers 1991, 861–862).

See also **minimum pension liability; projected benefit obligation (PBO); Statements of Financial Accounting Standards (SFAS).**

ACI   *See Advertising Council Inc.*

acid test ratio   Current quick assets (that is, cash and assets that are quickly converted to cash) divided by **current liabilities.**

The acid test ratio measures a company's ability to pay its debts immediately. Because most companies cannot liquidate their inventories at a moment's notice, these items are usually excluded from the ratio, although by the strict definition, inventories are listed as **current assets.** Accordingly, accountants use the following formula:

$$\text{Acid test ratio} = \frac{\text{cash} + \text{marketable securities} + \text{accounts receivable}}{\text{current liabilities}}$$

The acid test ratio is similar to the **current ratio,** but with this essential difference: It does not include current inventories and certain prepaid expenses in the numerator. Two companies can have the same current ratio, but differ widely in their acid test ratios.

EXAMPLE:

	Company X	Company Y
Current assets		
Cash	$ 1,500	$ 3,000
Marketable securities	5,000	10,000
Accounts receivable	4,000	5,500
Inventories	8,000	1,000
Prepaid expenses	2,000	1,000
Total current assets	20,500	20,500
Current liabilities	9,000	9,000
Current ratio	**2.28**	**2.28**
Acid test ratio	**1.17**	**2.06**

Even though the two companies have identical current ratios, Company Y has $2.06 worth of quick assets for every $1.00 of debt. It is, therefore, much more flexible in its ability to convert those assets into cash in order to pay its debts. With an acid test ratio of 1.17:1, Company X is not having financial woes, but it is close to the break-even point, should its creditors come calling.

See also **current ratio.**

acquisition   One organization's (or individual's) successful gain of a controlling interest of another company.

Usually the controlling interest means at least 50 percent of the voting shares of a company, which the acquiring company may try to garner by any means possible. In a hostile takeover bid, one company may offer to buy another company's shares at a price much higher than that offered on the general market.

EXAMPLE: Among the most celebrated acquisitions in business history, the Walt Disney Company's purchase of Capital Cities/ABC in February 1996 for just under $20 billion and SBC Communications' purchase of Pacific Telesis for $16.5 billion on April 1, 1997, sent clear signals to the business community and shareholders about just how big an acquisition could be. To speak of limits, however, is to speak prematurely, for such deals keep getting bigger.

ACRS   *See accelerated cost recovery system*

activity-based costing (ABC)   An accounting method that identifies costs and profits associated with a specific process, activity, or product line, thereby determining how much gain or drain it brings to the enterprise as a whole.

Also called *product-line costing,* ABC allows managers to account more accurately for expenses and profits associated with a particular product or process. Focusing their attention on **overhead** costs, managers can increase, reduce, or eliminate costs by redesigning the company's layout, reassigning personnel, or modifying the production process itself (Fess and Warren 1993, 876–879).

ABC appears to be much more popular in the United States than in Great Britain. Roughly half the companies surveyed in 1996 by the Institute of Management Accountants (IMA) reported using ABC for making decisions not just in accounting but also in marketing, engineering, and operations. However, the way in which this method is employed appears to differ dramatically between the United States and Great Britain. In 1994, the *Times 1000* found that only 50 companies in Great Britain had adopted ABC, usually for reducing costs rather than making decisions about redesigning processes and reassigning personnel (Cost reduction 1995; Financial executives 1997).

ABC probably works best in manufacturing settings where it is easier to measure how many machines and machine hours are allocated to producing an item. The method is less successful when the dividing line between two activities blurs.

EXAMPLE: Experiencing rapid growth through the mid-1980s, international carrier DHL discovered that its costs had risen equally fast, as much as 50 percent in some cases. Reasoning that salaries and benefits paid to DHL employees accounted for the majority of costs, managers determined to ride herd on the workers. Activity-based costing, however, revealed that management and information technology (IT) contributed more to the excessive costs than personnel did. Accordingly, DHL undertook a program to reduce costs by eliminating waste, not dismissing people (Cost reduction 1995).

activity-based management (ABM)   The organization and control of business processes and expenses based on analyses of profitability provided by *activity-based costing.*

See also activity-based costing.

ad response   A measure of consumers' reaction to an advertisement.

Marketers measure response by testing consumers' recall of an ad, by their recognition or awareness of a product's features, or by their purchasing behavior. The number of coupons clipped from a local newspaper and redeemed at the grocery story can be a gauge of an advertisement's success. In more complex programs, marketers issue identification cards to customers who agree to be monitored as they shop and to have their buying patterns tracked electronically. Analyzing those patterns of behavior, researchers determine whether the advertising did, in fact, influence decisions to purchase a product.

See also **motivation research.**

ADA *See Americans with Disabilities Act*

additional paid-in capital The excess above **par value** that investors pay for a company's stock.

Stockholders make two kinds of financial contributions to a company: the **paid-in capital** or the par value of the stock multiplied by the number of shares issued; and the additional paid-in capital, which often is considered a donation. Those contributions appear in the **stockholders' equity** section of the company's **balance sheet,** which is usually provided in its **annual report.** Paid-in capital, listed as **common stock,** is typically much lower than additional paid-in capital or "proceeds in excess of par value." If the company buys back its **treasury stock,** accountants report the amount as a reduction to additional paid-in capital.

EXAMPLE: A company issues 10,000 shares of its stock with a par value of $5 at a price of $7 per share. The additional paid-in capital amounts to $20,000 (10,000 shares × $2). The stockholders' equity section of the balance sheet might appear as follows:

CONSOLIDATED BALANCE SHEET (SELECTION)

	As of December 31	
Liabilities and shareowners' equity	**1997**	**1996**
Common stock, par value $5 (1 million shares authorized; 10,000 shares issued in 1997; 11,000 shares issued in 1996)	$50,000	$55,000
Additional paid-in capital	**$20,000**	**$ 6,875**
Treasury stock (1,000 shares at cost)	(6,000)	0
Total liabilities and shareholders' equity	**$64,000**	**$61,875**

ADI *See area of dominant influence*

adverse opinion An auditor's unfavorable report on a company's **financial statements** either because the organization inaccurately presents its financial condition or because its reports do not conform to **generally accepted accounting principles (GAAP).**

Adverse opinions sometimes result from a legal technicality. In New York and other states, the law requires insurers and mutual companies to issue public financial disclosures in accordance with statutory principles, not GAAP. The **American Institute of Certified Public Accountants (AICPA),** however, stipulates that accountants *must* issue an adverse opinion on any statement that does not conform to GAAP. New York mutual companies thus find themselves on the horns of a dilemma: Either they must pay for *two* accounting reports or they must explain why the statement prepared according to statutory principles carries an adverse opinion (SOP takes adverse view 1996).

See also **audit opinion; qualified opinion; unqualified opinion.**

advertising   The promotion of an idea, a product, or a service by an identified sponsor or organization that pays to have the message printed or broadcast by the mass media, including television, radio, newspapers, magazines, direct mail, **telemarketing,** billboards, transit cards, and the Internet.

AD SPENDING IN 1995 AND 1996
(Dollars in millions)

Rank (1996)	Media	Ad spending Jan.–Sept. 1996	Ad spending Jan.–Sept. 1995	Percent change
1	Network TV	$10,525	$ 8,830	19.2
2	Newspapers	10,358	9,611	7.8
3	Spot TV	10,008	9,355	7.0
4	Magazines	7,730	7,135	8.3
5	Cable TV networks	3,341	2,673	25.0
6	Syndicated TV	1,701	1,449	17.4
7	National spot radio	1,038	957	8.5
8	National newspapers	1,004	815	23.2
9	Outdoor	877	825	6.4
10	Sunday magazines	672	688	−2.4
11	Network radio	604	563	7.2
Total	All media	$47,858	$42,901	11.6

SOURCE: Competitive Media Reporting (webinfo@adage.com).

advertising agency   A company specializing in the production of advertising campaigns and strategies to help clients target and promote their products and services.

There are three types of advertising agencies: full-service, specialty service, and in-house.

Full-service agencies offer clients creative **advertising, public relations (PR), marketing research,** promotion advice, media buying, and publicity. Most of these agencies charge a **commission** on all media purchases they make for clients. For large accounts, this commission is the only compensation the agency receives, unless it also provides public relations and publicity. For those services, the client usually pays on a dollar fee basis, since no media charges are involved.

Specialty service agencies offer only one or two of the services that full-service agencies provide. Many agencies supply only research, copy, or media. Frequently, specialty service agencies, sometimes referred to as *boutique agencies,* operate within a single industry, such as fashion or health care. Some agencies also function as wholesale media buyers and offer a more efficient, less expensive method of buying television or radio time.

An in-house advertising agency actually operates as part of a client company; the marketing company thus has its own advertising agency. In-house agencies can perform any number of advertising services, although the company may still use outside agencies for large or complex projects.

EXAMPLE: In 1997, Omnicom Group—which includes a large advertising network made up of BBDO Worldwide, DDB Needham Worldwide, TBWA Chiat/Day, and a number of specialty advertising agencies—announced plans to purchase Fleishman-Hillard, Inc. The *acquisition* will result in what is said to be the world's largest public relations group (Omnicom 1997).

advertising allowance A manufacturer's discount offered to *retailers* who agree to market a product through special advertisements or in-store displays to attract customers (Kotler and Armstrong 1994, 506).

Advertising Council Inc. (ACI) A volunteer organization financed in part by contributions from over 350 corporations and dedicated to producing and distributing national nonpolitical, public-service advertising campaigns.

The group's most famous slogans include McGruff the Crime Dog's "Take a Bite out of Crime" and Smoky the Bear's "Only You Can Prevent Forest Fires." The ACI has also created ads for the U.S. Department of Transportation, warning that "Friends Don't Let Friends Drive Drunk" and for the United Negro College Fund proclaiming that "A Mind Is a Terrible Thing to Waste." Most recently, the council worked with the Women's College Coalition to develop an ad to combat stereotypes of female students as underachievers in areas such as math and science. It created the slogan "Expect the Best from a Girl. That's What You'll Get."

Established in 1942 as the War Advertising Council, the ACI adopted a strictly nonpolitical stance and raised $35 billion for war bonds, encouraged blood donations, inspired 50 million victory gardens, and recruited 2 million women for the armed forces through its mascot, Rosie the Riveter. Now funded entirely by businesses, advertising agencies, and the media, the ACI directs its attention to campaigns designed to improve the lives and education of children in the United States, to promote preventative health care, to preserve the environment, and to strengthen the family unit. Its volunteers include distinguished figures in advertising and the media.

The ACI's New York office is located at 261 Madison Avenue, New York, NY 10016. Telephone (212) 922-1500. E-mail adcouncil@prodigy.com. Update information is available at the ACI's home page at http://www.adcouncil.org.

advertising frequency The number of times during a specified period that a member of a targeted audience is exposed to an advertisement.

Ads in popular magazines have a high frequency rate because of repeated readings and exposure through skimming (pass-ons). Television or radio ads—depending on the time at which they are aired and the *market share* of the show with which they are associated—may reach a wider audience with only one or two repetitions. Frequently aired commercials can prove an effective strategy when a company faces stiff competition and when customers need to be reminded of a product's worth (especially a product that falls into the category of goods purchased often, such as soap or paper). If *brand* loyalty is weak or if customers hesitate to adopt a brand, frequent advertising can help drive them to the product or service.

Media experts measure the number of exposures E for an ad by multiplying its reach R by its average frequency F (Kotler 1994, 638–640).

EXAMPLE: During one month, *Business Week* has 1 million readers. An ad appearing in that month's issues reaches 200,000 readers once, 400,000 readers twice, and the remaining 400,000 three times. Its frequency is calculated according to the following equation:

$$\frac{(200,000 \times 1) + (400,000 \times 2) + (400,000 \times 3)}{1,000,000} = \frac{2,200,000}{1,000,000} = 2.2$$

Frequency rates are helpful in determining how effective an ad campaign is, but they prove less reliable as measures used in comparing two or more advertisement schedules. If, in the preceding example, the reach is estimated to be 10,000 readers and all other population figures are reduced proportionately, the frequency rate is still 2.2.

affiliated company A company that owns less than 50 percent of another company's *common stock;* also a company paired with another by virtue of the fact that they are both *subsidiary companies* of a third company. If the affiliated companies are small, they may share the same management team.

EXAMPLE: Smith Barney Investment Services, Commercial Credit, and Primerica Financial Services are affiliates because they belong to the Travelers Group.

affirmative action (AA) The philosophical and ethical basis of numerous pieces of legislation enacted since the 1960s, in which the intention is to "level the playing field" in education, business, and other areas of society for those minorities who have endured decades of discrimination.

Perhaps the most important of legislative acts was the Equal Employment Opportunity Act of 1972, which created a commission to investigate unfair and discriminatory practices in hiring and promoting, awarding of contracts, training apprentices, and the like. The intention of the law was to encourage or, if necessary, force employers, admissions boards, and others to take special steps to ensure a balance of majority and minority members roughly equal to that in society at large. The EEO Act thus grew out of and extended the 1964 Civil Rights Act (Title VII), which outlawed discrimination in the workplace but took no decisive action on correcting any imbalances that might be found there.

Since its inception in 1972, the EEO Act has prompted a number of diverse and difficult cases, many of which are fought in reaction to its original intentions.

afternoon drive time In radio advertising, the time segment between 3:00 P.M. and 7:00 P.M., Monday through Friday.

For advertising purposes, afternoon and *morning drive times* (6:00 A.M. until 10:00 A.M.) are considered *prime time.* Because they represent the hours of greatest reach, these periods for radio are analogous to television's prime time, which runs from 8:00 P.M. until 11:00 P.M. (EST).

age discrimination Any negative action in hiring, training, promoting, disciplining, compensating, rewarding, or terminating employment for an individual on the basis of age.

In 1967, Congress passed the Age Discrimination in Employment Act (ADEA) to combat the unfair practices directed against employees between the ages of 40 and 65. In 1978, new legislation entitled the Mandatory Retirement Act prohibited the forced retirements of employees before they reach age 70, but this law was superseded by the 1986 amendment to the ADEA that removed the age-70 cap altogether. The U.S. Department of Labor originally oversaw the implementation of the ADEA, but in 1979, Congress created the Equal Employment Opportunity Commission (EEOC) and charged it with overseeing all discrimination issues.

The ADEA applies to private companies with 20 or more employees, to employment agencies, to labor unions with 25 or more members, and to government agencies. In 1986, the Omnibus Budget Reconciliation Act included an amendment to the ADEA that removed the upper age limit of 70.

Age discrimination cases hinge on issues of disparate *treatment* or *impact*. The majority of those cases involve differential treatment: Older employees receive lower pay for the same work that their junior colleagues are doing, their health benefits are limited, they are excluded from training sessions that could help them advance within the company, or their employers intentionally overlooked them for promotions or higher compensation simply on the basis of their ages.

In cases of disparate impact, plaintiffs charge that regardless of whether it is intentional, the employers' actions created undue burdens for the employees or resulted in their being terminated. Evidence can be either explicit (for example, a letter in which a personnel manager cites a policy that the company refuses to hire people beyond a certain age) or implicit (the plaintiff presents statistical data showing that older employees at the company receive fewer promotions and salary increases).

Responding to these charges, employers cite any of the following defenses:

1. **Bona fide occupational qualifications (BFOQs):** Some jobs have unique requirements that necessitate age criteria. Some local police departments, for instance, have tried to impose an age limit of 55 on public safety personnel, arguing that employees must have the stamina and physical endurance to fulfill their job functions. Officers in New York and New Jersey, among other states, have challenged such requirements in court, arguing that these regulations constitute age discrimination. In 1995, however, the House of Representatives passed HR 849 to amend the ADEA so that it would "allow but not mandate" local and state governments to enforce restrictions that qualify as bona fide qualifications for work. Moreover, the bill grandfathers in policies that have been in place since March 3, 1983 (Quist 1995).

2. *Bona fide seniority system:* Employers can justify differential treatment of employees, whatever their ages, based on seniority systems. An older employee who claims to be the victim of age discrimination will find the case harder to prove if the company in question promotes employees primarily on the basis of length of service.

3. *Good cause:* An employee's behavior can result in a demotion, a reduction or suspension of salary, discharge, or other disciplinary actions. To justify disparate treatment, employers cite reasons such as falsification, theft, chronic absenteeism, poor judgment, and moral turpitude.

4. *Factors other than age (FOA):* Employers must justify that the unequal treatment an employee received was based on individual circumstances, not on age. Examples of such justifications include violation of a company policy, poor performance (the employee's or the company's), business-related lay-offs, and internal restructuring. An employee, of course, will seek to show that the FOA is really a smoke screen for age discrimination.

5. *Business necessity:* Conditions within a particular business sometimes necessitate policies that discriminate against employees, either old or young. A clothing store, for instance, that caters to a youthful customer might try to argue that it can hire only young people as sales personnel. This is perhaps the weakest of the five defenses, for it requires the company to prove that employing workers within a certain age group is a key to the company's survival.

A shift in age discrimination suits occurred in 1993, soon after the Supreme Court ruled in *Rathindra N. Ghoshtagore* vs. *Westinghouse Electric Corporation* that "neutral employer policies" that treat older employees more harshly do not necessarily violate the ADEA (Brennan 1997; McMorris 1977).

In some other countries, a tradition of age discrimination has worked in favor of older workers. Like many Japanese companies, Mazda for years promoted older workers, bypassing younger workers, because of unwritten policies to show respect to older people. In March 1997, however, the company announced that it would no longer discourage workers below the age of 40 from entering midlevel management positions (Mazda 1997).

aggregate plan   A guide for managing production and minimizing short-term variations by working with grouped (or *aggregate*) units such as machine hours, materials, and finished goods and services.

If managers look only at short-term changes in labor, materials, and production, they are likely to formulate a distorted business strategy that does not make the best use of the company's production capabilities and projected sales. Rather than distinguishing the minor differences between games, dolls, and puzzles, for instance, a toy manufacturer might create an aggregate plan based on the total number of *units* produced and sold, grouping all three lines of toys for the purpose of projecting changes in the workforce, **distribution channels,** and use of resources.

Although there will always be small deviations in **demand** and production, the aggregate plan helps managers set a clear strategy for meeting day-to-day changes. Depending on numerous factors such as market conditions, competitors, and available resources, managers pursue either a **level production** aggregate plan or a **chase demand** plan. The former sets production at a constant level over the course of the planning period, thereby stabilizing the workforce and costs of production. **Inventories** act as shock absorbers, fluctuating as demand varies. Although inventory costs often increase, the company enjoys predictable **fixed costs** such as salaries and avoids having to pay workers overtime.

In contrast, a chase demand aggregate plan calls for quick responses in **outputs** in order to keep up with demand. While inventory costs shrink, a chase demand strategy makes it more likely that the company will need to hire more workers during peak production but lay them off when demand falls.

In a service company, a chase demand aggregate plan requires that some employees work overtime or on split shifts. To keep up, the company may have to hire temporary or part-time workers and frequently experience a decline in quality. Because the service company has no way to stockpile inventories, it can sometimes find that a level production aggregate plan makes poor use of the workforce.

agile manufacturing   Computer-controlled manufacturing has taken a quantum leap forward with the introduction of the *intelligent agent*. Machines linked by software can request and receive information from each other as peers, as opposed to the traditional structured approach to control. Using the information asking and receiving process, better and faster decisions can be made and evaluated. It may also include a virtual reality component, which will allow the user to test the manufacturing process and feedback systems prior to making the precision parts. Instead of a sequential approach, the product is evaluated as it is being produced and corrective measures or improvements are made as information is obtained to improve reliability or quality. Much of the work is carried on by Sandia Corporation.

AGVS   *See automatic guided vehicle system*

AI   *See artificial intelligence*

AICPA   *See American Institute of Certified Public Accountants*

allowance for bad debts   In the *current assets* section of a *balance sheet,* the amount a company subtracts from its *accounts receivable* to show obligations that managers consider uncollectible.

   If a company has accounts receivable of $150,000 and allots 5 percent ($7,500) to uncollectible notes or accounts, the current assets section of its balance sheet would read as follows:

Accounts receivable	$150,000
Allowance for bad debts	($7,500)
Net receivables	$142,500

Using the allowance method, the company anticipates the percentage of its accounts that it believes will not pay for products or services rendered. (If, in fact, those accounts do pay later, or if the company understates its bad debts, it will need to make adjustments on its balance sheet at the end of the *accounting period.*)

   In reviewing a company's *financial statements,* it is important both to note the ratio of the bad debt allowance to total accounts receivable and to determine how much that ratio changes over the years. The allowance of 5 percent in the preceding example may seem reasonable, but if the company has traditionally set aside 12 percent of its accounts receivable as an allowance for bad debts, one could argue that either managers are attempting to inflate the company's net receivables or they have suddenly become much more successful in collecting what is owed the company.

alpha (1)   A factor for projecting the rise in a stock's price, if the stock's *beta* and market volatility are kept at zero.

   Alpha (α) is calculated by multiplying beta by the difference between the market return of an index or average and a risk-free return as might be found in U.S.

Treasuries. Alpha is therefore always tied to an index or average such as the Standard & Poor's 500 Index. An alpha of 1.0 indicates that the stock is expected to keep pace with the S&P Index, whereas an alpha of 1.15 means that the price of the stock is projected to rise at a rate of 15 percent above the index's growth.

alpha (2) A category of stocks on the London Exchange that are more strictly regulated than either beta or gamma stocks. Alpha stocks constitute approximately 80 percent of the total number traded on the exchange.

alternate weeks (A/W) A media strategy that directs a radio station, television station, newspaper, or magazine to run a commercial or print advertisement for one week, skip a week, then run it again for a week.

Also called *flighting,* the A/W strategy gives advertisers an extra week of exposure for the price they would pay for only two weeks of advertising.

AMA See *American Management Association* or *American Marketing Association*

American Academy of Advertising (AAA) A professional organization of educators and advertisers dedicated primarily to improving education about *advertising.*

At the 1958 convention of the Advertising Federation of America, a group of advertising educators led by Harry Hepner of Syracuse University formed the organization to promote professional education for advertisers and to stimulate research in advertising. Today, the AAA has over 600 members, primarily teachers of advertising in colleges and universities, and the organization publishes the *Journal of Advertising,* a quarterly publication for articles and essays on theoretical issues and empirical research in the field of advertising and mass communication.

For more information, contact Professor Robert L. King, AAA Executive Secretary, E. Claiborne Robins School of Business, University of Richmond, Richmond, VA 23173, or at http://www.utexas.edu/coc/adv/AAA/about.html.

American Advertising Federation (AAF) A national association of advertising professionals committed to maintaining standards for truthful and responsible *advertising.*

Founded in 1967 when the Advertising Federation of America merged with the Advertising Association of the West, the AAF has been influential in establishing the Federal Trade Commission (FTC).

American Association of Advertising Agencies (AAAA) Also known as the Four A's, the national organization formed in 1917 to help regulate the advertising industry by monitoring practices and setting standards for ethical *advertising.*

The AAAA acts as spokesperson for *advertising agencies* in dealings with government, media, and the public. In addition, it provides member organizations with a rich supply of research on advertising, media, *marketing,* statistical data, and foreign markets. The organization has 1,225 offices in the United States and over 1,800 offices in 119 foreign countries.

AAAA's headquarters are located at 405 Lexington Avenue, New York, NY 10174. Telephone (212) 682-2500. Fax (212) 953-5665.

American Depository Receipts (ADRs) Certificates that represent shares of stock in a foreign company.

Denominated in U.S. dollars, ADRs can be purchased or sold on American exchanges or over the counter through a stockbroker, an ADR mutual fund, or directly from a depository bank. Leading American depositaries include the Bank of New York, which has captured approximately 60 percent of all new ADR programs over the past six years, as well as J. P. Morgan and Citibank. There are currently in excess of 1,700 ADRs available from enterprises representing more than 60 countries.

Foreign companies place shares on deposit in the trust account of one of the aforementioned New York banks, which issues *depositary receipts* for those shares. The receipts, in turn, can be listed and traded on U.S. exchanges and over-the-counter markets just like shares of domestic companies.

It is virtually impossible to tell the difference between ADR **transactions** and those involving common shares of American companies. The stock certificate looks the same; broker **commissions** are identical; and quotations for listed ADRs appear in the *Standard & Poor's Stock Guide*, the *Wall Street Journal*, and *Value Line*.

ADRs present several advantages over investing in foreign companies through foreign stock exchanges:

- ADRs pay dividends in U.S. dollars.
- Settlement costs applicable in some foreign markets are eliminated.
- Financial reports are in English, and although their accounting assumptions differ from those used by most American companies, the reports are readable.
- Trading inconveniences and custodial fees associated with buying shares on foreign markets are eliminated.

American Institute of Certified Public Accountants (AICPA) Founded in 1887, the national organization that sets professional standards, monitors performance, and acts as liaison between members and various governmental and regulatory organizations.

Current membership in the United States exceeds 328,000 **certified public accountants (CPAs)**. The AICPA's main office is located at 1211 Avenue of the Americas, New York, NY 10036. Telephone (212) 596-6200. Fax (212) 596-6213. Other offices are located in Washington, D.C., and Jersey City, New Jersey. The organization maintains an informational Web site at http://www.alcpa.org.

American Management Association (AMA) An organization that acts as both a networking and an educational forum for its members and their colleagues. The AMA publishes materials on professional development and provides a variety of educational seminars designed to promote superior business skills as well as explore active best practices worldwide.

Founded in 1923, the AMA has a current membership of approximately 70,000. Although it maintains offices throughout the United States, the headquarters are located at 1601 Broadway, New York, NY 10019-7420. Telephone (212) 586-8100. Fax (212) 903-8168. E-mail cust_serv@amanet.org. The AMA Web site is located at http://www.amanet.org/aboutama.htm.

American Marketing Association (AMA) The world's largest society of marketing professionals, with over 45,000 members representing 92 countries.

Headquartered in Chicago, the AMA was founded in 1937 as a nonprofit organization. The organization seeks to promote the science and ethical practices of *marketing* as well as to assist members and students of marketing with career development. In addition to publishing *Marketing News, Marketing Research,* the *Journal of Healthcare Marketing,* the *Journal of Marketing Research,* and several other publications, the AMA offers books, pamphlets, and numerous bibliographic resources in marketing.

The AMA's main office is located at 250 South Wacker Drive, Suite 200, Chicago, IL 60606. Telephone (312) 648-0536 or 800-262-1150. Fax (312) 993-7542. The Web site is at http://www.ama.org.

See also **Advertising Council Inc. (ACI); American Advertising Federation (AAF); American Association of Advertising Agencies (AAAA).**

American Stock Exchange (AMEX)   One of the largest stock exchanges in the United States.

Before the American Revolution, traders gathered on the docks of New York City, where they bought and sold securities. These *transactions* shifted locale frequently in the early part of the nineteenth century, but keeping within the area of the southern tip of Manhattan. Known in the early years of the twentieth century as the New York Curb Market Association, the exchange moved indoors (at 86 Trinity Place), and in 1953 changed its name to the American Stock Exchange. By 1996, the AMEX listed 690 domestic companies and over 60 non-U.S. companies (including Canadian organizations). It had a combined market value of over $135 billion and traded over 5.6 billion shares, representing a record $91.3 billion.

Companies can qualify for one of four types of membership on the AMEX: The current 661 regular members transact business in both *equities* and *options,* whereas the 203 *options principal* members deal only in options. Both types occupy seats on the exchange, which range in price from a low of $650 (in 1942) to a high of $420,000 (in 1987). Associate and allied memberships do not have direct access to the trading floor, although associate members can communicate through wire access to the floor, where regular members can conduct business on their behalf.

Requirements for membership on the exchange are more lenient than those established by the **New York Stock Exchange** (**NYSE**). Although the AMEX considers many relevant factors such as the nature of a company's business, the reputation of its management, its record of earning power, and its potential for future success, the exchange sets the following minimum standards for regular membership:

- Pretax income: $750,000 for the latest *fiscal year* or for two of the past three years
- Market value of public *float:* $3,000,000
- *Stockholders' equity:* $4,000,000
- Stock price: $3.00
- Number of stockholders: 800 (this number may be as low as 400 under certain alternative arrangements)

In 1996, as determined by total *assets,* the top 10 leading companies on the AMEX were:

Rank	Company	Total assets ($ million)
1	B.A.T. Industries, PLC	70,254
2	Viacom Inc.	29,002
3	First Empire State Corporation	12,821
4	Imperial Oil Ltd.	7,722
5	Quebecor, Inc.	3,973
6	Telephone and Data Systems, Inc.	3,933
7	MAXXAM Inc.	3,883
8	New York Times Company	3,520
9	Brascan Ltd.	3,307
10	Hasbro, Inc.	2,999

SOURCE: *AMEX Fact Book* (New York: American Stock Exchange, Inc., 1997).

Americans with Disabilities Act (ADA)   The federal law (42 U.S.C.A. §§ 12101-213; P.L. 101-336), enacted on July 26, 1990, banning discrimination against people with disabilities.

The ADA extends civil rights protection to people with disabilities; thus, it is seen as a logical extension of two major predecessors: Title II and Title VII of the Civil Rights Act of 1964 provide direction for coverage and enforcement, whereas the Rehabilitation Act of 1973 is used for defining the term *disability* and determining what constitutes discrimination. The ADA, however, goes further than either of these two laws. Whereas the Civil Rights Act merely prohibits discrimination, the ADA forces businesses and schools to accommodate people with disabilities and to promote their economic independence. And whereas the Rehabilitation Act stipulated that only those companies doing business with the federal government had to comply with the regulation, the ADA extends its reach to both public and private businesses, regardless of whether they are under contract with the government (Allen 1993).

The ADA clearly excludes some mental and physical impairments from its list of protected disabilities: The use of illegal drugs and alcohol, for instance, is forbidden (although the recent adoption by California voters of a proposition legalizing the use of marijuana for certain medical conditions may soon call this clause into question); other impairments not covered by the ADA include kleptomania, pyromania, compulsive gambling, and, according to one source, "various sexual behaviors (including homosexuality)" (Hardwicke and Emerson 1992, 410). As this assertion suggests, there is still much ignorance about what constitutes a disability.

In the area of human resources management, critics of the ADA have described it as vague legislation or "law by adjective." That is, the law, as written, does not specify what constitutes a "*qualified* individual with a disability, who must be seen as performing an *essential* function at work" or what the legislators had in mind when they defined a disabled person as one who has "a major life activity that is substantially limited by a physical or mental impairment." Nor does the law specify to what extent a business must go in order to make a "reasonable accommodation" for an employee or a client with a disability; employers are exempt from the regulation if the accommodation presents an "undue hardship." The courts continue to hear cases debating the meanings of those terms, despite the extensive writings by the Equal Employment Opportunity Commission (EEOC) in an attempt to clarify the issues (LeRoy and Schultz 1995, 147–148).

In a document entitled "Myths and Facts about the Americans with Disabilities Act," the Civil Rights Division of the U.S. Department of Justice (1997) asserts that in a five-year period (the commission does not specify what five-year period), there were "only about 650 [lawsuits] nationwide." Diverging widely from this number, however, is the count provided by the EEOC, which tallies 69,203 claims filed against employers under the ADA. Although some 45,000 of those cases were dismissed by the EEOC either for lack of reasonable cause or because plaintiffs did not follow through, the agency ruled that reasonable cause did exist in almost 1,300 cases. Over the same four-year period plaintiffs received almost $105 million in damages (Fine 1997).

There is equally as much discrepancy in calculating how much it costs a business to make the physical changes in its structure to accommodate employees or customers with disabilities. Often these changes amount to little more than installing washbasins and towel holders in lower positions, whereas other companies undertake more extensive renovations. In 1995, a Harris poll found that of the companies that had figures to report, the median cost of the physical changes to accommodate each employee with a disability amounted to only $223 (Tiernan 1997). The Hilton Hotel chain, however, has spent $25 million to retrofit its hotel rooms and provide special services such as a shuttle bus system, special telephones for people with hearing impairments, and wider doorways and ramps to accommodate people in wheelchairs (Fine 1997).

In one ironic situation, Max Cleland, elected in 1996 to the U.S. Senate from Georgia, found that he could not get around the halls of the Capitol in Washington, D.C., because the very building where the ADA had been approved almost a decade earlier had never upgraded itself to accommodate those with disabilities. Although the Capitol is a pre–Civil War edifice, renovations to make it accessible to all did not begin until the 1970s. But those changes were designed primarily for visitors to the site, not for those who work there. In 1994, four years after the ADA was passed, Capitol architects undertook a systematic renovation that would make it easier for Senator Cleland and others to make their way through the halls (Foskett 1996).

The Department of Justice offers a toll-free, 24-hour-a-day fax service for anyone with questions about the ADA and compliance with the law. Call the ADA Information Line at (800) 514-0301 (voice) or (800) 514-0383 (TDD) to receive free faxes or other information about compliance with the law. The Web address is http://www.usdoj.gov/crt/ada/adahom1.html. The EEOC operates various field offices throughout the United States. (Check government listings in local directories.) Or write the EEOC at 1801 L Street, NW, Washington, DC 20507. Phone (202) 663-4900. Fax (202) 663-4912.

amortization   The gradual reduction of an *asset's* value through a charge against *revenues.*

During a specified *accounting period,* the cost value of either a *fixed asset* or an *intangible asset* can be spread out over its *useful life.* If the asset has physical substance and a useful life of more than one year, it is considered fixed, and the item can be amortized or depreciated. (If the asset is an item occurring in nature, such as an oil well or a uranium mine, the accounting term used is *depletion* rather than *depreciation.*) Many companies also amortize their intangible assets such as *copyrights,* patents, and *goodwill.* If a company's product has increased sales because it enjoys a reputation for high quality, or if its employees are highly skilled, these assets depend on favorable factors that are considered intangible and can be amortized for accounting purposes. *Generally accepted accounting principles* (*GAAP*) state that the amortization of an intangible asset cannot exceed 40 years and that *straight-line depreciation* must be used (Fess and Warren 1993, 396–398).

annual percentage rate (APR)   A measure of the true cost of *credit.*
The APR expresses as a percentage the ratio of the finance charge to the average amount of *credit* used during the term of a loan. There are four ways to calculate APR for installment loans:

1. *Actuarial method:* Lenders prefer this method because it gives the most accurate results, but it relies on complicated calculations that are best performed on a computer. Essentially, the actuarial method is the interest calculated at a fixed rate on the unpaid balance of the loan's principal, with each payment allocated first to interest, then to the remaining principal. Most home mortgages, for example, are calculated according to the actuarial method.

2. *Direct-ratio method:* Simpler to calculate than the actuarial method, the direct-ratio method can often understate the real APR. Its formula is:

$$APR = \frac{6MC}{3P(N + 1) + C(N + 1)}$$

   where: M = Number of payment periods per year
   N = Number of scheduled payments
   C = Finance charges
   P = Original proceeds

3. *Constant-ratio method:* This method approximates the APR, but usually overstates the true amount. The formula is:

$$APR = \frac{2MC}{P(N + 1)}$$

4. *N-ratio method:* This calculation comes closer to the APR than either the constant-ratio or the direct-ratio method. Its formula is:

$$APR = \frac{M(95N + 9)C}{12N(N + 1)(4P + C)}$$

EXAMPLE: A company borrows $1,000, which it must repay in 12 equal payments of $92. The finance charge comes to $104. The ARP under each of the four methods described above is calculated as follows:

Actuarial method: As calculated by computer, the APR is 18.67 percent.

Direct-ratio method:

$$\text{APR} = \frac{6 \times 12 \times \$104}{3 \times \$1,000(12 + 1) + \$104(12 + 1)} = 0.1856 \text{ or } 18.56\%$$

Constant-ratio method:

$$\text{APR} = \frac{2 \times 12 \times \$104}{\$1,000(12 + 1)} = 0.192 \text{ or } 19.20\%$$

N-ratio method:

$$\text{APR} = \frac{12[(95 \times 12) + 9] \times \$104}{12 \times 12 \times 13 \times [4(\$1,000) + \$104]} = 0.1866 \text{ or } 18.66\%$$

The **Consumer Credit Protection Act of 1968** requires lenders to disclose, often in bold print, both the annual percentage rate and the dollar amount of the finance charge so that borrowers can make meaningful comparisons between different loans.

annual report   A detailed statement that a company prepares at the end of its reporting year, which can be either a calendar year or a *fiscal year.*

Annual reports present a company's *income statement, balance sheet, statement of cash flows, statement of shareholders' equity, management's discussion and analysis of operations (MD&A)* notes to the *financial statements, audit opinion,* and selected other data such as stock price ranges, names and occupations of company directors, and information about corporate offices. The *Financial Accounting Standards Board (FASB)* also requires that companies include in their annual reports operations in different industries, export sales, foreign operations, major customers, and government contracts. The annual report is analyzed by stockholders, investors, creditors, analysts, employees, and other interested parties.

annuity   A contract sold by an insurance company that guarantees periodic payments to the buyer (annuitant) at some time in the future, usually upon retirement.

There are two general types of annuities: fixed and variable. With a fixed annuity, the annuitant receives payments of equal amounts; with a variable type, payments change according to the value of the underlying *investments* that make up the annuity. Whether fixed or variable, an annuity that continues until the annuitant's death is called a *perpetuity.*

See also *future value; present value.*

antitrust legislation   Laws passed to dissolve monopolies in an effort to promote competition, combat conspiratorial attempts to corner a business market, and ensure fair prices for products and services.

The U.S. Constitution (Article 1, Section 7) grants Congress the power to oversee interstate commerce. In response to the rapid rise in the late nineteenth century of corporate trusts, Congress passed the Sherman Antitrust Act of 1890, legislation designed to prevent conspiracies to restrain or monopolize trade either within the United States and its territories or between the United States and foreign nations. ***Corporations*** found to be in violation of this act could be fined as much as $10 million. After he became president upon the death of William McKinley in 1901, Theodore Roosevelt developed a reputation as the "trust buster," having initiated proceedings against over 40 U.S. companies that had formed monopolies. In one of the most famous cases to fall under the provisions of the Sherman Antitrust Act, the Supreme Court ordered the breakup in 1911 of the Standard Oil Company of New Jersey, which John D. Rockefeller had built through ***mergers*** with competitors or their annihilation.

The ***Clayton Antitrust Act of 1914*** further restricted a company's use of price discrimination whereby it might try to sell the same item in two or more locations for widely different prices. If the company could offer no *statutory defense*—for example, evidence that it had to beat a competitor's low price in one of the locations or that it cost more to ship the item to another location—that company could be brought to trial on grounds of antitrust violations. The Clayton Act also made anticompetitive ***mergers*** and ***acquisitions*** illegal, and it created the Federal Trade Commission (FTC) to oversee and enforce the act. The Clayton Act also prohibited the practice of *tying contracts*, that is, forcing buyers to purchase a second product when they bought one item from the company. And it sought to forbid the practice of *interlocking directorates*, in which someone serving on the board of directors of one company sits on the board of another company within the same industry (Wessels 1993, p. 362).

The Robinson-Patman Act of 1936 focused chiefly on unfair price cutting, a practice of large ***conglomerates*** that dominate a ***market*** and crush competitors who cannot meet the company's low prices. The major issue comes in deciding whether the company had the *intent* to undermine competition and thereby gain the upper hand in the market. If a seller can demonstrate that price differentials result, for example, from selling in large quantities, the courts are more likely to interpret the practice as bona fide competition (Kotler and Armstrong 1996, 380).

The ***European Community*** (***EC***) Court in Luxembourg rules in similar cases involving antitrust regulations, particularly two articles in the Treaty of Rome, which in 1957 established the European Economic Community. Article 85 establishes the principle that certain business practices are illegal in that they intend to create monopolies, whereas Article 86 speaks to the specific issue of market domination (Hoogvelt and Puxty 1987).

EXAMPLE: The EC Court is currently using Articles 85 and 86 to investigate allegations against Microsoft of commercial agreements that are allegedly deemed to be anticompetitive, as well as the possible abuse by Microsoft of its dominant position within Europe.

See also ***conglomerate.***

APEC The Asia Pacific Economic Cooperation organization, of which the United States is a member.

APR *See **annual percentage rate***

arbitrage The process of buying a security, currency, or ***commodity*** on one market and selling it on another.

Price differences between the two markets give arbitrageurs their profits.

EXAMPLE: Stock X trades on the London Stock Exchange for $10.00 per share and on the New York Stock Exchange for $10.50 per share. A broker buys 10,000 shares of the stock in London and simultaneously sells 10,000 shares in New York. The arbitrage profit (π) is calculated as follows:

$$\pi = Q(X_b - X_a)$$

where: Q = Quantity of shares traded
         X_a = Lower-priced shares
         X_b = Higher-priced shares

In this **transaction,** the arbitrageur's profit is

$$10,000(\$10.50 - \$10.00) = \$5,000$$

The higher demand will increase the stock's price on the London Exchange, while the lower demand will cause the stock to fall on the New York Exchange; thus, arbitrage results in rapid equalization. For that reason arbitrageurs must act with both speed and deliberation in order to seize the best opportunity.

arbitrage pricing theory (APT)   A theoretical measure of various factors affecting the relationship between a security's return and the general market return.

The arbitrage pricing theory (APT) differs from the **capital asset pricing model** (**CAPM**) in the greater number of variables it weighs in its calculation. Whereas the CAPM relies solely on a security's **beta,** or the ratio of its expected return to the return for the whole **market,** the APT factors in such variables as the rate of **inflation,** the position of the **gross domestic product** (**GDP**), the fact that stocks in the same category (e.g., utilities, technology, or banking) can move up or down as a group. The APT, in other words, seeks to measure the sensitivity of a stock to various market conditions, and thus to arrive at a more reliable measure of the stock's **rate of return** (Brigham and Gapenski 1994, 209–214; see also Ross 1976).

area of dominant influence (ADI)   A standard means of defining, for **marketing** purposes, a geographic area that receives a particular radio or television station's signals.

In 1965, the Arbitron Ratings Company completed a county-by-county survey to determine which radio and television stations people watched or listened to. It then established ADIs for various counties, assigning areas according to which stations people listened to most frequently. The Federal Communications Commission (FCC) later adopted ADIs as the standard definition for the radio and television industries. National advertisers use ADI to define both budget allocations and distribution territories when they create media campaigns. Although ADIs are in widespread use today, the advent of cable communications and the Internet will mean local programming and advertising will no longer hold so much power over customers in a given geographical area.

EXAMPLE: The area of dominant influence sometimes confuses telecommunication matters more than it clarifies them. In Davenport, Florida, FCC regulations are forcing Time Warner to drop from its cable lineup all local Orlando television stations in favor of local stations from Tampa, even though Davenport is geographically closer to Orlando. Area residents find that the Tampa stations infrequently report news items pertinent to local concerns and that weather forecasts are rarely accurate.

The FCC assigns viewing areas according to ADIs. The cable company must give first consideration to local stations within their viewing area who request space on the lineup to the detriment of stations outside that viewing area even if they are physically closer to subscribers. In this instance subscribers are so unhappy with the process that they are considering canceling their subscriptions (Northeast Polk 1996).

arithmetic return   A measure of ***investment*** return over either a single time period or multiple periods.

Arithmetic return is calculated by taking the average of a series of one-period returns according to the following formula:

$$\text{Arithmetic return} = \frac{\sum r_i}{n}$$

where: r_i = Return for each holding period
        n = Number of time periods

EXAMPLE: A company invests in a stock valued at $50 per share. The stock triples in price during one time period (t), then returns to its original price at the end of the following period.

The first step is to calculate the return r for each period the stock is held according to the equation

$$\text{Holding period return} = \frac{\text{current income} + \text{capital gain (loss)}}{\text{purchase price}}$$

Period 1:

$$\frac{\$0 + (\$150 - \$50)}{\$50} = 200\%$$

Period 2:

$$\frac{\$0 + (\$50 - \$150)}{\$150} = -66.7\%$$

The arithmetic mean is thus calculated:

$$\frac{200\% + (-66.7\%)}{2} = 66.65\%$$

The stock's arithmetic average return is the average of the 200 percent return during the first period and the −66.7 percent return in the second period. Although the arithmetic return is helpful in tracking successive ***rates of return,*** it can be misleading when used for calculating return over many periods because it does not take into account the time value of money. For extended rates of return, the geometric average return is more appropriate.

arm's-length transaction   A business ***transaction*** conducted between two or more parties at prices established by current ***market*** conditions.

Sales between related parties—for example, a parent company and its subsidiary, or two companies in alliance—are considered to be "at arm's length" if the prices, terms, and conditions are identical to those offered in the general marketplace. Tax laws disallow deductions or adjustments to business valuations if business transactions between related parties do not conform to market conditions. Examples of transactions not considered to be at arm's length include:

- Sales from a subsidiary to a parent company at cost
- Rent charged a subsidiary by a parent at substantially less than the market rate
- Loans from shareholders at *interest rates* less than market rates
- Loans from a corporation to its shareholders at no interest or at interest rates lower than those charged to the general public

ARR   *See accounting rate of return*

artificial intelligence (AI)   The fast-growing area of research in which scientists use computers to imitate human behavior and reasoning.

At MIT, CalTech, and other major centers, researchers are experimenting with robotics, *cybernetics,* game theory, and complex problem solving in ways that can harness the power of artificial intelligence for business, health care, defense, and financial markets. In their most widely used forms today, those problem solvers are called *expert systems,* which make use of large databases of information and directed paths to the best mutual funds in which to invest, the best strategy to use in a wartime emergency, or the best set of procedures to follow in a life-threatening crisis.

In more complex forms, artificial intelligence systems work with symbols rather than data, and they use rules, procedures, and networks rather than calculations and algorithms. In manipulating symbols, AI systems reason deductively, make assumptions, and learn from their mistakes; thus, they are well suited to handle decision making in cases where information changes rapidly while the process of reasoning remains constant. A much improved "Deep Blue," the RS/6000 CP supercomputer developed by IBM, challenged world champion Garry Kasparov to a six-match contest in May 1997. Hoping to avenge another computer's 4-2 loss to Kasparov in 1996, the new IBM computer can ponder 2 million chess moves in one second (Kaplan 1997).

ASB   *See Auditing Standards Board*

ASEAN   The Association of South East Asian Nations, a grouping of most nations in Southeast Asia. The goal is economic union.

AS/RS   *See automated storage and retrieval system*

asset   An economic resource for a company or an individual.

Assets include money, land, buildings, property and property rights, and machinery. An asset can belong to one of two categories: tangible or intangible assets. These classifications have important consequences for accounting and tax purposes.

Tangible assets have physical substance. Reported as *noncurrent assets* on a *balance sheet,* tangible assets include machinery, buildings, furniture, and fixtures. **Inventory,** securities, and cash are listed as **current assets.** For accounting purposes, physical assets such as buildings or machinery have a **useful life** of at least one year.

Intangible assets provide economic benefit but have no physical substance. Included in this category are patents, **copyrights, goodwill,** and **intellectual property** such as software. For accounting purposes, items listed as intangible assets also appear on the balance sheet and are amortized over an extended period. In the case of goodwill assets such as location and product reputation, **amortization** cannot exceed 40 years and must use the **straight-line depreciation** method.

asset turnover   In accounting, the ratio of a company's annual sales to its total average assets.

Asset turnover is one measure of the **productivity** of the company's assets, as calculated by the following formula:

$$\text{Asset turnover} = \frac{\text{sales}}{\text{total average assets}}$$

To calculate *average assets,* add the total of assets at the beginning of the year and at the end of the year, then divide by 2.

Asset turnover can also be used to measure the productivity of specific assets such as **inventory turnover** or **accounts receivable turnover.** In those cases, substitute the average annual inventory or average annual accounts receivable for total average assets in the denominator. Such ratios, however, need to be taken with a grain of salt since a high profit margin may indicate that the company is working close to **capacity** or that it is engaged in a low-volume, high-markup business. Moreover, the period chosen for calculating the average assets may not be representative of the assets' performance over the long term.

asset value business valuation method   A method for determining the valuation of business equity interests.

The asset value method assumes that all or a significant portion of a company's assets could be liquidated readily if so desired. This assumption makes this a favorite method of secured lenders for assessing the value of collateralized assets. Small businesses also look to this method as a starting point from which to make plus and minus adjustments. In this case, **book value,** not liquidation value, is normally used as an expression of **net asset value** (**NAV**).

The IRS also uses the asset value method to value **employee stock ownership plans** (**ESOPs**), special **recapitalizations,** and other tax issues.

One problem with using the asset value approach is that it looks at business assets as valuable in themselves, regardless of their impact on the business as an ongoing activity. Except in rare cases where **investments** in businesses are made for the purpose of liquidating the company, the only real value in business assets lies in their ability to enhance the company's earning power.

In general, valuations relating to **mergers, acquisitions,** or sales of companies or equity interests, and other purely business purposes use methods of valuation that more accurately can reflect future benefits to investors.

attractiveness test   *See **industry attractiveness test***

attribution theory   The behavioral theory that attempts to assign two types of causes—external and internal—to any behavior.

Externally caused behavior results from outside factors, often beyond the individual's control. If an employee is an hour late returning from lunch, the delay might be the result of a traffic accident or a breakdown of the public transportation system. An internal cause for the same event might be attributed to the individual's habit of stopping at a bar for several drinks. Many internal causes are as uncontrollable as the external ones, of course.

Whether a behavior is externally or internally motivated is a complicated issue, not always easily resolved. But in evaluating an individual's attitudes and behavior, psychologists do look closely at three factors: consistency, consensus, and distinctiveness:

- *Consistency* is the extent to which a person acts in the same way at different times. If an employee is usually late in returning from lunch, an observer will first attribute the behavior to internal causes. If the employee is rarely late, the behavior could be attributed to external causes.

- *Consensus* is the extent to which other people in the same situation act in the same way. If everyone in a department is repeatedly late returning from lunch (high consensus), the observer will probably attribute the behavior to internal causes such as poor morale. If, however, this is a one-time instance of tardiness, the observer is more likely to attribute the behavior to external causes.

- *Distinctiveness* is the extent to which an individual acts the same way in different situations. Does the employee arrive late every morning? Is there a pattern to the employee's breaks? Does the employee leave early every day? Do coworkers complain that the employee is a "slacker"? If any of these cases applies to the individual, the behavior shows a high distinctiveness, probably attributable to internal causes. If the lateness is unusual, the behavior has a low level of distinctiveness and is likely caused by external conditions.

audit   An examination of a company's compliance with accounting standards and policies.

There are four types of audits: financial, internal, management, and compliance. In a financial audit, an independent *certified public accountant* (*CPA*) examines a company's accounting records and procedures, then gives an *audit opinion.* In an internal audit, an auditor investigates the company's procedures to make sure that they meet corporate policies. As its name suggests, a management audit examines management's *efficiency.* A compliance audit determines whether a company is following specific rules and regulations, usually set by a government agency or the industry itself.

*See also **adverse opinion; qualified opinion; unqualified opinion.***

audit opinion   A report given by an independent *certified public accountant* (*CPA*) that states the auditor's opinion as to the reasonableness of a company's *financial statement.*

*See also **adverse opinion, qualified opinion, unqualified opinion.***

Auditing Standards Board (ASB)   The authoritative branch of the *American Institute of Certified Public Accountants* (*AICPA*) that creates and interprets *generally accepted accounting principles* (**GAAP**) through its Statement on Auditing Standards.

Formed in 1978, the board is responsible for developing and distributing to member CPAs its rulings on auditing standards and procedures. Fifteen members, including representatives from international, national, regional, and local accounting firms, compose the ASB.

automated storage and retrieval system (AS/RS)   A computerized system of storage racks with vehicles that load and unload the racks automatically.

automatic guided vehicle system (AGVS)   A transportation system that automatically sends materials by means of pallet trucks, carts, conveyor belts, and the like, to predetermined destinations without the aid of a human operator.

automatic merchandising   Sales made through a vending machine.

Automatic merchandising allows around-the-clock sales in locations where there is heavy traffic, such as taverns, college dormitories, office complexes, and factories. Although vending machine sales of cigarettes have declined sharply in recent years (from nearly 30 percent in 1970 to just over 2 percent in 1995), sales of candy, snack foods, and beverages have generated *revenues* approaching $11 billion (De Marrais 1996). Vending machines can also expand a marketer's distribution at locations—libraries, hospitals, and rest rooms, for instance—that otherwise would be closed to marketers.

Vending machines do have drawbacks, however, particularly the high cost of repairing and servicing them. Perishable goods such as milk and ice cream have to be replaced frequently, and in some areas vending machines are vulnerable to vandalism and burglary. To offset these high *operating expenses,* vending machine marketers set much higher prices for products than local stores do.

autonomation   The automatic shutdown of a machine, process, or line whenever the system detects an abnormality or error.

available market   In *marketing,* those consumers who have interest in a particular product or service, access to it, and enough income to buy it.

The key word in this definition is *interest.* The available market, in other words, is not the same as the *potential market,* which consists of all those consumers who potentially have interest in a given product or service.

EXAMPLE: In the razor blade market, all men and women who have reached puberty and are showing hair growth make up the *potential* market for companies such as Gillette, Schick, and Bic. Some in this group, however, have no interest in shaving; thus, they are not part of the *available* market for those companies.

Identifying the available market helps marketers understand more precisely where sales are being generated.

See also *penetrated market* and *served market.*

average cost method   A method of *inventory valuation* that uses the average cost of the goods on hand to determine both the value of *inventory* on the *balance sheet* and the *cost of goods sold* on the *income statement.*

EXAMPLE: During the year, a company makes the following purchases:

January	100 units @ $70	$ 7,000
March	200 units @ $80	16,000
April	50 units @ $90	4,500
July	100 units @ $100	10,000
October	100 units @ $110	11,000
Total goods for sale: 550		**$48,500**

The average cost for each unit of inventory comes to $88.18 ($48,500 ÷ 550 units). If *ending inventory* on December 31 is 175 units, the company enters it on the balance sheet as follows:

$$175 \times \$88.18 = \$15,432$$

Cost of goods sold is calculated in a similar manner:

Total goods purchased	550 units
Ending inventory	175 units
Units sold	375 units

Cost of goods sold: 375 × $88.18 = $33,068

The average cost method is a compromise between the *first-in, first-out* (*FIFO*) and *last-in, first-out* (*LIFO*) methods of inventory valuation.

B

baby boomers   People born between 1946 and 1964, representing a substantial increase in the population of the United States following the end of World War II.

In 1970, for instance, the population of the United States comprising those people 24 years old or younger was approximately 93.4 million or 46 percent of the total. By 1994, that segment had fallen to 36 percent of a total population that had increased by 60 million people (U.S. Bureau of the Census 1995). As many have recognized, in the first three decades of the twenty-first century there will be a smaller percentage of people in the 20-to-65 age bracket working to pay the Social Security benefits of huge numbers of baby boomers who begin reaching retirement age as early as 2006. By 2030, when the last of the baby boomers turn 65, it is projected that there will be only two workers for each retiree. That ratio contrasts dramatically with the five-to-one ratio of workers to retirees in 1960 (Goodrich 1997).

Add to this demographic the fact that U.S. citizens are now living longer and that their health care costs will surely rise in proportion to their numbers (or at least become more expensive), and the potential for catastrophic upheavals in the Medicare and Social Security systems boggles the mind. On the plus side, the "graying" of America, as the demographers have put it, has deep implications for business, especially for those who design, produce, market, and distribute products and services to older adults.

backbone   The complex of switches, channels, and fiber-optic cables that enables networks of computers and users to tap into high-speed communications technology.

Analogous to the human spinal cord, a backbone is the main line of communications, a central nervous system that may be local or extend hundreds of miles.

EXAMPLE: In March 1997, MCI Corporation announced a partnership with Northwest Iowa Telephone Company and Northwest Iowa Power Cooperative to provide communications services to rural customers, schools, and businesses in Iowa and possibly throughout the Midwest. MCI provides the high-speed, high-capacity backbone of communications, to which local customers gain access through fiber-optic networks and Internet hosts provided by the utilities (MCI delivers 1997).

backlog   Customer orders that have been received and recorded but either are not fulfilled or are in process.

Also called the *order board* or *open orders*, backlogs result from scheduling and production necessities: An item may not be stocked because there has been a unanticipated **demand** or because a customer has rigid specifications for building the product. Large items such as mainframe computers and aircraft are frequently backlogged because it is impractical to make and store them, then redesign them to meet customers' specific requests.

The term *backlog* originally referred to the log placed at the back of a fire for support and a supply of energy. By the late nineteenth century, particularly in the United States, the term was used to refer to any reserve supply. Its current meaning of orders in arrears arose in the early 1930s, according to the *Oxford English Dictionary*.

backorder   A customer order that remains unfilled.

Backorders result when **inventory** runs out, either because managers mishandled the **supply** or because they did not anticipate accurately the **demand** for the product.

EXAMPLE: Backorders for Tickle Me Elmo dolls.

backward integration   A strategy by which a company creates a **competitive advantage** for itself by controlling the **supply** of its raw materials or parts, or the suppliers themselves.

Backward integration can take any number of forms. A company, particularly if it orders frequently in large quantities, may enter into special contracts with its suppliers to be first in line for receipt of raw materials or parts. Or the company may purchase the suppliers, thereby exercising the tightest control over its sources. The Goodyear Company has recently initiated several projects aimed at expanding its facilities in Beaumont and Houston, Texas, which produce polymers such as styrene-isoprene-butadiene. Those polymers, in turn, are used by the Goodyear division in Akron, Ohio, to produce high-performance tires (Davis 1997).

Backward integration, while it can be an effective strategy, can be disastrous for a company that invests heavily in buying up its suppliers if there is a sudden drop in the **demand** for its products. It is by no means a sustainable strategy. A company's competitors might enter the fray for purchasing suppliers or the materials, thereby raising the costs to an organization such as the James River Corporation, which has seen its strategy lose luster for this reason.

See also **forward integration; vertical integration.**

backward scheduling   In manufacturing, a technique of assigning work on the basis of when the completed work is due.

Using this technique, managers would schedule jobs with the most distant due dates to be completed exactly when they are needed. They assign work to various stations in reverse order of their actual processing. When numerous jobs are being processed simultaneously, backward scheduling will identify potential **bottlenecks** and idle time at workstations.

EXAMPLE: At 9:00 A.M., a print shop receives three rush orders, which it labels X, Y, and Z. The first job, X, which needs to be completed by 5:00 that afternoon, involves printing, collating, and binding. The second job, Y, is due at 3:00 P.M. The customer wants a long document printed, tabbed, and bound. A third customer requests that a job, Z, needing only tabbing and binding, be completed in four hours.

The print shop has four workstations, each assigned to a separate activity:

Workstation 1: Printing
Workstation 2: Collating
Workstation 3: Tabbing
Workstation 4: Binding

The three jobs themselves can be summarized as follows:

Job	Hour due	Required processing (in order)
X	8	2 hours at Station 1, 1 hour at Station 2, 1 hour at Station 3, 1 hour at Station 4
Y	6	2 hours at Station 1, 2 hours at Station 3, 2 hours at Station 4
Z	4	2 hours at Station 3, 2 hours at Station 4

Forming a backward schedule, the print shop manager begins with job X because it is not needed for eight hours. She assigns work to various slots, beginning with the last operation to be completed, which happens to be at Station 4. Then she works backward, assigning work as needed:

Hour:	10:00	11:00	12:00	1:00	2:00	3:00	4:00	5:00
Station 1	Y	Y		X	X			
Station 2						X		
Station 3	Z	Z	Y	Y			X	
Station 4			Z	Z	Y	Y		X

This schedule shows that Job Z will be completed at 1:00 P.M., Job Y at 3:00 P.M., and Job X at 5:00 P.M., as promised. More significantly, it shows when each station will be idle: The three jobs make a 50 percent use of Station 1 and a 62.5 percent use of Stations 3 and 4, but Station 2 is nearly unused (12.5 percent). If no other jobs come in, the shop will average only 46.88 percent of its workstation capacity. Furthermore, the schedule reveals that a potential bottleneck will occur between 12:00 and 1:00, the hour when the print shop staff takes its lunch break, yet the very time when three of the four stations have to be working at full steam.

This model assumes that there is no significant amount of time needed to move between workstations. If binding takes place in another building, however, the print shop manager would need to take this factor into account, adding time to allow for shifting work to another location. If a station requires a half hour for setup, the manager will need to make adjustments accordingly.

balance delay   A measure of the inefficiency of a production line derived by subtracting from 1 a factor for *efficiency.* This efficiency factor results from a calculation involving three factors: *cycle time,* the total task time, and the number of workstations in the line.

Cycle time is the amount of time that can be spent at a workstation before having to move to the next one. Assigned tasks performed at the one workstation must be completed in that allotted time. Cycle time is determined by dividing daily production time by daily *demand.*

The total task time is the sum of all times for all tasks needed to produce a unit of output. The number of workstations needed is total task time divided by the cycle time. The resulting value is rounded *up* to the next highest *whole number,* simply because there cannot be a fractional workstation.

To calculate efficiency, use the following formula:

$$\text{Efficiency} = \frac{\text{total task time}}{\text{number of workstations} \times \text{cycle time}}$$

EXAMPLE: A company produces 200 units per day.

- The cycle time is (8 hours × 60 min./hr.) × 200 units = 2.4 minutes. The most time a unit can spend at any one workstation is 2.4 minutes.
- Total task time is set at 6.0 minutes. This is the time it takes to build each unit.
- Number of workstations required = 6.0/2.4 = 2.5. Because there cannot be a partial workstation, we round this number up to 3.
- Efficiency = 6.0/(3 × 2.4) = 0.83 or 83 percent. With three workstations and a cycle time of 2.4 minutes, there are 7.2 minutes of time available to complete each unit, which under normal circumstances will require only 6.0 minutes.
- *Balance delay* = 1 − efficiency, or 17 percent.

Adding more workstations decreases efficiency: A fourth workstation in this example decreases efficiency to 6/(4 × 2.4) = 0.625 or 63 percent. The balance delay in this case would become 37 percent.

balance of payments   A summary of the official statement of international ***transactions*** between the United States and foreign nations.

In effect, this balance depicts the international trade and capital positions for the United States. Balance of payments statistics reflect two accounts: The *current account* comprises the country's ***balance of trade*** in merchandise and services, as well as its ***investment*** income and payments or receipts for debts; the *capital account,* in contrast, reflects amounts of ***capital***—either ***fixed*** or ***intangible assets***—that U.S. concerns invest in foreign countries or that foreign investors make in the United States. If Citicorp, for instance, makes a loan to a third-world country and receives repayment of a loan from another country, both amounts appear in the capital account.

During the 1960s, balance of payments accounts were tied to fixed ***exchange rates*** between national currencies. In the 1970s, however, these accounts underwent significant changes when the U.S. dollar ceased to have a fixed relationship with other currencies and began to ***float.*** Two primary accounts emerged during this period: the current account contrasts exports of goods and services with imports of goods and services; the capital account contrasts the inflow of capital—direct investments and long-term lending by foreigners—with the outflow of capital, or investments made abroad by U.S. residents and long-term lending to foreigners.

In general, a deficit in the current account brings about a capital account surplus, and vice versa. Because the total of all items in the current account and the capital account must equal zero, a factor called the *statistical discrepancy* is inserted to make the two accounts square with each other.

The following table presents data in billions of dollars for the merchandise trade balance, the current account, and the capital account for the period from 1985 to 1997:

	Merchandise trade balance	Current account	Capital account	Statistical discrepancy
1985	−122.2	−124.0	106.5	17.5
1986	−146.1	−153.2	132.5	20.7
1987	−159.6	168.1	−160.4	−7.7
1988	−127.0	−128.2	145.8	−17.6
1989	−116.2	−104.2	55.6	48.6
1990	109.0	−91.9	67.0	24.9
1991	−74.1	−5.7	53.8	−48.1
1992	−98.1	−56.4	100.2	−43.8
1993	−132.6	−90.8	85.1	5.6
1994	−166.2	−133.5	136.8	−3.3
1995	−173.6	−129.1	144.0	−14.9
1996	−191.2	−148.2	101.3	46.9
1997	−198.9	−166.4	69.3	97.1

SOURCE: U.S. Department of Commerce, *Statistical Abstracts of the United States: 1997*, 788–789.

balance of trade   The net difference between the monetary value of a country's imports and exports of merchandise over a specified period of time.

The country's *current account* reflects a currency drain when imports exceed exports, and the country is said to have a ***trade deficit.*** If the reverse holds true, the country experiences a currency surplus. If specified for a particular country, balance of trade statistics show the disparity between each country's imports of the other's products and services, and they are instrumental in affecting economic policies between the two countries. When in the early 1990s the U.S. dollar fell dramatically against the Japanese yen, the balance of trade shifted in favor of the United States because prices of Japanese products skyrocketed while American-made products became much more affordable in Japan.

	Exports to Japan	Imports from Japan	U.S. balance with Japan	Yen/$
1985	22.1	65.7	−43.5	238.5
1986	26.4	80.8	−54.4	168.4
1987	27.6	84.6	−56.9	144.6
1988	37.2	89.8	−52.6	128.2
1989	43.9	93.5	−49.7	138.1
1990	47.8	90.4	−42.6	145.0
1991	47.2	92.3	−45.0	134.6
1992	46.9	97.4	−50.5	126.8
1993	46.7	107.2	−60.5	111.1
1994	51.8	119.1	−67.3	112.9
1995	63.1	123.5	−60.3	94.0
1996	67.6	115.2	−47.6	108.8

balance sheet   A published statement of a company's financial position at a specific time, usually at the end of the **accounting period.**

Also called a *statement of financial position*, the balance sheet presents a picture of the company's resources, the amount it owes its creditors, and the **owners'** or **shareholders' equity.** The balance sheet categorizes the company's **assets, liabilities,** and **equity** according to the fundamental **accounting equation:**

$$\text{Assets} = \text{liabilities} + \text{shareholders' equity}$$

The following categorization is typical for companies subscribing to SEC regulations and **generally accepted accounting principles (GAAP):**

CONSOLIDATED BALANCE SHEETS
(In millions except for per-share amounts)

	December 31	
	Year 2	Year 1
Assets		
Current assets		
Cash and cash equivalents		
Accounts receivable		
Inventories		
Marketable securities		
Prepaid expenses		
Total current assets		
Property, plant, and equipment		
Land		
Buildings and improvements		
Fixtures and equipment		
Transportation equipment		
Operating and other assets		
Land held for development		
Investments in leases, etc.		
Software, goodwill, and other intangibles		
Total operating assets		
Total assets		
Liabilities and stockholders' equity		
Current liabilities		
Accounts payable		
Accrued liabilities		
Salaries		
Other		
Accrued federal and state income taxes		
Current portion of long-term debt		
Deferred revenue		
Obligations under capital leases due within one year		

	December 31	
	Year 2	**Year 1**
Total current liabilities		
Long-term debt		
Long-term obligations under capital leases		
Deferred income taxes		
Shareholders' equity		
Preferred stock A		
Preferred stock B		
Common stock A		
Common stock B		
Additional paid-in capital		
Retained earnings		
Total shareholders' equity		
Total liabilities and shareholders' equity		

balanced scorecard   A term developed by Kaplan and Norton (1996) to designate both a systematic way of measuring an organization's performance and a means of translating strategy and vision into action.

Beginning in 1990, Kaplan and Norton participated in meetings with representatives from 12 major companies—Advanced Micro Devices, American Standard, Apple Computer, BellSouth, CIGNA, Conner Peripherals, Cray Research, DuPont, Electronic Data Systems, General Electric, Hewlett-Packard, and Shell Canada—to evaluate the traditional measures of performance, namely, the financial summaries that companies present to shareholders in ***annual reports*** and other communications. Those financial reports, however, measure only the company's performance in the past, not its future direction. Because of the pressures on companies to learn to compete in an increasingly technological age, the authors propose a *balanced scorecard* that measures, in addition to the traditional financial reports, a company's internal business processes, its ability to achieve its vision by learning and growing, and its appearance to its customers. More than a measurement process, however, the balanced scorecard, according to the authors, can enable an organization to create a responsive, transformative management system (Kaplan and Norton 1996, 7–19).

balloon   A large lump-sum payment at the end of the period covered by a mortgage that has over its life required a lower repayment of the debt.

Because of its lower repayment schedule, such mortgages are popular among young home buyers and business entrepreneurs. Presumably, after several years their salaries will increase, and they will be able to handle larger mortgage payments. A mortgage with a balloon payment at the end either does not amortize the loan or does so only partially by paying off the interest owed.

bandwagon effect   A tendency to want to join the newest and most visible fad, social cause, or political action out of fear of being left behind rather than out of principled commitment to the effort.

Many companies successfully resisted the bandwagon effect that accompanied recent trends such as ***downsizing*** and installing extensive information management systems. This is not to imply that such solutions are worthless, but only that managers who jump to them without considering alternatives are probably falling prey to bandwagon appeals that are designed to strike fear in the faint of heart.

bandwidth　In communications, the frequency range of transmitted data that various channels such as coaxial wire, ISDN lines, and fiber-optic cables can conduct.

Frequencies are measured in units of hertz (Hz), or one complete cycle of an electromagnetic wave. So-called narrowband channels, such as those used for telegraph messages, transmit between 45 and 150 *bits* of data per second and range below 300 Hz. Voice-grade bandwidth is typical for traditional telephone lines, which carry some 1,800 bits per second (or more if they are fax lines). But the high-frequency requirements of modern technology, such as high-resolution images used in teleconferencing, create the need for much wider bands that can transmit billions of pieces of data per second.

Bandwidth has been described as the number of lanes on the Internet highway: The wider the lane, the faster the traffic can flow. The image offers only limited help, however. More important is the capacity of broadband channels to transmit various *kinds* of data, not just more of one type of data. Because a broadband channel can carry not only data but also voice and video, it is an essential element in communications where complex images need to be transmitted.

Bank for International Settlements (BIS)　A consortium bank founded at the Hague Conference in 1930 "to promote the cooperation of central banks and to provide additional facilities for international financial operations."

Undertaking its duties on May 17, 1930, the BIS is the world's oldest international financial organization. Originally responsible for coordination of the collection and rescheduling of German reparations after World War I, it has conducted international *transactions* involving the European Payments Union (later the European Monetary Agreement, or EMA, which was disbanded in 1972), the European Coal and Steel Community, the *International Monetary Fund* (**IMF**), and other organizations. It now functions as the primary forum for international monetary cooperation. Its depositors are not individuals, but the *central banks* of the 32 member nations as well as over 100 other banks and international financial institutions, whose combined deposits in March 1996 exceeded $97 billion, approximately 7 percent of the world's foreign exchange reserves.

The BIS has survived as sort of an international financial ombudsman, a central bank for the central banks of its member nations. With consensus approval from those banks, the BIS sets standards for the global banking system.

In the late 1980s, the BIS recognized that overextended loan portfolios had resulted in the deterioration of *capital* ratios of banks throughout the world. In 1988, it sought to correct this disruption by issuing minimum standards for the capital/asset ratios of banks having significant operations outside their local *markets.* Those guidelines stated that by January 1, 1993, banks had to have a minimum ratio of capital to assets of 8 percent. Confirmed by the U.S. *comptroller* of the currency, those guidelines helped slow U.S. bank lending to businesses and consumers.

Currently the BIS board comprises representatives from 11 countries: Belgium, Canada, France, Germany, Italy, Japan, the Netherlands, Sweden, Switzerland, the United Kingdom, and the United States.

The address is Bank for International Settlements, Centralbahnplatz 2, CH-4002 Basle, Switzerland. Cable INTERBANK. Telephone (061) 280 80 80. Telex 962 487 biz ch. Telefax (061) 280 91 00 and (061) 280 81 00. The Internet address is http://www.bis.org.

banker's acceptance (BA)   A time draft countersigned, or accepted, by a bank.

BAs are used in the import-export trade to provide evidence that a bank has extended *credit,* usually as a *letter of credit* (*L/C*). BAs take one of two forms:

- *Documentary banker's acceptances* depend on the importer's credit to complete the sale. After the product is shipped, the sale is completed, and the exporter can sell the receivable at a discount to a bank.
- *Clean banker's acceptances* require that the exporter provide security for the issuing of credit. The importer or buyer provides no collateral.

BAs can be discounted and sold in the secondary *bond* market, where they have become popular investments, in part because they are readily negotiable and because they are not recorded on the bank's *balance sheet.* Thirteen states, including New York, however, prohibit local governments from investing in banker's acceptances, as well as money market funds and commercial paper (Roy 1997).

bankruptcy   A formal and legal declaration of financial insolvency, either by an individual or by an organization.

After the declaration is approved and all *accounts receivable* are collected, the courts order a payoff of business debts, followed by a liquidation of the remaining *assets,* which are often divided among the individual's or the company's creditors. In the case of some *partnerships,* the liquidation applies only to the assets of the company, not to the assets held by individual partners; in other cases, each partner may be held liable for the debts of other participants. Companies declaring bankruptcy file under either *Chapter 7* or *Chapter 11* proceedings.

As *Federal Reserve* chairman Alan Greenspan lamented to the Banking Committee of the House of Representatives in March 1997, bankruptcies declared in 1996 by U.S. individuals exceeded one million for the first time, a rise of 27 percent over the previous year's high. Personal bankruptcies have lost the taint of shame, and today many Americans consider the action merely a convenient, albeit public, way of dispensing with high credit card debts. They opt for the bankruptcy declaration rather than some other acceptable repayment plan, which may be less drastic and permanent.

Among U.S. businesses, over 53,000 declared bankruptcy in 1996. Filings under Chapter 7 increased 29 percent over those in 1995, whereas bankruptcies under Chapter 11 declined by 8 percent (Ahern and Stohr 1997).

bar code   A group of alternating bars and spaces representing encoded information, usually printed not only on product labels, but also on parts, containers, subassemblies and other elements of a product.

Bar codes are read by electronic scanners, which input the data into a computer system. The database keeps track of inventories, reorders, customer profiles, sales personnel, and other items of interest to marketers and managers.

EXAMPLE: A. O. Smith Corporation in Barrie, Ontario, supplies rear axle assemblies and engine-cradle modules to the Chrysler plant in nearby Bramalea. To perfect its *just-in-time* (*JIT*) inventory system, A. O. Smith insists on bar-coding practically all its parts. The bar codes record not only *inventory* data, but also information about when the part was constructed, which worker put it together, and who purchased it. Thus, if Chrysler finds a defective part and issues a recall, the Smith Corporation can pinpoint every detail of its production (Keenan 1995).

barrier to entry   Any factor, tangible or intangible, that prevents or deters a company from entering an industry or *market.*

Because it increases the costs or complexity of entering a new market or industry, a barrier to entry has an impact on a company's competitive strategy. Such barriers can come from a number of sources. Product *differentiation,* such as *brand* recognition and loyalty, may be prohibitively costly or time-consuming for a new entrant to overcome. *Economies of scale* and high switching costs for retooling equipment or retraining employees can force new entrants to incur higher costs than existing competitors that produce in large quantities and have well-trained workforces. Companies that seek to enter new markets often have difficulty gaining access to *distribution channels* (for example, they may not be able to secure shelf space). Relationships with key suppliers, proprietary technology, and government restrictions may further deter a company from undertaking new ventures.

Many companies aggressively create and maintain barriers to entry in order to secure the market for themselves. Soft drink companies, such as Coca-Cola and Pepsi, commit significant *revenue* to product differentiation. As a result, a potential new entrant would have to spend inordinate amounts on *advertising* in order to create a *brand image* that would draw customers away from Coke and Pepsi. Because of strong barriers to entry, the two soft drink companies have dominated the market and continue to discourage new competitors.

If an established company reacts to possible entrants by slashing prices on its products or increasing production, it may be successful in deterring upstarts. Or if the industry as a whole is experiencing a slow period, new competitors are unlikely to want to take their chances until conditions improve.

EXAMPLE: In early 1997, a group of nine small airlines, led by Frontier, formed the Air Carrier Association of America (ACAA) to combat the barriers to entry that they assert United Airlines has established to deter competition. According to executives at Frontier, United had dumped a large number of cheap seats on flights in and out of Denver's Stapleton Airport, offered contracts to business travelers, and engaged in unfair competition. United denied the charges (Williamson 1997).

*See also **barrier to exit.***

barrier to exit   Any factor that discourages a company from leaving an area of business or discontinuing a product line or operation.

Barriers to exit, like *barriers to entry,* have a significant effect on a company's strategy and position. If a company is considering a large *investment* in a new plant that promises a large increase in *market share,* it must consider the barriers to exit that competitors will face as the plant comes on line and begins to affect their market share. If those barriers are high, competitors are likely to resort to price cuts to maintain their share of the *market.* If their plants are old and fully depreciated, competitors may be prepared to lower prices enough only to cover *variable costs.* But those prices might remain artificially low for some time, thus keeping the company's new plant from becoming profitable.

Many barriers to exit originally served as barriers to entry. Investments in large-capacity factories, heavy *advertising* to build *brand* image or cultivate loyalty, and the development of an extensive distribution center are costly for any company to initiate, but having once undertaken them, the company may look upon them as reasons for staying in the business. Proponents of this line of reasoning find the notion of *sunk costs* hard to swallow. It is difficult, even under the best of circumstances, to walk away from such heavy investments in plants, technologies, and employees.

Barron's Confidence Index   A list of corporate *bond yields* published weekly by *Barron's*.

The index calculates the yields on ten top-grade *bonds* as a ratio to the Dow Jones average of 40 bonds. Using this ratio as a measure of confidence in the economy, investors who are worried will buy high-quality bonds with lower yields; those who feel secure about the economy will buy riskier bonds with higher yields. The spread as measured by Barron's Confidence Index indicates whether general economic optimism or pessimism dominates the investing community.

basis points   Interest charges used to measure the market in corporate *bonds.*

One hundred basis points equal one percentage point of interest. When speaking of a particular bond, issuers and traders use the phrase "spread over Treasuries" to contrast its rate against that earned or charged by a U.S. Treasury security of comparable maturity. Companies using municipal revenue bonds pay interest determined by basis points plus or minus interest percentages against the *prime rate.*

baud   A measure of the speed of data transmission equal to one *bit* per second.

Named for Emile Baudot, a French scientist who experimented in communications and whom Negroponte (1995, 22) calls the Morse of telex, the term *baud* has come to be widely used, thanks to the preponderance of the *modem* and *e-mail.* Converting data bits into wavelengths and back again, the modem has become an indispensable tool of the modern office. It operates at various speeds, anywhere from 2,400 baud to 57,600 baud (or bits per second), but as Negroponte (1995, 22–23) points out, the technology is still in infant stages. Futurists predict that with increased *bandwidth* and improved technology, a typical household or business might receive thousands, if not millions, of television signals, complex video and audio communications, and digitized information of encyclopedic proportions.

bear hug   Slang term for a corporate takeover.

bearer bond   Securities not registered to any particular holder but taken as evidence of ownership for anyone who happens to possess them.

Possession is all of the law, in this case, and whoever bears the bond receives the interest. Although once commonly used in the U.S. financial system because many investors found them more attractive, bearer bonds have now largely been replaced by registered bonds.

beginning inventory   The merchandise on hand at the start of an *accounting period.*

See also *ending inventory.*

behavioral response   A consumer's reactions—psychological, physical, and monetary—to *marketing* activities and campaigns.

When consumers purchase the advertised product, marketers reach their ultimate goal. But much of marketing has other strategic intentions such as generating awareness about an item, creating or changing attitudes about a particular **brand,** altering or meeting the criteria that consumers have to decide what to buy, changing and shaping attitudes, and promoting an intention to buy. **Image advertising,** for instance, seeks to shape positive feelings or dispositions about a product or **market.** Many stages precede the actual act of buying, and strategic marketing actions are directed toward these steps as well as toward the purchase itself.

behavioral segmentation   Subdivision of the **market** according to consumer behavior variables: user status, **brand** loyalty, product usage, benefits sought, usage occasions, lifestyle, social class, economic standing, and the like.

Although *descriptive* variables such as age, gender, income, and geographical location are useful in dividing markets into homogeneous groups, they do not give marketers much insight into consumer motivation. Behavioral variables are thus a much more powerful tool for segmenting markets.

Benefit segmentation, for instance, focuses on the primary benefits that consumers seek in a product. The marketer analyzes information about consumer desires and translates that information into **marketing** programs that will satisfy those desires. Although consumers look for as many benefits as possible from the products they buy, they make many of their choices on the basis of a single value, which will vary depending on the product. The person who looks for durability in blue jeans, for instance, may seek the lowest price in a fax machine, yet spare no expense in purchasing a personal computer.

See also **market segmentation; undifferentiated marketing.** *Compare to* **demographic segmentation; preference segmentation; psychographic segmentation; volume segmentation.**

bellwether   A security that the market regards as an indicator of future trends.

Bellwether stocks are widely held by institutional investors who exercise substantial control over mutual funds, stock market prices, and the movement of stock indexes. For years Sears was considered a bellwether stock of the retail products industry, but it has largely been replaced by Wal-Mart. AT&T, IBM, and General Electric, despite occasional fluctuations, command close scrutiny as bellwether performers. Long considered a bellwether security in the **bond** market, the U.S. Treasury 20-year bond has been frequently tied to movements in **interest rates.**

The term *bellwether* derives from the age-old practice of hanging a bell around the neck of a *wether,* or male sheep, which led the flock and served as a point of reference for the shepherd.

benchmarking   A process in which an organization assesses its current business practices by comparing them with the *best practices* of other organizations.

The concept of benchmarking is derived from the mark that surveyors placed or chiseled onto the side of a building or other stationary structure to indicate a reference point in tidal fluctuations. The mark was shaped like a partial arrow:

7

As this derivation suggests, the main purpose of benchmarking is to offer a point of reference, a measurement of fluctuation against a fixed and solid structure. This fundamental meaning is captured by the International Benchmarking Clearinghouse (IBC) Design Steering Committee of the American Productivity and Quality Center (APQC):

> Benchmarking is a systematic and continuous measurement process; a process of continuously measuring and comparing an organization's business processes against business process leaders anywhere in the world to gain information which will help the organization take action to improve its performance. (*Planning* 1992, 4)

The key phrase in this definition is "systematic and continuous measurement." While comparative performance measures are used to stimulate improved process performance, true benchmarking has nothing to do with mere copying.

It is generally acknowledged that effective benchmarking follows four basic steps: plan, do, check, and act. Planning what types of processes should be studied as well as which companies should be analyzed is followed by intensive primary and secondary research. Checking the results of the research and its applicability leads inevitably to the implementation of improved business processes.

Berne Convention (for the Protection of Literary and Artistic Works) of 1886 An international agreement, originally signed in 1886 and currently initialed by 80 countries, to safeguard *copyrights* of *intellectual property.*

The oldest international treaty of its kind, the Berne Convention established an agreement among member countries to grant the same protection to foreign authors that those countries grant to their own nationals. The protection covers literary and artistic creations such as novels, plays, music, fine art, motion pictures, and video games. Minimum standards include rights for authors (or their executors) to permit or prohibit copying or reproduction of their works in any manner or form for at least 50 years beyond the date of their deaths.

The terms of the convention are administered by the World Intellectual Property Organization (WIPO; Presner 1991).

best effort A sale or purchase of stock in which the underwriter pledges to seek the best price possible for the shares in question.

Best effort sales occur primarily in initial public offerings (IPOs; see *going public*) because of the risks and delays that such an arrangement brings to the issuing company. The more popular form of *underwriting* agreement is a *firm commitment* underwriting, whereby the underwriter buys all the offering shares and then resells them to the public. From the issuing company's perspective, this is clearly the less risky choice.

best execution The principle widely adopted by the *Securities and Exchange Commission (SEC)*, brokerage firms, and traders that investors should receive the highest price possible for securities they sell and the lowest price possible for those they buy.

Despite recent rulings from the SEC, stock traders disagree on the precise application of this principle, and it is frequently the case that an investor receives a buy or sell order from one stock exchange that differs markedly from that offered by another exchange. The **New York Stock Exchange** (**NYSE**), for instance, recently challenged the Cincinnati and Boston exchanges for favoring large brokerage firms over small investors (Eaton 1997).

beta   A measure of a particular stock or mutual fund's risk, as determined by comparing its return over an extended period with the return of the market as a whole, usually measured by Standard & Poor's 500 Composite Index or the Dow Jones 30 Industrials.

A perfect correlation or beta (β) between a stock and, say, the S&P 500 Index is 1.0: That is, for every dollar of the index's return, the security will rise by the same amount. If a stock has a beta of 2.0, it will rise at a rate twice that of the market; conversely, if it has a beta of 0.5, it will go up only half as fast. A security with a beta of 0 carries a return independent of the market and thus represents a relatively risk-free *investment.* An example is a Treasury bill.

Plotting on a graph the market return for Company X against the total market's return, we can perform a straight *regression analysis* and determine an average as represented by a line intersecting the two axes:

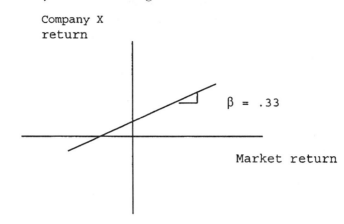

The security's beta is simply the slope of the line. In this example, a beta of 0.33 indicates that the stock of Company X will rise at a rate of only one third that of the market as a whole (Brealey and Myers 1991, pp. 183–186).

The betas of most securities fluctuate only slightly. However, betas do not represent a sure approach to estimating volatility: After all, a change of direction or the rise of new competitors can dramatically alter a company's stability and thus affect its stock's market risk.

See also **alpha.**

better-off test   An evaluation of the contributions that a newly acquired business unit brings to the parent company.

The better-off test stipulates that the new unit must either gain a significant *competitive advantage* for itself through its association with the parent company or offer a competitive advantage to the parent corporation.

See also **industry attractiveness test.**

Big Six   Colloquial name for the six largest CPA firms in the United States, all of which have recently taken on significant international identities.

The rankings of the accounting companies are relative and change over time, depending on criteria such as the number of accounts, *revenues,* or the number of employees. In alphabetical order, the Big Six are:

- Arthur Andersen & Company (Geneva and Chicago)
- Coopers & Lybrand LLP (New York)
- Deloitte & Touche LLP (New York)
- Ernst & Young LLP (New York)
- KPMG Peat Marwick (Amsterdam and New York)
- Price Waterhouse (London and New York)

Several *mergers* have been recently proposed but then annulled, signaling potential for consolidation in the future.

bill of lading An official document, issued by a carrier, that details the contractual terms such as time and place of receipt, for the delivery of goods.

Transfer of the bill to the recipient also transfers title to the goods.

bill of material (BOM) A list of all the parts, subassemblies, raw materials, and intermediates used to make a product.

Managers use BOMs to determine which items and what quantities need to be purchased as well as to set production schedules. In some cases, BOMs serve as purchasing requisitions.

See also materials requirements planning, (MRP).

bit An abbreviation for *binary digits*, the basic unit of information that computers encode as either an *on* (1) or an *off* (0).

Each letter of the alphabet, for instance, is designated by a unique string of eight ones and zeros. The letter *A*, for example, is encoded as 11000001, a sequence that is called a *byte* (for *binary digit eight*). Because computers rely on the binary system of ones and zeros, peculiarities in nomenclature arise: A kilobit (kb), for example, is not 1,000 bits, but 1,024 bits (2^{10}).

Computer *modems* are classified by *baud* rates, the number of bits of data they can transmit per second. The standard modem today, for instance, transmits information at the rate of 28.8 kbps (although that number is multiplied by a factor of 8 if the modem is transmitting *bytes* of information).

blackbirds Colloquial term for products or services announced by a powerful company or by the dominant company in an industry, which seeks to scare away potential competitors.

Real or imagined, blackbird products can act as strong deterrents to new competitors, despite the provisions of the Sherman Antitrust Act. A company may have no plans to offer such a product or service; nonetheless, it starts the rumor in the hope of scaring away small companies from its feast. Although an unethical practice, it may work once or twice; however, if the company continues to create blackbirds, it will soon lose credibility with its customers and lay a goose egg (suggested by a problem proposed on roscoe.law.harvard.edu/courses/techseminar96/antitrust/synopses/boundaries.html).

See also antitrust legislation; barrier to entry.

blank check offering   The initial public offering (IPO; see *going public*) of a *shell company,* one that has no operating structure and no *assets.*

The public offering usually promises that funds will be invested in acquiring equity interests in solid, high-growth companies, both start-ups and established businesses. But beyond that, the prospectus offers few details, and investors rely entirely on the word of the shell company's officers and the broker promoting the sale. Although the *Securities and Exchange Commission* (*SEC*) requires that the organization provide potential investors with information about company officers' integrity and current or past legal entanglements, the vagueness of the IPO easily leads to scams by unscrupulous brokers or people seeking to create a front for tax evasion.

Because of the frequent abuse, blank check IPOs developed a reputation for untrustworthy or unsavory dealings. Several states enacted legislation to prohibit them entirely, and the Securities and Exchange Commission (SEC) tightened regulations in ways that have, for all practical purposes, strangled blank check offerings.

blanket purchase order   A contract, usually good for one year, that may be used to buy an array of items carried by a distributor, such as office supplies or repair parts.

A blanket purchase order reduces the number of individual POs and often achieves a better price and more prompt delivery of goods.

bleed ad   An illustration or photograph reproduced in an advertisement so that it covers the entire page without leaving a margin.

Most magazines charge a premium for bleeding photographs since the process requires using printing plates larger than normal. Bleed ads allow an art director greater flexibility and space in designing the ad.

blind pool offering   A stock offering from a shell company, the prospectus of which, as a minimum, identifies the industry in which company officers will invest the *capital* received from the initial public offering (IPO; see *going public*).

In this respect, blind pools are the stock market equivalent of many private placement *limited partnerships.* And like *blank check offerings,* blind pools carry huge risks involved with acquiring equity shares and controlling interest in potentially high-return, small private companies. Unlike their unsavory counterparts, however, most blind pools are legitimate and, if properly constructed, help small companies finance large projects or business *acquisitions.*

A closely held company, for example, may wish to expand into new product lines by acquiring a business that already does this work well. Because the acquiring company already carries a full debt load, its owners do not want to make the company go public. Their solution is to form New Corporation, which will have no assets, and initiate an exempt IPO with a private placement. They write the prospectus to show that the IPO is intended strictly to raise *capital* for New Corporation to acquire the business. If the company or its underwriter can *float* the issue, the owners can use any capital raised in order to make the acquisition in the name of the new entity.

blue chip   A *common stock* with a long history of *dividend* payments and steady earnings.

In poker, blue chips have the highest value. In the stock market, blue-chip stocks are relatively low-risk issues that provide a steady stream of income; thus, they are favorites of long-term investors and custodians of mutual funds.

Although the companies that belong to this august group fall in and out of public favor from time to time, they generally represent prudent *investments* over the long haul. Companies currently considered blue chip include AT&T, General Electric, General Motors, and IBM.

body copy   The text of an advertisement, excluding headlines, logos, and captions.

The body copy should present the advertisement's sales message immediately to the intended audience. Although the headline may seek to startle, puzzle, or shock the reader, the body copy itself needs to explain the benefits of the company's product or service as succinctly as possible. Body copy is often subtle rather than aggressively direct, but if it is vague or obscure, it is unlikely to attract the target audience.

BOM   *See bill of material*

bona fide occupational qualifications (BFOQs)   Lawful discrimination in the form of specific requirements for particular jobs that the Equal Employment Opportunity Commission (EEOC) allows a company to issue.

bond   A debt obligation of a company, a government body, or other organization to pay a specified amount on a given date.

The bond is said to *mature* at the date specified, and the issuer pays the bondholder the full amount of the bond's *face value* (see *par value*). Interest-bearing bonds require that the issuer pay the bondholder interest on specific dates, usually semiannually.

Zero-coupon bonds, such as U.S. savings bonds, are issued at a discount. That is, the bondholder buys the bond at less than face value. Although bondholders do not receive any money from zero-coupon bonds until maturity, the IRS requires that each year they report as taxable income the amount of interest they would have collected.

Companies issue bonds to raise *capital.* From a corporate point of view, a bond issue has at least one advantage over a stock issue: The interest that corporations pay to bondholders is tax deductible, whereas stock *dividends* are not. When a company liquidates, bondholders are entitled to collect what they are owed before common or preferred shareholders, but they rank below secured lenders.

Bonds appear as part of *long-term liability* on a company's *balance sheet.* They adversely affect the *debt-to-equity ratio,* among other key measures of performance.

A number of organizations rate bonds for their creditworthiness. The best known of these independent evaluators is Moody's Investors Service, which uses a graduated scale of Aaa to C3 based on such factors as the bond issuer's ability to make timely payments, the strength of the enterprise, and the long-term value of the project being undertaken. In general, a bond rated by Moody's as Baa3 or higher can be considered investment grade. So-called junk bonds are rated Ba or lower at Moody's (Klott 1987, 78; U.S. Senate 1997).

bond buyback   A company's purchase of its own publicly traded bonds at a discount from the market price.

A company may use this strategy when market *interest rates* are rapidly rising, thus causing a decline in bond prices.

bond valuation   The calculation of a bond's true value by determining the *present value* of the bond's expected future *cash flows* and the *rate of return* that investors require as indicated by what they could receive with a comparable *in-vestment.*

Bond valuation requires knowledge of three key measures: (1) the amount of cash flow the investor will receive (equal to the total of the bond's periodic interest payments and its *face value* at maturity), (2) the date the bond matures, and (3) the investors' required rate of return.

bond yield   The return an investor receives on the original bond *investment.*

Yield is a function of four factors: *coupon interest rate, face value* (see *par value*), *market valuation,* and *maturity date.*

A bond issuer states that a bond will pay a set amount of interest each year, usually in two equal payments. The coupon interest rate is calculated by dividing these annual payments by the face, or par, value of the bond (usually $1,000). A bond that makes annual interest payments of $160, for example, carries a coupon rate of 16 percent ($160/$1,000 = 0.16). A bond's market value is determined by several factors such as the date of issue, the coupon interest rate, current market rates, market timing, and call provisions.

There are two types of bond yield:

- *Current* (or *simple*) *yield* fluctuates according to the bond's market price. It represents the interest a bond pays at a particular moment in time, as determined by the following formula:

$$\text{Current yield} = \frac{\text{coupon interest payment}}{\text{market price of bond}}$$

If a bond is selling for $877.60, for instance, and makes a coupon payment of $80 per bond, its current yield is

$$\frac{\$80}{\$877.60} = 0.091, \text{ or } 9.1\%$$

As long as the price of the bond remains the same, it will pay investors a yield of 9.1 percent. If, however, the price falls while the coupon interest rate remains steady, the yield increases. Say the bond price declines to $700. In that case, the current yield becomes

$$\frac{\$80}{\$700} = 0.1143, \text{ or } 11.4\%$$

Current yield, then, rises as bond prices fall. It drops when bond prices climb.

- *Yield to maturity* involves a more complicated calculation that recognizes three key factors: (1) the annual interest received, (2) the difference between the current security price and its maturity value, and (3) the number of years to maturity. This formula is expressed as follows:

$$\text{Yield to maturity} = \frac{\text{interest} + \dfrac{\text{par value} - \text{market value}}{\text{number of periods}}}{0.6 \,(\text{market value}) + 0.4 \,(\text{par value})}$$

(The 60 percent and 40 percent factors in the denominator adjust for slight differences from mathematical averaging over time.)

If a particular security, set to mature in six periods, has a coupon interest payment of $150,000, a *par value* of $2 million, and a *market value* of $1,295,923, its yield to maturity can be calculated as follows:

$$YTM = \frac{\$150,000 + \dfrac{\$2,000,000 - \$1,295,923}{6}}{0.6(\$1,295,293) + 0.4(\$2,000,000)}$$

$$= \frac{\$267,346}{\$1,577,554}$$

$$= 0.16946, \text{ or } 16.95 \text{ percent}$$

Jordan & Jordan (40 Exchange Place, New York, NY 10005) now provides a Web page at http://www.jandj.com/jordan/bondyeld.htm where bondholders can request information about bond yields. By entering the settlement date, the maturity date, and the price as a percentage of par value, a user can request that the service calculate the bond yield.

Another Web site, http://www.oir.com/sample/tables/ctgb.htm, provides bond yield correlations for eight countries during the past 20 trading sessions. The countries surveyed are the United States, Canada, Germany, France, the United Kingdom, Italy, Spain, and Japan.

book value (1)   The amount shown for an *asset* on a *balance sheet.*
The original cost of an item largely determines book value, which differs, often dramatically, from the *market value* of the item. The book value of a three-year-old delivery truck, for instance, may be $10,000, although the truck, when new, cost the company $25,000. Depreciated over three years at $5,000 annually, the truck has an *accumulated depreciation* of $15,000. The same truck may have a market value of $8,000, depending on its condition and the demand for it.

book value (2)   The amount shown as *stockholders' equity* on a *balance sheet.*
Book value frequently becomes the starting point for negotiating the price for the purchase or sale of a *privately held company.* It is also used in the calculation of *book value per share.*

book value (3)   The *net assets* of a company's securities or other properties.
Net assets are calculated according to the following formula:

$$NA = TA - IA - L$$

where: NA = Net assets
TA = Total assets
IA = Intangible assets such as patents, copyrights, and goodwill
L = Current and long-term liabilities.

See also net asset value (NAV).

book value per share   The *assets* of a company divided among its owners of *common stock.*
Book value per share indicates what each share of common stock is worth at any given point in time. The formula for calculating book value per share takes into ac-

count the amount a company would have to pay out if it paid all preferred *dividends* and liquidated all its preferred shares:

Book value per share =

$$\frac{\text{stockholders' equity} - (\text{preferred dividends} + \text{liquidation of preferred stocks})}{\text{common shares outstanding}}$$

In using this formula, it is important to compute an accurate value for the liquidation value of *preferred stock.* Some companies give holders of preferred stock liquidation premiums that exceed the par value of the preferred shares. Those premiums can significantly affect the *book value* of the common stock.

EXAMPLE: A company wishes to calculate the book value of its common stock. To do so, it collects the following data:

Total stockholders' equity		$10,000,000
Preferred stock		
Number of shares	200,000	
Dividend rate	8%	
Par value of each share	$20.00	
Total par value (200,000 × $20)		$ 4,000,000
Preferred dividend ($4,000,000 × 8%)		$ 320,000
Liquidation value per share	$25.00	
Total liquidation value (200,000 × $25)		$ 5,000,000
Common stock		
Number of shares	100,000	
Par value	$40.00	

The book value of the common stock is:

$$\text{Book value} = \frac{\$10,000,000 - (\$5,000,000 + \$320,000)}{100,000}$$

$$= \$46.80$$

In this example, the common stock's book value exceeds its *par value.*
    Book value can also be calculated for preferred stock:

Book value (preferred stock) =

$$\frac{\text{liquidation value (preferred stock)} + \text{preferred dividend}}{\text{preferred shares outstanding}}$$

With data from the preceding example, the per-share book value of preferred stock is:

$$\frac{\$5,000,000 + \$320,000}{200,000} = \$26.60$$

By comparing book value per share with market price per share, financial analysts can determine how the stock market views a company. Usually the market price, which represents what current traders are willing to spend for the stock, is *higher* than its book value. If, however, the book value per share exceeds the market price, the difference will present a good measure of just how low an opinion investors have of the company's stock.

bookkeeping   The recording of a company's financial **transactions** in journals and ledgers called *books of account.*

The most common form of bookkeeping occurs in a *T-account* format, so called because of its resemblance to the letter *T.* That is, the bookkeeper performs a *double entry,* recording both the **debit** and the **credit:**

Account Name	
Debit (Dr.)	**Credit (Cr.)**

Traditionally, the *left* side of the T-account is the place to record debits, such as cash receipts, whereas the *right* side is reserved for credits such as cash payments. Occasionally, the abbreviations *Dr.* (from the Latin word *debere,* "to owe") and *Cr.* (from Latin *credere,* "to entrust") are used to designate the left and right sides of a T-account.

Entries on the debit side of an account increase an **asset** or expense, while decreasing **liabilities, equity** (or net worth), and **revenues.** When cash is received, for example, it is debited to the Cash Account, an asset. Similarly, when goods that have been sold are returned, the entry will debit sales.

On the right side appear transactions indicating where cash receipts came from—for example, bank loans, **accounts receivable,** and the sale of **common stock.** In those instances, the amount equal to the cash received is credited to Bank Loans Payable (thereby increasing a liability), Accounts Receivable (thereby reducing an asset), or Common Stock Outstanding (thereby increasing net worth).

All books of account, regardless of the type of company or use of a computer, consist of three or more journals (Cash Receipts, Cash Disbursements, and General Journal are the most common) in which transactions are entered, and a general ledger, where the monthly totals from the journals are posted. A company may use many subledgers and a variety of journals, but almost every company, no matter its size or accounting system, has need to record cash receipts and disbursements, as well as to make entries in a general journal.

See also **credit; debit.**

borrowing base   **Assets** used by a company, **partnership,** or individual entrepreneur as collateral to secure short-term **working capital** loans from banks or other lenders.

A borrowing base comprises qualified **accounts receivable** (normally less than 90 days old) and **inventory** that can be sold readily. Most lenders will not include in the borrowing base any work in process or special materials purchased to customer order. Although the ratios vary with the nature of the business, the financial strength of the organization, and the disposition of the lender (for example, the degree to which the lender is averse to risk), companies may be able to borrow up to 85 percent of qualified receivables and up to 50 percent of shelf-item parts and raw materials, as well as finished goods ready for sale. The following table demonstrates how a borrowing base works:

	Borrowing base	Factor	Loan
Qualified accounts receivable	$2,000	85%	$1,700
Inventory of raw materials and parts	1,000	20%	200
Inventory of finished goods	1,500	50%	750
Maximum short-term loan			$2,650

bottleneck   That portion of a process, whether an individual task or a machine, which limits or determines the *capacity* and speed of the entire process.

If workers at every stage of an assembly line could handle the same number of items in the same amount of time, there would be no bottlenecks as long as the line kept moving. However, in a TV assembly operation, for example, those in charge of producing the receivers can assemble 40 sets an hour, whereas those workers responsible for making the TV cabinets can produce only 20 an hour. Because every set must have a cabinet, the entire process is limited to 20 sets an hour. The cabinet shop is the bottleneck.

To solve the problem and remove the bottleneck, managers might elect to reduce the size of the set production staff by 50 percent or increase the number of cabinetmakers by 100 percent, thereby doubling production. Other alternatives involve asking cabinetmakers to work overtime, subcontracting the extra work to a separate group of cabinetmakers, or redesigning the product so that sets do not need such elaborate cabinets.

Many managers (e.g., see Toth 1993) recommend various tools such as *flowcharts, cause-and-effect diagrams,* and **Pareto charts** to help identify where and why the bottlenecks occur, as well as what to do about them.

Bourse   French for *purse,* the English cognate; now the name for the French stock market centered in Paris, as well as stock markets in other EC countries.

brand   A name, logo, or symbol that differentiates a product or a line of products from all others in a **market.**

Branding offers owners and marketers numerous benefits. By differentiating products, brands can help create promotions and **advertising** campaigns designed around the specific features of the product.

Branding includes other kinds of identification:

- *Corporate brands* arose in the late nineteenth century and helped some large businesses become household words: General Electric, Ford Motor Company, American Telephone & Telegraph, and Coca-Cola are brand names people everywhere now recognize. And for good reason: AT&T leads the list of companies that spend the most on advertising their brands. Each year AT&T earmarks close to a half billion dollars to advertise its name and products.

- *Generic brands* constitute the "other." Cheaper and blander, the no-name brand appeals to the customer who wants a quick meal rather than a dinner or a hair soap rather than a luxury shampoo. In 1982, a young executive at Star Markets in Boston named Tom Stemberg developed the first line of generic foods sold in America (it was canned tuna). Although Star Markets' parent, the Jewel Companies of Chicago, had grave doubts about the venture, Stemberg's generic brands became overnight successes with customers. (Stemberg, by the way, went on to found Staples, the office supply store, and now serves as its CEO. Profiting from the experience at Star, Stemberg now markets tons of paper clips, notepads, and pencils under the Staples brand.)

See also **brand awareness; brand extension; brand mark; brand name.**

brand awareness   In marketing, a measure of consumers' knowledge that a particular **brand** exists.

Most marketing professionals consider brand awareness the first step in making a sale. Accordingly, marketing campaigns are designed to create that awareness in hopes of increasing the product's success on the market.

A study by Landor Associates, released in 1990 and due to be updated at the end of 1998, asked consumers in the United States, Japan, and countries in Western Europe to indicate their degree of awareness of family brands such as Sony, Mercedes-Benz, Kodak, and McDonald's. Surprisingly, no company appeared in the top-ten list of all three markets at that time. Several, however, had strong global name recognition: Coca-Cola, Kodak, Mercedes, and Sony, for example. But nowhere on the Landor study's lists did the names Procter & Gamble, Philip Morris, and General Foods appear, even though they produce some of the most powerful *brand names.*

The Landor study illustrates the important difference between a well-known family of brands and a famous brand name (which happens to be the name of the company). While average consumers might not know that Procter & Gamble manufactures Sudsy, Pampers, and Pringles, they are not likely to misidentify a Sony TV set or the black and yellow box that holds Kodak film (Kotler and Armstrong 1996, 285).

brand equity   Chiefly intangible factors that create value, such as how well known the item is, people's perceptions about how well the product is made, and what associations they have with the item.

The Waldorf-Astoria Hotel enjoys tremendous brand equity because its name has become part of the glamorous life of upper-crust New York.

brand extension   A marketing strategy that takes advantage of a well-known *brand name* for one product and seeks to associate it with another product.

Usually the new product is similar to the old: Procter & Gamble relied heavily on its immediately recognizable Tide brand when it launched Tide Liquid. Similarly, the company used brand extension when it created a new decaffeinated coffee and drew upon customers' familiarity with the Folgers name. Nabisco extended its popular Ritz crackers brand to Ritz Bits, a miniature cracker, as well as to Ritz Bits Sandwiches, which were made with peanut butter.

In other cases, the product categories differ markedly. Coca-Cola, for example, licensed the use of its product's name to a clothing line. In international markets, Spalding extended its brand name from sporting goods to fashionable street clothing and sunglasses.

Using brand extension has several strategic advantages. Because customers are already familiar with the brand name, the cost of introducing the new product is much lower than launching a wholly new brand. *Advertising* and other promotional expenditures are more effective because they produce greater consumer awareness and recognition for the extended brand. Moreover, because the new product's image is already established, marketers can avoid some of the risks involved in introducing it: Developmental costs are reduced; thus, the costs of product failure are lower.

Brand extension, however, has a downside. A brand extension that flops can cause consumers to lower their opinion of the original brand.

brand management   The focus, control, and direction of research, production, and *marketing,* all of which contribute to the successful launch of a new *brand* or the maintenance or revival of an old one.

In the 1990s, name brands have had a resurgence, not because the products themselves are appreciably better (although some are) and not because consumers are more discriminating (although many are). This rebirth can be attributed to *brand managers,* those gurus of R&D and marketing at savvy companies such as Procter & Gamble, General Foods, and IBM. Successful management of brands requires that a company "pull" customers by means of good ***advertising*** while it "pushes" ***wholesalers*** and ***retailers*** by means of promotions and special incentives to distribute and sell the products.

In a paper entitled "The Consumer and the Brand: An Understanding within the Framework of Personal Relationships," Susan Fournier, an assistant professor of business administration at Harvard Business School, identifies 15 types of relationships that consumers have with brands, ranging from a passing acquaintance to a deep commitment. For many consumers, selecting a product is analogous to choosing a mate or a friend, and this attitude can prove a source of great value to brand managers (Gifford 1997).

As companies reach for global markets, the work of brand managers will increase in importance.

brand mark   A symbol, design, logo, or distinctive feature that gives a ***brand*** instant recognition.

Brand marks, which are also called ***trademarks,*** help to differentiate a product from its competitors. They become part of a company's ***goodwill*** assets (that is, ***intangible assets***), and as such, their value will be reported on the company's ***balance sheet.*** Brand marks can be registered with the U.S. Patent and Trademark Office for a ten-year period (and renewed for any number of additional ten-year periods, provided the brand continues to be in use and there are no court orders against its use). A brand mark may be registered up to six months before it actually goes into use if an inventor or a company so desires. This preliminary registration can also be extended, up to a total of three years from the date of the original granting of trademark status (Hardwicke and Emerson 1992, 349).

EXAMPLES: The Ralph Lauren Polo horse; the Izod alligator; Charlie, the Star-Kist tuna; Tony the Tiger (for Kellogg's Frosted Flakes cereal); the Pillsbury Poppin' Fresh Doughboy; the Gerber baby; Aunt Jemima; and Betty Crocker. Distinctive script can become part of ***brand names*** as Coca-Cola, Ford, and IBM have devised. Even artwork and hot colors, such as seen in the bull's-eye on a Tide detergent box, can qualify as part of the brand logo or mark.

brand name   The words, letters, or numbers of a ***brand*** that can be spoken aloud, such as CBS, 3M, General Electric, Budweiser, or HP.

Whereas a ***brand mark*** often combines both graphics and words, a brand name is a word or set of words that function in the same ways as a person's name—that is, as a label without meaning except as a referent interpretable only in a context. Thus, *Edsel* can refer to either the son of Henry Ford and the president of the Ford Motor Company from 1919 until 1943, or to the short-lived automobile that has become symbolic of great failures in design and marketing. But out of context, the name formed by the letters *e, d, s,* and *l* has no meaning.

Brand names should be easy to pronounce (Sure deodorant), have a clear connection to the product (Downy fabric softener), and be memorable (Odor Eaters foot deodorant pads). Geographical terms usually prove poor choices for a brand name. The law cannot protect one manufacturer from competitors who use the same name location as part of the identification for their products.

EXAMPLE: Three companies now produce "Smithfield" hams. Even though the original company has been doing business in Smithfield, Virginia, since before the American Revolution, it could not legally protect its name when competitors began producing their own "Smithfield" hams.

Generic terms also make poor choices for brand names. Any word in the dictionary that can be used to describe a product may be considered generic and thus eligible for any company's marketing campaign.

EXAMPLE: Miller Brewing Company introduced its Lite brand, drawing on the useful connotations of the word *light*. The company, however, could not secure exclusive rights to the term and thus could not prevent Anheuser-Busch and Schlitz from introducing their own versions of light beer.

Some companies find that their brand names evolve into generic terms. From a marketing perspective, this evolution is hardly enviable, as the examples of Kleenex and Xerox demonstrate: Many consumers today simply refer to *any* brand of tissue as "Kleenex" or call *any* copying machine a "Xerox." When some brands become generic, promoting them can lead to greater sales of competing products.

On the other hand, the name brand can become so much a part of people's thinking that they use the term generically yet retain their *brand loyalty*. Thus, both *FedEx* and *Xerox* have become verbs in common parlance, and it is not unusual to hear someone promise to "fedex" a package for delivery the next day.

Marketers of brands can use a manufacturer's brand alone, a distributor's brand alone, or a combination of both. They can also choose among a family brand, an individual brand, or a generic brand strategy. Marketers who sell more than one item and use the same brand name for all their products—General Electric, for instance—use a family brand strategy. Companies relying on distributors' brands include Sears, which uses the name *Kenmore* for its appliances and *Craftsman* for its tools, and A&P food markets, which brand their own products with the name *Ann Page*.

Marketers use an individual brand strategy when they apply each brand name to only one product. Procter & Gamble, for instance, markets Tide detergent, Crest toothpaste, Folgers coffee, and Ivory dishwashing soap. Highly diversified companies often choose this strategy because they want to appeal to particular segments of the **market.** Sometimes a company uses both family and individual brands.

EXAMPLES: Pillsbury markets its Pillsbury's Best flour, biscuits, and cake mixes, but it also uses the Hungry Jack brand for another line of biscuits, pancakes, and waffle mixes.

Marketers use a generic brand strategy when consumers perceive little difference between the offerings of different companies. Examples include frozen peas, bleach, canned fruits, and bottled water. Generic branding reached its peak in the high-inflation period of the 1970s, but has lost much of its effectiveness in recent years due to customer suspicion of products that carry no company name behind them.

For good and ill, brand names frequently become associated with values and styles that move in and out of favor with consumers, and even the steadiest of companies will feel the pain of a customer's snub. Levi Strauss & Company, while it still commands an impressive lead in the jeans market, has lost ground to other manufacturers who appeal to young people's preference for the baggy look, the shredded pant leg, or the bejeweled pocket. The triumvirate of the blue jeans market—comprising Levi Strauss, the VF Corporation (maker of Lee jeans and Wranglers), and the Guess Corporation—takes seriously the threat posed by upstart companies such as JNCO, Menace, and Pacific Sunwear of California, which cater to the mid-teen market (Steinhauer 1997).

brand-switching matrix   A table showing the changes a group of customers made in their purchasing patterns over two fixed time periods.

EXAMPLE: Three companies make shampoo. Company A wants to know how its brand has fared against its two competitors' products in July and August. After surveying customers, it constructs the following brand-switching matrix:

		A	**B**	**C**
		Switched from August		
Switched	**A**	60%	20%	20%
from	**B**	19%	31%	50%
July	**C**	5%	45%	50%

Of the consumers who purchased Shampoo A in July (reading horizontally on the graph), 60 percent purchased it again in August, whereas 20 percent switched to Shampoo B and another 20 percent switched to Shampoo C. The shaded areas, reading diagonally from upper left to lower right, represent each brand's repeat purchase rate. In this case, Shampoo A retained a 60 percent share of its **target market,** whereas Shampoos B and C had repeat rates of 31 percent and 50 percent, respectively.

The numbers from left to right indicate the switching-in and switching-out rates for each brand. In this example, 20 percent of Shampoo A's July sales went to Shampoo B, while another 20 percent went to Shampoo C. In the next line, 50 percent of Shampoo B's July sales went to Shampoo C, indicating a significant drop-off in sales. In August, 45 percent of Shampoo C's July sales went to B, whereas only 5 percent went to A. These numbers suggest that Shampoo A has *brand loyalty,* but has a hard time prying customers away from either B or C.

break-even analysis   The calculation of the point at which *revenues* from sales equal the costs for producing the product. A company or a division shows neither profit nor loss for the period in question.

This calculation requires knowledge of both *fixed* and *variable costs* of a product. Fixed costs are those expenses that remain relatively stable no matter how many items are produced. Those costs would include rent, mortgage, insurance, and managers' salaries. Variable costs, in contrast, include expenses such as raw materials, utilities, and the labor costs associated with making a product or producing a service.

The break-even analysis is calculated according to the following formula:

$$U = \frac{NP + FC}{SP - VC}$$

where: U = Number of units sold
  NP = Net profit (set at zero)
  FC = Fixed costs
  SP = Selling price of the unit
  VC = Variable cost per unit

EXAMPLE: A manufacturing company plans to market a new cabinet, which it hopes to sell for $190. Managers estimate that variable costs—those for labor, wood, metal, paint, electricity, and so forth—will account for $110 per cabinet. Annual fixed costs (insurance, rent, taxes, administrative salaries, and interest) total $1.6 million. Using this data, managers calculate the break-even point, the number of cabinets that must be sold if the company is to cover all expenses associated with the new cabinet, but without clearing a profit:

$$U = \frac{0 + \$1,600,000}{\$190 - \$110}$$

$$= 20,000 \text{ units}$$

This example, of course, assumes that the manufacturing company makes *only* this cabinet and nothing else. The calculation becomes somewhat more complicated if the company's operating expenses include other lines, and managers would need to agree on which expenses fall into the category of **sunk costs.** For purposes of illustration, however, if we assume that the company intends to make only this one item and that all its variable costs amount to approximately $2,200,000 (20,000 units × $110 per unit), then we can construct the following chart to show the break-even point and difference between the company's total sales and total costs:

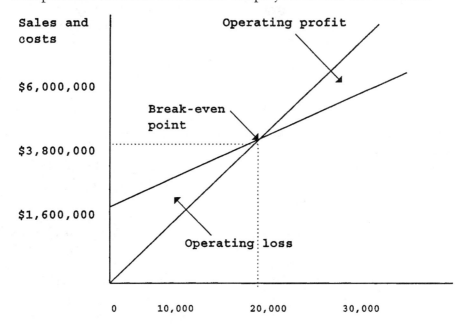

This chart shows that the company would need to sell 20,000 cabinets at $190 each to break even. After it passes that point, it will begin operating at a profit so long as total sales continue to outpace total costs.

The calculation for break-even analysis can be used to determine the number of units that the company must sell if it is to achieve a target profit (an amount greater than zero). Using the preceding formula and setting their target net profit at $4,400,000, managers can calculate the minimum number of units the company must sell:

$$U = \frac{\$4,400,000 + \$1,600,000}{\$190 - \$110}$$

$$= 75,000 \text{ units}$$

Bretton Woods Agreement   An international pact signed in July 1944, establishing guidelines for *exchange rates* between nations and for the formation of institutions that came to be known as the *International Monetary Fund* (*IMF*) and the *World Bank*.

Near the end of the Second World War, representatives from 44 countries met in Bretton Woods, New Hampshire (U.S.) to discuss international monetary policies. Thirty-nine nations actually signed the agreement (the most important holdout was the U.S.S.R.). Conference members set currencies in relation to one another and established the U.S. dollar as the standard by which all others would be linked or "pegged," with the dollar itself pegged against the value of gold. The IMF was set up as the *lender of last resort,* and in principle it was designed to have certain powers, much as a national *central bank* would have, to exercise control over debtor nations. Despite the good intentions of the participants, however, the IMF had neither the monetary reserves nor the independence nor the authority to act as such a lender (Panic 1995, 40–41).

As the dollar lost ground against other currencies, the U.S. *balance of payments* was adversely affected by the overvaluation of the U.S. currency and in 1971, the pact was partially dissolved (Hoogvelt and Puxty 1987). By 1973, the system was defunct.

broadband channel   *See bandwidth*

budget deficit and debt   The excess of expenditures over *revenue* and accumulated deficits.

The U.S. federal government has spent more than it has received in revenues in all but six years in the period since 1940: 1947 to 1948, 1951, 1956 to 1957, and 1960 (though it may post a surplus in 1998).

The budget deficit represents the shortfall in savings in the federal government sector, as has been the case for almost 40 years. Other sectors such as households, businesses, state and local governments, and foreign lenders must make up the difference. Moreover, cyclical forces exacerbate the deficit: When the economy suffers a recession, tax receipts decline, while expenditures for unemployment insurance, welfare assistance, and other such programs inevitably increase. These conditions cause the deficit to widen even further. The secular or structural deficit is the shortfall, exclusive of cyclical effects.

The following table shows the budgets and debt levels for selected years since 1945 in millions of dollars.

Fiscal year	Budget balance	Total federal debt
1945	–$ 47,553	$ 260,123
1950	–3,119	256,853
1955	–2,993	274,366
1960	301	290,525
1965	–1,411	322,318
1970	–2,842	380,921
1975	–53,242	541,925
1980	–73,835	909,050
1985	–212,334	1,817,521
1990	–221,194	3,206,564
1991	–269,359	3,598,498
1992	–290,402	4,002,136
1993	–255,013	4,351,416
1994	–203,104	4,643,705
1995	–163,899	4,921,098
1996	–145,636	5,207,298

SOURCES: U.S. Office of Management and Budget, *Historical Tables,* annual, in U.S. Dept. of Commerce, 1995, 333; *Economic Report of the President,* 1997.

buffer stock   The amount of a company's *inventory* in excess of the average demand on its goods.

Also called *safety stock,* a buffer stock is frequently set aside to protect against uncertainties in *supply* and *demand.* A company may carry the extra inventory to compensate for increases in demand over the reorder lead time or for increases in the reorder time itself. Those inventories buffer a company during periods when control over inventory levels is low. In some operational processes, managers may require a work-in-process buffer stock (also called a *decoupling inventory*) to keep the production rolling when one station creates a *bottleneck* or breaks down.

Since the rise in popularity of *just-in-time* (*JIT*) inventory, fewer companies want to bear the responsibility and costs of carrying the additional inventory.

See also ***inventory functions; work-in-process inventory.***

bundling   The grouping of several products into one package.

By bundling products, a company can often reduce the ***buying power*** of its customers. A computer company, for instance, might include a software package and maintenance agreement in a package with a personal computer. This practice makes it difficult for a buyer to determine the true cost of each element in the package and so compare prices against those of competing companies. Despite the reduction in buying power, many customers prefer bundling because it offers them the convenience of purchasing several products from one supplier rather than from many. Moreover, a customer can be relatively assured that the various products will work in tandem with each other—a certainty that is not available if one purchases goods from several vendors.

Bundling offers several other benefits. When it is expensive to identify and form relationships with new customers, bundling can provide a way to absorb those costs over a variety of products and services. The downside is that it is difficult to identify which products in the bundle are profitable and which are enjoying the coattails effect.

Antitrust legislation makes some kinds of bundling illegal. If a seller forces a buyer to purchase one item in order to receive a second, even though the buyer may prefer another seller's product, the practice, which is also called *tying*, may fall under the jurisdiction of the Sherman Antitrust Act (Section 1) or the Clayton Antitrust Act (Section 3).

EXAMPLE: The main problem with bundling is that it rides a fine line between developing integrated products and pursuing a market monopoly. Microsoft is currently the subject of a well-publicized investigation into its practice of bundling its own Web browser program, Internet Explorer, with its operating system, Windows 95. To date, the Justice Department appears to have demanded only that Microsoft provide PC manufacturers with two versions of Windows 95—one with its own Web browser and one without.

business combination   The association of two or more companies through either a merger, a consolidation, or an acquisition.

These three types of association share many features, and their differences are largely a matter of the legal nature of their combination. A statutory **merger** occurs when Company X buys all the stock of Company Y, which is then either dissolved or allowed to operate as a subsidiary of Company X. The shareholders of both companies must agree (by a two-thirds vote in most cases) to the conditions of the merger. Stockholders of Company Y are required to surrender their certificates, which are replaced by an equitable number of shares in Company X.

A statutory **consolidation** occurs when a third company, Company Z, buys the stock of both Company X and Company Y. Often this third company is formed for the purpose of carrying out the consolidation. The two companies, X and Y, cease to exist as independent entities, although one or both may become subsidiaries of Company Z.

An **acquisition** occurs when two or more companies combine in such a way that each company retains its legal identity.

EXAMPLE: SBC Communications of San Antonio, Texas, acquired Pacific Telesis of San Francisco on April 1, 1997, for $16.5 billion. The acquisition created the second-largest communications company in the United States, behind AT&T. Another "Baby Bell," Bell Atlantic, recently acquired NYNEX for $23 billion.

business cycle   The recurring pattern of macroeconomic activity and industry trends that affect the expansion or contraction of **markets,** a company's sales, **inflation,** employment, market **interest rates,** stocks and **bonds,** and other indicators of the economy's health.

A complete business cycle can be measured in two ways: from peak to peak or from trough to trough. The first is generally more popular, not to say upbeat, because it tracks the economy's progress from one peak through a recession and down to its lowest point (the trough), but then back up again to a new peak. Alternatively, some economists measure business cycles by tracking activity from one trough up through the recovery and its peak and back down again to the next trough.

Some economic activities are classified by their cyclical characteristics. Consumer spending for durable goods, for instance, is considered *procyclical:* Spending has a steeper decline than that for other economic activities during a recession; in contrast, when times are good, consumer spending rises at a higher rate than other elements in the economic recovery.

Other activities—for example, housing starts, the stock markets, and orders for **durable goods** such as refrigerators and automobiles—*lead* the economy at its cyclical peaks and troughs. In contrast, unemployment and inventory **investment** *lag* behind the overall economy. Still other activities, such as industrial production, personal income, and employment, are *coincident* with the movement of the overall economy.

business process reengineering   The radical redesign of an organization's operations and management to achieve **competitive advantage** and flexibility in a changing global marketplace.

The term *reengineering* came to the business lexicon largely through several publications in the early 1990s: Johnsson, McHugh, Pendlebury, and Wheeler published *Business Process Reengineering* in 1993, the same year that *Reengineering the Corporation,* by Michael Hammer and James Champy, appeared. The authors argue that reengineering is *not* restructuring, delayering a managerial bureaucracy, or **downsizing** an organization's staff. Rather, as Hammer and Champy (1993, 49) put it, reengineering is "starting over," creating the organization anew as if one were starting with a blank sheet of paper and redesigning all of the *core processes.*

A core business process is a set of linked activities that both crosses the boundaries of traditional functional operations and, when carried out in concert, fills the needs and expectations of consumers. As distinct from ordinary processes or organizational functions, the core business processes drive the company's success and competitive advantage. A core business process is not, however, a core technology, although the two are often confused. Every electronics company, for instance, must master the technology of "stuffing" boards with circuits and chips, and an electronics executive might identify that as one of the company's core business processes. But board stuffing is not a core process in the same way that altering the supply chain would be for the automotive industry. An electronics manufacturer would have much difficulty creating market advantage by differentiating its product on the basis of board stuffing alone, which is, in fact, merely the price of admission to market competition.

Reengineering the supply chain process in the automotive industry, however, could lead to staggering changes in market dynamics, and is thus a core *process.* The manufacturer of catalytic converters discovered an opportunity to reduce the cost of goods by 41 percent and reduce a 250-day inventory **float** that existed because the **original equipment manufacturer** (**OEM**) mismanaged the supply chain.

Most companies or industries have no more than five or six core business processes. Redesigning or enhancing any of those processes can lead to vast business improvements (Johnsson et al. 1993).

business strategy   *See corporate strategy*

buyback   *See countertrade*

buyer's remorse   A psychological phenomenon in which the purchaser of a large item, such as a home, comes to regret the *transaction,* which cannot be reversed.

One of the interesting things about buyer's remorse is that it occurs chiefly in situations when the transaction is irreversible.

buying decision process   In *marketing,* the steps that a consumer takes in determining whether to buy a product or service.

Drawing on the work of psychologists, marketers often divide the process into five stages:

- Recognizing the problem
- Searching for information
- Evaluating alternatives
- Making the purchase
- Evaluating the purchase

The process is evident in making purchases both great and small, from buying a personal computer to buying a house on a 30-year mortgage.

Marketers need to identify which of these five stages is most appropriate for their campaign.

buying power   The ability of consumers to pressure a company to reduce its prices for products and services.

Buying power is usually high in situations where (1) there are few consumers; (2) buyers are well informed about competitors' products, which are readily available; (3) the costs of switching from one product to another are low; (4) companies can pursue a strategy of *backward integration* and manufacture the product in-house; (5) the product is a substantial portion of the buyers' costs; (6) the seller competes on a cost basis; and (7) the seller is not profitable.

Bundling is one means of reducing buying power. An equipment manufacturer, for instance, might include an agreement to supply spare parts and labor for any piece of machinery it sells. Thus, it would force a consumer to rely on the equipment company for service and parts and thereby dissuade the consumer from switching to another supplier.

Companies can also reduce buying power by strongly differentiating their products from those of the competition, keeping in close contact with key customers, financing customers' purchases, and creating an *inventory* control system that automatically replenishes supplies and notifies the customer.

See also five forces model; supplier power.

buying roles   The six activities involved in the exchange process:

- *Initiator:* The person who first recognizes a need or desire that must be satisfied
- *Influencer:* The person who provides information on how to satisfy that need or desire
- *Decider:* The person who selects the alternative

- *Buyer:* The person who purchases the product or service
- *Consumer:* The person who uses the product
- *Evaluator:* The person who determines if the purchase was satisfying

Of course, one person may occupy more than one of these positions. In large organizations, each role may fall to a committee or a department, although ultimately a single individual may be responsible for completing that part of the exchange process.

byte *See **bit***

C

CAD *See computer-aided design*

CAE *See computer-aided engineering*

call An option to purchase shares if within a specified period the price of a stock rises above a certain price.

A call option is the reverse of a ***put option.*** If speculators believe that the price of a stock will rise to, say, $30 a share, they may purchase the option to buy that stock at a future date if the price (called the *strike*) goes that high or higher. The call option does not obligate the speculator to make the purchase, however.

call feature An agreement that stipulates the time and price at which a bond issuer may repurchase a ***bond*** before it matures.

Also called a *provision* or *call option,* this agreement allows corporations and municipalities to buy back bonds when ***interest rates*** fall, then to reissue the bonds at the lower rates. In order to do so, however, they must pay a *call premium,* approximately one year's interest if the bond is recalled in its first year. This premium declines as the bond approaches its maturity date.

CAM *See computer-aided manufacturing*

camera-ready In ***advertising*** and printing, a descriptive term indicating that an ad or a text is ready to be photographed and reproduced by the press.

Camera-ready copy is produced at a very high resolution, at least 1,200 dots per inch (dpi). A high-quality desktop printer can generate copy typically at no more than 600 dpi.

cannibalization The reduction in a product's sales that results when the same company introduces a similar product, which then competes and takes ***market share*** from the existing product.

Cannibalization usually occurs when the ***market*** for a product is relatively static. Hoping to jack up sales, a snack food company, for instance, introduces a new corn chip, which then competes with the same company's already successful line of potato chips. The new product's success thus comes at a great expense: The corn chip product cannibalizes the potato chip market as customers switch to the newcomer.

Even though a product may take business away from the company's other ***brands,*** the strategy can work if (1) the new item also takes market share away from competitors' products and (2) the total sales and profitability of the company's new product and those for the products it cannibalizes are significantly higher than the sales and profitability the company enjoyed before the new product was introduced.

EXAMPLE: Although McDonald's operates over 19,000 restaurants in some 100 countries, the company has pursued a strategy to increase sales by opening more and more *franchises*—one on every corner, if possible. Cannibalizing sales at existing franchises may help a new restaurant build a customer base, but eventually the strategy hurts the company. Likewise, the Benetton chain suffered a decline in sales when in the mid-1980s the number of its stores proliferated to a point at which the company had to close many of its U.S. outlets (Millman and Buck 1997).

capacity A measure of an organization's capability to produce output.

Capacity measures come in several forms: hours of operation, economic factors, *productivity,* use, and so on. A plant has a technical or design capacity; a steel mill can operate on 21 turns or work shifts per week. Although it is technically possible for the mill to operate at that capacity, the additional strain on equipment will hasten breakdowns; thus, managers may choose to operate the mill at 19 turns per week, reserving two turns for maintenance. The production lost by this schedule is compensated for by reduced wear and tear on equipment and fewer shutdowns.

Economic measures for capacity can increase if an organization uses the most efficient or lowest-cost resources. There is, of course, the drawback that raising capacity by such means can increase costs when products must be recalled.

Many hospitals measure capacity by the number of beds that are filled each day, although given the increased use of outpatient treatments, this measure can give an unrealistic picture of just how busy the hospital is or how many more patients it can handle.

EXAMPLE: Between 1994 and 1997, the General Motors Metal Fabricating Division in Lordstown, Ohio, more than doubled its daily shipping capacity to 920 tons by installing almost 400 robots in its production lines and hiring another 500 employees. By simplifying the production process and reducing the number of presses required to make parts, the division was able to add a second production line, thereby doubling capacity (Kubik 1997).

capital (1) Material wealth owned by an individual or an organization and used for the production of additional wealth.

This is the meaning that Karl Marx employs in his three-volume work, *Das Kapital* (1867–1894), the foundation for modern-day socialism.

capital (2) Available funds or cash, as in *working capital* or financing by "raising capital."

A company can raise capital by taking on *short-term debt* or *long-term liability,* as well as by issuing *common* or *preferred stock.*

capital (3) The amount on the *balance sheet* that represents ownership in a business.

Capital is thus the difference between *assets* and *liabilities.* In a corporation, capital equals *stockholders' equity.* In the following example, a small company issues a balance sheet showing assets and liabilities:

Assets		Liabilities and owners' equity	
Cash	$ 5,500	Accounts payable	$ 3,800
Accounts receivable	900	Total current liabilities	3,800
Inventory	2,300		
Prepaid expenses	600	Debt payable	3,000
Total current assets	9,300	Total liabilities	6,800
Machinery	2,500	Owners' equity	5,600
Automobile	1,200		
Less accumulated			
depreciation	(600)		
	3,100	Total liabilities and	
Total assets	$12,400	owners' equity	$12,400

In this company, capital is listed as **owners' equity** on the balance sheet at $5,600. It is calculated by subtracting total liabilities ($6,800) from total assets ($12,400).

capital asset   An asset purchased for use rather than resale.

Capital assets include both tangible and intangible items. The former category includes land, buildings, plants, and equipment, as well as investments in **subsidiary** and **affiliated companies.** Intangible assets include patents, **trademarks,** and **goodwill.**

capital asset pricing model (CAPM)   A theoretical measure of a security's risk and investors' required rates of future return, both for the security in question and for the market as a whole.

Nobel laureate William F. Sharpe developed the capital asset pricing model in 1964, and it was further refined by Lintner (1965). Using estimates for the **interest rate** (r_{rf}) on Treasury bills, which are assumed to be "risk-free" **investments,** and for the expected market premium ($r_{mkt} - r_{rf}$), investors can calculate the CAPM as a function of the statistical factor called **beta,** which expresses the relationship between the return on an individual security and the return on the market as a whole:

$$r = r_{rf} + \beta(r_{mkt} - r_{rf})$$

If U.S. Treasury bills have an interest rate of 6.5 percent and the current market risk premium ($r_{mkt} - r_{rf}$) is 6.9 percent, the CAPM would give the following calculation for Stock S, whose beta is 0.95:

$$r_s = 6.5 + 0.95(6.9)$$

$$= 13.06$$

Thus, Stock S can be expected to offer a return of 13.06 percent, almost twice as much as Treasury bills can provide, although there is no absolute guarantee that Stock X will perform at this rate.

Because the theory is a mathematical calculation using factors that are, in essence, unmeasurable—after all, the theory wants to measure *future* risk—it must rely not only on measures of *historical* performance but also on a number of assumptions about ideal investors and "perfect" market conditions. Those assumptions include the following:

- From a large collection of portfolios, all investors choose a portfolio based on its expected *rate of return* and standard deviation of *market risk.*
- All investors are averse to risk and require a premium kicker for any investment that does not have a guaranteed return.
- All investors have identical holding periods, as well as identical expectations about rates of return and *capitalization* rates.
- Investors will put their money in a few leading portfolios and avoid speculative issues.
- Investments in U.S. Treasury bills are free of risk.
- Investors can borrow and lend money at the exact same rate.
- No *transaction* costs will be incurred.
- There are no taxes.
- The market has perfect divisibility and *liquidity.*
- The future will be like the past.

Obviously these assumptions are not true in the sense that they correspond to conditions in the real world. But from a pragmatic point of view, the mathematical calculations must be based on such ideal conditions. Although the model can be applied to an individual stock, it is generally safer and more accurate to use the CAPM for estimating the volatility of a portfolio of, say, ten or more stocks (Blume 1975; Brealey and Myers 1991; Brigham and Gapenski 1994; Levy 1971).

Extensive empirical tests such as those by Fama and French (1992), have called the CAPM into question, particularly the theory that average stock returns are positively correlated with market betas. That correlation, which the CAPM takes for granted, has been shown to be weak at best during the period from 1941 to 1990 (Fama and French 1992; Jensen 1972; Roll 1977).

See also **arbitrage pricing theory (ABT).**

capital flight   The movement of *capital* out of or into a given market.

Capital moved out of Mexico and other Latin American countries to the United States during the "lost decade" of the 1980s. Because of economic conditions and the conversions to free-market governments, those nations in recent years have seen some of that capital flowing the other way.

Capital is, of course, mobile, especially with the advent of instantaneous banking now available through computers and electronic transfers. An axiom of financial markets is that "capital will always fly to the highest-return, lowest-risk investment."

EXAMPLE: After the breakup of the former Soviet Union, capital flight became a problem for the new Russian government, which saw huge sums of its wealth flowing through Latvian banks to the West. In response, the Yeltsin government established a special commission headed by Viktor Chernomyrdin, the prime minister, to investigate the bank deals through which rubles are converted into Western currencies. In one popular scheme, a legitimate Russian company contracts with a sham company to transfer funds from a Russian bank to a second sham organization, this one an "offshore" firm that has performed some "service" for the first company. The legitimate company avoids paying taxes on the funds, and a Latvian bank handles the transfer, converting the rubles into foreign currency. As soon as the deal is completed, the intermediary company is dissolved and the tax bill left unpaid (Mukhina 1997).

capital gains   Profit from the sale of *assets* such as stocks, ***bonds,*** and real estate.

In the United States, capital gains are categorized as either short term (less than one year) or long term (one year or more). For the past several years, federal and state governments have imposed a capital gains tax on individuals and organizations, which may be slightly higher for short-term as opposed to long-term gains. With no allowance for ***inflation*** and variations in the value of currency, the Internal Revenue Service requires that the tax be paid on the difference between original buying price and the final sale price. In 1997, Congress considered legislation that would do away with the capital gains tax for many individuals and most businesses.

capital lease   A lease in which the lessee acquires substantial property rights.

If any of the following conditions exists when the lease is signed, the lease must be considered a capital lease and disclosed in the ***financial statements:***

- Payments for the exclusive use of the ***asset*** approximate the asset's fair ***market value.***
- The lessee has sole access to the asset for all or a substantial part of its ***useful life.***
- The lessee can buy the asset at a discounted price at the end of the lease period.
- The lessee holds proof of ownership, such as a legal title to the asset.

If none of those four conditions are met, the lease is considered an ***operating lease.*** Thus, any mention of it as an asset or an obligation to make future payments will be disclosed in the notes to a company's financial statement.

Accountants consider a capital lease an installment purchase of an asset; thus, the ***balance sheet*** lists the asset as both an ***intangible asset*** (that is, the rights to the leased asset) and a ***liability*** (that is, the obligation to make lease payments). Both ***depreciation*** and ***interest expenses*** on the lease obligation must be disclosed on the ***income statement.*** The disclosure of lease payments on the balance sheet must show both the current and the noncurrent portions of the lease obligation (that is, that portion due within one year and that which is due in over one year from the statement date).

capital market theory   A set of complex mathematical formulas that identify how, under certain given assumptions, investors should choose ***common stocks*** for their portfolios.

Focused on publicly traded stocks, the theory has no direct bearing on valuing closely held companies; however, several of its intuitive parts are significant. One of the easiest to understand is the determination of required rates of return for different levels of risk aversion.

The capital market theory defines ***rate of return*** as the total return, including ***dividends,*** interest income, cash distributions, and the appreciation of the asset's ***market value.*** This part of the theory can be expressed by the following formula:

$$\text{Return} = \frac{\text{ending price} - \text{beginning price} + \text{cash distributions}}{\text{beginning price}}$$

EXAMPLE: An investor purchases 1,000 shares of Company X for $100 per share and holds the security for five years. During this period, the company pays annual dividends of $5,000, for a total of $25,000. At the end of the period, the investor sells the 1,000 shares for $200,000. The rate of return, therefore, is calculated as follows:

$$\text{Return} = \frac{\$200,000 - \$100,000 + \$25,000}{\$100,000} = 1.25 \text{ or } 125\%$$

The return of 125 percent over five years represents an annual return of 25 percent. As presented here, the calculation makes no allowance for **inflation** or the payment of taxes on **capital gains** and on short- and long-term distributions.

The capital market theory distinguishes *systematic* from *unsystematic* risk: The former refers to risks that the entire market (the "system") experiences, such as shifts in national and world economies, inflation, recessions, and the like. Unsystematic risks occur because of conditions in individual companies, within a single industry, or from a particular type of **investment** (e.g., minority versus controlling interests). Total risk is the sum of systematic and unsystematic risks.

The capital market theory assumes that the required investment premium is limited to systematic risk. On the surface, this makes little sense. In closely held companies, particularly small businesses, unsystematic risk associated with management skills, market position, and the development of products in heavy demand will have greater influence on a company's return than movements in the overall stock market. However, because the capital market theory was developed to value publicly traded issues, it assumes that investors have the ability to hold widely diversified portfolios, thereby eliminating or minimizing the risk attached to a single investment.

capital markets   Exchanges where corporate stocks and long-term debts are bought and sold.

The best-known example of a capital market is the **New York Stock Exchange** (**NYSE**), where the stocks and bonds of many large companies are traded. Securities not sold on one of the organized stock markets are said to be sold *over the counter.* In the *primary* market, new issues of securities are traded, whereas in the *secondary* market, previously issued securities are bought and sold.

See also **money markets.**

capital stock (1)   In financial investing, the shares that represent ownership of a company.

A company establishes the number and types of shares of stock that it may issue. Although this determination is made when the company issues its articles of incorporation, it may at a later date increase the number of shares through **stock splits** or reduce that number through **reverse splits.** Likewise, it may decide later, with the shareholders' approval, to issue preferred as well as common shares.

Information about the initial offering is referred to as the *authorized capital stock* and is shown in the company's **annual report.** When the stock is sold, it is called *issued capital stock.* If that stock remains in the hands of shareholders, it is further referred to as *outstanding shares;* if the company buys back some or all of the shares, they are then called **treasury stock.**

Capital stock usually grants its owners four privileges: (1) a portion of the business profits on a per-share basis; (2) a claim, usually reserved for owners of preferred shares, on the company's assets if it goes out of business; (3) the right to vote on issues that come before the company such as the election of directors, the appointment of auditors, compensation packages, and proposals by other shareholders; and (4) the right to maintain proportionate ownership in the event of additional stock issues and stock splits or reverse splits. Many companies have also begun reinvestment programs whereby shareholders can purchase additional shares at current market prices by reinvesting **dividends** and by making voluntary contributions (within specified limits each quarter).

capital stock (2)   In economics, the physical, nonhuman, but reusable, **inputs** to production.

The capital stock reflects the accumulated **investment,** minus replacement costs needed to make repairs or supply new parts, which are necessary to maintain the capital stock rather than to increase its value.

The application of capital in production is the main source of growth in **productivity.** As a general rule, the more **capital** that workers have to work with, the greater their output or productivity.

capital structure   The **common stock, preferred stock,** long-term debt, and **retained earnings** that a company maintains in order to finance its **assets.**

There is some disagreement over whether long-term debt should be included in a company's capital structure: Is it used to finance long-term assets, as proponents believe, or is it simply a **liability,** as opponents argue? If a company takes the point of view that long-term debt is due to creditors, it should not be included with the other forms of **capital.**

In one of the most significant contributions to financial principles, Modigliani and Miller (1958) proposed a theory stating that the **market value** of any company is independent of its capital structure; that is, a company's assets determine its value, not whether that company chooses to split risks by issuing both debt and equity securities.

See also **complex capital structure.**

capitalization (1)   The classification of an **asset** as an expense because it benefits a company in the long term (more than one year).

EXAMPLE: A company builds a new warehouse and capitalizes the labor costs by considering them part of the asset's value when it is listed on the **balance sheet.** A second company, which is also building a warehouse, might decide to expense the labor costs.

capitalization (2)   A company's **capital stock,** or all the securities such as **common** and **preferred stocks, debentures,** and **bonds,** which the company sells to individual and institutional investors.

CAPM   See **capital asset pricing model**

carpal tunnel syndrome (CTS)   A disorder resulting from muscular and neural stress of repetitive acts such as typing, computer data entry, and the operation of heavy machinery.

The carpal bones in the wrist form a tunnel through which nerves extend to the fingers. When repeated and severe vibration injures this tunnel, the sufferer experiences pain, numbness, or a tingling sensation in the hands and fingers. For office workers, machine operators, and others whose jobs involve repetitive motion, the ailment has become the source of discomfort, work hours lost, and hospital costs. In 1994, U.S. workers reported over 300,000 injuries resulting from repetitive motion. Costs to U.S. businesses for workers' compensation run as high as $20 billion a year (Fletcher 1997). Accordingly, human resources managers, employers, and insurers look for ways to decrease the workers' chances of injury.

Skeptics argue that there is little or no scientific evidence to explain, for instance, why two employees doing the same repetitive tasks do not both develop CTS, or why insurance claims for CTS sufferers increased so dramatically in the 1980s. In 1997, on the eve of the Virginia legislature's adoption of legislation providing employee benefits for injured employees, a Roanoke law firm, Woods, Rogers, and Hazelgrove, questioned the reliability of scientific studies on the ailment, pointing out that women are ten times more likely than men to contract the problem and suggesting that the plethora of CTS cases came as a response to extensive publicity about the ailment since the early 1980s (Sturgeon 1997).

EXAMPLE: In *Rotolo et al.* v. *Digital Equipment Corporation,* three plaintiffs sued Digital Equipment, claiming that use of the company's LK201 keyboard caused "cumulative trauma disorder" (CTD). In the landmark case, the jury awarded the plaintiffs $5.9 million for their injuries. Other courts, however, have ruled in favor of computer makers. IBM, for instance, won a case, *Piester* v. *IBM,* because the jury found no evidence suggesting that use of the standard QWERTY keyboard (named for the first six letters in the upper left line of the keyboard) actually caused the injury (Buckley 1997).

The Microsoft Company has assiduously avoided calling its "Natural Keyboard" an ergonomic device, presumably out of concern that customers will buy the product and be misled by suggested claims that it eliminates carpal tunnel disorders.

carrying costs Expenses that a company incurs when it holds items in *inventory.*

Also called *holding costs,* these expenses include amounts incurred for storing, insuring, cataloging, and maintaining items that have yet to be sold or are awaiting delivery. It also includes shrinkage, obsolescence, deterioration, and security of the inventory. Furthermore, a company loses money that could have come from interests on *investments* when it spends that money instead on maintaining a large inventory. Carrying costs increase proportionally as inventory grows. Primarily but not exclusively for that reason, *just-in-time* (*JIT*) inventory has become a popular alternative to maintaining extensive inventories.

cartel A group of sellers who have banded together to influence or regulate the prices of certain goods through their dominance of a particular *market.*

The most famous cartel is the **Organization of Petroleum Exporting Countries (OPEC)**, which comprises 12 nations, most of which are located in northern and central Africa and in the Middle East: Algeria, Gabon, Indonesia, Iran, Iraq, Kuwait, Libya, Nigeria, Qatar, Saudi Arabia, the United Arab Emirates, and Venezuela. Established in 1960, OPEC became strong enough to drive up oil prices sharply, causing an oil crisis in the United States and many other countries in 1973. That crisis helped push through legislation and policies governing oil reserves in the United States as well as the trans-Alaskan pipeline and other provisions to ensure that the one country with the highest per capita consumption of petroleum products would never run short again. Despite efforts of other countries to become less dependent on OPEC oil production, in the 1990s the cartel was responsible for approximately 40 percent of the world's total production, and projections for the first decade of the twenty-first century show that OPEC will produce almost half of that total (Energy Information Administration 1995).

Antitrust legislation has helped check the rise of cartels, which are declared illegal by the U.S. government. In a free-enterprise, capitalistic system, however, it is increasingly difficult to make a cartel work effectively. Because most cartels depend on price inelasticity, they cannot, short of totalitarian coercion, force everyone to charge the same price for an item or to restrict its trading. In the case of OPEC's attempt to control oil prices, the member nations did not anticipate the cost-saving measures that Americans took in response. Over the long term, the demand for petroleum products declined as people sought different, more efficient means of spending energy.

EXAMPLE: De Beers of South Africa controls approximately 80 percent of the world's diamond market. Its cartel, furthermore, recently signed an agreement with the Russian government, granting De Beers control of over 95 percent of Russia's rough diamonds (Rao 1997). De Beers was founded in 1881 by Sir Cecil Rhodes and named for the Boer landowners in South Africa. In the early twentieth century, Ernest Oppenheimer succeeded Rhodes as chief executive of the company and began building the cartel (Farrelly and Woolf 1997).

cash basis accounting   The immediate recording of cash receipts for the sale of goods and services, as well as cash expenses for goods and services purchased.

The alternative to *accrual accounting,* cash basis accounting does not use designations such as *accounts receivable, accounts payable,* and *accrued expenses.* For tax purposes, an organization will have to choose one or the other system of accounting and use it consistently until it formally declares a change of accounting bases. The *Securities and Exchange Commission (SEC)* does not allow public companies to use cash basis accounting (or a hybrid system), nor is this system recognized as a *generally accepted accounting principle (GAAP).* The IRS, however, does permit some small, privately owned businesses, especially those in the service sector, to use this accounting method.

Under a hybrid system, an accountant will record *inventory* on the *balance sheet* as it is paid for and will write it off to the *income statement* as items are sold. *Tangible assets* such as computers and office furniture appear on the balance sheet when they are paid for and depreciated. Similarly, bank loans and *long-term liability* are recorded on the balance sheet when the cash is received; they are reduced as payments are made on a monthly or quarterly basis. All other sales and expenses are recorded directly to the income statement when they are made or incurred.

cash cow   A company or product that generates a consistent supply of cash, *assets,* or value.

In 1970, the Boston Consulting Group (BCG) used the term in its *corporate portfolio matrix*, which it proposed as a guide to measuring how much each **strategic business unit** (**SBU**) contributed to an organization's overall value, its potential for growth and **market share** (Boston Consulting Group 1970). The BCG applied the term *cash cow* to any SBU that showed low but steady growth and high market share. According to the matrix, products or divisions in this category had only limited potential to continue generating such value in the long term. Because it added this distinction of limited future growth, the BCG obviously took liberties with the original meaning of *cash cow*, which traditionally has been seen as reliably productive.

In most business contexts, the term today refers simply to a product or business that provides a steady source of funds. If managers, however, neglect the cash cow, assuming that it will forever be fruitful, they are likely to regret soon that they milked it dry.

cash dividend   Money that a company pays to its stockholders.

Cash dividends, which may be paid on a monthly, quarterly, or yearly basis, are calculated either on a dollar amount per share for a company's **common stock** or on a fixed percentage of **par value** (or dividend rate) for its **preferred stock.**

EXAMPLE: A company has 1 million outstanding shares of common stock, for which it declares a $.10 per share dividend. It has also issued 500,000 shares of preferred stock, which has a par value of $10 and a dividend rate of 7 percent. In the current **accounting period,** the company's cash dividend would be calculated as follows:

Common stock
1,000,000 shares × $.10 = $100,000

Preferred stock
500,000 shares × $10 = $5,000,000
× .07 (dividend rate) =   350,000

Total cash dividend   **$450,000**

cash equivalent   Any **asset,** including **inventories,** Treasury bills, and other marketable securities, that can be quickly liquidated.

All cash equivalents are reported in the Current Assets portion of a company's consolidated **balance sheets.**

cash flow   The movement of cash as it comes in and goes out, or cash received minus cash paid out.

Sometimes a trickle, sometimes a tidal wave, cash flow can be measured for any operation or division in a company over a particular period of time. Income and proceeds from operations, **investments,** and financing usually are reported in the consolidated **statements of cash flows,** which are part of a company's **annual report.**

EXAMPLE: In its third quarter, a company makes $200,000 in cash sales and pays out $50,000 in wages, $70,000 in inventory, and $7,500 for a new computer and office supplies. Its cash flow for that quarter is calculated as follows:

Sales		$200,000
Expenses:		
Wages	$50,000	
Inventory	70,000	
Supplies and equipment	7,500	
Total expenses		127,500
Cash flow		**$ 72,500**

cash flow statement   *See statement of cash flows*

cash-to-current-liabilities ratio   A measure of a company's ability to pay short-term financial obligations with the cash it has on hand.

A ratio of 1.0 means that for every dollar a company owes in the short term, it has a dollar in cash on hand. ("On hand" means readily available in bank accounts and in investments that are immediately convertible to cash.) If the ratio is a great deal higher than 1.0, the company is probably not investing its cash intelligently. If the ratio is extremely small, the company could be in trouble if creditors come knocking.

The formula for the ratio is:

$$\frac{\text{Cash} + \text{cash equivalents} + \text{marketable securities}}{\text{Current liabilities}}$$

*See also **acid-test ratio; current ratio.***

caveat emptor   Latin phrase for "Let the buyer beware."

In commerce, the phrase encapsulates the principle that whoever contemplates purchasing a product or service is ultimately responsible for assessing its quality or worth.

caveat venditor   Latin for "Let the seller beware."

CD (1)   Abbreviation for *certificate of deposit.*

CD (2)   Popular abbreviation for *compact disc,* a piece of polycarbonate plastic, 4.5 inches in diameter, on which digital information is written. The original CDs were developed jointly by Philips and Sony in 1982 and first used in the music recording industry. While aficionados still swear by vinyl records, even die-hard fans will admit that the CD has replaced those relics from the nondigital past.

In the computer industry, CDs have become one of the most popular means of recording and storing digital information. While the 3.5-inch diskette is still widely used, chiefly by people who do not have CD-ROM drives on their computers, the CD can store many times the amount of information as a 1.44-megabyte diskette. Furthermore, the CD is not subject to the electromagnetic distortions, as is its smaller counterpart, because the digital information is "pitted" onto the surface of the disk, which is then covered with a shiny lacquer to protect it from damage.

cellular production   An organizational strategy that groups people, equipment, and processes on the basis of similarity in production needs in order to achieve the most efficient creation of products and services.

Analogous to the division of labor evident in the cellular structure of a beehive, for instance, cellular production in manufacturing seeks to classify the various processes an organization puts into place in order to create its products and services. Planners might survey the entire range of a company's products, grouping processes according to the particular skills people need to run them and according to the types of machines required to make those products.

EXAMPLE: A sporting goods manufacturer might divide its output according to its primary products:

Rackets	Inflatable balls	Noninflatable balls	Camping equipment	Remainder
Tennis	Footballs	Golf	Tents	Golf clubs
Squash	Basketballs	Baseballs	Campers	Waterskis
Racquetball	Volleyballs	Softballs	Cookware	Rollerblades
Table tennis	Soccer balls	Tennis	Car carriers	Helmets, etc.

The classification process in some companies will be clear-cut, whereas in others, as in the case of the sporting goods manufacturer, the groupings are not always consistent. For this reason, a separate category called "Remainder" serves as a catchall for what does not fit in elsewhere. The main cells, however, contain products that are similar in their demands on people's skills and types of equipment needed to manufacture them.

In those cells, where the products are all roughly similar, a machine can be set up and people can be trained to produce one item or all in a group. Some cells can produce an entire group of products or services with a single machine, whereas other cells may have dozens of machines and employ as many as 50 people.

Separate cells are usually managed as independent teams. Members of each cell team are responsible for conducting, scheduling, and inspecting the work of the entire group. In this regard, cellular production differs markedly from that performed by conventional job shops or by assembly lines. In assembly line production as might be found in an automobile plant or a car wash, the equipment does most of the work, and there is little chance of developing a sense of teamwork. In a job shop such as an automobile repair facility or a hospital, workers may feel a greater sense of being part of a team, but because everyone is working on a different task, few have a sense of the entire project. This is not the case, however, with cellular production, where all employees in a particular group are responsible for the entire job. According to its proponents, cellular production nourishes team building and provides challenges to meet deadlines and to improve the quality of each product or service.

The conversion from a conventional job shop to a cellular unit is usually inexpensive. Although some cells may require special equipment, the cell strategy does not usually require that the company make additional large investments, but only that it move the appropriate equipment and people into each production cell. If equipment cannot be moved, cellular production can be implemented by designating "virtual" cells, where the team has sole use of the machine even though it is not physically present.

*See also **job process system.***

central bank   At the top of a national hierarchical banking system, the bank responsible for overseeing the country's **monetary policies,** monitoring the value of its currency both at home and abroad, controlling the supply of **credit,** setting certain monetary rates such as the prime lending rate, and requiring member banks to hold certain amounts in reserve to meet creditors' demands.

The first central bank was the Bank of England, established in 1694. It has provided the model for other central banks, including the **Federal Reserve** System, headquartered in Washington, D.C.; the Banque de France in Paris; the Bank of Japan in Tokyo; and the Deutsche Bundesbank in Frankfurt.

Most central banks operate independently of federal fiscal policy. In the United States, for instance, the Department of the Treasury determines the division of government finance between taxation and government debt issues, but the Federal Reserve System determines whether the private sector will hold government-issued, interest-bearing paper that cannot be used to purchase goods and services, or whether it will hold non-interest-bearing coins and currency.

Central banks set policies that influence, if not determine, the growth of money and credit as well as the level of **interest rates** on short-term securities. By controlling the aggregate demand for money, most central banks extend their reach to influence long-term economic growth. It is often said that the chairman of the Federal Reserve System is the second most powerful person in the United States, after the president, a comparison that is borne out by the adage commonly heard in financial circles that "when Alan Greenspan, Fed chairman since 1987, sneezes, Wall Street catches a cold."

certainty equivalents   In corporate finance, a method of comparing the value of two **investments** with different levels of risk.

The goal is to determine the point at which an investor is indifferent to choosing between the certain return of a safe investment and the expected return of a riskier one.

EXAMPLE: A financial manager can invest in **junk bonds** predicted to have a one-year return of $1,000 or put the money in U.S. Treasuries that have a risk-free yield (r_f) of 6 percent or $800. The manager wants to know what the return must be from the riskier investment in order to equal the rate paid by the risk-free investment.

In order to calculate the different return rates for the two investments, the manager must first calculate the **present value** (**PV**) of the risk-free investment, using the following formula:

$$PV = \frac{C_1}{1 + r_f}$$

$$= \frac{\$800}{1.06} = \$754.72$$

The manager now needs to know the risk-adjusted rate, or the required return of the risky investment, which can be represented by the variable r_r in the formula

$$PV = \frac{\$1,000}{1 + r_r}$$

and setting this equal to $754.72, the *point of indifference,* so called because if the return on the risky investment is neither more nor less than that on the sure thing, then it makes no difference which investment the manager chooses (other than a few sleepless nights perhaps).

Given these parameters, the manager calculates the required rate of the risky investment as follows:

$$\frac{\$1,000}{1 + r_r} = \$754.72$$

$$\$1,000 = \$754.72 + 754.72r_r$$

$$r_r = \frac{245.28}{754.72} = 0.325 \text{ or } 32.5\%$$

In other words, the risky investment must pay a 32.5 percent return in order to be equivalent to the risk-free investment, which has a 6 percent return. The certainty equivalent method works best when the financial manager knows exactly what trade-offs he or she is willing to make. Otherwise, the risk-adjusted *discount rate* would be a more appropriate method for comparing investments.

certified public accountant (CPA)   Certification awarded by the *American Institute of Certified Public Accountants* (*AICPA*) to U.S. candidates who receive a college degree in accounting, pass the Uniform CPA Examination, and satisfy requirements set by individual states for length of experience in public accounting and in continuing professional education.

In the United Kingdom, Canada, India, Australia, and other countries once a part of the British Commonwealth, the certification is awarded by the Association of Certified Accountants. The Accounting Standards Committee (ASC) in Great Britain and elsewhere operates much as the *Financial Accounting Standards Board* (*FASB*) does in the United States: It establishes standards for conducting an *audit* and reporting its results. Whereas the FASB only makes recommendations, the ASC issues rulings with which companies must comply.

CPAs are licensed to issue *audit opinions* on a company's *financial statements.*

change in accounting estimate   A revision of an accounting forecast or assumption.

EXAMPLE: A company that purchased factory equipment five years ago with an estimated *useful life* of five years now determines that the equipment will last for an additional five years. Thus, the company reports the new estimate in its *financial statement* as a change in accounting estimate. Such changes in accounting estimates are shown over current and future years; the company does not restate the years before the change.

See also accounting change; change in accounting principle.

change in accounting principle   A switch from one accounting method to another.

EXAMPLE: A company moves from *straight-line depreciation* to the *sum-of-the-years'-digits* (*SYD*) *method* of accounting; thus, it must show the effect of the change in the current year's *financial statements.* This change usually appears in the entry called *cumulative effect of a change in accounting principle.*

Some changes in accounting principles, such as a new pronouncement by the *Financial Accounting Standards Board* (*FASB*), require a retroactive accounting to show what the effects would have been if the new principle had been in use for those years.

*See also **accounting change; change in accounting estimate.***

Chapter 7   The conventional form of *bankruptcy,* governed by special provisions in the 1978 Bankruptcy Act.

Under Chapter 7 provisions, a company or an individual can file with a court to liquidate its *assets* in a straight bankruptcy. A court-appointed trustee oversees this liquidation and distributes the proceeds to creditors. Such bankruptcy cases follow an established schedule in which all creditors are grouped into certain segments of the hierarchy: Those at the top are likely to receive the lion's share of the company's remains, while owners of *common stock* rank at the bottom of the hierarchy and are likely to receive nothing. Owners of *preferred stock* are not guaranteed any payment, but because they are just one step above the common shareholders, they are unlikely to receive much if anything.

Chapter 9   A provision of the 1978 Bankruptcy Act that covers the public sector, much as *Chapter 11* declarations are used by small and large businesses.

When a public entity such as Orange County, California, or Cleveland, Ohio, files for *bankruptcy,* it does so under Chapter 9 provisions.

Chapter 11   One of the dominant forms of *bankruptcy,* used by companies of any size and number of assets.

In contrast to *Chapter 7,* the alternative for companies declaring bankruptcy, the Chapter 11 provision of the U.S. Bankruptcy Reform Act of 1978 allows a sole proprietorship, a *partnership,* or a large *corporation* to continue its operations while managers negotiate a financial restructuring of the company's debts and an appropriate repayment plan. Usually the declaration of Chapter 11 is preceded by a court-ordered examination and the appointment of a trustee, who then works with the company's creditors to arrange an acceptable schedule for repaying debts.

In a Chapter 11 reorganization, the company's creditors are classified according to type, amount, and length of outstanding payments, and each is guaranteed to receive at least as much as would have been received if the company had simply declared itself insolvent and filed a Chapter 7 bankruptcy.

chart of accounts   A numbered list of the titles of all accounts used in a company's *bookkeeping* system.

The accounts that appear in the company's *financial statement* are listed first, usually in the order of *assets, liabilities,* and *owners' equity.* Those are followed by the accounts that appear in the *income statement,* namely *revenues* and expenses. Some companies assign identifying numbers to the accounts for the purpose of coding *transactions,* as the following list suggests:

100	Cash on hand
110	Cash in regular bank account
111	Cash in payroll account
120	Accounts receivable

131	Inventory—raw material
132	Inventory—work in process
133	Inventory—finished goods
200	Accounts payable—trade
210	Accounts payable—state
220	Accrued expenses
300	Long-term mortgage
400	Common stock
500	Sales
600	Cost of sales
700	Selling expenses
800	Administrative expenses
900	Interest

chase demand   An aggregate planning strategy that maintains a minimal *inventory* level while changing production levels to meet expected *demand* for a given period.

EXAMPLE: Using chase demand, a candy company plans on increasing production for the months of September and October in anticipation of the increased demand for candy at Halloween. The company makes changes in production by asking employees to work overtime and by hiring temporary workers to make up for the shortfall. To ensure its products' freshness, the company holds only a small inventory; thus, it has only the cost of a small *buffer stock* to prevent shortages when demand is greater than expected.

See also level production.

cherry picking   The purchase of products, normally sold by a single company in *bundling,* from a number of suppliers.

It is also a technique of producing a limited product line with those products having the biggest *profit margin* or the highest sales level. Producing only the high-demand or high-profit items is picking the best from the *product mix.* In large industries such as automobile production, however, the customer—an auto manufacturer, for example—has a lot of clout and can cherrypick from a vast number of suppliers for the best prices on component parts.

Chicago School   A group of economists at the University of Chicago in the 1960s who advanced the economic principles of *monetarism* and free trade and objected strongly to the federal government's intervening to fight *inflation,* unemployment, and rising prices.

Those associated with the Chicago School included Milton Friedman, George J. Stigler, Frank H. Knight, Henry C. Simons, and Friedrich A. von Hayek. In response to interventionists such as John Maynard Keynes, Friedman argued that the *Federal Reserve* should allow the supply of money to grow at a slow and steady pace rather than responding to the rate of inflation.

chief (or corporate) executive officer (CEO)   The top managerial position in a company's hierarchy.

The position of CEO came into its own in 1975, the year of the first reported use of the acronym, according to *Merriam Webster's Collegiate Dictionary.* (The concept of a "chief executive" is much older than that, of course.) Many CEOs now have replaced or absorbed the duties of their companies' presidents. Although in some companies the two positions, CEO and president, occupy the top levels of management, the CEO represents the ultimate authority in conducting the company's operations and authorizing both expenditures and planning.

In some cases the bifurcated structure of a company's executive branch results from a ***merger*** or an ***acquisition.*** The chief officers of the acquiring and the acquired companies frequently assume the titles of CEO and president, respectively, but it is the chief executive officer who ultimately controls the new entity.

chief financial officer (CFO)   The executive who manages all of a company's financial aspects.

CFOs are responsible for keeping accounting records, ***forecasting*** financial conditions, designing accounting systems, tracking the performance of corporate ***investments,*** raising ***capital,*** overseeing shareholder relations, and preparing SEC reports. In large companies, the CFO delegates some of those responsibilities to financial vice presidents, ***controllers,*** and treasurers, whereas in a small company, the CFO might perform all of those activities. He or she often sits on the company's board of directors.

chief operating officer (COO)   The executive who has oversight for the daily operations of a company.

In some organizations this position is identical (except in name) with that of president. In the company hierarchy, the COO reports to the CEO.

Child Protection Act of 1966   A federal law in the United States forbidding the sale of hazardous toys. An amendment, passed in 1969, adds a number of other consumer products such as anything that creates an electrical or mechanical hazard or the threat of fire.

Cigarette Labeling Act of 1967   A regulation approved by Congress requiring that tobacco manufacturers print on each cigarette pack and carton the statement, "Warning: The Surgeon General has determined that cigarette smoking is dangerous to your health."

Subsequent amendments to the act have resulted in various alterations of this message. Some packages, for instance, carry the following statement: "Surgeon General's Warning: Quitting smoking now greatly reduces serious risks to your health."

CIM   *See **computer-integrated manufacturing***

Clayton Antitrust Act of 1914   A U.S. federal law intended to strengthen the Sherman Antitrust Act of 1890, making it illegal to fix prices, tie contracts, or interlock boards of directors where the intention is "substantially to lessen competition or . . . create a monopoly in any line of commerce." The act stipulates that the Federal Trade Commission (FTC) can fix or modify existing quantity limits on various ***commodities*** as it sees fit.

CNC   Acronym for *computer numerical control.*

COBOL A computer programming language developed in 1959 primarily for business applications and still widely used today.

The acronym COBOL stands for *Common Business Oriented Language.* It has its widest applications on mainframes rather than personal computers, but one of its drawbacks is that its language and grammar are not easily transferred from one computer to another. In COBOL applications, programmers use English verbs such as *multiply, stop,* and *move* in writing commands that drive the programs.

cold call A pressure selling technique in which a salesperson approaches a potential customer with little or no warning.

In a bygone era, the classic example of the cold-call technique was the door-to-door salesperson, peddling brushes, vacuum cleaners, encyclopedias, or household products. Now that figure has been replaced by the high-tech telemarketer who calls potential customers, usually between 5:00 and 8:00 P.M., to pitch a new product. As the technology becomes more and more sophisticated, the degree of contact becomes increasingly impersonal. It is not unusual to receive an unsolicited fax late at night or to hear a recorded voice promoting the sales pitch. Those calls are truly cold because they are bloodless.

column inch The unit by which *advertising* space is sold in newspapers, magazines, books, and other publications.

Each page of a newspaper or magazine is divided into columns, generally three to eight. A column in the *New York Times,* for instance, is approximately two inches wide, and a typical page has six columns. Because a column inch measures the width of one column by one inch deep, the advertising space represented by a column inch in the *Times* covers about two square inches. If an advertisement fits into a space that is three columns wide by ten inches deep, the advertiser needs to purchase 30 column inches ($3 \times 10 = 30$). If the publication charges $25 per column inch, space for that ad will cost $750 ($25 \times 30$).

The current cost of one column inch of business recruitment advertising at the *New York Times* is $797. A full page ad in the *Times,* occupying 126 column inches and sold at a somewhat reduced rate, is therefore around $88,000 for a single appearance.

combination rate A reduced rate offered to advertisers who place an advertisement in more than one publication owned by the same publisher.

To qualify for the special rate, advertisements must be identical in copy, art, and size. In most cases the advertisements must run on the same day. A publisher of both morning and evening editions of the same newspaper may well offer combination rates to advertisers.

COMEX Acronym for the Commodity Exchange, Inc., 4 World Trade Center, New York, New York, where futures contracts in gold, silver, aluminum, copper, and others are traded.

comfort letter A letter that expresses the writer's opinion that certain legal or financial matters have been or will be properly executed.

The two most common uses of comfort letters occur in securities registrations and in legal agreements between two parties.

The **Securities and Exchange Commission (SEC)** requires that independent auditors include as part of a securities registration a comfort letter stating that they have no reason to believe that the information presented in the registration and the accompanying prospectus is incorrectly prepared. Because this letter does not guarantee that the information is accurate, it is frequently called a *cold* comfort letter.

The second use of a comfort letter arises when two parties in a legal contract reach an agreement about their intentions. The letter is thus called a *declaration of intent* because one party specifies the intention to take (or not to take) a specific action. The comfort letter is not legally binding since it remains outside the primary agreement.

commercial paper   Short-term (2 days to 270 days) securities, which are issued by typically high-quality corporations, banks, and other borrowing organizations to raise **working capital.**

Investors use commercial paper as a short-term **investment** while they wait for other opportunities to open up. Because it represents an unsecured debt, there is always some risk involved in the investment. It can, however, be sold at discount or allowed to bear interest. Issuers like commercial paper because of its maturity, its flexibility, and the absence of hard collateral. Both Moody's and Standard & Poor's rate commercial paper, thereby making it easier for investors to verify creditworthiness.

commission   A sales incentive plan in which salespeople receive a fixed or sliding percentage of the sales or profits they help generate.

Some salespeople work strictly on a commission basis; others combine commissions with a base salary. Commissions are typically found in such industries as clothing, insurance, investments, real estate, furniture, and retail sales.

A straight commission plan with no base salary offers several advantages: (1) It encourages sales representatives to work at maximum capacity; (2) it links selling costs with sales **revenues;** (3) it allows management to influence the activities of the sales team by placing different commissions on different products. Such plans, however, come with heavy costs. Because they receive no other compensation, salespeople resist nonselling (hence, non-income-producing) tasks such as providing customer service and filling out sales reports. Straight commission selling also leads to high-pressure tactics that can damage customer relations, and the sales floor too often becomes a dog-eat-dog world where cooperation and teamwork are chewed to pieces. From the employee's point of view, a straight commission pay plan looms as a serious threat to financial security if sales are seasonal, as in garden equipment, home air conditioners, and toys. Unable to predict sales and volume, those employees may find it difficult to secure credit or home mortgages.

In companies that pay a combination of salary and commission, managers use the plan to create incentives while they avoid placing undue burdens on the employees. A common arrangement is 70 percent salary and 30 percent commission. Using the combination plan, managers can control the nonselling activities of the sales force and provide some measure of job stability if sales decline.

commodity   A highly standardized product such as cement, wheat, steel, and eggs.

Consumers will often buy commodities from the manufacturer who offers the lowest price. A company can move away from offering a commodity in two ways:

- Differentiate the product from those of competitors. Frank Perdue fed his chickens a special meal containing marigold petals in order to give his chickens their distinctive golden color. Perdue then went on to star in a series of memorable advertisements in which he claimed that his birds were superior to other chickens on the market. Hugely successful, the ad campaign helped create the impression that Perdue chickens were of higher quality, a perception that gave Perdue enough *brand equity* to raise the price per pound 15 percent above that charged by competitors.

- The second strategy is to recognize that different buyers have different needs and to tailor various marketing programs for each. Companies can offer, for instance, longer payment terms, more reliable delivery, or a better technical assistance program in order to attract customers with something more than just a low price. The key to succeeding with this strategy is to identify which customers' needs are not being met and to design products or services accordingly, all the while watching what competitors are doing to attract the same market.

common stock   A share in the ownership of a public or privately owned *corporation.* In its charter, the corporation must state how many shares of common stock it is authorized to sell, but this figure can change with the approval of a majority of shareholders if they are asked to vote on a proposed *merger* or *stock split.* In its *annual report,* the company specifies how many of its authorized shares it has sold or *issued,* either in certificate form or as part of a *stock reinvestment plan.*

Investors who purchase shares of common stock are guaranteed certain rights; for instance, they may vote for company directors, approve the selection of an independent auditor, attend the annual meeting, submit proposals for adoption by other shareholders, and share in the distribution of the company's earnings. Merely having the right to share in those earnings, however, does not guarantee that there will be any earnings; indeed, the directors may declare that no *dividend* will be distributed at all.

Owners of common stock generally have fewer rights than owners of *preferred stock,* who do receive a guarantee that they can share in company earnings. If the company declares *bankruptcy,* owners of preferred stock stand first in line to collect the remains, whereas owners of common stock usually receive nothing. Compensating for the discrepancy in treatment, however, is the likelihood that the common stock price will increase at a faster rate than the preferred stock price.

See also capital stock; dividend; preferred stock.

common stock equivalent   A security that can be converted into *common stock.* For a security to be classified as a common stock equivalent, it must meet the requirements set forth in the *Opinions of the Accounting Principles Board, no. 15,* "Earnings per share" (New York: AICPA, 1969). Examples include convertible *preferred stocks, bonds,* stock *options,* two-class common stocks, *warrants,* and contingent shares. If the equivalent is term *dilutive,* it must be taken into account when the company states its EPS, or *earnings per share.* A company, for instance, with 1,000,000 shares of common stock outstanding and common stock equivalents that can be converted to 500,000 shares would need to divide its total earnings by 1,500,000 in order to give an accurate picture of its EPS.

See also complex capital structure.

common stock valuation   An estimate of a common stock's value over a specified period, based on the stock's current price and *dividend* payments.

Stockholders expect that their *investments* will yield both cash dividends and *capital gains.* If a stock selling at $50 per share today increases to $58 a share one year from now and currently pays investors $2 per share, those stockholders would realize a profit of $8 plus $2, or $10 per share (disregarding taxes they would have to pay on capital gains and dividend income). If they have an expected *rate of return* of, say, 12 percent, those investors can calculate the common stock valuation as follows:

$$\text{Price} = P_0 = \frac{D_1 + P_1}{1 + r}$$

$$= \frac{2 + 58}{1 + 0.12} = \$53.57$$

comparison advertising   A strategy by which a company presents its product as significantly better than a competitor's.

To be effective, the ad campaign must name the competing product or strongly imply its identity so that potential customers will recognize the benefits of the featured product.

EXAMPLES: MCI promises cheaper rates and better service than AT&T can offer; Sprint boasts that it can beat both. In an implicit reference to Hertz, car renter Avis proclaims proudly that because it is Number 2, "We try harder." Pepsi, in competition with Coca-Cola, promotes its "Pepsi Challenge" by offering an on-the-spot taste comparison of the two soft drinks. The University of California at Berkeley touts itself in a ranking of the top ten colleges and universities in the United States: UC-Berkeley claims that it has the highest number of students who graduated in the top 10 percent of their high school classes, while it maintains the lowest tuition charges of any school on the list (which includes Harvard, Yale, Duke, and Princeton).

competitive advantage   The combination of factors within a company that give it an edge over its competitors.

The concept has occupied the attention of practically every writer of business books and articles, but perhaps none to the extent that Michael E. Porter of Harvard Business School has shown. In *Competitive Advantage* (1985), Porter analyzes the reasons that many companies fail to achieve success by *sustaining* the advantages that their business strategies may have created for them. To keep from falling into mediocrity or competing at a disadvantage, Porter argues that a company will need to make a choice between *cost leadership* within the industry or differentiation of its products and services.

Those two goals are usually incompatible: If a company aims to sell its products at a price lower than its competitors can offer a similar product, it will probably need to pursue *economies of scale,* contract with suppliers of raw materials or component parts at the lowest possible cost, and persuade its customers that its products and services are equal to those offered by competitors or that, if they do exist, the differences between the products in question do not matter all that much. Wal-Mart, for example, has not only achieved the enviable position of cost leadership in many areas, especially in the rural South, but also has maintained that competitive advantage despite the arrival of many challengers.

Becoming the cost leader, however, is not for everyone, Porter argues. It makes no sense for Mercedes-Benz, Infiniti, or Cadillac to try to beat out other carmakers on price: None of them wants to cut costs if it means that their customers, who expect luxury, will grow dissatisfied with the quality of the automobile. Thus, each automaker will seek competitive advantage through ***differentiation,*** the attempt to make its product unique in the eyes of its customers. Most companies that opt for differentiating their products and services cannot simultaneously pursue the strategy of cost leadership: To make a product unique, a company usually has to spend a lot of money on it. While it is not impossible to be both the lowest-cost producer and the creator of the most highly differentiated product, the examples of such competitive advantage are rare (Porter 1985, 17–18).

competitive forces   *See five forces model*

competitor analysis   An evaluation of the intentions, actions, and market position of a company's competitors.

Corporate strategy is chiefly a function of managing a company's strengths relative to those of its main competitors within an industry. Gauging competitors' current positions and success in a particular ***market*** is relatively easy, since much of this information is available in ***annual reports,*** newspaper and magazine articles, and surveys of the inquiring company's own customers, who can evaluate the competition's products or services.

Much more difficult is the attempt to anticipate what direction a competitor will take, what new items are now in tests or are ready for a *product launch.* Some managers believe that it is almost impossible to obtain such private information, but it is often available to anyone who takes time to do the research. Good starting points are a company's sales force, its suppliers, distributors, and subcontractors.

complementary products   Products, such as cameras and film or computers and software, that must be used together.

Neither product can be substituted for the other, and the sale of one increases the sale of the other.

The development of complementary products poses several questions for managers setting strategy:

1. To what extent should a manufacturer be involved in the complementary products? In 1987, IBM partnered with Microsoft to develop a computer operating system, OS/2, that would run on its personal computers and be more flexible than its cumbersome predecessor MS-DOS. Although a powerful program for multitasking, it has not proven so popular as the various versions of Microsoft's Windows.

2. If the company decides to produce complementary products, should they be sold as a package or as individual items? ***Bundling*** products, as Microsoft can testify, can be profitable yet can lead to legal problems because of charges of unfair trade practices. The U.S. Justice Department in 1997 filed a suit charging Microsoft with such practices because the company had bundled its Internet Explorer with its operating system, the dominant driver in

the industry, which was installed on many of the personal computers sold in the United States. Although they were not forced to buy Microsoft's Explorer, the suit claimed that the bundling gave Microsoft an unfair advantage.

3. How should complementary products be priced in order to maximize sales and profits? Kodak, for example, once pursued a strategy of selling its cameras at a less profitable price, while it built a loyal base of Kodak film users. The increased profits from the sale of film helped balance the losses from the sale of cameras.

complex capital structure   The financing structure of a company with both *common stock* and *common stock equivalents.*

In this situation, a company must calculate two figures for *earnings per share:* (1) primary earnings per share and (2) fully diluted earnings per share. If the two figures differ by more than 2 percent, the company must disclose both in its *financial statements.*

*See also **common stock; common stock equivalent; simple capital structure.***

compound interest   The amount of interest earned when a financial institution or other agent adds one or more previous interest payments to the principal, then calculates the amount of the payment.

In other words, interest in subsequent periods is earned not only on the original amount of a *note receivable* or *note payable,* but also on the accumulated interest from previous periods. The interest may be compounded over any specified period—annually, quarterly, monthly, weekly.

EXAMPLE: A principal of $1,000 deposited in an account earning 3.5 percent interest compounded annually for three years is calculated as follows:

Principal		$1,000.00
1st-year interest	$1,000 × 0.035	35.00
2d-year interest	$1,035 × 0.035	36.23
3d-year interest	$1,071.23 × 0.035	37.49
Total		**$1,108.72**

compressed workweek   Any reduction in the number of days one works so long as the total number of hours at work remains approximately 40, the norm (at least in the United States) for full-time work.

In actuality, the average number of hours worked in U.S. manufacturing is just under 38 hours per week. Recently in many European countries and elsewhere, the average number of hours worked per week has significantly declined. The current averages for manufacturing are: 35.6 in Great Britain, 31.7 in France, 29.0 in Germany, and 35.0 in Italy (Tagliabue 1977).

In the last few decades many workers have opted for compressing their 40-hour workweek into four days or some other combination through flextime to qualify as full-time employees.

comptroller   Alternate spelling of *controller.*

This term derives from a misspelling that occurred around 1500 in England. Scribes apparently mistook the first syllable of the word *contrerolleur* as a form of the verb "to count," which in French is *compter.* According to the *Oxford English*

Dictionary, however, the word *contreroller* is derived from the prefix *contra-,* meaning "opposite." That prefix was reduced or simplified to *cont-,* which forms the basic meaning of the modern word *controller,* one who restrains an organization from destructive and chaotic forces, either internal or external.

Comptroller, although based in error, has a long history of official recognition in government and business.

computer numerical control   *See **numerical control** (NC)*

computer-aided design (CAD)   The use of computers in the design of products.

As computer technology continues to improve, graphic designers, builders, architects, and product developers of everything from cars to advertisements have turned to the design capabilities of CAD to help consumers visualize new products. An architect, for instance, can create a three-dimensional design for an addition to a customer's house, manipulate any of its parts by adding or deleting features such as windows, skylights, or doors, and even supply various carpet textures and colors on screen so that the customer can see the whole picture before buying it.

computer-aided engineering (CAE)   The use of computers to generate and test the engineering specifications of a product.

In the aerospace industry, engineers commonly use CAE to test the structural integrity of particular parts or subassemblies. Dassault, a French aircraft manufacturer, for instance, first developed software for creating *computer-aided three-dimensional interactive applications* (CATIA), computerized humanoid figures used in designing airplanes and helicopters. Boeing, Airbus, and other manufacturers now make widespread use of CATIA to determine, before a plane is built, whether a human being of average size and weight can squeeze into a compartment or extend a hand through a small opening. CAE innovations such as CATIA have helped narrow the gap between the startling ideas of designers and the actual capabilities of manufacturers and mechanics to make them real and practical (Belden 1977).

computer-aided manufacturing (CAM)   The use of computers to drive the manufacturing and assembly of a product.

There are two forms of CAM: direct and indirect. In direct CAM, manufacturers use computers or computer technology to control the processing equipment or handle the materials on the production line. Many automobile assembly lines employ robots, for example, in the construction of components. In indirect CAM, computers keep track of inventories, purchasing, planning, and other parts of the manufacturing process except for actual construction. The computer indirectly supports the activities needed for smooth line operations.

*See also **computer-integrated manufacturing** (**CIM**).*

computer-integrated manufacturing (CIM)   Another (and earlier) name for *computer-aided manufacturing* (**CAM**), which is now in wider use.

Through a computer system, CIM links a wide array of activities including engineering, designing, drafting, business planning, as well as shop-floor operations, inventory control, and ***materials requirements planning*** (**MRP**). CIM seeks to eliminate much of the ***overhead*** associated with the manufacturing process.

Computerized Maintenance Management Systems (CMMS)   Over 200 programs are available for scheduling preventative maintenance, maintaining records on equipment and vehicle maintenance, costing maintenance, analyzing expenditure patterns, and otherwise controlling the maintenance effort. Ranging from the simple to the complex and costing from $200 to $1.5 million, the software is available to allow better control over maintenance expenditure. A starting point for evaluation is the *Thomas Register's Guide to CMMS.* For under $100, a company can purchase the CD-ROM version and input its requirements to the search engine. In this manner many systems are eliminated and those that have the desired characteristics can be evaluated.

concurrent engineering   In the design of products and services, the incorporation of suggestions, requirements, and ideas from various stakeholders, including a company's functional areas such as manufacturing, its suppliers, and customers.

EXAMPLE: Concurrent engineering can create symbiotic relationships between companies, as exemplified by the Bose Corporation. Bose has implemented a system whereby its suppliers each maintain a full-time "implant" on-site at Bose. This supplier representative has full authority from Bose to attend engineering and design meetings and gather marketing and sales information, as well as full authority from its own company to conduct **transactions.** This system reduces a three-step process (planner-buyer-salesperson) to one, and facilitates the exchange of innovative suggestions in terms of design, engineering, and cost-effective **inventory** supply. (Hiebeler, Kelly, and Ketteman 1998, 94–96).

conglomerate   A collection or merging of several business entities, usually in different industries, under the authority of one executive officer and a board of directors.

Derived from the Latin word *glomus* ("ball"), a conglomerate is figuratively a number of strands wound up together. Mitsubishi, Matsui, and other groups of large Japanese companies in banking, mining, construction, and trade grew powerful in the nineteenth century, developing into monopolies with global reach. In the United States, R. J. Reynolds added to its vast cigarette business by acquiring numerous other companies including fast-food restaurants, oil companies, and liquor businesses. In 1985, the company purchased Nabisco Brands, as well as began selling off some of its other concerns, so that today it is a widely diversified holding company that manufactures and markets cigarettes, cereals, cookies, chewing gum, dairy products, condiments, and dog food.

Conglomerates usually do not fall under the jurisdiction of the **Clayton Antitrust Act of 1914** because they comprise businesses in various areas. From an economic point of view, they may appear attractive because the controlling company is able to spread its risk over its numerous business entities. But others question whether the same risk-spreading benefits cannot be more cheaply obtained by holding a portfolio of independent stocks.

Conglomerates can encompass businesses in many industries in many parts of the world. The first of the world's major conglomerates, the ITT Corporation, under the direction of Harold S. Geneen, comprised over 350 companies in 80 countries. Among Geneen's most famous **acquisitions** were Avis Rent-a-Car and the Sheraton Hotel chain. In January 1997, the Hilton Hotel Corporation began a hostile acquisition of ITT, but Starwood Lodging Trust, acting as a white knight, rescued ITT from the takeover and in 1998 gained control of the conglomerate.

conjoint analysis   A technique of analyzing data in which respondents rank various products according to their preferences for different combinations of those attributes.

Conjoint analysis hinges on three key management decisions: (1) which attributes to bundle in the survey's options, (2) what level of attributes to offer, and (3) what combinations of attributes are most likely to attract customers' attention.

EXAMPLE: An automobile manufacturer uses conjoint analysis by asking potential customers how they feel about various combinations of features and price. They may be asked, say, to compare a $32,000 car with all-wheel drive, antilock brakes, and a sunroof with a $40,000 model that adds air bags, leather interior, and a high-quality stereo system. Both models could be contrasted with a no-frills vehicle priced at $22,000. If the manufacturer has surveyed a representative sample, the conjoint analysis can provide fairly reliable data for determining the exact combination of features and price that the *target market* will find most appealing.

conservatism   One of the basic accounting tenets under *generally accepted accounting principles* (*GAAP*), which states that a company must recognize all losses as soon as they are quantifiable (even as estimates), but not record gains until they are realized.
See also matching concept.

consignment   A method of selling that allows the return of unsold and undamaged merchandise either from wholesalers to manufacturers or from retailers to wholesalers.

Newsstands frequently sell magazines on consignment, returning unsold copies to the distributor.

EXAMPLE: Even old software can be purchased on consignment. Software Sequels in Birmingham, Alabama, sells old versions of Microsoft Office, Wordperfect, and Lotus 1-2-3 for a fraction of their original costs, with the consignor receiving about 50 percent of the selling price. Customers can then use the older version to obtain updates at substantial savings over what they would have spent to buy the new product at retail (Milazzo 1997).

consolidation (1)   In accounting, the reporting of earnings of both a parent company and its *subsidiary companies* or *affiliated companies* as if they constituted a single entity.

The practice is widespread (and entirely legal) in many countries, including the United States, so long as the parent company owns at least 50 percent of the voting *common stock* of the subsidiary (this amount represents, in effect, control of that subsidiary). If the subsidiary engages in business operations that are vastly different from those of the parent company, such consolidation of earnings reports is not allowed by *generally accepted accounting principles* (*GAAP*).

consolidation (2)   A *merger* of two or more companies in which a new umbrella entity is created for the express purpose of acquiring the companies in question, which then cease to exist.

constant dollar accounting A method of measuring the items on a company's *financial statements* in terms of dollars with the same purchasing power—in other words, ignoring the impact of *inflation* or deflation.

Historic costs (HC) are converted according to the following formula using the *consumer price index* (*CPI*):

$$HC \times \frac{\text{average CPI for the current year}}{\text{CPI at the time of acquisition}}$$

Translating all accounts into constant dollars makes comparisons between years more meaningful because all *assets* will be stated in dollars of equivalent purchasing power regardless of when an asset was purchased.

Consumer Credit Protection Act of 1968 An act passed by Congress requiring truth-in-lending disclosure of all terms and conditions of finance charges in consumer credit *transactions* and loans.

Consumer Goods Pricing Act of 1975 A law passed by Congress that modifies the Sherman Antitrust Act, the *Clayton Antitrust Act of 1914,* and other pieces of legislation by prohibiting resale price maintenance (RPM) agreements between manufacturers and resellers in interstate commerce with the intention of creating monopolies and unfair competition.

consumer market All individuals and households that purchase or acquire goods and services for personal use.

Also called the *mass market,* the consumer market has four key characteristics: (1) a large number of buyers and sellers, (2) a wide geographic distribution, (3) small individual purchases, and (4) a wide variety of different products. Those characteristics lead to widespread distribution systems to link sellers and buyers. The distribution systems, by design, carry small amounts of various products across the country. An increasingly active communications system provides information to buyers and sellers, helping to eliminate price discrepancies among geographic areas and eventually leading to the development of new products.

EXAMPLE: SafeGuard Interactive, Inc., estimates the consumer market for data backup software products to be worth $200 million by the end of 1998. To reach this market, the company has begun selling its product through catalogs and at Web sites operated by Global, PC Connection, Online Superstore, and others (Kovatch 1997).

consumer price index (CPI) In the United States, the primary measure of *inflation* used in calculating Social Security payments, Medicare and veterans' benefits, federal pensions, tax brackets, wages based on cost-of-living adjustments, and the federal budget deficit.

Introduced in 1920, the CPI is the most important metric used by the U.S. government to measure inflation, a determination that has wide-ranging effects. For instance, the CPI affects cost-of-living adjustments to Social Security payments, and even a slight overstatement or understatement of the actual inflation rate can have a dramatic impact on how much retirees receive each month. Furthermore, the CPI is used in calculating the federal budget deficit, and according to the Congressional Budget Office, a 1 percent reduction in the CPI would reduce the deficit by $634 billion up to the year 2005. A slow rise in the CPI means a heavier tax burden for many Americans, who would find that their standard deductions and contributions to **401(k)** plans would not keep pace with the actual increases in the cost of living.

To estimate the CPI, the U.S. Bureau of Labor Statistics calculates the amount that urban consumers pay for specified goods and services. Recently, many economists have objected that the CPI overestimates the rate of inflation by approximately 1.1 percent a year (Kapoor, Dlabay, and Hughes 1996; McQuaid 1997).

Consumer Product Safety Act of 1972   The law that established the Consumer Product Safety Commission and gave it authority to set and enforce safety standards for consumer products.

The act excludes such products as tobacco, motor vehicles, pesticides, aircraft, boats, drugs, and food (many of these items are regulated under separate laws). It includes any product that creates an "unreasonable" risk of injury, which consumers cannot anticipate and against which they might have no other means of protection.

An independent regulatory board established on October 27, 1972, the Consumer Product Safety Commission (CPSC) comprises five members appointed by the president. Working with industry, the board has developed over 300 voluntary standards for products ranging from children's clothing to hair dryers. In 1993, the CPSC issued regulations to create child-resistant cigarette lighters. It has also regulated the packaging for prescription drugs and issued safeguards against lead paint.

The CPSC's hot line is (800) 638-2772. For more information, contact the Web site at http://www.cpsc.gov.

consumer-adoption process   In *marketing* theory, the steps that potential consumers follow in discovering, evaluating, and either adopting or rejecting a new product.

The process is said to comprise five stages: (1) *awareness*—the consumer becomes aware of the product's existence but has no information about it; (2) *interest*—the consumer seeks to learn about the product; (3) *evaluation*—the consumer decides whether to try the product; (4) *trial*—the consumer buys the product to confirm his or her estimate of its usefulness; (5) *adoption/rejection*—the consumer becomes a regular user of the product or rejects it (Boone and Kurtz 1995, 379–381).

continuous improvement   *See kaizen*

contribution margin (CM)   The amount by which sales exceed the *variable costs* (such as materials and labor) of a product or service.

The contribution margin represents the amount that a company can use to cover *fixed costs* (for example, rent, insurance) and generate a profit. Financial managers use this measure to decide, for instance, whether to keep, drop, or add a product line, manufacture or outsource a subassembly, or accept special orders.

To calculate the CM, subtract variable costs from total sales.

EXAMPLE: A manufacturer sells 100,000 widgets at $20 per widget for total sales of $2 million. Fixed costs amount to $700,000 or $7 per widget, and variable costs come to $1.2 million or $12 per widget. Thus, the company makes a profit of $100,000. After these sales and costs are accounted for, a customer offers to buy 1,000 widgets for $15 each. Assuming that the company has enough idle capacity to produce that many widgets without increasing its fixed costs, should the company accept the offer?

In order to make that decision, financial managers should look at the contribution margin of the additional 1,000 units:

Sales: 1,000 × $15	$15,000
Less: Variable costs, 1,000 × $12	(12,000)
Contribution margin	$3,000
Less: Fixed costs	0
Net income	**$3,000**

This analysis shows that the company can profitably sell 1,000 units at $15 each so long as it has idle capacity. The contribution margin of those widgets will add $3,000 to the company's profits without increasing fixed costs.

control chart   A tool used in quality control to monitor and make timely decisions about whether a particular process is in statistical control.

A process is said to be in *statistical control* if any variation results from purely random or accidental causes (Shirland 1993). In precision-oriented production lines, each unit should theoretically be exactly like the other items. While this standard may apply to the production of prescription drugs and computer processors, it is rarely the case when the products are sport utility vehicles, bottles of chardonnay, or rump roasts. Variations among products coming off the same production line can be attributed to random or known causes. Causes known and assigned can be corrected.

To allow for variation, manufacturers establish levels of tolerance, the maximum physical variation a product can have and still perform the function for which it was made. Anything exceeding those tolerances becomes an item for rejection or must be reworked to make it functional.

A control chart can be considered a meter or a gauge to measure variation and issue a warning if the number of defects increases beyond tolerable levels. Just as a tachometer measures RPM and warns the driver against excessive revving of an engine, so a control chart warns managers that a sample is out of statistical control.

In developing a control chart, managers define a set of statistical limits that are closer to the specification than to the physical tolerances. Setting the upper and lower *control limits* at $\pm3\sigma$ (standard deviations) and assuming a normal curve allows us to infer that the chance of a random failure or a unit falling beyond $\pm3\sigma$ is 3 per 1,000 units produced.

control limit   The upper and lower statistical limits that managers select for use in a *control chart.*

controller   The principal accounting executive for a large company.

Also called a *comptroller* (the two words are pronounced exactly alike), the controller reports and interprets financial data, computes taxes, develops the accounting system, coordinates both internal and external *audits,* manages the payroll, performs cost analyses, and prepares *financial statements* and budgets.

A controller differs from a treasurer, the primary financial officer of usually a small firm, in the areas of investment portfolio management and credit policies. The treasurer looks after the company's management of its cash and **credit.** He or she might write disbursement checks for stockholders, manage the firm's pension and insurance plans, and work with banks to obtain financing for new projects.

    See also **chief financial officer (CFO); comptroller.**

conversion ratio   A formula for calculating the number of shares of a **convertible security** that a shareholder receives when a conversion occurs.

    Conversion can affect the status of any security. A company can convert all pre-ferred shares into **common stock** shares, or vice versa, or it can exchange its shares of stock for equivalent stock of either an acquiring or an acquired company. The for-mula states that the face value of the security is to be divided by the conversion price that the holder pays for the common stock into which the security will be converted:

$$\text{Conversion ratio} = \frac{\text{face value of convertible security}}{\text{conversion price}}$$

If a $50,000 **bond** is convertible into common stock at a conversion price of $25 per share, the conversion ratio is computed as follows:

$$\frac{\$50,000}{\$25} = 2,000 \text{ shares}$$

In other words, the holder of the convertible bond can exchange it for 2,000 shares of common stock.

EXAMPLE: In a complex **recapitalization** move, Kaiser Aluminum Corporation sought to convert 100 million shares of its common stock into two types of stock: Class A shares would have full voting rights, but Class B would have only a one-tenth vote per share. Kaiser stockholders could expect that for each share of com-mon stock they would receive a one-third share of Class A stock and a two-thirds share of Class B. In addition, owners of certain preferred (nonvoting) shares could expect a conversion into shares of common stock under the plan's ratio of 0.8333 to 1.0. Because of ambiguities in the corporate certificate, a Delaware court blocked this attempt to restructure the company (Garmisa 1996).

convertible security   Stocks and bonds, such as **preferred stock** (subject to con-version), that can be converted into **capital stock** at an announced date.

    Using the **conversion ratio,** a company determines the number of shares it will issue.

EXAMPLE: A $10,000 convertible bond issue (ten bonds at $1,000 each) is con-verted at a ratio of one bond for each 30 shares:

$$\frac{\$10,000}{\$1,000} = 10 \text{ bonds}$$

$$10 \text{ bonds} \times 30 \text{ shares/bond} = 300 \text{ shares}$$

The bondholder, therefore, will receive 300 shares of stock for the original $10,000 bond issue.

    See also **bond; capital structure; earnings per share.**

coproduction   An agreement, often involving the exchange of equity interests, in which two or more companies combine resources to generate profits from the sale of products.

Resources can include management expertise, technology, production space, raw materials, as well as financial support. Aside from the direct gains resulting from the sale of products, each company realizes several other benefits. If the coproduction occurs between a foreign and a domestic company, the host might gain new technology and managerial expertise, whereas the guest could reap the benefits of direct investment in a foreign country without the risk of starting its own business from scratch.

EXAMPLE: Coproduction between Universal TV and various foreign groups has been so successful that it has become the cornerstone of the studio's international expansion strategy. More than $500 million in yearly incremental revenues is generated from coproduction and licensing deals with companies like the Kirch Group in Germany, France's Canal Plus, and a 50 percent partnership in Poland's RTL 7 satellite and cable channels.

copyright   The exclusive right to publish and sell a literary, musical, or artistic work (including films, photographs, television programs, and software), or any piece of written material that can be reproduced and sold.

Copyright laws protect the holder against unauthorized appropriations of the *expression* of ideas, concepts, and facts, not the ideas or facts themselves. Because it is in the public interest to disseminate these ideas and facts, the concepts themselves cannot be copyrighted. For instance, Einstein's original paper describing the theory of relativity cannot be published or copied without permission, but the theory itself belongs to the community of interested persons who may refer to it in any work.

Holders of copyright have certain privileges such as the rights to reproduce the copyrighted work, to profit from the sale of works derived from the original, to distribute copies, to perform the work publicly (in the cases of poetry, drama, musical works, and so forth), and to display the work in public (in the case of paintings and other artistic creations).

A work receives copyright protection as soon as it is created; it needs neither to be registered, as in the case of a patent, nor to be published. In the United States, at least for works created after January 1, 1978, each work remains under copyright for the life of the author plus 50 years. During that time, the concept of *fair use* is applied when the work is used for educational purposes (not for gain), such as occurs when teachers wish to copy portions of a work for classroom use or when librarians make single copies of a work for circulation to patrons. In recent years, however, even the privilege of fair use has come under greater scrutiny.

When the copyright expires, the work enters public domain and can be used by anyone.

Copyright Act of 1976   U.S. law granting legal protection to original works fixed in any tangible medium of expression. The act was rewritten in 1978.
     See also **copyright.**

copywriter   The creator of the concepts for and the text of an advertisement.

Usually a copywriter works with an art director on a project, creating the copy, concept, art, and design of an ad campaign. Some copywriters work full-time at *advertising agencies,* whereas others work as freelancers.

core competence A skill or aptitude, or more likely a collection of such skills, that enables an organization to integrate business processes in the creation and delivery of true benefits for customers, and to distinguish itself sufficiently from its competitors as well as block their attempts at imitation, and to establish *competitive advantage.*

As Hamel and Prahalad (1994) point out, most businesses have between 5 and 15 core competences, although something closer to the lower number is more realistic among companies that seek to establish dominance in their fields. A core competence need not be absolutely unique to a company, any more than Federal Express is the only company that uses package tracking to advantage; however, for a competence to be considered *core*, it must integrate the collective wisdom and expertise of the company's employees, suppliers, and customers (Varadan 1997).

EXAMPLE: Casio developed a core competence in display technology that allowed it to extend its products to *markets* that included computer monitors, automobile dashboards, calculators, digital watches, and miniature televisions. The company integrated its expertise in miniaturization, microprocessor design, material science, and precision casing (Varadan 1977).

corporate advertising The promotion of a corporate image rather than a focus on the products and services the business sells.

Advertisers may also advocate the corporation's point of view on an issue it wants to promote. Unlike product advertising, which reports to *marketing,* corporate advertising in a large business typically reports to *corporate communications.*

EXAMPLES: For over 25 years Texaco has sponsored broadcasts of the Metropolitan Opera on public radio and PBS stations. Citicorp backs the 1997–1998 concert tour of Central and South America by the New York Philharmonic Orchestra. And Mobil wins points with the public by offering the Pegasus Prize for literature, given annually to a writer in a country where Mobil has operations.

In addition to promoting the arts and making such performances available to wider audiences, these companies recognize the power that such associations have for their corporate images and customer base.

corporate communications A functional area responsible for managing a corporation's *public relations* (*PR*), its image or public face, and its relations with various public and private groups.

As public attitudes toward business have grown increasingly negative, corporate executives have come to appreciate the importance of combining communications activities under one manager. In many large companies, the corporate communications function reports directly to the CEO or president, has responsibility for creating a coherent image for public consumption, and promotes the corporation's identity, including its strategies and mission. Moreover, this executive oversees *corporate advertising, image advertising,* relations with employees, the media, and the community, as well as corporate philanthropy.

EXAMPLE: "What's in a name?" Juliet asks Romeo. Both Shakespeare and corporate America would answer: "Plenty."

Companies often change their names, at no small expense considering all the signage, the stationery, the corporate logos, the Web pages, and other means of communicating with the public. Esso (from "S.O." for Standard Oil of New Jersey) became Exxon in 1972 at a cost of $100 million (a lot of money in 1972). (SOURCE: Hoover's online library.) Similarly, North Carolina National Bank became NCNB, which then became NationsBank, and hundreds of other companies have taken the same route to fame and fortune.

In the first half of 1997, 100 companies changed their names, according to statistics compiled by Interbrand Schechter, Inc., more than in the entire 12 months of 1991. Over the span from 1991 to 1996, an average of 120 companies changed names annually. One of the most famous was Kentucky Fried Chicken's change to KFC in 1991, as part of the company's attempt to avoid using the word *fried* in its appeal to diet-conscious customers (Wong 1997).

corporate culture   The composite of an organization's values, customs, norms, and attitudes.

In fashion during the 1980s, the idea of a *corporate culture* has in the decade of the 1990s found many detractors. It was the subject of a best-selling book by Terrence E. Deal and Allan A. Kennedy, entitled *Corporate Cultures: The Rites and Rituals of Corporate Life* (1982), who detail the various manifestations of "culture" in their examination of corporate "rituals" (Case 1996). Those who believe sincerely in the term's validity speak of "how we do things around here." Skeptics, on the other hand, argue that business has appropriated an ambiguous term from anthropology and that a single entity such as a corporation cannot legitimately lay claim to the idea of uniform behavior, shared values, and a sense of an organization's history, no matter how tirelessly it promotes that unity.

corporate strategy   The plan of action an organization devises to achieve its goals.

In setting a corporate strategy, management needs to determine what the company does best, where its **core competences** lie, what business the company wants to engage in, and what contribution it intends to make. As a military metaphor, strategy is sometimes seen as a science, sometimes as an art, and sometimes as both simultaneously.

Derived from the Greek word *strategia* ("generalship"), the term connotes the marshaling of forces in a planned and organized fashion for the purposes of competing and winning. Corporate strategy is sometimes distinguished from business strategy in that the former refers to the competitive stance of the entire organization, whereas the latter involves decisions regarding individual products or services.

The decisions and planning that make up corporate strategy usually take effect over a long period of time and help define both the character and image of the company. Decisions to acquire sophisticated technology or to pursue a policy of **total quality management** (**TQM**), for instance, will have an impact on the company and its employees for many years. Other decisions—such as those involving product lines, manufacturing, and marketing—may have to change very quickly. Thus, it is important to find ways of integrating short- and long-term strategies so that they do not work at cross-purposes.

Short-term financial goals such as raising profits and achieving a high ***return on equity (ROE)*** may conflict with other goals such as increasing ***market share*** and sales growth over time. The best-devised strategies, therefore, delineate (1) the products or services that the company offers or plans to offer; (2) the ***markets*** in which it plans to compete; (3) the ***distribution channels*** it will use to reach those markets; (4) its profit objectives; (5) the method of financing that the company plans to use to attain its goals; (6) policy statements for the major functions within the company, including manufacturing, marketing, research and development, materials procurement, personnel, and labor relations; and (7) the company's size, organizational design, and culture.

corporation   The formal organization of a business, in accordance with the laws of the state (occasionally the federal government) in which it locates its headquarters, for the purpose of raising ***capital,*** producing goods or services, issuing shares of stock or ***bonds*** (or both), and conducting business.

As a legal entity, a corporation is entirely separate from the people who own it and from those who operate it. That is, the entity would continue to exist even if, for instance, all the executives and the board of directors were suddenly killed. Although the roots of the modern corporation can be traced back to the Roman empire, it was primarily during the age of exploration in the Renaissance that trading companies were formed to help colonize foreign lands and generate wealth for their owners. Examples include the East India Company and the Massachusetts Bay Company.

A corporation can borrow money, own property, enter into contracts with other organizations or individuals, incur or pay off debts, acquire other companies or be acquired by them. Since it is separate from its shareholders, the corporation is liable for its own debts.

See also **S corporation.**

cost accounting   The allocation of a business's operating expenses to the costs of the goods a company makes or the services it renders.

In cost accounting, all the actual expenses of making and delivering a product or service—including labor, materials, ***overhead,*** and in some cases selling and administration—are tallied and categorized so that managers can apply a variety of cost analysis techniques. These include ***direct costing,*** whereby managers determine all product costs that vary directly with production or sales volume, and standard costing, which compares actual costs with present ***standard costs.***

cost center   A unit within a company—whether a department, a piece of equipment, a business process, or an individual—to which ***direct costs*** can be attributed.

In addition to direct costs, many cost centers account for a portion of the company's ***fixed costs,*** or ***overhead.*** A factory, for instance, is a cost center.

Managers of cost centers seek to increase the difference between ***standard costs*** (the direct costs and overhead that management assigns to each cost center) and its actual costs.

The key to the effective use of cost centers is accurate assessment and assignment of direct costs and overhead. In many cases, cost allocation is a matter of historical convention rather than careful analysis. This can lead to a distorted perception of the profitability of various cost centers.

See also **management control systems.**

cost leadership A marketing strategy by which a company attempts to capture a *market* by offering the lowest-cost product or service.

In order to achieve cost leadership, a company must reduce its production costs, *overhead,* and other expenses, while it keeps quality and customer service at least at a level acceptable to consumers. While effective in gaining *market share,* however, the strategy has two primary drawbacks. First, the company may cut the price too much and lose money. Second, a cost leadership strategy diminishes *brand* loyalty: Customers will switch to another product if they can buy it at a lower price. Competitors, therefore, will have an opportunity to steal market share. Companies that have had success with cost leadership include Briggs & Stratton in small engines, Texas Instruments in calculators and computers, Black and Decker in electric and battery-powered tools, and DuPont in chemicals (Porter 1980).

cost of capital The *rate of return* available in the marketplace on *investments* comparable in terms of risk and other investment characteristics such as marketability.

Cost of capital, in practical terms, is the expected rate of return an investor requires before purchasing the rights to future streams of income as reflected in the business interest under consideration. Cost of capital is an integral part of the business valuation process. It is, however, determined by market forces, which are completely out of management's control. It represents the degree of risk that potential investors perceive: The lower the perceived risk, the lower the cost of capital.

See also ***capital asset pricing model*** (***CAPM***).

cost of goods sold In accounting, the expenses a manufacturing company incurs to make a product.

As a rule, these costs include labor, materials and parts, factory *overhead,* conversion costs, and other such expenses. *Gross profit* is the difference between sales and cost of goods sold. Cost of goods sold is listed on the *income statement* and is calculated as follows:

Sales			$10,000
Less:	Cost of goods sold		
	Beginning inventory	$2,000	
	Add: purchases	5,000	
	Cost of goods available for sale	$7,000	
Less: ending inventory		3,000	
Cost of goods sold			4,000
	Gross profit		$ 6,000

cost per thousand (CPM) In *advertising,* the cost of reaching a thousand people with an advertisement.

Data on circulation and program audiences is relatively easy to come by. Nielsen ratings for television, for instance, provide statistics on the number of viewers for individual programs, series, and time slots. Print media can calculate the number of issues of a magazine or newspaper printed and subtract the number sold or distributed in order to determine the size of an audience, potential or actual.

The abbreviation *CPM* reflects the use of the Roman symbol "M" for *mille,* or 1,000. In order to calculate a CPM, divide the cost to place an ad in any given medium (print, radio, television, etc.) by the number of people that medium reaches.

EXAMPLE: A full-page newspaper advertisement costs $160,000 and the paper has a circulation of 5,000,000.

$$CPM = \frac{cost}{audience\ size} = \frac{\$160,000}{5,000,000} = \$0.032\ or\ 3.2¢$$

Marketers use CPM, as a rule, to compare different outlets within the same medium—two newspapers, for instance. This comparison is valid, however, only if the two media reach the same target audience.

EXAMPLE: A calculator manufacturer attempting to reach an audience of businesspeople has an option of placing an ad either in the newspaper mentioned above or in a local business journal with a circulation of only 200,000 for $0.50 per thousand. A comparison of CPMs alone would suggest that the former option is the better choice. The business journal, on the other hand, probably is the better buy, given this advertiser's needs, because it reaches the target audience directly.

cost-benefit analysis A calculation to determine whether the results of a particular course of action are sufficient to justify the costs and risks in taking it.

EXAMPLE: In considering whether to expand nationwide, a regional restaurant chain conducts a cost-benefit analysis comparing all its projected expenses with the potential *revenues* such a move would bring in. After calculating those costs, managers determine that the setup expenses outweigh potential benefits by $10 million; thus, they decide not to pursue the plan.

Some costs and benefits, however, are not so easily measured in terms of expenses and revenues.

EXAMPLE: An automobile manufacturer finds that one of its cars has a defective parking brake, which can give way when vehicles are parked on a hill. If the manufacturer performs a strict analysis comparing the relative costs and benefits of a full recall as opposed to a small number of lawsuits, it might seem that the less expensive course of action would be simply to settle the lawsuits and avoid the costs of a recall. This simplistic reasoning, however, ignores the intangible costs to the manufacturer's reputation, not to mention the incalculable costs of injuries to human beings.

cost-of-entry test The calculation of the strategic impact of the *acquisition* or start-up of a new business unit.

The cost-of-entry test states that the cost of entering a new business must not exceed the future profits generated by that business.

EXAMPLE: In 1997, Wachovia Bank invested $222 million to acquire First United Bancorp of Boca Raton, Florida. With other recent acquisitions in Virginia, the North Carolina–based Wachovia has indicated its intentions of aggressively pursuing *markets* in other southeastern states, including the Carolinas, Georgia, and Florida. Although the cost of entry is high, the potential profits for Wachovia are much greater (Plunkett 1997).

cost-plus pricing In marketing, the strategy by which manufacturers or retailers add a standard *markup* to the cost of a product.

If a clothing manufacturer produces 1,000 pairs of pants that cost $19,000 ($19 each) and adds a markup of $5 per pair to the cost, the price to *wholesalers* is $24 per pair. The manufacturer collects a profit of $5,000 (20.8 percent). For cost-plus pricing to work, however, the seller must accurately predict the *demand* for its products at a given price. If the clothing manufacturer decided to sell the pants for $35 per pair, generating a profit of $16,000 or over 84 percent, but wholesalers balked at the high price and bought only 500 pairs, the company would make only $17,500. This amount, however, represents a loss of $1,500, since it cost $19,000 to make the pants in the first place.

When implementing cost-plus pricing, it is important to consider the series of markups that can take place throughout a distribution system. Assume the clothing manufacturer sells pants to a wholesaler for $24 a pair, and the wholesaler sells to a *retailer* for $30 a pair (yielding a 25 percent profit), and the retailer sells the pants for $60 a pair or a 50 percent profit. The final price to the consumer can vary considerably, depending on which channels are used and the markup each member of the channel makes.

See also distribution channel.

countertrade The exchange of goods, services, and perhaps currency for other goods or services.

Countertrade arrangements are grouped into three broad categories: barter, *parallel trade,* and buybacks.

Bartering, the oldest and most common form of countertrade, involves exchanging items without invoicing or any exchange of money. In the modern world, more sophisticated practices have evolved, but they all involve paying for merchandise or services with *commodities* of equal value, either with or without partial payment in currency or some other recognized valuable. In a celebrated instance of countertrade, two soldiers in Homer's *Iliad* (Book 6), upon discovering that they have common ancestors, honor each other by exchanging their armor as if the pieces were of equal value. One suit of armor is bronze, but the other is *gold.*

Parallel trade involves the execution of two separate contracts—one for the sale of goods by party A to party B, and a second contract for the sale of goods by party B to party A. The two contracts are necessary for insurance coverage and possible *credit* terms for each shipment. Each contract exists independently of the other and is individually enforceable. *Counterpurchase,* one form of parallel trade, involves actual cash transfers. Seller and buyer each pay the other for the goods received, using either a *letter of credit* (*L/C*) or cash payment. If buyer and seller are from different countries, payments from both parties may be in one currency, or they may be denominated in the currency used by the party originating the *transaction.*

Buyback countertrade agreements result from the sale of technology, a license, production lines, or even a complete factory. Full or partial payment consists of products manufactured in the production facility, or from the license or technology involved in the transaction. Buyback transactions frequently involve the importing of subassemblies, components, or other products, which a manufacturing exporter then turns into finished products. The most common use of buyback agreements relates to turnkey construction projects.

Coproduction is a specialized form of buyback countertrade used mainly for the transfer of technology or management expertise. For example, two companies form a *joint venture* (*JV*) to build a plant in Haiti. The U.S. company takes an equity interest in the facility. It may also furnish management support to run the facility. In either case, the U.S. and the Haitian companies coconstruct the facility and remain responsible for its operation. With equity interests, both parties benefit from the sale of products manufactured in coproduction: The Haitian partner gains by generating sales within Haiti and exporting products to other nations, but, most important, it gains by acquiring new technology; the U.S. company profits through exports either to the United States or to other nations.

In the United States, regulatory bodies such as the Internal Revenue Service (IRS) and the *Securities and Exchange Commission* (*SEC*) are generally opposed to countertrade, although there is little they can do to stop it. The U.S. government recognizes that countertrade is necessary for American companies to compete in world markets, but refuses to sanction it. Rules governing the practice are practically nonexistent. The *American Institute of Certified Public Accountants* (*AICPA*) prefers the regularity of its *generally accepted accounting practices* (*GAAP*) to the nonconforming practices of barter.

Countertrade contracts vary with each deal and from customer to customer. Form and content are limited only by the imaginations of those engaged in the trade. Some contracts are bilateral; others, multilateral. Some exchange goods for goods; others include a partial cash payment. For exports, the cash portion may be in the currency of either the buyer or the seller.

CPM *See cost per thousand or critical path method*

crashing a project Committing more dollar resources to shorten the time of activities on the critical path. This could be adding more people or changing equipment. The idea is to shorten the path. Care must be taken not to shorten the path to the point that the critical path is no longer the longest path, but has been displaced and another path is now longer. Such expenditures waste money. The selection of the activity to shorten is usually based on the return per dollar expended. Since the common measure is time, the lowest cost per day of reduced task activity is often chosen when looking at the activity to crash.

credit (1) An entry on the right side of a T-account (abbreviated "cr.").

In *asset* and *expense* accounts, a credit signifies a *reduction* in an asset or expenses, such as cash paid to employees. In contrast, in other kinds of accounts such as *liability, owner's equity, revenue,* and *net income,* credit indicates an *increase* through the issuing of *common stock,* a sale of property, net income, and the like.

See also bookkeeping; debit.

ACCOUNT TITLE	
Left	Right
Debit	Credit

BALANCE SHEET ACCOUNTS

Assets	=	Liabilities	+	Owners' equity
Dr. | Cr.		Dr. | Cr.		Dr. | Cr.
(+) | (−)		(−) | (+)		(−) | (+)

INCOME STATEMENT ACCOUNTS

Revenues	−	Expenses	=	Net income
Dr. | Cr.		Dr. | Cr.		Dr. | Cr.
(−) | (+)		(+) | (−)		(−) | (+)

credit (2)   The ability to borrow money or purchase an item with an obligation to pay later.

critical path method (CPM)   A project management tool developed by DuPont and Remington Rand in 1957 for project management and control. In any project there is a series of activities that must be performed in a certain sequence, yet all tasks need not be performed sequentially. Some tasks can be performed in parallel. CPM requires the project engineer to define the tasks, define the relationship among tasks (what must precede what and what can be done independently), convert it to a network or precedence diagram and make a time estimate for each activity. Upon doing this, the longest path through the network or precedence diagram is the critical path and therefore the project duration. Paths shorter than the critical path contain *slack.* This means there can be some delay in starting the activities that have slack without impacting on the duration of the project. CPM has a single time estimate for each activity, while its companion, ***Program Evaluation Review Technique*** (***PERT***), has three estimates of time for each activity.

critical ratio analysis   A tool used to prioritize inventories in a *flow process* system.

    The critical ratio analysis highlights items in an ***inventory*** that are in lowest supply. In a flow shop, goods are usually made-to-stock rather than made-to-order. The objective in managing a flow process is to replace stocks of finished goods before they run out. A cigarette manufacturer, for instance, must keep careful watch over inventories of tobacco, paper, and filters.

    In order to calculate a critical ratio for those items, the managers of the cigarette company must know three things: (1) the remaining amount of each material in stock, (2) the rate at which those materials are being consumed in the production process, and (3) the processing time of each type of inventory.

    The critical ratio is an extension of the **runout method,** which estimates how quickly an inventory will be depleted. Runout time is calculated by dividing the remaining amount of inventory by the rate at which it is used (that is, by its demand rate):

$$\text{Runout time} = \frac{\text{inventory remaining}}{\text{demand rate}}$$

EXAMPLE: For the cigarette company mentioned above, the runout time for each inventory item is calculated as follows:

Item	Inventory remaining (units)	Daily demand (units)	Runout time	Runout sequence
Tobacco	18	3	18/3 = 6 days	2
Paper	21	7	21/7 = 3 days	1
Filters	20	2	20/2 = 10 days	3

In other words, runout analysis indicates that the cigarette company will run out of paper in three days, tobacco in six days, and filters in ten days. If the inventories are ranked by this runout sequence, paper will be the first item to be depleted, followed by tobacco and filters.

The critical ratio improves on runout analysis by incorporating the processing time of each inventory into the analysis. For example, it might take four days to process a unit of tobacco into a batch of cigarettes, three days to process a unit of paper, and 15 days to process a unit of filters. The critical ratio is then calculated by dividing an inventory's runout time by its processing time:

$$\text{Critical ratio} = \frac{\text{runout time}}{\text{processing time}}$$

In the cigarette company, the critical ratios for each inventory are calculated as follows:

Item	Inventory remaining (units)	Daily demand (units)	Runout time (days)	Processing time (days)	Critical ratio	Critical sequence
Tobacco	18	3	6	4	6/4 = 1.5	3
Paper	21	7	3	3	3/3 = 1.0	2
Filters	20	2	10	15	10/15 = 0.67	1

When an inventory has a critical ratio above or near 1.0, as with the items tobacco and paper, there is usually no cause for immediate concern. Stock is being used more slowly than or at about the same rate as the processing time. If the critical ratio dips below 1.0, however, as is the case with filters, the inventory is being used faster than the remaining processing time. A shortage is therefore likely. The lower the critical ratio, the greater the priority managers should place on increasing that stock.

cumulative effect of a change in accounting principles In accounting, the *income statement* account showing the effect of switching from one accounting principle to another.

Accountants present two sets of calculations: One set reports the *retained earnings* at the beginning of the year under the old method, and the second set gives the retained earnings that would have been reported if the new method had been used since the beginning of the year.

See also **accounting change; change in accounting principle.**

current account *See* **balance of payments**

current asset   In accounting, an item with a useful economic life of one year or less, or the normal operating *cycle* of the company, whichever is greater.

Current assets are listed on the ***balance sheet*** and include cash and ***cash equivalents,*** marketable securities, ***accounts receivable, prepaid expenses,*** and ***inventory.*** Most companies list only current assets with a ***useful life*** of one year, but companies with a long operating cycle (say, a construction company working on a large project) might list current assets that have a useful life of five or six years.

current cost accounting   The measurement of ***assets*** in terms of their ***replacement costs.***

For inventories, current cost is the cost of buying goods of the same type and quantity as those in ***inventory*** as of the ***balance sheet*** date. In determining the current cost of property, plant, and equipment, the guiding principle is service potential. In other words, the replacement cost of a factory is not the cost to duplicate the entire factory; it is the cost of duplicating the factory's ***capacity*** using present technology.

EXAMPLE: A vintner owns several small wineries, but current technology is such that only large wineries are being built. That means the replacement cost of the small wineries would be that of a single, larger operation.

In current cost accounting, only inventories and ***fixed assets*** are adjusted to reflect their replacement value. The historic costs of all other assets and ***liabilities*** are assumed to show their current costs without adjustment. ***Owners' equity*** under current cost accounting is determined by subtracting liabilities from the adjusted total assets.

The only changes in an ***income statement*** caused by current cost accounting are in ***cost of goods sold*** and ***depreciation*** expenses related to current cost adjustments to the inventories and fixed assets on the balance sheet.

The often large discrepancy between historic cost accounting (what a necessary piece of equipment or a process originally cost the organization) and current cost accounting has raised many objections among accountants.

EXAMPLE: British Gas operates a pipeline network approximately 282,000 km long, which it calls "one of the largest, safest, and most efficient systems in the world." Leaks in the system result in an annual loss of only 1 percent, a figure the company plans to reduce to 0.8 percent by the year 2000. Generally, British Gas reports current replacement costs, offering historical cost analysis only for the sake of comparison. The company depreciates its network over a 60-year period, including any additions it makes and subsequently revalues. In 1995, for instance, British Gas made improvements on its gas mains and facilities that under a historic cost accounting policy showed a depreciation charge of £83 million. The current cost accounting method, however, revealed a depreciation charge of £378 million (Clatworthy, Jones, and Mellett 1997).

current liability   In accounting, a debt payable within one year or within the normal operating *cycle* of a company, whichever is longer.

Current liabilities include ***accounts payable, accrued expenses*** payable (such as salaries or taxes), short-term notes payable, and the correct portion of long-term debt. Current liabilities are shown on the **balance sheet** and must be paid either with a **current asset** or with the creation of another current liability such as a bank loan.

current ratio   A measure of a company's ability to pay its **short-term debts.**
   The higher the current ratio, the greater the company's ability to satisfy its creditors. To calculate the current ratio, divide **current assets** by **current liabilities:**

$$\text{Current ratio} = \frac{\text{current assets}}{\text{current liabilities}}$$

EXAMPLE: A company has $3.5 million in current assets and $278,000 in current liabilities. Its current ratio, therefore, is:

$$\frac{\$3,500,000}{\$278,000} = \$12.59$$

In other words, the company has $12.59 in current assets for every dollar in current liabilities. A ratio greater than 1 is desirable (although a company's ratio should be compared, if possible, with those of other companies in the same industry to determine whether it is high or low).

   Generally, companies with current assets consisting of low levels of **inventory** and high **accounts receivable** can operate with a lower current ratio than companies with high inventory and low accounts receivable. Inventories, of course, are not so easily converted into cash as accounts receivable. If a company's ratio is much higher than the industry norm, it might indicate that the company is not actively investing its current assets, as the preceding example might suggest. Although creditors might find this condition attractive, investors may infer that the company's managers are too timid to risk current assets in order to achieve higher returns.

   EXAMPLE: In the sometimes icy competition among Canadian beer makers, Molson Breweries in Ontario, Canada, has had both fizz and fizzle. Although it has enjoyed a **market share** of over 50 percent, the company has recently suffered some setbacks. A potential contract to brew and sell Coors Light in Canada has apparently fallen through. Molson has also had to sell off a number of its interests in tangential areas just to keep up with other beer makers. Already the company has sold off its stake in a chemical business (Diversey Corporation), and it may do the same with a 25 percent stake in Home Depot. Recently, Molson reported a current ratio of 1.30, 1.25, 1.37, 1.11, and 1.03 for the years from 1992 to 1996 (Shecter 1997).
   See also **acid test ratio.**

current yield   *See* **bond yield**

customized marketing   A marketing strategy whereby a company has clearly segmented customers for whom it produces specialized and tailor-made products and services.
   Aircraft manufacturers including Boeing and Airbus customize planes to fit the needs of a few major airlines or national governments. Customized marketing is also common in the upholstery, housing, and hairstyling businesses. The recent ad-

vances in computer technology, particularly the arrival of the Internet, will continue to have dramatic effects on customized marketing.

EXAMPLE: In 1995, Wal-Mart created its own Web site (www.wal-mart.com) and the next year added technology that allows a customer to go online and order directly from the discount chain. Although still a small part of its overall sales (approximately 1 percent of over $100 billion, according to 1996 figures), the site is expected to draw more visitors, who will be able to customize their purchases for items such as wallpaper, clothing, and home furnishings (Rubinstein 1997).

cybernetics   The study of messages and communication between human beings and machines, as well as between machines themselves, in an effort to understand how to control society, human beings, and technology.

Norbert Wiener, professor of mathematics at the Massachusetts Institute of Technology, believed that the engineering and mechanical advances that had been discovered during World War II (e.g., transmission of coded messages) could be turned to solving postwar problems in society at large. The computer, for instance, could imitate communications and control processes such as error correction and deductive reasoning.

Writing in 1948, Wiener coined the term *cybernetics,* using the Greek work *kubernetes,* meaning "governor." His book, *Cybernetics: Control and Communication in the Animal and the Machine,* created a stir among his fellow scientists and mathematicians, but the book was beyond the understanding of the general public. Accordingly, Wiener published *The Human Use of Human Beings: Cybernetics and Society* in 1950, to demonstrate how machines and human beings communicate with each other and how the control of messages is key to controlling society and solving societal problems (Wiener 1954, 25).

cyberspace   The imaginary or so-called virtual expanse said to "exist" between two or more computers, networks, or databases, which can share information and communications.

The term *cyberspace* was coined in 1984 by William Gibson in his science fiction novel, *Neuromancer,* in which he imagined all the computers of the world joined together in "unthinkable complexity" (Gibson 1984). The prefix *cyber-* is derived from the Greek word for "governor" or "steersman," and thus conveys the meaning of control, the ability to harness latent power in any system and use it to achieve any objective.

See also **cybernetics.**

cycle   In manufacturing, sales and marketing, investing, and other business areas, the recurrence of an event at a known frequency.

Cycle lengths are responses to such events as seasonal **demand** for products and services, the advent of new lines (as in automobiles and clothing), political and economic conditions on a large scale, the rise and fall of **interest rates,** and other uncertainties in employment, **inflation,** and the like.

cycle counting   A means of ensuring the accuracy of a company's **inventory** by tallying goods and materials on the basis of a cyclic schedule rather than once a year.

Cycle counting aims to find inventory items that are in error and to trigger research into the causes of the problem. Cycle inventory counts occur on a regular basis, with high-value items counted frequently, medium-value less frequently, and low-value not at all. Cycle counts can also count a small fraction of inventory every week.

EXAMPLE: Sequa Chemicals, Inc., located in Chester, South Carolina, bar-codes some 5,000 containers of chemicals used in textiles, paper production, and other industries. Rather than taking an annual inventory by hand, which used to force the company to shut down for three days and cost over $100,000, it now scans and tallies its inventory every eight weeks. Varying in cost from $2,500 to $4,000, the scanners have already paid for themselves in terms of the efficiency with which the inventories are now done (Allimadi 1993).

cycle time   The amount of time it takes to perform each task in a process.

Cycle time is frequently used to mean the time of the longest task in the entire process.

EXAMPLE: A company assembles suspension systems for a major auto producer. It performs this process at five workstations in a sequence, as represented in the following table:

Workstation	Task	Task time (in minutes)	Idle time (in minutes)
1	A	2.0	1.0
2	B	2.4	0.6
3	C	3.0	0.0
4	D	2.5	0.5
5	E	2.8	0.2

The cycle time for each task is the task time. This is the length of time to complete the individual task on one unit. The **bottleneck** in the operation shown above is station 3, where the task takes the longest amount of time (3.0 minutes). If five workers, one at each workstation, are assembling units, a unit comes off the line every three minutes. The last column shows the impact of this bottleneck: All stations except the third have some idle time. If everyone is working, the process can produce a maximum of 20 units per hour (60 minutes ÷ 3 minutes per unit) and up to 160 units per day (assuming employees work an eight-hour day). This is the production line's *technical capacity.* If, however, managers grant two 10-minute breaks, and the wash-up and start-up times consume another 10 minutes, then the real or *economic capacity* may be only 150 units per day. As much as 30 minutes per day, representing the production of 10 units, will be lost to those other activities.

To measure the **efficiency** of the operation, divide the time working in the cycle by the time of the longest task. Station 1, for instance, works in this process at 67 percent ($2.0 \div 3.0 = 0.666$). Station 2 works at 80 percent efficiency; Station 3 at 100 percent; Station 4 at 83 percent; and Station 5 at 93 percent. The entire line averages 2.54 minutes, which is 84.7 percent of capacity.

See also **balance delay; critical path method (CPM).**

cyclical inventory   Increases and decreases in stockpiles that occur in some industries, usually with a regular and predictable frequency.

Among those industries most vulnerable to cyclical inventory are agriculture, automobiles, paper, and clothing. In the paper industry, for instance, customers normally allow their stocks to be depleted if pulp prices remain high or show signs of increasing. The phenomenon is familiar to anyone who does the grocery shopping for the household, for there is the ever present temptation to buy in bulk or large quantities when prices are low and to put those items in the larder for that rainy day in the cycle of time (Mortished 1996).

D

days inventory   In accounting, a measure of the number of days it takes to sell the average amount of *inventory* on hand during a particular time period.

As a rule, the longer a company takes to sell its inventory, the greater the risk that it will not get full value for the goods. Companies that carry perishable or quickly obsolete items are particularly vulnerable to such losses. To calculate days inventory, divide 365 by the *inventory turnover* ratio, which is determined by dividing the *cost of goods sold* for a specified period by the average amount of inventory on hand for that same period:

$$\text{Days inventory} = \frac{365 \text{ days}}{\text{inventory turnover ratio}}$$

If a company has an inventory turnover of 5.25, its days inventory ratio is

$$\frac{365}{5.25} = 69.52$$

In other words, the company required nearly 70 days to sell the average amount of inventory it had on hand in the past year.

EXAMPLE: Logic Devices, a Sunnyvale, California, manufacturer of integrated circuits, has an unusual claim to fame: Although many computer companies in Silicon Valley have as much as 200 days of inventory, Logic Devices has enough items in stock to last a full 900 days, over ten times its quarterly *revenues.* In an industry where the technology changes so rapidly, that large a stockpile sends a troubled message to stockholders (Greenberg 1997).

debenture   An unsecured *bond,* one provided by a government or an organization that backs the issue only with its own creditworthiness.

The term derives from the Latin word *debentur,* meaning "they are owed," in reference to debts incurred by individuals or groups in the Middle Ages. Today's debentures frequently have a feature that allows a holder to convert the debts or *warrants* into *common stock* on a specified date or in the case of a default on interest payments or bond redemption.

debit   In accounting, an entry on the left side of a T-account signifying either an increase in an *asset* or expenses, or a decrease in a *liability* or *revenue.*

A debit is often abbreviated "dr." from the Latin verb *debere,* to owe.

See also bookkeeping; credit.

debt instrument   Any written contract or promise to repay a loan.

Examples of debt instruments include certificates of deposit (CDs), bills, promissory notes, ***banker's acceptances*** (**BAs**), and ***commercial paper.***

debt securities valuation   A process to determine the ***investment*** value of secured debts, those which specify the percentage of interest, the date of maturity, the principal, as well as any discounts.

Unlike ***debentures*** and equity investments, a debt security expressly describes the time and amount of income payments (interest) and the return of ***capital*** (principal) within the instrument itself. The risk of investing in debt securities is substantially less than that for equity investments.

Except for that difference in risk, both equity investments and debt securities use a similar method of valuation, based on the general theory of valuation, which states that the fair market value of a future stream of ***cash flows*** is equal to the present value of future cash flows. In addition, both recognize perceived risk in their ***capitalization*** rates.

Three factors influence or determine ***interest rates*** and repayment terms of any debt obligation:

- Current market risk-free rates, as reflected by the ***prime rate,*** the rate that banks charge their best customers, and by the rate paid on U.S. Treasuries nearly everywhere else
- Perceived risk of receiving interest and principal payments on schedule
- Collateral backing the loan (the quality of which detracts from or adds to the risk factor)

In addition to providing a base from which to negotiate with lenders for the lowest rate with the best terms, companies perform debt valuation for several other reasons. For instance, if they wish to invest excess cash in corporate or government bonds, they will need to know the correct valuation of the debt security. In addition, some buy/sell transactions involve the exchange of debt for ***equity.*** Privately held businesses are obliged by law to state the fair market value of debt obligations.

Moreover, a group in the process of making a ***leveraged buyout*** (**LBO**) must reclassify a company's old debts and take into account present values in order to allocate the purchase price among the participants. Companies may also recapitalize their ***balance sheets*** to increase the amount of leverage they have to work with, or in cases of ***bankruptcy*** they may have to rearrange debt securities, create new classes of them, or exchange them for equity issues.

If a debt security is traded in open markets, the present value of its future cash flows may be observed from the market price of the security at any given time. The application of a security's rate of interest to its future cash flows produces a present value equal to the security's observed market price. This is called the security's ***yield to maturity*** and is synonymous with the phrase *market rate of interest.*

For privately held companies whose debt securities are not traded in open markets, however, security valuation must be calculated by using the ***present value*** formula. Three factors are needed for this calculation: (1) the amount of future cash flows generated by the security; (2) the timing of those cash flows; and (3) an appropriate rate of interest or yield to maturity.

debt/equity swap   The exchange of debt securities for equity interests. Several types of debt/equity swaps have become popular.

1. The swap of a third-world country's external bank debt obligations traded in secondary markets for equity interests in a business that the government is "divesting" through its privatization program, a privately owned business, or a business that is being started from scratch. Of course, the acquiring company must use its own funds to acquire the ***debt instrument*** in the first place, but that is often a small price to pay for a bargain-basement investment.

EXAMPLE: A company purchases a third-world government debt instrument in the secondary market at a 50 percent discount from its face value. It then offers to exchange this obligation with the debtor government for local currency. The rate of exchange is equivalent to 75 percent of the debt. To make up the difference, soft currency is used to build or purchase a facility in the host country for half the cost that the company might have invested with U.S. dollars.

2. The swap of a company's debt obligations with lenders for equity interests in the company.

EXAMPLE: Assume that XYZ Corporation owes $1 million to Fidelity Commerce Bank (FCB) on a term loan evidenced by a ***demand note.*** XYZ falls into arrears but has high expectations that when new product lines are introduced in two years, the business will take off. FCB recognizes that if something is not done with the loans, bank examiners will classify them as nonperforming. If that happens, FCB will need to set aside additional revenues and lower its capital ratio. XYZ agrees to give a 20 percent equity share in the business to FCB in exchange for half the loan, thereby reducing debt service payments to a manageable level.

3. The swap of a company's trade obligations with a creditor for an equity interest.

EXAMPLE: A company strapped for cash owes a major supplier substantially more than it can pay. Rather than cutting off a valuable source of supply on the one hand and a good customer on the other, the two parties work out a debt/equity swap: The supplier exchanges part or all of its receivable for a minority share in its customer.

4. The swap of public bonds for a minority equity interest.

EXAMPLE: Alpha Corporation has $5 million in bonds outstanding. LPL, a limited partnership, offers to make a swap with Alpha, trading the bonds for $2.5 million worth of shares of ***common stock.***

In addition to these four types, debt/equity swaps are now being arranged among debtors and creditors to ensure the preservation of natural habitats, for environmental ventures, for college scholarships, and for a variety of other purposes.

debt-to-assets ratio   A measure of a company's obligations relative to its ***assets.***
In general, the lower the debt-to-assets ratio, the more financially sound a company is or is thought to be. To calculate the ratio, divide the company's total debt by its total assets. The more conservative attitude requires that ***current liabilities*** and ***noncurrent liabilities*** be combined rather than including only those liabilities formally classified as debt. The formula for the ratio is:

$$\text{Debt-to-asset ratio} = \frac{\text{current liabilities} + \text{noncurrent liabilities}}{\text{total assets}}$$

EXAMPLE: If a company has current and noncurrent liabilities totaling $780,000 and assets totaling $1,120,000, its debt ratio is:

$$\frac{\$780,000}{\$1,120,000} = 0.696$$

In other words, for every dollar that the company has in assets, it has approximately $0.70 in debt. Whether that ratio is good or bad depends on the standards of the particular industry. In general, however, companies with lower ratios are more solvent; those with higher ratios are vulnerable to creditors' claims on their resources.

debt-to-equity (d/e) ratio   In accounting, a measure of the amount of debt a company has in relation to its *owners' equity.*

Potential creditors may be reluctant to give financing assistance to a company with a high debt-to-equity ratio. This ratio, however, varies widely from industry to industry.

Debt-to-equity ratios are traditionally calculated according to the *book values* for a company's debt and its *stockholders' equity.* Their *market values* may give a more realistic measure, however, because they more clearly reflect current market conditions. For information on these values, see *Key Business Ratios* and Standard & Poor's *Industry Surveys,* which supply data on a variety of *balance sheet* ratios grouped by industry and time periods. To calculate the d/e ratio, divide the company's total *liabilities* by its shareholders' equity. For financing purposes, total shareholders' equity may be adjusted for certain classes of *preferred stock* and convertibles.

$$\text{Debt-to-equity ratio} = \frac{\text{total liabilities}}{\text{total shareholders' equity}}$$

EXAMPLE: Total liabilities for Company Z are $3,400,000, and total shareholders' equity has a book value of $2,500,000. The debt-to-equity ratio is:

$$\frac{\$3,400,000}{\$2,500,000} = 1.36$$

That is, for every dollar of the company owned by a stockholder, there is $1.36 owned to creditors. If the ratio is greater than 1.0, the company might not be able to meet all its obligations if it had to settle up immediately. A ratio greater than 1.0, however, does not necessarily raise many flags of warning unless the ratio is substantially higher. Just as important may be the company's ability to pay interest on loans it has taken, an estimation of which is provided by the EBIT (earnings before interest and taxes) formula.

decentralization   The diffusion of authority, responsibility, and decision-making power throughout the organization.

Decentralization represents a major departure from the classic pyramid of top-down authority and responsibility. Because it is layered with bureaucracy, the traditional structure is slow to respond to changes in an uncertain and highly volatile environment. Because lower-level managers often do not have the information or the authority to make quick decisions, processes slow down or stop completely while the decision is pushed higher up the pyramid. Top managers, however, overloaded with decisions, often make the wrong ones because they also lack the knowledge of frontline employees and actual processes.

In such situations, companies may find it advantageous to shift to a decentralized organizational structure. Consider, for instance, the following decentralized clothing company:

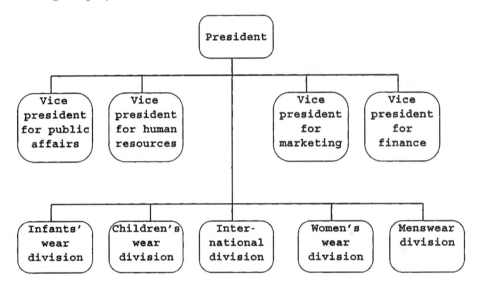

Decentralization

Organized around both product areas (e.g., mens- and women's wear) and **markets** (e.g., international), the clothing company comprises various divisions, each with resources enabling it to perform its special tasks. This "every tub on its own bottom" approach to organizational structure forces each division to concentrate on what it does best, to compete shrewdly and competently, and to avoid becoming embroiled in issues facing other divisions in the company.

In decentralized organizations, managers can better concentrate on specific products or services, sharing resources within the division as conditions warrant. Such a structure is especially effective when the business environment is complex and volatile, forcing rapid responses to changes in the marketplace. When a company divides itself into discrete, semi-independent units, it can, in effect, segment that environment and seek to reduce the complexity its managers face. As a result, managers may need less information than they would require if they tried to cope with the entire line of products and services the company offered.

Decentralization in its most extreme form begins to look like a house divided against itself. Inevitably, such a house must fall. Objections to decentralization include the charge that the structure wastes resources, both financial and human, when people or business units work in such isolation that they do not (or cannot) share information. If one product area in the preceding clothing store example, for instance, develops a practice for tracking customers and keeping them informed about new products and sales, sharing that practice with other areas would benefit the entire organization. Further, the division of products into mens- and women's wear overlooks the potential profits from unisex designs, nontraditional customers, and potential conflicts and overlaps with categories such as "international," which presumably would have their own mens- and women's-wear divisions.

See also **functional organizational design; matrix structure; organizational environment.**

decision making   The process of choosing a course of action among several alternatives.

As most theorists of business management agree, decision making permeates every aspect of the manager's role and is crucial in directing the activities of an organization. It is also one of the most difficult aspects of management, involving not only the ability to understand complex relationships but also to make inferences and to persuade others that one's decision is the right one. Merely to make decisions, however, is only part of what it takes to be a good leader or manager: One must be able to communicate effectively, motivate people, and take responsibility for the decisions one makes.

Various attempts have been made to isolate the steps involved in making effective decisions. For instance, the following six-step process can help managers see their way through unfamiliar terrain:

1. *Identify the problem.* One technique is to describe the problem, preferably in writing, as precisely as possible. Merely listing symptoms should be avoided.

2. *Collect reliable data.* The information should cover all aspects of the problem, including details on who, what, when, where, why, and how. For data to be reliable, it should come from known, representative sources or samples, which are as free from bias as possible. Reliable scientific evidence will come from empirical sources that admit retesting or reduplication. Less reliable, or completely unreliable, evidence comes from sources based on rumor, opinion, once-in-a-lifetime experience, and non-reduplicative testing.

3. *Enumerate possible solutions or alternatives.* Good managers spend a long time on this step, soliciting responses from as many people as possible, entertaining any alternative regardless of how absurd it may seem. This is not the time to dismiss any alternative before its time.

4. *Test possible solutions.* Feasibility often proves the most powerful criterion for evaluating an alternative: Can it be done? How much will it cost? Who will do the work? What are the risks? Other criteria include the suitability of the solution (Will the problem be solved permanently or only for the moment?) and the degree of acceptability (Will everyone agree that this solution is the best one?). The best managers recognize that clarifying those criteria in order to achieve as much consensus as possible does consume a lot of time and energy but is worth the effort in the long run.

5. *Choose the best alternative or course of action.* Here is another hidden assumption to thrash out. In selecting the solution (or combination of solutions) that works best, managers need to define *best* for the benefit of everyone affected by the decision: Best for whom? In the short or the long term? As a mere face-saving expedient or as a legitimate solution to a real problem?

6. *Implement the solution.* Although the primary focus is on solving the problem at hand, the ethics of making a decision raise complex questions about the work of managers and, indeed, about any step-by-step process, including this one. Merely solving the problem does not always make the decision the "correct" one.

EXAMPLE: In the 1840s the Western Railroad in Massachusetts faced the problem of building a line between Boston, Massachusetts, and Albany, New York, which had to cut through the Berkshire Mountains. Construction costs were high, the work dangerous, labor unreliable. Managers made the decision, common in those days because of expenses and other factors, to build a *single* line over certain sections of the railway that would handle trains traveling both east and west. The solution worked so long as conductors kept a strict watch on schedules, but it was also a solution tailor-made for disaster. In 1841, as many people had feared, two trains collided head-on near Springfield, Massachusetts, resulting in loss of life, property, and reputation for the struggling railroad (Chandler 1977, 96).

EXAMPLE: The Tylenol poisoning scare of 1982 ranks among the most exemplary cases of managerial decision making. Eight people in the Chicago area died after ingesting cyanide-laced Tylenol capsules. Although it was not responsible for the poisoning, Johnson & Johnson pulled all Tylenol capsules from store shelves and destroyed some 31 million bottles at a cost of $50 million. The company spent millions more repairing the damage done to its image and that of one of its most famous brands. No doubt company managers considered less costly alternatives, but they determined to give a higher priority to public safety and long-term profits for the company (Robbins 1994, 68).

decision support system   *See artificial intelligence; expert system*

decision tree   A type of flowchart that depicts the prescribed sequence of decision making and spells out each consequence of those decisions.

EXAMPLE: Consider the following decision tree for determining whether to launch a new product. Management decisions are represented by squares. Chance events, those outside the control of managers, are represented by circles. Lines represent the sequence of choices run between each decision and the chance events that the decision sets in motion.

A probability is assigned to each of the possible consequences of chance events. If, after receiving a favorable result from market testing, the company decides to launch the product, there might be, say, a 60 percent chance of strong sales, a 30 percent chance of weak ones, and a 10 percent chance of negligible sales. With those probabilities, the company can calculate the likely payoff if it pursues a launch or decides to abandon the product. Once all of the probabilities and payoffs have been evaluated, company managers can choose the course of action that appears to provide the most favorable outcome.

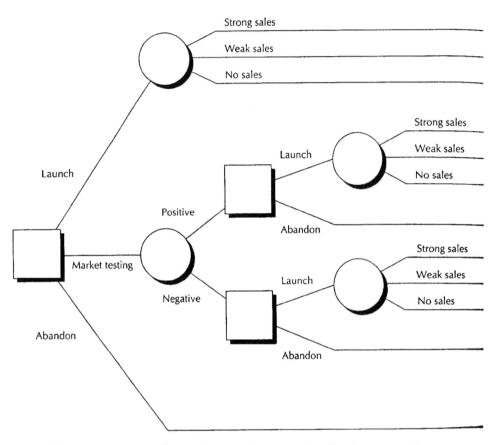

    Decision trees are obviously not substitutes for the decision-making process. They merely present a visible chain of events, options, and priorities. If probabilities are actually calculated and hung on the tree, managers can determine ahead of time what will be the fruits of their labor in terms of expected payoffs for the company. Of course, the success of that analysis depends on the accuracy of their **_fore-casting._**

    Drawing a decision tree has two primary advantages: First, because it visually depicts the relationship between decision and event, the chart forces managers to consider all the ramifications of their decisions; second, it places before managers, again in visible form, all the chance events and the uncertainties that accompany them.

decoupling inventory   *See **inventory functions***

deferred charge   *See **deferred expense***

deferred credit   *See **deferred income***

deferred expense   A charge incurred in one **_accounting period_** that will benefit future accounting periods.

Also called a *deferred charge,* such an expense is recorded as a **noncurrent asset** on the **balance sheet.** Examples include organization expenses to start up a business or a branch, establish a bond discount, refurbish a plant or facility, and build up other **intangible assets.** Those expenses should be positioned against the company's assets, typically its sales, in the same accounting period, as specified by the **matching concept** of financial accounting. For bond discount, the **amortization** is over the life of the bond. When the benefit period is indeterminable, as it is with organizational expenses, moving expenses, or plant rearrangement expenses, the asset may be amortized over an arbitrary period, but no longer than 40 years.

EXAMPLE:

Dr.	Cash	$ 9,000
Dr.	Deferred bond discount	$ 1,000
Cr.	Bonds payable	$10,000

The issuance of ten-year bonds at a 10 percent discount is recorded as follows:

Year 1

Dr.	Bond discount (income statement)	$100
Cr.		100

For tax purposes, business must use the amortization stipulated by the IRS code.

Compare to **deferred income.**

deferred income   In accounting, any item of income that has initially been recorded in the books of an account as a **liability** and will not be realized until future **accounting periods.**

Also called *deferred credit* or *deferred revenue,* this form of income is, at the time of its being received, "unearned." Any payment made in advance of the actual undertaking of work falls into this category. Thus, a consulting fee, a subscription to a journal, and a prepayment for medical services provide examples of deferred income.

EXAMPLE: A construction company receives payments according to the **percentage-of-completion method.** These entries record amounts due from the project:

PROJECT XYZ

Dr.	Unrealized receivable (noncurrent asset)	$5,000	
Cr.	Deferred income (revenues) from project		5,000

In a subsequent accounting period, these entries recognize sales from the project matched with related costs:

PROJECT XYZ

Dr.	Deferred income (revenues) from project	$5,000	
Cr.	Sales		5,000

The IRS code stipulates that a different treatment be used for deferred income. *See* **deferred income tax charge.** *Compare to* **deferred expense.**

deferred income tax charge   In accounting, income resulting from a temporary difference in the recognition of *revenues* and expense items.

A deferred income tax charge is an *asset* created when a company reports an expense in its *financial statement,* but actually takes a tax deduction on a later tax form. The difference is reported on the financial statement as a deferred income tax charge.

EXAMPLE: Warranty expenses are deducted from a company's books in the year of a sale, but deducted on the tax return of the year in which those expenses are actually paid.

EXAMPLE: A company has sales of $10,000. It estimates its warranty expenses as $1,000, but it has actually paid only $800 on the warranties. Assuming a tax rate of 40 percent, we can calculate and enter the deferred income tax charge as follows:

	Book income		Taxable income
Income	$10,000		$10,000
Warranty expense	1,000		800
Income before taxes	$ 9,000		$ 9,200
Tax expense ($9,000 × 40%)		$3,600	
Deferred income tax charge		80	
($200 × 40%)			
Tax payable ($9,200 × 40%)		$3,680	

*Compare to **deferred income tax liability.***

deferred income tax liability   In accounting, an estimate of the amount of future taxes on income that has been earned and recognized for accounting purposes, but not yet recognized for tax purposes.

In other words, reported income—also called *book income*—will be greater than taxable income. The difference is shown in the *financial statement* as a deferred tax liability. Eventually the two amounts will be reconciled.

EXAMPLE: A company with income of $50,000 used *straight-line depreciation* for a charge of $5,000 in its financial reporting and a method of *accelerated depreciation* amounting to $7,500 for taxes. Assuming a tax rate of 40 percent, we can calculate and enter the deferred income tax liability as follows:

	Book income		Taxable income
Income	$50,000		$50,000
Depreciation	5,000		7,500
Income before taxes	$45,000		$42,500
Tax expense ($45,000 × 40%)		$18,000	
Tax payable ($42,500 × 40%)		17,000	
Deferred income tax charge		$ 1,000	
($2,500 × 40%)			

*Compare to **deferred income tax charge.***

deferred revenue   *See **deferred income***

defined benefit pension plan   A program outlining pension benefits employees will receive at retirement.

The pension benefits are calculated through a formula that takes into account an employee's years of service and compensation level as that employee nears retirement. In establishing a defined benefit pension plan, a company must ensure that its *pension fund* has sufficient assets to pay what has been promised. Typically a company's reported pension expenses will be different from the amount actually paid, resulting in a deferred pension *liability* or *asset.*

*See also **defined contribution pension plan; funded pension plan.***

defined contribution pension plan   A program stipulating the annual dollar amount that an employer contributes to an employees' pension plan.

To calculate the contribution it should make, the company uses a formula that takes into account years of service, age, and salary level for each employee. Under a defined contribution pension plan, the employer makes no guarantee of future benefits to employees, as with **defined benefit pension plans.** Rather, there is simply a fixed dollar amount placed into the **pension fund** each year.

*See also **defined benefit pension plan; funded pension plan.***

Delphi analysis   A *forecasting* technique in which members of a panel, working independently and anonymously, make their predictions, then come together either as a group or through the coordination of a group facilitator to discuss results and work out a consensus.

Working anonymously and independently offers several advantages. Foremost, it avoids *groupthink*, or the phenomenon of peer pressure to conform to the will of the collective body. Furthermore, the technique can help reduce tension and disagreement within a group, particularly if there are some group members who have strong personalities or who appear overbearing in defending a point of view. In addition, the Delphi analysis can take place at various times and locations, thus making it feasible to bring together a group of experts from distant locations through telecommunications.

The Delphi technique, however, does have certain disadvantages. Its success depends on the quality of the coordinator's analysis that summarizes and reconciles the various points of view from the experts, on the willingness of panel members to discuss and modify their predictions, and on the manner in which information is presented to the individual members.

demand   In economics, the amount of a good or service that consumers stand ready to buy at different prices, other factors being held constant.

Those other factors include (1) tastes and preferences; (2) income; (3) prices of related or similar goods, such as substitutes or complements; (4) number of buyers; (5) scarcity of similar items in demand; and (6) future expectations about market price.

The most common way to visualize demand in economic analysis is to trace the relationship between changes in a product's price and the amount that people are willing to pay. Economists assume that rational consumers will tend to buy more as prices fall and vice versa. Any changes in the other factors—often called *changes in market conditions*—cause consumers to reevaluate the amount they are willing to pay for the demanded item.

EXAMPLE: The recent demand for sport utility vehicles (SUVs) caught just about everybody off guard. Purchases of such vehicles as the Ford Explorer, the GMC Jimmy, and the Toyota 4Runner soared in 1997 to record highs. Luxury carmakers, not to be outdone or left in the outback, introduced cushier versions of these four-wheel-drive trucks: Lincoln came out with its Navigator, and even the venerable Cadillac announced a new model for its 1998 lineup.

demand forecasting   An estimate of expected *demand* for a product or service.

Demand forecasting offers a company three main strategic applications: (1) to determine whether it should enter a *market*, (2) to plan short-term changes in a production schedule such as workforce and materials requirements, and (3) to plan for the long-term *capacity* needs of its facility. If there is not sufficient demand to justify the costs of entering the market, the company should reject the opportunity.

Both formal and informal methods of forecasting demand exist. Informal methods include educated guesses and a "feel" for the new market. Formal methods rely on either quantitative or qualitative data. Quantitative forecasting is broadly split into two categories: (1) historical data such as past sales in order to predict future demand and (2) current data, such as *test markets* and surveys, which can be used to augment historical data. The use of historical data (sometimes called *autoprojection*) is usually cheaper. In its simplest form, it merely calculates an average of past sales and on that basis comes to its prediction. In more complex forms, it relies on multiple *regression analysis* to determine the factors influencing sales.

The use of test markets and other surveys—sometimes called *causal* methods—adds cost and complexity to the task of forecasting demand, although this method is better for long-term predictions.

EXAMPLE: Procter & Gamble tested its new olestra-based Pringles by giving away 2,000 cans of the chips to people visiting the Capitol in Washington, D.C. The company also conducted extensive taste tests in grocery stores throughout the Washington area. After reports began circulating that olestra was dangerous for people who had gastrointestinal problems, the company expanded its research by conducting tests on some 3,000 people, only a small percentage of whom showed signs of intestinal distress. This seemed a small price to pay for confirming a product that it had spent over 25 years and $200 million to develop (Hellmich 1996).

demand lending   A stipulation in a loan contract that grants the lender the right to call the loan at any time, to make revolving loans only at its discretion, and to require that all business receipts be applied immediately to the loan's repayment.

Demand loan documents carry a wide array of covenants requiring the lender's consent for nearly any action the borrower wishes to take, particularly actions outside the normal course of business such as making an *acquisition* or purchasing an expensive piece of machinery or real estate. *Demand notes* are the norm, however, for smaller companies, whose financial status may be in question. They are increasingly used for larger companies if they show a spotty earnings history or are burdened with large debts.

EXAMPLE: Tee-Comm Electronics, Inc., a satellite television company in Milton, Ontario, fell into receivership when the Bank of Montreal called for immediate payment of a loan worth more than $34 million. After reaching a high on the

Toronto Stock Exchange of $18.75, shares of Tee-Comm fell to $0.68 in May 1997 (Dalglish 1997).

demand note   A promissory note with no set maturity date, but with a clause stipulating that the lender may demand payment at any time.

Like other loan agreements, a demand note specifies the amount of the loan and the *interest rate.* Where the demand note differs is the date for repayment. Although the note may spell out terms for repaying the loan, including a specified due date, it also includes the unilateral right of the bank or other lender to call for the entire remaining payment at any time, without the consent of the borrower.

Most business loans to small companies are secured by demand notes as well as by other forms of collateral. In 1996, the *Securities and Exchange Commission* (*SEC*) proposed a subordinated agreement rule to govern *secured* demand notes issues to borrowers who put up cash and securities as collateral against their loans. Under this agreement a lender retains rights to receive payment and interest only after payment of prior loans and claims have been made.

The SEC also proposed a margin rule stipulating that a broker or dealer cannot extend *credit* to a borrower in excess of 40 percent of the current *market value* of the securities the borrower uses for collateral to the demand note (Reyes 1996).

demand rate   *See critical ratio analysis*

demographic segmentation   In marketing, the division of a *consumer market* by age, ethnicity, gender, marital status, income, education, geographical location, or other characteristics.

Demographic segmentation recognizes that segments of the consumer base are closely linked with preference patterns. Certain products, in other words, appeal to older individuals, whereas others appeal to the younger set.

EXAMPLE: The typical buyer of a Cadillac is 63 years old and has a substantial enough income to support the purchase and maintenance of a luxury car, long known for its solid, if not stolid, performance. In the mid-1990s Cadillac introduced its Catera, a sporty model, hoping to appeal to a younger group of wealthy, active consumers. This marketing strategy was only partly successful, however. It turns out that the average owner of the new model is 58 years old (Brown 1997).

Marketers depend on profiles and statistics provided by such sources as the U.S. Department of Commerce, the Bureau of the Census, and the Labor Department to identify the particular mix of consumers in each segment of the U.S. market. Similar data sources exist for other areas of the world (see Part II, section 14: "Demographics, Marketing Data, and Marketing Research").

In the *industrial market,* or business-to-business market, the demographic divisions concentrate on company size, industry, and geographic location.

See also market segmentation; undifferentiated marketing. Compare to behavioral segmentation; preference segmentation; psychographic segmentation; volume segmentation.

dependent demand   *See derived demand*

depreciation   An accounting method of spreading the cost of a *fixed asset,* such as a plant, a computer, or a piece of machinery, over the term of its *useful life.*

The basic concept behind depreciation is that the value of every **asset** is reduced through use or obsolescence. Depreciation establishes a relationship between the asset's ability to generate **revenue** and the reduction of its value over time. This relationship stands in accordance with the **matching concept** in accounting.

A company that buys a fixed asset must make three managerial decisions with regard to depreciation, each of which will have a direct effect on the company's income and calculation of taxes. As a general rule, the higher the rate of depreciation, the lower the company's income.

First, company managers must elect to use one of three widely used depreciation methods in computing its tax returns: the **double declining balance depreciation,** the **straight-line depreciation,** or the **sum-of-the-years'-digits method.** Once chosen, this method must continue to be used on all subsequent tax returns.

Second, company managers need to determine how to estimate the asset's expected useful life. Vehicles and computers, for instance, are governed by very different criteria for such determinations: A truck purchased for making deliveries may have a useful life of several years if it is driven modestly and infrequently. A computer, on the other hand, may become obsolete in two or three years, or less, as technology advances so rapidly.

Third, managers must decide how to estimate the asset's **salvage value,** the amount they can expect to receive for the item once it has reached the end of its useful life and is sold or disposed of.

derived demand   A condition in marketing whereby the demand for one product or service results from the demand for another.

The demand in the **industrial market** is created by demand in the **consumer market.** As consumer demand for sweaters goes up in winter, for instance, so too does the demand for the wool, dye, and yarn used to make them. Demand for industrial goods is often more volatile than that in the consumer market, however. In some cases, particularly when purchases are costly or require a long lead time, an increase of 10 percent in consumer demand can cause industrial demand to rise by 100 percent. Decreases can be equally dramatic.

EXAMPLE: Gillette markets its razors at a very low price, knowing full well that consumers will need to purchase replacement blades for them. A package of five blades can cost as much as the razor itself.

EXAMPLE: Makers of automotive batteries know well the effects of derived demand. Exide Industries is the market leader in India for the production of original-equipment automotive batteries, and when lots of vehicles are produced, Exide enjoys a brisk business, as it has found in the mid-1990s. If vehicle production falls off, however, Exide knows that in about three years the demand for replacement batteries will rise, for that is about how long an original-equipment battery lasts (Krishnakuma 1997).

design capacity   The **output** level at which a facility was technologically designed to run.

EXAMPLE: Growing at nearly double the average for the computer industry, Dell Computer Corporation in 1996 opened a second manufacturing facility in Austin,

Texas, employing approximately 1,000 people. The new facility will double Dell's capacity for producing made-to-order computers for individuals, businesses, educational institutions, and government (Woods 1996).

design for manufacturability   A team approach to manufacturing in which those who design a product are paired with those who actually build it.

Manufacturability—variously known as *concurrent* or *simultaneous engineering,* or *design for producibility* or *assembly*—has significant advantages over traditional manufacturing in which R&D engineers build their design or **prototype,** then pass it along to the assembly line in the production department without ever receiving input from those frontline workers. A manufacturability team, on the other hand, comprises designers, manufacturing engineers, marketing representatives, finance managers, R&D personnel, materials suppliers, and others who have an interest in the project (including customers). The inclusion of these parties often helps speed the project to completion, avoiding delays that the traditional approach may encounter.

The manufacturability approach, however, does have some disadvantages. The fires of imagination are often drowned by the waters of cold reason. Designers, in other words, are limited by the practical considerations imposed by other team members. On the other hand, those designers may profit from information about availability, costs, and safety concerns about some materials they wish to use. Each member of the team probably has to sacrifice some independence and creativity in order to reduce the problems normally encountered in bringing a new product to market.

development banks   Banks that function as coordinating and intermediary organizations to raise **capital,** attract **investment,** and provide technical assistance for the economic development of nonindustrialized areas.

Four multination development banks are owned and funded by governments in each region, by governmental agencies from industrialized nations, by the World Bank, and by large international banks:

- The Asian Development Bank (for Asia and the Pacific Basin)
- The African Development Bank and Fund (for Africa)
- *The Inter-American Development Bank* (for Latin America)
- The European Bank for Reconstruction and Development (for Eastern European countries)

In addition, regional development banks concentrate on specific, closely knit regions encompassing several countries (such as the Eastern Caribbean or Central America). Local development banks also promote investments in specific countries. All development banks direct their attention to attracting new investment in infrastructure and private-sector businesses to a country or region.

differentiated marketing   A marketing strategy that segments the **market** in order to tailor products and services for each significantly different segment.

Differentiated marketing often results in greater sales volume, although companies must be careful to guard against **cannibalism,** the infiltration of one product's market by another item the company produces. This strategy is also responsible for increasing costs because it threatens the savings resulting from **economies of scale.**

EXAMPLE: Anheuser-Busch offers various beers to appeal to all sorts of tastes and preferences: Budweiser, Bud Light, Bud Dry, Michelob, Michelob Light, Michelob Dry, Busch, Busch Light, Busch Dry, and so on. The company's product line, in effect, comprises regular beer, premium beer, low-calorie beer, and no-aftertaste beer. In short, it attempts to meet the varieties of specialized preferences in the marketplace.

differentiation   In marketing, the emphasis a manufacturer or a company puts on an important benefit of its product, creating for it a sense of value that its competitors can match only at great expense and difficulty.

Differentiation is a common strategy in a *market* characterized by strong competitors with relatively equal products. A company might cultivate its strength as a service leader, for instance, by offering an unusually comprehensive warranty and presenting it to customers as an advantage over its competitors. A company can also establish differentiation by associating a particular image with a product, although there are few substitutes for true quality in a product.

EXAMPLE: As part of its *mission statement*, Ben & Jerry's Homemade, Inc., cites its intention to produce and distribute premium-quality ice cream and related items "in a wide variety of innovative flavors." The company's innovative flavors have made it a hit with consumers, as indicated by its net sales totaling $174 million in 1997. Chocolate Chip Cookie Dough, Cherry Garcia, and Chunky Monkey are a few of the off-the-wall and extremely popular combinations.

diffusion of innovation curve   A timeline of acceptance and adoption of a new product by different segments of the population.

In each product category, innovators are the first to adopt a new product. Next come the early adopters, followed by an early majority, late majority, and laggards. Characterized by their willingness to take risks with new products, innovators constitute about 3 percent of the population. Early adopters make up only about 13 percent: More cautious, they act as the opinion leaders in a particular *market.* That is, they make reasoned, deliberate decisions about acceptance of a new product.

Comprising approximately 34 percent of the population, the early majority give new products careful consideration but tend to adopt the product before the general public does so. The late majority makes up a second 34 percent of the population. Generally suspicious of new products, they prefer to buy them only after they have been out a while and had all the bugs taken out. The laggards, constituting about 16 percent of the population, are bound to tradition, dislike change, and adopt new products only after they have been on the market long enough to establish their own legitimacy.

diluted earnings per share   Any adjustment that lowers a stock's per-share earnings, resulting from the inclusion of *convertible securities* or *common stock equivalents* if they have an effect of 3 percent or more on those earnings.

Normally, a company's primary per-share earnings are calculated by dividing the number of outstanding shares by the company's total earnings during a specified period (quarter, year). Many companies, however, issue *warrants,* convertible stocks or bonds, and other common stock equivalents that can be converted to common stock at any time. The *fully diluted* report provides perhaps a more realistic picture of what the company's earnings really are, if in the most extreme case all the shares are issued as promised.

direct cost   In accounting and manufacturing, any expense that the organization incurs in the creation, development, production, and distribution of a product or service.

Examples of direct expenses include the cost of raw materials and assembly line labor, and some transportation costs (for example, those incurred by the company to have raw materials shipped to the factory). Managers need to determine which costs are direct and which are **indirect costs,** although the distinction is often subjective. A supervisor's salary, for instance, is usually considered an indirect cost, but in that occasional crisis when the supervisor must fill in for an absent worker, his or her salary becomes a direct cost.

direct costing   An accounting method that considers only the **variable costs** that can be linked directly to a product or service.

Fixed factory **overhead** becomes a period cost and is deducted along with the selling and administrative costs of that period. Under direct costing, the value of a company's **inventory** is calculated as the following example illustrates:

Direct materials	$ 10,000
Direct labor	90,000
Variable factory overhead	66,000
Product cost	$166,000

Variable factory overhead includes those costs associated with running the factory that can be directly related to a particular product, such as the cost of electricity to run machines.

Direct costing is not allowed for either external reporting or income tax reporting; it is used for internal management only. Some of its internal uses include **break-even analysis, inventory valuation,** income determination, and short-term **decision making.**

direct labor cost   *See direct cost*

direct marketing   The use of various media—telephone, print, mail, door-to-door, or the Internet—to elicit an immediate sale or response from a consumer.

Direct marketing campaigns have four central elements: (1) a two-way interaction with the **target market,** (2) an opportunity for the consumer to respond, (3) a communication that can take place at nearly any location, and (4) a measurable response. The platform for direct marketing is the direct conversation with the consumer, which most frequently occurs over the telephone. Telemarketers, for example, contact potential consumers directly, especially between the hours of 6:00 P.M. and 9:00 P.M., in order to sell their products or solicit contributions. Mail-order sweepstakes and "personal" invitations to apply for a new credit card provide further examples of direct marketing through print media. By returning the completed application or mailing back a sweepstakes entry, the individual completes (or begins) a two-way interaction with the marketer.

The real value of direct marketing lies in its ability to measure all responses it generates. Any response—or nonresponse—can be linked with an individual consumer, and the marketer can identify what worked to elicit that response. With those pieces of information, paired with a profile of the consumer, the direct marketer can determine exactly which communications strategies best generate sales.

EXAMPLE: True Value Hardware Stores contracts with a direct mail company that uses deed filings, credit card reports, and magazine subscriptions to identify potential consumers who are changing their addresses. The company then mails out 40,000 letters each month to welcome newcomers to a neighborhood. Although the response rate varies between 3 percent and 9 percent, the letter represents the initial contact with many consumers who will become loyal customers (Goldbogen 1997).

direct material cost   *See direct cost*

direct method   *See funds provided from operations*

direct numerical control (DNC)   *See numerical control (NC)*

disclaimer   An explicit warning issued by a seller to a potential consumer to beware of possible defects or limitations in a product or service.

In the United States, the Uniform Commercial Code (UCC) guidelines, particularly §2-316, assumes that the consumer and the seller do not always exist on equal footing with respect to their knowledge of the law or of the quality of the product or service they are negotiating. The most frequent disclaimer, therefore, is a simple "as is" warning, visibly and prominently affixed on the price sticker or on the item for sale. Unless specified otherwise, there is no warranty or guarantee of quality for such a product, and the principle of *caveat emptor* is understood to be in effect (Hardwicke and Emerson 1997, 164).

*See also **Magnuson-Moss Warranty/Federal Trade Commission Improvement Act.***

disclosure   An explanation, required by law, of a company's financial position and operating results.

The disclosure statement may appear either in footnotes or as a supplement to its *financial statement* or *annual report.* If the company has any information—for instance, an impending lawsuit, a proposed purchase or sale of a major asset—that would cause potential investors to reconsider their plans to buy shares of that company's stock, it should make a full disclosure in a print publication.

discount rate (1)   The *interest rate* charged by the *Federal Reserve* for loans to member banks.

The discount rate is a major index in national *monetary policy.* As the Federal Reserve lowers the discount rate, member banks pay less for funds they have borrowed. Thus, they are theoretically in a position to pass along those savings to their consumers and business customers. In this way, the Federal Reserve can increase the demand for borrowing and can stimulate the entire economy by encouraging the public to assume more debt.

There is a downside, of course. Recent history points to the fallacy in using this leverage alone to prick the economy into new life. Even though the discount rate declines, banks have often kept high the interest rates they charge to their loan customers.

discount rate (2)   The rate applied to a future stream of an organization's earnings or *cash flow* to calculate *present value. Discount rate* and *capitalization rate* are used interchangeably to designate the premium charged by investors as compensation for the perceived risk or uncertainty in receiving forecasted future benefits.

discounted cash flow   A method used to reduce a forecasted stream of cash flows to its *present value.*

Discounted cash flow is the fundamental principle underlying business valuations, which analysts, investors, appraisers, the IRS, and others use to determine the present value of the resource. For hotels, real estate–based companies, and other businesses, the *internal rate of return* method can effectively calculate the *discount rate* to be used in discounted cash flow analyses.

These analyses are frequently used for the following purposes:

- To calculate the expected future benefits to investors in either debt obligations or equity interest
- To determine the price of a partnership interest in a buyout agreement
- To value debt obligations for *debt/equity swaps*
- To value minority interests
- To designate the value of partial interests in an entrepreneurial business for divorce settlements
- To assess estate taxes

discretionary income   The portion of a person's income that remains after paying taxes, rent, mortgage loan installments, food costs, utility charges, tuition, medical (including veterinarian) bills, insurance payments, and all the myriad other necessary expenses that demand to be paid.

Most Americans spend their discretionary incomes on nonessential items; a few save this extra money and invest it.

See also disposable income; Maslow's hierarchy of needs.

dispatching   The release of a work order from a production and planning department to the manufacturing or operations department.

Work orders can specify the sequencing of tasks and the assignment of various people to workstations. Dispatching can be either manual or computerized.

display advertisement   A print advertisement often placed in the editorial section of a publication.

Newspapers and other print media tend to group advertisements by categories: Banks and brokerage houses advertise in the financial section; the sports section sports practically everything from tires and batteries to used cars and hair replacements. Display advertising, however, is not grouped by such classification and specialized interests.

disposable income   The portion of a person's income that remains after the taxes are paid.

Disposable income, as opposed to *discretionary income,* can be spent on both essential and nonessential items, or it can be saved. Essential items include food, housing, and clothing.

distribution channels   The various routes that products and services take as they travel from the manufacturer or producer to consumers.

Also called *marketing channels*, these routes include all the intermediaries—trucking companies, railroads, airlines, storage facilities, retail outlets, distribution centers, and so on—that deliver products and services into the hands of consumers. As goods move through the channels, they may stop at any number of intermediate points, depending on the nature of the products and the shipment. Perishable goods, for instance, make fewer stops en route from field to market, whereas automobiles shipped from Japan to the United States or Germany may endure a number of delays. In some cases, the path the product takes may differ from that taken by its ownership, or title, because some intermediaries do not take title, or legal ownership, to the product. They simply facilitate exchanges.

In most cases, the legal ownership of the product also changes hands. Each exchange adds to the cost of the product for the end user, except in cases where a *liquidation* occurs. In addition to the exchange of cash for the goods, information is exchanged as products pass from one owner to the next. Communication backward through the channel can be useful in giving the manufacturer clearer insights into consumers' preferences and needs, but the flow of information can run the other way, too. In the form of promotion, manufacturers can promote their products and stimulate exchange not only to **consumer markets** but also to channel members.

Distribution channels typically include an independent producer that manufactures the goods; **wholesalers** buy and distribute the goods to various sellers; agents who do not take title can facilitate (or complicate) the exchange; and **retailers** offer the product for sale to consumers. Each member of the channel, except for the consumer at the end, seeks to maximize profits, occasionally at the expense of the entire system.

See also **cost-plus pricing; push strategy.**

diversification   The spreading of risk among several different product lines, **markets,** or industries; or for investors, the spreading of risk among various types of **investments** of different returns, maturities, and business interests.

Business **conglomerates** demonstrate the principle of diversification by offering a varied line of products and services. The International Telephone and Telegraph Company (ITT) acquired companies in numerous industries, both in the United States and in 80 foreign countries, to develop into the first major international conglomerate with extensive diversification.

Investors, both institutional and individual, seek to diversify their portfolios, essentially following the old warning not to put all of one's eggs into the same basket. Maintaining a portfolio of traded stocks, corporate and government bonds, real estate, mutual funds, foreign stocks, venture capital, and precious metals represents a diversified investment strategy.

See also **conglomerate.**

diversity   An increase in the heterogeneity of an organization's personnel through the inclusion, voluntary or forced, of different groups.

Since the civil rights movement of the 1960s, these groups have been defined in terms of race, ethnicity, and gender. For many other companies, diversity has come to include people from other groups such as gays, lesbians, the elderly, people with disabilities, and so on. Traditionally, diversity was managed as a "melting pot" in which managers assumed that different people would somehow assimilate and become more homogeneous. Today, most managers recognize that employees do not leave their preferences and values at home when they come to work. The challenge posed by diversity, then, is to accommodate different groups by addressing their lifestyles, values, work styles, and family needs without compromising the goals and operations of the organization.

dividend   The distribution of a company's earnings to stockholders.
Cash dividends are most common, although dividends can be issued in various other forms such as stock or property.

dividend payout ratio   In accounting, a measure of the percentage of *net income* paid in *dividends.*
The ratio is calculated by dividing dividends per share by *earnings per share.* If a company has a net income of $200,000, for instance, and it pays a dividend of $50,000 on 50,000 outstanding shares of its *common stock,* its earnings per share amount to $4.00, and its dividend per share is $1.00. The dividend payout ratio is the relation between those amounts according to the following equation:

$$\frac{\$1.00}{\$4.00} = 0.25 = 25\%$$

In other words, this company distributes 25 percent of its income in dividends to its shareholders. The higher the payout ratio, the higher the percentage of earnings distributed to shareholders. Many investors look for companies with such high ratios, but there are plenty of others who are more interested in *capital gains.*

EXAMPLE: The Coca-Cola Company announced in early 1997 that it would continue to lower its dividend payout ratio to 30 percent. Much of the remaining 70 percent of earnings is to be returned in the form of investments in its business, the repurchasing of its stock, and marketing its products.

DNC   *See numerical control (NC)*

double declining balance depreciation   In accounting, a method of *accelerated depreciation* in which 200 percent of the *straight-line depreciation* rate is applied to the declining balance of the asset's *book value.*
An *asset* has no estimated *salvage value* when double declining balance depreciation is used because it is not included in the asset's book value.

EXAMPLE: An asset is worth $1,000, has a *useful life* of ten years, and has a straight-line depreciation rate of 10 percent. Double declining balance depreciation uses a rate of 20 percent (10 percent × 200 percent). The annual depreciation charge is calculated as follows:

Year	Original cost	Beginning book value		Double declining rate		Depreciation expense
1	$1,000	$1,000.00	×	20%	=	$200.00
2	1,000	800.00	×	20%	=	160.00
3	1,000	640.00	×	20%	=	128.00

Year	Original cost	Beginning book value		Double declining rate		Depreciation expense
4	1,000	512.00	×	20%	=	102.40
5	1,000	409.60	×	20%	=	81.92
6	1,000	327.68	×	20%	=	65.54
7	1,000	262.14	×	20%	=	52.43
8	1,000	209.71	×	20%	=	41.94
9	1,000	167.77	×	20%	=	33.55
10	1,000	134.22	×	20%	=	26.84
11	1,000	107.38	×	20%	=	21.48
12	1,000	85.90	×	20%	=	17.18
13	1,000	68.72	×	20%	=	13.74
14	1,000	54.98	×	20%	=	11.00

Under double declining balance depreciation, depreciation continues until the book value of the asset becomes inconsequential or the asset is disposed of. In order to avoid this situation, many companies switch to the straight-line method for the later years of an asset's life. Doing so allows them to depreciate the entire cost of the asset over a specified number of years. If the company had switched to the straight-line method in the preceding example, the calculations for the final five years of the asset's life would have been as follows:

Year	Original cost	Net book value		Straight-line rate	Depreciation expense
6	$1,000	$327.68	×	20%	$65.54
7	1,000	262.14	×	20%	65.54
8	1,000	196.00	×	20%	65.54
9	1,000	131.06	×	20%	65.54
10	1,000	65.52°	×	20%	65.54

°The final figure is $0.02 low because all of the depreciation calculations were rounded to the nearest penny.

See also **accelerated depreciation; depreciation.** *Compare to* **straight-line depreciation; sum-of-the-year's-digits method.**

double entry bookkeeping   *See bookkeeping*

Dow Jones Industrial Average (DJIA)   In the United States, the oldest and most widely quoted average used to measure and report value changes in a representative stock grouping.

As of March 1997, the DJIA comprises the following 30 **blue-chip** U.S. stocks: AT&T, AlliedSignal, Alcoa, American Express, Boeing, Caterpillar, Chevron, Coca-Cola, Disney, DuPont, Eastman Kodak, Exxon, General Electric, General Motors, Goodyear, Hewlett-Packard, IBM, International Paper, Johnson & Johnson, McDonald's, Merck, Minnesota Mining and Manufacturing (3M), J. P. Morgan, Philip Morris, Procter & Gamble, Sears, Travelers, Union Carbide, United Technologies, and Wal-Mart. The member stocks are selected by the editors of the *Wall Street Journal* and are listed in the "Money and Investing" section of the *Journal* each day.

On May 26, 1896, the day that Charles H. Dow took the first "average," he simply added up the prices of stocks on his list (including General Electric, which has been there, off and on, ever since), and divided by the total number of stocks he had chosen (12). The first average was 40.94.

The Dow has since broken through many so-called barriers, usually marked in the thousands, although these numbers mean very little in themselves. They are, however, extremely important as emotional and symbolic milestones, and investors are known to wait breathlessly for the average to break through the, say, 8000 mark (which it did in 1997). Theoretically, there is no upper limit on how high the DJIA can rise.

Casual investors continue to rely on the DJIA and other averages and indexes to judge market movement and value. Since institutional investors now carry a very large piece of the total value of each of the DJIA companies, the validity of this average for serious investors is being increasingly challenged.

downsizing   Euphemism for company layoffs, usually a large number of them, in association with an attempt to reengineer the company.

The term *downsizing* has come into the business vernacular as practically a synonym for *reengineering*, which it was never intended to be. In the attempt to become "lean," a trend of the 1980s and 1990s, companies began a slash-and-burn tactic that left many employees, particularly middle managers, jobless. Downsizing, as Jim Champy points out in *Reengineering Management* (1995, 114–115), is not at all the same thing as reengineering, which redefines the work processes for those who remain in the company. Downsizing, especially if used alone without reengineering, may temporarily relieve one kind of a company's expenses (salaries), but rarely rescues that company from its financial or operational woes. In real terms, downsizing reduces not a company's costs, but its expertise and its capacity to produce.

Downsizing, of course, is not to be equated with corporate firings. Some employees are encouraged to take early retirement; others are not replaced once they retire or leave the company. Still others, however, do receive **pink slips,** often without much warning.

EXAMPLE: In early 1998, Xerox announced plans to lay off 9,000 employees (in association with a major restructuring of the corporation and its processes). In perhaps the most famous instance, AT&T announced 10,000 layoffs in September 1995.

due diligence   The process by which an investor, underwriter, lawyer, or auditor gathers and verifies the accuracy of data.

In business **acquisitions, mergers,** or divestitures, the gathering of data prerequisite to preparing pro forma **financial statements** and **cash flows** is called *due diligence*. In an initial public offering, due diligence refers to the efforts made by an underwriter to ascertain the background and financial viability of the issuing company and to determine the uses to which the proceeds of the issue will be put. In the banking community, due diligence relates to the investigative efforts of the lender to determine the borrower's financial viability and the adequacy of collateral the borrower offers.

dumping   In international marketing, the practice of charging less for a product than it originally cost to manufacture and sell in a company's home country.

   This technique is used to eliminate a surplus or quickly gain *market share* in a new country or a new *market.* In most cases it is considered an unfair trade practice and is subject to numerous laws both in the United States and other countries.

EXAMPLE: When Japanese television manufacturers entered the U.S. market with several lines of low-priced television sets, the American manufacturer Zenith accused them of dumping. Under the Antidumping Act of 1974, the U.S. Customs Bureau can institute tariffs if it finds evidence of such unfair practices.

Dun & Bradstreet reports   A source of *credit* information, available to subscribers, that includes data on a company's management, the nature of its business, product lines, number of employees, credit history, banking relationships, legal or criminal proceedings, current debts, and record of payments to suppliers.

durable good   A tangible product that has an expectancy of a long and useful life.

   Durable products such as television sets, refrigerators, and washing machines require personalized selling and service, provide relatively high profit margins for the seller, and usually are sold infrequently and with a long-term guarantee, an extension of which might also be sold.

   The Department of Commerce classifies goods with a *useful life* of three years or longer as durable goods.

E

E commerce *See electronic commerce*

EAR Export Administration Regulations of the United States Bureau of Export Administration. All exports of U.S. goods, services, or technology from any location are controlled. Failure to comply with these regulations may result in civil and criminal penalties.

earnings per share A measure of a company's profit shown in terms of each share of *common stock.*

There are two types of earnings per share: primary and fully diluted. A company with a *simple capital structure* reports only primary earnings per share. The calculation for primary earnings per share is given as:

$$\frac{\text{Net income} - \text{preferred dividend}}{\text{Weighted-average common stock outstanding}}$$

Companies with a *complex capital structure* must report both primary and fully diluted earnings per share when the amounts differ by more than 2 percent. Fully diluted earnings per share are calculated as follows:

$$\frac{\text{Net income} - \text{preferred dividends}}{\text{Weighted-average number of common shares} + \text{common stock equivalents}}$$

See also **common stock equivalent.**

EBIT Acronym for *earnings before interest and taxes.*

ECO *See engineering change order*

economic order quantity (EOQ) A method of determining the optimum amount of materials that needs to be ordered on a regular basis.

The EOQ itself is that quantity that balances the cost of possession with the cost of acquisition. There are two assumptions that must be met in order to apply EOQ: (1) **Demand** is constant (say, 100 units per day); (2) all costs and unit prices are constant.

EXAMPLE: The Richmond Company performs electrical repair work on a contract basis. It uses approximately 24,000 light sockets annually, for which the company's accountant estimates a $50 charge to place an order and a 2 percent inventory carrying cost based on the value of the **inventory.** Richmond now pays $1.50 per socket. Wanting to maintain a cost balance, the accountant decides to explore the EOQ as a way of balancing costs of possession and ordering. The following exhibit presents a ten-day ordering cycle to replace the number of sockets depleted from the inventory:

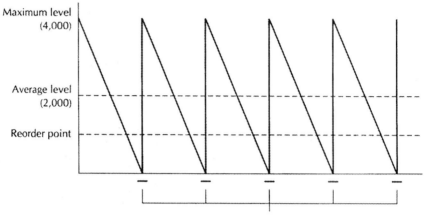

Economic Order Quantity: Exhibit 1

The EOQ is based on the following formula. The total cost of inventory is the sum of ordering and inventory carrying costs and the product purchased.

Let D = annual demand for the product, O = ordering cost, and C = unit cost. Let I = inventory carrying costs as a percentage of unit cost. This is done so that each unit of product bears its fair share of inventory carrying cost (a $1.00 item costs the same proportionally as an item that costs $100,000). Finally, let Q = the economic order quantity or the optimal-size order, and TC = cost to order plus cost of product plus cost to possess. Thus,

$$TC = \frac{(D/Q)}{O} + CD + \frac{(Q/2)}{CI}$$

This equation is the mathematical representation of Exhibit 2,

where: D/Q = Number of orders placed
CD = Total cost of product purchased
$Q/2$ = Average inventory as illustrated in Exhibit 1
CI = Dollar value of inventory carrying costs

The total cost equation is that of a curve. We seek the minimum point on that curve and thus must use calculus to find that point. We take the first derivative of the function as seen in the following:

$$\frac{dTC}{dQ} = -\frac{DQ}{Q^2} + \frac{CI}{2}$$

Setting the first derivative equal to 0 and solving for Q, we find the following:

$$Q = \sqrt{\frac{2DO}{CI}}$$

Looking at the Richmond Company's problem, we see that the EOQ for sockets is

$$Q = \sqrt{\frac{2(24{,}000)(50)}{(1.50)(12)(.02)}}$$

$$= \sqrt{\frac{2{,}400{,}000}{0.36}}$$

$$= 2{,}582 \text{ units}$$

Thus, the Richmond Company should order 2,582 (or 2,600 rounded) units each time it places an order. With that data, Richmond's accountant calculates nine orders per year (rounded), and the orders must be placed every six weeks. The lead time from the local supplier is estimated to be one week. Thus, the reorder point, that quantity of stock needed to supply Richmond during the reorder lead time, is 433 units, or one week's usage. The accountant rounds this number to 500 and advises the stock clerk to put in a requisition when the stock level reaches 500 units.

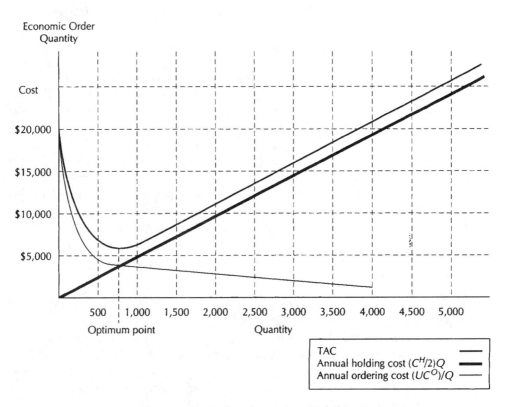

Economic Order Quantity: Exhibit 2

The total cost of that policy over and above the investment in sockets is the cost of ordering (nine orders at $50) and the cost of possession (1,300 units average inventory multiplied by an annual cost of 24 percent (2 percent each month × 12 months) of $1.50, or $0.36. This yields $450 + $468, or $918. Therefore, buying with the EOQ adds $0.038 to the cost of each socket. The total unit cost of each socket is thus $1.54 (rounded up from $1.538).

economies of scale   The lowering of costs through the production of larger volumes.

If a manufacturer estimates that the setup costs for a new product are $2,000 and the company runs one unit on this setup, the unit cost is $2,000. If the same company runs 2,000 units on the setup, the cost drops significantly to only $1.00 per unit. Economies of scale arise primarily from spreading *fixed costs* such as plant and equipment, administration, insurance, sales, and labor over a greater number of products.

EXAMPLE: A pencil factory uses $1 million in fixed costs to produce 20 million pencils per year. Management considers adding colored pencils to the company's product line, estimating that 5 million such pencils can be produced by using available *slack* in the company's fixed expense categories. In other words, producing colored pencils will not increase fixed expenses at all, and the resulting economy of scale will have the following effect:

Present fixed cost allocation: $1,000,000/20,000,000 = $0.05 per pencil

Proposed fixed cost allocation: $1,000,000/25,000,000 − $0.04 per pencil

The profitability of each pencil will increase one cent.

Economies-of-scale strategies are, however, limited. Because of the inherent inefficiencies of increasing facility size (such as increased bureaucracy, long lines of authority, and poor communications), the disadvantages of economies of scale can quickly outweigh their economic advantages.

Managers frequently use economies of scale to justify the production or expansion of a company's products or services. These new products, however, can create production and marketing requirements that can cause the company to lose its competitive edge. When considering economies of scale, one must consider the source of the economies: sometimes from off-peak available capacity, sometimes from the use of common technology, sometimes from higher volume. If the source of the economy creates a diseconomy of scale—through either decreased efficiency or loss of competitive focus—the company should not pursue the idea.

See also economies of scope.

economies of scope   The lowering of costs through the production of a wide variety of products or services.

The basic concept behind economies of scope is the same as for *economies of scale:* spreading *fixed costs* over more products or services. The primary difference is that the increase in scale for economies of scope is achieved through the production of small batches of a wide variety of products rather than larger batches of the same product.

Edge Act   Federal legislation passed in 1919 that enables national banks to conduct foreign lending operations through federal or state-chartered subsidiaries called *Edge Act corporations.*

Edge Act corporations are the U.S. version of private banking. They have become a popular medium for investing in foreign securities and private businesses.

These institutions are allowed to own banks in foreign countries and to invest in commercial and industrial firms, a flexibility denied to U.S. commercial banks.

In an effort to help U.S. banks compete with foreign banks, moreover, the Edge Act permits the **Federal Reserve** System to set reserve requirements on foreign banks that do business in the United States. To put some teeth in this law, the International Banking Act, enacted in 1978, specifically instructs the Federal Reserve Board to eliminate any banking regulations that put U.S. (i.e., Edge Act) banks at a competitive disadvantage with foreign banks operating in the United States.

Private banks, including Edge Act banks, have managed the financial affairs of wealthy individuals for many decades, offering an array of services including investment advisory services, corporate finance, trust services, custodial services, company formations, and professional portfolio management.

Private banks have nothing to do with teller cages, money machines, home mortgages, checking accounts, and the myriad other services offered by commercial banks. Instead, they specialize in one-on-one services, providing virtually any financial assistance investors need for managing offshore portfolios. Private banks also sell short-term bank instruments at competitive rates to investors awaiting other long-term opportunities.

EDI   *See electronic data interchange*

effective capacity   The quantity that a facility or a process can produce under normal operating conditions.

A factory with a *design capacity* for manufacturing 100,000 toasters per year might have an effective capacity of only 85,000 units. Factors influencing effective capacity include the availability of skilled labor and raw materials and the condition of factory machinery. Even though the toaster factory theoretically can produce 100,000 units, it cannot in actuality do so if the skilled labor and the component parts are lacking.

See also capacity.

effective interest rate   The real rate of interest on a loan.

The effective interest rate is stated as an annual percentage that is applied to the entire life of the loan. Effective interest rate is calculated as

$$\frac{\text{Face value (nominal) interest on a loan}}{\text{Net proceeds of the loan}} = \text{effective interest rate}$$

EXAMPLE: A company borrows $100,000 at 13 percent, the nominal interest rate, to be repaid in one year. The interest comes to $13,000. The effective interest rate, in this case, is the same: $13,000/$100,000, or 13 percent.

The effective rate takes on greater significance when a loan is discounted, a common practice in which interest is deducted from the proceeds of the loan at the beginning of its term. Banks issuing discounted loans often require a compensating balance, a deposit to offset the unpaid loan. Compensating balances, which earn no interest, can also significantly affect the effective interest rate paid on a loan.

If in this example the $100,000 is discounted, the effective interest rate then becomes:

$$\text{Proceeds} = \text{principal} - \text{interest} = \$100,000 - \$13,000 = \$87,000$$

$$\text{Effective interest rate} = \frac{\text{interest}}{\text{proceeds}} = \frac{\$13,000}{\$87,000} = 0.1494, \text{ or } 14.9\%$$

Thus, when the loan is discounted, the effective interest rate becomes 14.9 percent, a significant increase over the original 13 percent. If a compensating balance is required (say, 10 percent), the effective interest rate becomes even higher:

$$\text{Proceeds} = \text{principal} - \text{interest} - \text{compensating balance}$$
$$= \$100,000 - \$13,000 - \$10,000 = \$77,000$$

$$\text{Effective interest rate} = \frac{\text{Interest}}{\text{Proceeds}} = \frac{\$13,000}{\$77,000} = 0.1688, \text{ or } 16.9\%$$

The true cost of the loan, therefore, is 16.9 percent, not what was originally presented as an interest rate of 13 percent.

effective tax rate   The actual tax rate paid by a company.
Effective tax rate is calculated by dividing the amount of tax by taxable income:

$$\frac{\text{Tax}}{\text{Taxable income}}$$

EXAMPLE: A company with taxable income of $500,000 pays $200,000 in taxes; thus, its effective tax rate is 40 percent ($200,000 ÷ $500,000).

efficiency   A measure, expressed as a percentage, of how well a process functions.
Efficiency is calculated by dividing the total time taken to complete a job by the product of the longest *cycle time* of the entire process and the number of workstations:

$$\frac{\text{Total task time}}{\text{Cycle time} \times (n \text{ workstations})}$$

EXAMPLE: A department store must process 600 credit applications a day. To finish on time, managers divide the work into the following seven tasks, each with its own workstation:

	Task	Time (min.)	Preceding task
1	Open applications.	0.25	None
2	Read enclosed letter, note special requirements.	0.45	1
3	Process page 1 of application.	0.32	1
4	Process page 2 of application.	0.30	1
5	Determine credit limit from standardized tables.	0.50	3, 4
6	Supervisor checks credit limit, notes applicant's address, and determines type of letter to be sent.	0.75	2, 5
7	Assistant prepares and mails form letter.	0.35	6
	Total	2.92	

The total time for the process is 2.92 minutes. The longest cycle time is 0.75 minute, the amount of time the supervisor requires for checking credit limits. With this information, managers can calculate the efficiency of the process as follows:

$$\frac{2.92}{0.75 \times 7} = 0.5562$$

The efficiency rate, therefore, is approximately 55.6 percent.

Efficiency can be improved by changing the staffing of the workstations to lower the cycle time of the process. If a second supervisor, for example, is hired, the work at workstation 6 can be done twice as quickly, reducing task time to 0.38 minute. The longest time in the process would then be 0.50 minute for determining the applicant's credit limit. This figure then becomes the cycle time used in the efficiency calculation:

$$\frac{2.92}{0.50 \times 7} = 0.8343$$

This calculation gives an efficiency measure of 83.4 percent.

A more theoretical approach to increasing efficiency is **line balancing.** This process calculates the minimum number of workstations needed for 100 percent efficiency and assigns them equal cycle times. Cycle time is calculated with the average daily **output** rate (in this case 600 applications). This approach assumes that the number of applications processed is equal to the number of applications received. If more than 600 applications come in per day, a **backlog** will be created. If fewer than 600 come in, there will be unnecessary **idle time.** Cycle time is then calculated by dividing the available work time (eight hours) by daily demand.

$$\frac{\text{Available work time}}{\text{Daily demand}} = \text{cycle time}$$

In the example, cycle time is

$$\frac{8 \text{ hours} \times 60 \text{ minutes}}{600 \text{ applications}} = 0.8 \text{ minute per application}$$

In other words, in order to process 600 applications per day, the credit department must complete one every 0.8 minute. Managers can determine the minimum number of workstations required by dividing the total task time by the cycle time:

$$\frac{\text{Total task time}}{\text{Cycle time}} = \text{number of workstations}$$

In the example, at least four workstations are needed, or

$$\frac{2.92}{0.8} = 3.65$$

Although the actual number of workstations required is 3.65, it is impossible to set up 0.65 of a workstation. Thus, the number is *always* rounded up. It may be, however, that the work cannot be divided into exactly four workstations, and five, or even six, may be needed. If this is the case, each additional workstation will diminish the efficiency of the process. For example, with four workstations,

$$\frac{2.92}{4 \times 0.8} = 0.9125, \text{ or } 91.3\% \text{ efficiency}$$

With five workstations,

$$\frac{2.92}{5 \times 0.8} = 0.73, \text{ or } 73\% \text{ efficiency}$$

In practice, an efficiency measure anywhere between 80 and 90 percent is desirable. Anything less than 80 percent means too much idle time. Any more than 90 percent indicates the process cannot adapt to a short-term increase in demand.

See also *productivity.*

efficient capital markets   In finance, a theory that market prices reflect the knowledge and predictions of all investors.

In that this knowledge of financial markets is so widespread and readily available (thanks to computers and telecommunications), price changes, according to the theory, are the result of unpredictable, random events.

In other words, because so much information is available, predictions are made of the expected performance for each security, and prices are set accordingly. Price changes, then, are the result of unpredictable events (after all, if they were predictable, they would have been incorporated into security prices in the first place) that are essentially random in nature. The efficient market theory underlies the controversial proposition that a monkey selecting stocks by throwing a dart at the financial pages of a newspaper has as good a chance of outperforming the market as any professional investor.

electronic commerce   Broadly defined as business (business to consumer, or business to business, or government to business) conducted via electronic communications methodologies, such as the Internet, intranet, corporate connections via *modem,* and other means.

electronic data interchange (EDI)   The transmission of standard business forms and information between or within companies that are linked by a special high-speed, secure networking system.

In contrast to *e-mail,* which handles nonstandard communications across telephone lines and *modems,* EDI offers instantaneous transmission of such items as purchase orders, credit approvals, and shipping and distribution data. An electronics facility, for instance, can use EDI to link up with its suppliers and customers, creating a web of interchanges that allow the free flow of information to all of the company's stakeholders who have an interest in the production of an electronics component.

e-mail   Current lingo for *electronic mail.*

In contrast to "snail mail," as many people call regular postal delivery, e-mail is instantaneous, or nearly so, because it is transmitted across telephone or TCP/IP (Transmission Control Protocol/Internet Protocol) lines.

emotional appeal   An *advertising* message approach that tries to appeal to a consumer's psychological, social, or emotional needs, rather than practical or rational concerns.

Marketers of undifferentiated products often use emotional appeals to gain consumer interest. Also, many marketers of products that have strong psychological components—cosmetics, travel, and clothing, for instance—use emotional appeals.

Emotional appeals fall into two categories: positive and negative. Popular negative emotional appeals include fear, guilt, and shame, which are used to motivate people to do things they should, such as using condoms and dandruff shampoo, and to stop doing things they should not, such as smoking or drinking and driving. Positive emotional appeals include love, happiness, humor, delight, and excitement. These emotional appeals can be applied to almost any product or service.

EXAMPLE: In an effort to change its image from a rather stodgy, albeit upscale, automaker, the Oldsmobile Division of General Motors hired RSA USA, Inc., the *advertising agency* operated by brothers Tony and Ridley Scott, to produce 60-second ads for the 1998 Intrigue. Opening in some 6,000 cinemas in July 1997, the ads made a strong emotional appeal to a young audience who may not have known whether they were watching an ad or a trailer for an action movie (Dretka 1997).

employee discharge   Firing an employee.

Traditionally, employee-employer relations were *at will*. In other words, either party could terminate the employment for any reason and at any time without providing advance notice to the other party. In the past several decades, however, an increasing number of employees have initiated wrongful discharge suits against their employers. Although there is no federal law that governs this practice, many states have been active in creating employee protection legislation. For example, of the 51 cases that went to court between October 1979 and January 1984 in California, 70 percent were won by employees. In those cases, the average jury award to the employees was $178,184. The 19 highest awards averaged $553,318. Even when employers won a wrongful discharge suit, their legal fees were close to $100,000.

Significant costs, therefore, attend upon the wrongful discharge of an employee. Because of those costs, it is important to clarify the legal basis for wrongful discharge suits. The three most common types of suits rest on one or more of the following infractions: (1) public policy violations, such as falsifying documents, in which an employee is fired after refusing to break a law; (2) breach of good faith, which generally means that the discharge is arbitrary or capricious; and (3) breach of contract, in which an employment contract, either written or implied, is broken.

employee stock ownership plan (ESOP)   A benefit plan that gives employees shares in the company.

The shares may come with voting rights, although in most cases they represent a special class of nonvoting *common stock* shares. The rules governing ESOPs change with revisions to the IRS code.

An ESOP is a legal entity that receives either company shares donated in the names of employees or cash that is used to purchase shares from the company. *Corporations* are allowed a tax deduction for part or all of their donations. ESOPs may borrow funds from a financial institution and use the money to acquire additional shares in the company.

Besides motivating employees by granting them shares of their company, ESOPs are used as the acquiring mechanism (through bank loans) for a management buyout of part or all of the company, a widespread event of the 1980s. They may also be used as an anti-takeover defense.

empowerment   The deeper involvement of workers in the work they do, thereby increasing both their responsibilities and their motivation as well as sense of satisfaction with their jobs.

EXAMPLE: The Ritz-Carlton Hotel chain empowers workers by authorizing each one to spend up to $2,000 to solve a guest's problem—any problem related to accommodations at the hotel (Peters 1994, 78).

ending inventory   The merchandise on hand at the end of an *accounting period.*
Ending inventory appears on the *balance sheet* and is an integral part of the calculation of *cost of goods sold* on the *income statement.*
See also beginning inventory; cost of goods sold.

engineering change order (ECO)   A revision to a design or blueprint made by an engineering department to modify or change a part's design. They are sometimes called ECPs (engineering change proposals).
Requests for ECOs can come from a quality control department or a manufacturing department, or they may be the result of customer dissatisfaction with the product or its costs.

EOQ   *See economic order quantity*

EPS   Earnings per share. *See common stock valuation; expected return*

equity   In accounting, the monetary value that represents an ownership interest in a business.
It is also referred to as *stockholders' equity,* net worth, and *owners' equity.* In a corporation, *common stock* represents the amount of equity owned by each party. If a company liquidates, equity owners are entitled to the residual value (if any) of company *assets* after creditors (debtholders) and owners of *preferred stock* have been paid.

equity interest valuation   The process of determining the value of a business of interest.
Regardless of the size or type of company, or which valuation method is used, the business valuation process itself remains relatively constant. It includes four major steps:

1. *Forecasting* the company's *cash flow* for a specified number of years
2. Estimating the cost of *capital* to be included in the valuation analysis
3. Determining the continuing value of a business beyond the valuation date
4. Analyzing and interpreting the results of calculations and assumptions

The greatest confusion usually occurs in estimating the cost of capital and determining the continuing value of the business. Determining the cost of capital involves choosing a *discount rate* (also referred to as a *capitalization rate*) to discount a stream of future earnings or cash flows to *present value.* Theoretically, a discount rate should represent the expected return on alternative investments with comparable risk.

Continuing value represents the stream of future benefits beyond the cash flow forecast period. Companies that have a solid position in the marketplace should continue to produce profits and cash flow to perpetuity. Only in companies where continued success depends on the special managerial or technical skills of one or a few owner-managers may continuing value not be pertinent.

Although there are several theories for calculating continuing value, the following simplified approach works well in most cases:

Step 1. Arbitrarily choose a finite period—for instance, 50 years, 75 years, or 100 years—that is long enough to make the end year insignificant for weighing investment options.

Step 2. Extrapolate the cash flow from the last year in your finite forecast period as typical for every year thereafter. In other words, multiply the last forecast year's cash flow by the number of years in the continuing period.

Step 3. Assume the same discount factor applies ad infinitum.

Step 4. Calculate the present value of the continuing cash stream.

Step 5. Add this present value to the sum of the annual present values derived within the forecast period.

equity kicker   A stock derivative attached to a debt instrument that gives the holder the right to acquire equity interests under certain circumstances or by specific dates.

Stock *warrants,* rights, and *options* are the most common derivatives attached to *bonds, debentures,* and *preferred stock.* The convertibility feature of debentures, which permits the holder to exchange them for common shares, is another type of equity kicker.

A few examples of conditions that trigger the exercise or conversion of equity kickers include the following:

- Default on debt obligations
- A specific date in the future
- Sale or merger of the company
- Secondary public offerings
- Any action by the company that would dilute the value of the debt obligation

ERG theory   An explanation of motivation, proposed by the psychologist Clayton Alderfer, who argued that *E*xistence, *R*elatedness, and *G*rowth are the key factors in determining what makes people behave as they do.

Similar to *Maslow's hierarchy of needs,* Alderfer's theory points to three categories: (1) needs related to one's existence, such as food, water, and shelter; (2) needs associated with the experience of relatedness, such as interpersonal and social relationships; and (3) needs for growth, such as learning, creating, and excelling at a task.

Although some theorists, including Abraham Maslow, have argued that there is a hierarchical relationship between these needs (that is, existence needs must be satisfied before growth needs), Alderfer maintained that the progression (or regression) from need to need is governed by desire and frustration. The theory is based on three premises: (1) The less a need has been satisfied, the more intensely it is pursued; (2) once a lower-level need has been satisfied, there is increased desire for higher-level ones; and (3) if a higher-level need is frustrated, an individual will seek to satisfy lower-level ones.

ESOP   *See employee stock ownership plan*

eurobond   A corporate *bond* denominated in U.S. dollars or other hard currencies and sold to investors outside the country whose currency is used.

Eurobonds have become an important source of debt capital for both large and small companies throughout the world. Normally, a eurobond issue is syndicated by a consortium of international investment banks. This provides wide exposure to investors in different countries.

For example, a British company may sell a eurobond issue through a consortium led by the merchant bank (investment bank) Morgan Grenfell to German investors who buy from an overseas affiliate of a new York bank, to Swiss investors who buy through a Swiss syndicator, and to French investors who buy from Swiss accounts. Such a wide exposure normally enables a company to pay a competitive rate while ensuring that the issue will be fully subscribed.

eurocurrency   A currency on deposit outside of its country of origin (for example, a dollar on deposit at an international banking facility in the United States, or a yen on deposit in the Japan offshore market).

Such deposits are also known as *external currencies, international currencies,* or *xenocurrencies.* The term *eurocurrency* is preferred in most circles, however, and dates to the original banks in the market, the Banque Commercial pour l'Europe du Nord, which carried a cable code EUROBANK. The eurocurrency market has become a major force in international finance, reaching more than $1.3 trillion per day.

Companies with international interests find that borrowing from and making deposits in eurobanks located in offshore banking centers results in less cost, more flexibility, and greater creativity in structuring financial instruments than domestic banks provide.

eurodollar   U.S. currency held on deposit in banks located outside the United States, mainly in Europe.

Eurodollars are commonly used for settling international *transactions* outside the United States. Certain securities—debt as well as equity—are denominated in eurodollars. Thus, interest, principal repayments, and *dividends* are paid out of U.S. dollars deposited in foreign bank accounts.

The market for eurodollar-denominated securities remains strong despite local European currency fluctuations. Many U.S. companies raise *capital* in European markets when U.S. market rates are unfavorable. This action can be an especially attractive avenue for companies making an initial public offering that splits into two branches—one to be traded on U.S. exchanges, and one to be traded on a European exchange.

European Community (EC)   Former name of the *European Union (EU)*.

European Union (EU)   An economic alliance, formed under the Treaty of Rome in 1957 as the European Economic Community (EEC). This organization, also known as the Common Market, originally comprised six nations: Belgium, the Federal Republic of Germany (then West Germany), France, Italy, Luxembourg, and the Netherlands. Nine other European nations have followed, including Austria, Denmark, Finland, Greece, Ireland, Portugal, Spain, Sweden, and the United Kingdom.

The EU offers members a number of benefits, albeit still controversial ones, such as freedom of passage for citizens of member nations across international borders (without passports), standards governing the sale and transportation of goods and services, removal of tariffs, a common currency, and the security of established trading partners among member nations. Under the Treaty of Maastricht, signed in 1991 by the 12 members that then constituted the EU, member nations would have to demonstrate financial solvency and currency stability in order to gain entry into the economic and monetary union (EMU; Honore 1997).

These economic connections will support the planned confederation of member nations into a free trade zone resulting in the potential political unification of most of Europe. Whether this political unity ultimately results is anyone's guess, especially in light of the strong feelings of nationalism and the presence of at least 11 major languages that make communication across borders difficult. Still, as an economic force, the EC represents one of the largest trading blocs in the world, encompassing approximately 375 million people.

The address for the European Union is EU, Rue de la Loi 200, 1049 Bruxelles, Belgium.

events marketing   The tying of a promotional message with an event of interest to a *target market.*

Sporting events (the Olympics, the Super Bowl, Wimbledon), cultural events (rock concerts, the Academy Awards, the Kennedy Center honors, Metropolitan Opera performances) are among the most popular events for this approach to marketing.

EXAMPLES: In 1997, Sprint sponsored a Rolling Stones concert tour of some 30 cities. General Motors offered $1 billion for rights to be the exclusive automobile sponsor of the 1998 winter Olympic games in Nagano, Japan, the 2000 summer games in Sydney, Australia, and subsequent games in the first decade of the twenty-first century (Howes 1997; Sickinger 1997).

excess earnings business valuation method   A means of determining the value of business equity interests.

The excess earnings method (EEM) is used by the IRS for estate and gift tax purposes and is a popular method for calculating the selling price of microbusinesses and certain professional practices.

The EEM was originally defined by IRS Revenue Ruling 59-60 ("the Ruling") and later modified by Revenue Ruling 68-609. The Ruling requires people to:

1. Determine a value for all net *tangible assets.*
2. Establish a *normalized* earning level.
3. Estimate an appropriate **capitalization** rate applicable to that portion of the expected return based on or supported by net tangible assets.

4. Multiply the net tangible asset value by that rate to determine the amount of value generated by net tangible assets.

5. Subtract the amount in #4 from the normalized earnings from #2. The result is defined as *excess earnings*. Theoretically, this is the amount of earnings that could be expected above a fair return on net tangible assets.

6. Establish an appropriate capitalization rate to apply to the sum of excess earnings (presumably resulting from **goodwill**) and earnings resulting from **intangible assets** such as patents, leases, and **copyrights.**

7. Add this value to that derived in #1 to arrive at a total business valuation.

Despite the theoretical fallacies in the excess earnings approach, its simplicity and ease of calculation give it merit. For example, assume the following conditions for a small, privately owned business that keeps its books as an **S corporation:**

• Value of net tangible assets (equipment, vehicles, furniture, fixtures, scales, building, land) totals $1,000,000. This value should be established by an independent appraisal using the fair market value approach.

• Normalized (that is, before extraordinary items) current year's net income (before taxes since this is an S corporation) equals $400,000.

• Using industry statistics, accountants determine that the return on net tangible assets should be 15 percent.

• Based on normalized net income, 30 percent will be used to capitalize excess earnings.

The value of this business, therefore, can be calculated as follows:

Net tangible asset value		$1,000,000
Normalized earnings	$400,000	
Less: Earnings attributable to net tangible assets ($1,000,000 × 0.15)	150,000	
Excess earnings	$250,000	
Capitalized value of excess earnings ($250,000 ÷ 0.30)		75,000
Total value of business		**$ 925,000**

This method has strong appeal in buying and selling small businesses, since the only items to be negotiated are the **rate of return** on net tangible assets (which can usually be substantiated by industry statistics) and the capitalization rate for excess earnings.

exchange rates   The prices at which one country's currency can be converted into that of another country, often calculated with a service charge for the convenience.

Although perceptions in the currency markets of the security of a country's economic base certainly affect exchange rate movement, fluctuations are less a function of specific currency market manipulations than a fallout of a number of economic forces experienced on a worldwide level such as **inflation** rates, **interest rates,** unemployment, political unrest, financial market aberrations, and **commodity** prices. Furthermore, currency rates respond wildly to major economic shocks: local wars, **cartel** maneuverings, natural disasters, and anticipated actions, political and economic, of world powers, such as blockades.

In a global economy, exchange rates play a critical role in virtually every aspect of financial management. Companies that import or export or that compete against companies that do should watch exchange rates closely and, if necessary, enter into *futures* currency contracts or trade in financial futures to maximize profit potential, although this is a greater risk.

Eximbank   *See **Export-Import Bank** and **Eximbank's City-State Agency Cooperation Program***

Eximbank's City-State Agency Cooperation Program   A cooperative program launched in 1989 between Eximbank and various city and state export finance and development agencies to help small and midsize businesses understand and use Eximbank's programs.

By working with Eximbank as the funding medium, state and local agencies offer counseling and financial assistance to help small and midsize companies create new jobs (and a higher tax base) through export markets.

Eximbank has now opened both its loan guarantee and its foreign credit insurance programs to local agency participation in the belief that this action will free up export financing for the small exporter and silence critics of Eximbank's traditional preference for large corporations and foreign buyers.

The City-State Agency Cooperation program started as an Eximbank ***marketing*** tool. City and state agencies market Eximbank guarantees and ***Foreign Credit Insurance Association*** (***FCIA***) credit insurance through direct mail, calls to local banks and merchants, seminars, and a modest ***advertising*** campaign. They also provide technical support to smaller companies. According to Eximbank officials, this "makes exporting more accessible and creates less confusion and wasted time for local banks." Each city and state promotes a slightly different program. All, however, have the same objective: getting more small and midsize businesses and lenders involved in export trade.

*See also **Export-Import Bank** (**Eximbank**).*

expectancy theory   An explanation of motivation in terms of (1) the expectation that an act will be linked directly to a predetermined reward or satisfying outcome and (2) the attractiveness of that outcome to the person who performs the action.

A small cutlery company, for instance, might promise its salespeople a monthly bonus based on a percentage of all sales over a designated quota. Expectancy theorists would predict that those employees would become motivated to exceed the quota because of a clear link that the company has established between sales performance and the reward. The motivation might increase if the reward is substantial and appealing. If, however, the company promises that all salespeople who exceeded the quota would be placed in a lottery for a set of steak knives, motivation would be nil or even counterproductive. In the second case, there is no direct link between performance and reward; moreover, for employees of a cutlery manufacturer, a set of steak knives has little attraction as a bonus.

Not all rewards, of course, are equally attractive to people; thus, it is a mistake to assume that all salespeople at the cutlery manufacturer will be equally motivated by the promise of a reward, monetary or otherwise. In interviews, therefore, a manager should try to determine what motivates those salespeople and to ensure that the goals are within their power to achieve (Witchel 1997).

expected return   The profit that shareholders expect to make on their *investment* in a company's stock.

This profit comes in two forms: *dividends* paid on a regular or sporadic basis, and *capital gains* or profit representing the amount of money the investors originally put into the company, subtracted from the amount that they sell the stock for. These items are expressed by the formula:

$$\text{Expected return} = r = \frac{\text{dividends} + (\text{SP} - \text{PP})}{\text{PP}}$$

where: SP = Selling price
         PP = Purchase price

The expected return is also called the *market capitalization rate.* Another way of expressing this concept is:

$$r = g + \frac{D_1}{P_0}$$

where: g = Expected rate of growth in dividends
        D_1 = Present annual cash payment or dividend a company pays on its common stock
        P_0 = Stock's present value

EXAMPLE: In 1996, General Motors paid a dividend of $1.60 per share on its $1⅔ *common stock,* based on per-share earnings of approximately $6.00. The *payout ratio* is calculated as the dividend amount divided by *earnings per share* (**EPS**), or approximately 27 percent. Assuming that GM puts the other 73 percent of its earnings—called the *plowback ratio*—back into the company, and that its *return on equity* (**ROE**) is approximately 20 percent, it is possible to estimate the *growth rate of dividends* (*g*) as follows:

$$g = \text{plowback ratio} \times \text{ROE}$$

$$= 0.73 \times 0.20 = 0.146 \text{ or } 14.6\%$$

Now, given the 1996 average stock price of $52.34, it is possible to estimate the value of *r* as follows:

$$r = \frac{1.60}{52.34} + g = 0.031 + 0.146 = 0.177 \text{ or approximately } 18\%$$

expediting   Rushing a job through the production process.

As jobs fall behind schedule or are designated as important, managers use expediters to speed them through operations. Expediters were once widely used (and still are in many companies). Their use makes it very difficult to maintain a good production schedule. By labeling particular jobs as "hot" and assigning them to an expediter, managers can disrupt the schedule. Expediters must gather all necessary materials quickly in order to complete a particular task. The interruption in normal procedure often creates a *backlog* for other jobs, which may have to be expedited in the future.

experience curve   *See learning curve*

expert system   A type of *artificial intelligence* in which computerized systems give users access to a particular area of expertise and make decisions or solve complex problems according to preprogrammed rules and "reasoning" capacity.

Present-day computers, as sophisticated as they are, do not reason as human beings do. They are programmed with relatively strict rules of "either/or" behavior and are incapable of including information gained from intuition, feelings, and emotions, all of which play an important part in human decision making. That said, expert systems can process vast quantities of data, survey alternative solutions, evaluate the success of those solutions, and even predict the costs that a company will incur if it chooses one decision over another (Turban, Wetherbe, and McLean 1996).

EXAMPLE: A bank might develop an expert system for evaluating loan requests. Programmed with various rules and procedures, the system would provide junior loan officers a tool to use in processing loan requests. If—and it is a big "if"—all the loan requests have similar characteristics and contain no special circumstances (such as customer loyalty to the bank), the expert system can evaluate requests with the same skills as senior loan officers might bring to the process.

export order–backed securities   A securitized obligation used extensively by subsidiaries of multinationals to finance long-term export orders from developing countries.

These securities are used primarily because the underdevelopment of local banking systems and government export-credit institutions precludes straightforward export credit. Many of these securities are issued and traded on foreign exchanges in emerging capital markets. Some longer-term export orders also securitize debt issues on American exchanges.

Export order-backed securities attract investors for several reasons:

- Interest rates exceed market rates by one to three percentage points and sometimes more.
- Active trading on booming local exchanges offers a good potential for *capital gains.*
- Many issues carry secondary guarantees from such multilateral agencies as the World Bank's Multilateral Investment Guarantee Agency (MIGA), local development banks, or export-credit agencies backed by the home-country government.

Export Trading Company Act of 1982   An act of Congress intended to encourage export trade by U.S. companies. Banks are permitted to engage in commercial operations such as the purchase and sale of goods, and corporations are permitted to engage in activities in export markets that include price fixing, allocation of markets, and allocation of supply.

Export-Import Bank (Eximbank)   Federal bank created under the Export-Import Bank Act of 1945, as amended through October 15, 1986.

Originally, the bank's primary objective was to compensate U.S. exporters for subsidies granted competitors by foreign governments. Eximbank has reached far beyond this goal, however, to become the primary source of export credit and guarantees for U.S. companies.

Except in unusual circumstances, Eximbank will not support exports to communist countries or finance the sale of military products or services. Moreover, to qualify for Eximbank assistance, companies must provide evidence that exported goods or services have at least 50 percent U.S. content.

Upon completion of an application to Eximbank, companies may qualify for assistance under several programs, the most popular of which are the commercial bank guarantee program, the foreign credit insurance program, a cooperative financing facility with overseas banks, and the discount loan program with U.S. banks. Applicants should be aware, however, that to receive Eximbank financing or guarantees, they must be willing to deal with a vast quantity of paperwork required for processing an application and to be patient while the bank processes the loan request.

externality   Any incidental by-products, either positive or negative, associated with a particular course of action.

Pollution is a classic example of a negative externality. When a company discharges waste into a river, it increases the costs to people or companies downstream that use the river and its water. Positive externalities might be gained by landscaping the grounds of a factory, and they might include increased employee morale, improved community relations, and increased property values, both for the plant and for the surrounding area. Placing a precise price on externalities is key to their management. The company responsible for polluting the river must consider government fines and penalties, legal suits by users of the river, and possibly even the cost of cleaning the river. More and more, companies are being held responsible for the full costs of the externalities associated with their manufacturing activities or other operations.

EXAMPLE: Perhaps the most famous externality is the Exxon *Valdez* oil spill off the coast of Alaska in 1989, an accident that dumped 11 million gallons of crude oil into Prince William Sound. In 1995, a lagoon at Maready Farms in Beulaville, North Carolina, ruptured, spilling almost 9 million gallons of chicken waste into the Cape Fear River. The lagoon functioned as a catch basin for water used to wash the floors of chicken houses at the farm, which had a production rate of some 60,000 eggs per day. Largely as a result of this accident, Carlisle Poultry of Burgaw County decided to sell the chicken farm.

extraordinary item   In accounting, an economic item that is both unusual and infrequent.

Extraordinary gains and losses are reported on a company's *income statement* between entries for income from discontinued operations and the *cumulative effect of a change in accounting principles.* Extraordinary items include the write-off of an *intangible asset,* gains on life or property insurance, restructuring charges, acts of God (such as losses from an earthquake or flood), and gain or loss from the early retirement of debt. Write-off and write-down of inventories and receivables, such as a warehouse full of unsalable merchandise or an uncollectible debt, are not considered extraordinary items because they are related to normal business activities.

401(k) An employee retirement plan that allows employees to set aside a portion of their income each year and place it in a special retirement investment account where the contributions and interest accumulate tax free until they are withdrawn.

   The amount employees can put aside is adjusted for *inflation* periodically. In 1996, the IRS allowed a maximum contribution of $9,500 which is not counted as income for tax purposes. Depending on the mix of investment vehicles, the contributions continue to collect interest until the employee retires (minimum age of 59½), or until the employee withdraws the funds before retirement. In the latter case the employee must pay a penalty of 10 percent on top of the tax that is due, depending on the employee's particular tax bracket.

   Most companies, through an arrangement with an investment or insurance company, provide various funds such as a guaranteed fixed-rate income fund, a money market fund, and a selection of bond and stock portfolios. Employees may choose which of these funds to invest in and, in some cases, may switch contributions from fund to fund without penalty. Many employers contribute to their employees' 401(k) funds, typically at a rate of $.50 for every dollar the employee contributes, but no more than 6 percent of the employee's salary.

face value *See bond*

facilitating good Any item that accompanies or adds value to a service.

   From one point of view, advertising is a service, although from another, advertisements are products. To avoid confusion as to whether an advertising campaign is a service or a product, advertisements are considered facilitating goods. In many service companies, such as an accounting firm, there may be no facilitating goods. These companies provide what is referred to as *pure services.*

factoring The selling or transferring of *accounts receivable* to another company, called the *factor,* which then acts as principal in collecting from a customer what is owed.

   Receivables are sold "without recourse," a phrase meaning that the first party relinquishes all responsibility for collecting the account. Receivables may be factored on either a *notification* or a *non-notification* basis. In the former, customers are notified to remit directly to the factor; in the latter, they remit directly to the first party without having any knowledge that their accounts have been sold.

   Factoring may involve a discount arrangement, whereby the company sells receivables for immediate cash at the face amount, less a discount (usually 15 to 25 percent) and less allowances for estimated claims and returns, plus an *interest rate* on uncollected balances. The interest rate typically ranges from 2 percent to 5 percent above the *prime rate.*

A second option is called *maturity factoring,* whereby the factor performs the entire credit and collection function and remits the collection proceeds to the company—less discounts, allowances, and *commissions* ranging from 0.05 percent to 3 percent.

Fair Package and Labeling Act of 1966 An act that requires manufacturers to state on a label who made the contents of a package, what those contents are, and how much the package contains.

fair use *See copyright*

FASB *See Financial Accounting Standards Board*

FCIA *See Foreign Credit Insurance Association*

Federal Deposit Insurance Corporation (FDIC) Agency created by the Banking Act of 1933 to guarantee deposits in qualifying U.S. banks and financial institutions.

The impetus behind creating the FDIC was the need to calm the public's fears of another financial crash such as the disaster of 1929. Originally, the FDIC insured accounts for up to $2,500; today, the limit on each individual account is $10,000.

Federal Energy Regulatory Commission (FERC) The independent agency within the U.S. Department of Energy that regulates the interstate transmission of natural gas, oil, electricity, and hydroelectric power.

Created in 1977 to replace the Federal Power Commission, FERC oversees the construction of natural gas pipelines (but not oil pipelines), the interstate transportation of oil and natural gas across state lines, and the transfer of wholesale electric power. The U.S. president appoints five representatives to the commission, no more than three of whom may belong to the same political party. In fiscal year 1996, FERC operated with a budget of over $130 million.

For additional information, call (202) 208-0200 or visit the Web site at http://www.ferc.fed.us.

Federal Reserve The main overseer of the banking system and the institution responsible for *monetary policy* in the United States.

The Federal Reserve has both centralized and regional responsibilities, as reflected in its organization. The central agency is the Federal Reserve Board, located in Washington, D.C. The board comprises seven governors, each of whom is appointed by the U.S. president and confirmed by the U.S. Senate for 14-year terms. In 1997, the members are Alan Greenspan (chairman), Alice M. Rivlin (vice chairman), Edward W. Kelley, Jr., Susan M. Phillips, and Laurence H. Meyer.

Created by the Federal Reserve Act of 1913, the 12 Federal Reserve districts are located in Boston, New York, Philadelphia, Cleveland, Richmond, Atlanta, Chicago, St. Louis, Minneapolis, Kansas City, Dallas, and San Francisco. (See Appendix 19 for addresses and Web site.) These 12 districts were, for a time, more powerful than the central Federal Reserve in Washington. Today, each district is controlled by its member banks, which include all national banks in the region. State banks are invited to join, but only about 10 percent actually become members.

Among its primary duties, the Federal Reserve issues Federal Reserve notes and coins, buys and sells U.S. Treasury securities, sets the *discount rate* and general monetary policy, and regulates banking activities both in the United States and abroad (Flaherty n.d.).

Federal Trade Commission Act of 1914   The legislation that established the Federal Trade Commission (FTC) and charged it with promoting "free and fair competition in interstate commerce in the interest of the public through the prevention of price-fixing agreements, boycotts, combinations in restraint of trade, unfair acts of competition, and unfair and deceptive acts of practices" (§5).

FIFO   *See first-in, first-out*

finance lease   A long-term rental commitment by both lessor and lessee that usually runs for the entire *useful life* of an *asset.*

The total of monthly, quarterly, or annual payments approximates the purchase price of the asset, plus finance charges. Large pieces of production equipment, heavy-duty trucks, store fixtures, and production facilities are assets that typically fall under a finance lease.

From the lessor's perspective, rents must be sufficient to cover the original equity investment in the asset, any debt service payments for financing its purchase, all administrative costs, and a profit. Projected *cash flow* is also a major factor in setting monthly rentals. Cash flow to a lessor is the sum of (1) the actual rent charged, (2) the tax benefits of the lease, and (3) the residual value of the asset after the lease expires. Projected tax savings and the estimated *market value* of the asset at the end of the lease term should increase the lessor's cash flow and reduce the rent charged.

Most finance leases are *net* leases, under which the lessee remains responsible for the maintenance of the asset, property and other taxes, and insurance premiums. The lessor's role is strictly that of a financier whose responsibility extends to financing the asset purchase but stops short of any liability arising from its use.

financial accounting   The recording, interpretation, and reporting of a company's historical cost *transactions.*

A company records these transactions in *bookkeeping* journals and ledgers. To interpret them, it uses, among other analytic tools, a series of ratios such as the *acid test ratio, current ratio, inventory turnover, debt-to-equity (d/e) ratio,* and so on. Financial reports include *financial statements (balance sheet, income statement, statement of cash flows),* as well as special internal monetary reports that are unique to each company.

Publicly held companies must follow financial accounting principles set by the *Financial Accounting Standards Board (FASB)* and the *American Institute of Certified Public Accountants (AICPA).* Together, these principles are known as *generally accepted accounting principles (GAAP).* The *Securities and Exchange Commission (SEC)* takes ultimate responsibility for establishing financial reporting guidelines for publicly owned companies, but it permits the FASB and the AICPA to set ground rules.

Financial accounting methods use ***accrual accounting, cash basis accounting,*** or a hybrid of the two. Accounting systems are manual, computerized, or a combination of both.

Financial Accounting Foundation   The body that oversees and finances the ***Financial Accounting Standards Board*** (***FASB***).

Financial Accounting Standards Board (FASB)   The independent institution that establishes and disseminates ***generally accepted accounting principles*** (***GAAP***) and recording practices, published as FASB Statements or rulings.

The ***American Institute of Certified Public Accountants*** (***AICPA***) and the ***Securities and Exchange Commission*** (***SEC***) both recognize the statements issued by the FASB, established in 1973 to set standards governing private-sector preparation of financial reports. All practicing CPAs are required to adhere to FASB rules in the preparation of accounting and financial reports.

In July 1997, Edmund L. Jenkins began a five-year term as chairman of the FASB. One of his primary objectives is to direct the board in developing greater consistency between international standards and those adopted by most U.S. accounting firms.

financial communication   An organization's attempt to enhance and promote its image with the public, with Wall Street brokers, and with financial analysts and reporters.

The company may set as one of its goals the increase of its stock price, or it may wish to keep analysts and shareholders aware of activities that affect its financial performance. Financial communication professionals also take care to develop the company's ***annual report*** and other public announcements. Reporting to the head of ***corporate communications,*** those professionals in charge of financial communication have an ongoing relationship with the organization's ***chief financial officer*** (***CFO***).

EXAMPLE: Corporate relations personnel have become increasingly aware of shareholders' dissatisfaction with merely a list of the names and positions of corporate directors. In the 1990s, the public has demanded at least a photograph and a short biographical statement. Tina Warren, director of corporate communications at Coca-Cola Beverages, Ltd., in Toronto, notes that the more specific information about board members now occupies a two-page spread strategically located in the annual report (McGovern 1997). Although not required by law, this additional information seeks to put a human face on management, which shareholders and employees have long seen as impersonal and inaccessible.

financial futures   Contracts on U.S. Treasury securities, eurodollars, stock indexes, foreign currencies, and the like, with the intention of creating a hedge against ***interest rate*** and ***exchange rate*** fluctuations.

Futures contracts involve agricultural, industrial, or financial issues, particularly the buyer's or seller's expectation of what prices will be at some future time. If people believe the price—say, of Treasury bonds—will rise, then they will buy contracts that allow them to make deliveries when the maturity date arrives. If they think the price will fall, they try to sell contracts for those issues.

Coming into vogue during the 1980s, futures shift the risk of price changes from hedgers, those who wish to avoid the risks, to those speculators who think they can make a profit from them. What will be the interest rates in 12 or 18 months? A large number of buyers and sellers of interest rate futures will peer into their crystal balls to come up with their expectations *today* about whether those rates are going up or down. Their views are not predictions actually, and they are far from being scientific since there are so many unknowns that can affect the future of interest rates. Rather, in expressing their views, these futures dealers are selling (or buying) an intuition, a best guess, about what shape the yield curve will take in the months to come.

In the United States, there are some 50,000 futures brokers, registered stockbrokers who have passed a test offered by the National Futures Association (Burns 1997). The financial futures market is an offshoot of *commodity* markets that have traded in futures for years. The basic principles in buying and selling foreign exchange futures are identical to those underlying futures contracts in the interbank foreign exchange market; that is, the intention is to insure against future currency fluctuations without paying the cost of an insurance policy.

EXAMPLE: An investor wants to invest $100,000 in short-term securities in the next six months. She expects interest rates (or exchange rates) to decline by that time; accordingly, she speculates on what the future interest rate will be and buys contracts for six-month U.S. Treasury bills now. If, after six months, the rates have fallen, she can buy Treasury bills at that time and sell the futures contracts, thereby making a profit on the transaction.

financial highlights   A section of an *annual report* that shows selected financial data for the current *accounting period* (quarter, year) in comparison with data from a corresponding period.

The comparison is thus an abbreviated annual report, listing such major items as company sales, *dividends, earnings per share,* and other financial data that the company believes will interest shareholders and investors at large.

financial public relations   A branch of the public relations field that specializes in corporate disclosure responsibilities, investor relations, and relationships with the financial community.

Financial public relations firms help a *corporation* manage its financial image with the public, particularly at the critical time when the company makes an initial public offering (IPO; see *going public*). Financial public relations specialists promote a favorable company image to attract investors and interpret SEC regulations and compliance requirements for company personnel.

financial statement   The *balance sheet, income statement,* or *statement of cash flows.*

All three of these statements are included in a company's *annual report.*

finished goods inventory   The amount of goods on hand that can be sold to customers.

Finished goods inventory is listed as a *current asset* on the *balance sheet* and is used to calculate the *cost of goods sold* on the *income statement.*

EXAMPLE: Harley-Davidson, Inc., manufactured approximately 131,000 motorcycles in 1997, producing some 31,000 of which in the third quarter alone. As popular as these vehicles are, the company prefers to keep a finished goods inventory to maintain a hold on the U.S. market and to make inroads on the European market (Todd 1997).

finite loading   The assignment of no more jobs to a workstation than that station can complete in a particular time period.

Finite loading usually refers to a computerized operation that revises the priorities within a shop in order to level the workload for each workstation.

*Compare to **infinite loading.***

first mover   A company or individual who takes the risk and initiative to enter a new *market* first, thereby gaining a ***competitive advantage*** at least for a time.

The term is hardly new. In his discussion of the laws of motion, Aristotle posited the existence of a "first mover," which itself remained unmoved even as it caused other objects to move. And in the depiction of the earth-centered universe, the Alexandrian astronomer Ptolemy in the second century asserted that the earth was surrounded by ten concentric circles of heavenly bodies (including the sun, moon, and stars). The last and largest of these circles he called the *primum mobile* ("first mover"), which made one complete revolution around the earth every 24 hours, causing the other bodies to complete their revolutions in the same time period.

Applied to business, the term *first mover* has appeared in numerous contexts, perhaps the most important being competitive advantage. Porter (1985), for instance, discusses both advantages and disadvantages that can come to early entrants in a market. First movers can often set industry standards and develop relationships with distributors, suppliers, and buyers that later entrants cannot match. If the ***learning curve*** is steep or long, the first mover can gain advantage by mastering techniques before its competitors realize what is happening.

The disadvantages, however, can be just as startling. A company can spend large sums to investigate and enter a market where it finds itself unable or unwilling to create and meet ***demand.*** The company incurs all the costs of initially developing and marketing its products, creating a demand for them, establishing ***distribution channels*** for both supplies and finished products, and obtaining patents and regulatory approval. Having blazed a path, first movers can sometimes set themselves on fire. Followers can then enter the new market at much lower costs and risk.

EXAMPLE: IBM, already an established manufacturer of business machines, capitalized on its status as the first mover in the computer industry when in 1964 it introduced its System 360, a line of mainframe computers and peripheral devices. Once the System 360 reached the market, IBM managers pursued a strategy of investing large sums in research, development, and production. It also expanded its international marketing division and created many more ranks of managers. As a result of its first-mover efforts, IBM became the dominant force in the computer industry for many years.

first-in, first-out (FIFO)   An ***inventory valuation*** based on the concept that merchandise is to be sold in the order of its receipt or used in production in the order received—oldest goods used first.

EXAMPLE: An electronics store buys 100 units in January and 50 units in February. FIFO prescribes that the units purchased in January will be sold before those purchased in February. Under FIFO principles, *cost of goods sold* is based on the cost of older inventory.

For the sake of illustrating a company's purchasing, assume that prices are rising (if the reverse is occurring, the following effects are also reversed):

Month	Units	Cost	Amount
January	100	$ 70	$ 7,000
February	50	80	4,000
March	200	90	18,000
April	100	100	10,000
May	100	110	11,000
	Total goods available for sale		$50,000

When inventory is valued under FIFO, it closely approximates the true *replacement cost*. If *ending inventory* on June 30 is 175 units, the *fiscal year*'s ending inventory is computed as follows:

	Units	Cost	Amount
Most recent purchase (May)	100	$ 110	$11,000
Next most recent purchase (April)	75	100	7,500
Total inventory			$18,500

Cost of goods sold is calculated by determining the price of the inventory in the order in which it was purchased. FIFO cost of goods sold closely approximates the physical flow of goods since most companies sell their oldest merchandise first. FIFO cost of goods sold is calculated in this manner.

Total goods purchased	550 units
Ending inventory	175 units
Units sold	375 units

Cost of goods sold

Earliest purchase (January)	100 units	@ $ 70 =	$ 7,000
Next earliest (February)	50 units	@ $ 80 =	4,000
Next earliest (March)	200 units	@ $ 90 =	18,000
Next earliest (April)	25 units	@ $100 =	2,500
Cost of goods sold	375 units		$31,500

To illustrate all the ramifications of using FIFO, it must be compared with the other common method of inventory valuation, *last-in, first-out* (**LIFO**). The LIFO method is the opposite of FIFO. Inventory is valued on the basis of the *oldest* units available, and the cost of goods sold is based on the *most recent* purchases.

EXAMPLE: End-of-the-year LIFO inventory valuation of the same 175 units is

Earliest purchase (January)	100 units @ $70 = $ 7,000
Next earliest (February)	75 units @ $80 = 6,000
Total inventory	$13,000

Inventory under LIFO is significantly lower ($5,500) than inventory under FIFO. Since inventory valued by LIFO is stated using older costs, the inventory amount that a LIFO company reports on its *balance sheet* may have no relation to the inventory's replacement costs. When inventory is based on newest costs, cost of goods sold must be based on the more current costs, resulting in a higher figure, or

Total goods purchased	550 units	
Ending inventory	175 units	
Units sold	375 units	

Cost of goods sold

Most recent purchase (May)	100 units	@ $110 =	$11,000
Next most recent (April)	100 units	@ $100 =	10,000
Next most recent (March)	175 units	@ $ 90 =	15,750
Cost of goods sold	375 units		$36,750

Cost of goods sold under LIFO is $5,250 higher than it would be if calculated under FIFO. This difference, in turn, affects net income on the **income statement.** If we assume that the company had sales of $50,000, for instance:

	Income statement LIFO	Income statement FIFO
Sales	$50,000	$50,000
Less: Cost of goods sold	36,750	31,500
Net income	$13,250	$18,500

Each method has both advantages and disadvantages. FIFO shows *current* inventory costs on the balance sheet and, by using lower historical costs for costs of goods sold (assuming inflation exists and prices have been rising), maximizes net income on the income statement. This method is used primarily in periods of low inflation. LIFO, on the other hand, shows *historic* inventory costs on the balance sheet and, by using current costs reflecting the impact of higher inflation for costs of goods sold, reduces net income, thereby reducing tax obligations. As prices decrease, the opposite effect occurs. In other words, its proponents believe that LIFO better matches current prices to current costs. FIFO proponents, however, believe that the LIFO calculation misstates **inventories** by using current costs.

FIFO and LIFO are both permitted for income tax calculations, although once a company chooses a method, it cannot change it without securing permission from the Internal Revenue Service (IRS). If a company chooses LIFO for tax purposes, it must also use LIFO in its published *financial statements.*

EXAMPLE: In 1991, with $14,000 and some used computers, Fred Radcliffe and Tom Wise started Radcliffe Systems, Inc., a small business in Mississauga, Canada, specializing in keeping track of other people's inventories. One of their customers, the Seagram Company, depends on the service to identify the oldest containers of whiskey blends and ship those out first (Picton 1997).

Seagram's use of FIFO is similar to that of grocers, for instance, who are eager to sell items, particularly perishable ones, that have been sitting on shelves the longest.

fiscal policy   The federal government's use of spending and taxation to affect the level of macroeconomic activity.

The theory that weak economic activity requires *stimulation* in the form of tax cuts, spending increases, or a combination has long been a political and economic staple. Conversely, it is argued, excessively robust economic activity should be suppressed by such *restrictive* fiscal policies as tax increases and spending cuts.

In practice, fiscal policy has been problematic because of institutional delays in enacting a policy response to altered economic circumstances. Fiscal policy changes are usually proposed by the president and approved by Congress. Following the changes in the federal tax code in 1986, the prospect of fiscal stimulation has been limited, and a greater burden has been placed on ***monetary policy.***

fiscal year   A period of 12 consecutive months used by an organization to account for and report the results of its operations.

The term is derived from the Latin word *fiscus,* originally "basket." During the Roman Empire, the word designated that part of the state treasury under direct control of the emperor; hence, it came to mean money or wealth.

For many businesses the fiscal year is the same as the calendar year, running from January 1 through December 31. Other businesses, however, use particular economic events or patterns—for instance, a harvest, a building cycle, or a large influx of tourists—to determine their ***accounting periods.*** A department store with highest sales occurring in December and a large ***inventory*** of goods in January (because of returns) might choose, for instance, to operate according to a fiscal year beginning on February 1.

five forces model   A theoretical depiction developed by Michael E. Porter to describe the competitive forces in the environment in which a business operates.

A professor at Harvard Business School, Porter published the theory in 1980 in *Competitive Strategy.* The following diagram depicts in a simplified fashion the five major threats posed by elements within an organization's environment.

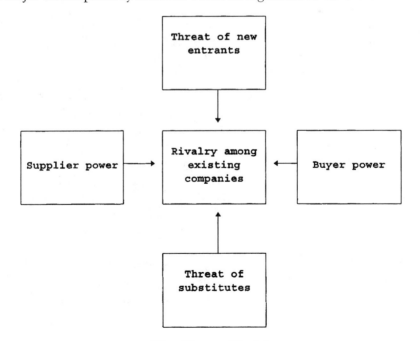

Five Forces Model

SOURCE: Michael E. Porter, *Competitive Strategy: Techniques for Analyzing Industries and Competitors* (New York: Free Press, 1980), 4.

The total strength of these five forces determines the potential for profitability for an industry or a company (where profit is measured by return on invested **capital**). This potential will vary from industry to industry. In industries such as paper, tires, and steel, for instance, where the forces are strong, no individual company distinguishes itself with high returns. In industries where the forces are relatively weak—for instance, cosmetics, toiletries, and oil field equipment—individual companies can do quite well in their returns.

In developing a competitive strategy, managers can use the five forces model as a guide to analyzing the factors that affect profitability, allowing them to defend the company against the threats those forces pose.

See also **barriers to entry; barriers to exit; buying power; supplier power.**

fixed asset   In a business operation, any purchased item that has physical substance and a *useful life* greater than one year, and that is not to be sold to customers.

Totaled on the **balance sheet,** fixed assets include buildings, machinery, and real estate. All fixed assets, except land, are subject to **depreciation.**

fixed costs   Charges that remain constant regardless of increases or decreases in sales activity.

Typical fixed costs include rent on a factory, which for a given time remains constant no matter how many items that factory produces. Although such costs themselves do not change, the ratio of fixed costs to units produced will vary depending on volume.

EXAMPLE: A company rents a factory for $10,000 a month. The total costs remain the same, month after month, as do other fixed costs such as salaries paid to managers and executives, non-overtime pay for regular employees, insurance, and interest. If all such costs amount to $100,000 per month and the factory produces 10,000 widgets, the fixed cost per widget is $10.00 ($100,000 ÷ 10,000). If the factory increases production to 100,000 widgets, the ratio of fixed costs to units produced drops to only $1.00 per item.

EXAMPLE: General Motors Corporation owns a large minority interest in American Axle in Saginaw, Michigan, which acquired GM's aging facility, the Saginaw Steering Gear plant with some 6,500 workers. American Axle also acquired GM's contractual agreement with the United Auto Workers (UAW) to pay workers an average of $22 an hour, representing a large fixed cost. There are compensatory benefits, however: Over 90 percent of American Axle's $2.2 billion in revenues for 1996 was directly attributable to GM, largely because the company has the benefit of a "last look" on work GM puts out for bids (Sherefkin 1997).

Compare to **variable costs.**

fixed interval reorder system   *See periodic inventory review system*

flexible manufacturing system (FMS)   An automated process incorporating the computerized handling of materials, robots, and other machinery to produce a range of products designed to meet various customers' specifications.

Many such systems require few human beings to participate in the production process, although no system is so automated to dispense with humans altogether. Communicating with a large database, a host computer controls and programs machines to measure, lift, load, assemble, test, and ship a relatively limited range of products. To justify its name, the system must be flexible enough to avoid a completely new setup when programmers order a switch from one product to another. The use of "soft automation" allows for smaller lots and runs, as well as greater responsiveness to customers' needs.

Flexible manufacturing systems are expensive, but they can offer consistency in quality, minimal expenses in labor, and large savings in time and *variable costs.*

flighting   *See alternate weeks* **(A/W)**

float (1)   In finance, the amount of a corporation's outstanding stock that is available for public trading.

The less the float, the greater the volatility in share price. To build up float, smaller companies issue large numbers of shares at a low *par value.*

float (2)   In banking, the term refers to the time span between the deposit of a check in the payee's bank and its clearance by the payor's bank. If the banks are separated by great geographical distance, as in two separate countries, the float can be several days. Since the advent of modern communications technology, however, transfers between banks can be instantaneous. The main purpose of a modern-day float, therefore, is to enable banks to invest added money for their own accounts, although in the United States there are now laws limiting the float to a period of two or three days.

flow process   A production system using specialized equipment, assembly line tasks, and an uninterrupted flow of materials.

The flow process, used in companies called *flow shops,* exists in many industries where relatively fixed *inputs,* operation times, and *outputs* are the norm. Nearly any industry in which repetitive manufacturing occurs can make efficient use of *process flow scheduling* (*PFS*) as an alternative to *materials requirements planning* (*MRP*). Automakers, computer manufacturers, and steel producers, for instance, use flow processes because of their low per-unit costs, high-volume output, and lower labor costs.

There are two broad types of flow processes: (1) In the assembly line, such as a computer manufacturer uses, the process is designed to combine a number of components—disk drives, microchips, and processors—into a completed product; (2) in the production line, such as a potato chip maker uses, raw materials are transformed into a finished product.

Although the operation of a flow process is relatively simple, the equipment is highly specialized, expensive, and costly to maintain and repair. Even a minor change in the product can result in a large investment in new machines. An entirely different set of equipment may be required, for instance, when a paper clip company decides to add a new type of clip to its product line. Because changes in the rate of production are also difficult to achieve, many companies are reluctant to make product design changes, thereby weakening their *competitive advantage.*

From another viewpoint, the flow process system can offer a business several advantages. Because such systems require fewer skills for operation and supervision, lower wages can be paid. As with most standardized processes, materials can be purchased in large quantities, thereby cutting costs. Because processing time remains constant, in-process inventories can be kept to minimum levels. Managers can route materials, schedule production, and meet delivery dates more efficiently.

Taylor and Bolander (1995) categorize four increasingly larger and inclusive components in process flow scheduling: At the lowest level is the equipment, which is grouped into process units. Those units, in turn, constitute process "clusters" that are united by virtue of the fact that they have common production schedules. Various clusters can be grouped into process stages, and in very complex processing operations these can be joined to form a "process train."

flow shop   *See flow process*

flowchart   A schematic design showing the movement of an item through a chain of command or a series of activities in an established process.

focus group interview   A gathering of a small number of people, usually between 8 and 12, who are questioned by a group facilitator or moderator to gain their views on a particular problem or product.

Frequently used in exploratory research, focus groups help researchers define a problem and suggest further questions that can help planners design better products or services. Because focus groups are small and not always representative, their responses cannot be generalized to the larger population; however, they can aid researchers to determine what questions to ask of the larger group and how to phrase questions more effectively.

*See also **research validity, external.***

EXAMPLE: The auditing firm KPMG Peat Marwick conducted focus interviews with about 50 randomly selected teachers and students from the Orange County (California) School District, as well as the parents of many students in the system. Not surprisingly, the auditors heard little else but complaints from teachers about overcrowded classrooms and special treatment administrators reserved for themselves; parents complained about school security; and the students moaned about the lack of adequate recreational space, the unequal distribution of textbooks, and the inability of some teachers to set disciplinary standards (Berry 1998).

focus strategy   A means of gaining *competitive advantage* by concentrating on one particular aspect of a product (such as service or durability) or a *market* (such as distribution or geographic area) that is important to a specific type of customer.

As markets demand increased product variety to satisfy ever changing demands, many broad-line producers have found their competitive positions threatened by focused competitors who target particular consumers.

Although a focus strategy can help increase *market share,* it does present three significant risks. First, in that it relies on a particular type of consumer, product, *distribution channel,* or geographical region, a focus strategy may lose effectiveness as the market evolves. Second, the size of the *target market* available to a competitor pursuing a focus strategy can limit the growth potential for a company. Third, because growth is limited, it may be difficult to take advantage of the cost reductions offered by *economies of scale* or *economies of scope.*

EXAMPLE: For years, manufacturers of sport utility vehicles (SUVs) presented advertisements aimed at skiers, campers, and outdoor sports enthusiasts. As the market for these vehicles broadened to include people with families, chores, and dinner plans at fancy restaurants, the advertisers turned their attention to presenting ads depicting the Ford Explorer or the GMC Jimmy, for instance, as vehicles for any situation, in the city or in the backwoods.

focused factory A plant dedicated to producing a limited number of products as determined by a company's competitive strategy.

This strategy places precise limits on the volume, technologies, and markets that a plant must manage.

Food and Drug Act of 1906 Legislation that prohibits the interstate manufacture, transport, or sale of adulterated, unsafe, or fraudulently labeled foods or drugs.

forced conversion The obligation to convert a security into shares of *common stock.*

A forced conversion occurs when an issuer calls in a *convertible security.* Investors generally have a choice of three responses: (1) Accept the call price, (2) convert the security into common shares, or (3) sell their holdings. These conversions occur when the *market value* of the underlying common shares has driven the selling price of the convertible security above its call price.

forecast error The difference between forecasted and actual *demand.*

EXAMPLE: In 1995, America Online offered unlimited time online for a flat fee of $19.95 per month. Having completely misread the public's interest in such a service, AOL found its lines jammed with customers trying to take advantage of the service even at times previously thought unpopular. As a result of this embarrassing forecast error, AOL had to install millions of dollars worth of computers, servers, and additional lines, not to mention costly advertising and promotions to pacify irate customers, in order to accommodate the vast increase in demand.

forecasting The estimation of sales of products or services in order to plan for manufacturing, selling, and distribution.

Foreign Credit Insurance Association (FCIA) A group of insurers, principally the Great American Insurance Company of Cincinnati, Ohio, providing short-term policies covering losses that result from commercial causes (such as insolvency) or political events (such as war or inconvertible currency).

The FCIA is an agent of the *Export-Import Bank* (*Eximbank*)*,* which details the insurer's primary goals: (1) to protect exporters against failure of foreign buyers to pay credit obligations for commercial or political reasons; (2) to encourage exporters to offer foreign buyers competitive terms of payment; (3) to support exporters' prudent entry into foreign markets where risks are high; and (4) to give exporters and their banks greater financial flexibility in handling overseas accounts receivable (Tuller 1992).

The FCIA offers various insurance policies covering losses from small amounts to more than $1 million. Applications can be obtained from FCIA Management Company, Inc., 40 Rector Street, 11th Floor, New York, NY 10006. Telephone (212) 306-5000, or by the Internet at http://www.island-metro.com/trade/fcia.htm.

foreign currency translation In accounting, the process of converting the *functional currency* of a foreign *subsidiary company,* branch, representative office, or other affiliated entity in U.S. dollars for presentation on a *financial statement.*

Subsidiaries and branches in foreign countries usually prepare financial statements in local currencies. To consolidate these statements with the one prepared by the parent U.S. company, accountants must translate or convert the foreign currencies to U.S. dollars. In addition, companies without foreign currency debt often engage in *transactions* such as exporting, importing, and assuming debts that are denominated in foreign currencies. For financial purposes, these companies must record the monetary amounts of such transactions in U.S. dollars.

Two issues loom large in foreign currency translation: (1) What *exchange rate* should be used? (2) What entry should be made to record the resulting gain or loss? That is, should the amount be included under income, deferred to a future accounting period, or charged directly to *stockholders' equity?*

When the functional currency is the currency of the foreign unit, companies must follow the *all-current* method of translation. That is, all sales (*revenues*) and expenses for the year are translated at the *average* exchange rate for that year. *Balance sheet* accounts are translated at the exchange rate in effect at the *end* of the *accounting period.*

The only translation gain or loss reported in *net income* is that occurring from transactions during the year. For example, collections of foreign receivables are assumed to be part of the parent company's equity investment and are accumulated in a separate account in the stockholders' equity section of the balance sheet. If the foreign unit is sold, the cumulative translation adjustment is offset against the gain or loss on the sale.

EXAMPLE: A foreign subsidiary of a U.S. company is located in Russia, a high-inflation country where, since the breakup of the Soviet Union, the ruble has undergone several devaluations. Accountants at the U.S. parent company would not use the current exchange rate because it would severely distort the company's consolidated statement. Instead, they would choose an appropriate rate reflecting the real cost of the asset when it was acquired. Similarly they would select historic rates for cost of sales and *depreciation,* with average rates for other line items. A separate line item called *gain or loss on translation* effectively adjusts *retained earnings* for the difference and is used on the *income statement.* Such accounting procedures are precisely the ones that many shareholders and legislators hope to see enacted in order to account for the effects of *inflation* on *capital gains* and losses from the sale of securities.

foreign direct investment (FDI)   In international trade, the investing by companies of one country in businesses or projects located in another country.

Increased competition has led many companies in the United States and elsewhere to seek cheaper materials and labor in foreign countries in Latin America, Eastern Europe, Asia, and elsewhere. Foreign direct investments in Latin America and Eastern Europe, for instance, continue to be made through government privatization programs, which represent one stage in the conversion of controlled economies to free-market economies as government-owned businesses are sold. *Debt/equity (d/e) swaps* serve as one means of financing this type of investment.

foreign exchange   The conversion of one country's currency into that of another country.

From the end of World War II until about 1972, foreign exchange rates—the rates at which currencies were exchanged—were fixed and allowed to fluctuate only within narrow ranges. Since the early 1970s, the U.S. dollar and other currencies have been allowed to *float* in much wider variations, thus adding much uncertainty to the financial markets and increased opportunities for speculators and traders. Nonfinancial managers whose businesses have international scope are also interested in these rates of exchange.

The following table shows exchange rates between the U.S. dollar and several foreign currencies, expressed in foreign currency units per dollar, except for the British pound, which conventionally is shown in dollars per pound.

		1970	1975	1980	1985	1990	1995	1997
Great Britain	£	2.40	2.22	2.32	1.30	1.78	1.58	1.65
Canada	Can$	1.01	1.02	1.17	1.37	1.17	1.37	1.44
France	Ffr	5.52	4.29	4.23	8.99	5.45	4.99	5.99
Germany	DM	3.65	2.46	1.82	2.94	1.62	1.43	1.79
Italy	lira	623	653	856	1,909	1,198	1,629	1,703
Japan	¥	357.6	296.8	226.6	238.5	144.8	94.1	130.1
Mexico	peso	—	—	—	—	2.81	6.42	8.05

Current conversion rates, provided by the Federal Reserve Bank of New York, are available on the Internet at http://www.dna.lth.se/cgi-bin/kurt/rates or at http://www.rubicon.com/passport/currency/currency.htm.

Foreign Sales Corporation (FSC)   An offshore company eligible for IRS incentives that encourage U.S. companies to enter into export *transactions.*

Legislation passed in 1984 created, as of January 1, 1985, the Foreign Sales Corporation (FSC), which replaced the old Domestic International Sales Corporation (DISC) as a means of reducing current tax liabilities on export sales. The main advantage over the old DISC is that FSCs actually reduce the tax bite: DISCs merely deferred taxes, and under the provisions of the ***General Agreement of Tariffs and Trade*** (***GATT***), they were considered illegal subsidies for exporters. Whereas a DISC was strictly a company on paper, an FSC must be physically incorporated outside the United States, have a legitimate office, and maintain accounting records. As long as the FSC is incorporated in a qualifying country, and both the FSC and the domestic parent corporation comply with IRS accounting and documentation requirements, an FSC can save a U.S. exporter 15 percent to 30 percent of taxes on income generated through export sales. (Benefits are prorated on a daily basis.)

Other requirements will help companies determine whether an FSC is the right strategy for them. FSCs may have no more than 25 shareholders at any time and no preferred stock outstanding. Each FSC must have at least one board member who is a non-U.S. resident at all times during the tax period. The FSC may not be a member of a group of which a DISC is a member, and it must elect to be treated as an FSC. In addition, the FSC must maintain an office in an approved country and keep records both at the foreign location and at the U.S. site.

Having a reciprocity agreement with the U.S. Treasury, some 30 countries currently qualify for FSC incorporation and operation. These include American Samoa, Australia, Austria, Barbados, Belgium, Bermuda, Canada, Cyprus, Denmark, Dominica, Egypt, Finland, France, Germany, Grenada, Guam, Iceland, Ireland, Jamaica, South Korea (Republic of Korea), Malta, Morocco, Netherlands (but not the Netherlands Antilles), New Zealand, Northern Mariana Islands, Norway, Pakistan, the Philippines, Sweden, Trinidad and Tobago, and the Virgin Islands. Puerto Rico is excluded from the qualifying countries. Most FSCs have been established in the U.S. Virgin Islands, but there is growing competition from Barbados, Guam, American Samoa, and Bermuda (Mandell 1995).

Companies may set up either large FSCs—used by nearly all of the Fortune 500—or small FSCs. To be classified as "small," the FSC's annual export sales of the parent company must be $5 million or less. Administrative complexities and reporting requirements are significantly less for small FSCs. From a practical perspective, however, exporters with less than $50,000 in export sales find it too expensive to set up and maintain their own FSC. Recognizing this disparity, several state and trade organizations have started their own FSCs called *shared FSCs*. Those entities enable any company, with any amount of export sales, to take advantage of tax-saving allowances.

Smaller exporters find it impractical to set up a foreign office, staff it, and maintain local accounting records. FSC management companies in all qualified foreign countries handle those administrative details at a low cost. Most large U.S. banks, law firms, and accounting firms with foreign offices provide the service, as do independent FSC management companies.

forward contract   A formal agreement to exchange a certain amount of one currency for another at a specified future date.

All foreign currency transactions involve the delivery of an amount of one currency in exchange for another. This exchange must take place at the same time, either when the contract is executed or at some agreed-upon time in the future. Current *foreign exchange* rates are called *spot prices*. Those occurring at some time in the future are referred to as *forward prices*, and the contracts serving as evidence of those transactions are called *forward contracts*.

Currency deals can be made on any business day agreeable to both parties in the transaction. The date may be placed far into the future, so long as both parties agree, although seldom do forward contracts extend beyond a year. Spot prices generally refer to a delivery date within the next few days, although common usage limits the time period to two business days.

EXAMPLE: Assume that a U.S. company contracts to ship products to a customer in Great Britain in six months. The price is $1,000. Payment is to be made against a *letter of credit* (*L/C*) denominated in U.S. dollars. The exchange rate at the date of the contract is U.S.$1.00 = 0.60 pound sterling.

The importer's treasurer believes that in six months the dollar will weaken to 0.50 pound sterling, so that the shipment of goods will cost the British company 500 pounds rather than 600. The British treasurer places an order for a forward contract in the exchange market to become effective in six months. If the treasurer is right, the British company will purchase the same goods for a 13 percent discount. The forward cover has no effect on the U.S. exporter, who still receives $1,000.

If the treasurer anticipates the reverse—that is, that the U.S. dollar will strengthen—she may contract to purchase dollars at the current spot price to secure a higher yield on return.

forward integration   A company's expansion into areas in the value chain that typically occur after the company has completed its primary task of producing a product or service.

Such downstream areas might include shipping companies, advertisers, sales and distribution centers, customer services, resellers, wholesalers, and other merchandisers. True *integration* occurs when the producing company participates directly in those downstream activities by partnering with salespeople or customers, for instance, to achieve greater value for both sides. If a publisher, for instance, who was normally concerned with the development, selection, marketing, and distribution of books, were to open a number of bookstores, it would be pursuing a strategy of forward integration.

EXAMPLE: Intel Corporation, maker of the famous Pentium processors that function as the command-and-control centers of many PCs and networks, has made several forays into the world of hardware vendors. In 1997, the company announced a new product, its "Create & Share" camera pack that includes a PC camera, software for editing images, and hardware interfaces that allow users to turn their PCs into electronic cameras and create pictures at their will. This and other products, which in effect represent for Intel a forward integration, are highlighted on the company's Internet product site at http://www.connectedpc.com (Natarajan 1997).

forward scheduling   A method of determining the starting times for the various workstations involved in a particular job on a first-come, first-served basis.

Jobs are scheduled for workstations as they are expected to become available. The projected completion date is then given to the customers. Forward scheduling is used when the delivery date for a job is set directly by a company's operations department, rather than marketing or sales.
Compare to **backward scheduling.**

four P's   In *marketing,* the four main categories of activities: product, price, place (that is, distribution), and promotion.

A marketing manager attempts to manipulate these four decision areas, or tools, in order to maximize consumer satisfaction and, thereby, sales.

EXAMPLE: Graf Canada, Ltd., and its parent company Graf and Company of Switzerland make high-performance ice skates for hockey players, figure skaters, and speed skaters. Exporting more than 65 percent of the 90,000 pairs of skates it produces each year, Graf still faces icy competition from Nike and CCM, who have a strong hold on the North American market. As part of its marketing strategy, Graf has elected to stay in the mid- to high-end range, offering products that are technologically advanced and much lighter than models produced by the competition.

Through years of working with wholesalers and distributors, Graf has developed strong relationships that, in effect, determine the place where the company conducts its business. In terms of promotion, the fourth "P," Graf recognizes that it cannot go head to head with Nike and other strong advertisers (Maclean 1997).

fragmented industry   The absence of a single, dominant competitor or *market* leader among companies engaged in the same products or services.

Fragmented industries are often made up of small- to medium-sized companies, usually privately owned by people with a variety of goals and aspirations that make them willing to accept the smaller returns associated with such an environments matrix. In some cases, however, those businesses can sustain reasonably high profit levels, especially when they focus on smaller geographical regions with select customer segments. Travel agencies, beauty salons, and restaurants are good examples of this phenomenon.

EXAMPLE: In photoprocessing, the development of inexpensive, easy-to-use film-processing equipment helped to fragment the industry. Traditionally, the market had been controlled by a few dominant companies with large, centralized laboratories that could take advantage of the *economies of scale* created by the large volume of film processed at each lab. When the new equipment became widely available, a number of small businesses specializing in one- to two-hour photoprocessing emerged, and the industry became fragmented. In order to combat this fragmentation and gain some control over the market, the incumbent companies aggressively bought the smaller ones. Eventually, the industry became concentrated again, and the larger companies asserted their control over the market.

franchise   A business operated by a licensee who, in return for an often sizable investment and payment of royalties and marketing fees, agrees to use another company's *trademarks, brands,* logos, and technology, and to operate a business in the name of the grantor.

Franchising in the United States accounts for as much as one third of all retailing, estimated to be worth $750 billion a year. In 1994, the number of franchises in the United States topped 663,000, representing a 50 percent increase in the decade since 1984 (Lundegaard 1996). A licensee may produce and market a company's products, as illustrated by many auto dealerships that agree to sell one manufacturer's product line. In other businesses, the franchisee receives business information, technology, instruction in producing and marketing products or services, and numerous other benefits from the franchiser. McDonald's, for example, has established franchises worldwide and provides everything from fish fillets and french fries to plastic straws and cups.

Studies conducted at Imperial College in London reveal that almost 30 percent of franchisees are disappointed in the franchise experience, although the success rate for franchises is estimated by the International Franchise Association in Washington, D.C., to be as high as 95 percent (Pitfalls 1996). Statistics on the success of franchises are inconclusive and often contradictory: According to Lundegaard (1996), an Arthur Andersen study of 1991 found that the original owners of 86 percent of franchises opening in the period from 1986 to 1991 were still in business in 1991; in contrast, Tim Bates, a professor at Wayne State University in Detroit, put the number at only 62 percent for the same period.

S.C. Promotions in Denver, Colorado, now stages the "Own a Business Expo" at convention centers in some 70 cities, attracting over a half a million would-be entrepreneurs in 1996. There is as much disagreement about the costs of starting a franchise as there is about how successful they are. Shael Buchen, president of S.C. Promotions, puts the average between $2,000 and $4,000, with the range extending from a mere $99 to over $30,000 (Romell 1996). John Gruber, president of Franchise network of the San Joaquin Valley in California, says that half the franchises are under $50,000 (Pollock 1996).

full-cost method   In accounting, the reporting of all exploration costs incurred by companies in extraction industries such as oil and gas production.

This accounting method requires that the costs of all exploration efforts, both successful and unsuccessful, be capitalized and reported on the **balance sheet** as natural resource assets.

*See also **successful efforts method**.*

functional currency   In accounting, the currency used in the **financial statements** of an operating entity.

Financial Accounting Standards Board (FASB) Statement 52 lays out specific characteristics for determining whether the U.S. dollar or the local currency of the foreign unit is the functional currency.

The U.S. dollar is the functional currency under the following conditions:

1. **Cash flows** from foreign entities (receivables and payables) are denominated in U.S. dollars and readily available for remittance to the parent company.
2. Sales prices are influenced by worldwide competitive factors and are affected on a short-term basis by **exchange rate** changes.
3. Cost factors (materials, labor, technology, supervision, and other components of the business) are obtained primarily from the United States.
4. Financing is denominated in U.S. dollars, or ongoing cash transfers are made by the parent to finance the foreign unit.
5. A high volume of the intercompany transactions and extensive operational interrelations between parent and foreign units occurs. For example, the foreign unit produces products in a foreign free-trade zone for shipment back to the United States.

In some instances, the rules are ambiguous. In those cases, management must judge which functional currency best captures the economic effects of a foreign unit's operations and financial position.

*See also **foreign currency translation**.*

functional organizational design   The traditional hierarchy of an organization's managerial component, usually depicted in a chart showing boxes or cells, each representing a managerial position and connected to each other by lines indicating who answers to whom in the organization.

A typical functional hierarchy is sometimes described as a "stovepipe" design because its functional units or departments remain virtually independent of each other. The following diagram suggests this relationship.

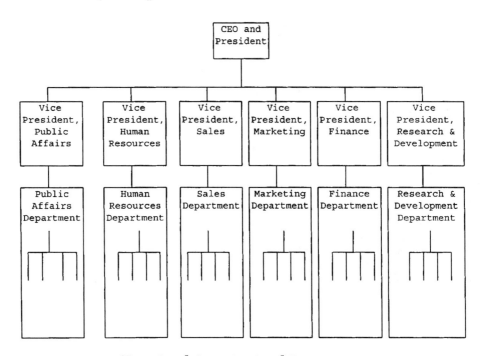

Functional Organizational Design

Functional organizations are fully hierarchical, and managers are divided into specialized functional areas. For instance, in the preceding diagram, the marketing staff—represented by the ladder in the lower rectangle—reports to the manager of the marketing department, who reports to the vice president for marketing, who reports to the company's CEO and president. This structure works well when the company's environment is relatively stable. When the company faces uncertainties and the market is volatile, however, the functional or "vertical" organization shows serious weaknesses. Lower-level managers and frontline workers, for instance, often lack the information they need to make decisions and keep the organization productive. Decisions keep being pushed higher and higher in the organizational structure, with the result that top-level managers become overloaded with responsibilities and changes in the environment.

See also **decentralization; matrix structure; organizational environment.**

funded pension plan   A retirement plan in which an employer contributes money to a **pension fund,** which in turn is managed by a trustee who oversees the payment of benefits to employees.

See also **defined benefit pension plan; defined contribution pension plan.**

funds provided from operations   In accounting, the first entry in a **statement of cash flows.**

Funds are usually defined as **working capital** or cash. A high level of funds provided from operations shows that a company's **net income** consists mostly of liquid funds, which can be easily reinvested in the company's operations or distributed to stockholders. There are two ways to determine funds provided from operations: *direct* and *indirect*. In the direct method, accountants start with the amount of cash received from operations (sales) and make adjustments to that figure in the following categories:

1. ***Dividends*** and interest received by the company (increase)
2. Receipts of cash such as insurance and lawsuit settlements or refunds from suppliers (increase)
3. Cash payments for wages and other goods and services (decrease)
4. Taxes paid (decrease)
5. Interest paid (decrease)
6. Other payments such as customer refunds, lawsuit settlements, and contributions to charity (decrease)

Recommended by the FASB, the direct method is computed according to the following formula:

Cash from operations − payments of cash for operations

= funds provided from operations

Most companies, however, prefer to use the *indirect* method, which begins with net income and adds noncash expenses (***depreciation*** and ***amortization***). Next, accountants subtract the effects of noncash income adjustments such as deferred taxes, undistributed earnings of ***affiliated companies,*** gains on sales of equipment, and provisions for losses. Finally, changes in **current assets** and **current liabilities** (***inventory, accounts payable,*** accruals, and taxes) other than cash are incorporated, and the final figure for funds provided from operations is calculated:

Net income ± noncash revenue and expense adjustment

± adjustments for receivables, payables, taxes, and inventories

= funds provided from operations

future value   The value of an ***investment,*** based on the rate of interest paid at set time periods, at some point in the future.

Future values incorporate both the earned rate of interest and the amount of interest compounded on interest already earned. Interest may be compounded annually, monthly, weekly, or even daily. The more frequently interest is compounded, the higher the future value of the investment.

future value of an annuity   A measurement of the value of a series of ***annuity*** payments at some point in the future (assuming that all payments are invested at a constant rate).

A pension fund manager might be interested in determining, for instance, the future value of the annual employee payments that go into a company's pension fund.

GAAP *See generally accepted accounting principles*

Gantt chart A graph, developed by management scientist Henry L. Gantt around 1917, showing the sequencing of tasks and resources used in a process.

Gantt charts illustrate a timeline with different sections blocked off to represent different tasks, workstations, projects, employees, and so on. Gantt charts can be used for a number of purposes, from tracking a particular job to planning and scheduling a series of different projects.

EXAMPLE: Consider a company with three jobs, scheduled as follows:

Job	Date due	Required processing (in order)
X	May 10	1 day at station 3, 5 days at station 2, and 2 days at station 1
Y	May 8	2 days at station 2, 3 days at station 3, and 1 day at station 1
Z	May 6	1 day at station 3, 2 days at station 1

If **backward scheduling** were used to determine the order of each process, the following Gantt chart might be generated.

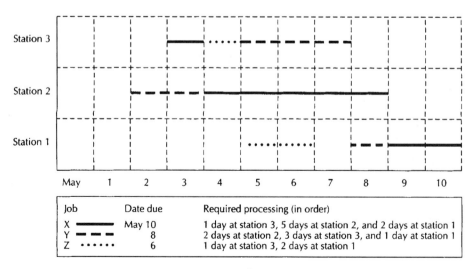

Gantt Chart

With the Gantt chart, management can quickly determine the staff and materials requirements for each station on any particular day (in the example, none of the workstations is scheduled to operate on May 1, and all three stations must run simultaneously on May 5 and 6, and must be staffed and supplied accordingly).

Although the Gantt chart is an effective means of visualizing job and facility status, it is not, in and of itself, a scheduling technique.

General Agreement on Tariffs and Trade (GATT)   A multilateral treaty, the basic aims of which are (1) to liberalize and promote world trade via multilateral trade negotiations, (2) to place world trade on a secure basis, and thereby (3) to contribute to global economic growth and development.

1. *Background:* The General Agreement was negotiated in 1947. It came into force in January 1948. At the time, the 23 nations that signed the General Agreement were in the process of drawing up a charter for a specialized United Nations organization called the International Trade Organization (ITO). It was assumed that the General Agreement would be managed by the ITO.

   However, when the charter for the ITO was not passed by the required two thirds of the U.N. General Assembly, plans for the ITO were abandoned. Thus, the General Agreement became the only international instrument that formed the foundation for international trade that was accepted by most of the world's trading nations.

2. *GATT Principles and Rules:* The General Agreement is the only multilateral, international organization that lays down specific rules for international trade. In addition, GATT also functions as the principal international body for negotiations about the reduction of tariff and nontariff barriers.

   The General Agreement is complex, and sometimes so are its rules (embodied in the Articles of the GATT). However, all of them are based on the following fundamental Principles of International Trade:

   PRINCIPLE 1: *Trade without Discrimination*—All parties that are signatories of the GATT are bound to grant to each other treatment as favorable as they grant to any other nation in the application of import and export tariffs. This is the famous "most-favored-nation (MFN) clause."

   PRINCIPLE 2: *Protection through Tariffs*—Tariffs are the only internationally acceptable means for protecting domestic industry. Commercial measures (e.g., nontariff barriers) are not an acceptable means for protecting domestic industry.

   PRINCIPLE 3: *A Stable Basis for Trade*—A stable and predictable basis for international trade is provided by the "binding of the tariff levels" negotiated and agreed among the Contracting Parties to the GATT. (Tariff schedules in which "bound" items are listed for each country form an integral part of the GATT.) Provisions exist for the renegotiation of bound tariffs.

   PRINCIPLE 4: *Consultation, Conciliation, and Peaceful Settlement of Differences*—It is expected that all signatories to the GATT will consult with each other in trade matters and will aim to resolve differences in a peaceful manner, including the use of the GATT for hearings on and arbitration of disputed trade matters.

3. *GATT Headquarters:* The Secretariat of the GATT is located in Geneva, Switzerland.

4. *GATT Institutions:* The supreme GATT institution is the Session of Contracting Parties held annually. Consensus is used for arriving at decisions, although voting is used on difficult issues.

   Thus, when GATT members act collectively (either via consensus or vote), they are called "Contracting Parties" in all GATT documents and in all other documents that make reference to the status of member nations that act in accordance with their legal obligations under the GATT.

   Between sessions of the Contracting Parties, the GATT Council of Representatives is authorized to act.

5. *GATT Committee Work:* Apart from the United Nations Conference on Trade and Development (UNCTAD), the Trade Negotiations Committee (TNC of the Group of Negotiations on Goods (GNG) oversees the work of 14 major GATT Standing Committees (or Groups) before, during, and after each round of multilateral trade negotiations. These are as follows:

   a. Negotiating Group on Nontariff Measures

   b. Negotiating Group on Natural Resource–Based Products

   c. Negotiating Group on Textiles and Clothing

   d. Negotiating Group on Agriculture

   e. Negotiating Group on Tropical Products

   f. Negotiating Group on Subsidies

   g. Negotiating Group on GATT Articles

   h. Negotiating Group on Multilateral Trade Negotiations (MTN) Agreements and Arrangements

   i. Negotiating Group on Safeguards

   j. Negotiating Group on Trade-Related Aspects of Intellectual Property Rights (TRIPS)

   k. Negotiating Group on Trade-Related Investment Measures (TRIMS)

   l. Negotiating Group on Dispute Settlement

   m. Negotiating Group on the Functioning of the GATT System (FOGS)

   n. Group of Negotiations on Services

   In addition, Working Parties (i.e., ad hoc committees) are established (1) to investigate urgent, current issues; (2) to deal with requests for accession to the GATT; (3) to verify that agreements concluded by member nations are in conformity with the GATT; and (4) to study any issues on which member countries may later wish to make a joint decision.

   Further, in accordance with Principle 4, Panels of Conciliation are established (on an ad hoc basis) to investigate disputes between member countries (Presner 1991).

general and administrative expenses   All costs connected with the performance of general and administrative activities.

General and administrative expenses include, among others, legal and audit expenses, office expenses, office rent, office utilities, office equipment, and *depreciation.* Such items are reported as *operating expenses* on the *income statement.*

generally accepted accounting principles (GAAP) The policies, standards, and rules followed by accountants in the preparation of *financial statements,* and in recording and summarizing *transactions.*

GAAP are based on (1) formal statements from an authoritative organization, such as the *Financial Accounting Standards Board* (*FASB*) or the *American Institute of Certified Public Accountants* (*AICPA*); (2) less formal industry guides, such as those issued by the AICPA; and (3) general industry practice and tradition.

generic appeal An *advertising* strategy that promotes awareness of a product category without mentioning specific *brand names.*

Generic appeal advertising is usually sponsored by an industry group that represents each individual company or by the leading producer in an industry.

EXAMPLE: The American Dairy Association sponsors commercials that promote the drinking of milk. Noted athletes such as Pete Sampras, Michael Johnson, and Brett Favre sport a white "milk mustache" that proclaims their commitment to drinking milk.

generic competitive strategies A popular theory in strategic management that splits business strategies into three "generic" types: *cost leadership, differentiation,* and *focus strategy.*

In other words, the theory suggests that companies should rely on either low costs, a unique product, or a product that appeals to a particular *market* segment. Although the notion of simply choosing among these three options can be appealing, it often leads to an overly simplified view of strategy. When this happens, strategy is in danger of becoming a single-minded quest for a "big move" that will create a significant *competitive advantage.* A more sophisticated approach to strategy recognizes that competitive advantage is the result of many individual sets of actions that build over time. In some activities, such as sales or service, it might be best to differentiate products in a way that appeals to customers, thus allowing a price premium. In other activities, however, such as standardizing product components, it might be best to pursue a strategy of cost leadership.

generic product An unbranded, inexpensive, plainly packaged version of a common product such as cigarettes, cotton balls, or canned green beans.

Generics are usually of standard quality or lower quality than most nationally advertised brands. The drop in quality is offset by a price that can be 30 percent to 50 percent lower than that of branded items. The company can offer a global lower price because the generic uses lower-quality ingredients, inexpensive labeling and packaging, and little advertising.

For a generic product to prove successful, consumers must perceive it as not markedly inferior in quality from its branded competitors. Research has shown that generics' success has been greatest in the categories of canned fruit and vegetables, paper and plastic products, and soaps and detergents. They do not fare so well in pet products, soft drinks, and other products where consumers readily perceive differences. The other key to an effective generic product strategy: The price must be significantly lower than that of competing branded items.

See also **brand name.**

EXAMPLE: Hi-Tech Pharmacal Company, based in Amityville, New York, sells its generic liquid creams and ointments under the names H-T, Tussin, and Rx Choice to over 200 wholesalers and retailers, among them Kmart and Rite Aid Drug Stores. In an industry where many generic pharmaceutical companies have not done well, Hi-Tech Pharmacal presents a success story with growing yearly sales and increasing numbers in its workforce. Founded in 1930 by Reuben Seltzer as Success Chemical Company in Brooklyn, the company originally specialized in hair colorings and cough medicines. Under current chairman and CEO, Bernard Seltzer, Hi-Tech Pharmacal focuses on products that no longer require FDA approval and generates savings as high as 70 percent for customers (LI Business Spotlight 1996).

ghost shopper   An incognito *marketing* specialist who goes from store to store to monitor the presentation and salesmanship accorded a company's products and those of its competitors.

Many large companies, including General Electric, Gillette, Del Monte, and J.C. Penney, employ ghost or mystery shoppers. This practice is also extensively used by *franchise* organizations to monitor adherence to quality standards.

global marketing   The activity of a global *corporation* that seeks to achieve long-run, large-scale production efficiencies by producing standardized products of good value and long-term reliability for all consumers (or industrial users) in all segments of all markets; the marketing of a standardized product on a worldwide basis, with little allowance for or acceptance of regional or local differentiation of the marketing-mix strategies.

EXAMPLE: Coca-Cola, the quintessential global corporation, markets an identical-ingredient formula and primary package worldwide. Of necessity, the labeling on the bottle, and on the secondary containers, varies from country to country. From example, *Disfrute Coca-Cola* is used in Spain and *Buvez Coca-Cola* is used in France (although, according to French grammar, this direct translation has proved contentious in itself and should be *Buvez du Coca-Cola* or *Buvez le Coca-Cola*). But every country's marketing program contains the same core message, the same core consumer promise, and the same core perception of benefit. (In the Coca-Cola corporate culture, it is called "One sight, one sound.")

At the physical level of corporate control of the global marketing effort is the commitment to global standardization. Every week from every plant where Coke is bottled globally, a random sampling of the product arrives in Atlanta for quality control testing, aimed at ensuring that the product is identical regardless of where it originates (Presner, 1991).

EXAMPLE: In 1997, McDonald's and the Walt Disney Company announced a pact that will pair the two marketing giants in a new global venture. McDonald's will open restaurants in all of Disney's theme parks and profit from Disney's global film and video business in some 93 countries. The first restaurant will open in 1998 in Dinoland at Walt Disney World in Orlando, Florida (Stewart 1996).

going private The shift of a company's shares from public ownership to private ownership.

This shift is generally accomplished through the company's repurchase of shares or through purchases by a private investor outside the company. Usually, a company goes private when its shares are selling at a market price significantly below *book value.* The company can buy the assets very cheaply. Another common reason for going private, or removing its shares from the market, is to eliminate the possibility that the company might become the target of a takeover attempt.

EXAMPLE: In 1985, Levi Strauss & Company went from a publicly held to a private company, assuming a leveraged buyout debt of $1.5 billion. When Elise Haas, a major shareholder, died in October 1990, the company announced that it would buy $450 million worth of the stock she owned. CEO Robert Haas observes that there are a number of advantages that the move to private status affords: no shareholder meetings, no worries about how Wall Street will respond to plant closings and quarterly reports (Motamedi 1991).

Compare to **going public.**

going public The sale of a portion of a privately held company's common shares to the public as a means of raising equity capital.

Equity capital may be raised by selling **common stock** in two ways: (1) to the public at large, which of course is a *public issue,* and (2) to a select group of buyers, in which case it is referred to as a *private placement.* Furthermore, both public issues and private placements may be sold nationally (interstate) or within only one state (intrastate). Public issues can also be divided into segments, or *tranches,* with one tranche sold in U.S. markets and another sold internationally.

The first time a company sells stock to the public, the issue is called an *initial public offering* or *IPO* (see **going public**). Once a company's stock begins trading in public markets, further new stock issues are called *secondary* issues. The significance of these distinctions relates to regulatory requirements, cost, stock appreciation potential, flexibility, and market acceptance. Prior to developing specific plans to sell common stock, companies must weigh each of these factors in light of capital needs, previous profitability, and management capabilities. As a start, precisely how much new **capital** is needed, what percentage of ownership current shareholders are willing to relinquish, and the uses to which the new capital will be applied must be determined.

goodwill In accounting, the value of ***intangible assets,*** such as reputation, name recognition, and customer relations, that give a company an advantage over competitors.

Goodwill appears in a company's ***financial statements*** only if it has been paid for in a ***business combination*** using the ***purchase method.*** Under this method, goodwill is the difference between the purchase price of a company and the fair ***market value*** of the company's assets. Once goodwill is recognized on the ***balance sheet*** as an intangible asset, it must be amortized for the period during which it provides economic benefit, not to exceed 40 years. The amortization expense is not tax deductible.

EXAMPLE: In acquiring Orion and Goldwyn, MGM assumed about $500 million of goodwill, representing a considerable financial burden against earnings for several years (Collier 1997).

government market   All federal, state, county, and municipal offices and departments.

The government market typically makes purchases that revolve around highways, streets, parks, education, public safety, and public health. When dealing with the government, a marketer must be familiar with two major buying procedures: competitive bidding and negotiation. In competitive bidding, the government sends potential suppliers requests for proposals (RFPs) containing specifications for the product; the quantity, terms, and condition of delivery; terms of the contract; and due date of the bid. On the due date, the contract goes to the lowest bidder (unless, that is, the government agency determines that the lowest bidder cannot fulfill the order; in that case, the contract goes to the next-lowest qualified bidder). In negotiation, the government considers only a small number of companies. This purchase process usually involves very large, risky contracts that attract few competitors.

*See also **consumer market; industrial market.***

greenmail   The purchase and subsequent resale of a large amount of the stock of a company that has been targeted for a takeover.

The targeted company must buy back its shares at a significantly higher price, in return for which the suitor agrees to end the attempted takeover.

The term *greenmail* appears to have been coined in 1985 in reference to a sale of Phillips Petroleum Company stock in order to thwart a hostile takeover of the company by Carl Icahn. While not quite the same thing as blackmail, the deal was tinged by the color of money, and a new business term was invented (Wilson 1997).

gross domestic product (GDP)   The main and broadest measure of U.S. economic activity.

GDP measures the output produced and income earned within the United States (exports are shown on a net basis, that is, exports minus imports). In 1991, the United States switched its official measure of ***productivity*** from the gross national product (GNP) to the gross domestic product (GDP) in order to present a more realistic measure that would be in keeping with reporting practices of other countries. Whereas the GNP measures production by U.S. citizens wherever they do business, the GDP covers only those activities that take place within the geographical borders of the United States.

GDP measures economic activity in two ways, although each arrives at the same total. The income accounts measure the various income payments to the factors of production. The *product* accounts measure the value of the goods and services produced in a year. The two approaches must be equal: The payments to the factors of production must equal the costs of production, the value of output. Totals for 1996 for the major components for the two approaches are shown in the following table.

U.S. GROSS DOMESTIC PRODUCT AND PERSONAL INCOME, 1996
(Amounts in billions of dollars)

Gross domestic product (GDP)	7636.0
Gross national product (GNP)	7637.7
Less: Capital consumption allowances	830.1
Equals: Net national product	6807.6
Less: Indirect business tax and nontax liability	604.8
Business transfer payments	33.6
Statistical discrepency	−59.9
Plus: Subsidies less current surplus of government enterprises	25.4
Equals: National income	6254.5
Less: Corporate profits with inventory valuation and capital consumption adjustments	735.9
Net interest	425.1
Contributions for social insurance	692.0
Wage accruals less disbursements	1.1
Plus: Government transfer payments to persons	1042.0
Personal interest income	735.7
Business transfer payments to persons	26.0
Personal dividend income	291.2
Equals: Personal income	6874.2

SOURCE: Bureau of Economic Analysis, U.S. Dept. of Commerce.

Since GDP provides a measure of overall economic activity, it is a useful benchmark to which businesses can compare their own activity. In addition, companies can gauge the cyclical nature of their own businesses by comparing it to that of the GDP.

gross profit   The excess of sales over *cost of goods sold.*

When gross profit is expressed as a percentage, calculated by dividing gross profit by sales, it is called *gross profit margin.*

group   A gathering of individuals in a company to perform functional duties, complete a task, or enhance personal interests and friendships.

The understanding of different groups and their individual characteristics is central to the management of any large organization.

Functional groups are created by a company's structure. For example, in a marketing department, there might be various sales groups, some designated by geographical regions and others in charge of particular products or brands. Most functional groups have an implicit, or often an explicit, hierarchical structure. In a sales group, for example, there might be a district sales manager with authority over the other sales representatives. Functional groups tend to exist for long periods of time. Their goals, leaders, interactions, performance requirements, and interdependencies are generally determined by the company.

Task groups are usually formed for the purpose of completing a particular job. Once the job is completed, the task group usually disbands. Accordingly, these groups are often designated as ad hoc groups. For example, task groups are frequently used in the aerospace industry to design, build, and test a particular product, such as a missile or an airplane. There is usually an assigned leader who follows a master schedule and tries to complete the project within set time, cost, and quality requirements. Task groups are often used to diagnose and resolve particular problems. For example, a university might establish a task group to develop recommendations on its curriculum.

Interest and friendship groups are formed on the basis of shared interests, beliefs, and activities. For example, within the functional group of sales representatives at a particular company, there might be a friendship group that plays tennis on weekends. These groups are usually quite informal and can have members from a number of different functional or task groups within an organization. For example, people from different departments might be on the same softball team or work together for a charitable cause. As a result of the overlapping memberships between friendship, functional, and task groups, there is the possibility that the goals of the groups might not be in line with the goals of the company as a whole. The issue for management, then, is to be aware of these differences and to work to eliminate or reduce them so that they do not conflict with the goals and policies of the company.

group cohesion   The extent to which group members are attracted to each other and are inclined to remain in the group.

Although a high level of group cohesion might intuitively seem to be an attractive goal, it does not always correspond with high *productivity.* Research has shown that the impact of cohesiveness is mitigated by the performance-related norms (see *group norms*) within a given group.

Performance-related norms	Group cohesiveness	
	High	**Low**
High	High productivity	Moderate productivity
Low	Low productivity	Low to moderate productivity

In other words, a cohesive group with a high level of performance-related norms will be more productive than a less cohesive group with the same norms. But when the level of performance-related norms is low, a more cohesive group will have lower productivity than a less cohesive group.

group norms   Established standards of acceptable behavior within a group.

All groups have norms, implicit or explicit. For example, golfers do not talk while putting on the green; tax accountants know to keep up with changes in tax laws that affect their clients; hospital personnel do not discuss a patient's condition where they might be overheard by people not concerned with the case. Norms give group members direction about what to do and what not to do in various situations. When norms are widely accepted and agreed to within a group, they can be an important means of influencing group members' behavior with a minimum of outside control.

group technology   An engineering philosophy that simplifies production by organizing materials according to families that require the same design and production procedures.

Group technology is often a component of **computer-integrated manufacturing (CIM).** For example, a computer manufacturer might separate molded plastic parts, electronics, mechanical parts, and so on. This separation would allow the company to group workstations according to the different procedures demanded by each family of parts. As a result, the company would be better able to work with small batches and to provide a greater degree of **differentiation** between products.

growth/market share matrix   A framework, developed by the Boston Consulting Group, that allows managers of diversified companies to visualize the differences in **cash flow** potential and growth for a number of different businesses within their portfolios.

Depending on its position on the matrix, each business is assigned a particular category that describes its standing within the company's portfolio. In other words, the growth/market share matrix shows which businesses represent investment opportunities, which should be used as sources of funds for other activities, and which are candidates for elimination from a company's portfolio. The basic structure of the growth/market share matrix is as follows.

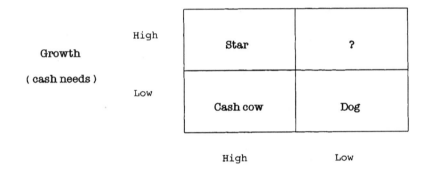

Growth/Market Share Matrix

The four categories are stars, question marks, cash cows, and dogs. Stars are businesses that have both market dominance and strong growth. They may or may not have the cash flow to be self-sufficient, but they promise large cash returns in the future. Question marks have high growth, low market share, and require significant amounts of cash to maintain their position in the market. Many question mark businesses are in emerging industries, and the question is whether they will ever develop a strong enough market position to earn a solid return. Cash cows typically have high market share, slow growth, and generate more cash than they use or can reasonably reinvest. These businesses are a good source of cash that can be used to increase the market position of the question mark businesses. Dogs have a poor market position and offer little chance for significant growth. They neither generate nor require substantial amounts of cash. Usually, any cash generated must be reinvested along with additional outside **capital.** This requirement has earned them the title of *cash traps.*

H

hard currency   Currency in which there is wide confidence in world markets, as opposed to *soft currency,* which is not accepted as legal tender outside the country of origin.

Hard currencies can be exchanged for other hard currencies as well as soft currencies throughout the world. Soft currencies cannot be swapped. Hard-currency countries include, among others, the United States, Great Britain, Germany, France, Switzerland, Italy, Canada, Japan, and Australia. Soft-currency countries are best exemplified by Russia, where the Russian ruble has no value outside the Commonwealth of Independent States (nations comprising the former Soviet Union).

When a company from a hard-currency country does business in a soft-currency country, some form of *countertrade* is usually required to close the deal. Exceptions occur when a soft-currency country has sufficient hard-currency reserves in its *central bank* to finance imports by national companies. This is the current status of most Latin American countries as a result of *International Monetary Fund* **(IMF)** loans, U.S. government guarantees, and improving foreign trade environments.

harvesting   The maximization of short-term *cash flow* and earnings.

Harvesting is generally accomplished by cutting operating costs such as reducing the sales force, reducing new *investment,* reducing the product range, eliminating smaller customers, cutting back on the number of distributors, or taking advantage of any remaining strengths, such as the ability to raise prices.

Businesses that are candidates for harvesting are usually subject to some combination of the following conditions: (1) The business has a small *market share* that can be increased only at great cost; (2) the business does not make a contribution to a company's profits, reputation, or market position; (3) the business is in a saturated *market* that offers little growth potential; or (4) there are more attractive investment opportunities that require the cash currently devoted to the business that will be harvested.

The decision to harvest a particular business carries considerable risk. For example, RCA was premature in harvesting its television manufacturing business, a market that had been thought to be mature with little growth potential, just when Japanese competitors were investing heavily in videotape, which revitalized the television market.

Hazardous Substances Labeling Act   An act passed in the United States in 1960 that controls the labeling of packages that contain hazardous household substances.

holding period return   The return on an ***investment,*** held over a period of time.

A holding period return is computed by dividing the investment's current income, less ***capital gains*** or losses, by the investment's purchase price, or

$$\text{Holding period return} = \frac{\text{current income} - \text{capital gains or losses}}{\text{purchase price}}$$

Say stock X and stock Y were each held for one year:

	Stock X	**Stock Y**
Purchase price	$50	$50
Cash dividend	8	5
Selling price	47	55
Capital gain (loss)	(3)	5

The holding period return for each stock is

Stock X: $\dfrac{\$8 - \$3}{\$50} = 0.10$

or 10 percent

Stock Y: $\dfrac{\$5 + \$5}{\$50} = 0.20$

or 20 percent

Holding period return is frequently used by financial managers (along with return records and risk measures, such as ***beta***) in making investment decisions.

horizontal integration   A growth strategy in which a company buys a competitor who performs a similar value-adding activity—such as retailers buying out other retailers, or manufacturers buying out other manufacturers.

Horizontal strategies can help a company broaden its product line or appeal to a new segment of the ***market.*** General Motors did both when it purchased Saab in Sweden. Many major U.S. brewers have also boosted their ***market share*** by buying up smaller breweries.

EXAMPLE: Boeing's merger with McDonnell Douglas in 1996 represents a case of horizontal integration in that both companies specialized in putting together thousands of parts rather than in manufacturing each one themselves. McDonnell Douglas made the F-15 and F/A-18 fighter planes, whereas Boeing is constructing the F-22, which is not yet in full production. One of the merger benefits is that Boeing can make use of McDonnell Douglas's engineering and toolmaking capacities in order to eliminate some of the ***backlog*** that has occurred at its own plants (Enter McBoeing 1996).

See also ***vertical integration.***

horizontal marketing strategy   A marketing strategy in which two or more nonrelated companies at the same level in the channel of distribution join forces to take advantage of a new marketing opportunity.

EXAMPLE: H&R Block and Hyatt Legal Services made an arrangement that allowed Hyatt's legal clinics to rent office space from H&R Block's tax preparation offices. The deal allows Hyatt to penetrate the market quickly through H&R Block's nationwide chain of offices, whereas H&R Block gets the benefit of steady rent income in an otherwise highly seasonal market.

See also **vertical marketing system.**

housing starts and residential construction An important economic activity in the United States, accounting for roughly 3 percent of total **gross domestic product** (**GDP**) in any year.

This is a highly cyclical activity for a number of reasons: (1) The expenditure involved is large. (2) As a result, building is often financed through borrowing (mortgages). (3) Because of both of these factors, the decision to build can be postponed.

Four aspects of residential construction are individually monitored by the Department of Commerce. *Housing permits* are the authorizations to build new housing units, typically required by local governments. Thus, the issuance of a housing permit is usually the first stage in construction and is regarded as a leading cyclical indicator. *Housing starts* represent the start of construction, when the foundation of the home or apartment building is dug. *Housing completions* measure the end of construction, whereas records of *new home sales* look at the end of the entire process.

Residential construction is incorporated into the estimates of GDP as construction progresses, using the payments that are made as construction proceeds as the main measure. This reflects the actual impact on the economy.

The following chart presents both single-family and multifamily housing starts:

HOUSING STARTS: 1978–1997

Year	Single-family	Multifamily	Total
1978	1,433,000	587,000	2,020,000
1979	1,194,000	551,000	1,745,000
1980	852,000	440,000	1,292,000
1981	705,000	379,000	1,084,000
1982	663,000	400,000	1,062,000
1983	1,067,000	635,000	1,703,000
1984	1,084,000	665,000	1,749,000
1985	1,072,000	669,000	1,742,000
1986	1,180,000	625,000	1,806,000
1987	1,146,000	474,000	1,621,000
1988	1,081,000	407,000	1,488,000
1989	1,003,000	373,000	1,376,000
1990	895,000	298,000	1,193,000
1991	840,000	174,000	1,014,000
1992	1,030,000	170,000	1,200,000
1993	1,126,000	162,000	1,288,000
1994	1,198,000	259,000	1,457,000
1995	1,076,000	278,000	1,354,000
1996	1,160,900	315,900	1,476,800
1997	1,113,100	390,900	1,474,000

SOURCE: U.S. Bureau of the Census, http://www.nahb.com/starts.html.

humorous appeal   An *advertising* strategy that relies on the power of humor to persuade consumers to purchase a product.

Humorous ads tend to attract a lot of attention and generate affection for the sponsor, but they may also obscure the message of the ad. In other words, the audience may be laughing too hard to notice the product.

EXAMPLE: Ameritech unveiled a lighthearted advertisement emphasizing the clarity of its telephone connections over those of rival Cellular One. Using Ameritech's cellular connections, Harry proposes to his girlfriend, while another suitor, Tom, tries to do the same thing over his Cellular One phone. Trouble is that the latter is beset by lots of static and, unable to make himself heard clearly, Tom loses the girl. Thus, Harry meets Sally (or whatever her name is) in cellular phone bliss (Pate 1995).

See also ***emotional appeal.***

hygiene factors   Those factors in the workplace such as salary, company policies, and working conditions, that, when inadequate on a job, result in employee dissatisfaction.

When hygiene factors are adequate, however, they do not bring about appreciable levels of employee satisfaction. In other words, hygiene factors are the bare minimum workplace conditions either by company policy or legal mandate. When they are present, workers are placated. When they are absent, workers are dissatisfied.

idle time   Any time spent not actively working on a process due to setup, lack of material, lack of scheduling, maintenance, and so on.

Management must be aware of idle time and, whenever possible, attempt to eliminate it.

image advertising   An advertising strategy designed to promote a particular image for a company, product, or brand.

Image advertising is different from other product advertising in that it does not focus on gaining immediate sales. Instead, the advertisements build a mood, focusing on beauty, love, excitement, reliability, or strength. No statement is made about the product or company except those created by the images.

EXAMPLE: A natural gas company could create an image campaign highlighting its concern for the environment in order to promote natural gas as an environmentally sound alternative to other energy sources.

incentive plans   Any rewards that motivate employees.

Incentive plans are an important tool by which top management can influence the actions of executives in order to achieve corporate goals. In establishing an incentive plan, it is important to emphasize consistency with the company's overall strategy. When considering an incentive plan in terms of its consistency with *corporate strategy,* there are four potential problem areas:

1. *Company-divisional relationships:* Corporate management's role in multidivisional firms can vary a great deal. In some companies, management works directly with division managers. In others, management simply acts as a resource center and divisional managers are essentially independent. The incentive plans for each different structure must incorporate that structure's particular characteristics. For example, a company with a series of independent divisions might base incentives on some measure of profitability (which encourages each manager to treat his or her division as an independent company), whereas a company with more interdependent divisions might base incentives on some other performance measure, such as overall sales (which encourages each division manager to coordinate his or her actions with headquarters to achieve corporate goals).

2. *Interdivisional relationships:* Incentive plans affect how divisional managers work together. If there is a need for cooperation between divisions, the in-

centive plan will be quite different from the situation where divisions work independently.

3. *Risk taking versus risk aversion:* Companies in emerging **markets** might want to encourage rapid growth by fostering a risk-taking entrepreneurial spirit in their managers. In these companies, incentive plans should be structured to reward this kind of behavior. Companies in mature markets, however, may emphasize the maintenance of market position over any significant attempts to gain **market share.** In these situations, incentive plans should reward behavior that avoids risk and solidifies market position, such as improving customer relations.

4. *Short-term versus long-term:* Incentive plans have a great impact on managers' trade-off decisions. For example, if incentives are based on quarterly production figures, a factory manager might choose to skip the scheduled maintenance on a particular piece of equipment in order to produce more units of **output.** This decision to pursue short-term gains, possibly at the expense of a serious equipment malfunction at some point in the future, is directly motivated by the incentive plan. In this situation, it might have been preferable to have an incentive plan that emphasized long-term **productivity** rather than short-term goals.

income from continuing operations   In accounting, an **income statement** entry describing after-tax **revenues** and expenses arising from the business's ongoing operations.

Nonrecurring gains and losses, such as the **write-off** of uncollectible **accounts receivable,** are included in income from continuing operations.

income statement   A formal statement of the elements used in determining a company's **net income;** also called a *profit and loss statement.*

Every company must include an income statement in its **annual report.** Generally, the categories reported in an income statement are as follows:

Sales
Less: cost of goods sold
Gross margin
*Less: operating expenses, selling expenses, and general and administrative
    expenses*
Income from operations
Add: other income
Less: other expenses
Income before tax
Less: provision for income taxes
Income from continuing operations
Income or loss from discontinued operations (net of tax)
Income before extraordinary items or cumulative effect
Add or less: extraordinary items (net of tax)
Add or less: cumulative effect of a change in accounting principle (net of tax)
Net income

Most companies do not follow this format exactly, as one can see with the income statement from the Hewlett-Packard Company for 1997:

HEWLETT-PACKARD COMPANY AND SUBSIDIARIES
Consolidated Statement of Earnings

For the years ended October 31 (in millions except per share amounts)	1997	1996	1995
Net revenue:			
Products	$36,672	$33,114	$27,125
Services	6,223	5,306	4,394
Total net revenue	**$42,895**	**$38,420**	**$31,519**
Costs and expenses:			
Cost of products sold	$24,217	$22,013	$17,069
Cost of services	4,102	3,486	2,945
Research and development	3,078	2,718	2,302
Selling, general and administrative	7,159	6,477	5,635
Total costs and expenses	**$38,556**	**$34,694**	**$27,951**
Earnings from operations	$4,339	$3,726	$3,568
Interest income and other, net	331	295	270
Interest expense	215	327	206
Earnings before taxes	4,455	3,694	3,632
Provision for taxes	1,336	1,108	1,199
Net earnings	$3,119	$2,586	$2,433
Net earnings per share	**$2.95**	**$2.46**	**$2.31**
Weighted average shares and equivalents outstanding	**$ 1,057**	**$ 1,052**	**$ 1,052**

incremental cost   The cost difference between two or more business alternatives.

EXAMPLE: If a toy company can make rubber balls in either red or blue, it might analyze the incremental costs of the two options:

	Red	Blue	Incremental costs
Materials	$10,000	$8,000	$2,000
Labor	5,000	5,000	0

In other words, there is a $2,000 incremental cost associated with the materials required to make the red balls.

independent demand   Demand for an item that is not based on demand for the end item. Maintenance, repair, and operating (MRO) items tend to be independent demand items. The need for them is independent of when they are used.

Independent demand is separate from **derived demand,** in which the demand for a product is predicated on the demand for another product. An automobile creates the demand for fine tires.

EXAMPLE: Clothing, books, and automobiles are all subject to independent demand, whereas the fabric, paper, and metal that make them up are subject to derived demand.

indexing   The practice of relating **investments** or contracts to widely known compilations or indexes.

For investors, indexing can be accomplished by weighting a portfolio in the same manner as a broad-based stock index to match the index's performance. Indexing can also mean the act of investing in a mutual fund (known as an index fund) that buys and sells stocks in the same weighting as a compiled index.

When related to business activity as opposed to investing, indexing means tying increases in selling prices to national indexes (such as **inflation** rates) or tying labor contract wage increases to indexes such as the cost-of-living index. As the index changes, prices and/or wage rates change in the same proportion.

indirect cost   An expense that cannot be traced back to a specific unit of production or item sold.

Management salaries, rent, and utilities, for instance, are indirect expenses.

indirect method   *See* **funds provided from operations**

industrial goods   All goods or services that are used in the production of other goods or services subsequently supplied to ultimate consumers.

Industrial goods fall into one of three categories: raw materials and components, capital goods, and services and supplies. Each of these categories is involved differently in the manufacturing process.

Raw materials and components are goods that are incorporated completely into the manufacturing process. Flour that is made into bread, tires that go on a car, and leather that becomes a pair of shoes are all examples of raw materials or components. Usually, raw materials are viewed as **commodities,** so the marketing strategies used for them center on low price. Components, such as engine subassemblies or computer parts, however, are marketed based on price and service.

Capital goods, which include factory buildings, office computers, and tools, are only partially involved with the finished product. Companies producing capital goods usually rely on marketing strategies that emphasize personal selling and service.

Supplies and services are not incorporated into the finished product at all, but rather are used to support the production of finished goods. Supplies and services, which are usually purchased on a **straight rebuy** basis, include typing paper, lubricating oil, and repair services. Since there is a great deal of standardization and little brand loyalty among these products, companies selling supplies and services must emphasize price and service in their **marketing mix.**

industrial market   All individuals or companies that produce or acquire goods or services that are incorporated into the production of other finished goods or services subsequently sold to consumers; also called the *business* or *producer market.*

The main difference between the industrial market and the ***consumer market*** is that the industrial market does not buy goods for final consumption. The industrial market has four types of buyers: manufacturers, ***wholesalers,*** institutional consumers, and ***retailers.*** Manufacturers buy goods for use in the production of their own final products. Wholesalers purchase goods from manufacturers and distributors and sell them to retail outlets. Institutional consumers are large-volume buyers and include government as well as private businesses such as restaurants, nursing homes, hospitals, hotels, and churches. Retailers offer products to the ultimate consumer for final consumption. Each of these different buyers offers the industrial marketer a different ***target market.***

     See also ***consumer market; government market.***

industrial policy   The course of action set by a government to influence the development of domestic industrial sectors in particular and the direction of national industrial growth in general.

     A government's industrial policy may comprise such instruments as subsidies (direct and indirect), tax incentives, regional development programs, training programs for workers, and research and development (R&D) assistance.

     EXAMPLE: Canadian industrial policy has come under frequent attack from various U.S. industrial sectors. Americans have claimed that, under the guise of assisting domestic industry, the Canadian government has really been subsidizing the development of competitive export industries. Such alleged activities are contrary to both the Canada-U.S. Free Trade Agreement and the ***General Agreement on Tariffs and Trade*** (***GATT***).

     The U.S. Omnibus Trade Act of 1988 (Section 301) prohibits foreign governments from engaging in export targeting. The rationale is that since export targeting uses government leverage to enhance export effectiveness, it is implicitly unfair and thus deserving of action by the U.S. Trade Representative (Presner 1991).

industrial production   The ***output*** of U.S. factories, mines, and utilities.

     This output constitutes the production of *things*—the goods portion of goods and services. (The only goods excluded are those produced in agriculture, fisheries, and forestry.) The ***Federal Reserve*** Board has measured industrial production since the 1920s. In fact, industrial production is an older measure of U.S. output than GDP.

     Details of production are compiled for a wide variety of industries, and these provide a precise benchmark for firms that operate within the covered industries. For instance, a textile firm can contrast its own recent activity with that for the industry as a whole. Production trends in a particular industry—one that is a client industry, for instance—may also point to future ***demand*** for a firm's products.

     Industrial production is a coincident indicator of economic activity: It traces the behavior of the ***business cycle*** nearly exactly.

industry attractiveness test   A method of evaluating the strategic impact of entering a new industry.

     The attractiveness test states that the industry chosen for ***diversification*** must be structurally attractive or be able to be made attractive. In other words, the new industry must offer returns that exceed the ***cost of capital*** required for entry. If those returns do not exist, the company must be able to restructure the industry or create a sustainable **competitive advantage** that generates returns above the industry average. The industry attractiveness test can also be used by current participants in an industry.

See also **better-off test; cost-of-entry test.**

infinite loading   The process of scheduling work on a workstation or resource as if it had a limitless capacity to handle any and all jobs.

This process wreaks havoc on a production schedule and should be avoided.

Compare to **finite loading.**

inflation   An increase in the general price level.

Inflation can be regarded as either an increase in the *cost of living* or an erosion in the value of money—a loss of purchasing power. A crucial emphasis is that inflation is a generalized rise in prices as opposed to upward pressure on the prices of particular goods because of specific supply-demand imbalances.

Increases in the rate of inflation often reflect an excess in aggregate demand relative to output, **demand pull** inflation. Moreover, expectations of increasing inflation exert an upward effect on **interest rates.** Thus, financial markets—particularly the credit and money markets—often translate signs of increased economic activity into portents of building inflationary pressures and rising interest rates.

Increases in specific costs can, by raising costs of production generally, lead to inflation that is called *cost push* inflation. This has long been noted to be a connection between wage costs and inflation. In the 1970s, however, sharp increases in oil and energy costs also led to higher inflation.

Along with the **unemployment rate,** inflation represents the other major (and usually opposite) example of poor economic performance because it also reflects a macroeconomic inefficiency.

inflation accounting   A method of financial reporting that incorporates the financial impact of changes in the price level.

Constant dollar accounting and **current cost accounting** are both inflation accounting methods.

informal organizational structure   The network of social relationships that develop within an organization as people work together.

The informal structure of a company is often quite different from its formal structure. Whereas many formal structures rely on strict superior-subordinate relationships, informal structures frequently circumvent this hierarchy. In many cases, the informal structure of an organization is equally as important as its formal structure. For example, in a situation where a company faces a great deal of uncertainty—say the possibility of a takeover by a competitor—employees frequently work within the company's informal structure to gather information and create a sense of cohesiveness and loyalty within the organization that could not have been developed through any formal policies or statements.

It is important to note, however, that the informal structure of a company usually relies on rumor, innuendo, and gossip rather than facts. As a result, much of the information that flows through the informal structure is incomplete or even false.

Of course, information that flows through formal channels may not always be complete or accurate, either.

in-house advertising agency   *See advertising agency*

initial public offering (IPO)   *See going public*

innovation   A new product or service.

An innovation is distinct from an invention in that it is simply the *introduction* of something new, whereas an invention is the design or *creation* of something new. An innovation may be an invention, a combination of existing elements that forms a new and unique product, or a service that has not previously been offered.
See also **product life cycle.**

inputs   The factors that are combined in the production of a product or service. At their most basic, inputs are the raw materials of a manufacturing process.

EXAMPLE: If a construction company is building a house, the inputs naturally include cement, wood, brick, wire, pipes, and glass. Inputs, however, also include other factors that are not so readily identified as the components of a finished product. For the construction company, inputs also include the facilities in which the carpenters work, the administrative system that directs their activities, the equipment and tools used to build the house, the labor and knowledge that the carpenters bring to the job, the supplies used by the carpenters and construction company, and, perhaps most important, the time to complete the project.

Managing inputs, then, is much more complicated than simply organizing raw materials. It requires careful attention to the materials, equipment, facilities, labor, supplies, knowledge, and time required to finish a process.

insertion order   Directions to a publisher for the exact placement and terms of a print advertisement.

An insertion order states the size of the ad, its position on the page, its position in the publication (in the sports section of the newspaper, for example), its price, and the dates on which the ad will appear. A copy of the advertisement is usually enclosed with the insertion order.

intangible asset   In accounting, an item or right that has no physical substance yet provides an economic benefit.

Examples include patent rights, **goodwill,** and a **copyright.** Intangible assets are shown on the **balance sheet** and must be amortized over a period not to exceed 40 years.
See also **asset.**

intellectual property   A collective term used to refer to ideas or works in the classes of industrial property or copyright.

These terms are defined as follows:

1. *Industrial property* means legal rights in the form of patents, technological inventions, **trademarks,** industrial designs, and "appellations of origin."
2. **Copyright** means legal rights in the form of literary works, musical works, and artistic works and in films, books, and performances of performing artists

in live form and in any recorded format, including photographs, television, or another visual medium.

To qualify for inclusion in either one or both of the preceding classes, ideas and/or works must (1) be put into an appropriate formal documentary form and (2) have been filed with the appropriate national authority for the purpose of registering the material to obtain the domestic (and possibly international) legal protection for the works of the authors, owners, or inventors.

The key body that promotes and coordinates international efforts to protect intellectual property and under whose aegis a number of international agreements are administered in this regard is the World Intellectual Property Organization, or WIPO (Presner 1991).

Inter-American Development Bank   *See development banks*

interest expense   In accounting, the ***income statement*** entry showing the period costs of borrowing money.

interest rate   The payment borrowers make for the use of the funds that they borrow and the payment that lenders demand for the use of the funds they lend (termed *interest*), expressed as a percentage of the principal (loan amount).

This percentage is the interest rate. Interest rates typically are expressed in whole percentages and basis points. A basis point is one hundredth of a percentage point. Thus, the U.S. Treasury 30-year bond had an interest rate of 7.09 percent in February 1993, 25 basis points less than the 7.34 percent average rate for January 1993.

There are four main components to market interest rates: (1) the risk (or default) premium, (2) the maturity premium, (3) an inflation premium, and (4) the "real" rate.

The *risk* premium is a recognition that different classes of borrowers have greater or lesser risk of default. Interest rates are higher for riskier borrowers; they are lowest for the U.S. Treasury, which is considered a "risk-free" borrower. The difference in interest rate between any other borrower and the U.S. Treasury for the same maturity is called a *quality spread.* The *maturity* premium reflects the fact that, in general, a longer loan will have a higher interest rate than a shorter loan. The *yield curve* shows the change in interest rates as maturities are extended for a given class of loans. The ***inflation*** premium is a recognition that inflation may erode the purchasing power of the funds lent. Thus, interest includes compensation for the inflation *expected* over the length of the loan. The remaining portion of an interest rate reflects the *real* rate of interest that must be paid to induce the lender to forgo the use of the funds. (*Note:* This is not simply the interest rate less *current* inflation, but rather interest rates less the average *expected* inflation over the length of the loan. Subtracting the current inflation rate provides an *inflation-adjusted* interest rate. Often, since future interest rates are assumed to conform to an average of past rates, lenders use some such average as a proxy for expected inflation.)

The following table provides examples of these concepts for four widely different years: 1982, 1986, 1992, and 1996.

	Percentage			
	1982	**1986**	**1992**	**1996**
U.S. Treasury bonds	13.00	7.68	7.01	6.54
AAA corporate bonds	13.79	9.02	8.14	7.37
Quality spread	+0.79	+1.34	+1.13	+0.83
U.S. Treasury 3-year note	12.92	7.06	5.30	5.99
U.S. Treasury 10-year bond	13.00	7.68	7.01	6.44
Maturity spread	+0.08	+0.62	+1.71	+0.45
U.S. Treasury 10-year bond	13.00	7.68	7.01	5.99
Consumer inflation°	9.78	3.84	3.64	3.30
Inflation adjusted rate	3.22	3.84	3.37	2.69

°Average inflation rates for previous five years used as a proxy for inflation expectations.

intermittent production   *See job process system*

internal rate of return   The *discount rate* at which the *net present value* (that is, the value of all future cash flows, in excess of the original investment, expressed in today's dollars) of an *investment* equals zero.

Internal rate of return is frequently used by financial managers to decide whether to commit to an investment. In most cases, an investment opportunity is accepted when the internal rate of return is greater than the **opportunity cost** (that is, the projected return on an investment of similar risk) of the **capital** required for the investment. Internal rate of return is expressed mathematically as

$$\text{NPV} = P_0 + \frac{P_1}{1 + \text{IRR}} + \frac{P_2}{(1 + \text{IRR})^2} + \frac{P_3}{(1 + \text{IRR})^3} + \cdots + \frac{P_n}{(1 + \text{IRR})^n} = 0$$

where: NPV = Net present value of the investment
$P_0, P_1, \ldots P_n$ = Cash payments in periods $0, 1, \ldots n$, respectively
IRR = Internal rate of return

The actual calculation of IRR is basically a matter of trial and error. Many business calculators are programmed to perform the calculations.

EXAMPLE: Consider a project that generates the following cash flows:

P_0	P_1	P_2
−$8,000	+$4,000	+$8,000

The project's internal rate of return is expressed as

$$-\$8,000 + \frac{\$4,000}{1 + \text{IRR}} + \frac{\$8,000}{(1 + \text{IRR})^2} = 0$$

The first step in determining IRR might be to assume that it is zero. That is,

$$-\$8,000 + \frac{\$4,000}{1.0} + \frac{\$8,000}{(1.0)^2} = 0$$

The net present value of the investment (with an IRR of zero) is $4,000. Since the NPV is positive, the IRR must be greater than zero. The next step might be to try 25 percent, or

$$-\$8,000 + \frac{\$4,000}{1.25} + \frac{\$8,000}{(1.25)^2} = \$328.21$$

The net present value of the investment (with an IRR of zero) is $320. Since the NPV is still positive, the IRR must be greater than 25 percent. The next step might be to try 26, 27, or as luck would have it, 28 percent:

$$-\$8,000 + \frac{\$4,000}{1.28} + \frac{\$8,000}{(1.28)^2} = \$9.00$$

For practical purposes, an NPV of $7.81 is equivalent to zero (a financial calculator or a few more calculations would give a more precise IRR of about 28.0776 percent) and the IRR of the investment is 28 percent.

If the opportunity cost of the capital required for the investment is less than 28 percent, the investment has a positive net present value when discounted at the opportunity cost of capital. Say the opportunity cost of capital for the investment in the example is 20 percent; its net present value is

$$-\$8,000 + \frac{\$4,000}{1.20} + \frac{\$8,000}{(1.20)^2} = \$888.89$$

This is a strong indication that the investment should be pursued. If the opportunity cost of capital is greater than the investment's IRR (say 35 percent) the investment has a negative present value, or

$$-\$8,000 + \frac{\$4,000}{1.35} + \frac{\$8,000}{(1.35)^2} = -\$647.47$$

This is a strong indication that the investment should not be made.

See also **net present value (NPV).**

International Monetary Fund (IMF)   A multinational organization under the aegis of the United Nations set up by the Bretton Woods Agreement in 1944.

The original purpose of the IMF was to stabilize *exchange rates* after World War II through the coordination and regulation of member-country currency movement.

Today, the IMF no longer coordinates and regulates, although it does promote stability through surveillance and consultation with member countries. The IMF also provides minimum short-term loans to member countries for resolving balance-of-payment difficulties. Today the IMF is one of the most powerful and important financial institutions in the world. Its major activity in recent years has been to support the building of infrastructures in developing countries. The IMF's major thrust in this regard is to act as a police force, exercising approval authority over specific projects and investing developers prior to the awarding of financial assistance by development banks.

To obtain IMF approval, countries must reduce inflation rates, dramatically reduce budget deficits, curtail money supplies, and achieve at least a modicum of political stability. Critics cite the potential for high unemployment and social unrest that such stringent policies could bring, but so far the IMF has held its ground.

International Monetary Market (IMM)   A division of the Chicago Mercantile Exchange; the premier market for foreign currency.

Other activities include trading futures in U.S. Treasury bills, certificates of deposit, and **eurodollar** deposits.

inventory   Any goods available for use or resale at any given time.

Inventory is recorded at the lower of cost or **market value** and reported on the **balance sheet.** There are three types of inventory in a manufacturing company: **raw materials, work-in-process,** and **finished goods.** Inventory can include both goods that are out on **consignment** and goods that are in transit.

See also **beginning inventory; ending inventory.**

inventory forms   The five broad categories into which inventories are classified: **raw materials inventory; work-in-process inventory;** maintenance, repair, and operating inventory; **finished goods inventory;** and goods in transit.

Raw materials inventories are any items to be used directly in the production of a final product. Steel, flour, paint, wood, and plastic are all commonly considered raw materials; but the definition extends to any other materials, such as spark plugs, circuitry, and engines that may have been purchased from an outside organization for use in a product.

Intermediaries include spare parts and supplies that are not necessarily incorporated into a final product but are an integral part of its manufacture. Examples include packing material, paper, and lubricants.

Work-in-process (WIP) inventory consists of all items that have left the raw materials stage but are not yet finished goods. They are incomplete from a product perspective.

Maintenance, repair, and operating (MRO) inventories are those materials, such as tools, lubricants, or spare parts, that are held in order to keep a process flowing smoothly. They often do not go into the product.

Finished goods inventory is made up of completed products. Once an item is completed, it is transferred from work-in-process inventory into finished goods inventory, after which it can be sent to distribution centers, or sold to **wholesalers, retailers,** or customers. Goods in transit are inventory moving to the next user.

inventory functions   The four broad operational reasons that companies retain inventories: anticipation, buffer cycle, decoupling, and transit.

Anticipation inventories are held in anticipation of a predicted or known future increase in **demand.** Rather than operate at peak **capacity** during one period and then shut down in a subsequent period, anticipation inventories can be allowed to accumulate before a period of peak demand and then sold or used during or afterward. Clothing manufacturers, for example, build up anticipation inventories in the months before Christmas, when demand for their products will be high. This strategy allows for more level production throughout the holiday season, with little **idle time** in the months to follow.

Buffer stock is created to protect against unexpected surges in demand or imbalance between stages of production. Any inventory held over and above the average demand requirement is considered buffer inventory. High buffer inventories allow companies to continue to serve customers throughout unexpected increases in demand. Excessive buffer inventories, however, can be quite expensive to maintain. Because conditions and demand vary a great deal from industry to industry, there is no rule of thumb as to what constitutes an excessive buffer inventory. However, an appropriate analysis might be to compare a company's buffer inventories with historical demand patterns within its industry.

Cycle inventories are the result of ordering materials in large batches rather than on an as-needed basis. Cycle inventories are frequently seen when the costs associated with ordering materials are greater than the costs of holding the material.

EXAMPLE: If the annual demand for a particular component is 24,000, management might decide to order a single shipment of 24,000 parts and maintain a large inventory rather than place 12 orders of 2,000 and maintain a smaller inventory.

Decoupling inventories act as cushions between two processes that operate at different speeds.

EXAMPLE: In a bakery, where a mixer can turn out cookie dough five times faster than the preceding workstation can assemble ingredients, a decoupling inventory of preassembled ingredients might be maintained in order to keep the mixer operating at its desired speed.

Decoupling inventories also serve to separate the different operations in a process so that, if an element in a process breaks down, all subsequent workstations could continue to operate, at least for a short time. Without decoupling inventories, each workstation must produce at exactly the same rate; if one operation breaks down, the entire process comes to a halt.

Transit inventories, also called *pipeline* inventories, are, as the name suggests, in transit from one place to another and are generally unavailable for use. Transit inventories may keep a steady stream of material flowing through the production process in contrast to a single shipment. For example, in the automotive industry, Toyota uses transit inventory to keep floor stock at a bare minimum, even though its suppliers are thousands of miles away.

inventory turnover   In accounting, a measure of the number of times that the average amount of inventory on hand is sold within a given period of time.

In other words, the inventory turnover ratio shows how many times a company "emptied its warehouse" over a particular period of time. This ratio is calculated by dividing the **cost of goods sold** for a specified period of time by the average amount of inventory on hand for that same time period (average inventory is calculated by adding **beginning inventory** and **ending inventory** for a given time period and dividing the sum by 2), or

$$\text{Inventory turnover rate} = \frac{\text{cost of goods sold}}{\text{average inventory on hand}}$$

A high inventory turnover rate might indicate that a company has low inventory levels, which may cause a loss in business. A low ratio might indicate that a company has low inventory levels, which may cause a loss in business. A low ratio might indicate that a company is overstocking its merchandise. This could be a reaction to a coming shortage or the result of an obsolete product line. Of course, inventory turnover ratios vary a great deal, and what is considered high in one industry might be considered low in another. Occasionally, "sales" is used in the numerator of the ratio instead of "cost of goods sold." This results in a less useful figure, but the technique may be necessary in order to make a comparative analysis.

See also ***days inventory.***

inventory valuation   In accounting, the costs assigned to inventory.

These costs are reported on the ***balance sheet*** and used in the calculation of ***cost of goods sold*** on the ***income statement. Generally accepted accounting principles*** (***GAAP***) allow several methods of inventory valuation.

See also ***average cost method; first-in, first-out*** (***FIFO***)***; last-in, first-out*** (***LIFO***).

investment   The addition businesses make to ***capital.***

Investment consists of additions to the *fixed capital stock,* both residential (residential construction is included in investment because it is so long-lived; the ***useful life*** of a house is assumed to be at least 50 years) and nonresidential, and *changes in business inventories.* (Purchases of shares of stock are *not* investments in the economic sense unless it is newly issued stock. Otherwise, individuals are simply exchanging one form of wealth—money—for another—the shares—and no new capital is being created.)

The more conventional notion of investment is the expenditure on fixed business capital—plant and equipment. However, much of the investment in business capital is for replacement as previous capital wears out or becomes obsolete. This is the reason for the word *gross* in ***gross domestic product.*** Investment in net new capacity—the addition to capital—requires that businesses have positive expectations for future economic activity in general, and for the prospects for their own firms in particular. Thus, investment is quite cyclical.

IPO   Acronym for *initial public offering. See* ***going public***

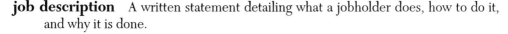

J

job description   A written statement detailing what a jobholder does, how to do it, and why it is done.

job enrichment   A method of increasing worker satisfaction by giving employees increased roles in the production operation, such as quality control, workstation scheduling, and planning.

EXAMPLE: Rather than just assembling the motor of a blender, the worker may also install and inspect it. The process aims to give the worker a greater degree of autonomy and accountability by assigning him or her a *complete* task rather than a small portion of a larger job. Job enrichment constitutes an expansion of the job responsibilities.

job process system   A production system designed to produce small batches of unique products.

Also called *intermittent production,* the job process system is used in companies that are essentially "job shops." Usually each product in a job shop takes a different path through the organization, uses different materials and parts, takes a different amount of time, and requires different operations. Bakeries, physicians' offices, television production companies, supermarkets, and automobile repair shops use job processing. Service companies such as ***advertising agencies*** and tax preparation companies, which offer custom services to individual clients, are frequently well suited for the job process.

The four main characteristics of a job process are (1) a large variety of ***inputs,*** (2) a significant amount of transport of either materials or staff, (3) grouping of equipment and staff according to function, and (4) considerable variation in the time it takes to complete a given job. The advantage of a job shop is the ability to produce a wide variety of products.

Since most job shops perform a wide variety of tasks, general-purpose equipment can be used. General-purpose equipment is usually much less expensive and more easily available than special-purpose equipment. Because the equipment is widely used, there is a larger base of experience to draw upon in terms of operation and maintenance. In addition, since there is a large market for used general-purpose equipment, it is easier to dispose of; thus, the expense of obsolescence is reduced.

Because jobs come through in small batches that require different operations, workers in a job shop are likely to take more responsibility for, and pride in, their work. The pace in a job shop is not dictated by a constantly moving production line; thus, it is possible to establish incentives to encourage *productivity.* Moreover, because there is no line that is constantly moving, if one part of the operation stops, the other parts can continue working as long as there is significant in-process *inventory.*

Job process systems have significant disadvantages as well. As a result of the variety in products, processes, and scheduling, it is nearly impossible for management to control a job shop when demand is high. As a result, *expediting* is frequently necessary to track down particular jobs and push them through the operation. Naturally, this can be a very expensive and inefficient situation.

Inventories can also be a disadvantage in a job shop. Typically, a job shop maintains significant inventories of a variety of materials and supplies. **Work-in-process inventories** also tend to build up. The total effect of all of these inventories is a significant expense and loss of space.

Because various inventories must travel between workstations, materials-handling costs also tend to be high. Since jobs take different paths through the organization, it is usually impossible to invest in inexpensive materials-handling equipment, such as conveyor belts. Instead, more expensive materials-handling equipment, such as forklifts or carts, is used. Because this equipment is typically quite large, more space— beyond that needed to house the inventories—must be used, in the form of wider corridors and aisles.

Johnson's rule for dual workstations   A method developed by scheduling researcher S. M. Johnson in 1954 to determine the quickest possible time to push a number of jobs through a process with two workstations in the same order.

The rule states: If the shortest time for a job is on the first workstation, schedule it as early as possible, or first. If the shortest time for a job is on the second workstation, schedule it as late as possible, or last. Delete that job and repeat the process.

Johnson's rule seeks to ensure maximum workstation utilization by methodically processing a large number of jobs, thereby avoiding lengthy delays for any particular job.

EXAMPLE: Say a physician and a nurse travel among rural schools conducting routine vision tests of students. An initial screening has been given to all students, and those who show a vision problem are then given a more comprehensive test by the nurse and an ophthalmologic examination by the doctor. If five students have been selected through the initial screening to receive further examination, it is desirable to conduct the comprehensive tests and examinations as quickly as possible so that the doctor and the nurse can move on to another school. From the initial screening, the nurse estimates that the testing and examinations (beginning at 8:00 A.M.) will require the following allotments of time (in minutes):

Student	1	2	3	4	5
Testing	60	15	10	20	30
Examination	10	30	60	15	30

According to Johnson's rule, the student with the shortest time in the second task is student 1. That student should be scheduled last. The student with the shortest time in the first task is student 3, so that student is scheduled first.

Thus far, the schedule is as follows:

3				1

The three remaining students have these requirements:

Student	2	4	5
Testing	15	20	30
Examination	30	15	30

The next-shortest time is 15 minutes, but it appears as both the shortest time for the first task (student 2) and the shortest time for the second task (student 4). Usually this sort of situation calls for arbitrary scheduling, but since the 15 minutes is split between the first and the second tasks, it is a simple matter to invoke Johnson's rule and schedule student 2 after student 3, while student 4 will come before student 1. Student 5 is then scheduled in the only remaining spot:

3	2	5	4	1

The entire schedule can then be illustrated on a **Gantt chart:**

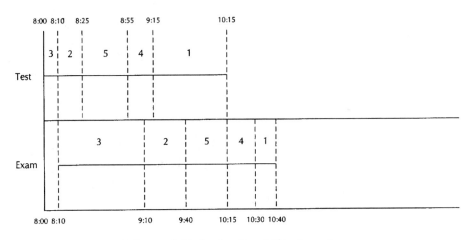

Johnson's Rule for Dual Workstations

All five students will have been screened and examined by about 11:40. Although Johnson's rule will result in an optimum schedule, it is not the only optimum schedule. It is important to note, however, that none of the students will finish sooner than the one determined by Johnson's rule.

joint venture (JV)   A legal form of business organization between companies, whereby there is cooperation toward the achievement of common goals between entities that were, prior to the JV, separate.

There are three types of JVs: (1) contractual, (2) equity, and (3) hybrid.

1. *Contractual JVs:* Under this type of arrangement, the JV is not created as a separate legal corporate entity. It is an enterprise in the form of an unincorporated association, created to carry out clearly defined activities and to attain specific goals over a specific period of time.

There is a clear separation between the companies that agree to cooperate within this type of JV framework: Each of them is responsible for its own liabilities.

2. *Equity JVs:* This arrangement is an enterprise comprising at least two partners and having the following characteristics:

- Formation of a legal **corporation** with limited liability and the joint management of it by the JV partners
- Pooled **equity** in the corporation from which an equity ratio is determined (for example, 50-50, 49-51, 30-21-49)
- Profits and losses shared between the partners in proportion to their equity in the JV

3. *Hybrid JVs:* This commercial agreement is, as its name suggests, a cross between contractual JVs and equity JVs. From the equity JV format, the hybrid JV retains the form of a separate legal entity, but one that is not necessarily a limited liability corporation. From the contractual JV format, the hybrid type retains the specificity of time-limited activities and objectives (Presner 1991).

EXAMPLE: Over 30 companies from the United States, Great Britain, China, and Japan are teaming up to build roads, airports, power plants, and telephone companies in the Najin-Sonbong free-trade zone of North Korea. Marphy Overseas Ltd. of the United States, for instance, plans to invest $100 million to dredge the seabed in Ungsang harbor so that it can develop a lumberyard to process timber (Over 30 Companies 1996).

EXAMPLE: Manheim Auctions of Atlanta, Georgia, and the automotive dealer services unit of Automatic Data Processing, Inc., in Roseland, New Jersey, have entered into a joint venture to enable customers to use the Internet to search, sell, and finance used cars. The new venture, called AutoConnect (*www.autoconnect.net*), will allow dealers to post listings at no charge. Customers will pay a fee to have the company take care of all the financing and insurance paperwork (Frook 1997).

journal entry   A record of the accounting impact of a business **transaction.**
An entry includes the date of the transaction, a short explanation, and the account(s) debited and credited.
See also **bookkeeping; credit; debit.**

Journal of Marketing   *See American Marketing Association*

Journal of Marketing Research   *See **American Marketing Association***

junk bonds   Debt securities rated below investment grade by credit-rating agencies.
During the 1980s, many companies, large and small, raised **capital** for business **acquisitions** and other expansions with junk bonds. The *below investment grade* credit rating means that the risk of receiving either interest payment or the return of principal is very high. This high risk, plus the absence of any collateral, forces junk bonds to carry very high **interest rates** relative to market rates.
Investors put more than $68 billion into junk bonds in 1996, up from $1 billion invested in 1991. According to a CNN report in 1996, AMG Data Services, which

tracks investments, reported that 15 percent of the money invested in mutual funds during one week in February went to junk bonds, which on average offer a return of approximately 12.5 percent (SOURCE: http://cnnfn.com/yourmoney/mutual-funds/9702/20/highyield_pkg/index.htm).

just-in-time (JIT)   An approach to dealing with materials *inventories* that emphasizes the elimination of inventories waiting to be put into the production process. Inventory loses its identity as rapidly as possible.

Just-in-time was originally developed in the mid-1970s by the Toyota Motor Company in Japan. The basic concept behind JIT is that materials and supplies are replenished exactly when they are needed and not before or after. More than an approach to dealing with materials, just-in-time describes an attitude that affects each part of a company's operations, from suppliers to interdepartmental relations to customers. The Japanese interpretation of JIT is to attempt to make products "flow like water" through a company. JIT is best suited to companies with a repetitive production process, such as automobile production, but it can be successfully adapted to companies that use the *job process system* or *cellular production.*

By replenishing materials exactly when they are needed, the cost of having expensive materials sitting idle while waiting for production (and of having equipment wait for late materials) is eliminated.

Because of its broad nature, JIT has become a major part of many companies' competitive strategies. Wilson (1996) argues that Henry Ford developed a production system that shared many of elements of JIT long before the Japanese put their philosophy into practice at Toyota and other companies, although he concedes that that the parallels are not exact. Ford produced essentially a single product, which was the key factor in the efficiency of the assembly line production, but he could not match the advantages that contemporary JIT systems (such as that at Toyota) have in supply chain management and transportation: Ford's suppliers were simply too far away, and the means of transportation were too unreliable to achieve the level of *efficiency* that today's companies can demonstrate (Wilson 1996).

Traditional operations generally have market priorities that dictate the acceptance of all customer orders by providing a variety of products or features from which a customer can choose. For example, some automobile companies offer customers their choice of a variety of options, such as air-conditioning, power windows, and antilock brakes. These individual orders tend to complicate production, which increases both errors and costs. JIT companies, on the other hand, set strict limits on both the *target market* and the variety of products. This does not, however, mean that items produced by JIT companies do not have the features most customers want. JIT automobile manufacturers, for example, tend to include popular features such as air-conditioning, power windows, and antilock brakes as standard equipment. Doing so simplifies production and lowers costs, which, in turn, gives the JIT company its competitive edge.

Traditionally, companies contract with multiple materials suppliers. This strategy is intended to ensure a wide variety of materials at low prices by forcing suppliers to compete against each other.

Relying on frequent small deliveries of high-quality materials, JIT requires an approach that integrates suppliers into the production team, often by single-sourcing to one vendor. As a member of the team, vendors frequently help design and engineer the materials and parts they will ultimately purchase. Clearly, the quantity of materials ordered must be large enough to make this involvement attractive to the vendor.

The most significant cost savings with single-sourcing for JIT is the elimination of cost associated with carrying inventories.

Single-sourcing is not, however, without considerable risks. By maintaining low inventory buffers and relying exclusively on a single supplier, a JIT company is vulnerable to expensive work stoppages and shortages if, perhaps through no fault of its own, the supplier cannot deliver as needed. Additionally, there is perhaps some loss of incentive for a supplier to continue to improve quality or costs once an exclusive contract has been granted.

Inventory management is the central element in just-in-time. In Japan, where space and materials are extremely scarce, a large inventory of any type, from raw materials to finished goods, is considered a waste of valuable resources. Traditional systems, however, view inventory as an essential component in continuing smooth operations.

EXAMPLE: The Bose Corporation, maker of high-fidelity audio systems and speakers, has taken the JIT philosophy and practice one step further. Bose invites its suppliers (at their own expense) to become "in-plant" personnel at the Bose site, in order to carry out transactions, participate in design and prototyping, refine services, and collect information on marketing and distribution. This system, which Bose calls "JIT II," overcomes many of the transportation problems that Henry Ford experienced (see discussion above) in that personnel from suppliers such as Roadway Trucking and ocean freight lines now sit in a command center at Bose and "direct traffic," so to speak, in order to ensure that materials arrive precisely when they are needed (Hiebeler, Kelly, and Ketteman 1998, p. 48).

EXAMPLE: The major U.S. automakers have implemented many JIT principles in recent years, but occasionally find that strikes cripple production schedules. In March 1997, a strike at a General Motors brake plant in Ohio forced 27 out of 29 assembly plants to close and cost GM $15 million. In April of that year, over 1,800 autoworkers at an engine facility owned by Chrysler went on strike, causing five plants to shut down. Such costly shutdowns might suggest to some critics that automakers need to develop backup suppliers and a safety stockpile, but those measures defeat the purposes of JIT and prove to be largely impractical (Johnson 1997).

K

kaizen The Japanese word for "continuous improvement," the enhancement of a product or service through constant study, revision, and improvement in both product and process.

EXAMPLE: When the Toyota Motor Company made numerous engineering improvements to its 1997 Camry line—including suspension refinements, enlarged rear door openings, and a more rigid chassis and frame—it actually *lowered* the price of the car $1,000 while doing so. Many of the changes required fewer parts and simpler installation through use of *kaizen* thinking, making the cars easier and quicker to build. Toyota then implemented similar steps with every car it manufactured both in Japan and North America—just the type of continuous improvement thinking that over a seven-year period earned Toyota facilities numerous gold medal honors from J. D. Power and Associates (*Toronto Sun* 1996).

In the past, upgrades to U.S.-manufactured goods meant a price increase for consumers. But by emphasizing **total quality management (TQM),** many U.S. companies now insist on their *kaizen*-like measures, allowing them to pass along similar savings to customers.

kanban A materials control system that utilizes cards to authorize the production and routine replenishment transactions for materials.

The basic concept of a *kanban* system is to authorize materials for use only if they are needed. This pulls products through the production system rather than pushing them through before they are required, which necessitates storage. The *kanban* process works as a domino effect; once final assembly is authorized, this triggers the sanction of subassembly production, which in turn activates the authorization of parts assembly, and so on down the line. *Kanban,* which means "card" in Japanese, was originally developed by the Toyota Motor Company as part of its **just-in-time (JIT)** manufacturing system.

The most popular modern *kanban* method relies on two types of cards: a withdrawal *kanban* and a production *kanban.* Each card usually shows only the part name and number, the work centers involved, the container capacity, and a storage location. In another technique, an emptied container returned to the supplying operations signals the need for more production. A number or color marking on the container alerts workers to which material (and how much) is required. A very simple system, *kanban* is nonetheless extremely successful.

EXAMPLE: At Toronto-based Cimco, Canada's oldest and largest industrial refrigeration manufacturer, *kanban* cards saved the company more than $1 million by greatly reducing **inventory,** as detailed in a July 1994 article in *CMA* magazine. Cimco's cards are laminated to stand up to rough shop conditions, sometimes include detailed engineering drawings, and hold all pertinent information required for production. As the article explains, the *kanban* cards move along the production line with materials, helping the system to automatically replenish inventory to minimum levels daily using a five-step process:

1. When shelf stock reduces to the reorder point marked by the card, an operator transfers the card to a yellow box at the aisle end of the shelf.
2. At the end of each day, all cards throughout the plant are taken to a central location, where each production team has its own red box.
3. Each card is placed in the red box of the appropriate parts producer.
4. The next morning, each team picks up its cards and meets briefly to determine how different parts can be produced within the production time specified on the cards.
5. All finished parts are taken to the internal customer's site (also indicated on the card), and the card is placed back in its proper point in the Cimco stack.

In addition to the cost savings, use of the *kanban* system enables Cimco to cut both its lead time and production time in half. Workers can easily keep exact counts of parts (once a big problem) and prepare for unusually large orders by pulling cards to get the required parts ready ahead of time. Reordering often requires simply sending a fax of the information from the *kanban* card to the supplier, and machine operators manage the work flow themselves with no need for floor supervisors. Delays and errors are all but eliminated.

keiretsu   Corporate conglomerates whose members combine their marketing, financial, and other capabilities into a loose federation capable of wielding more power in the domestic and international business environment; a Japanese term.

Drawing on the loyalty and cooperation deeply rooted in Japanese culture, *keiretsu* emerged following World War II when occupying Allied forces in Japan outlawed the old business *zaibatsu.* Strictly hierarchical, *keiretsu* member companies use each other's resources to gain business they might never attain independently.

There are three major types of *keiretsu* in Japan: (1) bank-centered *keiretsu,* (2) supply-centered *keiretsu,* and (3) distribution *keiretsu.*

1. Bank-centered *keiretsu* are massive industrial combines of 20 to 45 companies centered around a bank. This structure enables the companies that compose the core of the *keiretsu* to share financial risk and to allocate investment in economically advantageous ways worldwide. There are seven major bank-centered *keiretsu* in Japan: Sumitomo, Mitsubishi, Mitsui, Dai Ichi, Kangyo, Fuyo, and Sanwa. The group comprises 182 companies in all.
2. Supply-centered *keiretsu* are groups of companies vertically integrated along a "supplier chain" dominated by a major manufacturer known as a *channel captain.* These *keiretsu* characterize the automotive and electronics industries. They are well known for the pressure tactics used by channel captains

to enforce time, cost, and delivery-schedule compliance by suppliers (and to extract price concessions from them) under strategies such as ***just-in-time*** (***JIT***) supply systems.

Examples of important supply-centered *keiretsu* are the NEC group (electronics) and the Canon and Nikon group (semiconductor diffusion). Many of the companies in the supply-centered *keiretsu* are linked to the bank-centered *keiretsu*: Twenty-five percent of the NEC group is owned by Sumitomo banks, making the NEC group Sumitomo's principal electronics company. Canon is the $8 billion diversified electronics company in the Fuyo bank-centered *keiretsu*, and Nikon is in the Mitsubishi *keiretsu*. Together, Canon and Nikon hold more than 60 percent of the world market in the production of semiconductor capital equipment.

3. Distribution *keiretsu* are webs of relationships tying Japanese **wholesalers** and **retailers** to a particular manufacturer who acts as the channel captain.

The Japanese Fair Trade Commission (JFTC) issued guidelines on January 17, 1991, to enforce Japan's Antimonopoly Law against distribution *keiretsu* manufacturers who have engaged in systematic protectionist trading practices to restrict competition and exclude foreign companies from entering the Japanese market. Some of these protectionist trading practices include:

- Payment of rebates by manufacturers to retailers as rewards for not carrying products made by competitors.
- Payment of special rebates to wholesalers for handling the goods of a single manufacturer ("tied selling").
- "Joint boycotts" in which rival manufacturers collude to keep out their competitors.
- Cutbacks in manufacturers' shipments to punish retailers (or to punish wholesalers who, in turn, will punish retailers) who reduce prices below a level established by the manufacturers ("resale-price maintenance"; Presner 1991).

EXAMPLE: Alone, the Mitsubishi Trading Company is already the world's single biggest company with annual sales of $180 billion, making it the globe's 22nd-strongest economic power following 21 entire countries. The five-branch *keiretsu* Mitsubishi leads, however, is considerably bigger, with 150 total companies, combined **revenue** of $306 billion, and clout in the auto, chemical, electric, and other industries. The group includes Mitsubishi Trading, Mitsubishi Motors, Mitsubishi Electric, Mitsubishi Heavy Industries, and Mitsubishi Chemical. As its leader, Mitsubishi Trading dictates the *keiretsu*'s manufacturing pace—often enforcing competitive measures such as ***just-in-time*** (***JIT***) inventory systems (Longwood 1996; Swoboda 1996).

Sometimes viewed by other countries, including the United States, as isolationist, *keiretsu* are overseen by the Japanese Fair Trade Commission to help guard against protectionist tactics. As complaints have increased in recent years, accompanied by a softening of the Japanese economy, the power of *keiretsu* has decreased. It is not uncommon for companies now to buy supplies outside the group or borrow from an unrelated bank (When the Mask Cracks 1997).

Keogh plan   A tax-deferred pension account designed for use by employees of unincorporated businesses or for those who are self-employed.

Under a Keogh plan, an individual may make annual contributions of the lesser of (1) 15 percent of earned income or (2) $30,000. By IRS definition, earned income is the net income shown on Schedule C of a personal tax return (Form 1040).

Self-employed persons who use an *S corporation* to bill management service fees to a second wholly owned company (as many single-practitioner management consultants do) cannot use these fees as earned income. Only Schedule C income is considered earned by the IRS: Income distributed from S corporations is reported on Schedule E. To use a Keogh plan, one must fit the category of a self-employed person, which means filing Schedule C.

Keynesian economics   A body of economic ideas, named after the economist John Maynard Keynes, which focuses on the core idea that government involvement in the economy is the most intelligent, reliable, and expedient way to moderate the effects of extreme fluctuations in the business cycle.

The modus used by government is called *fiscal policy*—government's authority to tax and its power to redistribute wealth by way of government expenditures.

Keynesian economics have also been termed liberal economics, demand-side economics, fiscal economics, fiscalism, or, eponymously, Keynesianism (Presner 1991).

labor force   The measure of the number of persons who are either employed or unemployed.

In its effort to determine the employment status of the working-age population, the Bureau of Labor Statistics (U.S. Department of Labor) compiles this measure each month. The labor force is measured so that the **unemployment rate** can be estimated. The data are drawn from a sample of households that are statistically representative of the United States as a whole. Those who were employed in the previous four weeks are so classified. The category *unemployed* comprises (1) those who lost a job or left employment in the past four weeks and (2) others who actively sought employment in the past four weeks. The total of the employed and unemployed constitute the labor force, and the unemployment rate is equal to the percentage of the labor force that was unemployed. The following table presents totals, in thousands, for the labor force and its components and the unemployment rate for the second and third quarters of 1997, as well as a detailed look at the months August, September, and October. Unemployment rates for this period are also provided.

U.S. WORKFORCE EMPLOYMENT DATA, SECOND AND THIRD QUARTERS 1997
(Figures in thousands, except percentages)

Category	Quarterly averages 1997 II	III	Monthly data 1997 Aug.	Sept.	Oct.	Sept.–Oct. change
Household data			**Labor force status**			
Civilian labor force	136,157	136,413	136,480	136,467	136,361	−106
Employment	129,462	129,742	129,804	129,715	129,894	179
Unemployed	6,695	6,671	1,677	1,752	1,467	−285
Not in labor force	66,678	66,954	66,884	67,102	67,407	305

Category	Quarterly averages 1997		Monthly data 1997			Sept.–Oct. change
	II	**III**	**Aug.**	**Sept.**	**Oct.**	
Household data			**Unemployment rates**			
All workers	4.9%	4.9%	4.9%	4.9%	4.7%	0.2%
Adult men	4.1%	4.1%	4.1%	4.1%	4.1%	0%
Adult women	4.4%	4.3%	4.4%	4.4%	4.0%	−0.4%
Teenagers	15.9%	16.5%	16.4%	16.7%	15.3%	−1.4%
White	4.1%	4.2%	4.2%	4.3%	4.1%	−0.2%
Black	10.2%	9.4%	9.3%	9.6%	9.5%	−0.1%
Hispanic	7.7%	7.6%	7.2%	7.6%	8.0%	0.4%

SOURCE: Bureau of Labor Statistics (http://www.stats.bls.gov/news.release/empsit.t03.htm).

last-in, first-out (LIFO)   In accounting, a method of *inventory valuation* based on the concept that merchandise is sold in the reverse order of its receipt.

In other words, if an electronics store bought 100 stereos in January and 50 in February, LIFO will account for the sale of the February units before the sale of the January units.

In periods of *inflation,* LIFO results in *cost of goods sold* figures that are based on the most recent current costs, and inventory figures that are based on older, historic costs. This leads to *lower net income* than would have resulted from the *first-in, first-out* (*FIFO*) method because LIFO matches current costs against *revenue.* However, the inventory figure on the *balance sheet* will be *lower* under LIFO than under FIFO because inventory is based on older costs.

See also average cost method; first-in, first-out (FIFO); LIFO liquidation; LIFO reserve.

latent market   A group of people who have a similar need or desire for a product that does not yet exist.

One example of a product with a large latent market is a painless dentist's drill. Identifying a latent market is often the first step in a successful marketing plan.

EXAMPLE: The Coca-Cola Company realized that a latent market existed for a low-calorie soft drink. The company quickly developed Tab and went on to capture and hold on to the majority of the new diet cola market.

EXAMPLE: Lucent Technologies recently developed a $15 million monitoring facility, called the Network Reliability Center, to provide new telephone companies with the technical backup and monitoring system they need to succeed in the deregulated world of telephone communications. Although referred to as a "latent" market, it is expected to generate as much as $500 million in annual revenues by the year 2000 (Smith 1997).

layout   The physical grouping of centers of economic activity (that is, materials, workstations, machines, groups of people, and inventory storage areas) within a production facility.

lead time   The time from the determination of the need for an item to its receipt.

Components of lead time include order preparation time, supplier notification, supplier production time, packing and shipping time, and receiving and inspecting time. Lead time is an important consideration in materials planning and process scheduling. The availability of *inventory* at the supplier's facility reduces that lead time.

leadership   The functions, behavior, and personality characteristics of people with responsibility, influence, and authority over groups. There is a vast literature that focuses on what leaders do and differences among them.

For example, one popular distinction is between two extremes of leadership behavior: authoritarian and democratic. Authoritarian leaders delegate very little authority and tend to make the bulk of the decisions affecting a group. Democratic leaders, in contrast, delegate a great deal of authority and allow group members to make many of their own decisions. Between these two leadership extremes lie a number of different leadership styles.

Although it is widely acknowledged that effective leadership behavior is frequently the result of a particular business situation (for example, if a project must be completed within a very limited time frame, an authoritarian leadership style might be effective, whereas in a situation with little time pressure that requires extensive coordination among different individuals and departments, a more democratic style might be appropriate), there is a common misperception that democratic leaders are superior to authoritarian leaders. Most research does not support this inference. For example, in one study, teams of three people were presented with a series of problem-solving tasks. The teams with authoritarian leaders were instructed simply to follow orders. The teams with democratic leaders were encouraged to offer suggestions and question their orders. There was no difference in *productivity* between the groups.

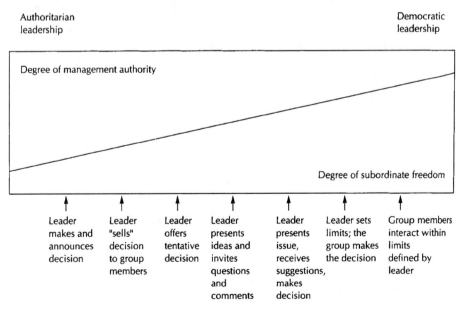

Leadership

leading, coincident, and lagging indexes (LCLg) National indicators that constitute an analytic system for assessing current and future economic trends, particularly cyclical expansions and recessions.

These indexes are grouped as leading, coincident, and lagging, according to their tendency to change direction before, during, or after the general economy turns the corner—either from recession to expansion or from expansion to recession. The leading index reflects business commitments and expectations, the coincident index reflects the current stage of the economy, and the lagging index identifies business cost trends.

Formerly compiled by the Bureau of Economic Analysis, U.S. Department of Commerce, since December 1995 the indexes have been compiled by the Conference Board. They are reported in a monthly publication, *Business Cycle Indicators,* that contains the composite indexes and over 250 additional economic series. The Conference Board also has a Web site devoted to the indexes (http://www.tcb .indicators.org).

The concept of economic indexes is that profits are the prime mover of an economy based on private enterprise and that recurring **business cycles** are caused by changes in the outlook for future profits. Such outlook is reflected in the leading indicators and in the ratio of the coincident index to the lagging index (which ratio is itself a leading index). The components of each index are as follows.

Leading index

- Average weekly hours of manufacturing production workers (average weekly hours)
- Average weekly initial claims for unemployment insurance benefits
- Manufacturers' new orders for consumer good and materials industries in 1992 dollars (manufacturers' orders)
- Vendor performance (percent of companies receiving slower deliveries)
- Manufacturers' new orders for nondefense capital goods in 1992 dollars
- New private housing permits (building permits)
- Stock prices of 500 common stocks (index: 1941–1943 = 10)
- Money supply (M-2) in 1992 dollars (money supply)
- *Interest rate* spread, ten-year Treasury bonds less federal funds rate
- Index of consumer expectations (1966: 1 = 100)

Coincident index

- Employees on nonagricultural payrolls (employment)
- Personal income less transfer payments in 1992 dollars
- Industrial production index (1992 = 100)
- Manufacturing and trade sales in 1992 dollars

Lagging index

- Average duration of unemployment in weeks
- Ratio, manufacturing, and trade inventories to sales in 1992 dollars
- Change in index of labor cost per unit of output in manufacturing (six-month percent)
- Average *prime rate* charged by banks in percent

- Commercial and industrial loans outstanding in 1992 dollars
- Ratio, consumer installment credit outstanding to personal income
- Change in *consumer price index (CPI)* for services, six-month percent

In the business cycles since World War II, the leading index declines for nine months and the coincident/lagging ratio declines for 13 months, on average, before the onset of recession. Also, the leading index turns up four months before an expansion and the coincident/lagging index two months prior.

These indexes are only a rough guide to the direction of the economy; however, they can be useful in preparing pro forma forecasts and developing strategic plans.

EXAMPLE: The following figures present an economic snapshot of the Washington, D.C., area in terms of leading, coincident, and lagging indexes:

LEADING, COINCIDENT AND LAGGING INDEXES
Washington area economic indicators, current and previous months

Economic indicator	Estimates			Percent change	
	Sept. 1996 preliminary	Aug. 1996 final	Sept. 1995 final	Aug. 1996 to Sept. 1996	Sept. 1995 to Sept. 1996
Washington area business cycle indicators					
Coincident index (1987 = 100)	103.2	103.8	103.4	−0.58%	−0.23%
Leading index (1987 = 100)	97.0	97.2	96.2	−0.21%	0.80%
Washington area coincident index components					
Total wage and salary employment ('000)°	2,427.7	2,411.9	2,419.0	0.70%	0.40%
Consumer confidence (South Atlantic)°	146.0	150.8	134.7	−3.18%	8.39%
Airport domestic passengers ('000)†	1,109.4	1,126.5	1,178.1	−1.52%	−5.83%
Nondurable goods retail sales ($'000,000)†	1,527.5	1,620.3	1,581.9	−5.73%	−3.44%
Washington area leading index components					
Total residential building permits°	2,252.0	3,319.0	2,513.0	−32.15%	−10.39%
Consumer expectations (South Atlantic)°	99.4	105.8	98.3	−6.05%	1.12%

Economic indicator	Estimates			Percent change	
	Sept. 1996 preliminary	Aug. 1996 final	Sept. 1995 final	Aug. 1996 to Sept. 1996	Sept. 1995 to Sept. 1996
Washington area leading index components					
Initial unemployment claims[1]	2,846.0	3,522.1	3,681.9	−19.19%	−22.70%
Help wanted index[°]	46.0	44.0	42.0	4.55%	9.52%
Durable goods retail sales ($'000,000)[1]	1,245.0	1,309.2	1,186.7	−4.90%	4.91%
Washington area labor force total labor force ('000)[°]	2,572.4	2,592.0	2,612.4	−0.76%	−1.53%
Unemployment rate[°]	3.8%	3.8%	4.1%	—	—
Washington area wage and salary employment					
Construction ('000)[°]	117.9	116.7	117.7	1.03%	0.17%
Manufacturing ('000)[°]	93.6	93.2	93.4	0.43%	0.21%
Transportation and public utilities ('000)[°]	117.8	118.3	114.3	−0.42%	3.06%
Wholesale and retail trade ('000)[°]	471.4	472.9	466.5	−0.32%	1.05%
Finance, insurance, and real estate ('000)[°]	132.8	133.8	134.2	−0.75%	−1.04%
Services ('000)[°]	904.8	903.3	885.7	0.17%	2.16%
Total government ('000)[°]	588.5	570.8	606.4	3.10%	−2.95%
Federal government ('000)[°]	344.7	347.1	358.9	−0.69%	−3.96%
National indicators					
Total retail sales ($000,000)[1]	158,063	162,584	157,698	−2.78%	0.23%
Nondurable goods retail sales ($000,000)[1]	89,870	92,049	91,577	−2.37%	−1.86%
Durable goods retail sales ($000,000)[1]	68,194	70,535	66,121	−3.32%	3.13%
Leading index (1987 = 100)	103.5	103.4	101.2	0.10%	2.27%
Coincident index (1987 = 100)	121.9	121.6	118.3	0.25%	3.04%

Economic indicator	Estimates			Percent change	
	Sept. 1996 preliminary	Aug. 1996 final	Sept. 1995 final	Aug. 1996 to Sept. 1996	Sept. 1995 to Sept. 1996
National indicators					
Lagging index (1987 = 100)	102.8	102.5	102.2	0.29%	0.59%
U.S. consumer confidence— present (1987 = 100)	129.0	129.5	110.0	−0.39%	17.27%
U.S. Consumer confidence— expected (1987 = 100)	100.4	100.3	88.8	0.10%	13.06%
U.S. CPI—durables (1987 = 100)	119.4	119.1	118.1	0.23%	1.10%
U.S. CPI—durables (1982–1984 = 100)	129.2	128.9	127.8	0.23%	1.10%
U.S. CPI— nondurables (1987 = 100)	134.1	133.1	130.2	0.70%	3.00%
U.S. CPI— nondurables (1982–1984 = 100)	144.1	143.1	139.9	0.70%	3.00%
Federal funds rate	5.30%	5.22%	5.80%	—	—
FHA 30-year mortgage rate	8.58%	8.56%	8.03%	—	—
3-month T-bill	5.09%	5.05%	5.28%	—	—
10-year Treasury bond	6.83%	6.64%	6.20%	—	—

SOURCE: http://www.econreporter.com/metrowatch/washdc/sept96/washdctable.htm.
°Unadjusted data.
†Seasonally adjusted data.
‡Seasonally adjusted constant (1987) dollars.

learning curve The predictable improvements (in cost, labor hours, or machine hours) in a production process that result from increased knowledge and experience.

Also called *experience curves,* learning curves were first observed in the assembly of air frames in the 1930s, when it was found that the labor hours required to assemble each plane declined as production increased. Specifically, each time ***output*** doubled, the amount of direct labor hours needed declined by a steady percentage. In other words, the fourth plane required only 80 percent as much labor time as the second, the eighth only 80 percent as much as the fourth, and the fiftieth only 80 percent as much as the twenty-fifth.

As World War II began and aircraft production increased, managers incorporated the effects of the learning curve into their production plans. They manufactured more airplanes than would have been possible had production estimates been based on more conventional assumptions of level performance and constant costs.

Since the learning curve takes into account any increases in workers' knowledge and skills, it stands to reason that operations paced by workers are more affected by the learning curve than operations paced by machines. For example, in aircraft manufacture, about 75 percent of the labor time is assembly; the rest involves workers doing machine work. In this highly worker-paced operation, an 80 percent learning rate is fairly common. When the proportion of assembly work to machine work is about 50/50, the learning rate is closer to 85 percent. If the ratio is one-fourth assembly and three-fourths machine work, the learning rate is about 90 percent. In other words, in a worker-paced operation, the direct labor on the fourth unit will take 80 percent as long as the second. In an operation where there is a balance between worker-paced and machine-paced procedures, the direct labor on the fourth unit will take 85 percent as long as the second. In a largely machine-paced operation, the direct labor on the fourth unit will take 90 percent as long as the second. It is possible to mathematically predict the impact of learning on labor time and costs.

The learning curve works primarily on direct labor content in the product or service.

learning organization   An organization that displays the capacity to continually adapt to changes in its business environment. This concept has been popularized by Peter Senge in his book *The Fifth Discipline.*

leasehold improvement   Any refurbishment made to a leased property, such as painting the interior of a rented office building.

Leasehold improvements are generally accounted for as ***intangible assets*** (although some companies list them under property, plant, and equipment) on the ***balance sheet*** and must be amortized over the life of the improvement or the term of the lease, whichever is shorter.

letter of credit (L/C)   A popular bank instrument stating that a bank has granted the holder an amount of ***credit*** equal to the face amount of the L/C.

In other words, a bank guarantees payment of its customer's draft up to a stated amount for a given period of time. In effect, collection risk moves from the seller to the bank. In international trade, L/Cs guarantee payment and are called *documentary letters of credit*. The holder of the L/C presents it along with other authenticating documentation to the drawer's bank and demands payment of the face amount.

Domestically, a letter of credit may serve as a guarantee that the payee will perform an act or make a payment. Used in this manner, it is called a *standby L/C*. The term *standby* means that the holder cannot draw against the L/C unless the payee fails to perform or pay as agreed upon by contract. Standby L/Cs are used by the construction industry as a substitute for surety bonds or in the banking industry as backup guarantees to a revenue bond issue or to secure loans from a large money center bank.

Letters of credit come in a variety of forms and carry a wide range of provisions. They can be revocable or irrevocable, confirmed or advised, straight or negotiated, payable at sight or over an extended period of time. A letter of credit may be transferable, assignable, or restricted.

level production   An aggregate planning strategy that maintains a uniform *output* and allows *inventories* to vary with demand changes. Inventory absorbs changes and the workforce remains constant.

A furniture manufacturer, for instance, may maintain a stock of its most popular items in order to ensure a steady supply of its products. A level aggregate production plan increases inventory but stabilizes employment. In a service company, where there is usually no way to inventory service, any attempt at a level production plan ends with a poorly utilized workforce in staffing to meet peak demand. Service organizations use part-time personnel and flexible work schedules to overcome this utilization problem.

leverage   In accounting and finance, the amount of long-term debt that a company has in relation to its *equity.* The higher the ratio, the greater is the leverage. Leverage is generally measured by a variation of the *debt-to-equity (d/e) ratio,* which is calculated as follows:

$$\frac{\text{Long-term liabilities}}{\text{Total stockholders' equity}}$$

Optimal leverage depends on the stability of a company's earnings. A company with consistently high earnings can be more leveraged than a company with variable earnings because it will consistently be more likely to make the required interest and principal payments.

leveraged buyout (LBO)   The purchase of controlling interest in a company using debt collateralized by the target company's *assets* to fund most or all of the purchase price. This debt is subsequently repaid out of the *cash flow* of the acquired company.

During the 1980s, LBOs were the financing mode of choice by buyers and lenders alike. From the buyer's perspective, all or controlling interest in a company's shares could be made with very little down payment. If the value of the company's assets was equal to or greater than the purchase price, an LBO could be made with zero equity contributions. From the lender's perspective, the highly expansionist economy of the times created rapidly appreciating assets that provided more than adequate loan security. LBOs were also a very popular device used by controlling shareholders of public companies to borrow funds against the company's assets in order to buy up large blocks of its stock, thereby taking the company private.

By the 1990s, the frenetic LBO fever of the 1980s had subsided. LBOs are still a popular way to finance business *acquisitions,* but today lenders demand a much greater equity contribution relative to borrowed funds.

leveraging   The advantage gained by using debt financing to create *asset* appreciation.
The theory behind leveraging is that the earnings from a company or the appreciation of an asset acquired with a very high amount of debt financing and very low amounts of equity contributions can be used to repay the debt obligation and interest. In this way, small equity interests can be "leveraged up," thereby causing an increase in the value of original investments.

Buying a house or condo with a small down payment and a high mortgage is a good example of leveraging. As the mortgage gets paid down and the value of the dwelling appreciates, equity interests multiply geometrically.

liability   An obligation payable in money, services, or goods.

Liabilities are reported on the **balance sheet** and include **accounts payable, accrued expenses,** and debt. Liabilities are classified into current (due within one year) and noncurrent (due in more than one year).

LIFO   *See* **last-in, first-out**

LIFO liquidation   A method of accounting for the sale of years-old **inventory** valued under LIFO.

Because this inventory is based on historic costs that can be significantly less than current inventory costs, the sale of these inventory "layers" can greatly reduce **cost of goods sold** and increase **net income.** Assume that a company makes the following purchases and sales:

Year	Beginning inventory	Purchases	Sales	Cost of goods sold	Ending inventory
19X0	$ 0	100 @ $10 = $1,000	50	$ 500	50 @ $10
19X1	500	100 @ $11 = $1,100	50	550	50 @ $11
19X2	1,100	100 @ $12 = $1,200	50	600	50 @ $12
19X3	1,700	100 @ $15 = $1,500	50	750	50 @ $15
19X4	2,450	100 @ $18 = $1,800	50	900	50 @ $18
19X5	3,350	25 @ $20	200	2,725	

In 19X5, when sales suddenly increase, the company has to sell 175 units of its older inventory. Under LIFO, this inventory is valued at its historic cost, so the cost of goods sold is calculated as follows:

Cost of goods sold = 25 units @ $20 + 50 units @ $18

$$+ \text{50 units @ \$15} + \text{50 units @ \$12} + \text{25 units @ \$11}$$

$$= \$200 + \$900 + \$750 + \$600 + \$275$$

$$= \$2,725$$

By contrast, if 19X5 purchases have equaled or exceeded sales, cost of goods sold would be:

$$\text{200 units @ \$20} = \$4,000$$

LIFO reserve   In accounting, the difference between the reported LIFO cost of **inventory** and its current cost, as approximated by FIFO.

Generally, companies that use LIFO will report a LIFO reserve in order to facilitate the adjustment of the inventory stated on the **balance sheet** to more current costs.

See also **first-in, first-out (FIFO)**; **last-in, first-out (LIFO)**; **LIFO liquidation.**

limited partnership   A business structure that combines certain features of both **corporations** (e.g., limited liability) and standard **partnerships** (e.g., profit and loss pass-through).

A limited partnership consists of one or more general partners, normally the business owner(s), and one or more limited partners, usually investors. General partners manage the business of the partnership and are liable for its obligations in the same manner as in a standard partnership. Limited partners have no liability for the activities of the business, much the same as preferred shareholders in a corporation. The term *limited* designates limited legal liability in the same way that the corporate shield protects shareholders from liabilities of a corporation.

For many years, limited partnerships have been a popular medium for financing business *acquisitions.* Typically, the acquiring company is set up as a general partner with individual investors and perhaps a venture capital firm, as limited partners. Limited partnerships are also used extensively to raise *capital* for start-up businesses, especially those involved in real estate development, oil and gas exploration, and other activities with long-term *capital gain* potential.

Recently, *privately held companies* have used limited partnerships as vehicles to raise significant amounts of equity capital for new businesses in such diverse industries as hotels, car dealerships, equipment and vehicle rental companies, resort complexes, movie theaters, booksellers, specialty farms, beer distributors, boat chartering companies, travel agencies, and technical schools.

Limited partnerships are also used in multiple corporate hierarchies for structuring offshore tax shelters and for shielding corporate real estate investments. And small business owners/managers find a limited partnership an excellent vehicle to use in various estate-planning techniques.

The income tax shelter advantages of limited partnerships were effectively eliminated in 1986. Since then, "at risk" rules and *passive activity loss* (PAL) provisions severely restrict the ability of limited partners to deduct start-up losses on their personal returns. Nevertheless, enough tax benefits still remain to encourage limited partnership investments in potentially high-growth business start-ups.

line balancing A method of assigning and grouping tasks to particular workstations in order to minimize both the number of workstations and the total amount of *idle time* within the system at a given level of production. The cycle time (demand/time) is the key factor, and operations are grouped to ensure that the process is completed within that cycle time.

EXAMPLE: Say a bank is processing credit applications. It is required to process 600 applications per day. The job can be divided into the following seven tasks:

	Preceding	Time	Task
1	Open applications	0.25	none
2	Read enclosed letter, noting any special requirements	0.45	1
3	Process page 1 of application	0.32	1
4	Process page 2 of application	0.30	1
5	Determine credit limit from standardized tables	0.50	3, 4
6	Supervisor checks credit limit, notes applicant's address and type of form letter to be sent	0.75	2, 5
7	Assistant prepares and mails form letter	0.35	6
	Total	2.92	

Line balancing determines the minimum number of workstations needed for 100 percent **efficiency** and assigns them equal **cycle times.** Cycle time is calculated with the average daily **output** rate (in this case, 600 applications). This assumes that the number of applications processed is equal to the number of applications received. If more than 600 applications come in per day, a **backlog** will be created. If fewer than 600 come in, there will be unnecessary idle time. Cycle time is then calculated by dividing available work time (eight hours) by daily demand:

$$\frac{\text{Available work time}}{\text{Daily demand}} = \text{cycle time}$$

In the example, cycle time is:

$$\frac{(8 \text{ hours} \times 60 \text{ minutes/hour})}{600 \text{ applications}} = 0.8 \text{ minute per application}$$

In other words, in order to process 600 applications per day, an application must be completed every 0.8 minute.

The minimum number of workstations required is calculated by dividing the total task time by the cycle time determined above.

$$\frac{\text{Total task time}}{\text{Cycle time}} = \text{number of workstations}$$

In this example, at least four workstations are needed:

$$\frac{2.92}{0.8} = 3.65$$

Although the actual number of workstations required is 3.65, it is impossible to set up 0.65 of a workstation, so the number is *always* rounded up. However, it may be that, because of the order in which tasks must be performed, the work cannot be divided into exactly four workstations, and five, or even six, may be needed. If this is the case, each additional workstation will diminish the efficiency of the process. Consider the bank example.

With four workstations:

$$\frac{2.92}{4 \times 0.8} = 0.912, \text{ or } 91.2\% \text{ efficiency}$$

With five workstations:

$$\frac{2.92}{5 \times 0.8} = 0.73, \text{ or } 73\% \text{ efficiency}$$

Assuming that the bank decides to use five workstations, the line can be balanced by using the LOT rule, which requires the generation of a list of all tasks whose predecessors have been completed. Each task is then considered individually, and the task with the *longest operation time* is placed in a workstation. Any other tasks that can be added to the station without exceeding the station's cycle time should be included in that workstation. The procedure for the credit application process is as follows:

Station	Tasks	Tasks available	Time Assigned (min.)	Idle time
1	1, 2, 3, 4	1, 2	0.70	0.10
2	3, 4	3, 4	0.62	0.18
3	5	5	0.50	0.30
4	6	6	0.75	0.05
5	7	7	0.35	0.45

The first tasks to assign are those that have no preceding task. Thus, task 1, with a time of 0.25 minute, is assigned to workstation 1. Tasks 2 (0.45 minute), 3 (0.32 minute), and 4 (0.30 minute) are then available. According to the LOT rule, task 2 should be the first considered. Since it can be included in station 1 without exceeding the 0.80-minute cycle time, it is assigned to that station. At this point it is impossible to add any more tasks without exceeding the cycle time, so the "extra" 0.10 minute is noted as *idle time.*

Tasks 3 and 4 are the next available tasks that can be assigned to station 2. Their total time is 0.62 minute, with an idle time of 0.18 minute. Task 5 cannot be included in this station because its time of 0.50 minute would exceed the cycle time of the station. Because of this, and the fact that it cannot be combined with any subsequent tasks, task 5 is the only task in workstation 3. Similarly, workstation 4 contains task 6 and workstation 5 contains task 7.

In other words, workstation 1 is responsible for opening applications, reading the enclosed letter, and making note of any special requirements. Workstation 2 is responsible for processing pages 1 and 2 of the application. Workstation 3 is responsible for determining the applicant's credit limit. Workstation 4 is responsible for checking the credit limit, noting the applicant's address, and determining the type of form letter that will be sent. Finally, workstation 5 prepares and mails the letter.

liquidity   In accounting, the ability of **current assets** to meet the financial obligations of **current liabilities.**

A liquid company is less likely to default on debt and is more able to take advantage of **investment** opportunities than an illiquid company.

*See also **acid test ratio; current ratio.***

list broker   An agent who arranges the sale or rental of a mailing list.

Direct mail advertisers and market researchers use these lists in order to reach a particular **target market.**

EXAMPLE: The Direct Marketing Association in New York reports that Americans receive over 3.8 million *tons* of junk mail each year—fliers, advertisements, catalogs, solicitations, magazines, free offers—each piece directed, more or less precisely, to the people who will be most interested in it. Although the technology for matching recipient and offer is not perfect, it is much more sophisticated than it used to be, and a list broker such as Specialized Marketing, Inc., in Somers, New York, can now pair up the user of a gas card with products he or she would be most likely to buy if given the chance (Ossorio 1994).

load   The amount of work scheduled for a specific work center within a given time period. A work center's load is usually expressed as standard hours of work.

load profile   In manufacturing, a summary of future *capacity* requirements based on work orders (either planned or released) for a given time period.

loading   The assignment of jobs to particular work centers.

    Although capacity planning will determine that there is enough *capacity* to meet the master production schedule, it does not usually make any specific work center assignments. For example, some equipment might be better suited for certain jobs, or a particular team of workers might be less heavily loaded than other workers. Thus, there is usually a most efficient (or less costly) assignment of jobs.

logistics   Those actions and business practices that manage the movement of goods or services throughout the supply chain.

logo   *See brand mark*

London Interbank Offered Rate (LIBOR)   The base lending rate that banks charge each other in the London eurocurrency market.

    The rates are set each day at 11:00 A.M. (London time) after five major banks—the National Westminster Bank, the Bank of Tokyo, Deutsche Bank, Banque Nationale de Paris, and Morgan Guaranty Bank—report their individual bid-and-offered rates for $10,000. These rates are then averaged and rounded to the nearest $\frac{1}{16}$ of a percentage point. HSH Associates compiles a list of rates for the past ten years or so at its Web site http://www.hsh.com/indices.libor.html. In September 1997, for instance, LIBOR rates for adjustable-rate mortgages were 5.672 (one-month), 5.782 (three-month), 5,852 (six-month), and 6.008 (one-year). The following graph shows the movement of the six-month LIBOR for the period from 1990 to 1997.

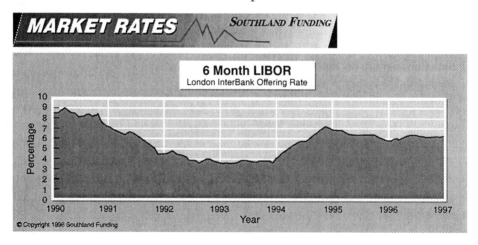

SOURCE: http://www.southland1.com/market/libor.htm.

    LIBOR is the European equivalent of the U.S. *prime rate,* although it is not calculated the same way. LIBOR is an actual market rate determined by the supply and demand of *eurodollars* in London's *capital markets* and charged by one bank to another bank. The U.S. prime rate is a fictitious rate set by money center banks based on the cost of doing business plus a profit.

    With increasing frequency, the globalization of the financial system forces U.S. lenders to quote *interest rates* based on LIBOR rather than prime. Generally,

LIBOR runs slightly less than prime. Borrowers approve of LIBOR because it represents an actual market rate, not a fictitious estimate.

long bond   Thirty-year U.S. Treasury bonds or other bonds that mature beyond ten years.

Long-bond *interest rates* and yields run higher than those for short-term securities because investors perceive the risk of tying up money for long time periods to be greater than for short periods. Long-bond rates are frequently used as a risk-free benchmark for business valuations. They also serve as a barometer of the health of the U.S. economy, with declining long-bond rates signaling a rising economic base. Rates for long-term mortgages are also tied to the rates of long bonds, which offer an alternative *investment* opportunity for long-term lenders.

longitudinal panel   A group of participants in a market research study who are questioned at various points over a period of time.

See also omnibus panel.

EXAMPLE: The National Purchase Diary Panel consists of a consumer panel of 13,000 families who record their purchases of each of a number of products each month.

long-term asset   In accounting, an *asset* with future economic benefits that are expected for a number of years.

Long-term assets are reported on the *balance sheet* as *noncurrent assets* and include equipment and buildings.

long-term liability   In accounting, an obligation that is due in a period of more than one year.

Long-term liabilities are reported on the *balance sheet* as *noncurrent liabilities* and include mortgages and long-term debt.

See also liability.

loss leader   A retailing strategy of putting low prices on selected items in order to attract customers or reduce *inventory.*

Also called a *traffic builder,* this strategy does attract customers; however, it is not popular with manufacturers who feel that the heavy discounting of their products dilutes the image of their *brands.*

EXAMPLE: In 1994, Dwayne Goode, owner of American Drugs, Inc., in Conway, Arkansas, sued Wal-Mart over the giant retailer's practice of selling some items at a much reduced price (often, according to Goode's suit, below cost) in order to attract customers to the store, where they might purchase other, more expensive items. Wal-Mart defended its strategy of loss-leader pricing by arguing, in essence, that all's fair in love and retailing. As the suit made its way through the courts, Goode made a regular practice of driving from Conway to Little Rock, where he visited the local Wal-Mart, buying up as many sale items as he could carry in his car. Then he would return to Conway and sell those items on his own drugstore shelves (Kristof 1994).

See also retailer.

lot tolerance percentage defective (LTPD)   The percentage of defective goods in a single lot of incoming materials that a company is willing to accept as defective. It is the poorest acceptable quality in a single lot.

See also acceptable quality level (AQL); type II error.

lower of cost or market   A rule applied to the valuation of *inventories* and *investments*.

Conservatism dictates that these accounts be stated at the lower of cost or market. Doing so could result in an unrealized loss in the *financial statements.*

EXAMPLE: A company has inventory with a historical cost of $1,000 and a *replacement cost* of $900. That means it must report inventories at $900 and declare an unrealized loss. When the reverse is the case (that is, inventory has a historic cost of $900 and a replacement cost of $1,000), inventory is reported at $900 and there is no recognition of any gain. The lower of cost or market rule applies to all financial reporting, regardless of the method of *inventory valuation.*

M

Magnuson-Moss Warranty/Federal Trade Commission Improvement Act
Legislation passed in 1975 that requires clear disclosure of consumer product warranty terms prior to sale of an item.

The Federal Trade Commission (FTC) is empowered to determine the manner in which product warranties must be made available to consumers. The act also provides for consumer redress, including class action suits.

makegood   A credit an advertiser gets from a publisher or a broadcaster to make up for an erroneous advertisement or one that doesn't reach the promised audience.

Makegoods must be negotiated between the advertiser and the medium, but they usually involve rerunning the ad or commercial.

In print advertising, makegoods may be given when the publisher makes a mistake in the printed copy (such as an incorrect address) or when the advertisement is placed in a position in the publication other than the one specified by the advertiser.

In broadcasting, makegoods are given when the television or radio station fails to deliver the audience size or composition it promised for a particular commercial or when the commercial does not run as scheduled.

EXAMPLE: A lackluster fall television season in 1997 left TV executives grappling with a two-pronged problem: Shortfalls in key viewing segments threatened to limit *revenue* growth that could be used to offset cash makegoods, while significantly greater up-front ad sales left precious few spots available for rerunning commercials (Levin 1997).

make-to-order (custom made)   Goods or services produced according to customer-provided specifications, prints, or designs.

Make-to-order items are usually turned out in small volumes with a great deal of variety between products. Consumer-oriented firms such as upholsterers, carpenters, and interior designers traditionally provide make-to-order items. If the item fails to work properly, the customer who provided the specifications is legally responsible for nonperformance.

EXAMPLE: The Monsanto Company is using client/server technology at its Pensacola, Florida, fiber plant to produce carpet fiber according to the type, color, weight, density, and amount specified by individual customers. "We are making something for a customer rather than making it and then seeing who we can sell it to," says a Monsanto official (Weston 1996).

*See also **job process system; make-to-stock.***

make-to-stock   Goods produced to the manufacturer's specifications and stored as *inventory* in anticipation of future *demand.*

Make-to-stock items are usually turned out in large batches, with only slight variations between individual products.

See also *make-to-order.*

management by objective (MBO)   A management method that emphasizes specific, jointly agreed-upon goals for each employee.

With MBO, all affected parties, from upper management to supervisors to shop floor workers, participate in the goal-setting process, which ensures that everyone's concerns are considered in devising realistic objectives.

Each objective should be as explicit as possible, with tangible performance measures and a set time frame clearly stated. For example, instead of simply planning to improve quality or cut costs, zero in on a specific target—such as reducing returns to less than 2 percent of sales over the next six months or cutting costs by 10 percent within the next *fiscal year.*

A critical component of MBO is performance feedback, which should occur at every level. For example, if the sales force is charged, say, with increasing sales of a line of products by 5 percent during the current quarter, the vice president of sales will study weekly sales figures for each product, while each district manager keeps tabs on the performance of individual sales representatives. The sales reps themselves will monitor their own personal progress toward the goal.

Rewards such as pay raises and promotions are based on the evaluations of employees' progress toward meeting their goals.

management control systems   The combination of planning, strategy, penalties, and rewards that shape management behavior.

All companies need controls, if only because the necessary act of dividing activities and responsibilities among organization members means that overall corporate goals and strategies will likely be altered slightly by the needs of various individuals. Thus, it is important to encourage consistency by holding managers accountable.

Management control systems are almost always based on some form of financial measurement. A specific financial objective, such as increasing sales or profit, can clarify the issues and decisions faced by managers, even if it does not have the desired effect. There are four broad types of financial responsibility, each with its own set of objectives:

1. *Cost centers* are activity areas within a company where *direct costs* can be measured and to which part of the company's overall *fixed costs* can be allocated. In a factory production department, for example, *standard costs* of direct materials and labor are specified; it is the manager's objective to minimize the difference between actual and standard costs.

2. *Profit centers* are areas that are treated as separate businesses for the purposes of management and financial control. Profit center managers are responsible for creating the best possible combination of costs and *revenue,* with the objective of maximizing profits. Profits can be measured in various ways within the management control system; for example, the sales manager of a product line division is responsible for *gross profit,* whereas profit fig-

ures for the division's **marketing** manager might include deductions for promotional expenses and factory **overhead.**

3. *Revenue centers* are areas that have no control over prices or costs. A sales department is generally thought of as a revenue center, where the goal of the manager may be to widen his or her margin of revenue without exceeding the expense budget.

4. *Investment centers* are areas within a company where the manager is responsible for purchasing the various **assets** used by the company. Investment center managers must balance the need for current profits with the need to make investments that increase future profits. Their objective is generally to maximize the department's **return on investment** (**ROI**).

In establishing management control systems, fairness and goal congruence are crucial. Fairness dictates that each manager's financial objectives accurately gauge performance, taking into account all the factors within his or her control while excluding those beyond control. Goal congruence prevents managers from working at cross-purposes by aligning the company's various management control systems so as to serve overall corporate goals and strategies.

EXAMPLE: XYZ Widget sets a goal of increasing first-half output by 10 percent and, to accomplish this goal, it establishes a set of monthly production requirements for its factories. The Midwest factory supervisor, concerned with meeting May's production targets and cutting monthly costs, decides to put off preventative equipment maintenance. In June, equipment breakdowns cause the factory to lose five days of production. Although the Midwest plant's May output increased by 10 percent, the June loss more than offset the earlier gain.

The XYZ system lacks congruence between overall company strategy and the Midwest manager's short-term cost-cutting goal.

See also **incentive plans.**

management information system (MIS)   A formal, usually computerized, means of supplying managers with the information needed to make decisions.

Originally, the MIS was focused on providing accurate internal information, such as sales and **inventory** figures. The systems were designed to speed up business processes in order to contain costs and improve administrative efficiency. In recent years, however, the MIS network has been expanded to include an external component, integrating a flow of information from customers, distributors, and suppliers.

EXAMPLE: The MIS system for Mrs. Fields cookies includes computer terminals in every store. Each morning, store managers enter a sales projection based on the previous year's performance and answer a series of questions posed by the computer. Questions include "What day of the week is it?," "Is it a normal day, a sale day, a holiday, a school day, or other?," and so on. If it is, say, a Wednesday and a school day, the computer analyzes the store's hour-by-hour, product-by-product performance on the three previous school-day Wednesdays. Using that information, the computer then comes up with a plan for the day that includes how many customers should be served each hour, what types of cookies should be made, and when batches should be mixed and baked.

As the day progresses, the MIS utilizes computerized cash registers to keep track of hourly sales and revise sales projections. It also will make suggestions; for example, if the number of customers is satisfactory but the average check is too small, the system might recommend setting out a tray of samples to encourage more purchases.

When used effectively, the MIS can be a valuable source of **competitive advantage,** as well as a way to improve communication and coordination among various departments and individuals.

management's discussion and analysis of operations (MD&A)   A section in an **annual report** that summarizes the reasons for changes in a company's operations, **liquidity, capital** resources, and **working capital.**

The MD&A, which is required by the **Securities and Exchange Commission** (**SEC**), is designed to help readers of **financial statements** understand the effects of changes in business activity and accounting methods.

manufacturing margin   In accounting, the excess of sales over the variable cost of goods sold (Fess and Warren 1993, 922).

EXAMPLE: XYZ Computer Corporation produces computers that have a variable cost of $1,000 each. It sells these items at $1,500. If the company sells 3,000 computers a year, its sales amount to $4,500,000. But its variable cost of goods sold is $3,000,000. The difference is the manufacturing margin, which in this case is $1,500,000.

manufacturing resource planning (MRPII)   Complex, computer-based planning system that integrates a wide range of company functions such as engineering, **materials requirements planning** (**MRP**), **marketing,** purchasing, production scheduling, business planning, and finance.

MRPII is a broadening of the scope of production planning, bringing in other functional areas whose input impacts the production decision. The major purpose is to integrate primary functions into the planning process.

Because these systems can also assess the impact of production schedules on resources such as equipment and labor, production planners are able to decide when to shift orders, reduce workloads, or increase **capacity** with part-time workers, overtime, and so on.

marginal cost   The increase or decrease in total cost that results from producing one more or one less unit; also called **incremental cost.**

In manufacturing, marginal cost typically declines as production volume rises. That is because **economies of scale** arise when **fixed costs** are spread over a larger number of units, thereby reducing the per-unit cost. Conversely, spreading fixed costs over fewer units raises the per-unit cost.

EXAMPLE: A toy maker receives an order for 100,000 units of a plush, tail-wagging, stuffed dog. The total cost—including materials, labor, electricity to run the machinery, and an allowance for fixed costs such as rent and insurance—is $300,000, or $3.00 per dog.

The customer considers increasing the order by another 10,000 units. Since the fixed costs of producing the stuffed dogs are already covered, and since many of the other costs are related to preparing for the manufacturing run, making another 10,000 dogs will add only $10,000 to the toy maker's total cost. The marginal cost for the extra dogs, then, is $1.00 apiece ($10,000 ÷ 10,000 dogs).

Selling the additional dogs for more than $1.00 each will increase total company profit, even though that price does not cover the total cost of producing each dog. But the toy maker must charge *at least* $1.00 per dog for the additional production because the marginal cost is also the lowest possible sales price before overall company profitability begins to suffer.

Marginal cost analysis can be a handy tool for deciding whether to increase or decrease production.

See also **marginal revenue.**

marginal revenue The extra *revenue* received from selling one more unit of production.

Marginal revenue is the difference between total revenue before the sale of the extra unit and total revenue after the sale. So long as the price of a product or service remains constant, marginal revenue equals price.

EXAMPLE: A radio manufacturer that sells car radios for $250 each receives $250 in marginal revenue if one more radio is sold.

Sometimes, however, additional output can only be sold at a reduced price. So before deciding whether to make more radios, the radio manufacturer must look at *marginal cost.* If marginal cost exceeds marginal revenue, making additional radios is obviously not a wise move.

See also **contribution margin** (**CM**).

marginal revenue = marginal cost rule A rule in economics that says a company should produce up to the point where the cost of an additional unit of *output* (its *marginal cost*) is just equal to the *revenue* earned by selling the additional unit (its *marginal revenue*).

Moreover, if the producer has the power to set the price of its product, it should do so at a level where consumers will demand this optimal level of output.

By following this rule, a company can maximize its profit and minimize its loss. However, if the market price falls below the company's average *variable cost,* this rule is negated. In such a situation, the best thing a company can do is shut down.

See also **shutdown situation.**

market All people who have a specific, unsatisfied need or want and are willing and able to purchase a product or service to satisfy that need.

EXAMPLE: The market for automobiles consists of anyone of legal driving age who has a need for transportation, access to roads, and enough money to make an outright purchase or make payments on a car.

Marketers look at consumer interests and income to help determine the most likely buyers for any given product. Many consumers might like to have an in-ground swimming pool, but only those who can afford one are part of the market. A pool builder might look at research data detailing consumer interests and income levels in a specific town or neighborhood, learn who is interested in buying a pool and who can afford one, then target its *marketing* effort directly to those people.

See also **available market; penetrated market; potential market; served market; target market.**

market aggregation   *See* **mass marketing**

market capitalization rate   *See* **expected return**

market life cycle   The stages through which a **market** passes as it comes into being, flourishes, and eventually disappears.

Four distinct stages comprise the market life cycle: emergence, growth, maturity, and decline. A market *emerges* when a consumer need is first realized and met.

EXAMPLE: Recognizing that the need to make multiple copies of documents was imperfectly satisfied by carbon paper and mimeograph machines, the forerunner to the Xerox Corporation acquired the rights to xerographic imaging in 1947. A year later, the company produced and marketed its first copying machine. A new market had emerged (SOURCE: "A Brief History of Xerox" from the Xerox Web site).

The *growth* stage of a market is marked by increasing sales and competition. Competitors attempt to discover and fill various niches and segments of the market. In the copier market's growth stage, competitors offered portable and color copiers to attract different market segments. When each segment has been served and competitors begin to eat into one another's sales, the market has reached *maturity.* A market is in *decline* when **demand** for current products wanes or a new technology encroaches on the old. Eventually, the old technology will fall by the wayside and a new market will emerge.

Different **marketing** strategies are appropriate at each stage of the life cycle. In the emergence stage, when there is little or no competition, a company has three options:

- Design a product that appeals to a small segment of the market; this allows small companies to avoid conflict with larger would-be competitors.
- Launch two or more products simultaneously to capture several market segments; this is appropriate when consumer preferences are all very different (see **diffusion of innovation curve**).
- Target the mass market by designing a product with the widest possible appeal; this is most effective for large companies with substantial resources and distribution capabilities.

Companies entering a market during the growth stage also have three possible strategies:

- Pursue a niche strategy (*see* **niche marketing**) in one small segment.
- Compete directly with the market pioneer.
- Attempt to serve multiple niches in small segments of the market.

When a market enters maturity, competitive strategies focus on finding new product innovations or reducing prices in order to gain **market share.** In the decline stage, competitors must decide whether to move to another market or work to increase market share as other companies seek greener pastures.

The whole concept of "life cycle" has taken on a different cast in the computer and communications industries, which are notorious for how quickly products seem to become obsolete. Just ask anyone who bought last year's "most powerful" personal computer model or the cellular phone with "the clearest reception." But not only consumers feel the crunch. In a 1996 survey by *OEM* magazine, nearly three fourths of the respondents expected product development cycles to speed up and market life cycles to shrink. Yet fewer than half expected R&D expenditures to increase (Lieberman 1996).

See also **product life cycle; product maturity.**

market risk   The result of factors such as the state of the economy, **interest rates,** and **inflation** that affect the prices of all stocks; also called *systematic risk.*

Market risk—as opposed to **nonmarket risk** (or *nonsystematic risk*), which involves the risks faced by individual companies—accounts for the fact that stocks tend to move as a group in a particular direction. An individual stock's sensitivity to the conditions that constitute market risk is measured by its **beta.** A stock with a beta of 1.0 carries the same risk as the total risk of the market as a whole. A stock with a beta of 2.0 is twice as sensitive to market fluctuations as is the stock with a beta of 1.0. That means that if the market drops 10 percent, the stock with a beta of 2.0 will drop 20 percent.

See also **alpha; capital asset pricing model (CAPM).**

market risk premium   The *rate of return* investors demand from a security with a given level of **market risk.**

In its broadest terms, the market risk premium is the difference between the average return of the overall market and the going rate of interest. The market risk premium for an individual security is calculated using the **capital asset pricing model (CAPM).**

market saturation   *See product maturity*

market segmentation   Dividing a large, diverse **market** into smaller parts that share common characteristics.

Companies sometimes develop different versions of a product to appeal to each segment's specific wants and needs. But even if the product doesn't vary, marketers will usually develop separate promotional programs for each subgroup. The **marketing mix** will be designed to suit relatively homogeneous segments. Sneakers, for example, are worn by everyone from toddlers to grandparents. The basic structure of the shoe worn by a teenage boy might well be identical to that worn by his father, but the exterior will vary dramatically with the addition of decorative trims, colors, and laces. And so, too, the **advertising** will be tailored to appeal to the different age groups.

Markets can be broken down in numerous ways, as marketers try to find distinctive groups of consumers within the total market. For generic products such as paper clips, no special groups exist, so relying on **undifferentiated marketing,** or only one **marketing** program, makes sense. At the other extreme, consumer **demand** for products such as clothing, furniture, automobiles, and so on is highly diverse. In those instances, a marketer can choose to serve all, many, or some of the market's varying needs and desires.

Markets can also be segmented descriptively by using geographic and demographic variables such as age, ethnicity, gender, educational level, marital status, income, and so on, as well as behaviorally, based on consumer attitudes, lifestyles, product usage, and other fluctuating elements.

EXAMPLE: Avon Products, Inc., the world's leading direct seller of cosmetics and beauty-related products, has developed marketing strategies and tactics based on the values, trends, and buying patterns of consumers in the Hispanic, African-American, and Asian-American market segments. Information gleaned from ***marketing research*** led Avon to hire a separate ***advertising agency*** specifically to address issues raised by the Hispanic community. To appeal to African Americans, the company has added cosmetic color shades appropriate for darker skin tones and also offers more Afrocentric gift items, such as books on Kwanza. As part of its push in the Asian-American market (Chinese, Japanese, and Korean subgroups are being targeted), Avon uses a multi-Asian language brochure and Asian language radio commercials in some areas of the country (Chapman and McFarland 1995).

For market segmentation to work successfully, five criteria must be met. The segment must be:

- Identifiable and measurable
- Big enough to be profitable
- Reachable, so that marketers can communicate easily and effectively with the target group
- Willing and able to purchase
- Stable, not likely to change rapidly

Market segmentation has both advantages and disadvantages. On the plus side, segmenting allows marketers to direct a larger share of promotional spending to the most promising areas and to vary ad campaigns for different target groups. Moreover, consumers aren't forced to make compromises when they purchase a product because segmentation produces a better match between what the consumer wants and what a marketer offers.

The downside is that as the marketer investigates more and more segments, research costs mount—and so do production costs, because production runs are shorter and ***economies of scale*** are lost. Also, the marketer may have to sacrifice sales in one segment as it concentrates on serving another.

*See also **behavioral segmentation; cannibalization; demographic segmentation; psychographic segmentation; volume segmentation.***

market share The ratio of one company's sales to total sales by all competitors in a given ***market.***

Market share is arrived at by dividing the sales of the company in question, either total number of units sold or their dollar value, by the corresponding total for all competitors taken together.

EXAMPLE: About 15.1 million new cars and light trucks were sold in the United States in 1997. General Motors Corporation, which sold approximately 4.7 million of those, garnered a 31 percent market share (4,700,000 ÷ 15,100,000 = 0.31, or 31 percent; Kerwin and Vlasic 1998).

Market share, which is calculated for a specific period, often a year, is a good indicator of a company's competitive standing because it allows for direct comparison with others in the same market. A company may pat itself on the back for an annual sales increase of 10 percent, only to learn that the market as a whole posted a 50 percent gain; clearly, the company's competitors had a much better showing. Savvy companies continually monitor competitors' market share to benchmark their own progress.

market value (1) The price at which a security, product, or service can be sold.

market value (2) In accounting, the ***replacement cost*** of an item, as used in the ***lower of cost or market*** rule.

marketable security An ***equity*** or debt security that can be easily sold or converted into cash.

Marketable securities may be short-term obligations, such as Treasury bills and ***commercial paper,*** or traded stocks and ***bonds.*** Companies invest in marketable securities as a way to earn some return on cash that would otherwise be temporarily idle. They are usually carried at cost as a ***current asset*** on the ***balance sheet.***

marketing The process of planning and executing the strategy involved in getting ideas, goods, and services to the consumer.

Everything from conception of the product or service to positioning, pricing, and promotion to distribution and after-sale relationship is a facet of marketing. In short, *marketing* means using an understanding of consumers to satisfy their needs while also meeting the goals of the company. It differs from mere salesmanship (persuading someone to buy something), because it involves making an effort to figure out what a customer desires and then helping the company find a way to profitably meet those desires.

Nearly every part of a company's operations has something to do with marketing. When management decides to offer a new product based on market research, it is practicing marketing. So, too, the design department that incorporates features with specific consumers in mind. Even the friendly receptionist who goes out of his or her way to make customers glad they called is practicing effective marketing.

EXAMPLE: Pushing hard to overtake competitors in the race for U.S. ***market share,*** Taiwan's leading bicycle manufacturer, Giant Manufacturing Company, has put together a package of marketing moves. Attempting to shed what it believes is an undeserved image as a mediocre import, Giant has sponsored high-profile racing teams and secured endorsements from well-known downhill racers. Product offerings have been perked up with the inclusion of desired high-tech features on more of its models. In addition, the company has added new models in the high-end (over $1,000) mountain- and road-racing bike category.

And the result of this revamped marketing strategy? Giant appears to be reaching its ***target market*** and winning converts: U.S. sales jumped 30 percent in 1997, lifting Giant's market share and propelling it into the ranks of the top-five specialty-bike marketers in the United States (Moore and Engardio 1998).

marketing channels *See **distribution channels***

marketing mix   Tools and techniques a company uses to achieve *marketing* goals in its *target market.*

Four elements compose the marketing mix:

- *Product,* which includes quality, assortment, service, guarantee, packaging, and warranty
- *Distribution,* which comprises **wholesalers, retailers,** sales representatives, warehousing, **inventory,** and transportation
- *Price,* which includes consumer and competitor reactions as well as cost
- *Promotion,* which covers **advertising,** publicity, and personal selling

Each element is equally important, although some may get more emphasis than others in particular marketing situations and strategies. In marketing a **commodity** such as nails, where buyers base purchases primarily on cost, pricing policy would be the central element in the marketing mix. Products such as perfume, on the other hand, rely heavily on promotion and advertising to attract customers.

In most cases, however, successful marketing requires an organization to competently juggle all four elements in the mix. Not only must a company offer an appealing product at an acceptable price, but it must be able to promote the product in a way that attracts the desired customer segment. Moreover, without an efficient distribution system that can deliver the product to the right place, at the right time, and in the amounts needed, all the product, pricing, and promotion effort will be for naught.

EXAMPLE: Few companies can match the expertise displayed by Nike, Inc., in balancing the four elements of the marketing mix. The company pins its brand image worldwide on top-quality athletic shoes that promote fitness and performance. This theme drives everything from product development and styling to advertising, merchandising, and pricing.

Yet despite its global focus, Nike knows that sales are made locally. Thus, managers at the local level are given discretion to decide how best to implement the fitness and performance image. And although Nike makes a wide assortment of shoes, it varies its product offerings according to which sports are popular in which countries. Nike also uses geographically popular athletes to endorse its products and tailors its message to fit the **market.** Distribution outlets and pricing strategies also vary according to the market. Nike's combination of standardized market image and flexible implementation has helped make it the world's leading athletic apparel maker (Roth 1995).

*See also **four P's.***

marketing myopia   A condition in which a company is so involved with selling that it loses sight of the true nature of its product.

The term was coined by Theodore Levitt, professor of marketing at Harvard Business School.

A company suffering from marketing myopia eventually finds itself overshadowed by competitors.

EXAMPLE: The railroad industry is frequently cited as a classic example of extreme shortsightedness. Nearly a century ago, railroad company executives failed to recognize that their product was transportation. Consequently, while they were busy focusing on the railroad business, automobiles and airplanes largely swallowed the passenger market, leaving the rails with only a tiny segment of that market. By defining their industry by product rather than by customer, the railroad companies lost an enormous opportunity for growth.

Marketing News A publication of the ***American Marketing Association.***

marketing orientation Making the needs and desires of the ***target market*** the guiding light of the company.

Companies with a marketing orientation go to almost any lengths to satisfy their customers more effectively than do their competitors.

EXAMPLE: Lands' End, Inc., the Dodgeville, Wisconsin, mail-order firm, prides itself on bending over backward to satisfy its customers. Gary Comer, who founded the company in 1963, developed eight principles of doing business that still guide the company today. The principles guarantee high quality, fair pricing, and customer satisfaction no matter what.

And does the company live by its credo? Customer anecdotes indicate that it does. For instance, a question about sizing of a particular clothing item featured in the Lands' End catalog can easily lead to a discussion with the telephone representative about the customer's lifestyle, body type, and preferences as to fit (looser here, tighter there), with the telephone rep apparently well versed as to specific product features. And in the end, there's always the assurance that "you can send it back if it's not right."

marketing plan A document that some companies use to outline their ***marketing*** strategy and tactics.

The marketing plan is a useful tool for organizing and managing a marketing effort. A good plan contains eight sections as follows:

- The *executive summary* gives a short overview so managers can easily grasp the plan.
- An *analysis of the current marketing situation* presents key background information concerning product, ***market,*** technology, competition, distribution, price, and promotion.
- An *analysis of opportunities* summarizes the issues, opportunities, threats, strengths, and weaknesses facing the product.
- The *objectives* lay out the goals for sales, ***market share,*** and profits.
- The *marketing strategy* presents the overall approach that will be used to meet the objectives.
- The *plan of action* specifies how the plan will be implemented.
- The *financial projections and costs* state the budget and anticipated consequences.
- The *control mechanisms* explain how the plan will be monitored.

marketing research Systematic, objective gathering of information for use in dealing with specific ***marketing*** issues.

Marketing research, first used in the 1920s, has become an indispensable information-gathering tool for marketers in the ever more challenging, premillennial marketplace. Today's savvy consumers are busier, better informed, and much less homogeneous than in the past. More than three quarters of large companies rely on in-house departments, made up of anywhere from one to several dozen researchers, to define the size and scope of potential *markets* and to figure out how best to take advantage of them. The remaining 25 percent or so must go to outside marketing research companies, of which there are three types: (1) syndicated service companies that collect and sell periodic consumer and trade information, (2) customer research companies that design and execute specific research projects, and (3) specialized marketing and research firms that offer a specific service, such as facilitators for *focus group interviews,* to other research firms and departments.

Whereas traditional research companies came under fire in the past for using unscientific methods, shading results in favor of clients, and designing loaded questions, today's high-tech, single-source research is revolutionizing the field. This method, pioneered by Information Resources, Inc., combines consumer characteristics with scanner data that accurately measure in-store buying behavior to more precisely define *target markets.*

Here's how it works: Researchers put together panels of consumers in representative towns across the country. Each panel member gets a magnetic card to present at the supermarket checkout counter; the card records the items that the particular consumer bought. Each panel member also fills out an extensive questionnaire on demographics, media behavior, lifestyle, and attitudes. Marketers then build databases with the behavioral and demographic information, which they ultimately use to tailor *advertising* and promotions to individual and narrowly defined groups of consumers. With hundreds of cable television channels available, as well as special interest publications, direct mail, promotional newsletters, and myriad other communication methods, these finely tuned marketing efforts can be delivered directly to the desired markets.

But it's not just supermarkets that are building databases. A survey by *Business Week* showed that 56 percent of the manufacturers and retailers polled were using some means—scanners, telephone surveys, warranty cards, fill-in coupons, and so forth—to build databases on their customers. As the numbers continue to grow, scenarios like the following will be commonplace.

EXAMPLE: A gambler enters her favorite casino and presents her VIP guest card to the greeter. While she enjoys a VIP-style welcome, her card is put through a scanner that records the date and time of the visit. Throughout the night as the gambler uses her card, the casino is automatically compiling a record of which games are played, how much is spent, how much is won and lost, and other data. The VIP card entitles the casino guest to free meals, coupons, and a line of credit. In exchange, the casino gets valuable information about how its products and services are used. The research is fast and unobtrusive, but, more important, it's accurate (Bush 1995).

See also *primary data; secondary data.*

markup The difference between what a *retailer* pays for a product and the price at which that product is sold.

The markup helps determine a retailer's profit. Boutiques and specialty stores (such as Giorgio of Beverly Hills and Ermenegildo Zegna) might pursue a high-markup, lower-volume strategy, while discounters and mass merchandisers (such as Wal-Mart and Target) go for lower markups and higher volumes. Full-service retailers (such as Nordstrom) would fall somewhere in between.

Maslow's hierarchy of needs   A theory developed by psychologist Abraham Maslow to explain why people are driven by particular needs at particular times.

In order of importance, Maslow's needs are:

- Physiological (food, drink, shelter)
- Safety and security
- Social (love and a feeling of belonging)
- Esteem (self-respect and prestige)
- Self-actualization (fulfillment of potential)

According to Maslow, a person is motivated to satisfy the most important need first. When that need is satisfied, it is no longer a motivator, and the person will then try to satisfy the next most important need. Also, more than one need can be satisfied by the same action. That means, for instance, that a person can meet both physiological and social needs by having dinner with a group of close friends.

Understanding Maslow's theory helps marketers to design products and strategies with attributes that appeal to the different levels of needs.

EXAMPLE: The immense popularity in the United States of large, sport/utility-type vehicles can be attributed to consumers' dual need for safety/security and esteem/prestige.

See also ***motivation research.***

mass marketing   Pitching a product to the widest possible range of buyers; also called *market aggregation.*

A company that makes a ***commodity*** item such as paper clips can produce, promote, and distribute a single, standard product to the entire ***market.*** Generally, however, mass marketing has become far less common because technology and aggressive ***marketing*** tactics now allow manufacturers to more precisely target products to specific segments of the population. Yet, because mass marketing can still maximize production efficiency and minimize cost, companies will continue to use mass distribution and promotion techniques where possible.

EXAMPLE: Kaiser Permanente Health Systems settled on a carefully devised mass marketing campaign to attract Medicare patients to a new health maintenance organization in suburban New York. Using print and television advertising, visits to health fairs and senior centers, and direct and ***telemarketing*** efforts, Kaiser wooed potential consumers with a message carrying nearly universal relevance: "If you love someone, you have a special responsibility to take care of yourself" (Rand 1996).

See also ***undifferentiated marketing.***

master production schedule (MPS)   A detailed plan for product manufacturing. The MPS covers a period extending at least one quarter beyond the overall schedule for procuring materials and producing the items the manufacturer needs to fulfill its commitments to **retailers, wholesalers,** or customers.

*See also **materials requirements planning (MRP).***

matching concept   A basic tenet of ***financial accounting*** that pairs expenses with the **revenues** derived from them.

The matching concept mandates that, except for issues covered under the **conservatism** principle, expenses must be recorded in the same **accounting period** in which associated benefits, usually sales, are realized. This principle underlies the entire system of ***accrual accounting*** in which revenues are recognized when they are earned and expenses when they are incurred, regardless of when the cash is actually brought in or paid out. By the same token, the matching principle dictates that companies write off **noncurrent assets** (those with a **useful life** of more than one year) in the accounting period during which the benefits of the assets are realized. **Depreciation** of **fixed assets** and **amortization** of **intangible assets** are two examples of such an event.

materiality   An accounting concept aimed at determining what information must be disclosed in the ***financial statements*** of a ***publicly held company.***

In effect, materiality dictates that insignificant events need not be reported, but that all important information must be fully disclosed in the **annual report.**

The problem with the materiality concept lies in its imprecision and the fact that materiality is relative; what is deemed insignificant to a multinational corporation with **revenues** in the hundreds of billions of dollars might well be significant indeed to a company whose revenues and profits are measured in the millions. Lacking explicit guidelines, accountants must rely on their own judgment about what is or is not material. It's generally accepted that an item is material if disclosing it would cause the average investor to behave differently.

materials requirements planning (MRP)   A computerized management planning system that seeks to closely coordinate material needs with the schedule.

Using the ***master production schedule*** (**MPS**) and customer orders, the product structure, **lead times,** and **inventory** levels, MRP attempts to have the correct materials available, in the needed quantities to support the MPS. It is a push system that allows the material planning and buying operations to get what is needed, when it is needed, and in the correct quantity.

EXAMPLE: A large manufacturer of power tools with a product line that includes nearly 20,000 items significantly improved materials ordering and handling and reduced excess inventory, past-due receipts from suppliers, and engineering change orders by implementing MRP.

MRP is based on accurate forecasts of short-term (monthly, weekly, or even daily) **demand,** which allow managers to calculate the exact materials requirements for each particular product or subassembly and identify potential shortages or delays.

MRP systems usually depend on an extensive computer system to keep track of the materials required and used in each phase of production.

Implementing a successful MRP system thus requires a great deal of discipline and the maintenance of communications channels between every participant in the production process.

matrix structure   A formal organization arrangement that establishes dual authority on cross-functional projects. In other words, employees have two bosses. The matrix structure was originally developed in the aerospace industry because of the need to be responsive to specific changes in technology, products, and markets. By using the matrix structure to focus on a particular product or **market,** it is possible to concentrate the resources needed for a quick response.

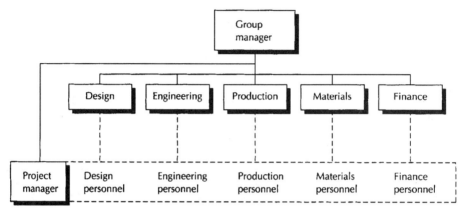

Matrix Structure

EXAMPLE: In the matrix structure diagram, authority is divided between the project manager and the individual managers of the design, engineering, production, materials, and finance functions. An employee in the production department for this particular project thus would report to both the production manager and the project manager.

Dual authority can make matrix structures complicated to manage. Great potential for conflict exists between project managers and managers of traditional functional areas. In order to head off conflicts, it is important to establish clear communication links between managers and encourage the development of interpersonal skills. Despite these difficulties, in situations where it is important to maintain a full-time focus on a particular product or market, a matrix structure can offer several important advantages, including:

- A reduction in information and technological requirements
- A concentration of specialized skills
- An opportunity for management to concentrate exclusively on a particular project or market

maturity date   The date on which the principal amount of a **bond,** note, or other debt instrument becomes due and payable.
   See also **bond yield.**

MBO   *See* **management by objective (MBO)**

MBTI   *See* **Myers-Briggs Type Indicator**

mechanization   The replacement or augmentation of human skills with mechanical ones.
   A factory that installs robots to assemble products is mechanizing the process. Mechanization may significantly improve **productivity** and ensures uniformity of

output. It also decreases setup time and the amount and quality of labor needed. In some cases, such as producing microchips, it is the only practical option.

medium-term notes   Promissory notes with a term of nine months to 15 years, although most are for 1 to 7 years. They are usually issued by companies rather than financial institutions.

MERCOSUR   A trade agreement among nations in Latin America. Presently it includes Argentina, Brazil, Paraguay, and Uruguay.

merger   A combination of two or more companies.

The combination may be accomplished by the exchange of stock for stock, which results in the combining of accounts (called a tax-free *pooling of interests*); by forming a new company to acquire the *assets* of the combining companies (called a *consolidation*); or by a purchase, in which the amount that is paid in excess of the acquired companies' *book value* cannot be allocated to the acquired assets and thus is treated as *goodwill* on the books of the purchaser. Although consolidations and statutory consolidations are technically not mergers, the terms are commonly used interchangeably.

*See also **business combination.***

methods-time measurement (MTM)   A system for studying individual motions, such as reach, grab, and position, in an effort to improve *efficiency.*

The *micromotions* of industrial workers are measured and timed using predetermined time values called *therbligs.* (One therblig equals 0.0006 hour, or about two seconds.) In an MTM study, a repetitive job is videotaped, the individual motions are isolated and timed using MTM values, and a figure for the time required to perform a job is calculated. Allowances are then factored into the time for fatigue, cleanup, and so on, and a time standard is developed. Videotaping allows for repeated viewing of the job as well as measurement of frames per second.

micromarkets   The splintering of *market* segments into smaller and smaller fragments based on age, sex, lifestyle preferences, geography, education, and so on; sometimes called *micromarketing* or *regional marketing.*

Marketers partition the mass market into ever smaller, more homogeneous groupings so they can achieve a better fit between *marketing* programs and preferences in the marketplace.

Although developing special marketing plans for micromarkets is effective, it can prove costly because marketers relinquish *economies of scale* as they focus on ever smaller segments.

*See also **market segmentation; niche marketing.***

minimum lease payments   The rental payments made against a *capital lease.*

The value of both the *asset* and the *liability* generated by a capital lease is determined by the discounted value of future minimum lease payments.

*See also **present value.***

minimum pension liability   An obligation that is reported on a company's *balance sheet* when the *accumulated benefit obligation* (*ABO*) of a *pension plan* is greater than the fair market value of the plan's *assets.*

In other words, if the assets in the pension plan don't cover the benefits workers eventually are entitled to, based on their current salary and service levels, then the shortfall must be shown as a *liability* on the balance sheet.

*See also **projected benefit obligation** (**PBO**).*

minority interest   An ownership interest of less than 50 percent of a company's stock.

In consolidated *financial statements,* minority interest is shown as a line item in the *noncurrent liability* section of the *balance sheet.*

MIS   *See management information system*

mission statement   A short declaration of the central purpose, strategies, and values of a company.

Essentially, a company's mission statement should answer the question, "What business are we in?" A good mission statement, however, goes beyond the obvious—"This hospital is dedicated to providing health care"—and deals with vital issues such as the company's raison d'être, or its guiding aim. It also briefly explains what strategy the company intends to use to fulfill that central purpose, as well as listing the basic principles that guide the actions of the company members.

When a mission statement is considered in these broad terms, its value becomes more apparent: It's easier for individual employees to make better sense of their day-to-day activities when they understand not only a company's goals but also its purpose, the strategies that will be used to achieve those goals, and the core values that underlie its actions. Thus, a good mission statement gives meaning to work that might otherwise have little point beyond the attainment of specific short-term goals such as getting a paycheck or meeting a sales quota. Sharing a sense of mission also engenders loyalty, cooperation, commitment, trust, and focus among employees.

EXAMPLE: Edge Learning Institute, a $6 million employee-training firm in Tempe, Arizona, credits its mission statement with giving it the focus needed to expand.

The company, which conducts corporate seminars to improve employees' communication skills and work habits, was seriously considering a plan to mass-market training videos to help meet burgeoning *demand* for its services. With a long list of prestigious Fortune 500 clients, its principals couldn't fit any more seminars into their already overcrowded schedules. But then the top executives realized that *mass marketing* was at odds with Edge's vow "to use the human touch when providing individuals and organizations with information." So, instead, the partners developed a network of *franchises* that provide the Edge Learning training methods.

The result: With four franchises up and operating and eight more under negotiation, Edge Learning *revenues* are now increasing at a 15 percent annual rate. "Our mission statement . . . has proved to be an invaluable corporate compass that guides all our business decisions," says company president, William Cole (Stern 1997).

modem   A modem converts the digital signals generated by a computer or terminal into audio signals for transmission over the phone lines, and then turns the audio signals received in a transmission back into digital pulses that can be understood by the receiving computer or terminal (Negroponte 1995, 22).

*See also **baud.***

modified accelerated cost recovery system (MACRS)   The most recent version of the *accelerated cost recovery system* (*ACRS*) for depreciating *fixed assets* for tax purposes.

In 1986, Congress amended earlier ACRS legislation containing the so-called 3-5-10 rule that allowed a company (or individual) to deduct a higher percentage of an asset's cost in the early years of its *useful life,* defined as 3, 5, or 10 years. The amendment expanded to eight—3, 5, 7, 10, 15, 20, 27.5, and 31.5 years—the number of classes of an item's useful life. Assets placed in service after 1986 fall under MACRS. Those placed in service after 1980 and before 1987 fall under ACRS.

Both pieces of legislation were designed to encourage *investment* by letting companies recover the cost of acquiring productive assets more quickly with relatively greater *depreciation* deductions early in the *asset's* life.

modularity   A production method in which interchangeable subassemblies are used to facilitate the manufacture of a variety of slightly different products.

EXAMPLE: Ford's modular automobile engine plant in Michigan is designed to build a number of different engine models. Some 25 percent of the parts previously required were eliminated, and the remaining 350 engine parts are standardized (for example, the combustion chamber is the same for the 12 engines). Variations among the motors are created by assembling the parts in different ways. The standardization of parts means the engines share about 75 percent of their parts. In the past, this modular approach has sharply reduced the time and expense involved in developing new engine variations.

monetarism   The school of economic thought that holds that the money supply is the chief determinant of macroeconomic activity both within a country and between countries and groups of countries.

The key tenets of monetarism, which is widely associated with the American economist and Nobel laureate Milton Friedman, are as follows:

- Change in the money supply directly affects and determines, over the long run, the levels of industrial and agricultural production, employment, and the price of goods and services.
- *Fiscal policy*—that is, taxes and expenditures—has little significant effect on *business cycle* events such as *inflation,* deflation, recession, and depression. Therefore, *monetary policy,* or the way a nation's central monetary authority uses the money supply and *interest rates,* is the preferred way to control a national economy.
- Economic stability can best be promoted by the government's following a simple money rule: Increase the money supply at a constant annual rate linked to the growth of the gross national product.
- Reduced government economic involvement equates with increased personal economic freedom, which, in turn, equates with increased personal political freedom.

*See also **Chicago School.***

monetary aggregates   The three main measures of "money" in the U.S. economy, as defined by the *Federal Reserve.*

The three—M1, M2, and M3—are sometimes referred to as "money supply" measures, but this is inaccurate, because the aggregates signify neither **demand** nor supply exclusively. Rather, they represent the equilibrium between the demand and the supply of money.

M1, which is the narrowest, most basic of the aggregates, consists of all the bills and coins in circulation, plus traveler's checks, demand deposits, and other accounts that can be immediately transferred to checking accounts. In other words, M1 represents cash and everything else that can be quickly converted for spending.

M2 is a broader concept that includes M1 plus savings and small (under $100,000) time deposits, money market deposit accounts, money market mutual fund balances, and some special financial deposits such as overnight repurchase agreements and **eurodollar** deposits.

M3 is the broadest of the Federal Reserve's measures, and it comprises M2 plus larger time deposits and institutional money market mutual fund balances.

The three aggregates differ in terms of **liquidity,** with M1 being the most liquid, and also in the sense that M2 and M3 both contain components that are interest rate–sensitive—such as money market deposit accounts and time deposits. The size of these nontransaction components can vary with fluctuations in **interest rates.** (Interest rate changes can have some residual effect on M1, but it is much less pronounced.)

Whereas most economists once monitored the monetary aggregates for clues to **inflation,** the economic import of any changes has diminished somewhat in recent years. This is due to differences in the way people save (more money now goes into higher-yielding forms of wealth) and to the fact that a greater proportion of lending now takes place outside the traditional banking system (via credit cards, automobile leasing agreements, and so forth).

monetary policy   In the United States, the efforts by the **Federal Reserve** System to regulate the **monetary aggregates** in order to influence the nation's economy.

The Federal Reserve tries to make enough money available in the banking system to feed a healthy and growing economy but not so much as to fuel **inflation**— all while maintaining orderly financial markets. The methods the Federal Reserve uses to achieve this balancing act have changed over the years, but basically it moves through open market operations, in which it buys and sells government securities, thus expanding or contracting funds in the banking system; changes in bank reserve requirements, which dictate how much cash or other liquid assets Federal Reserve member banks must keep on hand; and changes in the federal funds rate and the **discount rate,** which is what banks pay to borrow money from the Federal Reserve.

A sluggish economy might prompt a loosening of reserve requirements, a buyback of government securities, or a cut in borrowing rates, all of which would free more funds to circulate in the system. If, on the other hand, the economy is growing too fast and inflation appears to be heating up, the Federal Reserve might sell more securities to pull money out of the system, boost the bank reserve requirements, or raise **interest rates,** all of which would put a brake on economic activity.

EXAMPLE: In the first quarter of 1997, with the U.S. economy continuing to hum along after more than six years of economic expansion, Federal Reserve policy-makers became concerned that inflation might be heating up. To head off any such tendencies, they tightened monetary policy slightly by raising the federal funds rate to $5\frac{1}{2}$ percent from $5\frac{1}{4}$ percent (Humphrey-Hawkins Report 1997).

See also fiscal policy; monetarism.

money center banks   Institutions in the world's major financial centers whose dealings have a significant impact on the national and international economy.

Money center banks—such as Chase and Citibank in New York, Deutsche Bank in Frankfurt, Barclays in London, Crédit Lyonnais in Paris, and Dai-Ichi Kangyo in Tokyo—are the primary buyers of government securities and large lenders to both governments and corporations worldwide. These banks also provide regional and local banks with access to *foreign exchange* and depository services.

money markets   The arena for trading short-term (less than one year) debt instruments.

The market for short-term lending and borrowing is not a specific place, but rather a group of dealers who are linked electronically, much like the over-the-counter *NASDAQ Stock Market.* U.S. Treasury bills, *banker's acceptances* (*BAs*), certificates of deposit, and *commercial paper* are among the low-risk securities traded on money markets.

morning drive time   In radio advertising, the time segment between 6:00 A.M. and 10:00 A.M., which delivers one of the largest audiences of the day.

See also afternoon drive time.

motivation research   The attempt by marketers to understand and measure the emotional and psychological factors, the often subconscious motivations, that drive people to purchase products and services.

Because it resorts to nonscientific methods of investigation such as free association and fantasy, motivation research has developed a reputation for being too "touchy-feely" and "pretty goofy," according to Kotler and Armstrong (1996, 155). Nevertheless, this kind of research has its defenders and is frequently used with focus groups and others in helping marketers determine what really drives the customer.

EXAMPLE: American Express once asked a group of people to draw pictures of the typical users of the Gold Card and the Green Card. There was general agreement among respondents that Gold Card members were broad-shouldered, active men, whereas Green Card members looked more like couch potatoes, stereotypes that the company was able to use in marketing its credit cards. No doubt the study revealed more about the respondents' unwarranted assumptions and biases than it did about the true character of Gold or Green Card members, but this motivational research still had a tremendous effect on the company's marketing efforts (Kotler and Armstrong 1996, 155).

MRP   *See materials requirements planning*

MRPII   *See manufacturing resource planning*

MTM   *See methods-time measurement*

multiple sourcing   The purchase of a good or service from more than one supplier.

Myers-Briggs Type Indicator (MBTI)   A widely used personality test.

The test, which was developed by the mother-daughter team of Katherine Briggs and Isabel Briggs Myers in the 1940s, consists of 100 questions that ask how people would act or feel in a variety of situations. Based on the theoretical work of Swiss psychologist Carl Jung, it characterizes people as:

- Introverted or extroverted (I or E)
- Sensing or intuitive (S or N)
- Thinking or feeling (T or F)
- Perceiving or judging (P or J)

Once these characterizations are determined, they are combined to identify one of 16 different personality types. For example, someone who tests as ENTP (extroverted, intuitive, thinking, and perceiving) is a conceptualizer. He or she is good at many things, quick and ingenious in solving problems, but with a possible tendency to ignore routine work.

The MBTI is not, nor should it be, used to screen or judge employees. Rather, it is a tool for improving employee self-awareness. Proponents of the test argue that this increased self-awareness leads to improved communication, which, in turn, leads to increased *productivity.* Although there is little evidence that the MBTI actually improves productivity, it is widely used just the same by organizations as diverse as Apple Computer, Citicorp, Honeywell, and the U.S. armed forces.

NAPM index *See National Association of Purchasing Management index*

NASDAQ Stock Market The computerized market for trading over-the-counter (OTC) securities.

The NASDAQ is the world's largest electronic, screen-based market, with the capacity to handle a billion shares a day. Using sophisticated technology, the approximately 5,500 stocks listed on NASDAQ are updated simultaneously on the *New York Stock Exchange* (*NYSE*) and all regional exchanges, providing both buyers and sellers the best possible price at all times. The system supplies a wealth of information about a stock, including its trading history, daily trading volume, *dividends* paid, the high and low prices for the day and for the past 52 weeks, the daily closing price, and the price change from the previous day's close.

Minimum initial listing requirements for the NASDAQ are as follows:

- Publicly held shares numbering 1 million
- At least 300 round-lot (usually 100 shares) holders
- *Market value* for the shares of $5 million
- Net *tangible assets* of $4 million
- Market *capitalization* of $50 million or fiscal-year *net income* of $750,000
- Three market makers

Requirements for continued listing on the exchange are somewhat less stringent, that is: two market makers, net assets of $2 million, and market capitalization of $35 million or fiscal-year net income of $500,000.

At one time, the NASDAQ was thought of primarily as the venue for smaller, riskier companies and those unable to meet the listing requirements of physical markets like the NYSE and the *American Stock Exchange* (*AMEX*). But that is no longer true, as the NASDAQ—which is heavily weighted toward technology issues—trades giants such as Microsoft and Intel.

See also National Association of Securities Dealers, Inc. (*NASD*).

National Association of Purchasing Management (NAPM) index This index is compiled from surveys conducted each month of purchasing executives in over 350 industrial manufacturing companies. The report has been issued by the NAPM since 1931 (except during World War II), but it received new prominence in the early 1980s, when, with assistance by the U.S. Department of Commerce, the cyclical characteristics of the components and summary diffusion index were refined.

For each measure, the percentage of respondents reporting a decrease, no change, or an increase in the activity from the prior month are reported. The diffusion index is calculated by adding one half of the percentage of respondents indicating "no change" to the percentage indicating an "increase." Nine indicators are measured each month: new orders, production, employment, order **backlog,** speed of supplier deliveries, inventories, prices, new export orders, and imports. Five of the components are included in a weighted composite diffusion index that has the property of a leading indicator. These five and their weights are new orders (30 percent), production (25 percent), employment (20 percent), supplier deliveries (15 percent), and inventories (10 percent).

The index is reported on the first business day of the following month (for example, the index for February 1998 was reported on March 2, 1998). In general, a reading of 50 or higher indicates an expanding economy, a reading between 44 and 50 suggest that the overall economy is expanding, but that the manufacturing sector is declining, while a reading below 44 suggests the economy is recessionary.

EXAMPLE: Details for the NAPM index for February 1998 are shown as follows.

	% Decrease	% No change	% Increase	Index
New orders	20	52	28	55.9
Production	17	59	24	55.3
Employment	14	69	17	50.9
Supplier deliveries	7	90	3	52.1
Inventories	19	66	15	46.9
Composite				53.3

National Association of Securities Dealers, Inc. (NASD) Largest self-regulatory organization in the U.S. securities industry.

Every broker or dealer involved in the public securities business in the United States is required to be a member of the NASD, which is subject to oversight by the **Securities and Exchange Commission (SEC).** The NASD develops rules and regulates members' activities through its **NASDAQ Stock Market** and NASD Regulation subsidiaries.

NC *See numerical control*

net asset value (NAV) The value of a mutual fund's shares as determined by taking the closing **market value** of all securities owned plus other **assets** such as cash, deducting **liabilities,** and then dividing the result by the number of shares outstanding.

NAV indicates what price an investor would receive if he or she sold back shares to the fund.

net income In accounting, what remains after all expenses have been subtracted from **revenue;** also called *net profit.*

Net income is often referred to as "the bottom line" because that is where it appears on the **income statement.**

net present value (NPV) In corporate finance, the **present value**—that is, the value of cash to be received in the future expressed in today's dollars—of an **investment** in excess of the initial amount invested.

NPV is calculated as follows:

$$\text{NPV} = P_0 + \frac{P_1}{1+r} + \frac{P_2}{(1+r)^2} + \frac{P_3}{(1+r)^3} + \cdots + \frac{P_n}{(1+r)^n} = 0$$

where: NPV = Net present value of the investment
$P_0, P_1, \ldots, P_n$ = Cash payments in periods 0–n
r = Investors' required *rate of return* (the rate of return offered by a comparable investment)

Generally, P_0, the cash payment at time zero (today), is a cash outflow and thus a negative number.

EXAMPLE: Consider an investment with the following *cash flows:*

P_0	P_1	P_2	P_3
−$100,000	+$40,000	+$40,000	+$50,000

Let's say the investor's required rate of return is 12 percent. In that case, the investment's net present value is

$$-\$100,000 + \frac{\$40,000}{1.12} + \frac{\$40,000}{(1.12)^2} + \frac{\$50,000}{(1.12)^3} = \$3,191$$

The investment is worth $3,191. If an investment or project has a positive NPV, it should be pursued. If the NPV is negative, the investment should be rejected.

New York Stock Exchange (NYSE)   The largest marketplace, in terms of dollar volume, in the United States; also known as *the Big Board.*

About 51 million individual investors and 10,000 institutional investors are buyers and sellers of securities issued by more than 2,920 listed companies on the NYSE. As the following minimum listing requirements indicate, they are among the world's largest *publicly held companies:*

- Publicly held shares numbering 1.1 million
- *Market value* of $18 million for those shares
- Annual pretax earnings of $2.5 million
- Number of shareholders: 2,000 round-lot (usually 100 shares); 2,200 total
- Net *tangible assets* of $18 million

In addition, other requirements serve to keep smaller companies from listing, such as the degree of national interest in a company, its relative position and stability in its industry, and whether it is part of an expanding industry in which it is likely to maintain its relative position.

In recent years, however, the NYSE has relaxed some listing requirements to accommodate several larger companies that are valued more on the basis of *cash flow* than on reported income. It will now consider companies that have no reported profit but that have market *capitalizations* of at least $500 million and *revenues* of at least $200 million. Such companies must meet an adjusted *net income* standard that looks at earnings before deductions for investing or financing activities.

The exchange can request delisting if a company fails to meet stringent reporting requirements, if trading in its securities is inactive, or if the company no longer meets initial listing requirements.

See also American Stock Exchange (AMEX); NASDAQ Stock Market.

new-product development The process required to bring a new product to *market.*

The procedure usually includes eight steps:

- Idea generation
- Idea screening
- Concept development and testing
- Marketing strategy development
- Business analysis
- Product development
- Market testing
- Commercialization

Although individual companies may add or skip steps according to their particular circumstances, each step presents an opportunity for marketers to decide whether an idea should be pursued or dropped.

EXAMPLE: A magazine publisher that wants to expand its stable of publications might generate ideas by involving both employees and customers in a series of brainstorming sessions with top management (step one). After the company screens out the more improbable concepts (step two), it zeroes in on one idea—say a magazine for active senior citizens—as a viable option for concept development and testing (step three). This step includes positioning the product for a potential *target market:* In this case the magazine might be travel-oriented and appeal to wealthier retirees, or it could concentrate on health issues and have a broader appeal. Each of the possible concepts is then tested with a sample group of appropriate consumers.

Next, the company comes up with a strategy for marketing the most promising product concept—say, the travel magazine. The strategy describes the target market, estimates potential sales and *market share,* and develops future profit goals (step four). With a strategy in place, it's time for management to conduct a business analysis in which it estimates sales, costs, and profits (step five). If all these figures look promising, the concept is turned into an actual physical product (step six). *Prototypes* of the magazine are first tested on a small group of consumers before full-scale test marketing begins (step seven). Depending on how promising the test marketing looks, management may decide to take the plunge with the last and most expensive step, namely, putting the new product out into the marketplace (step eight).

The process takes its toll on potential ideas. Out of every 3,000 ideas, for instance, it's estimated that only two products ever actually see the light of the marketplace—and only one of those succeeds. To raise the odds of success, however, market gurus recommend that would-be entrepreneurs focus on consumer needs, capitalize on trends, and get to market fast.

EXAMPLE: In 1994, Michael Miller realized that his own passion for gardening was shared by many other **baby boomers.** Statistics showed that the market for garden equipment was expanding by 8 percent a year. A search for marketable ideas turned up an easy-to-use tool for one of the gardener's most hated tasks: weeding. In short order, Miller and his stepfather arranged to license the technology, form a company called Hound Dog Products, and get their $25 Weed Hound into stores like Target and Home Depot. The Weed Hound was a howling success, racking up $3 million in **revenues** in 1996 (Mandelker and Gilbert 1997).

newsboy problem   Term used to describe the dilemma involved in overstocking or understocking a perishable product.

Too much stock will obviously satisfy all the **demand,** but, at the same time, unsold, suddenly worthless **inventory** has to be discarded, which cuts into profits. Too little stock solves the inventory surplus but prevents the company from satisfying available demand and raising profits. With a perishable that loses all of its value in a relatively short time, there is no possible way to carry inventory or make up for a lost sale. The term *newsboy problem* derives from the fact that newspapers are considered perishable because they are of little or no value if they aren't sold on the publication date.

EXAMPLE: A newsboy buys copies of the morning edition of a daily paper at 5:00 A.M., then sells them on a corner outside a New York City subway station between 6:00 A.M. and 9:00 A.M. He buys his papers for 15 cents apiece and sells them for 25 cents. Some mornings he runs out of papers by 8:30, but other mornings he still has several unsold papers at 9:00. His problem is how to determine the optimal number of newspapers to purchase each morning in order to make the highest profit.

To solve the problem, he tracks the number of papers sold each day for 100 days. (Tracking time may vary from situation to situation, but it should be long enough to get an accurate measure of average demand.) On days when he sells all his papers before 9:00, he stays at his corner post and records the number of unfilled requests. Here's how his numbers break down:

Demand (newspapers)	Frequency (days)	Relative frequency
47	10	10%
48	25	25%
49	35	35%
50	15	15%
51	15	15%

His lowest level of demand was 47 newspapers and his highest was 51, so he knows his daily order should fall somewhere between the two. He needs to determine which of the five possible order quantities will maximize his profits. To do this, he devises a payoff table for which the profit is calculated at each quantity and demand level. Each entry is figured as follows:

$$\text{Demand} \times \$0.25 - \text{orders} \times \$0.15 = \text{profit}$$

So if he buys 50 papers and sells 48, his profit would be $4.50 (48 times 25 cents, or $12.00, minus 50 times 15 cents, or $7.50, equals $4.50).

Here is the payoff table for his newspapers:

| | Demand | | | | |
Order quantity	47	48	49	50	51
47	$4.70	$4.70	$4.70	$4.70	$4.70
48	$4.55	$4.80	$4.80	$4.80	$4.80
49	$4.40	$4.65	$4.90	$4.90	$4.90
50	$4.25	$4.50	$4.75	$5.00	$5.00
51	$4.10	$4.35	$4.60	$4.85	$5.10

Using this table, he knows what his profit will be for any particular order quantity and demand level. Since he also knows the relative frequency for each demand level, he can thus determine his expected daily profit for each possible order quantity. For example, if he decides to order 47 papers a day, his expected daily profit will be

$$10\%(\$4.70) + 25\%(\$4.70) + 35\%(\$4.70) + 15\%(4.70) + 15\%(4.70) = \$4.70$$

If he orders 51 papers per day, his expected daily profit will be

$$10\%(\$4.70) + 25\%(\$4.80) + 35\%(\$4.90) + 15\%(\$5.00) + 15\%(\$5.10) = \$4.90$$

The expected daily profit for each order quantity is as follows:

Order quantity	Expected daily profit
47	$4.70
48	$4.63
49	$4.79
50	$4.86
51	$4.90

It is clear that he will maximize profits by ordering 51 papers per day. Even though he will sell all of his papers only 15 percent of the time, his expected long-term return is higher than it would be if he took a more conservative approach and ordered fewer papers.

The same newsboy process can be applied to any situation in which a company seeks to balance between buying too much material and running a **stockout** with its potential loss of sales. It is too much versus too little with a perishable product.

niche marketing   A strategy whereby companies specialize in serving a small segment of the **market** that is of little interest to major competitors.

Some companies specialize in specific customer groups.

EXAMPLE: OshKosh B'gosh, Inc., received such enthusiastic response to a catalog picture of a child in its denim overalls that it decided to specialize in children's clothing.

Other niche producers include the microbreweries that flourish by marketing full-bodied beers to consumers who are willing to pay extra for what they perceive to be better taste. Another niche in the marketing universe is the one created by consumers who don't care about the bells and whistles and are happy with a basic service at a lower cost.

EXAMPLE: The paging industry continues to prosper despite long-standing predictions that cellular phones would relegate pagers to the same category as the buggy whip. Why? Not everyone who wants or needs to stay in touch also wants or needs to be always and instantly reachable. Pagers let their users decide when and how to respond. What's more, not everyone wants the cellular phone's price: Whereas the typical pager costs $12 to $14 a month, a cellular phone runs three to four times as much (Kanell 1996).

noncurrent asset   In accounting, an *asset* with an expected *useful life* of more than one year.

Noncurrent assets are reported on the *balance sheet* and include *fixed assets* such as machinery, buildings, and land.

See also *current asset.*

noncurrent liability   In accounting, a financial obligation due in more than one year.

Noncurrent liabilities are reported on the *balance sheet* and include long-term debt and *capital lease* obligations.

See also *current liability.*

nondurable good   A tangible product such as food that does not last a long time and is usually consumed quickly.

Because nondurables are purchased frequently, they lend themselves to a *marketing* strategy that emphasizes heavy promotion, low *markups,* and wide availability.

nonmarket risk   The result of factors that negatively affect one particular company's securities; also called *nonsystematic risk.*

Poor management, an inefficient production process, and an unexpected drop in *demand* are examples of factors that contribute to nonmarket risk. The portion of a security's return that is attributable to nonmarket risk is measured by *alpha.*

See also *beta; market risk.*

North American Free Trade Agreement (NAFTA)   A multilateral accord that removed most trade barriers between the United States, Canada, and Mexico.

As of January 1, 1994, NAFTA created the *North American Free Trade Zone* (*NAFTZ*), and thus expanded the previous Canada-U.S. Free Trade Agreement market of 275 million people to one of almost 365 million people.

The countries eliminated many tariffs and other trade barriers immediately and pledged to phase out most of the rest within 15 years. For example, *advertising* was freed of restrictions immediately, while all curbs on bank ownership were to be ended by the year 2000, and duties on American-made automobiles were to be eliminated over 10 years. Duties on agricultural products are subject to the 15-year phaseout. Mexico's state oil company kept its monopoly over most of that industry, however.

Intellectual property protections were strengthened, and border-crossing restrictions were eased to allow businesspersons to travel more freely among the three countries.

Disputes are resolved by special panels of judges.

note payable   A promise to pay a specified amount of money at a future date.

A note payable may involve borrowing from a bank, purchase of goods or services, or refinancing an *account payable.* Notes payable are reported on the *balance sheet* as either *current* or *noncurrent liabilities,* depending on whether the payment is due in one year or less.

See also ***note receivable.***

note receivable   The right to receive money owed at a future date.

Notes receivable are reported on the *balance sheet* as either *current* or *noncurrent assets,* depending on whether payment will be received in one year or less.

See also ***note payable.***

NPV   *See **net present value***

numerical control (NC)   Technology that allows a machine to operate automatically through coded numerical commands.

Originally, these commands were on punched paper cards or tape that directed a machine in much the same way a player piano is controlled. In later years, however, computers have become the main tool in numerical control, and, in many instances, NC is referred to as *computer numerical control,* or *CNC.* Numerical control can offer a more attractive alternative to complete automation because it allows for a variety of operations, speeds, materials, and so on.

Numerical control is expensive, with initial costs running between $20,000 and $500,000, but it offers many important advantages, including better equipment utilization, fewer manual operations, lower labor costs, consistent machining speeds and times, automatic tool selection, and uniform quality. NC also offers the potential to develop a machining center that is easily adaptable to multiple processes.

EXAMPLE: As part of its effort to build commercial airplanes faster, Boeing Company's Fredrickson, Washington, plant has replaced 54 large floor-assembly jigs, used for drilling holes in wing ribs, with a numerical control machine. The NC machine is faster and more accurate, and can more easily reposition the holes when an engineering change is ordered (Maharry 1997).

O

OECD *See **Organization for Economic Cooperation and Development***

OEM *See **original equipment manufacturer***

off-balance sheet In accounting, items not reported in *financial statements* that nevertheless affect a company's operations.

Liabilities such as pending litigation or guarantees of future performance, for example, are not reported on a company's *balance sheet,* but they may have a significant impact on future results.

Off-balance-sheet financing, such as the *sale/leaseback* of real estate holdings, is arranged so as not to affect a company's borrowing capacity. But if the financial instruments used in off-balance-sheet financing present credit or market risk, *generally accepted accounting principles (GAAP)* require disclosure of pertinent information.

offshore financial center A place where banking facilities accept deposits and make loans in currencies different from the currency used locally.

U.S. dollars on deposit in London, for example, or yen loaned from a New York bank, or deutsche marks on deposit in Singapore all qualify as offshore *transactions.* (Incidentally, the currencies involved in such transactions are often called *eurocurrency* and the banks located in offshore centers are called *eurobanks,* even though they may have no ties to Europe.)

Banks operating offshore are exempt from their home-country banking regulations, such as those relating to reserve requirements, legal lending limits, deposit insurance fees, *interest rate* ceilings, *capital* export controls, limits on bank *asset* growth, *liquidity* ratios, multiple taxing authorities, and *capital asset* ratio requirements. In addition, all offshore financial centers, including those in the United States, offer tax preferences—usually, but not always, in the form of tax-free remittances of earnings to banking subsidiaries' parent companies.

Most major banking centers—such as New York, San Francisco, Miami, Toronto, Tokyo, London, Paris, Zurich, and Singapore—maintain offshore banking facilities. In the United States, the offshore unit is called the International Banking Facility (IBF) and is available at all *money center banks.* Offshore financial centers like the Bahamas, Cayman Islands, Panama, Channel Islands, and so forth promote their *tax haven* status along with their international banking facilities.

EXAMPLE: Remember when mention of the South Pacific brought to mind author James Michener, coconuts, and trade winds? Well, if tiny islands like Vanuatu have anything to say about it, grass skirts and colorful shirts will be replaced by brief-cases and business suits, and the lure of these island paradises will revolve around their appeal as offshore tax havens.

Vanuatu is seeking to capitalize on the emerging Asian economies by marketing itself as an offshore financial center for companies from China, Indonesia, and Hong Kong. Features such as no income tax, no exchange controls, no money transfer reporting, and no interest withholding tax have proved popular with the new-money crowd. The island's collection of foreign banks, trust companies, and accounting and law firms adds about $4.4 million a year to the economy.

Trouble has been brewing in paradise, however, with the disclosure of a number of financial scams in the region. Though unrelated to Vanuatu's offshore banking activities, officials fear a spillover of negative publicity (Seneviratne 1997).

omnibus panel   A group of *marketing research* participants involved in various studies for a company over a period of time.

EXAMPLE: A panel of 1,100 people is used by Gillette Company's Parker Pen sub-sidiary to evaluate new writing instruments as they are developed.

See also **longitudinal panel.**

OPEC   *See* **Organization of Petroleum Exporting Countries**

operating expenses   In accounting, the costs of the selling and administrative activ-ities of a business.

Operating expenses are reported on the *income statement* and are usually cat-egorized as selling and general and administrative expenses.

operating income   In accounting, *revenue* less *cost of goods sold* and normal *op-erating expenses.*

Operating income is reported on the *income statement* and does not include items such as interest income and expense, *dividend* income, income taxes, and extraordinary items.

operating lease   A lease that provides for short-term use of property or equipment.

For example, companies may lease office space on an annual basis or individu-als may lease an automobile for two or three years.

An operating lease does not meet any of the four requirements of a *capital lease,* namely, (1) payments for the exclusive use of the *asset* that approximate the asset's fair market value, (2) sole access to an asset for all, or a substantial portion, of its *useful life,* (3) the opportunity to buy the asset at a discounted price at the end of the lease period, and (4) proof of ownership, such as legal title to the asset.

Operating leases do not have to be reported as a long-term *liability* in a com-pany's *financial statements* and are frequently used as *off-balance-sheet* sources of financing. Such usage can be perilous, however, when internal auditors do not maintain proper controls.

EXAMPLE: In the early 1990s, the Morrison Knudsen Corporation found itself in severe financial distress, and an out-of-control leasing program was partly to blame.

Having taken on $38.8 million of "noncancellable" annual lease obligations over a three-year period—none of which appeared on the corporate **balance sheet,** of course—the engineering and construction firm wound up with implied debt of around $246 million, five times the debt responsibility shown on the balance sheet (McNeil 1996).

operations   Most closely identified with service organizations. Operations involves the set of steps to provide that service. An insurance company has a set of operations to provide policies to customers. In contrast, the term *production* is more closely associated with the manufacture of physical goods.

opinion leaders   People who have expertise or influence in the eyes of consumers in the **target market.**

Often, marketers can quickly achieve market acceptance of a product by first targeting opinion leaders.

The advice of opinion leaders is valued both for its power to influence as well as to predict the behavior of others.

EXAMPLE: Fifteen years after a large Pacific Northwest utility achieved notoriety for its record-setting default on $2.25 billion of municipal **bonds,** it turned to opinion leaders to help it decide if a name change might finally erase its negative image.

The problem for the Washington Public Power Supply System (WPPSS) is that the pronunciation of its acronym, "whoops," instantly reminds people of the 1983 debacle. As part of a study by a Seattle-based public affairs firm, 63 opinion leaders from business, government, and the news media were asked about the infamous moniker. But the results were inconclusive, with many feeling that the utility could never escape the name association, while others thought that time had already obscured much of the notoriety (Ferris 1997).

opportunity cost   The amount that is sacrificed when choosing one activity over the next best alternative.

For example, if a person decides to stop working in order to attend school on a full-time basis, the opportunity cost is the sum of the expenses incurred to attend school plus the amount of salary that is lost by not working. Or, if a salaried person decides to leave his or her job in order to start a business, the forgone salary is considered to be the opportunity cost of this entrepreneurial activity.

In industry, one expression of opportunity cost is found in the so-called hurdle rate used by financial analysts in deciding whether to pursue a particular **investment** project. The hurdle rate is the minimum acceptable **rate of return** needed to justify the investment in a capital project. If a company's managers can demonstrate that the rate of return on a particular project will exceed the hurdle rate, they are saying, in effect, that the project's benefits outweigh the opportunity cost, or what the funds would earn in the next best alternative investment.

Looking at opportunity cost offers a quantitative way to make informed choices between competing businesses, as well as personal options.

option   A right that is granted, in exchange for an agreed-upon sum, to buy or sell property or **assets.**

If the right is not exercised within the specified period of time, it expires and the holder forfeits the money. Options are used most frequently in securities trading, although they are also common in *foreign exchange,* financial futures, and **commodities** trading. Companies also offer stock options as incentive compensation for their key employees.

Instead of exercising options, most investors prefer to buy and sell them in the open market before they expire, thereby cashing in on increases in trading value. One of the interesting features of trading in options is the amount of leverage option buyers enjoy. Buyers put up a relatively small amount of money to control a large number of common shares, potentially *leveraging* sizable profits or losses.

Organization for Economic Cooperation and Development (OECD)   An international group established in Paris in 1961 to act as a global forum to stimulate world trade and economic development.

The OECD grew out of the Organization for European Economic Cooperation (OEEC), a group of European participants formed in 1948 to guide the rebuilding of Europe after World War II. It differs from other governmental organizations in that it lacks both supranational legal powers and funds with which to provide loans or subsidies. The group's only function is to facilitate direct cooperation among its members, essentially on trade and investment policies, so as to head off conflicts.

The OECD consists of 29 of the world's developed countries working together to create an environment conducive to economic growth. At last count, its members included Australia, Austria, Belgium, Canada, the Czech Republic, Denmark, Finland, France, Germany, Greece, Hungary, Iceland, Ireland, Italy, Japan, Korea, Luxembourg, Mexico, the Netherlands, New Zealand, Norway, Poland, Portugal, Spain, Sweden, Switzerland, Turkey, the United Kingdom, and the United States. (Source: OECD Web site.)

Organization of Petroleum Exporting Countries (OPEC)   An international *cartel* of 11 oil-producing and exporting countries.

OPEC, which was officially established in Caracas, Venezuela, in 1960, is headquartered in Vienna, Austria. Its 11 members are Algeria, Libya, Nigeria, Indonesia, Iran, Iraq, Kuwait, Qatar, Saudi Arabia, the United Arab Emirates, and Venezuela. OPEC's stated aim is "to coordinate and unify petroleum policies among member countries in order to secure fair and stable prices for petroleum producers; an efficient, economic, and regular supply of petroleum to consuming nations; and a fair return on capital to those investing in the industry." The cartel attempts to carry out its aims by setting a ceiling on production so that oil will not flood the market and drive down prices.

For a ten-year period in the 1970s and early 1980s, OPEC wielded enormous world power by maintaining a tight grip on the production of crude oil. A relatively brief (five months) but effective embargo on oil shipments to the United States and the Netherlands set the stage for a string of price increases that saw crude oil soar from around $2.00 a barrel in 1973 to its peak of $42.00 a barrel in 1982. The United States was targeted because of its support for Israel in its 1973 war with Arab states, and the Netherlands was put under embargo because of its strategic geographic position.

OPEC's price increases pushed the nonindustrialized and non-oil-producing developing countries in Africa, Asia, and Latin America into severe **balance-of-payments** deficit positions. In the United States, vehicle owners were driven to despair, first by the long lines of motorists waiting to buy gasoline during the embargo and then by the price spiral that shocked a populace long used to seeing fuel charges that were among the lowest in the world.

Eventually, however, the cartel's grip began to loosen as conservation, alternative sources of energy, and fuel-efficient vehicles caught on. That attitudinal change, coupled with increased crude production from non-OPEC sources and a breakdown in discipline among cartel members (who exceeded quotas and lowered prices), signaled the end of OPEC's heavy-handed ways.

World crude oil prices have been subject to market fluctuations since 1983, but generally have remained at around half of their previous highs. OPEC, whose member countries supply more than 40 percent of the world's oil and control about three quarters of the proven crude oil reserves, continues to pursue a united production and pricing approach. However, it has never regained the power it once held. (SOURCES: OPEC Web site: http://www.opec.org/members.htm; WTI Crude Monthly Averages chart from WEN Web site: http://www.wen.co.za/wen/charts/oil/COMAWT.htm.)

organizational buying   The process whereby large organizations establish their need for *industrial goods* and services and then choose between alternative *brands* and suppliers.

Organizations purchase goods and services for a variety of reasons not common to the *consumer market,* namely, to make profits, lower costs, and satisfy employee needs. Organizational buying is usually a group decision, with each member assuming particular responsibilities and bringing a different set of criteria to the decision. Although each organization has its own set of formal purchasing policies and requirements, product, design, cost, and service will generally carry great weight in the decision making.

Marketers must assess all of these factors in determining their strategy for *marketing* to an organization. The potential payoff for an effective marketing effort is enormous because organizational buying usually involves large volumes.

EXAMPLE: A daily newspaper decides that it could increase profits by upgrading its computerized printing equipment. Members of the editorial staff, the advertising department, and the print shop meet to give their opinions on what is needed and to consider several different options. The marketer that succeeds in winning the contract for the printing equipment will understand what motivated the purchase decision, the process by which it was made, and the individual concerns of each member of the purchasing committee.

organizational environment   The elements that affect, and sometimes dictate, how a company is organized.

In designing a company's organizational structure, two environmental dimensions must be considered: static-dynamic and simple-complex.

The static-dynamic dimension of a company's environment describes factors that either change frequently or remain relatively constant over time.

EXAMPLE: A factory where the sales team's product requests are fairly constant and the materials department is usually able to supply a steady stream of raw materials is operating in a static environment. However, if the sales team frequently changes its orders and the materials department has difficulty supplying raw materials, the factory environment is dynamic.

The simple-complex dimension describes whether the decision-making factors in the environment are similar and few in number, or different and many in number.

EXAMPLE: A factory where only the sales department, which orders products, and the materials department, which supplies raw materials, have any say in decisions is operating in a simple environment. If, on the other hand, the programming and planning department has to consider a number of different environmental factors, such as suppliers, marketing, or customers, when it makes a decision, the environment is complex.

Most companies today operate in a dynamic-complex environment that is characterized by frequent change and a lot of uncertainty for managers. An appropriate organizational design is particularly vital in this type of environment.

EXAMPLE: AT&T moved from a static-simple environment to a dynamic-complex environment when the telephone industry was deregulated in the 1980s. To cope with the additional competition in the telephone market, it shifted from a *functional organizational design* to a much more decentralized model. The change was motivated by the need to obtain more *market* information and respond quickly to the actions of competitors.

ORGANIZATIONAL ENVIRONMENT

	Fairly low uncertainty	**High uncertainty**
Complex	• Many environmental factors • Environmental factors are not similar • Environmental factors remain basically the same *Example:* Food products industry	• Many environmental factors • Environmental factors are not similar • Environmental factors are prone to constant change *Example:* Commercial airline industry
	Low uncertainty	**Fairly high uncertainty**
Simple	• Limited number of environmental factors • Environmental factors are similar • Environmental factors remain basically the same *Example:* Soft-drink industry	• Limited number of environmental factors • Environmental factors are similar • Environmental factors are prone to constant change *Example:* fast-food industry
	Static	**Dynamic**

*See also **decentralization; matrix structure.***

original equipment manufacturer (OEM)   Companies that put together final products using components produced by other manufacturers.

EXAMPLE: Many of the computer industry's major OEMs, such as IBM, Hewlett-Packard, Novell, and Sun Microsystems, have distribution agreements with Netscape Communications that allow them to load the Netscape client software into their machines. In this way, Netscape is guaranteed that its product will end up in millions of homes and businesses (Netscape 1997).

outputs   A company's product or service.

Generally, products tend to be associated with physical goods, such as a Sony Walkman, whereas services are tasks performed for a customer, such as those provided by a security service or repair facility.

outsourcing   The purchase of parts from outside suppliers.

Many American small-appliance manufacturers use a great deal of outsourcing. The various parts and subassemblies for, say, a toaster or a blender are manufactured by a number of different companies; the so-called manufacturer does only the assembly and selling.

When a company is heavily outsourced, it is referred to as "hollow." Outsourcing is usually a good idea if the outsource can provide the parts or components at lower cost or higher quality. Outsourcing is an economic decision. Many American companies are becoming assemblers with very little *vertical integration.*

outstanding common stock   The shares held by investors.
  *See also **earnings per share; equity.***

overhead   The costs of operating a business—such as insurance, heat, light, supervision, and maintenance—that cannot be directly linked to the products or services produced.

These costs are usually organized into several groups (perhaps factory, department, or general overhead) so that they can be allocated to various areas of the company.

owners' equity   Item on the *balance sheet* that shows the claims of the owners on the *assets* of a company; also called shareholders' equity.

Owners' equity is derived by subtracting *liabilities* from *capital* investments and *retained earnings.*
  *See also **equity.***

P

paced line   A production line that moves at a constant rate of *output.*

The classic example is an automobile assembly line on which workers install engines, doors, windows, hoods, and so on as a conveyor moves cars past various workstations. A line may be operator-paced, meaning that its speed depends on the proficiency of the operator, or it may be machine-paced so that its rate of output is determined by the speed at which the machines operate. A paced line does ensure a smooth production flow as well as accurate measurements of the labor content of the products produced since output is x units per hour.

Pac-Man defense   A countervailing strategy employed by the object of an unwelcome *acquisition* offer.

Named after the electronic video game that was popular in the 1980s, the Pac-Man defense involves a tables-turning bid in which the original target company threatens to take over the acquirer and begins buying its shares.

paid-in capital in excess of par value   Accounting terminology describing what shareholders paid for a company's shares over and above the stock's stated value.

Also called *additional paid-in capital,* this amount is that which owners have contributed directly to the business by buying issued stock. Since the *par value* on *common stock* is usually a nominal, essentially meaningless amount, investors almost always contribute additional *capital.*

par value   The face value of a security.

The par value of a $1,000 *bond,* for example, is one thousand dollars. The interest, or coupon rate, paid on a bond is a percentage of the bond's par value. In other words, a 12 percent bond pays 12 percent of its par value annually through periodic coupon payments. In the same manner, the *dividends* paid on *preferred stock* are typically a percentage of the stock's par value. With *common stock,* par value has little meaning. It is generally a set amount, such as $1 per share, and is used to calculate the dollar value of the common shares on a company's *balance sheet.*

The par value of a security has no relation to its market price, which may be significantly higher or lower than par.

parallel trade   A form of *countertrade* that involves the execution of two linked, but distinct and individually enforceable, contracts.

The first of the contracts calls for the sale of goods by party A to party B; the second calls for the sale of goods by party B to party A. Both contracts are requirements for insurance, and sometimes credit, on each shipment.

EXAMPLE: A cosmetics distributor in New Jersey sells face creams to an import company in Singapore. The contract calls for payment in U.S. dollars. Under another contract, the importer agrees to sell textiles with the same dollar value to the cosmetics firm. If both companies live up to the terms of their contracts, they can accomplish the parallel trade with a book transaction, meaning that no money need ever change hands.

Parallel trade that involves an actual cash transfer is known as a *counterpurchase.* In a counterpurchase, the seller and the buyer each pay the other—using a **letter of credit (L/C)** or a wire transfer—for the goods received. Both of these cash payments may be denominated in the currency used by the party that originates the deal.

para-site   Familiar name for an Internet site that profits from the use of unauthorized material or links to other sites.

EXAMPLE: Six large media companies—Dow Jones & Company, Inc.; Cable News Network, Inc.; Times-Mirror Company; the Washington Post Company; Time, Inc.; and Reuters News Media, Inc.—used the term *para-site* in their suit against TotalNEWS. Although TotalNEWS had ceased its practice of linking to media sites owned by the six companies, an out-of-court settlement in June 1997 formally barred such use in the future.

Implications for other Internet sites are unclear at the moment, since the settlement determined no legal precedence (Atwood 1997).

Pareto chart   A rank ordering of priorities based on Pareto's law.

Pareto's law is attributed to Vilfredo Pareto, a nineteenth-century Italian sociologist and economist who theorized that income distribution in society is not a random occurrence, but rather something that hews to a consistent pattern throughout human history. Using a complex mathematical proof, Pareto concluded that 80 percent of a nation's income benefits only 20 percent of the population.

Stated another way, Pareto's law holds that 20 percent of potential causes account for 80 percent of eventual outcome. Thus, in a business setting, 20 percent of the customers would contribute 80 percent of the sales, a small part of the workforce would probably produce most of the **output,** and 80 percent of the difficulty with any given process might be attributable to 20 percent of the potential causes. Pareto's theory is also called the *law of the trivial many and the critical few* or the *80-20 law.*

Pareto efficiency   A desirable situation in which at least one party is better off and no one is worse off as a result of a **transaction.**

This concept, attributed to the nineteenth-century Italian sociologist and economist Vilfredo Pareto, is also called the *Pareto optimum.*

participative design   *See concurrent engineering*

partnership   An unincorporated business in which two or more people pool their funds and their skills, agreeing to share in all profits and losses.

A partnership may contain both *general* and *limited* partners. General partners are responsible for managing the partnership's day-to-day activities, and they are personally liable for any debts. Each general partner is also responsible for the actions of the other partners. That means that if one of the partners—say, an engineer in a consulting firm—makes a mistake that leads to a lawsuit, all the partners are potentially liable.

Limited partners contribute nothing to the venture other than money and are not active participants in its operation. Their liability extends no further than their investment.

See also **limited partnership.**

pay for performance   A management *incentive plan* that links monetary reward to specific levels of performance.

Incentive plans have long been a key component of executive compensation, but a growing trend in the 1990s saw salary increases, cash bonuses, stock options, and the like more closely tied to quantifiable performance results.

payout ratio   *See expected return*

PBO   *See projected benefit obligation*

P/E ratio   *See price/earnings ratio*

penetrated market   Those customers who have already purchased a product.

Knowing the penetrated market allows a marketer to gauge its position against its competitors. The penetrated market is not usually the object of a major *marketing* effort, but it can be an important element in a campaign to build loyalty to a particular company or product. The penetrated market might be illustrated in the following manner:

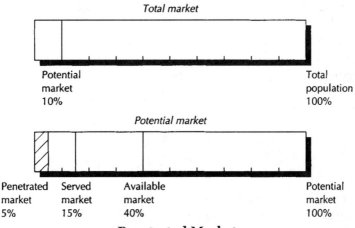

Penetrated Market

See also **available market; potential market; served market.**

penetration pricing   A *marketing* strategy of putting a low price on a new product to generate the greatest possible *demand.*

The idea behind this approach is that a low price will lead to such high volume that total profits exceed what could be earned with a higher initial price. The marketer hopes to reach the entire *market* instead of just the people who are willing to pay a higher price to sample a new product.

EXAMPLE: Providers of digital satellite service (DSS) television are giving the cable TV industry a run for its money for a variety of reasons, not the least of which is their willingness to employ penetration pricing. Satellite service providers such as DirecTV and USSB are even subsidizing the makers of the DSS equipment as part of their plan to build *market share.* Although DirecTV and USSB are sacrificing *revenue* now, they are betting that once they've captured a subscriber base, they will be able to hold onto it (Gaare 1997).

Marketers often use penetration pricing when the market is not divided into price segments—that is, there is no "elite" market willing to pay a high price. Thus, this strategy is appropriate for products that do not symbolize high status or in markets that are not price sensitive.

Marketers also use penetration pricing in situations where competitors can enter rapidly and drive the price down. Finally, penetration pricing can prove effective when the company has large-scale production plants that can reap the benefits of *economies of scale.*

The strategy does have its downside, however. Marketers can never assume that their market position is secure, even when they offer an attractive low price, because competitors will often meet it. That, in turn, can cut into the hoped-for high volumes and result in losses during a product's launch, when it is still gaining consumer acceptance. And because low-price strategy means that the break-even point is automatically pushed to a higher volume level, penetration pricing is inherently riskier than a high-price strategy.

*See also **perceived-value pricing; skimming; target return pricing.***

penny stocks   Shares in young public companies that are not listed on any exchange and typically trade at a very low price.

Penny stock prices range from under $1 a share to as much as $10 a share, usually following the heavy promotions that accompany an initial public offering (IPO; see *going public*). Penny stocks tend to be much riskier and more volatile than stocks traded on the *New York Stock Exchange* (*NYSE*) and the *American Stock Exchange* (*AMEX*). That is because they are thinly traded, which makes it easier for a single market maker to control the prices, and because they are issued by companies that have not yet developed into stable businesses with established track records of sales and profits. Experts warn the unsavvy investor against the scams and shell companies often associated with the penny stock market.

EXAMPLE: The Better Business Bureau, in conjunction with the North American Securities Administrators Association, offers a consumer bulletin that highlights the dangers of trading in penny stocks. Calling penny stocks "a booming, multibillion dollar national growth industry," the bulletin notes an alarming increase in the number of fraudulent offerings and warns the unsophisticated investor to beware the high-pressure *telemarketing* techniques often employed by abusive promoters.

The bulletin concedes that a number of the low-priced stock offerings are perfectly legitimate, but points out that the relative lack of meaningful information about many of these firms poses a serious hazard to the investor. (SOURCE: BBB Web site.)

Penny stocks are traded over the counter, many in Denver, Salt Lake City, or Vancouver, British Columbia. These markets have traditionally been hot ones for penny stocks of speculative oil, gas, and gold-mining ventures.

See also **pink sheets.**

pension fund   The money set aside by companies, labor unions, government bodies, and other organizations to meet the obligations of a retirement plan.

Pension funds are administered by trustees who invest the fund dollars and pay out the benefits to retired employees. Because these funds invest billions of dollars annually, they are a major factor in the U.S. securities markets.

See also **defined benefit pension plan; defined contribution pension plan.**

pension plan   A contract in which an employer agrees to provide benefits to retired employees.

Accounting for a pension plan involves the recognition of both the **projected benefit obligation** (**PBO**) and the cost of funding those benefits.

See also **defined benefit pension plan; defined contribution pension plan.**

perceived-value pricing   A way of setting prices that is based on the buyers' perception of value rather than the seller's costs.

Accurately estimating the consumer's understanding of the product's or service's value is the key to perceived-value pricing.

EXAMPLE: In the beauty business, the actual cost of providing a shampoo and a haircut varies little from salon to salon. Many upscale salons, however, recognize that their patrons attach great value to a good haircut. So they charge higher prices than many of their competitors to reflect the value their particular customers place on the service, not the costs the salon actually incurs.

percentage of sales   A way of budgeting product promotion expenditures based on a fixed percentage of past or predicted sales.

Marketers use this technique because it directly relates expenditures to sales.

EXAMPLE: A furniture manufacturer expects to do $10 million worth of business in the coming year. It decides to allocate 3 percent of its estimated sales figure to *advertising,* so it budgets $300,000 for that purpose.

Many marketers, however, discount the percentage-of-sales method as a classic case of putting the cart before the horse. The reason? It is based on the premise that advertising is the direct result of sales, rather than on the more conventional wisdom that says sales are the direct result of advertising.

percentage-of-completion method   A method of accounting that recognizes the costs and *revenues* in each year of a long-term construction project based on the value of the work performed.

Percentage-of-completion allows a company to spread earnings from long-term projects over the entire span of the project, rather than declaring all of them at its beginning or end. Companies engaged in the construction of high-rise buildings, bridges, ships, and other things that involve a design/development and construction/production process stretching over several years prefer this method because it gives a realistic estimate of the expenses incurred and the revenues earned at any particular time.

The amount of revenue to be recognized at any particular point is calculated by multiplying the percentage completed by the contract price:

$$\text{Percentage completed} \times \text{contract price}$$

EXAMPLE: A construction company has a $3 million contract to build a bridge that is to be completed in three years. After the first year of construction, it recognizes revenue that it calculated as follows:

$$33\% \times \$3,000,000 = \$1,000,000$$

Rather than using milestone dates to measure a project's completeness, many companies divide the costs incurred to date by the total estimated costs:

$$\frac{\text{Cost incurred to date}}{\text{Total estimated costs}}$$

Say the construction company estimates the overall cost of building the bridge at $2,000,000. At the end of the first year, the company has spent $900,000. It calculates the percentage of completion as follows:

$$\frac{\$900,000}{\$2,000,000} = 0.45, \text{ or } 45\%$$

Measuring costs shows that the project is now 45 percent completed, so the construction company would declare revenue of

$$45\% \times \$3,000,000 = \$1,350,000$$

See also **matching concept.**

perfect competition   A **market** so competitive that its participants have virtually no control over the price.

This is an economic term that describes a market in which participants must act as price takers, buying and selling at the price determined by the forces of **supply** and **demand.** The characteristics of such a market include:

- A large number of relatively small-scale buyers and sellers
- Easy entry into, and exit from, the market
- A standardized product among all suppliers
- Complete knowledge about the market price among both buyers and sellers

A perfectly competitive market is a theoretical idea that is rarely achieved. The agricultural sector of the economy comes the closest, with the prices of foodstuffs such as corn, wheat, beef, pork bellies, and soybeans determined primarily by the forces of supply and demand. Although the markets for **foreign exchange,** stocks, **bonds,** and certain precious metals are sometimes cited as perfectly competitive, many economists argue that large traders may, from time to time, exercise a strong influence over these prices simply by trading or withholding from the market large amounts of their holdings.

performance bond   A third-party guarantee that one party to a contract will carry out terms and payments to the other party as promised.

A surety bond issued by a surety insurance company is the most common form of performance bond, especially for construction companies. Other guarantors include the Small Business Administration (SBA), which guarantees payment of SBA-approved loans; the **Export-Import Bank** (**Eximbank**), which guarantees payment by foreign buyers of export orders; commercial banks, which guarantee performance against an export **letter of credit** (**L/C**) or standby letters of credit against deliveries; and individuals, who guarantee payment of bank loans of small companies or individuals.

periodic inventory review system   A method for reordering *inventory* at specific intervals rather than as needed.

Also called a *fixed interval reorder system,* this method fixes a specific reorder period but allows the reorder quantity to vary according to needs. Such systems are most appropriate when tracking inventory is difficult and the cost of *stockouts* or of maintaining safety stocks is low. The amount to be reordered is calculated by subtracting on-hand and on-order inventory from the maximum level of inventory and then adding in the *demand* expected during the delivery *lead time.*

Reorder quantity = maximum inventory

– on-hand and on-order inventory + demand during lead time

On-hand inventory, or the amount currently in stock, can be a negative number in situations where *backorders* are allowed. On-order inventory, which is the amount purchased but not yet delivered, is deducted from maximum inventory to ensure that a merchandise order is not duplicated. Expected demand during the inventory lead time is added to compensate for the number of units that will be sold (and then need to be replaced) between the time the order is placed and when it is delivered.

perpetuity   *See annuity*

personal communications channels   A framework for directing a sales effort to an individual.

Personal communications channels take three forms:

- *Advocate channels,* where company salespeople, perhaps from *telemarketing,* directly contact potential buyers in the *target market*
- *Expert channels,* where people who are not associated with a company but who have knowledge and experience with a particular product communicate with target buyers

EXAMPLE: The golf pro at the country club gives lessons to one of the members. After assessing the golfer's game and watching him make do with an old and inferior set of clubs, the pro recommends clubs particularly suited to the golfer's style and ability.

- *Social channels,* where family, friends, and neighbors talk with potential buyers in the target market

Savvy marketers will work to identify the personal communications channels in a target market and use them to advantage, because they know that one-on-one communication beats a nonpersonal *advertising* message hands-down.

personal consumption expenditures   The estimate of total consumer spending.

Consumer spending constitutes the largest of the major components of *gross domestic product* (**GDP**), typically equaling between 60 and 65 percent. There are three major categories within personal consumption expenditures:

- **Durable goods.** This category refers to purchases of goods with a ***useful life*** of more than three years, such as motor vehicles, furniture, and appliances. Because these goods are long-lasting and generally expensive, their purchase can be postponed in times of economic uncertainty. Thus, durable goods spending tends to be the most cyclical portion of consumer spending.

- **Nondurable goods.** This includes purchases of food, apparel, gasoline, and heating oil. This category is less cyclical because these items are necessities.

- *Services.* This is the largest component of consumer spending, accounting for about half of the total. Housing, household operating expenses (such as those for utilities), transportation, and medical care make up this category. Spending on housing includes both the actual amount paid by renters and an imputed amount that homeowners implicitly pay to themselves in their role as consumers of housing. (Note that new-home purchases are treated as an ***investment*** under residential construction. The use a person derives from living in a house is properly classed as consumption.)

PERT   *See **program evaluation and review technique***

PIMS   *See **Profit Impact of Market Strategies***

pink sheets   A daily publication that provides the trading prices of thousands of unlisted small-company stocks.

    The bid and asked prices of smaller public companies that cannot qualify for listing on the **NASDAQ Stock Market** (or that do qualify but choose to avoid NASDAQ regulations) are carried in this daily circular printed on pink paper (hence the name, *pink sheets*). Pink sheet stock trades are negotiated directly between buyers and sellers via telephone or computer. A private Jersey City, New Jersey, company, National Quotation Bureau, Inc., prints the quotes and the names of the brokerage firms trading in about 16,000 over-the-counter stocks, 11,000 of which are not listed on the NASDAQ.

    Pink sheets are sold to brokers by subscription only and are not distributed to the general public. This reduces market coverage and makes it more difficult for potential investors to research these companies or obtain current price information without going through a broker. Furthermore, pink sheet prices are not necessarily actual trading prices; rather, they are paid announcements by brokerage firms advertising their willingness to buy and sell certain securities.

    Pink sheet listings are subject to far fewer regulations than are NASDAQ-listed stocks. The National Quotation Bureau requires only that listing brokers be registered with the **Securities and Exchange Commission** (**SEC**) and that traded securities be either registered or exempt from registration. Only one market maker is needed to get a stock listed. Volume must be reported only when single-day trades total more than $10,000, or 50,000 shares. Furthermore, the bureau does not require asset or **shareholders' equity** minimums. Many of the shares carried in the pink sheets are **penny stocks.**

    Shares of both new and established companies trade off the pink sheets for several reasons: Although these companies may have been in business for a while, they have, for one reason or another, encountered obstacles to the development of market niches or profitability records sufficient to attract the level of investor attention necessary to drive up share prices. In addition, small companies that previously were closely held might go public with a small percentage of shares, raising *capital* for a specific purpose with little concern for ongoing trading values. Finally, shares of companies in a state of change, as in a turnaround mode, may also be listed on pink sheets while they work out their financial difficulties.

EXAMPLE: Not all pink sheet stocks have a checkered past, however. Among the tried-and-true moneymakers sprinkled throughout the pink sheets are well-known names like the mapmaker Rand McNally and Houlihan's Restaurant Group. And some lesser-knowns, like the Providence Journal Company, have also proved to be big winners for savvy investors. Value strategist Mario Gabelli snapped up a block of stock in the privately owned newspaper conglomerate and then watched it appreciate 85 percent in three years (Capell 1996).

pink slip   The notice an employer gives to an employee who is being terminated.
The term dates from about 1925, when a pink discharge notice was inserted inside an employee's final pay envelope.

planning horizon   The length of time that the *master production schedule* extends into the future.

plant within a plant (PWP)   A manufacturing strategy to improve *productivity* and management control by establishing independent business units within a larger facility.

PLC   *See **public limited company***

point-of-purchase (POP) advertising   A strategy that uses eye-catching displays near the location where customers pay for a product in an attempt to trigger impulse buying.

EXAMPLE: Cosmetics maker Aveda is trying new techniques to separate its POP displays from the crowd that traditionally adorns makeup counters. First of all, it is going with a standardized look that will be coordinated across all Aveda retail outlets, providing instant recognition. And rather than the usual pictures of gorgeous women, Aveda's creative team will use props on shelves to create "mini in-store windows" (Rudd 1997).

Point-of-purchase advertising can include not only window and counter displays, but freestanding end-of-aisle racks, banners hung throughout the store, and computer screens that spew out textual and graphical product information at the touch of a button. Usually, a manufacturer distributes these displays to the merchants that sell its products and often discounts the merchandise to compensate *retailers* for giving up valuable floor or shelf space to the POP display.

poison pills   A strategic tactic by the target company in a hostile takeover to make the union much less attractive.
Poison pill devices usually take effect automatically if an unwelcome *merger* or *acquisition* is completed. Examples might include activation of bylaw clauses that require the immediate sale of major *assets,* or the payment of all company obliga-

tions, or the disbursement to current executives of so-called golden parachute compensation packages. Such packages are so lavish that they reduce the value of the acquisition.

pooling of interests   A method of accounting for a ***business combination*** that assumes a simple joining of the two companies' resources, talents, risks, and earnings streams.

Under the pooling method, the two ***balance sheets*** are added together to produce a new consolidated balance sheet for the surviving entity. All ***assets*** and ***liabilities*** are entered at their ***book values.*** Essentially, the pooling method assumes that the two companies combined their financial resources in order to continue operations in the same manner as before, and that nothing of real economic substance has occurred.

Twelve conditions must be satisfied in order to use the pooling-of-interest method in a business combination. If the conditions are met, the pooling method must be used; if any condition is lacking, then the ***purchase method*** must be used. The 12 conditions are as follows:

1. Each company must be autonomous and not have been a subsidiary of another company within the two years before the combination.
2. Each company must be independent; that is, it may not own more than 10 percent of another combining company's ***common stock.***
3. The combination must take place in a single ***transaction*** or be completed in a specified plan within one year.
4. The acquiring company must issue voting common stock in exchange for 90 percent or more of the common stock of the other company.
5. Neither company may change its voting common stock interests in anticipation of the combination within the two years preceding the transaction.
6. Each company can repurchase voting shares of common stock only for purposes other than the business combination.
7. The ownership interest of each individual common stockholder must remain the same relative to any other common stockholder of the combined company.
8. Stockholders' voting rights may not be restricted.
9. The combination may not be contingent on the issuance of other securities or considerations.
10. The combined company may not retire or reacquire any of the voting shares issued in the combination.
11. The surviving company can make no financial arrangements for the benefit of the former shareholders of a combining company (such as guaranteeing loans secured by the stock issued in the combination).
12. The combined company cannot dispose of a significant part of the acquired assets (except to eliminate duplicate facilities) within two years of the combination.

Companies favor the pooling method for two reasons: First, the acquired company's assets are all transferred to the parent's ***financial statements*** at their book value, which allows the parent to match lower *depreciation* expenses with the *revenues* generated by the combined companies. This allows a company to report more revenue on the *income statement* than when a combination is effected under the purchase method, which results in larger depreciation expenses because the subsidiary's assets must be declared at fair market value. Second, pooling of interests does not involve *goodwill,* which, when generated by the purchase method, must be amortized over a period not to exceed 40 years. Finally, companies prefer the pooling method because it combines the *retained earnings* of the two companies as if they had always been a single entity. In other words, a company with a poor earnings record can improve its financial standing by combining with a company with a good earnings record. This can result in financial statements that show consistent earnings growth and attractive *debt-to-equity* and *dividend payout ratios.*

portfolio analysis   *See growth/market share matrix*

potential market   All consumers who have an interest in a given product.

> EXAMPLE: In the case of baby formula, the *market* consists of the parents of all infants, but the potential market is limited to those who are considering alternatives to breast-feeding.

> *See also available market; penetrated market; served market.*

power   The ability to motivate people to do something they would not otherwise do. Different situations require the exercise of different types of power, so managers should be familiar with each type and its potential applications. The five generally accepted bases of power are:

- *Legitimate.* Also called *position* power, this derives from the manager's position within the corporate hierarchy. A company president has more legitimate power, for example, than does a vice president, and the VP, in turn, has more than the department manager. A follower's response to legitimate power is related to the manager's position, not to any personal traits such as knowledge, expertise, or past performance.

- *Reward.* This power is based on employee expectations. In many companies, for instance, employees who comply with all company rules and policies and receive positive performance appraisals will receive annual salary increases. Rewards are not always financial, however, nor are they always controlled by managers. In some cases, a particularly well-thought-of worker can exert reward power simply by maintaining friendly relations with coworkers.

- *Coercive.* This type of power is based on the fear that exists when employees believe that a manager has both the ability and the inclination to punish them. In a corporate setting, coercive power can take the form of demotion, discharge, temporary disciplinary measures, or a pay cut. Because excessive use leads to distrust and fear, a wise manager turns to coercion only when all else fails.

- *Expert.* Competence begets expert power. A manager who is widely perceived as able to analyze, implement, and guide the set of tasks assigned to a group of workers will often have this type of power.

- *Referent.* Also called *charismatic* power, this type is related to the degree to which an employee identifies with a manager. Employees follow requests or orders simply because this particular manager asks them. The underlying factors that produce referent power are trust, affection, similarity, and acceptance.

PR   *See **public relations***

predatory pricing   The illegal practice of selling to consumers at below cost in order to drive other competitors from the marketplace and increase **market share.**

Predatory pricing is initially quite costly to the supplier since each product sold is sold at a loss. But once most competitors are weeded out and only one or a few suppliers remain, the product price can be inflated enough to earn a supercompetitive profit and recoup the earlier losses.

Prohibited by the Sherman Antitrust Act, predatory pricing is thought by some observers to be rare, largely because recovery is difficult at best. A **market** in which supercompetitive profits are commonplace will quickly attract new entrants, thus intensifying competition and blocking full recovery of the earlier losses (material suggested by an antitrust case against Netscape at the Web site www.roscoe.harvard.edu).

preference segmentation   A division of the **market** into distinct sectors according to consumer preferences.

Three basic patterns—homogeneous, diffuse, and clustered—will emerge when sampling consumers on important attributes for any given product. Homogeneous preferences indicate a market where all consumers value roughly the same attributes. In such a market, all **brands** would be similar and positioned in the center of the market.

Diffuse preferences show a market at the other extreme, one with no particular grouping pattern because consumers have widely varying ideas about desirable product features. In this situation, a brand positioned in the center of the market would appeal to the most people, but a brand that stakes out its own niche could gain the loyalty of customers not satisfied with the centered brand.

And, finally, clustered preferences indicate a market with several distinct segments. A company entering such a market has various options: It might try a centered brand, hoping to attract all the groups, it might concentrate on attracting the largest segment within the market, or it might develop several products to go after each of the different segments.

preferred stock   A type of **capital stock** that gives its holders preference over common stockholders in the distribution of earnings or rights to the **assets** of a company in the event of liquidation.

Preferred stock usually pays a set **dividend.** For example, a 5 percent preferred stock pays a dividend that equals 5 percent of the total **par value** of outstanding shares. (However, adjustable-rate preferred stock pays a varying amount based on changes in a specified **interest rate** such as the **prime rate.**) Preferred stocks generally do not have any voting rights.

Preferred stock also may carry a variety of features. It may be callable by the company, dividends may be cumulative, common stock **warrants** may be attached, or it may be convertible to ***common stock*** under certain conditions, to mention only a few variations.

*See also **convertible security.***

prepaid expense   Goods or services that are paid for but not completely used or consumed by the end of the ***accounting period.***

Prepaid expenses are reported as ***current assets*** on the ***balance sheet*** and might include ***advertising,*** insurance, and real estate taxes.

present value   The current value of a future payment or stream of payments.

The concept of present value rests on the belief that a dollar invested today will increase in amount as time passes because a profit will be earned on the invested dollar. Thus, money available today is more valuable than an equal amount that will not be available until some future date.

Present value is calculated by applying a discount to the future payments based on what one could reasonably expect to make on the invested amount. So, if $100 could be invested today at 10 percent interest, compounded annually, for a period of ten years, the ***discount rate*** would be 10 percent and the present value would be approximately $38.55.

The present value method forms the cornerstone of business or ***equity interest valuations*** and is also referred to as the *discounted cash flow method* or the *discounted earnings method.* It is widely used by companies and investors to determine the fair market value of a potential ***investment.*** Although it is extremely time-consuming to calculate the present value manually, ***annuity*** tables, programmable calculators, and computer programs make the calculations easy and fast.

present value of an annuity   A method of measuring the value, in current dollars, of the ***cash flows*** from an ***annuity.***

Basically, the present value of an annuity is the total payment that would have to be made today in order to equal the annuity.

press release   A prepared statement that is distributed to the media.

Press releases can be used for any number of situations, from the hiring of a new employee to the introduction of a new product.

pretesting   The testing of the copy, design, research, marketing strategy, or any other part of an ***advertising*** campaign before its launch.

There are three broad methods of pretesting. The first is direct rating by consumer panels that are asked to look at various ads and rate them. A high rating does not guarantee an ad's success, but it does suggest that the ad may prove effective. Another method is portfolio testing, whereby consumers study a series of advertisements and then are asked to recall individual ads and their content. The level of consumer recall is an indicator of an ad's ability to stand out and communicate its message. The third method, laboratory testing, uses complicated equipment to measure consumers' physiological reactions such as changes in blood pressure, heartbeat, and perspiration levels as they view an advertisement.

price controls   The use of government powers to keep the price of a product or service either above or below its equilibrium point.

When the government tries to keep a product's price above equilibrium, it is said to be establishing a *price floor.* For many years, the federal government's farm subsidy program either paid farmers not to use a certain amount of their land or bought up the surplus products that resulted from the price floor. This helped to bring the market price above the equilibrium level. (The 1996 Farm Bill began a seven-year phaseout of cash subsidies.)

When the government tries to keep the price of a product below its equilibrium level, it is said to establish a *price ceiling*. The U.S. government has exercised price controls in this manner several times during the twentieth century. During World War II, the prices of a number of essential goods were subject to price ceilings. In late 1971 and early 1972, the government established various degrees of price control over certain goods and services. In both instances, the intent was to control or prevent inflation in the aggregate economy.

price elasticity of demand   The effect that changes in price have on sales of a product or service.

Price elasticity is calculated by dividing the percentage change in quantity demanded by the percentage change in price. Past sales figures are usually used to estimate price elasticity.

$$\frac{\text{Percentage change in quantity demanded (sales)}}{\text{Percentage change in price}}$$

EXAMPLE: A watchmaker sells 100 watches a year for $1,000 each, which gives him an annual income of $100,000. If he raises the price of the watches by 4 percent, to $1,040, and then sells only 80 watches in a year, his demand has dropped 20 percent, which means the price elasticity for the watches is a negative five ($-0.20 \div 0.04 = -5$). The watchmaker's annual income will fall to $83,200. If demand drops by 4 percent after a price increase of the same magnitude and he sells 96 watches, the price elasticity is a negative one ($-0.04 \div 0.04 = -1$). The watchmaker's income will fall only slightly, to $99,840. If demand drops by 2 percent, to 98 watches, following the 4 percent price hike, the price elasticity is a negative one half ($-0.02 \div 0.04$). The watchmaker's income will rise to $101,920 (98 watches × $1,040). In a scenario such as the latter, when a big price change brings about only a small change in ***demand,*** the state of demand is called *inelastic*. The more inelastic the demand, the more the seller can make by increasing the price.

Three factors determine the price elasticity of demand:

- Are there substitute products? The more alternatives there are, the more price elastic the product tends to be.
- Is the product a necessity? A necessity tends to be price inelastic because the buyer has to have the product regardless of price.
- What portion of the budget goes to purchase the product? If the product takes a significant slice of the budget pie, demand tends to be more price elastic. Thus, cars and houses are more price elastic than are small, routine purchases such as milk and breakfast cereal.

price/earnings (P/E) ratio   A measure of a company's ***investment*** potential.

Literally, a P/E ratio is how much a share is worth per dollar of earnings. The price/earnings ratio is calculated as follows:

$$\frac{\text{Market price per common share}}{\text{Primary earnings per common share}}$$

A company's P/E ratio depends on investors' perceptions about a company's potential. Factors such as risk, quality of management, outlook for growth, earnings history, and industry conditions all come into play.

EXAMPLE: With the run-up in stock prices during the long-running bull market of the 1990s, investors bid up the prices of many **blue-chip** stocks to historically high levels relative to their earnings. Many observers wondered whether these stocks had become overvalued (Fitch and McDonald 1997).

*See also **earnings per share.***

primary data   Original information gathered for a specific research project.

EXAMPLE: A bank that is studying customer satisfaction gives a questionnaire to customers to fill out while they wait for a teller. The information collected in the questionnaires is part of the study's primary data because it was collected solely for the purposes of the customer satisfaction project.

Primary data differs from **secondary data,** which is usually obtained from previously published sources.

prime rate   The base rate that banks use in calculating interest charges on loans to their best, most creditworthy commercial customers.

The prime rate is a benchmark that helps determine the interest charged on a host of lending instruments. If the prime rate is at 6.5 percent, for example, a top-tier company like General Electric might borrow at that rate, whereas a smaller company might negotiate a loan at prime plus two percentage points, or 8.5 percent. Consumer loans on such things as homes, automobiles, and credit cards are also linked to the prime rate.

Banks claim that the prime rate is determined by a complicated formula that takes into account their cost of money—that is, the interest they pay out—as well as their expenses for salaries, supplies, rent, **depreciation,** and so on. Theoretically, the sum of these costs plus a reasonable **profit margin** equals the prime rate. In practice, however, it does not work quite that way. **Money center banks** establish an **interest rate** labeled *prime,* which is based, in effect, on what the traffic will bear. All correspondent banks around the country then follow suit, regardless of what their respective cost structures may be. It obviously does not cost a bank in rural Wyoming as much to operate as it does a bank in midtown Manhattan, yet both use the same prime measure to establish interest rates.

Contrary to popular opinion, the **Federal Reserve** does not set the prime rate. Although changes in the short-term borrowing rates that the Federal Reserve charges its member banks may have an indirect effect, the prime rate is entirely the doing of the money center banks.

The following chart represents the movement of the prime rate for the years from 1975 to 1997.

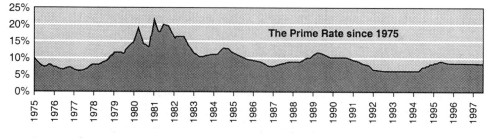

SOURCE: http://www.primerate.com.

private label   A product manufactured by a supplier and sold by a *retailer* under its own store or company label.

EXAMPLE: These days, private-label products run the gamut from wine to peanut butter. Where once they tended toward the generic, now they include premium and gourmet brands as well as foods for the health conscious. Shoppers at A&P grocery stores in the Northeast can satisfy their sweet tooths with a Master Choice chocolate bar, while Kroger customers can assuage their consciences with the chain's Healthy Indulgence line of products.

Private-label brands contributed $33.9 billion of the $180.2 billion total of grocery store sales in 1996, according to the Private Label Manufacturers Society. Why have private labels become so popular? For one thing, they help develop customer loyalty, and for another, they provide a greater margin of profit for the retailer (Fasig 1997).

When a retailer contracts with a manufacturer for a private-label product, it usually places a large order. That fact makes private labeling attractive to most manufacturers, but it can have drawbacks. First, a manufacturer has no control over the *advertising,* package design, and *brands* under which its products will be sold. Second, when competitors lower their prices, a manufacturer may lose profits on its own products by continuing to produce at the required volume for the private label. Finally, if the manufacturer produces its own brand, it can be expensive to maintain separate *inventories* in both packaging materials and finished goods.

private placements and limited exempt offerings   Procedures that permit a company to sell unregistered stock.

Exempt offerings generally fall into one of two categories: a private placement or a limited offering. It should be noted that these are exemptions from the Securities Act of 1933—a federal law—and do not necessarily apply under the securities laws of all 50 states. In most cases, however, states that do require formal registrations generally have more lenient requirements than does the *Securities and Exchange Commission (SEC).*

Private placements are used to raise a limited amount of *equity* capital in a relatively short time at the lowest cost. Because private placements are exempt offerings, issuing and ongoing costs are substantially lower than in public offerings. Although federal antifraud securities regulations must still be complied with, companies do not have to file formal registration statements.

In addition to cost savings, private placements enable a company to raise equity capital when an uncertain economic or market climate may prohibit an effective public offering. Or perhaps the company lacks the two or three years of steadily increasing earnings that are usually required before a successful public offering can be made. For some companies, it might be desirable to take advantage of the more lenient public disclosure requirements in order to keep company skeletons buried.

Investors in private placements may be relatives, friends, business associates, or strangers. An underwriter is usually necessary unless personal contacts with ready cash to invest can be attracted. Certain brokers specialize in keeping tabs on private investors who are anxious to make equity investments in closely held companies.

privately held company A company whose ownership shares are not publicly traded.

Privately held companies come in a variety of business forms, including ***corporations, partnerships,*** proprietorships, ***joint ventures,*** and limited liability corporations. They can be big and small, well known and obscure.

EXAMPLE: Warren Buffett's Berkshire Hathaway is one of the better-known privately held companies in the United States, while the German media empire, Bertelsmann, is no slouch in Europe. Both were ranked by *Fortune* magazine in 1997 as residing among the world's most admired companies (Fisher 1997).

The accounting principles for privately held companies are identical to those for public companies with one exception: The reporting requirements of regulatory agencies such as the ***Securities and Exchange Commission*** (***SEC***) and of public stock exchanges do not apply to them. Privately held companies do not have to disclose full ***financial statements*** to the public at large, but they do make them available to lending institutions, private investors such as venture capital funds and limited partners, and, in some instances, state regulatory agencies.

See also ***publicly held companies.***

pro forma In accounting, a ***financial statement*** in which the amounts stated are fully or partially estimated.

The term *pro forma* comes from the Latin phrase meaning "for the sake of form" or "as a matter of form."

A company making a ***change in accounting principle*** must prepare pro forma financial statements estimating what the previous year's earnings would have been if the new principle had been in use. Other instances of pro forma reporting might involve proposed debt issues or ***mergers*** and ***acquisitions.***

EXAMPLE: CKS Group, Inc., an integrated marketing services and technology holding company, filed pro forma consolidated ***income statements*** for both the quarter and the year ended November 30, 1997. In a series of footnotes, the company explained how its year-earlier results would have looked had a subsequent pooling-of-interests ***business combination*** been in effect at the time (CKS Group 1997).

Companies typically disclose the underlying assumptions of any pro forma statement.

process control A feedback mechanism that continuously monitors and corrects a manufacturing process.

Process control is the activity of monitoring a process, receiving feedback on the performance of that process, and providing corrective action if a deviation becomes unacceptable. The thermostat on a home-heating system is a process control device.

product attributes   The characteristics that describe a good or service.

Marketers use these features to attract consumers. But they must be careful when planning the campaign to create a fit between the product's attributes and the needs or desires of the *target market.*

EXAMPLE: Not surprisingly, milk buyers rate "freshness," as demonstrated by visible and readable codes, their number one product attribute at the dairy case, according to a study commissioned by Dairy Management, Inc. But one Midwestern retailer did profess surprise at finding out that cleanliness in the dairy aisle grabbed customers' attention while the presence of a *brand name* did not (Zimmerman 1997).

Consumers vary in the attributes that matter to them, and they will pay more attention to a product if it has the attributes that address their needs. The *market* for a product can often be segmented according to the attributes that are important to different groups of consumers.

See also ***product positioning.***

product concept   The way in which a product is positioned to be perceived by consumers.

A *concept* is distinct from an *idea* for a possible product that the company might envision itself offering to the *market.* A product idea can generate several product concepts.

EXAMPLE: A cosmetics company that develops a new skin cream has several options for its product concept. It might position the cream as a soothing aftershave lotion for men, or as a moisturizing night cream for women, or as a lotion to keep a baby's skin from chafing. Each concept would find a different *target market,* different competitors, and a different marketing strategy. Analyzing the appropriate strategy for each concept will move the company forward toward designing a *marketing plan* for the final product.

product life cycle   The process through which a product enters, grows, saturates, and then leaves a *market.*

The product life cycle usually consists of four stages: introduction, growth, maturity, and decline. Each demands a different marketing approach.

In the introduction phase, sales are slow and profit is nonexistent, so a marketing strategy might rely on heavy *advertising* and *sales promotions* in order to create product awareness and stimulate sales.

EXAMPLE: When Zeneca Pharmaceuticals developed Accolate, the first new asthma medication to appear in more than 20 years, it first targeted physicians and organizations supporting asthma sufferers so as to give the product credibility within the medical community. This initial phase was followed by direct-to-consumer *marketing* using direct mail and national advertising, all aimed at creating awareness and educating consumers about the product's benefits and how to obtain it.

During the growth phase, both sales and profits dramatically improve and the marketing focus shifts; the company may continue to advertise heavily—now focused on the ***brand*** rather than the product—while phasing out promotions. Advertising in the growth phase becomes increasingly focused on creating brand preference.

EXAMPLE: The market for mountain bikes has mushroomed in recent years, growing into a billion-dollar business. To create brand ***demand*** and increase ***market share,*** top manufacturers like Trek and GT have mounted aggressive advertising campaigns.

The maturity stage is marked by flattening sales and stabilizing, then decreasing, profits. The marketing strategy for a mature product might concentrate on taking away market share from competitors, primarily through price reductions. Another tactic might be to begin targeting an entirely new group of buyers, perhaps by relaunching the product.

EXAMPLE: At the Walt Disney Company, old products never die, nor, apparently, do they fade away. Disney is the master of breathing new life into mature products. Some Disney classics have been rereleased into theaters to charm a whole new generation of viewers, while others, both old and new, have been recycled into the video market. Disney also creates sequels, as with *Aladdin,* that are then released only in video format. Another tactic the company uses to get even more mileage out of an aging product is to produce add-ons, such as musical videos and audiotapes that include only part of a film (Hedden 1997).

A product enters decline when sales start to fall rapidly. An appropriate strategy for this stage might be to stop marketing to smaller market segments and further reduce the product's price. Marketers can also look globally to find new ***target markets,*** as makers of baby formula did when breast-feeding came back into vogue in the United States in the 1980s. But sometimes a dying market can be rejuvenated if marketers are savvy enough to pick up on changing attitudes.

EXAMPLE: The cigar industry seemed to be on its last legs in the 1980s. Smoking in general had lost its cachet because of the health risks, and cigar smoking in particular was out of favor because it was thought to be especially malodorous. But then the industry began to detect a whiff of discontent among Americans who were fed up with having every pleasure declared off-limits for one reason or another. Capitalizing on what they sensed to be a growing rebellion, cigar makers positioned their product as a relatively inexpensive indulgence that could still be enjoyed in an increasingly stressful world. Some makers even limit customer purchases to one cigar a day, enhancing the perception that their product is a very special treat (Hedden 1997).

See also ***market life cycle.***

product maturity Typically the longest phase in the ***product life cycle*** and identified with market saturation.

Many of the products on the market today—soft drinks, automobiles, fast foods—are in the maturity phase. That means that the majority of marketing managers must deal with a mature product.

Marketers divide maturity into three subphases:

- *Growth maturity,* in which sales increase but the rate of growth declines and new **distribution channels** are lacking.
- *Stable maturity,* in which per capita sales are level and future sales are dependent on population growth and replacement **demand.**
- *Decaying maturity,* in which the absolute level of sales declines and consumers move on to other products.

Marketers employ two broad strategies—market modification and product modification—in handling a mature product. Companies try to modify a **market** by increasing the number of users or increasing the rate of usage among current users. Three ways of increasing the number of users for any given brand are to:

- Enter new market segments, which is what Johnson & Johnson did when it began promoting its No More Tears baby shampoo to adult users.
- Challenge a competitor and try to take its customers, as Coke and Pepsi do in their ongoing back-and-forth battle to woo away each other's users.
- Try to convert nonusers, as the overnight air freight industry has done by proving to former nonusers that its service has benefits that other forms of transportation do not.

To increase customer usage of a **brand,** marketers can:

- Develop new uses for a product, which Arm & Hammer did by promoting baking soda as a multipurpose deodorizer instead of just a cooking ingredient.
- Encourage more frequent use, which some cereal makers do by promoting their product as a snack food.
- Advocate more usage per occasion, as when shampoo makers added the word *repeat* to the directions on the side of the bottle.

A marketer can modify a product by improving features, style, or quality. Feature improvement aims to expand a product's convenience, flexibility, safety, or some other **product attribute.**

EXAMPLE: Carmakers follow this strategy when they add new features such as four-wheel drive, antilock brakes, power door locks, and air bags. The drawback with this approach is that new features are easily imitated by competitors.

Style improvement increases a product's aesthetic appeal in hopes of luring new users.

EXAMPLE: Hush Puppies added funky new shoe colors to attract young, upscale buyers.

This approach has the potential to create a strong identity for a product, but determining which customers will like a new style and which will dislike it and move to another product is difficult. In the case of Hush Puppies, the company managed to pull off its new look without alienating older buyers. (SOURCE: *Advertising Age* Web site, http://www.adage.com)

Quality improvement attempts to attract customers by boosting a product's performance. As long as a company can actually improve quality (a toothpaste that cleans better as opposed to one that only has a "a new minty-fresh taste"), this strategy can revitalize a mature product.

See also **market life cycle.**

product mix The combination of products that a company offers to the **market.**

EXAMPLE: General Foods' product mix includes coffee, desserts, cereals, household products, pet foods, and other grocery items. Within the product mix are broad groupings called *product lines,* which are similar in terms of use or characteristics. Each of the General Foods product-mix members represents a separate product line.

Product mixes differ in the number of product lines they contain. If a mix includes a large number of product lines, it is said to be wide or broad. If it contains only a few product lines, it is narrow or limited. The number of product lines is known as the *variety,* while the depth within the product line is called the *assortment.*

EXAMPLE: Gaines Meal, Gaines Biscuits, Gaines Bits, and Gaines Variety constitute the assortment in the General Foods dog-food product line.

A marketer can focus on changing an existing product line, on adding and deleting items from the product mix, or on changing the assortment offered.

product positioning How a company places a product in the mind of the consumer or **market**—that is, which elements it chooses to emphasize—in relation to competitive products in the **target market.**

EXAMPLE: A perfume manufacturer might position its product as the rarest and most exotic scent in the world. All elements of the **marketing mix** contribute to this image: The perfume is made from exotic ingredients, packaged in a beautiful bottle, and given an appropriate name, say, Black Orchid. To enhance its image of rarity, the manufacturer distributes it in small amounts to exclusive boutiques. All the **advertising** for Black Orchid emphasizes its exotic qualities and precious ingredients. And, of course, it carries a high price tag as befits a scent made up of the rarest ingredients on earth. The product positioning gives Black Orchid a cachet that its competitors cannot easily match.

See also **product attributes.**

production function An economic concept describing the relationship between a firm's **inputs** and its **outputs.**

The short-run production function relates a firm's variable inputs to output while keeping at least one of its inputs fixed. As additional amounts of the variable inputs are added to the production process, the firm eventually encounters the law of diminishing returns.

The production function is computed by the following equation:

$$Q = f(L,C,T \ldots)$$

where Q represents the company's output (the variable amount), expressed as a function of labor (L), capital (C), technology (T), and any number of other independent variables or inputs. For purposes of illustration, assume that technology (*T*) is held constant and that the only inputs are labor and **capital.** Experience tells the managers that with one unit of labor (1*L*) and one unit of capital (1*C*), the firm can produce, say, 4 units of a product or service (4*Q*). Two units of labor (2*L*) and two units of capital (2*C*), however, quadruples this output (16*Q*). Using various combinations of labor and capital (and assuming an increase in returns to scale, as in the example), managers could determine the optimal output at any given time. It would, of course, not be in the company's best interest to enter production in which a great deal of capital had to be poured into the mix in order to compensate for a shortage of labor, or conversely, one in which a great deal of labor had to be brought in to make up for low contributions of capital to the production process.

In the long run, a firm is free to change all of its inputs. As it increases all of its inputs, a firm may encounter increasing returns to scale, constant returns to scale, or decreasing returns to scale. In the first situation, the output increase is proportionately greater than the increase in the firm's inputs. In the second situation, the output increases by the same proportion. In the third situation, the output increases by a smaller proportion than do the inputs.

See also **economies of scale.**

production plan   The formal statement of a company's production strategy.

A production plan is distinct from an **aggregate plan** in that it frequently deals with specific products or families of products. Production plans usually detail a company's expected resource requirements, labor requirements, changes in **inventories, capacity** limitations, and changes in the rate of production.

productivity   A measure of **efficiency** calculated by dividing **output** by the total number of hours worked.

$$\frac{\text{Output}}{\text{Worker hours}} = \text{productivity}$$

A company can increase its productivity by increasing output, decreasing worker hours, or doing both simultaneously.

Other measures of productivity can be devised simply by using a different denominator. Capital productivity, for example, is calculated by dividing output by dollars invested. Materials productivity is determined by dividing output by **inventory** spending, equipment productivity by dividing output by machine hours, and energy productivity by dividing output by kilowatt-hours. Each of these is considered a partial-factor measure of productivity that serves to highlight a particular area of management concern.

When more than one factor is used, such as labor and inventory, the resulting measurement is called *multifactor productivity*. In analyzing multifactor productivity, it is important to examine each factor separately in terms of percentage improvement. When all factors—labor, capital, materials, equipment, and energy—are used, the resulting measure is called *total factor productivity*. It is frequently used in making productivity comparisons such as those between companies or between time periods. In calculating multifactor and total factor productivity, all usages might also be converted to a common factor such as dollars.

profit center A separate unit or department within a company that is responsible for its own costs, *revenue,* and thus profit.

A profit center is one of the four broad types of financial responsibility used in *management control systems.* Profit center managers are generally free to make their own decisions regarding key issues such as price, *marketing,* and *product positioning.*

Profit Impact of Market Strategies (PIMS) A database designed to analyze business performance as it relates to *market* characteristics and strategies.

The database contains information on characteristics such as total size or growth and strategic measures such as *market share, research and development (R&D) costs, advertising* expenditures, breadth of *product line,* quality, and *vertical integration.* PIMS analysis can be used in a variety of situations, including estimating the value of a company's shares in different competitive situations, the likely returns from different strategic actions, and the impact of horizontal and/or vertical integration on long-term profitability.

profit margin An accounting term describing the ratio of a company's income to its sales.

There are two types of profit margin: *gross profit* margin and net profit margin. Gross profit margin shows the percentage return that a company is earning over the cost of the merchandise sold. It is calculated by dividing gross profit, or sales less *cost of goods sold,* by the total sales.

$$\frac{\text{Gross profit}}{\text{Sales}}$$

Gross profit is before outlays for *operating expenses* such as selling and administrative expenses, taxes, and interest.

Net profit margin, also called *return on sales,* shows the percentage of *net income* generated by each sales dollar. It is calculated by dividing the *income statement* figure for net income after taxes by total sales.

$$\frac{\text{Net income after taxes}}{\text{Sales}}$$

The net profit generated by a company may be held to support future operations or distributed to shareholders.

Program Evaluation Review Technique (PERT) A visual technique for planning, scheduling, analyzing, and evaluating large projects.

The PERT allows managers and employees to see (1) which tasks in a project have a direct effect on total project time and (2) how best to schedule each task in order to meet the project's deadline at minimum costs.

The PERT method is appropriate for projects that meet the following three criteria: (1) The project must consist of distinct tasks, which, when completed, mark the end of the job; (2) the individual tasks must be independent of each other and, within the sequence of the project, may be stopped and started; and (3) the individual tasks must be performed in sequence. The foundation of an office building, for instance, must be in place before the roof is put on.

The visual aspect of the PERT is a diagram showing the constituent tasks that make up a project. After identifying each task (each may be designated with a letter or some other symbol), managers list the items in sequential order and assign an appropriate length of time to each. Actually, *three* times are assigned to each task: t_o represents an *optimistic* estimate, t_m is the *most likely* estimate, and t_p is a *pessimistic* estimate or worst-case scenario for completing the task.

EXAMPLE: Managers at a foundry must install a particle scrubber system to meet environmental requirements and avoid fines levied by the Environmental Protection Agency. They determine the following eight tasks and assign optimal, expected, and pessimistic times to each:

Activity	Task	Preceding tasks	t_o	t_m	t_p
			\multicolumn{3}{c}{Times (in weeks)}
A	Purchase components	—	1	3	5
B	Reinforce floor and modify roof	—	2	3	4
C	Fabricate collection stack	A	3	5	8
D	Build frame	B	1	2	3
E	Modify scrubber	C	1	2	8
F	Control panel	C	2	4	12
G	Install scrubber	D, E	1	2	3
H	Inspect and test	F, G	1	2	3

The next step in the process is to develop the network to see the relationships among these activities. Note that because tasks A and B have no preceding events, they and their subsequent tasks can be undertaken concurrently, as represented in the diagram by parallel lines of activities:

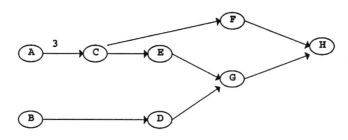

The PERT Method

The next step is to determine the average or mean times for each activity by using the following formula:

$$\text{Mean (expected) time } t_e = \frac{t_o + 4t_m + t_p}{6}$$

After these times are computed, the next step is to calculate the *critical path*, the longest path through the network. In the example, managers identify three paths: A-C-F-H, A-C-E-G-H, and B-D-G-H. When they compare these three, they find that the longest path, A-C-F-H, takes 15.17 weeks of effort.

After determining the longest path, managers next calculate the variance of individual tasks along the critical path. They use the following formula:

$$\text{Variance } \sigma^2 = \left[\frac{(t_p - t_o)}{6} \right]^2$$

The results are shown in the following table:

Activity	Mean time	On critical path?	Variance
A	3	yes	16/36
B	3	no	—
C	5.17	yes	25/36
D	2	no	—
E	2.83	no	—
F	5	yes	100/36
G	2	no	—
H	2	yes	4/36
	Total		145/36

The total of the variances is 145/36 or 4.03. Because the *standard deviation* (σ) is the square root of the variance, the managers are able to calculate σ as 2.007 weeks. Rounded off, this calculation comes to 2.0 weeks. Given that this project will consume 15.17 weeks on average, managers can predict with some statistical certainty that the chance of completing it in 17.17 weeks (that is, the mean plus one standard deviation) is 68 percent. Two standard deviations would give 4.0 weeks; thus, the time to completion would equal 19.17 weeks in 95 percent of the instances.

If this example is considered a PERT problem, the managers can use simpler computations. Adding up the mean times for the three paths, they produce the following analysis:

$$\text{A-C-F-H} = 14 \text{ weeks}$$

$$\text{A-C-E-G-H} = 14 \text{ weeks}$$

$$\text{B-D-G-H} = 9 \text{ weeks}$$

Since the project takes 14 weeks, any activities along the last path B-D-G-H can be delayed up to 5 weeks and all activities can still be completed on time. For instance, activity B can start up to 5 weeks after A has begun, and the paths will still converge on time without creating **bottlenecks.**

projected benefit obligation (PBO)   The *present value,* as calculated by an actuary, of the future amount owed by a company to its *pension plan* on the basis of future service and compensation levels.

See also **accumulated benefit obligation** (*ABO*).

prototype   A working model of a product designed for use in many testing areas.
Prototypes can take a number of forms, from a computer simulation to a full-scale working model.

EXAMPLE: General Motors developed several prototypes of an electric car it called the Impact. One was a clay model that was used in wind tunnel tests to determine the car's air drag; another was a complete working model that was tested at the company's Motor Technical Center in Warren, Michigan.

PSA   *See public-service advertisement*

psychographic segmentation   The division of a *market* into segments based on how consumers live, as reflected by their values, attitudes, and interests.
In researching lifestyle patterns, marketers focus on consumer activities and opinions.

EXAMPLE: Carmakers are turning to emotion-based *advertising* in a big way in an attempt to change customers' perceptions of their brands. And since *baby boomers* account for 65 percent of the new-car market as well as the lion's share of luxury-car sales, it is crucial that marketers understand the motivations of this over-40 age group.

In 1997, Strategic Directions Group randomly selected 3,000 of them for a psychographic segmentation study on car-buying habits. By analyzing the consumers' core values and their beliefs about themselves and about car uses, the researchers were able to divide the respondents into four groups: Accessorized Americans, Stylish Fun, Reliables, and Uninvolved.

And how did the various carmakers fare with each group? It seems that GM cars appeal equally to the Stylish Fun segment and those who are Uninvolved, while Lincoln drivers break down about equally as Accessorized Americans and members of the Stylish Fun crowd. Saturns appealed equally to the Reliables and the Uninvolved. Ford and Dodge owners are scattered about equally over all the segments, but Toyotas definitely appeal more to the Reliables.

And as for the luxury-car market, the affluent Stylish Fun were far and away the biggest group (Why we kick 1997).

*See also **behavioral segmentation; demographic segmentation; market segmentation; volume segmentation**.*

public limited company (PLC)   Under the 1985 Companies Act in Great Britain, a public company must so identify itself or use the acronym "PLC."
The acronym is roughly equivalent to the abbreviation "Inc." for "incorporated."

public relations (PR)   A form of communication designed to increase public understanding and acceptance of a product, service, or company.
Public relations personnel usually take advantage of nonpaid channels of communication by issuing news releases. This technique gives public relations campaigns an air of legitimacy that paid *advertising* frequently lacks. Most PR campaigns deal with broad issues rather than specific products or services. Besides press releases, PR departments use tools such as speeches, employee training seminars, and public-service activities to achieve their goals. Corporate sponsorship of

U.S. Olympic athletes is a well-known public-service activity devised by PR departments. The downside is that communications cannot be controlled by the company.

Many public relations campaigns are mounted to counter negative images that arise from unfavorable information or news about a company's product or **brand.** Adverse publicity has taken its toll on a number of companies and industries in recent years, among them: the beef industry, which suffered from the scare brought on by mad cow disease in Europe; the Chrysler Corporation, which had to deal with consumers panicked over news that the rear door on its big-selling Caravan and Voyager minivans was prone to fly open in rear-end collisions; and contaminated fruit and vegetable imports from South America.

EXAMPLE: Children's health problems are ranked as one of the worst things that can happen to a company, so shudders ran down the corporate spine of the makers of Odwalla juices when *E. coli* bacteria were found in the product. Sixty-one people became sick, and one child died in the outbreak that began in the fall of 1996.

To counter the negative publicity and save the Half Moon Bay, California, juice maker from collapse, Odwalla, Inc., president Greg Steltenpohl and his staff embarked on a public relations offensive that included a new crisis-communications tool: the Internet. After quickly holding a press conference to announce a recall of all products containing unpasteurized apple juice, the company set up an Internet site to serve as the public face of Odwalla's response to the crisis and to link anxious consumers to other health-related Web sites that could provide answers and information about the risks and treatments for *E. Coli*–related illnesses (Rapaport 1997).

See also *financial public relations.*

publicly held company   A corporation with shares outstanding that are owned by the general public.

Ownership is conferred by the purchase of some form of *capital stock* offered for sale on a public exchange. Publicly held companies must file their *financial statements* with the *Securities and Exchange Commission* (*SEC*).

See also *privately held company.*

public-service advertisement (PSA)   An advertisement with a message that focuses on the public good.

Most public-service advertising is sponsored by nonprofit organizations and is printed or broadcast using donated space or time. Organizations such as the United Way and the American Red Cross have sponsored a number of public-service advertising campaigns.

EXAMPLE: UNICEF unveiled the first global public-service campaign designed to focus on children's rights. Called "Cartoons for Children's Rights," the first of 100 public-service announcements were to be delivered to participating broadcasters early in 1998. Top animators from more than 25 countries joined to focus attention on a child's right have viable health care, an education, and life free of war, sexual abuse, homelessness, and poverty (UNICEF 1997).

pull strategy   A *marketing* approach in which the manufacturer promotes the product directly to consumers in the hope that they will request, or pull, it from *distribution channel* members.

With this approach, the flow of *demand* for a product is backward: Consumers put pressure on the intermediaries to carry it. Manufacturers of packaged goods often use this strategy. Heavy promotional spending by companies such as General Foods, Procter & Gamble, and General Mills pulls their products through the distribution system. The pull strategy is most effective when the product is readily differentiated from others, appeals to the mass market, and carries a low price.

*See also **push strategy.***

purchase method   A way of accounting for a ***business combination*** that treats the ***assets*** of the ***subsidiary company*** as if the parent company had purchased them in an ***arm's-length transaction.***

The purchase method is used when any of the 12 conditions required for the ***pooling of interests*** method are not met.

Under the purchase method, the assets and ***liabilities*** of the newly acquired subsidiary are transferred to the parent company's books at their fair market value as of the date of ***acquisition.*** If the subsidiary's purchase price is greater than the fair market value of its assets, the excess is considered ***goodwill.*** Goodwill must be identified as an asset on the parent company's ***balance sheet*** and amortized over a period not to exceed 40 years.

*See also **amortization.***

purchasing   In manufacturing, those activities that relate to the acquisition of goods and services needed to support all aspects of the production of finished products and plant operation.

purchasing, high and low involvement   The degree of mental effort expended by consumers in deciding to buy a product.

Marketers have noticed that the way consumers learn depends on how much they care about or are interested in a given product. Automobile and home purchases, for instance, are important to consumers, but most purchases aren't. Cotton balls, facial tissues, toothpaste, and many other products elicit low consumer involvement.

With low-involvement products, consumers learn passively. Instead of actively seeking information so they can evaluate a product before they buy it, consumers pick up bits and pieces of data randomly. Television ads can effectively convey information to a passive audience: The medium is attention-grabbing and frequent repetition of commercials helps consumers acquire random information.

With high-involvement products, by contrast, consumers are already interested, so marketers can offer more rational and logical arguments to induce people to buy their products or ***brand.***

*See also **buying decision process; buying roles.***

push strategy   A promotional approach in which a manufacturer uses its sales force and trade promotions to actively sell a product to ***distribution channel*** members such as ***wholesalers*** and ***retailers,*** who, in turn, aggressively sell the product to consumers.

Manufacturers do not entirely ignore direct promotion to consumers when they employ a push strategy, but they pay more attention to promotion aimed at getting cooperation from distributors and retailers. A push strategy works particularly well for ***durable goods,*** high-priced items, and products with limited ***markets.***

    *See also **pull strategy.***

put option   A contract that gives the holder the right to sell an ***asset*** at a certain price before a certain date. A buyer of a put option expects that the value of the underlying asset will fall before the contract's expiration date.

    *See also **call.***

PWP   *See **plant within a plant***

Q

qualified opinion   An auditor's report of a company's *financial statements* when it fairly presents the company's financial position, results of operation, changes in financial position, or conformity with *generally accepted accounting principles* (*GAAP*) except for some particular limitation.

In other words, the auditor has been unable to obtain objective or independent evidence of a particular *transaction* or policy, or has doubts about whether the enterprise can continue as a going concern.

EXAMPLE: Although some may not find it surprising, even the Internal Revenue Service is not exempt from auditors' qualified opinions on its financial reporting. In a report prepared by Gregory M. Holloway, director of Governmentwide Audits, and submitted to the U.S. Congress by Acting Comptroller General James F. Hinchman, auditors conducting an examination of the IRS's financial statements for 1996 found the organization had failed to provide evidence of responsible record keeping to address problems that the auditors had pointed out in their 1995 report. Furthermore, the IRS could not guarantee internal controls for safeguarding *assets* from material loss and could not assure compliance with laws covering the use of budget authority. In its opening statement, the board of auditors reported that "because the IRS could not provide us with supporting documentation for its reported administrative accounts receivable balances, we cannot determine if the Statement of Administrative Financial Position's presentation of accounts receivable and net position is reliable" (Government Accounting Office Report 1997).

See also adverse opinion; unqualified opinion.

quality circle   An organized activity in which workers from different segments of a production line meet regularly to discuss and solve quality problems related to their work efforts.

Developed in Japan in the early 1960s, quality circles give employees the opportunity to provide feedback on quality issues and participate in quality problem solving. Quality circles can also serve to educate employees about the various techniques (such as statistical process control and fishbone diagrams. The overall focus of quality circles is problem solving. Although in recent years, quality circle problem solving has expanded beyond the production process to virtually all areas of company operations, the technique has declined in popularity, largely because quality circles have not produced the high-performance results of self-managed teams. Ed Lawler, a professor at University of Southern California, attributes the decline to the fact that quality circles do not actually participate in work processes, but operate in activities parallel to them (Dumaine 1994).

A number of leading U.S. companies, including Ford Motor Company, American Airlines, General Electric, and 3M, have, in the past, used quality circles. Today, it is more likely for companies to use integrated teams of highly skilled employees and managers with authority to make decisions and solve problems as they occur.

quality of earnings   In accounting, the extent to which the **net income** a company reports is sustainable in the future.

High quality of earnings often reflects conservative accounting policies. Financial ratios such as **earnings per share, current ratio,** and **inventory turnover** are all effective tools for determining a company's quality of earnings.

EXAMPLE: In an attempt to rid itself of low-yielding investments, Dime Bancorp of New York reported in 1996 that it would sell $1.4 billion in mortgage-backed **bonds** and buy back 3 million shares of **common stock,** all in the interest of improving the bank's quality of earnings (Dime 1996).

quality of work life (QWL)   Programs designed to meet the sociotechnical problems emerging in the workplace.

Effectively combining people (*socio-*) and machinery (*technical*) on the job can be a serious challenge. QWL efforts are realized in many programs such as **job enrichment, quality circles,** and empowered teams.

quantity discount   A price reduction to buyers based on the amount of product purchased.

Quantity discounts encourage customers to buy more from one seller rather than buying the same product from multiple sources. It is a competitive tool whereby the seller lowers the price based on lower production costs associated with larger production runs.

quarterly report   A financial report released every three months.

Quarterly reports usually include unaudited **balance sheets, income statements,** and **statements of cash flows,** along with an overview of the company's current business situation in the periods between its **annual reports.**

queue time   The time a person or a job has to wait before a particular facility is available.

For example, a customer might spend 15 minutes in a bank waiting for a teller to complete a transaction or five minutes waiting for an automatic teller machine to come back from a computer crash. Queue time is a factor in all businesses. In a factory, partially finished products wait to be processed; at an airport, planes queue up for takeoff.

There are two broad types of queuing systems: single stage and multiple stage. Single-stage systems have jobs lining up for a process such as making a deposit at a bank. Multiple-stage systems have a single job waiting for a series of processes. In a plant, for instance, products line up for various operations in the process. A delay at one station may back up the whole system and cause downtime for many parts of the process.

The management (and reduction) of queue time is an important issue for many companies. This is why the rule is, "feed the bottlenecks." Operations that are **bot-**

tlenecks should always be running at ***capacity.*** Adding or reducing service facilities can effectively control queue time during rush hours or slow periods, as in the grocery store that opens or closes checkout clerks to handle customer demand. In some businesses, queue time can be controlled by separating customers into homogeneous groups.

Reducing psychological queuing time can also be an effective means of improving a queuing system. For instance, most physicians' offices provide reading material to keep patients entertained or distracted while they wait. The physician is the bottleneck and the ***revenue*** producer, so the physician is never idle.

R

R&D *See research and development costs*

rate card A brochure that details the costs for ***advertising*** on or in a particular communications medium.

Rate cards are available from any newspaper, magazine, television station, or radio station.

rate of return The annual percentage of income earned on an ***investment.***

There are dozens of ways to calculate rate of return depending on the type of investment (***bond,*** stock, real estate, operating ***assets***), the purpose of the investment (income generation, ***capital gains,*** operating ***efficiency***), and the maturity of the investment (short, intermediate, or long term).

The rate of return on fixed-income securities is typically calculated as the current yield—that is, the annual interest or ***dividend*** payments divided by the price of the security. ***Yield to maturity*** is also frequently used, especially for determining the rate of return for business valuation purposes.

The rate of return on common shares is usually calculated as the annual dividend divided by the purchase price per share (called the *dividend yield*). The return may also include the appreciation gain (actual or expected) realized upon the sale of the shares (called *total return*).

A variety of rates of return are utilized in the analysis of the financial performance of companies (called *ratio analysis*). The most popular include ***return on investment,*** return on equity, return on total assets, and return on sales. All of these ratios are calculated by dividing the income over a period of time (usually one year) by the average investment for the period.

Internally, companies use the internal rate of return in the capital budgeting process to weight the cost/benefit of "make-versus-buy" or "buy-versus-lease" decisions for financing capital equipment additions.

raw materials inventory The raw materials on hand at either the beginning or the end of an ***accounting period.***

Raw materials inventory represents items that will be components of manufactured goods. The ending balance for a given accounting period is reported on the ***balance sheet.*** Raw materials inventory is also used in the calculation of ***cost of goods sold*** on the ***income statement.***

*See also **finished goods inventory; inventory forms; work-in-process inventory.***

reach   The number of people exposed to a specific advertisement at least once during a particular time period.

If 80 percent of the *target market* will see or hear an ad, it is said to have wide reach. *Advertising* with a wide reach, such as a commercial on a very popular television show or an ad in a widely read magazine, can be effective in situations where (1) a company is introducing a new product, (2) a product is purchased infrequently, and (3) the target market is not clearly defined.

realized gain or loss   In accounting, the difference between the *book value* of an *asset* and the amount received from its sale.

Realized gains and losses are reported on the *income statement* (usually as an element of taxable income). Occasionally, a company can report a realized loss even when there has been no sale. For example, when a long-term *investment* permanently declines in value, the value of the investment should be written on the *balance sheet* and the amount of the decline in value should be reported as a realized loss on the income statement.

See also **conservatism.**

reasonableness test   A method of evaluating accounting information.

EXAMPLE: A company's current travel and entertainment expenses might be compared with those of previous years, the expenses reported by competitors, or industry norms. If the travel and entertainment expenses are comparatively high, they might not appear reasonable and should be investigated.

rebate   A price refund or reduction the manufacturer gives to a consumer after the purchase of a product.

Rebates are frequently used in the automobile industry to increase sales at the end of a model year and make room for new models.

recapitalization   The revision to a company's capital structure.

Recapitalizations may involve the exchange of debt obligations for equity interests (an increasingly common tactic for cash-poor companies).

Recapitalizations may also involve the exchange of one type of debt security for another, such as convertible *debentures* to *bonds.* Under certain circumstances, it makes sense to recapitalize by trading *preferred stock* for common or common shares for preferred.

Although *bankruptcy* reorganizations tend to be the major incentive for companies to recapitalize, a variety of other reasons could trigger the action. Three of the most common are:

- Reducing debt service to allow for additional borrowings
- Cleaning up a *balance sheet* prior to a *merger* or sale of the company
- Increasing tax deductions by substituting interest payments for *dividends*

receivables   In accounting, any money due a company from customers or others.

Receivables are classified on the *balance sheet* as trade receivables and nontrade receivables. Trade receivables are due from customers for products or services and are either *accounts receivable* or *notes receivable.* Nontrade receivables include advances to employees, expected insurance settlements, *dividends* receivable, and interest receivable. All receivables are classified as either current (due within one year or the normal operating cycle of the business) or non-current (due within more than one year or more than one normal operating cycle).

reference group   In *marketing,* the group that serves as a reference point when an individual evaluates his or her purchasing behavior.

Primary groups are small and intimate enough to allow all members to communicate with one another face to face. Examples of primary groups include one's family, a group of close social friends, and coworkers. Larger, less intimate secondary groups—trade unions, religious organizations, and professional associations, for instance—also influence consumer behavior.

The products or *brands* that are visible in social settings or consumed conspicuously are more heavily influenced by reference groups than other, less noticeable products. Reference groups, for example, probably do not play much of a role when a person chooses a desk lamp, but the groups' members notice, evaluate, and influence a consumer when it comes to buying a set of golf clubs.

*See also **buying roles; opinion leaders.***

regional banks   Large banks such as Mellon, First Chicago, Norwest, and Crocker, that function regionally in a fashion similar to *money center banks* at the national level.

Federal and state laws prohibiting interstate banking encouraged the growth of banks to meet the needs of large regional businesses. Within the last decade, however, legislation in several states has allowed these banks to expand statewide and to acquire banks in other states. Large regional banks have also become involved in foreign loans and many have staffed multinational personnel to handle international accounts. Regional banks serve as correspondents for smaller local banks in the same way that money center banks act as correspondents for regional banks.

regression analysis   A statistical technique used to show how a dependent variable relates to one or more independent variables or predictors.

Once the relationship is determined, it can serve as a model for making predictions. The relationship itself is often expressed as a *regression equation* in the form $Y = a + bX + e$, where Y is the dependent variable, X is a vector of independent variables, a is a constant, and e designates a term for random error (Brigham and Gapenski 1994, 200). If a manager wants to measure, for instance, the degree of satisfaction (the dependent variable) the members of a sales force have when their pay (the independent variable) increases or decreases, he or she might think in terms of the regression equation to predict how people would react if a system of rewards and bonuses were introduced.

Roberts and Chonko (1996) conducted studies on the relationship between salespeople's satisfaction with their pay and their intentions to look for another job. Not surprisingly, they found that as pay decreased, the salespeople became more intent on finding work elsewhere; thus, the study revealed an inverse relationship between the two variables.

EXAMPLE: The management of a department store is considering a move into a new location and uses regression analysis to help it select the best site. It wants to see if it can predict store sales (the dependent variable) by some of the characteristics, such as age, income, and education of the population (the independent variables) of each possible location. The data for each of the independent variables is fed into a computer, which performs the mathematical process of a regression and produces this equation:

$$\text{Sales} = \$500 + 2(\text{age}) + 4(\text{income}) + 3(\text{education})$$

The regression shows that there is a positive relationship between the age, income, and education of a population and store sales. In other words, a store located in a community whose population has a high income, is older, and has a higher level of education will have more sales than a store located in an area with lower levels of these characteristics.

Regulation A   A regulation established by the **Securities and Exchange Commission (SEC)** that allows small companies to make a public stock issue—called a *direct public offering (DPO)*—of up to $5 million in any 12-month period.

Regulation A, which originated under the Securities Act of 1933, allows a company to "test the waters," that is, investigating how much interest investors might have in such a venture without going to the expense of making the offering public. Under SEC guidelines, the regulation has a complex set of rules, the major features of which are as follows:

- The company files a *notification,* not a *registration,* statement. DPO candidates must still, however, make the same disclosure statements.
- Notification is filed with a regional SEC office, not Washington.
- An offering circular, not a full prospectus, is required, with the amount of disclosure similar to that required under an S-18. This document specifies the amount of potential risk, presents financial reports, names the company's directors, offers a history of the company, and sets forth marketing plans, products, and services.
- Uncertified *financial statements* may be used.
- It cannot be used by a company if affiliated persons or underwriters have been convicted of securities violations or postal fraud.

SOURCE: The Elysian Group, Inc. Web site: dpo@elysiangroup.com.

Regulation D   A federal securities law passed in 1992 to permit small businesses to sell up to $1 million of securities in a 12-month period and to be exempt from filing registration statements with the **Securities and Exchange Commission (SEC).**

Most states allow Regulation D filings; a few do not (as of 1998, three states did not recognize Regulation D offerings: Arizona, Nebraska, and Washington). The major provision states that security sales may be made only to "accredited" investors, who by definition fall into the following categories:

- An individual with an annual income of at least $200,000 in each of the two most recent years
- An individual investor (including spouse) with a net worth of at least $1 million
- An individual purchasing up to $150,000 of the security, as long as the investment does not exceed 20 percent of the investor's net worth
- Insiders of the issuing company—directors, executive officers, general partners

- Institutional investors (e.g., banks and insurance companies)
- Plans established by state government or their subdivisions for the benefit of their employees and that have assets in excess of $5 million, such as state employee pension funds
- Nonprofit organizations with assets exceeding $5 million
- Private business development companies defined by the Investment Advisors Act of 1940

Moreover, the issuing company must provide proof that each investor meets one of these requirements. Such proof must be in writing and attested to by the investor. Several other lesser restrictions also apply.

relationship marketing   A type of marketing in which consumers, distributors, and suppliers interact with each other personally, thereby allowing marketers an opportunity to build trusting, long-term relationships with each of them.

Most of the largest airlines now have frequent flier programs that depend on relationship marketing: Through the offer of bonus miles, an airline company encourages its customers to use the services or products of a hotel chain, a car rental agency, a restaurant, or some other company associated with travel. In another example, a catering company might establish good relationships with suppliers, thereby ensuring that it can consistently obtain the highest-quality ingredients in order to provide good meals for clients. Ideally, relationship marketing simplifies the interactions between a company, its suppliers, and its clients and creates a win-win situation where everyone involved saves time and money.

Relationship marketing recognizes the importance of building a stream of purchases over a buyer's lifetime; all contacts are made to create a perception that "we care."

EXAMPLE: In 1997, McCann-Erickson CEO and chairman John Dooner singled out relationship marketing as one of five focal points for his company's strategic planning and future initiatives. In October of that year, the network of ***advertising agencies*** formed a new relationship marketing unit with Scherer Team, one of the largest advertising concerns in Germany (McCann's 1997).

remanufacturing   In manufacturing, the process of restoring worn-out products to acceptable, resellable condition.

Remanufacturing is distinct from repairing or rebuilding a product in that a remanufactured product is considered to be equal in quality to brand-new. The U.S. Congress voted to award the Rochester Institute of Technology in New York over $2 million to help the Pentagon and private industry learn how to remanufacture products, particularly military vehicles and systems. The U.S. Department of Defense, with its private-industry suppliers, is the largest remanufacturer in the world (Machacek 1997).

EXAMPLE: Kodak remanufactures its single-use camera after the customer takes pictures and returns the camera to the manufacturer. Up to 85 percent of the original parts can be reused, in order to produce a new camera (Machacek 1997).

EXAMPLE: Safari-Kar International, located in San Bernardino, California, remanufactures Jeeps that the U.S. Postal Service has used for its deliveries. The vehicles are returned to their mint condition, and even their odometers are reset to 00000, a practice that the National Highway Traffic Safety Administration has approved. Safari-Kar now sells these "new" vehicles for about $6,500 each, making them formidable competitors in the sports utility vehicle market (Remanufactured Jeeps 1995).

repeat rate   The number of times a person buys a product within a specified period of time.

    The repeat rate for microwave popcorn, for example, is higher than for deodorant because the popcorn is consumed more quickly. Repeat rates are an important tool in evaluating new products and their *marketing* campaigns. A high repeat rate after a product launch with little *advertising* indicates that any additional advertising should produce much higher sales. A low repeat rate indicates that the product might need heavier promotion—or that it is a failure.

replacement cost   In accounting, the current cost of replacing an existing *asset.*

    EXAMPLE: If a company purchased a truck for $20,000 five years ago, its replacement cost today might be $30,000.

repurchase agreement   A short-term *investment,* also called a *repo* or *RP,* that serves as an alternative to *commercial paper,* certificates of deposit, or Treasury bills.

    Banks sell repos under an agreement to buy back the security at a specified price. The buyback date may be fixed or open and subject to call at any time. Typically, repos are collateralized with U.S. Treasury securities, making investment risk virtually zero. This enables banks to pay *interest rates* below the current market rate.

research and development (R&D) costs   In accounting, the cost of developing new knowledge and incorporating that knowledge into a new product.

    Generally, R&D costs are considered as expenses in any given *accounting period.* However, there are two cases in which they can be capitalized and treated as *assets:* (1) the purchase of materials and equipment for use in development and (2) the purchase of intangibles, such as patents and thus *copyrights.*

    One prominent exception is the computer software industry, which has been exempted from these rules because the research and development process is its primary activity. Computer software development companies are permitted to capitalize all R&D costs as soon as they develop a marketable *prototype.* However, all further development costs associated with a new product must be expensed as incurred.

research validity, external   A criterion by which a research project is evaluated.

    External validity hinges on whether the results of a research project can be generalized to an entire population.

    EXAMPLE: A detergent company conducts an experiment to test a new package design in which volunteer shoppers purchase detergents in an artificial store setting. The results, however, may fail to predict shoppers' responses to the new packaging in a real store. In other words, the study lacks external research validity.

    Compare to **research validity, internal.**

research validity, internal   A criterion by which a research project is evaluated. Internal validity depends on the consistency of the various procedures and methods used in a research project.

EXAMPLE: If several different questionnaires were used in a citywide survey, chances are good that the results of each questionnaire would be slightly different and the research would lack internal validity.

Compare to **research validity, external.**

reseller market   Individuals and companies that procure goods in order to rent or sell them to others at a profit.

The reseller market is a subset of the **industrial market.** Most **wholesalers** and **retailers** are resellers.

EXAMPLE: A supermarket operates in the reseller market when it buys food from producers across the country, places it all under one roof, and offers it for sale.

response rate   The percentage of responses generated by a **direct marketing** campaign.

If an insurance company sends 1 million fliers to potential customers and receives 30,000 phone calls about its offer, the response rate is 3 percent (30,000 divided by 1 million). Usually the response rate for any direct mail marketing campaign does not top 5 percent. **Telemarketing** and personal selling can attain much higher response rates.

response time   The time required to produce a product or service.

A rapid response time gives an important competitive edge, both in terms of customer service and expansion into new products or **markets.** A National Science Foundation study of the American and Japanese robotics industries, for instance, showed that Japanese firms are about 25 percent faster than their American counterparts in the development of new robots. The study also found that Japanese robotics companies tend to spend about 10 percent less in the development and **marketing** of new robots. The main difference between the American and Japanese firms was that the Japanese spent five times more than the Americans in the development of more efficient production methods, whereas the Americans spent more money and time on marketing.

retailer   Any company or individual that sells merchandise to a final consumer.

Retail sales are highest for food stores, followed by car dealerships, department stores, gasoline stations, restaurants, and bars. Retailers vary enormously in size. The number of employees can be as few as one, as with a small shop with a single owner, or as many as 500,000, as in the case of Sears, Roebuck and Company.

EXAMPLE: Federated Department Stores, Inc., was formed in 1929 as a holding company for Filene's F&R Lazarus, and Abraham & Straus and Shillito's. Bloomingdale's joined the group soon thereafter. The company moved to Cincinnati in 1945 and later added Macy's, Stern's, and others, to become the largest retailer in the United States (Madore 1997).

retained earnings   The total earnings of a company, less **dividends,** since its inception.

Retained earnings are reported in the ***stockholders' equity*** section of the ***balance sheet*** and calculated as follows: Take the unadjusted beginning balance and add (or subtract if a loss) prior period adjustments to determine the adjusted beginning balance; then add ***net income*** and subtract dividends to obtain the ending balance.

return on assets (ROA)   *See **return on investment***

return on equity (ROE)   *See **return on investment***

return on investment (ROI)   In accounting, a measure of the earning power of a company's ***assets.***

A high return on investments is desirable. ROI is broadly defined as ***net income*** divided by investments. However, the term ***investments*** has three distinct interpretations in financial analysis, each of which leads to a different calculation of return on investment: return on assets, return on ***owners' equity,*** and return on invested ***capital.***

Return on assets (ROA) is calculated by dividing net income after taxes by average total assets (average total assets is found by adding the ending balance of total assets for the previous year with the ending balance of total assets for the current year and dividing by two).

$$\frac{\text{Net income after tax}}{\text{Average total assets}}$$

ROA shows how much a company has earned on the investment of all the funds, including ***current liabilities, noncurrent liabilities,*** and owners' equity committed to the company. Because ROA does not discriminate among the various sources of investment funds, it is frequently used by top management to evaluate the performances of various divisions within a company. This allows equal comparison between divisions that have control over their assets, but little say in how those assets are financed.

Return on invested capital (ROIC) shows how well a company has used the funds given to it for a relatively long period of time. Invested capital equals noncurrent liabilities plus shareholders' equity. ROIC is calculated by dividing net income after taxes by the sum of noncurrent liabilities and ***stockholders' equity.***

$$\frac{\text{Net income after tax}}{\text{Noncurrent liabilities + stockholders' equity}}$$

Some companies use ROIC to evaluate divisional performance. This is appropriate only in situations where divisional managers have significant impact on asset purchases, inventory levels, ***credit*** policies, and cash management.

Return on owners' equity (ROE) measures the return that a company has earned on the funds invested by shareholders. The ratio is calculated by dividing net income after taxes by stockholders' equity.

$$\frac{\text{Net income after tax}}{\text{Stockholders' equity}}$$

Present and prospective stockholders frequently use ROE, although it is also employed by management, which is responsible for operating the business in the best interests of its owners.

EXAMPLE:

CONSOLIDATED BALANCE SHEET
HEWLETT-PACKARD COMPANY AND SUBSIDIARIES
October 31
(In millions except par value and number of shares)

	1997	1996
ASSETS		
Current assets		
Cash and cash equivalents	$ 3,072	$ 2,885
Short-term investments	1,497	442
Accounts and notes receivable	8,173	7,126
Inventories:		
Finished goods	4,136	3,956
Purchased parts and fabricated assemblies	2,627	2,445
Other current assets	1,442	1,137
Total current assets	$20,947	$17,991
Property, plant, and equipment:		
Land	$468	$475
Buildings and leasehold improvements	4,672	4,257
Machinery and equipment	6,636	5,466
	11,776	10,198
Accumulated depreciation	(5,464)	(4,662)
	6,312	5,536
Long-term investments and other assets	4,490	4,172
Total assets	$31,749	$27,699
LIABILITIES AND SHAREHOLDERS' EQUITY		
Current liabilities:		
Notes payable and short-term borrowings	$ 1,226	$ 2,125
Accounts payable	3,185	2,375
Employee compensation and benefits	1,723	1,675
Taxes on earnings	1,515	1,514
Deferred revenues	1,152	951
Other accrued liabilities	2,418	1,983
Total current liabilities	$11,219	$10,623
Long-term debt	3,158	2,579
Other liabilities	1,217	1,059
Commitments and contingencies		
Shareholders' equity:		
Preferred stock, $1 par value		
(authorized: 300,000,000 shares; issued: none)		
Common stock and capital in excess of $1 par value		
(authorized: 2,400,000,000 shares; issued and outstanding:		
1,041,042,000 in 1997 and 1,014,123,000 in 1996)	1,187	1,014
Retained earnings	14,968	12,424
Total shareholders' equity	16,155	13,438
Total liabilities and shareholders' equity	31,749	27,699

NOTE: The preceding table is for illustrative purposes only and omits necessary notes that accompany the financial statements. For complete details, see the 1997 Annual Report of the Hewlett-Packard Company.

revenue   Gross income received before any deductions for expenses, discounts, returns, and so on.

Revenue is also called *sales* in most companies. A much less common usage refers to interest income, ***dividends,*** royalties, refunds, and claim settlements as revenue. Generally, however, each type of income carries its own designation—sales, income, fees, claims, and so on.

revenue recognition   In accounting, the process of recording ***revenue.***

Most companies recognize revenue at the time of sale, regardless of when cash will be received. When revenue is recognized, related expenses must be matched to it within that ***accounting period*** (see ***matching concept***). Many service businesses use ***cash basis accounting,*** which allows them to recognize revenue only when cash is received. However, this method is not considered a ***generally accepted accounting principle*** (***GAAP***).

See also ***cash basis accounting; percentage-of-completion method; successful efforts method.***

reverse split   A procedure whereby ***corporations*** buy back a portion of their outstanding stock, thereby increasing the value of each remaining share outstanding while simultaneously reducing the number of shares.

The main reason companies engage in such a maneuver is to raise the price of their traded shares prior to entering into ***mergers,*** business ***acquisitions,*** or ***joint ventures*** (***JVs***), or as a preliminary step to making a new stock issue.

EXAMPLE: Atrix International (NASDAQ symbol: ATXI) announced a one-for-four reverse split in 1997 in order to lift its stock price above the minimum $1.00 bid requirement set by the ***NASDAQ Stock Exchange*** for listing small ***capitalization*** companies. The move reduces the number of shares of ***common stock*** from about 5.7 million to about 1.4 million (Atrix 1997).

reverse takeover   In corporate finance, a situation in which a small company, in an effort to expand rapidly, takes over a much larger company.

Reverse takeovers are usually financed by stocks, ***junk bonds,*** and other securities designed to raise a lot of cash over a short period of time.

reward systems   The types of rewards within an organization.

There are a number of different types of rewards that can be offered or received within a company, and they can be divided into two basic categories: intrinsic rewards and extrinsic rewards. Intrinsic rewards are related to the pleasure that a person feels while on the job. Examples include being able to participate in ***decision making,*** receiving more interesting work assignments, being given opportunities for personal growth, and receiving more responsibility. Extrinsic rewards involve the environment that surrounds the work itself. The most obvious extrinsic reward is compensation, or salary. Extrinsic rewards can be further divided into direct compensation and indirect compensation. Examples of direct compensation include bonuses, profit sharing, and overtime. Examples of indirect compensation include paid vacations, tuition reimbursement, and health insurance.

The distribution of rewards can be viewed in terms of the individual, the group, or the organization. There is a great deal of latitude between the three levels, but it is generally felt that if rewards are to be directly linked to performance, they should be given on the individual level.

EXAMPLE: General Motors and the United Auto Workers agreed on a unique rewards system for autoworkers at GM's Saturn plant in Tennessee. The system is based largely on levels of acceptable risk and lower base wages for employees. When the plant opened in 1992, Saturn workers accepted base wages at approximately 95 percent of what other GM workers were being paid for the same skills and work. The remaining 5 percent was "at risk," to be determined by sales and profitability. In 1992, each worker received approximately $1,800, an amount determined by the profitability of the assembly plant. In 1997, the rewards system became even riskier: The base wage was approximately 88 percent of the amount paid to other GM employees, whereas 12 percent was at risk. About $2,100 was paid out in that year.

In both 1995 and 1996, Saturn workers in Tennessee were delighted to see their paychecks increased by some $10,000 each year, as a result of those risky reward systems (Bohl 1997).

rollout market entry   A strategy for new-product introduction in which a product is sequentially launched in a number of different geographic areas over an extended period of time.

Rolling out spreads the substantial costs of a new-product launch over a longer period of time and provides an opportunity to fine-tune the *marketing mix* as the rollout progresses.

rough-cut capacity planning   A method of examining the *bottleneck* areas in a manufacturing process to determine if sufficient *capacity* is available to meet a production schedule.

The basic idea behind rough-cut capacity planning is that if sufficient capacity is available in the bottleneck areas, more than sufficient capacity will be available in the nonbottleneck areas.

Rule 147—Intrastate Offering   A federal securities regulation that applies to stock offerings within a company's state of residence.

To qualify for an intrastate exemption, all securities must be offered and sold to persons residing within the state in which the issuing company is incorporated and in which it does a significant portion of its business. These securities, once issued, must remain in the state. The instructions do not govern how these provisions should be monitored, however, just that issuers are held responsible.

Rule 147 does not impose any maximum amount on the offering or on the number of investors. The nonsolicitation rules of Regulation D do not apply either. It should be noted that Rule 147 is a federal regulation and relates only to federal offering requirements. This does not mean that intrastate offerings are exempt from state regulations. Nearly all states have their own sets of disclosure and other requirements that must be met. Although some have adopted common regulations, most remain unique.

To meet the federal compliance requirements under Rule 147,

- The issuing company must reside in the state or territory in which the private placement is made.

- The issuing company must do business in the state in which all offering solicitations and sales are made. "Doing business" is defined as follows: (1) At least 80 percent of gross revenues is received from sales within the state, (2) at least 80 percent of the issuing company's assets are located within the state, and (3) at least 80 percent of the offering must be used within the state.
- All investors to whom securities have been solicited or sold must be residents of the state.
- Resale of securities is restricted to residents of the state; this restriction is noted on the face of the stock certificate.
- No sales of securities can be made within six months before or after the offering.

runout method   A method of estimating how quickly an *inventory* will be depleted. Runout time is calculated by dividing the remaining amount of inventory by the rate at which it is used (demand rate):

$$\frac{\text{Inventory remaining}}{\text{Demand rate}} = \text{runout time}$$

See also **critical ratio analysis.**

S corporation (Subchapter S corporation) A tax strategy that permits certain qualifying **corporations** to elect to be taxed as **partnerships.**

Since S corporations have no legal standing, all laws, regulations, and restrictions bearing on C corporations apply here as well. The only significant difference is in the tax treatment of corporate earnings and distributions.

For tax purposes, all income and losses of a corporation pass through to its shareholders, retain the same character as they had in the corporation, and are reported on individual Form 1040 tax returns. Such a pass-through must be in the same proportion as each shareholder's stock holdings bear to the total shares outstanding. Except in the case of a C corporation converting to an S corporation, with the potential for being liable for tax under the *built-in gains* provisions, the corporation is not taxed.

To qualify for S status, a corporation and its shareholders must meet the following criteria:

1. The corporation must be a domestic corporation and not part of an affiliated group of corporations.
2. The corporation cannot own 80 percent or more of the stock of another corporation.
3. The corporation may not have more than 35 shareholders, with a husband and wife treated as a single shareholder.
4. Nonresident aliens are not permitted to be shareholders.
5. All shareholders must be individuals, estates, or certain defined trusts. They cannot be corporations or partnerships.
6. An S corporation may have no more than one class of stock issued and outstanding. All shares must bear the same rights relative to profits and **assets** of the corporation, except that stock may be segregated into voting and nonvoting shares for the purpose of establishing employee incentive stock option plans.

EXAMPLE: Your S corporation employs three key managers who have expressed an interest in obtaining an **equity** share of the business. But you, as principal shareholder, do not want to share voting powers. As an employee incentive, your company could award nonvoting shares of **common stock.** These shares would be subject to an agreement that if an employee leaves the company, these shares must be sold back to the company at a predetermined price, perhaps **book value** or book value plus a small premium. Not only do key managers get a financial stake in the business, but also knowing what the buyback price will be should motivate them to help increase the company's book value.

An election to be taxed as an S corporation must be filed on IRS Form 2553, within 75 days of the beginning of the year to which the election applies. All shareholders of the corporation must agree to the election and so affirm on the application. The S election terminates when any event occurs that would have made the corporation ineligible in the first place. The termination date is the date the event occurs.

The deduction of S corporation losses by shareholders is limited by

- The adjusted stock basis, as defined for each shareholder
- At-risk rules
- Passive activity loss (PAL) rules

S-1 registration   A document filed with the **Securities and Exchange Commission (SEC)** that details the specific purpose of a proposed public offering of securities.

Although the S-1 is used by most companies, and in fact must be used by those companies not qualifying under "simplified registrations" such as the S-18 or Regulation A, it is the most complex and requires the most extensive disclosure. It also requires three years of audited **financial statements.**

SEC regulations identify exactly what items must be included and how financial statistics must be displayed. In addition to a variety of minor items, the following major topics must be included:

1. The name of the registrant, the title and the amount of securities being offered, and the date; an estimate of the minimum/maximum range of offering price and number of shares; the share price to the public; **underwriting** discounts and **commission;** proceeds to the issuer or other persons; and notices about stabilization of offering price

2. A statement of whether any securities being registered are from current stockholders, the names of these security holders, their relationship with the company, and the number of shares owned before and after the offering

3. An estimate of risk factors (those factors that make the issue speculative or of high risk) and the ratio of earnings to fixed charges

4. Use of proceeds and any dilution of shareholder interest

5. The company's **dividend** policy, including its dividend history, policies currently followed, restrictions on dividend payments (if any), a statement of whether future earnings are to be reinvested in the company rather than paid out in dividends, and a description of the company's debt and **equity** position (its **capitalization**) before and after the offering

6. A management discussion and analysis that provides enough information for investors to analyze the company's **cash flow** position

7. A business description that discloses everything an investor needs to know to make an informed judgment about investing in the shares

8. Disclosure of all pertinent information about directors, officers, and key employees

9. Company financial statements and the related **audit opinion** certificate

S-18 registration   A simplified registration, specifically designed for smaller companies, that can be used by any U.S. or Canadian companies not subject to continuous reporting requirements of their respective countries (except investment companies and certain insurance companies).

The total stock offering in any 12-month period cannot exceed $7.5 million. Under this simplified version, the differences from the standard S-1 registration are these:

1. An audited **balance sheet** for one year rather than three
2. **Income statements** and statements of changes in financial condition for the past two years instead of three
3. No management discussion or analyses of financial condition and no selected financial data section

safety stock   *See **buffer stock***

sale/leaseback   A **transaction** whereby a company sells some or all of its hard **assets** to a leasing company for cash and then leases them back over a period of time.

A sale/leaseback is a popular mechanism for raising immediate **capital** against hard asset collateral while still maintaining control over the assets. This technique continues to be especially popular with companies that have a hard time raising new bank **credit** because of either overleveraged **balance sheets** or poor credit ratings.

Manufacturing businesses with substantial amounts of machinery and equipment and older hotels that need cash infusions for remodeling or for new appointments are the main users of this technique. Leases can be structured to include all equipment, furniture, and certain building fixtures, such as a central air-conditioning system. These operating leases stay open-ended, allowing the lessee to add and delete assets at will without rewriting the lease. When an asset needs replacing, the lessor merely buys the new asset and adds its rental payment to the existing lease.

The biggest disadvantage in equipment sale/leaseback arrangements, other than losing the value of owned assets for future collateral, is the very high rental payments required by lessors. Since many companies going this route have poor bank credit ratings and a sale/leaseback presents their last chance to raise capital, lessors price the leases accordingly.

Sale/leasebacks are also popular for real property. Because real property tends to appreciate rather than depreciate over time, very often the lease value of a building far exceeds its existing mortgage.

The sale/leaseback technique for commercial and industrial buildings is not restricted to companies with poor credit ratings or those that cannot raise capital elsewhere. For example, assume a company took out a 20-year mortgage for 80 percent of a building's value. It has made mortgage payments for 10 years, and the mortgage balance has decreased 30 percent.

If the property has risen in value 3 percent per year, its **market value** today is 38 percent higher than when the mortgage was placed. By combining a 30 percent decrease in the mortgage loan with a 38 percent increase in the asset's market value, an **equity** increase of over 40 percent results. For a property originally worth $100,000, a sale/leaseback would result in a cash infusion of $82,000!

sales promotions   According to the ***American Marketing Association (AMA),*** those ***marketing*** activities, other than personal selling, ***advertising,*** and publicity, that stimulate consumers to buy and that boost dealer effectiveness. Annual expenditures for these activities, which have become increasingly important in recent years, now top total spending on advertising.

Sales promotional tools fall into three broad categories: consumer promotion, trade promotion, and sales force promotion. Consumer promotions are targeted directly to potential customers and can include coupons, contests and prizes, rebates, samples, warranties, and demonstrations. Trade promotions operate within ***distribution channels*** and offer programs such as cooperative advertising, display materials, and complimentary goods. Sales force promotions target the people selling a product and include contests, bonuses, and sales rallies.

sales representative   The personal link between a company and its customers.

Sales representatives, or *reps,* serve a variety of functions—from contacting new customers and selling products to conducting market research and servicing products.

sales response function   The relationship between sales and a particular ***marketing*** tool.

Say a manager wants to see the effect of a small price change on sales volume. The manager might set up a sales response function that graphs any sales changes that are due to the price change.

salvage value   In accounting, the expected price that an ***asset*** will bring when it is no longer needed by a company; also called *scrap value.*

In calculating ***depreciation*** expense, an asset's salvage value is deducted from its cost (except for declining balance methods).

EXAMPLE: A company buys a truck for $20,000. Its estimated ***useful life*** is ten years and its estimated salvage value is $5,000. If straight-line depreciation is used, the depreciation expense would be the cost of the truck, less the salvage value, divided by its expected useful life, or

$$\$20,000 - \$5,000 = \$15,000$$

$$\frac{\$15,000}{10 \text{ years}} = \$1,500 \text{ annual depreciation expense}$$

sampling   The selection of a subset of a given population as the subject for a ***marketing research*** study.

EXAMPLE: A newspaper interested in its customers' reactions to a new home delivery system randomly selects 200 subscribers, lets them try the new system, and measures their responses.

The key to selecting a sample is to make sure that the characteristics of the sample are representative of the population as a whole and of a sufficient size to render the results convincing. Random sampling creates truly representative samples. Relatively small numbers of people or items may be chosen in order to give results for large populations (for example, polling experts can predict the winner of a statewide election based on the returns of only a few precincts that are known to be representative and indicative of past results).

sampling frame   A list of individuals or units from which a sample will be drawn.

> EXAMPLE: An electronics company wants to survey customers who bought its high-end stereo system within the past three years. It might create a list of all those who returned warranty cards within that time period. The list will not include everyone who bought the stereo, but it should be comprehensive enough to generate a representative sample.
>
> *See also **sampling.***

saving   Personal income that is not spent.

> Personal income can be regarded on a pretax or after-tax basis. After-tax income is referred to as ***disposable income.*** Since taxes are an enforceable obligation, individuals are only free to dispose of their after-tax income. In general, there are two ways in which after-tax income can be disposed of: It can be spent (that is, ***personal consumption expenditures***) or it can be saved.
>
> The preceding description provides an important insight into the nature of saving in the U.S. economy. Saving is measured as a residual. This measurement recognizes the primary role of consumption. Individuals decide how to spend their income. Whatever is left is treated as saving. This treatment is quite different from what would happen if the various instruments people use as savings vehicles—deposits, money market mutual funds, NOW accounts, and so on—were totaled.
>
> In the following table, totals for personal income (PI), taxes, disposable personal income (DPI), personal consumption expenditure (PCE), saving, and the saving rate (as a percentage of disposable personal income) for selected years are shown.

DISPOSITION OF PERSONAL INCOME
(Billions of dollars, except saving rate)

	1960	1965	1970	1975	1980	1985	1990	1995
PI	409	553	831	1,307	2,265	3,380	4,664	6,112
Taxes	49	62	109	156	312	437	621	794
DPI	360	491	722	1,151	1,953	2,943	4,043	5,318
PCE	332	445	664	1,025	1,748	2,667	3,748	5,072
Saving°	21	35	58	100	154	189	176	247
Saving rate (%)	5.7	7.0	8.0	8.7	7.9	6.4	4.3	4.6

°There is a further small residual, when PCE and Saving are subtracted from DPI, that reflects personal transfers (gifts) to foreigners and net interest payments by persons.

scientific management   Classical management theory began in the United States after the Civil War, with the popularity of scientific management. The leading proponent of the philosophy was Frederick Winslow Taylor, who prepared a report for the American Society of Mechanical Engineers to answer U.S. President Theodore Roosevelt's call for more efficient workers and the conservation of national resources. This report was published in 1911 as *The Principles of Scientific Management.*

Although Taylor could never be credited with a deep understanding of human nature, he did bring into sharp focus the need for efficient working conditions and personnel policies that would encourage people to get the most done at the lowest cost. Taylor posed questions such as whether a first-class shoveler at the Bethlehem Steel Company would do his best work with a large or a small shovel, whether he would shovel more tonnage if he shoveled in loads of 10, 15, 20, 30, or 40 pounds, and whether he should work at regular intervals but vary the shovel load. Taylor determined that the optimal shovel load was 21 pounds (Taylor 1911, 31–35).

While such precise measurements today seem antiquated and naïve, the concept of scientific management has continued to have a great impact on the relationship between managers and workers, particularly with the advent of robotics and *computer-aided manufacturing* (**CAM**). Based on the task concept, which states that all work must be carefully planned and presented to employees (usually through detailed written instructions), scientific management views employees as extensions of the task they perform. *Time studies* and motion studies are still frequently used in scientific management systems to break down each element of a worker's task and make it as efficient as possible. Compensation under scientific management is based on production. Workers who do not meet a particular production requirement are paid less than workers who meet or exceed the production requirement.

SEC   *See Securities and Exchange Commission*

secondary data   Information previously collected for another purpose and applied to a current problem.

A starting point for most *marketing research,* secondary data are usually found through a library search.

EXAMPLE: A mail-order clothing company wants to know which fabrics and colors have the greatest appeal to women over 40. Its researchers look for previous studies of recent trends in color or fabric preference. These studies can provide background and give direction for the current project.

Compare to **primary data.**

secondary market   The capital market where previously issued securities are traded.

The market may be (1) the *New York Stock Exchange* (**NYSE**), the *American Stock Exchange* (**AMEX**), or the *NASDAQ Stock Market;* (2) an informal market such as over-the-counter *pink sheets;* or (3) a *foreign exchange.* The secondary market provides a medium within which securities can be bought and sold by investors and traders. Proceeds from the sales go to investors and dealers, not to the issuing company, as is the case in a *primary market.*

secondary offering   A public sale by institutional investors, large corporations, and investment bankers of previously issued securities.

Frequently, syndicates will purchase large blocks of an initial issue of securities at a fixed price and then resell them in the open market. The issuing company gains by having an assured market for its securities; the syndicate gains by the spread between purchase and sale prices.

Section 936   A section in the U.S. Internal Revenue Code that grants special privileges to branches or subsidiaries of U.S. companies doing business in Puerto Rico.

Certain U.S. corporations that derive a significant portion of their income from Puerto Rican business activities are called *936 companies* and are effectively exempt from U.S. income tax on that portion of their income derived from sources within Puerto Rico. Beginning in 1988, selected provisions applied to subsidiaries of U.S. companies in the U.S. Virgin Islands as well.

Funds repatriated to the mainland U.S. parent company by 936 companies are subject to a *tollgate tax* at a maximum rate of 10 percent. As long as these funds remain in Puerto Rico, they are tax free. As a result, more than $10 billion of Section 936 funds, referred to as *qualified possession source investment income* or *QPSII (quipsy)* funds, have been generated, to be lent to qualifying U.S. companies for investment in projects within Puerto Rico or in qualifying projects in any Caribbean Basin Initiative (CBI) country that has executed a Tax Information Exchange Agreement with the United States. Because of the tax-free nature of these funds, loans currently carry below-market *interest rates* of 85 percent of the *London Interbank Offered Rate* (*LIBOR*).

Investments in the following CBI countries qualify for Section 936 financing: Jamaica, Barbados, Grenada, Dominica, Trinidad and Tobago, the Dominican Republic, and Costa Rica. Other countries are in various stages of consideration.

Caribbean Basin Partners, Ltd. (CBBP) is a good example of how 936 financing has caught on. CBBP is a *partnership* of Section 936 corporations that invests debt and *equity* in eligible small- and midsize private-sector projects with job-creating potential. It grants loans ranging from $1 million to $10 million for ten years, up to 75 percent of the financing requirement.

Securities and Exchange Commission (SEC)   The federal government agency responsible for regulating financial reporting, use of accounting principles, trading activities, and auditing practices of *publicly held companies.*

SEC requirements (issued as Accounting Series Releases and Staff Accounting Bulletins) encourage full financial disclosure in order to protect the interests of investors. Generally the SEC defers to the opinions released by the *Financial Accounting Standards Board* (*FASB*) and the *Auditing Standards Board* (*ASB*).

securitization   The use of contractual *cash flows* as collateral to debt issues.

When borrowing from a bank, companies execute a contractual obligation to repay the loan. Securitization creates the same type of contractual obligation to repay investors as loan documentation does to repay banks.

Whereas bank loans are collateralized with balance sheet *assets* (receivables, *inventory,* machinery and equipment, or buildings and land), securitized *bonds,* notes, and *commercial paper* are collateralized (securitized) with contractual cash flows from either *balance sheet* or *off-balance-sheet* assets. Future cash flow contracts that qualify as collateral include construction contracts, credit card receivables, mortgage obligations, export orders, or any other quality future cash flow contract.

Companies sell pieces of paper (securities) to investors that represent rights to these cash flows. Examples of such securities include bond issues, commercial paper, euronotes, short-term or medium-term notes, certificates of deposit, *euro-bonds,* pass-through and pay-through securities, and property income certificates. *Privately held companies* frequently use short-term promissory notes to evidence securitized debt obligations.

From a company's perspective, liquid *secondary markets* for these securities offer management the opportunity to restructure risks as economic events dictate.

For investors, securitized debt carries less risk than straight commercial paper or bonds. In most cases, it offers better returns than current market rates. And *liquidity* is assured by an active secondary market.

Securitization is essentially another form of transaction finance and is ideally suited to financially weak companies that need to finance specific *transactions* independent of other balance sheet debt or credit history.

Securitized obligations are also referred to as *asset-backed securities.*

segment reporting   In accounting, the presentation of the activities and operations of various parts of a company, such as product lines, countries, divisions, and sales territories.

Segment reporting is required in the *annual report* of a company if it meets any of the following criteria: (1) revenue of the segment is 10 percent or more of total *revenue;* (2) the segment operating profit (excluding unallocable general corporate revenue and expenses, income taxes, and interest expense) is 10 percent or more of total operating profit; and (3) a segment's identifiable *assets* are 10 percent or more of total identifiable assets. Any segment that has been reported in the past should be reported again, even if it no longer meets any of the established criteria.

Financial Accounting Standards Board (*FASB*) Statement No. 14 requires that *publicly held companies* provide segment *disclosures* regarding operations in different industries, foreign operations, major customers, export sales, and government contracts. These disclosures are not required if a company derives at least 90 percent of its revenues from one industry. *Privately held companies* do not have to make these disclosures. Segments must represent at least 75 percent of a company's total revenue. Generally, no more than ten segments are shown. Although sales or transfers between segments are not included in a company's consolidated *financial statements,* they are included in segment reports.

segmentation   *See market segmentation*

self-managed work teams   Groups that control how the goals assigned to them are to be accomplished and how to allocate their various tasks.

In most cases, self-managed work teams have collective control over the pace of work, scheduling of breaks, determination of work assignments, and inspection procedures. Totally autonomous work teams might even be able to select their members and evaluate each other's performance.

EXAMPLE: In California, General Motors (in a *joint venture* with Toyota) is manufacturing Chevrolet Novas and Toyota Corollas with self-managed work teams. In addition to being able to define their own jobs, the teams are given a great deal of responsibility for quality control. They conduct daily audits—a task that once fell to a separate department—and can use *stop line* cards that allow them to halt production immediately if they spot a problem.

Self-managed work teams have three key features: (1) Group members must have a variety of skills that allow them to perform a number of different functions, (2) members must perform functionally interrelated tasks and be collectively responsible for the end product, and (3) there must be some kind of evaluation of the performance of the group as a whole.

senior debt Debt securities that hold first-position claims to a company's *assets.*

If the company were to be liquidated, senior debtholders would receive proceeds from the sale before junior debtholders, preferred shareholders, or common shareholders. The same pecking order applies in a bankruptcy proceeding; that is, interest and principal payments against senior debt will be made before any payments on other debt or *equity* holdings.

Because of its priority position, senior debt normally carries a lower *interest rate* than junior obligations. Conversely, since junior obligations such as *junk bonds* carry very few rights to the company's assets, higher interest rates must compensate.

sequencing The order in which jobs are assigned to work centers.

These decisions can have a great impact on a company's operations in terms of being within (or exceeding) *capacity* requirements and completing jobs on time. To assist in the sequencing process, a number of priority rules, or *heuristics,* have been developed that can help one to decide which jobs should be scheduled first. Of course, priority rules vary from company to company, but some of the more common are the following:

1. *First come, first served.* The first job to arrive at a particular work center is done first. The underlying concept behind this rule is fairness. It is frequently used in service companies, such as auto repair, where the customer arrival is part of the process.

2. *Shortest operation time.* Short jobs are done first. This action moves them through the operations process more quickly, which can help to generate *revenue* quickly. Longer jobs must wait until the proper facilities are clear before they can begin.

3. *Longest operation time.* Jobs that take the most time are done first.

4. *Due date.* Jobs with an earlier due date (regardless of processing time) are given priority.

5. *Static slack.* In this case, *slack* is calculated as a job's due date minus the time of its arrival at a given work center. Jobs with the smallest amount of static slack are scheduled first.

6. *Static slack per remaining operation.* Jobs with more operations to be completed should be scheduled before jobs with fewer remaining operations.

7. *Covert.* Jobs with the highest ratio of cost of delay (d) over processing time (t) are given priority.

8. *By customer importance.* Good customers are given priority.

served market The portion of the market that a company decides to pursue. The served market is also called the *target market.*

EXAMPLE: For a company that manufactures video games, the **market** consists of anyone who owns a television. The **potential market** is defined as households with children and a television. The **available market** is limited to households with children, a television, enough income to make the purchase, and a store nearby that carries the game. The served market consists of households with a television, access to a toy store, sufficient income to buy the product, and children within a specific age range (between 11 and 15, for example).

*See also **available market; market; penetrated market; potential market.***

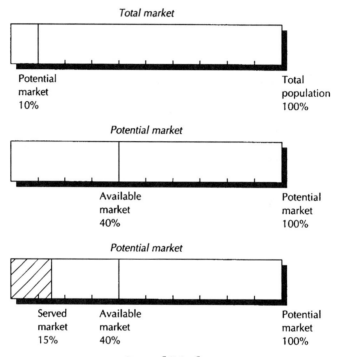

Served Market

setup costs   Any costs associated with the manufacture of parts or materials.

Setup costs include the costs of equipment downtime during a new setup, setup labor, and the cost of materials or parts used to test the new setup in accordance with the desired **output.** It is the "make ready to produce" cost.

seven-S framework   A framework developed by McKinsey & Company consultants to assist in understanding the interrelated strategic elements that determine a company's success or failure.

Proponents of the seven-S framework, which was widely popularized in the best-selling book, *In Search of Excellence,* by Tom Peters and Robert Waterman, argue that the effectiveness of a company is determined by the interplay of each of the following seven factors, rather than changes in corporate structure or organization:

- *Strategy*—the path chosen by a company to achieve its goals
- *Structure*—how the company is organized
- *Staff*—the company's human resources

- *Superordinate goals*—the basic values and goals of a company
- *Skills*—the particular capabilities of a company
- *Style*—the manner in which management presents itself to employees
- *Systems*—the procedures, both formal and informal, that govern daily activity

(Peters and Waterman 1982, 9–11)

In attempting to make major changes within a company, it is important to consider each of the seven S's. Usually, the *hard* S's, such as strategy and structure, receive a great deal of management attention, sometimes at the expense of the *soft* S's, such as staff and superordinate goals. Change that does not consider each of the seven S's is likely to fail. Successful change incorporates each of the S's and attempts to find a balance that will create consistency throughout the company.

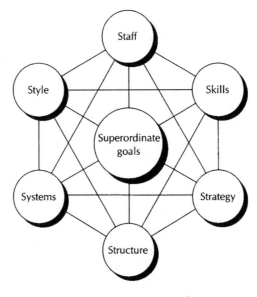

Seven-S Framework

SOURCE: Peters and Waterman 1982, 10. "Shared Values" is replaced by "Superordinate Goals."

sexual harassment   Any verbal or physical abuse based solely on the victim's gender and sexual status.

Sexual harassment laws apply equally to males and females, heterosexuals and homosexuals. Most laws are directed toward superior-subordinate relationships, but they apply to peer relationships and relationships between nonemployees and employees as well. Sexual harassment is widespread in the workplace and carries extremely high costs, both financially and personally. For example, in 1985, Cecily Coleman reached an out-of-court settlement with the American Broadcasting Corporation (ABC) for $15 million after bringing sexual harassment charges against the company resulting from unwanted sexual advances of former ABC vice president James D. Abernathy. Also in 1985, the Equal Employment Opportunity Commission (EEOC) received a record 7,273 sexual harassment complaints. Studies have shown that up to 70 percent of female employees have experienced sexual harassment on the job. For example, one study in California showed that up to one third of all Los Angeles working women have, at one point, lost or quit their jobs because of sexual pressures in the workplace.

Many incidents of sexual harassment go unreported, for reasons such as the following:

1. Victims do not feel that they will be believed. In many cases, sexual harassment is instigated by managers or supervisors who have more interaction with and authority in dealings with higher management. These factors tend to discourage victims from reporting sexual harassment because they feel that their word will not compare favorably with the word of a trusted manager.

2. Victims cannot give a detailed account of particular incidents. Since sexual harassment often takes place in the context of casual interactions, victims frequently do not record incidents until actions become blatant.

3. Victims may be accused of inviting or encouraging harassment. A victim's reluctance to report harassment may be caused by guilt or uncertainty regarding exactly which actions crossed the line from casual interaction to sexual innuendo. Laughing at sexual jokes, wearing revealing clothing, and even being too friendly can often cloud the issue of the initiation of sexual harassment and discourage employees from making formal reports.

4. Victims do not trust higher management to be objective. There is a common perception, due for the most part to the fact that most sexual harassment is initiated by men and most upper management positions are held by men, that complaints of sexual harassment will not be taken seriously.

5. Victims fear punishment. Frequently, victims of sexual harassment fear reprisals, such as dismissal, denial of promotions or raises, poor performance evaluations, and so on, if they make a formal complaint.

6. Victims do not want to cause problems. In many cases, the victim of sexual harassment is hesitant to report the problem because there is a reluctance to harm the employment situation or reputation of the person harassing them.

Sexual harassment has become a legal issue only since the mid-1970s. The first sexual harassment suit was filed in Arizona in 1975; two female employees quit their jobs as a result of repeated sexual advances, both verbal and physical, from their supervisor. The court ruled that the company was not liable for the actions of the supervisor, that the supervisor's actions were simply his own proclivity, served no policy, and did not benefit the employer. This rationale held until 1977 when the District of Columbia Circuit Court of Appeals found that, in situations where sexual harassment affects job conditions (that is, creates economic harm such as loss of job or denial of salary increase or promotion), it is sex discrimination under Title VII of the 1964 Civil Rights Act.

In 1980, the EEOC released guidelines regarding sexual harassment. The guidelines define sexual harassment as follows:

> Unwelcome sexual advances, requests for sexual favors, and other verbal or physical conduct of a sexual nature constitute sexual harassment when (1) submission to such conduct is made either explicitly or implicitly a term or condition of an individual's employment; (2) submission to or rejection of

such conduct by an individual is used as the basis for employment decisions affecting such individual; or (3) such conduct has the purpose or effect of unreasonably interfering with an individual's work performance or creating an intimidating, hostile, or offensive working environment.

The guidelines go on to state that cases of sexual harassment will be reviewed on an individual, case-by-case basis.

In determining whether alleged conduct constitutes sexual harassment, the Commission will look at the record as a whole and at the totality of the circumstances, such as the nature of the sexual advances and the context in which the alleged incidents occurred. The determination of the legality of a particular action will be made from the facts, on a case-by-case basis.

The District of Columbia Circuit Court of Appeals again advanced the legal thinking on sexual harassment in 1981, when it ruled that sexual harassment suits did not have to hinge on economic harms. The court held that sexual propositions and insults were damaging to the emotional and psychological terms of employment regardless of whether they resulted in tangible economic harm.

In 1982, the Eleventh Circuit Court established the quid pro quo (that is, the giving of something for the receipt of something else) theory of sexual harassment. This theory states that sexual harassment affects not only its victims but also other employees, owing to the fact that a victim who acquiesces to sexual advances in the workplace might receive promotions and salary increases at the expense of other employees.

The result of these various rulings and policies on sexual harassment has created a system of collective law that outlines four distinct factors that constitute sexual harassment: (1) It is offensive and unwelcome, (2) it involves authority with the power to produce an intimidating work environment, (3) it is repetitive and one-sided (with the exception of cases of sexual assault), and (4) it makes the victim feel powerless to stop or evade the behavior. Specific examples of clearly unacceptable behavior include the following:

- Verbal comments, compliments, and insults of a sexual nature, such as sexual jokes or pressuring for dates
- Comments such as "You get me hot" and "I like it when you wear those tight outfits" and "You know what you have to do if you want to get ahead around here"
- Nonverbal actions such as staring luridly, leaving sexual notes around the workplace, displaying suggestive photographs, pinching, unsolicited back or neck rubs, and physical obstruction, such as rubbing against an employee in a hallway

SFAC   *See **Statements of Financial Accounting Concepts***

SFAS   *See **Statements of Financial Accounting Standards***

share of voice   A measure of ***advertising*** effectiveness based on the percentage of advertising expense that a company pays within a chosen market.

EXAMPLE: A toy company accounts for 20 percent of all the advertising expenditures in the doll market, so it can claim a 20 percent share of voice. With a 20 percent share of voice, the company should expect approximately a 20 percent *market share.* If the market share is less than 20 percent, the company is probably spending inefficiently on advertising. If the share is greater than 20 percent, the company is spending efficiently and might consider increasing its advertising budget.

shelf registration   A provision in regulations set by the *Securities and Exchange Commission* (*SEC*) that permits companies to comply with the registration requirements for a public securities offering up to two years before making the actual offering.

With the registration essentially complete and on *the shelf*, corporations can make the issue when market conditions offer the highest share-price potential. Although shelf registrations must be continually updated and regular reports filed with the SEC, most companies find these a small price to pay for the ability to choose the proper timing for the issue. It is much less costly to file a shelf registration with updated reports than to refile full registrations if the first one proves untimely.

Shelf registrations are becoming increasingly popular with companies issuing *medium-term* notes where the outlook for two to five years is the crucial determinant for timing the issue.

Shippers Export Declaration   The principal document by which exporters report compliance with the Export Administration Regulations and U.S. customs regulations.

shop floor control   In manufacturing, a system for using information from a factory shop floor to monitor the status of various workstations and product orders.

Shop floor control has five key functions: (1) assigning priorities to product orders; (2) maintaining order-by-order quantity data on *work-in-process inventories;* (3) providing *output* information used in *capacity* control; (4) informing management of the status of each product order; (5) providing data that can be used for the measurement of *efficiency, productivity,* and *utilization* of the labor force or equipment.

shortage   In economics, a condition that exists when the quantity demanded of a good or service exceeds the quantity supplied at a given price.

When this situation occurs, it indicates that the market price is below its equilibrium level. As a result, consumers may experience long lines, waiting lists, or difficulty in finding products for sale in the stores. When a shortage exists, the market price rises, thereby clearing the market of the excess *demand.*

short-term debt   In accounting, a debt that is due within one year.

Short-term debt is reported as a *current liability* on the *balance sheet* and includes the portion of a long-term debt due within one year.

shutdown situation   In economics, a situation in which a firm would be better off to close down its operations than to continue to produce.

It occurs when the price of the product falls below its average variable cost of production. In such a situation, the *revenue* earned per unit of sale (the unit price of the product) is not enough to cover a firm's unit variable cost. Therefore, there is nothing left to contribute toward a firm's *fixed cost.*

Expressed another way, the shutdown situation occurs when the price is so low that a firm's operational losses exceed its total fixed cost. By shutting down, the firm minimizes its losses by having to pay only for the total fixed cost. When the price just equals a firm's average variable cost, it is referred to as the *shutdown point.*

simple capital structure   In accounting, a *capital structure* with no securities that can be converted into *common stock.*

See also *capital structure; common stock equivalent; complex capital structure; earnings per share.*

simple interest   The interest paid on the principal of a loan when there is no compounding.

Simple interest is calculated as

$$I = P \times I_t \times n$$

where: I = Simple interest rate
P = Principal amount
I_t = Interest rate per time period
n = Number of time periods

EXAMPLE: The simple interest on $100,000 at 11 percent borrowed for eight months is

$$\$100{,}000 \times 11\% \times 8/12 = \$7{,}333$$

In other words, the interest payments on the first eight months of this loan amount to $7,333.

single-sourcing   The purchase of a good or service from one supplier wherein the buyer selects one supplier from several candidates.

Traditionally, manufacturers sought to maintain at least two suppliers for each component part. This practice served to ensure a continuous supply and, more important, encouraged price competition between suppliers.

With the advent of *just-in-time* (*JIT*), manufacturers have adopted single-sourcing in order to establish close relationships with a small number of suppliers. These relationships frequently lead to higher quality, shorter lead times, and a greater degree of cooperation between the manufacturer and the supplier.

sinking fund   Money set aside for periodic payments in order to reduce a financial obligation.

Sinking funds are reported on the *balance sheet,* usually as *investments* or other *assets.* For example, if a company issues a sinking fund *bond,* it makes periodic payments to a trustee who then invests the money in order to be able to retire the bonds upon their maturity.

Six Sigma   A unit of statistical measurement, devised as a goal of quality control in 1985 by Dr. Mikel Harry and others at Motorola.

The concept of sigma or standard deviation is used to describe the number of defects in a certain number of parts per million produced. In industries where defects in parts present severe problems, this measurement of quality control has taken on increased significance in the past decade or so. The idea is to reduce the probability of the occurrence of a *random* defect to *n* in a million, where *n* is often less than 100.

EXAMPLE: If a defect is thought of in terms of a misspelled word in a written text, *four sigma* would be equivalent to one misspelled word occurring on a random basis in approximately 30 pages of text. *Five sigma* would measure an astounding increase in quality: only one randomly occurring misspelling in all the volumes of an encyclopedia. *Six sigma* would be the equivalent of only one misspelling in an entire library. (SOURCE: http://www.public,iastate.edu/~chu_c/coiurse/tqm/t6a.htm.)

skimming   In *marketing,* a pricing strategy in which the initial price is set high with the goal of selling the product first to people who want it and are willing to pay a premium for it. When this *market* is saturated, the marketer drops the price to appeal to consumers who are more price sensitive. In this way, total *revenue* is maximized.

For skimming to prove effective, three conditions should exist: (1) The people who want the product should be largely indifferent to price, and a number of price segments should exist. (2) Consumers should know little about the costs of producing and marketing the product. In this way, they are unlikely to know they are paying a premium to acquire it. (3) The likelihood of competitors entering the market and initiating price cutting is slim.

Skimming has a number of advantages. For one, it helps the marketer recover the costs of *new-product development* more quickly. For another, the initial high price can create a prestige image for the product. Moreover, marketers recognize that it is easier to lower prices than increase them. So skimming makes sense when the marketer does not yet know how much *demand* there will be for the product.

The disadvantages of a skimming strategy include the following: A price that is set too high initially may hurt sales and even lead to the product's early demise. Skimming also attracts competitors who see high profits being generated and want to get in on the action. Another drawback is that the skimming strategy often makes it necessary for marketers to revise the *marketing mix* to serve new *target markets* that emerge as prices drop. *Advertising,* for example, is likely to become more important than personal selling, and the distribution pattern will probably shift from specialty stores to mass merchandisers. *Compare to **penetration pricing; target return pricing.***

slack   The time difference between the scheduled deadline for a job and its estimated completion date.

If a job is finished ahead of schedule, it is said to have *positive slack time.* If a job will be finished behind schedule, it is said to have *negative slack time.*

Slack also refers to the amount of time that a task can be delayed without delaying an entire project.

*See also **critical path method** (**CPM**).*

societal marketing   A *marketing* strategy aimed at understanding and satisfying the needs and desires of the *target market* in a way that maintains or improves both the consumer's and society's well-being.

EXAMPLE: Ben & Jerry's Homemade, Inc., is a classic example of a company that uses societal marketing. The company has established a nonprofit foundation that is dedicated to world peace and donates a percentage of its profits to the organization. Ben & Jerry's marketing subsequently carries two messages: Enjoy our ice cream and help further world peace.

soft currency   The currency of a country that cannot be freely converted into a *hard currency,* thereby restricting its use to the country of origin.

Exporters to developing countries having soft currency frequently resort to *countertrade* arrangements as opposed to direct payments. Although some Eastern European and Latin American countries are making efforts to convert to hard currency, most continue to have insufficient dollar or other hard currency reserves to make the switch. Soft currency countries include most of Latin America, Eastern Europe, Africa, Commonwealth of Independent States, and certain Middle Eastern and South Asian countries.

span of control   The number of subordinates a manager is able to direct effectively.

Traditionally, spans of control were kept small—usually under 6. The trend today, however, thanks to improved training, communication, and information technology is to increase span of control up to 10 or 12.

spending multiplier   A sequence of spending increases leading to income gains leading to spending gains.

Personal consumption expenditures are the largest portion of *gross domestic product* (*GDP*), but they have a vital importance quite apart from their size. Ultimately, it is consumer spending that fuels economic growth. Increases in *disposable income,* however, can be either spent or saved. On average, U.S. consumers have spent some 90 to 94 percent of disposable income in the post–World War II era. This spending, in turn, generates additional income to the factors of production used to produce the consumer goods and services purchased. This additional income, then, fuels further rounds of spending and income. Thus, the spending multiplier is the increase in aggregate demand outside the consumption-income stream—such as increases in nonresidential *investment,* exports, or government spending—set off by the spending-income sequence just described.

spin-off   A form of divestiture that involves the implementation of accounting and legal steps to segregate the *assets* of a business unit—a division, subsidiary, branch, or product line—into a separate corporate entity.

The parent company then sells stock in the new entity, either to the public through an initial public offering (IPO; see *going public*), management groups, as through an *employee stock ownership plan* (*ESOP*), or private investors. A spin-off to private investors or management groups usually involves the outright sale of 100 percent of the equity interest. Public offerings are normally for a minority interest.

Assets of the spin-off business unit include the product engineering drawings, name, and patents (if any), as well as its raw materials, *work-in process inven-*

tory, and *finished goods inventory;* its customer list, order **backlog,** and receivables; any machinery, test equipment, or vehicles associated with the line; and land and buildings, if the business occupies a separate facility. Not infrequently, buyers retain most of the production workers as well as the supervisory and sales personnel responsible for the product line.

Legally, a spin-off is a sale of assets. The same bulk sales laws that apply when all of a company's assets are sold also apply to spin-offs. The tax recognition of **capital gains** and ordinary income is also the same. In addition, the built-in gains provisions of the tax code may apply if the selling entity has switched from a C corporation to an **S corporation.**

spoilage   Any production that does not yield salable products.

There are four types of spoilage: spoiled goods, defective goods, waste, and scrap. Spoiled goods do not meet a company's production standards and are either sold at a reduced price or discarded. Because defective goods do not meet production standards, they are either sold at a reduced price or reworked and then sold. Waste is any unplanned material lost in production. Scrap is a planned by-product of the manufacturing process that can be sold. It is the residue of the manufacturing process or worn-out tooling or fixtures.

spot   *See advertising*

spreadsheet   A table of figures, organized by rows and columns, commonly used for accounting and financial calculations.

Most spreadsheet calculations are performed by computer programs such as Lotus 1-2-3, Excel, Supercalc4, and Multiplan. These programs are frequently used for the preparation of **financial statements,** cost and performance reports, and worksheets, but they are especially good for making projections, such as determining the impact a different sales level will have on a company's profits.

standard cost   A predetermined cost representing the ideal or norm achievable by a company.

Standard costs form the basis of a standard cost system used extensively in manufacturing companies. At the beginning of each year, companies normally review standards for material price and usage, labor efficiency and wage rate, and **overhead** rates based on budgets.

In a standard cost system, all **inputs** to **inventory** are valued at standard and the variations from actual costs are written off to the **income statement** as variances. **Cost of goods sold** is always stated at standard cost. A partial income statement using a standard cost system would be as follows:

Sales		$10,000
Standard cost of sales		
Materials	$2,000	
Labor	1,000	
Overhead	3,000	
Total standard cost of sales		6,000
Standard gross profit		$ 4,000

Variances		
Material price	50	
Material usage	70	
Labor efficiency	120	
Labor wage rate	50	
Overhead efficiency	100	
Overhead budget	200	
Total variance from standard		590
Total cost of sales		6,590
Gross profit		$ 3,410

Since variances from standard are recorded when cost elements are put into inventory, they are written off in the current **accounting period.** Also, when variances from expected performance are recognized shortly after they occur, the company can take faster corrective action.

statement of cash flows   A formal statement of the cash received and disbursed by a company.

The statement of cash flows is divided into three sections: operating activities (usually a source of cash), investing activities (usually both a source and a use of cash), and financing activities (usually a source and use of cash). When cash is received or paid for more than one activity, it is allocated to that activity that is the prime motivation for the cash flow. For example, many companies consider cash spent on new equipment to be an **investment** activity rather than an operating activity.

In recent years, analysts have emphasized the statement of cash flows. The information contained in a statement of cash flows is vital since most stockholder and creditor interests are settled in cash. Cash flows information can help determine a company's ability to generate future cash from operations, pay dividends, and pay maturing debts and obligations.

See also **funds provided from operations.**

statement of shareholders' equity   A separate element of an **annual report** detailing the individual components of **stockholders' equity** and the changes that took place within the past year.

Stockholders' equity includes **preferred stock, common stock,** paid-in **capital, retained earnings, treasury stock,** unrealized losses on long-term **investments,** and **foreign currency translation** gains and losses.

Statements of Financial Accounting Concepts (SFAC)   The reports published by the **Financial Accounting Standards Board** (**FASB**) showing the basic concepts of **financial accounting,** reporting, and **disclosure.**

SFAC are issued in order to clarify or establish a basic accounting concept.

Statements of Financial Accounting Standards (SFAS)   The rules established by the **Financial Accounting Standards Board** (**FASB**) regarding **financial accounting,** reporting, and **disclosure.**

The standards deal with nearly every aspect of **financial accounting,** such as pensions, leases, **depreciation,** and presentation of **financial statements.**

stock dividend   A dividend of *common stock* granted to shareholders rather than cash.

Stock dividends are frequently used when companies are short of cash or when the market price of the stock is undervalued. Shareholders gain because the additional stock received is not taxed until sold, in contrast to cash dividends, which are taxed when received.

stock index   An indicator used to report and measure any changes in value of representative groups of stocks.

There are a number of different indexes, ranging from the National Association of Securities Dealers Automated Quotations system (NASDAQ), which represents all over-the-counter stocks, to more narrow indexes that concentrate on stocks in a particular market sector or industry. Some of the more widely used indexes are the AMEX Major Market Index, which is a price-weighted average of 20 *blue-chip* stocks; the AMEX Market Value Index, which measures the performance of more than 800 issues traded on the *American Stock Exchange* (*AMEX*); the *Dow Jones Industrial Average* (*DJIA*), which tracks the performance of 30 stocks traded on the *New York Stock Exchange* (*NYSE*); the New York Stock Exchange Composite Index, which relates all stocks traded on the NYSE to an aggregate market value as of December 31, 1965; and Standard & Poor's Composite Index of 500 Stocks, which is a market-value-weighted index of 500 stocks, most of them traded on the NYSE but including some AMEX and over-the-counter issues.

stock split   The issuing of new shares of *common stock* by reducing *par value,* and the market price, of the stock.

Stock splits generally serve to encourage *investment* by lowering the price of a stock.

EXAMPLE: A company has 1,000 shares of $40 par value stock, so its total par value comes to $40,000. If the company issues a two-for-one stock split, there will now be 2,000 shares with $20 par value. The total par value remains the same ($40,000). Usually, when a company issues a two-for-one stock split, the market price will drop by half.

*Compare to **reverse split**.*

stockholders' equity   In accounting, the ownership interest of stockholders in a company.

*See also **equity; owners' equity**.*

stockout   A situation in which a company cannot fill a customer order due to a lack of product.

Stockouts are the result of insufficient *inventory,* changes in product scheduling, or an unanticipated increase in *demand.* Stockouts can lead to *backorders* if the customer is willing to wait. Stockouts can also lead to order cancellation as well as losses of future business if the supplier is thought to be unreliable in meeting delivery schedules.

storyboard   In *marketing,* a visual representation of the script of a television commercial or show.

The storyboard, which resembles a comic strip, shows the key actions described in the script. Storyboards are used to present different script ideas to advertisers and can act as a guide in the actual production of a commercial.

straight rebuy   A buying situation in the *industrial market* where the purchaser re-orders goods or services, such as office supplies or maintenance, on a routine basis.

Competitors find it difficult to penetrate this market, since the purchase usually involves few decision makers with little time.

straight-line depreciation   In accounting, a method of *depreciation* that gener-ates equal depreciation expenses for each period because it assumes that the *asset* provides constant economic benefits.

Straight-line depreciation is simple to calculate and widely used. Straight-line depreciation charges are calculated by dividing the cost of the asset less its *salvage value* by the estimated economic life of the asset, or

$$\frac{\text{Cost} - \text{salvage value}}{\text{Life of asset}}$$

EXAMPLE: If a company buys $1,000,000 of new factory equipment that has a *useful life* of five years and a salvage value of $100,000, its depreciation expense would be calculated as

$$\frac{\$1,000,000 - \$100,000}{5 \text{ years}} = \$180,000$$

See also *accelerated depreciation. Compare to* *double declining balance depreciation; sum-of-the-years'-digits (SYD) method.*

strategic business unit (SBU)   A collection of product lines or product groups within a company with similar *markets,* competitors, or strategic problems.

In most cases, the individual units were, at one point, managed independently. The creation of SBUs, then, often cuts across established organizational structures. The key advantage of strategic business units is the ability to run a set of strategi-cally similar businesses under the same management. This reduces the distinction between strategy formulation and strategy implementation and eliminates a great deal of otherwise redundant effort as the manager of each individual unit attempts to cope with its environment.

strategic planning   Those actions that lead to the definition of a company's mission, the formulation of its goals, and the development of the specific strategies that will be implemented to meet those goals.

There are four basic characteristics of strategic planning:

1. It involves decisions by managers at all levels.
2. It deals with the allocation of large amounts of resources, such as *capital,* labor, or *capacity.*
3. It focuses on the long term, but increasingly strategic planning focuses on both the short and the long term.
4. It deals with a company's interaction with its environment.

subordinated debt   Any debt that, in the event of a company's liquidation, is not re-
payable until more senior claims have been settled.

Some subordinated debt may have greater claim on the *assets* of the liquidated
company than other subordinated debt. For example, a subordinated *debenture*
ranks above a junior subordinated debenture.

Compare to senior debt.

subsidiary company   A company in which a majority interest is owned by another
company. A majority interest is defined as ownership of between 50 and 100 percent of the company's shares.

successful efforts method   A method of accounting for exploration costs by companies in extractive industries, such as oil and gas.

The costs of a successful project are capitalized, whereas the costs of unsuccessful efforts are treated as an expense. The capitalized costs are amortized on the
basis of the reserves produced.

See also full-cost method.

sum-of-the-years'-digits (SYD) method   In accounting, a method of *accelerated depreciation.*

Sum-of-the-years'-digits depreciation charges are calculated by assigning numbers $(1, 2, 3, 4, \ldots, n)$ where n is the estimated *useful life* of an *asset.* SYD is then
calculated using the following formula:

$$SYD = \frac{n(n+1)}{2}$$

The annual depreciation charges are then calculated by

$$(\text{Cost of the asset} - \text{salvage value}) \times \frac{\text{remaining useful life}}{SYD}$$

EXAMPLE: An asset costs $1,000, has an estimated useful life of five years, and a
salvage value of $100. The SYD is calculated as

$$\frac{5(5+1)}{2} = 15$$

The annual depreciation charges are as follows:

REMAINING USEFUL LIFE

Year	Cost-salvage value		SYD		Depreciation
1	$900	×	5/15	=	$300
2	900	×	4/15	=	240
3	900	×	3/15	=	180
4	900	×	2/15	=	120
5	900	×	1/15	=	60
			Total		**$900**

Sum-of-the-years'-digits depreciation generates higher depreciation charges in
the earlier years of an asset's life than in later years. The method is appropriate in

situations where an asset provides greater economic benefits at the beginning of its life than at the end.

See also **accelerated depreciation.** *Compare to* **double declining balance depreciation.**

sunk costs   In accounting, a cost that has already been incurred and cannot be affected by any present or future decisions.

EXAMPLE: A machine purchased five years ago for $100,000 now has a current *book value* of $30,000. The $30,000 book value is a sunk cost. It is not affected by, nor should it affect, any future decisions about the machine's replacement.

supplier credit   Credit extended to a buyer from an exporter.

An exporter may choose to extend supplier credit independently, or it may obtain outside financing from government agencies, banks, or a number of other sources. Whenever an exporter records a receivable, the credit extension is considered a supplier credit.

supplier power   The ability of a supplier to influence or control buyers.

As an element of the *five forces model,* which determines the profitability of an industry, supplier power is an essential part of any strategic analysis. Powerful suppliers can severely reduce the profitability of an industry, say, by raising prices or reducing the quantity of their goods. For example, the chemical companies that act as suppliers to contract aerosol packagers have been able to exert their supplier power in the form of higher prices. The aerosol packagers, faced with intense competition from their own customers, many of whom created in-house packaging operations, are then limited in their ability to raise prices. As a result, profitability is reduced.

There are generally five conditions in which supplier power is high:

1. If the industry is controlled by a small number of companies and is more concentrated than the industry it sells to. When suppliers are selling to fragmented buyers, they will have considerable control over prices, terms of purchase, and quality.

2. If the suppliers are able to pursue a strategy of *forward integration,* such as developing the capacity to produce the finished product. For example, a textile company that sells to clothing manufacturers might increase its supplier power by beginning to manufacture its own line of clothing.

3. If the supplier does not face the threat of substitute products. For example, the sugar industry had a great deal of supplier power before the development of artificial sweeteners. Once substitute products entered the market, the industry's supplier power was reduced.

4. If the suppliers' products are differentiated or carry high switching costs. In many cases, if it is expensive to switch from one supplier to another, supplier power is very high. For example, supplier power might be enhanced if a company initiates a comprehensive *inventory* control system for its customers. Once the system is in place, buyers would face the formidable cost of developing a new inventory control system with a different supplier.

5. If the purchasing industry is not an important customer to the supplying industry. When a particular industry or company represents a small fraction of a supplier's sales, that supplier is likely to exert a great deal of supplier power.

supply In economics, the amount of a good or service that people stand ready to sell at a list of possible prices, other factors being held constant.

These other factors are (1) costs, (2) technology, (3) number of sellers, (4) future expectations about market price, and (5) weather conditions (particularly for the supply of agricultural products).

Economists expect that people are ready to sell more of their good or service as the price rises and to sell less as the price falls, other factors being held constant. When any of these other factors changes, the entire relationship between price and quantity supplied changes. For example, if bad weather in Florida destroys part of the orange crop, there would be a decrease in the market supply of oranges. As a result, there would be a smaller quantity of oranges supplied, regardless of the prices that are being offered for this product.

supply chain A network of facilities that procure raw materials, transform them into intermediate products and then finished goods, and transport them through a distribution system. It spans procurement, manufacturing, and distribution. No longer are these entities viewed as discrete elements but as functions that are grouped and the relationships between them understood. The supply chain can be local, regional, or global, and activities in one part of the chain can impact on other parts. The basic research goes back to Forrester at MIT in the late 1950s and his concept of *industrial dynamics.*

surplus In economics, a condition that exists when the quantity supplied of a good or service exceeds the quantity demanded at a given price.

When this situation occurs, it indicates that the market price is above its equilibrium level. As a result, sellers may experience a build up in *inventories.* When a surplus exists, the market price falls, thereby clearing the market of the excess supply.

SWOT analysis An acronym for "Strengths, Weaknesses, Opportunities, and Threats," a SWOT analysis is a strategy analysis framework that helps managers build a corporate and business strategy that emphasizes a company's strengths and opportunities.

Strengths are also known as *core competences.* They include proprietary technology, skills, resources, market position, and patents. For example, a young company might properly consider the enthusiasm of its employees, who work 12 to 14 hours per day, as a strength.

A weakness is a condition within a company that can lead to poor performance. Common weaknesses are obsolete equipment, a heavy debt load, a poor product image, weak managerial skills, and so on.

Opportunities are current or future conditions in the environment that a company might be able to turn to its advantage. For example, in the medical industry, the increasing age of the population might be seen as an opportunity.

Threats are current or future conditions in the environment that might harm a company. For example, if there is an increase in the gas tax, demand for recreational vehicles will probably fall.

SWOT analysis can help managers grasp their strategic situation, but it is important to assign probabilities to both opportunities and threats in order to evaluate their likelihood.

synergy   The concept that the combination of two or more different businesses, activities, or processes will create an overall value that is greater than the sum of the individual parts.

Synergy is frequently discussed in ***annual reports*** and company press releases, where its value is generally limited to a rationalization for a particular action. For example, when General Motors purchased Hughes Aircraft, there was a great ballyhoo about the synergy between the two. Cars were going to convert to electricity, and Hughes offered a great deal of expertise in that area. However, any actual synergy between the two was limited largely to the annual report.

Essentially two types of relationships can produce real synergy. The first is the ability to transfer particular skills between the various units of each company. For example, a cosmetics business unit, which has expertise in the marketing of beauty products, might be able to transfer ideas about the packaging and promotion to a newly acquired business unit that manufactures and sells shampoo. The second occurs when the two companies can share meaningful activities, such as a sales force or research department. For example, Procter & Gamble uses a common sales force and distribution system for both disposable diapers and paper towels.

T

10-K The annual filing made by *publicly held companies* to the *Securities and Exchange Commission (SEC).*

The 10-K usually contains more financial information than an *annual report,* with audited *financial statements, disclosures* on sales, *operating income, segment reporting,* and general business information.

10-Q The *quarterly reports* made by *publicly held companies* with the *Securities and Exchange Commission (SEC).*

Form 10-Q is not so comprehensive as Form 10-K. It contains interim financial reports (usually not audited), the appropriate *disclosures,* and comparative figures for the same period of the previous year.

tangible asset In accounting, an *asset* with physical substance and an expected life of more than one year.

Tangible assets are usually reported as *noncurrent assets* on the *balance sheet* and include equipment, machinery, furniture and fixtures, and buildings.
Compare to **intangible asset.**

target market The portion of the *market* that a company decides to pursue actively.
See also **served market.**

target return pricing A pricing strategy in which a marketer tries to obtain a predetermined percentage return on the *capital* it uses to produce and distribute a product.

Under this approach, the marketer determines a dollar amount for the *return on investment (ROI)* it wants to achieve. It then treats this amount as a *fixed cost;* that is, the amount is added to the other fixed costs—management salaries, rent, insurance, and so on—when it adds up the total cost of producing a set number of the product. When the marketer divides the total costs, including ROI, by the quantity it will produce, the resulting number is the price. That price ensures that the marketer will recapture the cost, plus the targeted return, if it sells all the products it produces at that price.

One advantage of using this pricing strategy is its simplicity. If a company sells all the items it plans to sell, it will achieve its target return. The strategy, however, ignores the *demand* side of the equation—that is, consumers may not buy the amount of product the marketer planned. It also excludes the competitors' pricing strategies; thus, the targeted return is not guaranteed.

Until the early 1980s, the U.S. automobile industry used target return pricing. The Big Three auto companies all relied on *pricing committees* that decided how many cars the automaker expected to sell, totaled up the costs, threw in a healthy profit, and simply divided these costs by expected sales. If costs rose or fell, the automakers would simply boost the price to make up the difference. Double-digit **inflation** in the late 1970s, though, and fierce competition from Japanese automakers combined to make a mockery of forecasted demand. That is when American auto producers turned to **sales promotions** such as **rebates,** savings certificates, contests, extended warranties, and even money-back guarantees to lure buyers into the showrooms.

tax haven   A country with tax-preference laws for foreign companies and individuals. Three classes of jurisdictions are referred to as tax havens:

1. Those that have no relevant taxes (such as the Cayman Islands, the Bahamas, Bermuda, Turks and Caicos Islands)
2. Those that levy taxes only on internal taxable **transactions,** but none at all or very low taxes on foreign source income (such as Hong Kong and Panama)
3. Those that grant special tax privileges to certain types of companies or operations (e.g., the Channel Islands, Liechtenstein, and Luxembourg)

The principal functions of tax havens are (1) to avoid or postpone taxes, (2) to avoid exchange controls, and (3) to act as a shield against confiscation, nationalization, and other forms of expropriation. Tax avoidance does not mean tax evasion, which is strictly illegal in all developed countries.

Tax havens are also known as *safe havens,* a concept that dates back many centuries. The most efficient and useful tax havens are also **offshore financial centers,** replete with cadres of offshore banking facilities, trust organizations, lawyers, and accountants. Many tax havens have also branched out into the rapidly expanding captive insurance business.

Modern tax havens or offshore financial centers began as safe havens for **capital** that might otherwise have been expropriated by politically unstable or war-torn governments in Europe and Latin America (and later in the Middle East and Africa)—not as methods of avoiding taxes. Switzerland is a prime example. As private enterprise expanded, currency areas changed, and corporate taxes escalated, safe havens (tax havens) became the raison d'être for places such as Bermuda, the Bahamas, and the Cayman Islands.

team   *See group*

team building   The creation of a high level of interaction between group members, and sometimes between groups, in order to foster openness and trust.

Team-building activities usually include goal setting, role analysis to delineate each member's responsibilities, and the development of relationships between team members. Of course, team-building activities vary from group to group.

technology transfer   The making available of know-how (patents, industrial design, operational systems) from one trading partner to another.

Technology transfer transactions can take two basic forms: commercial and noncommercial.

- Commercially transferred technology is done via direct **investment,** including direct sale, the licensing of intellectual property, the contracting for consultancy services, and turnkey projects.
- Noncommercially transferred technology takes the form of technical assistance funded by official government agencies (e.g., the Canadian International Development Agency). It is otherwise called *official development assistance* (ODA) and can be provided either noncontractually (i.e., free of charge) or on concessional terms.

Technology transfer also refers to a component of a type of **countertrade** transaction called direct offsets, in which an exporter agrees either to make available technical assistance to the importer or to conduct research and development (R&D) in the host country as a condition of winning the export contract.

EXAMPLE: A group of the Sahel nations agreed to Canadian exports of irrigation equipment provided that the companies funded local R&D in agronomy and hydrology aimed at reducing and ultimately eliminating their dependence on external agricultural inputs (Presner 1991).

telemarketing   A major tool in **direct marketing,** in which the consumer either calls or is called by a seller, listens to a sales pitch and a description of a product, and decides whether to place an order.

Telemarketing can prove effective in both the **consumer market** and the **industrial market,** where it can reduce significantly the amount of time-consuming, face-to-face personal selling between dealers and customers.

As a rule, telemarketing is considerably more expensive than other forms of direct marketing, but the higher cost is often offset by a much higher **response rate.**

television rating   The percentage of households with televisions watching a given broadcast.

In 1998, approximately 98 million households in the United States had television sets. The Nielsen Media Research Company is the best known of those tracking what people are watching. Estimates are gleaned from a representative sampling of about 5,000 homes and 13,000 people who have agreed to participate in the research by allowing their television sets to be fitted with metering equipment. Information from these meters is fed into Nielsen's computers, which tabulate statistics on who is watching what program or commercial and when. (SOURCE: http://www.nielsenmedia.com.)

*Compare to **television share.***

television share   The percentage of households with televisions *in use* that are tuned to a particular broadcast.

EXAMPLE: Say 50 percent of the households with televisions have their sets on, and 80 percent of these are tuned to the Super Bowl. In that case, the broadcast of the game has a share of 80. Television share tells the marketer the number of people watching a particular show as opposed to the number of people watching different shows at the same time.

*Compare to **television rating.***

tender offer   An offer to buy shares of a **corporation,** usually at a price in excess of market.

When a company or group of investors aims to purchase controlling interest in a corporation, it submits a tender offer to present stockholders for the purchase of their shares. Usually, but not always, the tender offer includes an offer price in excess of the current trading price of the shares in the market as an incentive for shareholders to sell.

Tender offers may be rendered in a friendly or a hostile takeover bid. In a hostile bid, the target company's board of directors may choose to block the offer with an offer of its own to purchase outstanding shares.

The **Securities and Exchange Commission (SEC)** requires full **disclosure** from any investor or group of investors accumulating 5 percent or more of a company's outstanding shares.

test market   A controlled **marketing research** experiment carried out in a carefully chosen part of the marketplace, usually a representative test city, designed to predict the sales and profit of a particular element of a marketing strategy.

Marketers can design test markets to examine nearly every aspect of the **marketing mix,** ranging from a new-product **rollout market entry** to a subtle change in an existing **advertising** campaign.

Test markets have two significant drawbacks: They are expensive, and they give competitors time to react and respond to any new products or marketing strategies.

EXAMPLE: A soft drink company wants to introduce a new raspberry-flavored soda. It conducts a test market by introducing it for a short period in several small markets—say, Spokane, Washington; Knoxville, Tennessee; and Peoria, Illinois—all popular test markets. By analyzing sales and consumer reaction to the new soda, the company can decide whether to move forward with a full-scale introduction of the product.

throughput time   The total amount of time it takes for a product or service to move through the production process. Also called *total processing time.*

EXAMPLE: An insurance company training a sales staff might divide the process into the following tasks:

Item	Task	Time (in days)
1	Prepare phase 1 of training	4
2	Select salespeople	2
3	Send salespeople to training	2
4	Train salespeople	10
	Total	18

The throughput time for this entire process is 18 days.

time study   A process by which the amount of time required to perform a given task is computed.

The methods include direct time study, where the worker is timed with a stopwatch, and **methods-time measurement (MTM),** where the job is videotaped or filmed and analyzed using predetermined time values or historical data. A time study is distinguished from a motion study by the fact that motion studies aim to improve *productivity,* whereas time studies seek only to measure productivity. Time studies are usually viewed by workers with some suspicion, if not outright hostility. The dislike is based upon an ultimate use of the studies—setting production standards for labor.

total quality management (TQM)   A philosophy of total organizational involvement in improving all aspects of the quality of product or service provided by the organization.

TQM recognizes that it is very expensive to maintain quality by inspections and much more efficient to build quality products in the first place. As a result, responsibility for quality is placed at the source—that is, with the workers who actually produce the products. This is not to say that quality control departments are not an important part of TQM. Rather, they are refocused on different responsibilities, such as training employees in quality control techniques, conducting audits of the quality of the company's parts and suppliers, making final tests of finished goods, and implementing quality control concepts throughout the company. There are many aspects to TQM, including employee *empowerment* in *decision making,* the use of teams in the organization, individual responsibility for products or services, and a strong customer service orientation. The philosophy is to prevent defects from occurring, not to catch them after they have occurred.

See also ***self-managed work teams; team building.***

Toy Safety Act   An act passed by Congress in 1984 granting the government the power to recall dangerous toys quickly.

trade credit (domestic)   The payment terms granted to a buyer by a supplier.

Typically, suppliers grant discounts of 1 percent to 2 percent to buyers willing to pay the entire invoice within 10 to 15 days, but demand payment in full within 30 days. For large orders or orders for special or scarce materials, suppliers may, under certain circumstances, grant trade credit for 60 days, 90 days, or longer.

Trade credit is normally the least expensive and easiest way to finance short-term *working capital.* Assuming a company's credit rating remains satisfactory, suppliers grant trade credit without any *interest rate* or collateral. Occasionally, however, they insist that the *commodities* purchased be used to secure the credit. This happens frequently when selling to a company in *bankruptcy.*

trade credit (international)   The credit granted to buyers of exported goods and services.

Short-term trade credit may be *supplier credit* or *buyer* credit. Supplier credit is that credit extended to the buyer of exported products by the seller (the supplier-exporter). When such credit is extended directly by the seller, it is similar to domestic trade credit, except that sellers normally insist on a *letter of credit* (*L/C*) as collateral. If a letter of credit is used, the buyer essentially pays for the goods immediately upon shipment, thereby eliminating the need for 30-day, 60-day, or 90-day terms.

Supplier credit may also be granted through a third party—banks, *Export-Import Bank* (*Eximbank*), or the buyer's home-country export credit agency.

Buyer credit is that credit extended directly to the buyer from a third party, that is, a grantor other than the seller. Buyer credit is frequently needed when the shipment of export orders extends over a long time period—perhaps one or two years. Such credit is usually granted by banks or export credit agencies in the buyer's home country, or by Eximbank or other U.S. government agencies. The credit may carry guarantees, or it may stand alone.

Another difference between supplier and buyer trade credit is that supplier credit is recorded as a receivable on the exporter's books, whereas buyer credit is not.

trade deficit   An imbalance in merchandise trade that results in an excess of imports over exports.

The United States managed to keep its merchandise (goods) trade account close to balance through the first 25 years of the post–World War II era. In the 1970s, trade deficits became more common, but in most years the United States managed to keep the *current account* close to balance by running a surplus on the service and *investment* income accounts.

In the 1980s, a rapid appreciation in the dollar's *foreign exchange* value made U.S. exports expensive in foreign markets, whereas foreign imports became inexpensive in dollar terms. As a result, the foreign trade deficit widened sharply. This widening began to narrow only after the dollar began to decline in foreign exchange value in 1985, but the deficit remained wide in the early 1990s. The following table shows levels for merchandise exports, imports, and the trade balance for selected years:

U.S. EXPORTS AND IMPORTS
(Amounts in billions of dollars)

	Exports	Imports	Balance
1990	394.0	495.0	−101.0
1991	421.7	485.5	− 63.8
1992	448.2	532.7	− 84.5
1993	465.1	580.7	−115.6
1994	512.6	663.3	−150.7
1995	575.9	749.4	−173.6
1996	612.1	803.2	−191.2
1997	678.3	877.3	−198.9

SOURCE: Office of Trade and Economic Analysis, U.S. Dept. of Commerce.

trade finance   The financing of imports and exports.

Trade finance may relate to the granting of *credit* for the sale of goods or services, or it may refer to the financing of the production of goods to be exported. Financing may be short term (less than 12 months), medium term (one to seven years), or long term (more than seven years). It may be sourced either from the exporter's country or from the importer's country. *Supplier credit* and buyer credit are both part of trade finance.

Commercial and political risk insurance forms an integral part of trade finance. All industrialized countries and many near-industrialized ones have government export credit insurance programs. In the United States, the **Foreign Credit Insurance Association (FCIA)**, an arm of the **Export-Import Bank (Eximbank)**, insures U.S. exports against both political and commercial risk.

The following are major sources of trade finance:

- Commercial banks—in either the supplier's or the buyer's home country
- Government-sponsored export credit programs
- Private export credit organizations
- Major corporations through **joint venture (JV)**
- Private-sector, nonbank, trade finance organizations

trademark   The right of a seller to exclusive use of an identifying symbol, or **brand.**

The Trademark Act of 1946 defined these marks as "names, symbols, titles, designations, slogans, character names, and distinctive features used in advertising." All trademarks are brands, but not all brands are trademarks. A trademark can include both a **brand name** and a graphic design. *Ford* is a brand name, but when the word is printed in a certain kind of script, it becomes a trademark. When the identifying symbol is applied to a service, it is called a *service mark*.

transaction   The exchange of something of value between two parties to the satisfaction of both.

EXAMPLE: A chef pays a fisherman $5 for a live lobster. The chef receives the lobster, and the fisherman collects the $5.

Any transaction includes three key elements: (1) at least two items of value to the participants (the lobster and the $5), (2) mutually acceptable conditions (an agreed-upon price of $5 and a lobster that is indeed alive), and (3) a time and place of agreement (in this case, a fish market). If any of these three elements is unacceptable to either the chef or the fisherman, a system of regulations called *contract laws* comes into play. These are designed to protect both parties in a transaction and can be invoked by either side.

Compare to **transaction, barter; transaction, monetary.**

transaction, barter   A *transaction* in which the value exchanged is some item or service other than money.

Barter transactions frequently take place in the television industry. For example, a producer of a program offers a show to a television station at little or no cost, with the provision that several minutes of commercial time within that show be reserved for the producer. The show's producer then sells the reserved time to advertisers. No money changes hands in these deals, but both parties get something of value: The television station gets a show to air, and the show's producers get to sell some advertising time.

See also **transaction.** *Compare to* **transaction, monetary.**

transaction, monetary   A *transaction* in which one of the values exchanged is money (for example, a consumer pays $300 for a stereo).

See also **transaction.** *Compare to* **transaction, barter.**

transfer price   The price charged when one segment of a company provides goods or services to another segment of the company.

EXAMPLE: An automobile manufacturer has one division that manufactures engines and another that manufactures spark plugs. The spark plug division will sell its products to the engine division at a set transfer price.

transformation process   The process of adding value via the production process.

EXAMPLES: A refinery transforms crude oil into gasoline. A bakery transforms flour and other ingredients into bread. A hospital dispenses medical care to improve the health of its patients.

The transformation process has six key characteristics that are generally of interest to management:

1. *Efficiency.* Generally measured as units of *output* per unit of *input.* An efficiency rate of 80 percent to 90 percent is usually desirable. When comparing the efficiency of two different transformation processes, it is important to choose the correct measures for inputs and outputs. For example, a department store might measure efficiency in terms of sales dollars per square foot, whereas a hotel might measure efficiency in terms of room occupancy.
2. *Capacity.* The maximum load that an operating unit can handle. Capacity may be stated in terms of input or output of the unit being measured.
3. *Effectiveness.* The production of the correct outputs. Effectiveness differs from efficiency in that it is known as "doing the right thing," whereas efficiency is known as "doing the thing right."
4. *Response time.* The amount of time required to meet a user's or a customer's requirement.
5. *Quality.* The ability of an output to meet a specification of the product; the adherence to specifications. The performance of the product over time is its *reliability.*
6. *Flexibility.* The ability of the transformation process to produce different outputs.

transit advertising   Any advertisement appearing on vehicles such as buses, taxis, and subways.

Allowing advertisers to reach specific geographic *markets* with a high repetition rate, transit advertising usually takes three forms: (1) car cards located inside vehicles, (2) outside posters located on the sides or backs of vehicles, and (3) station posters located in terminals.

treasury stock   Shares of *common stock* that have been issued to the general public but are repurchased by the issuing company.

The shares then can either be resold at a later date or canceled. No *dividends* are paid on treasury stock, and it does not have any voting rights. Treasury stock is accounted for in two ways: the cost method and *par value.* Under the cost method, treasury stock is shown on the *balance sheet* as the cost of the reacquired shares. Under the par value method, treasury stock is reported on the balance sheet at the par value of the reacquired shares. Under either method, retained earnings are reduced by the amount of the treasury stock.

turnover ratio　A measure of the activity of a given **asset.**

There are several types of turnover ratios. Each is calculated by dividing sales or **cost of goods sold** by the particular asset in question. Examples include **fixed asset** turnover, which shows how well fixed assets were employed to generate sales:

$$\frac{\text{Sales}}{\text{Fixed assets}}$$

Accounts receivable turnover indicates how well accounts receivable were managed by showing how long they were held before collection:

$$\frac{\text{Sales}}{\text{Average accounts receivable}}$$

Inventory turnover shows the number of times that the average amount of inventory on hand has sold within a given period of time (*see also* **days inventory**):

$$\frac{\text{Cost of goods sold}}{\text{Average inventory on hand}}$$

two-bin system　A method of inventory control in which low-value parts or materials are stored in two bins, one large and one small. When the large bin is emptied, an order is placed for more materials, and the contents of the small bin are used to satisfy **demand** during the replenishment period.

A two-bin system requires no detailed inventory records. In some systems, it is the responsibility of the worker who uses the last part in a bin to notify stores to requisition more units. In others, a complete requisition or release is kept in the bottom of the large bin, to be sent to a supplier to place the order.

type I error　The rejection of a *good* lot on the basis of finding more than x defective units in a sample of n units.

A type I error is called the *producer's risk* because the producer ships an acceptable lot, only to have it rejected by the receiver. An acceptable lot is one with a percent defective that is equal to or below the **acceptable quality level (AQL)**.

See also **acceptable quality level (AQL)**; **type II error.**

type II error　The acceptance of a *bad* lot based on the inability to detect sufficient defective units within a sample to reject the entire lot.

A bad lot is one containing more than **lot tolerance percentage defective (LTPD)**. Type II errors are of great concern to companies wanting to avoid selling defective products. A pharmaceutical firm selling chemotherapy drugs would want to avoid type II errors on incoming materials at all costs. The consequences of selling defective drugs would be disastrous. Emphasis on avoiding type II errors for incoming materials is related to the impact that poor materials may have on the final product.

See also **lot tolerance percentage defective (LTPD)**; **type I error.**

underwriting   The guarantee an investment bank gives a company issuing securities that the bank will purchase the securities at a fixed price, thereby eliminating the risk of not selling the whole issue and receiving less cash than expected.

An investment bank that acts as an intermediary in the process of raising ***capital*** through public issues takes a risk by *underwriting* the issue. Investment banks may also sell the issue on a ***best effort*** basis, whereby the issuing company assumes the risk and simply takes back any securities not sold during a fixed period of time.

undifferentiated marketing   A ***marketing*** strategy that looks at the entire ***market*** as a whole, with no segmentation.

Also called *aggregate* or ***mass marketing,*** this strategy can help a company capture the whole market with one offer.

EXAMPLE: In its early days, the Coca-Cola Company practiced undifferentiated marketing by offering one drink in one container with one taste for the entire market.

unearned revenue   In accounting, any advance payment for future goods or services.

Since the payment creates an obligation to provide the goods or service, unearned revenue is reported as a ***liability*** on the ***balance sheet.***

unemployment rate   The proportion of the workforce who have either lost employment in the past month or who actively sought jobs unsuccessfully in that time.

The Household Survey of Employment is intended to assess the employment status of the working-age population, specifically, to distinguish between those who are employed and those who are unemployed. Unemployment represents one of the most important signs of an economy that is underperforming.

Unemployment can take four forms:

1. *Job losers* are workers who have lost their jobs either temporarily—and, therefore, are on layoff—or permanently. These people represent the most widely understood notion of the unemployed.

2. *Job leavers* are those who have voluntarily left a job to relocate or to acquire new skills. An increase in the number of job leavers is regarded as a sign of confidence in the strength of the economy. Workers would be unlikely to leave employment if they thought labor markets would be weak.

3. *Reentrants* to the labor force are people who formerly were active in the labor force, but who left—most often women leaving to rear families—and are now returning.

4. *New entrants* to the labor force are people seeking employment for the first time.

The unemployment rate is equal to the number of unemployed divided by the total **labor force** (employed plus unemployed) and expressed as a percent. The rate is a lagging indicator of economic activity, for when a recession begins, the unemployment rate may respond with a lag. More important, even after recovery starts, the unemployment rate may rise as reentrants and new entrants, believing jobs may be more readily available now that economic growth is returning, swell the labor force.

unfunded   In accounting, the condition of a reserve for future contingent payments wherein the balance is insufficient to meet the obligation.

The term is used to describe an accrual for vacation pay that is not backed up with actual cash reserves. It also describes the condition of the reserve set up under an employee **pension plan** that is not backed by cash deposits with a trustee or otherwise. In general, any reserve that represents an allowance for future payments and that is not backed by cash deposits is referred to as an *unfunded reserve*. Those reserves that are partially funded with cash deposits but not in an amount sufficient to meet the full future obligation are said to be *underfunded*.

units of production method   In accounting, a method of **depreciation** in which depreciation expenses are allocated by the use of the **asset** in production.

EXAMPLE: A candy company buys a packaging machine for $200,000 that it estimates will be able to put wrappers on 5 million candy bars during its life. In other words, the machine will depreciate by $0.04 ($200,000 ÷ 5,000,000 candy bars) every time it puts a wrapper on a candy bar. The machine's annual depreciation expense is then calculated by multiplying the depreciation per unit ($0.04) by the number of units produced during the year.

unqualified opinion   The report on a company's **financial statements** made by an auditor who presents the company's financial position, the results of operations, and any changes in financial position, in conformity with **generally accepted accounting principles (GAAP)**.

An unqualified opinion is sometimes called a *clean* opinion.

See also **adverse opinion; qualified opinion.**

useful life   The amount of time that a piece of machinery, a vehicle, or other *fixed assets* can be expected to last.

Useful life is an estimate used in accounting methods that estimate **depreciation.**

See also **double declining balance depreciation; straight-line depreciation; sum-of-the-years'-digits (SYD) method.**

utilization   The reduction in attainable **output** because of equipment failures, breakdowns, human error, materials problems, changes in **demand,** and so on.

Utilization is generally less than 85 percent of an operation's **effective capacity.** For example, if a factory operating three shifts experiences a drop in demand and a subsequent drop in utilization to, say, 65 percent, the factory should probably switch to using just two shifts.

V

value chain   The collection of activities within a company that allow it to compete within an industry.

The concept of the value chain was popularized by Harvard Business School professor Michael E. Porter, who argues in his book, *Competitive Advantage* (1985), that the activities in a value chain can be grouped into two categories: *primary activities,* which include inbound logistics such as materials handling, operations, outbound logistics such as distribution, marketing and sales, and after-sales service; and *support activities,* which include human resources management, company infrastructure, procurement, and technology development.

Each of the primary activities involves its own support activities. For example, operations must be concerned with the management of the human resources in the production department, its position within the structure of the company, the procurement of equipment and maintenance services, and the development of technologies to assist in the operations function.

By considering each activity within a company in terms of the value chain, it is possible to isolate a potential source of **competitive advantage.** For example, the development of a clear, simple system of invoices that can easily be compared with the goods received by a customer may simplify the customer's procedures, reduce the customer's costs, and increase the attractiveness of the supplying company.

Value Line Investment Survey   An **investment** advisory service that tracks over 1,700 stocks in 91 industries.

Regular updates report the current status of each company in the survey with respect to **market share** price and price/earnings and other financial ratios. For each company, the survey also presents historical financial trend data, descriptions of the company's business, major subsidiaries and locations, major institutional shareholders, names of top officers, and insider shareholdings.

Value Line has developed a unique feature whereby each stock is rated on timeliness of purchase and safety of investment. With the aid of a complex computerized model, Value Line projects which stocks will have the best and the worst performance over the succeeding 12 months. Each stock is also assigned a risk factor that measures the volatility of its price relative to market averages.

value-added tax (VAT)   A tax based on the value added to a product during each stage of its manufacture and to the sale price of the finished product.

The United States does not have value-added taxes, but they are used extensively throughout Europe and Canada. Opponents of implementing a value-added tax in the United States argue that it is merely a disguised national sales tax. Proponents point out that since the manufacturer pays a tax at each stage of production (which is deducted from the tax due on the sale of the finished product), consumers pay less than they would under a national sales tax. In fact, however, by paying a VAT at each production stage, manufacturers would certainly pass on this extra cost to consumers in the form of higher sales prices, which would also increase the base against which the final VAT would be applied.

variable, dependent   In a research project or scientific experiment, a value that *changes* as a result of some separate factor.

EXAMPLE: A greeting card manufacturer wants to examine the impact an *advertising* campaign has had on sales of Mother's Day cards. Sales of Mother's Day cards would be the dependent variable. Sales depend on a number of factors, including price, effectiveness of the advertising campaign, quality of the greeting cards, position in the *marketing* campaign, and a host of social pressures on the consumer.

Compare to variable, independent.

variable, independent   In a research project or scientific experiment, a value that *causes a change* in a separate factor.

EXAMPLE: If a snack food manufacturer wants to test the impact that a new package design has on sales, the package design would be the independent variable.

Compare to variable, dependent.

variable cost   In accounting, expenses that vary directly with changes in business activities.

For example, the cost of raw materials increases and decreases as the volume of production units changes. Total variable cost rises with the number of units produced. Per-unit variable costs remain constant.

variable costing   *See direct costing*

variable pricing   A pricing strategy that creates a flexible price for different customers or different times.

Industries with many small, independently owned companies, such as the antique business, frequently use variable pricing. This pricing strategy can be risky since a customer may leave after discovering that another customer has paid less.

variable-rate bonds   In corporate finance, *bonds* with an *interest rate* that is periodically adjusted according to changes in the prime interest rate offered by banks to their best customers.

Variable-rate bonds are frequently issued when future interest rates and *inflation* are difficult to predict.

venture capital   The main source of financing (primarily equity capital) for start-up businesses, R&D ventures, companies bringing out new product lines, and turnaround companies.

Also known as *risk capital,* venture capital used in investing is, by definition, full of risks. These *investments* command virtually the highest *rate of return* available in financial markets, and venture investors normally expect a return on investment principal of five to ten times in less than seven years, in addition to **dividends** and interest during that period.

Except in rare cases, a company's **cash flow** during the start-up period is insufficient to pay such high returns each year. Therefore, most, if not all, of the cumulative gain must come from an initial public offering (IPO; see **going public**) from the company. This becomes a decisive factor in the timing and pricing of initial public shares.

Venture capital investors make the basic assumption that, as a company's products are accepted in the marketplace, sufficient investor interest will be generated to make an IPO feasible. The resultant trading market should then enable the original venture investors to reap substantial appreciation on their investment when they cash in their holdings. In the right situation, they may keep their holdings to see whether the market will drive the share price up, but only when the spread between the offering price and the venture fund's expected gain is fairly wide.

A company that sells equity shares directly to venture investors avoids the costly exercise of using underwriters or public stock markets and simultaneously gets cash into the company much faster than through the convoluted process of issuing public shares.

Companies use venture capital—both equity and debt—for three broad purposes:

- As *seed capital* to cover initial market research, testing equipment, facility rent, basic operating supplies, experimental materials, perhaps the payroll for a few employees, and, at least partially, the entrepreneur's living expenses. Such expenditures occur during the setting up, development, and testing stages of a new product, process, or business.

- As **working capital** at the end of the development stage when the product or process nears market potential. This additional financing pays for the materials, labor, **overhead,** and selling expenses required to produce and sell the products in quantities that meet market demand.

- As *acquisition capital* to fund the purchase of an ongoing business by an established company or group of entrepreneurial investors.

vertical integration   Expansion by moving forward or backward within an industry. Frequently, vertical integration can create an effective **barrier to entry** by allowing a company to achieve cost efficiencies over its competitors because it can exercise greater control over its resources and distribution. In some cases, however, vertical integration can mask the profitability of various business segments. For example, in the brewing industry in the United Kingdom, brewers commonly pursued vertical integration by opening their own pubs. As a result, many companies consistently overstated the profits of their brewing operations and understated the profits of the pubs.

*See also **backward integration; forward integration.***

EXAMPLE: If a brewery were to expand its operations either to include the cultivation of barley and hops (backward integration) or to open a series of taverns (forward integration), it would be pursuing a strategy of vertical integration.

vertical marketing system (VMS) A *distribution channel* in which the manufacturer, *wholesaler,* and *retailer* act as a single system.

Usually controlled by one member, a vertical marketing system eliminates the conflict that can occur among independent channel members.

EXAMPLE: A clothing company might buy its own warehouses and trucks and open a chain of boutiques in order to bring the manufacturing, wholesaling, and retailing of its product under the same management.

Vertical marketing systems are now the dominant method of distribution in the United States, serving between 70 and 80 percent of the market.

With a vertical marketing system, goods flow more smoothly through the channel. Since distribution members are all working together, conflicts are largely eliminated. Companies can also achieve some *economies of scale* with this system: All members of the channel, for example, can use the same *marketing research,* accounting programs, and *advertising* personnel. Nonetheless, inefficiencies are introduced in the process of restructuring the channel, and creating the new channel can require a sizable financial *investment.* Legal restrictions may also interfere with setting up a VMS, since the government might view some vertical systems as reducing competition. Despite these drawbacks, companies in the United States and other developed countries are establishing increasing numbers of these systems.

VMS *See vertical marketing system*

volume segmentation The division of the *market* into groups based on product usage patterns (for instance, distinguishing among light, medium, and heavy users).

Marketers who examine product usage rates often find evidence of the 80/20 principle; that is, 20 percent of the market accounts for 80 percent of the sales. This rule of thumb cannot be applied to every product, but it does suggest the importance of a small group of buyers to the health of many companies.

The beer industry, for instance, has found that the 80/20 principle is true for its market. The high-volume consumer segment is attractive to beer marketers. It is male dominated, younger, generally blue-collar, less well educated than many of the peers in the same age group. And its members drink copious amounts of beer.

Two studies, conducted 20 years apart, examined purchase and consumption behavior for 16 categories of products. The researchers assigned consumers to a *light half* and a *heavy half* on the basis of annual per capita purchase rates compared with the median for the category. If a household's purchasing rate was greater than zero but less than the median for the product class, it was classified in the light half. If the rate was greater than the median, it was classified in the heavy class. The researchers found that certain product categories, such as cola, frozen orange juice, and bourbon, contained segments in which one heavy-half household was equivalent to eight light-half households—clearly demonstrating the value of volume segmentation.

*See also **market segmentation.** Compare to **behavioral segmentation; demographic segmentation; psychographic segmentation.***

W

warrants   A security that gives its holder the right to purchase a set number of shares of a company's *common stock* at a specified price (usually higher than the market price).

Warrants, more formally called *subscription warrants,* are usually issued along with a *bond* or *preferred stock.*

See also equity kicker.

wholesaler   A member of a *distribution channel* that purchases or receives goods from a manufacturer, then sells them to a *retailer.*

See also retailer.

word-of-mouth advertising   Any *advertising* communicated from a satisfied customer to another potential customer.

Word-of-mouth is not advertising in its strictest sense because the advertiser has not paid for the communication. Nonetheless, it can be a powerful *marketing* force.

working capital   In accounting, a measure of a company's ability to service its financial obligations.

Working capital is *current assets* less *current liabilities.* Sources of working capital are (1) *net income,* (2) an increase in *noncurrent liabilities,* (3) a decrease in *noncurrent assets,* and (4) an increase in *stockholders' equity.*

work-in-process inventory   Any partially completed goods on hand at the end of an *accounting period.*

Work-in-process inventory is classified as a *current asset* on the *balance sheet.* In an actual cost system, the beginning and ending work-in-process amounts are used in the calculation of *cost of goods sold* on the *income statement.*

EXAMPLE: A car without an engine would be classified by an automobile manufacturer as work-in-process inventory. Its value as a product simply reflects the costs of the product up to that point in time.

Compare to finished goods inventory; raw materials inventory.

write-down   In accounting, a reduction in the *book value* of an *asset.*

An asset is written down when there is strong indication that the asset's value is diminished.

EXAMPLE: If a portion of a company's ***inventory*** were to become obsolete, the total value of the inventory would have to be written down.

write-off   In accounting, the reduction of the entire value of an ***asset*** as either an expense or a loss.

EXAMPLE: If a company's uninsured warehouse is destroyed in a fire, the warehouse would have to be written off as a loss or expense.

yield to maturity *Rate of return* used to value debt securities.

The calculation of yield to maturity results in one of three possible conditions:

- The market-determined yield to maturity is equal to the security's *interest rate*, in which case the security's fair market value equals its face amount.

- The yield to maturity is less than the interest rate as indicated by the market yields of similar issues, in which case the security's fair market value is greater than its face value.

- The yield to maturity is greater than the interest rate, in which case the security's fair market value is less than its face value.

Although the interest rate determines the amount of *cash flows* from the security, the yield to maturity indicates the fair market value of that cash flow at any point in time.

The yield-to-maturity calculation recognizes (1) the annual interest received, (2) the difference between the current security price and its maturity value, and (3) the number of years to maturity. The formula to calculate the yield to maturity can be expressed as follows:

$$\text{Yield to maturity} = \frac{\text{interest} + (\text{par value} - \text{market value})/\text{number of periods}}{0.6(\text{market value}) + 0.4(\text{par value})}$$

The 60 percent and 40 percent factors in the denominator adjust for the slight differences due to mathematical averaging over time.

EXAMPLE: Assume the following conditions:

- The coupon interest payment is $150,000.

- The par value of the security is $2,000,000.

- The market value can be estimated as the present value of principal payments, or $1,295,923.

- The number of periods is six.

The solution for *yield to maturity* can be calculated as follows:

$$\text{Yield to maturity} = \frac{\$150,000 + (\$2,000,000 - \$1,295,923)/6}{(0.6 \times \$1,295,923) + (0.4 \times \$2,000,000)}$$

$$= \frac{\$150{,}000 + \$117{,}346}{\$777{,}553 + \$800{,}000}$$

$$= 16.95\%$$

Amortization lookup tables provide the same solution for those who do not care to do the math.

Z

zero defects   A quality philosophy wherein a company attempts to produce goods that are 100 percent perfect. Part of the philosophy requires suppliers to provide defect-free *inputs.*

zero-coupon security   A debt security that does not carry periodic interest payments but instead is sold at a deep discount from its face value.

    At the maturity date, the holder's gain is calculated as the difference between the face value of the security and the original purchase price. This difference is treated as interest income by the IRS, and, since it is assumed to be earned over the life of the security, it is taxed annually.

Part II

Sources of Business Information

SOURCES OF BUSINESS INFORMATION

In many business situations, it's best to "go to the experts." The experts are here. "Sources of Business Information" is a listing of hundreds of books, databases, sites on the World Wide Web, periodicals, trade associations, government agencies, and research institutes that can provide the most current information available on almost any business topic, ranging from trade opportunities in Asia to competitor intelligence to environmental issues.

The listings are organized under 48 headings, starting with "General Business Sources." This first section, perhaps more than any other, contains sources that offer an incredible wealth of information. These listings offer a comprehensive cross section of business data that can be applied to almost any situation. Each of the other 47 headings relates to a specific topic. They are arranged in alphabetical order, beginning with "Accounting and Financial Reporting" and ending with "Venture Capital/Sources of Capital."

Each individual listing includes the title/name of the source, its author(s), a concise description of the information offered, date/frequency of publication or updating, and the publisher's or provider's name. Published sources of information—whether print or electronic—are listed within each section alphabetically by title. Many sections within "Sources of Business Information" also contain descriptions of the services provided by relevant government organizations and trade and professional associations. These descriptions, within the relevant sections, follow the listings of published sources.

"Sources of Business Information" concludes with a "Directory of Publishers, Vendors, and Database Providers" containing complete contact information—address, telephone number (toll-free when available), fax number, and World Wide Web address (when available). Contact information for government agencies and trade and professional associations is included within the entry rather than in the "Directory of Publishers, Vendors, and Database Providers."

Essentially, "Sources of Business Information" is a "source of sources." If you need business information, you can find out where to get it (and how to get it as quickly as possible) here.

1

GENERAL BUSINESS SOURCES

ABI/INFORM®

An index to more than 1,000 journals for business and related fields, this database contains abstracts and full texts of articles from approximately 500 periodicals. ABI/INFORM covers all phases of worldwide business and administration, including accounting, banking, finance, data processing, economics, energy, the environment, health care, human resources, insurance, international trends, labor relations, law, management, marketing, public administration, and transportation. It also indexes company news and analysis, market conditions and strategies, international trade and investment, and economic conditions and forecasts. Coverage: 1971–present.

Available online, on CD-ROM, and on magnetic tape through UMI's database licensing program. Also available online through BRS Information Technologies, BRS/AFTERDARK, DataStar, DIALOG, ESA-IRS, HRIN (Human Resource Information Network), and ORBIT Search Service.
Updated weekly by UMI/Data Courier.
Hourly online charge: $75.00.
For more information, contact UMI, a Bell and Howell Information Company, 300 North Zeeb Road, Ann Arbor, MI 48106.
(800) 521-0600
(800) 343-5299 (Canada)
(313) 761-4700
http://www.umi.com

American Statistics Index (ASI)
Statistical Reference Index (SRI)

ASI and SRI are indispensable guides to business and industry statistics. ASI is a guide to all statistics published by the federal government and covers all types of statistical reports and publications (not restricted to those published by the Government Printing Office). The Congressional Information Service, Inc. (CIS) publishes ASI in two separately bound parts: an index section and an abstracts section. As of 1997, cumulative indexes are available for the years 1974–1979, 1980–1984, 1985–1988, 1989–1992, and 1993–1996. The ASI database is accessible online through DIALOG and is updated monthly.

SRI is a guide to statistics published by groups and associations other than the federal government, such as universities, state governments, business organizations, and independent research centers. The resource compiles statistical reports from more than 1,000 agencies, universities, and research centers, as well as from periodicals, foreign reports, and the like.

Researchers can use the index to find comparative data in geographic, economic, and demographic categories, or to locate works by specific authors and agencies. Abstracts of articles and reports can be ordered from the issuing source.

Both ASI and SRI are available at most larger libraries (in many cases the indexed publications are also on microfiche), or they can be ordered directly from the Congressional Information Service. ASI and SRI are also available on CD-ROM.
Published monthly, with annual compilations, by the Congressional Information Service.
For more information, contact CIS, 4520 East-West Highway, Bethesda, MD 20814-3389.

(800) 638-8380
(301) 654-1550
Fax: (301) 654-4033

AT&T Toll-Free 800 Directory

The AT&T directory is divided into two sections. The White Pages contain alphabetical listings by name of approximately 150,000 businesses, organizations, and government agencies that provide 800 service to the public. These listings also include section numbers that indicate under what product and service heading a listing may be found in the Yellow Pages, which contain listings alphabetically by subject.
Updated twice a month by AT&T.
For more information, contact AT&T at http://www.tollfree.att.net.

The Burwell World Directory of Information Brokers

Formerly titled the *Directory of Fee-Based Information Services,* this directory lists more than 1,800 information retrieval services in 46 countries and covers a variety of fields including market research, competitor intelligence, corporate benchmarking information, foreign country research, legal research, online database research, document retrieval/delivery, patent/trademark research, and library/information management consulting.
Published annually by Burwell Enterprises, Houston, TX.
For more information, contact Burwell Enterprises at http://www.burwellinc.com.

Business Dateline®

This database focuses on hard-to-find regional business news in the United States and Canada and covers topics such as city economics, labor markets, state regulations, and corporate news. It draws its information from more than 450 business news sources, including city business journals (e.g., *Crain's New York Business*), regional business magazines (e.g., *Northern Ontario Business*), wire services (e.g., *Business Wire*), and daily newspapers.

Current material is from 1994 to the present. Material from 1985 forward is available on tape and online through DIALOG.

Available online, on CD-ROM, and on magnetic tape through UMI's database licensing program. Also available online through DIALOG, Dow Jones News/Retrieval, HRIN (Human Resource Information Network), MEAD Data Central's NEXIS, OCLC's EPIC Service, and VU/TEXT.
Updated weekly by UMI/Data Courier.
For more information, contact UMI, 300 North Zeeb Road, Ann Arbor, MI 48106.
(800) 521-0600
(800) 343-5299 (Canada)
(313) 761-4700
http://www.umi.com

Business Index

This microfilm resource provides a cumulative index to more than 800 regional business newspapers and periodicals dating back to 1979. It indexes the following national newspapers: *Christian Science Monitor, Los Angeles Times, New York Times, Wall Street Journal,* and *Washington Post.* Searches can be made according to subject, author, or company names. Many subject headings employ business slang and jargon, which make the index more accessible to the general user.

Business Index is available at most large libraries, or it can be ordered (along with a microfilm reader) directly from Information Access. *Business Index* is also available on CD-ROM.
Updated monthly by Information Access Company/Predicasts.
For more information, contact Information Access Company, 355 Lakeside Drive, Foster City, CA 94404.
(650) 378-5200
Fax: (650) 378-5368
Info@informationaccess.com

Business Information Sources

Lorna M. Daniells

Widely considered to be the most comprehensive guide of its type available, *Business Information Sources* (commonly referred to as "Daniells") lists an incredible variety of business information sources. Lorna Daniells, who has acted as both Head of Reference and Business Bibliographer at the Harvard Business School's Baker Library, presents the book in two sections. The first section concentrates on general business reference sources, the kinds of libraries with business reference services, indexers, government publications, abstracts, databases, handbooks, cassettes and other recordings, and loose-leaf services. Chapters within this section also list sources for current information on business trends and statistics (domestic, foreign, and by industry).

The second section concentrates on specific management functions, such as finance, accounting, international management, and marketing. Entries in this section include books written for practicing managers, textbooks, periodicals, and professional associations.

Business Information Sources is available at most larger libraries.

Third edition published in 1993 by the University of California Press, Berkeley.

Business Organizations, Agencies, and Publications Directory

Jennifer Arnold Mast and Kimberly N. Hujt, editors

This directory provides information on the agencies, associations, publications, and databanks that help users find business information. The directory contains 26,000 entries describing 39 types of business information. The entries are arranged in five broad categories: (1) U.S. and international organizations, (2) government agencies and programs, (3) facilities and services, (4) research and educational facilities, and (5) publications and information services. The directory is avail-

able in the following alternative formats: computer diskette, online, and magnetic tape. Available online from OCLC EPIC.

Ninth edition published in 1997 by Gale Research, Detroit.

Business Periodicals Index

An index of 345 English-language business periodicals dating back to 1958, the *Business Periodicals Index* covers broad subjects such as accounting, advertising, communications, corporate acquisitions, foreign trade, marketing, and finance. In many cases it includes publications that might not be entirely business-oriented, such as *Telecommunications, Automotive News,* and *Journal of Consumer Affairs.* Usually, the articles cited by the *Business Periodicals Index* are geared for the general reader and avoid overly technical issues.

The Business Periodicals Index is published monthly, with periodic cumulations, and is available at most large libraries. As of 1998 it includes 679,000 records, and it adds more than 80,000 records each year. The index is also available on computer disk, CD-ROM, and online. Available online from OCLC EPIC, and WILSONLINE.

Price (1 disk): $1,495.00 for annual subscription ($1,125.00 for educational institutions). Additional charges for multiple users on LANs.

Updated monthly, with annual cumulations by H. W. Wilson Company.

For more information, contact the H. W. Wilson Company, 950 University Avenue, Bronx, NY 10452-4224.

(800) 367-6700

(718) 588-8400 (outside U.S. and Canada)

Fax: (800) 590-1617

(718) 590-1617 (outside U.S. and Canada)

E-mail: custserv@hwwilson.com

http://www.hwwilson.com

Canadian Business and Current Affairs

Coverage in this resource includes descriptions of companies and industry information based on more than 150 full-text English-language business periodicals, 600 other periodicals, and 8 news sources devoted to Canadian business and current affairs. It also contains references to filing notices with the Ontario Securities Commission. Available online through the Internet from Micromedia's Voyageur ERL server, on the Web at WebSPIRS, or through subscription.

Updated monthly by Micromedia, Ltd.
For more information, contact Micromedia, Ltd. at (416) 362-5211.

Directories in Print

Charles B. Montney, editor

This annual directory lists more than 4,000 different directories for nearly every conceivable subject, such as education, engineering, banking, agriculture, public affairs, and health. Included are descriptions of databases, buyer's guides, membership lists, registers, handbooks, indexes, who's who, factbooks, yearbooks, and annuals. Each entry includes the publisher's name, address, telephone number, frequency of publication, and price.

Directories in Print is available at most large public libraries. It is also available in the following alternative formats: computer diskette, online, and magnetic tape. Available online through DIALOG.

Published annually by Gale Research, Detroit.

Directory of Business Information

Lawrence Rasie

This volume is a general guide to thousands of sources, libraries, and databases relevant to all aspects of business. Part I lists general business sources; Part II guides the reader to three essential business areas (the economy, some 350 major industries, and 2,500 leading companies); Part III focuses on new businesses, small businesses, international businesses; and Part IV covers state and regional issues relevant to business.

Published in 1995 by John Wiley & Sons, New York.

Directory of Special Libraries and Information Centers

Janice A. Demaggio and Debra M. Kirby, editors

This directory provides information on holdings, services, and personnel of special libraries, research libraries, information centers, archives, and data centers. The directory lists more than 20,000 sources of in-depth information on many general topics, as well as business and finance. Entries are arranged alphabetically and contain information on library holdings, services, personnel, addresses, fax and telephone numbers, and electronic mail addresses.

The directory has three parts: Volume I, *Directory of Special Libraries and Information Centers;* Volume II, *Geographic and Personnel Index;* and Volume III, *New Special Libraries.* In addition to the print version, the directory is available on computer diskette and magnetic tape.

Twenty-second edition published in 1998 by Gale Research, Detroit.

Dow Jones Interactive

This service combines Dow Jones News/Retrieval (DJNR), the Wall Street Journal Interactive Edition, Business Newsstand, the Dow Jones Publications Library, and numerous other sources and databases. Searching and browsing are in most cases offered free of charges, though there are additional charges (varying by provider) for the printing of full texts. The services include:

Dow Jones Publications Library, a collection of more than 70 million articles in over 5,000 publications, searchable in seconds online.

Company & Industry Center, which provides full-text reports from market analysts and researchers.

Business Newsstand, which allows free searching and browsing, but charges $2.95 for each article downloaded or printed.

Historical Market Data Center, a survey of historical pricing and data on financial issues worldwide, including dividends, securities, and exchange rates.

The Wall Street Journal Interactive Edition, a frequently updated version of the *Journal,* available 24 hours a day.

Dow Jones Web Site Reviews, which rates some 1,000 of the most useful sites on the Internet.

Top Newspapers, a daily listing of the full texts of articles from the *Wall Street Journal* (plus international editions), *New York Times, Washington Post, Los Angeles Times,* and *Financial Times.*

Dow Jones Business and Finance Report, updated continuously throughout the day.

Dow Jones International News, which covers 6,000 companies and provides information on the world's financial markets, with daily updates.

Dow Jones Text Library, based on the *Wall Street Journal, Barron's, the Washington Post,* McGraw-Hill business journals, and 200 other periodicals. The Text Library offers reports on more than 7,000 companies and 50 industries. It is updated daily.

DowQuest contains the complete text of more than 400 general and specialized business publications, which form a subset of those sources listed in the Dow Jones Text Library. This source is updated weekly.

Dow Jones Enhanced Current Quotes, Dow Jones Historical Quotes (with stock quotations dating back to 1979), *Dow Jones Real-Time Quotes* (stock quotations without delay), and *Dow Jones Futures and Index Quotes* (with delay) are available on DJNR, FT Profile, and Prodigy.

As of October 1997, Dow Jones Interactive is available at two pricings. Enterprise offers (1) various combinations tailored to each corporate customer, and (2) standard pricing, which is $29.95 per year (first year free).

For more information, contact Dow Jones and Company.
(800) 369-7466
(609) 452-1511
http://www.dowjones.com

The Economist Atlas of the New Europe

The Economist Atlas shows the major political, economic, and physical aspects of the world's rapidly changing geography. It contains political and physical maps, updated to reflect such changes as the reunification of Germany; thematic maps and charts on topics such as foreign debt, balance of trade, food and hunger, the environment, and education; and 200 country and regional profiles in map, chart, and narrative formats.
Published in 1992 by Henry Holt and Company (U.S. and Canada) and Economist Books (United Kingdom).

The Economist Pocket World in Figures

This text provides factual coverage of a wide variety of topics relating to 170 nations, including demography, economic strength, agriculture, industry, energy, commodities, transport, finance, trade, employment, education, and the environment. The book's country-by-country and regional comparisons encompass more than 200 economic subjects, with information on subjects as diverse as government debt, GDP growth, alcohol consumption, standards of living, inflation, and advertising spending.
Published in 1998 by John Wiley & Sons, New York.

Encyclopedia of Associations: National Organizations of the U.S.

Deborah M. Burek, editor

The *Encyclopedia of Associations* is an invaluable resource for obtaining information on the associations connected with various businesses and industries. For example, groups associated with the candy industry listed by the *Encyclopedia* include the National Confectioners Association of the United States, the National Candy Wholesalers Association, and the National Candy Brokers Association. Each entry includes the association's address, telephone number, a short description of its goals and activities, the number of members, budget, and any association publications or conventions.

This three-volume work is available at most libraries, or it can be ordered directly from Gale (which also publishes directories of international, local, and regional associations). The *Encyclopedia* is also available in the following alternative formats: computer diskette, magnetic tape, and CD-ROM. Available online from DIALOG.

Thirty-third edition published in 1997 by Gale Research, Detroit.

Encyclopedia of Business Information Sources

James Woy, editor

The *Encyclopedia of Business Information Sources* lists almanacs, directories, databases, periodicals, trade associations, and statistical sources covering a wide range of business topics and specific industries. The book is arranged alphabetically, and each entry includes a full bibliographic citation, addresses, and telephone numbers of the respective publications, as well as the price of various publications.

The *Encyclopedia of Business Information Sources* can be found at most libraries. *Twelfth edition published in 1997 by Gale Research, Detroit.*

F&S Index™

This online service provides an index to 2,500 business publications. It contains more than 3.5 million citations and provides titles, sources, and dates of articles, plus a one- or two-line citation. The files cover worldwide company, product, and industry information.

The *Index* is available online from DIALOG, BRS, and Data-Star. Also available in print as *F&S Index United States, F&S Index Europe,* and *F&S Index International.* These print products are published monthly, with quarterly and annual cumulative editions.

Updated weekly by Information Access Company.
For more information, contact Information Access Company, 355 Lakeside Drive, Foster City, CA 94404.
(650) 378-5200
Fax: (650) 378-5368
http://www.informationaccess.com

Gale Directory of Online, Portable, and Internet Databases

An expansion of the *Cuadra Directory of Databases,* (acquired by Gale Research in 1991), this source provides information on numerous publicly available databases and database products. Information is provided regarding more than 15,300 databases, 3,600 producers, and approximately 2,000 online services, vendors, and distributors. Volume 1 covers 6,500 online databases; Volume 2 profiles approximately 6,400 database products, including CD-ROM, diskette, magnetic tape, handheld, and batch access databases, as well as Gale's *CyberHound's Guide to Internet Databases.*

As of April 1997 there were 21,044 records included. Available in print format, on CD-ROM, online, and tape.

Updated semiannually by Gale Research, Detroit.
Internet contact:
http://www.krinfo.com/dialog/databases/html2.0/bl0230.html.

Guide to Special Issues and Indexes of Periodicals

Miriam Uhlan and Doris B. Katz, editors

This guide details, in alphabetical sequence, 1,748 U.S. and Canadian periodicals that publish special issues (e.g., directories, buyer's guides, statistical outlooks, and other features or supplementary issues appearing on a continual, annual, or other basis). Each entry lists the special issues, the subscription address and subscription price of each periodical, and the price of each special issue.

Fourth edition published in 1994 by the Special Libraries Association, Washington, DC.

The Information Bank Abstracts

This database provides a source of general news abstracts, dating from January 1969, for articles in the *New York Times*, the *Wall Street Journal*, and other news sources. It is available online from NEXIS.
Updated daily by the New York Times Company.
For more information, contact LEXIS-NEXIS, P.O. Box 933, Dayton, OH 45401-0933.
(937) 865-6800
(800) 227-9597
http://www.lexis-nexis.com

Information Industry Directory

Joseph C. Tardiff and Mary Alampi, editors

This two-volume resource contains nearly 4,800 entries covering producers and vendors of electronic information and related services. The directory provides details on information producers and vendors, online services and networks, CD-ROM/optical publishing products and services, information-retrieval software, transactional services, library networks, information consultants, mailing list services, information-on-demand services, document delivery, consultants and service companies, and professional and trade associations and publishers. Each entry includes full address and contact information, complete description of organization services, and areas of specialization.

The directory is also available on computer diskette and magnetic tape.
Eighteenth edition published in 1997 by Gale Research, Detroit.

The Irwin Guide to Using the Wall Street Journal

Michael B. Lehmann

This book helps readers "to be their own economist." It shows how to use the information contained in the *Wall Street Journal* to analyze business trends and economic conditions.
Fifth edition published in 1997 by McGraw-Hill, New York.

Louis Rukeyser's Business Almanac

Louis Rukeyser

An extensive collection of business facts and statistics, this almanac profiles 57 different industries, from advertising to video games, and covers topics such as tax fraud, mergers and reorganizations, and the labor movement.
Revised edition published in 1992 by Simon and Schuster, New York.

Management Contents (MC)

This database focuses on business practices and management techniques, with general coverage in the areas of marketing, accounting, and human resources. Regarded as an excellent source with a practical bent, it provides an index and abstracts of articles from more than 120 U.S. and international management journals. MC is available online through DIALOG.
Updated monthly by Information Access Company/Predicasts.
For more information, contact Information Access Company, 355 Lakeside Drive, Foster City, CA 94404.
(650) 378-5200
Fax: (650) 378-5368
http://www.informationaccess.com

National Fax Directory 1998: How to Contact More Than 180,000 Major Fax Users in the U.S.

Mary Alampi and Sheila Dow, editors

This directory lists fax contact numbers for approximately 180,000 major corporations, institutions, and agencies in the United States, including law firms, government agencies, financial institutions, and manufacturers. It is divided into two sections: the alphabetical section, where all entries are listed in a single alphabetical sequence; and the subject section, where entries are alphabetically organized by subject.

Published and updated annually by Gale Research, Detroit.

The New Internet Navigator: A User's Guide to Network Exploration

Paul Gilster

The revised third edition of *The Internet Navigator* shows how to access the Internet's vast resources and explains how to use many of the tools for expediting electronic file transfers, searches, and network exploration. It lists information about local service providers and offers a useful guide to people who already have some experience with the Web.

Published in 1995 by John Wiley & Sons, New York.

The New York Times Index

This is a biweekly index, with quarterly cumulations, of articles published in the *New York Times*. Entries are organized by subject and include a brief summary of each article, along with the date and page of publication. The index is available in most large libraries, or it can be ordered directly from University Microfilms International. The index is available in print, microfiche, microfilm, CD-ROM, and online. (Full text of the *New York Times* is available on CD-ROM and online through NEXIS.)

Published biweekly by University Microfilms International, with three quarterly cumulations and an annual index issued as the fourth quarterly.

For more information, contact UMI at http://wwwlib.umi.com.

Newsletter Database™: The News behind the News

This online database contains the full text of more than 600 full-text business and industry newsletters published in the United States, Europe, Latin America, the Middle East, and Asia. The source provides expert opinions, analyses, and information on business activities in the global economy. Available online

from Data-Star, DIALOG, and Dow Jones News Retrieval.

Published and updated daily by Information Access Company/Predicasts.

For more information, contact Information Access Company, 355 Lakeside Drive, Foster City, CA 94404.

(650) 378-5200

Fax: (650) 378-5368

http://www.informationaccess.com

Newsletters in Print: A Descriptive Guide to Subscription, Membership, and Free Newsletters, Bulletins, Digests, Updates, and Similar Serial Publications

Louise Gagne, editor

This directory provides information on more than 10,000 newsletters. Entries are arranged in seven broad categories, including ones for business, industry, information, and communications. Also available online though DIALOG as part of Gale Directory of Publications.

Tenth edition published in 1997 by Gale Research, Detroit; new editions are published biennially.

Profound

The Dialog Corporation has constructed this comprehensive online service that provides nine databases with over 20 million articles, reports, forecasts, and other published materials. The site can be accessed at http://www profound.com and is available to registered subscribers.

PROMT™: Predicast's Overview of Markets and Technology

PROMT™: Predicast's *Overview of Markets and Technology* is a multiindustry database for information on companies in 65 industries, products, applied technologies, and markets. With coverage dating back to 1973, it contains more than 2.5 million abstracts and full-text articles and is currently increasing by over 600,000 records each year. The

sources for the database include U.S. and international trade and business journals, newspapers, regional business publications, corporate news releases, highlights from corporate annual reports, U.S. and international investment analysts' reports and industry studies, and government publications. Available online from Data-Star, DIALOG, and NEXIS. Also available in print version, published monthly, with quarterly and annual cumulative indexes.
Updated every business day by the Information Access Company/Predicasts®. For more information, contact Information Access Company, 355 Lakeside Drive, Foster City, CA 94404.
(650) 378-5200
Fax: (650) 378-5368
http://www.informationaccess.com

Standard Industrial Classification Manual

Although this manual is not exactly a source of general business information, it contains the standard classification system developed by the U.S. Office of Management and Budget, and it provides two-, three-, and four-digit Standard Industrial Classification (SIC) codes for classifying major groups, industry groups, and specific industries. It is used by both the federal government and the private sector to collect and analyze industry data.
Published in 1993 by Jist Works.

The Standard Periodical Directory: 1998

This is an annual directory of more than 85,000 periodicals published in the United States and Canada. Titles are organized by subject, and the directory includes a number of business and industry categories. Each entry includes the publication's title, the name of the editor of the publication, the publisher's name and address, frequency of publication, circulation, subscription price, and whether the periodical is available through an online database.

The *Standard Periodical Directory* is available at most large public libraries. It is also available on computer disk.
Published annually by Oxbridge Communications, New York.

Statistical Abstract of the United States: 1997

Prepared by the Economics and Statistics Administration of the Bureau of the Census, the *Statistical Abstract* is the standard summary of statistics on the social, political, and economic organization of the United States. It serves as a convenient statistical reference and as a guide to other statistical publications and sources. Some of the sections of particular interest to businesspeople include population; state and local government finances and employment; federal government finances and employment; labor force, employment, and earnings; income, expenditures, and wealth; purchasing power; cost of living; banking, finance, and insurance; manufacturing, and domestic trade and services.
Published annually by the U.S. Department of Commerce.

Statistics Sources, 1998: A Subject Guide to Data on Industrial Business, Social, Educational, Financial and Other Topics for the United States

Jacqueline Wasserman O'Brien and Steven R. Wasserman, editors

This two-volume set provides guidance to more than 2,000 sources of statistical information, including U.S. and international, print and nonprint, and published and unpublished sources. For each country, *Statistics Sources* gives the name of the major statistical sources as well as the national statistical office. For each subject, listings of print and electronic sources are complemented by the names and addresses of key live sources.
Published annually by Gale Research, Detroit.

Ulrich's International Periodicals Directory: 1998

This directory is a listing of more than 100,000 periodicals from around the world, broadly classified by subject. For example, the "Business and Economics" section includes entries for accounting, investment, small business, and general business publications. There are additional categories for specific industries and trades, such as construction, computers, or clothing. Each entry gives the periodical's title, name and address of its publisher, circulation, language of text, subscription price, and whether it is available through an online database.

Ulrich's can be found in most large libraries, or it can be ordered directly from R. R. Bowker (Reed Reference Publishing). The directory is also available on computer disk, CD-ROM, and online. The online directory is available through DIALOG. *Published annually by R. R. Bowker, New Providence, NJ.*

The Wall Street Journal

The *Wall Street Journal* is the leading business and financial information newspaper in the United States. In addition to its interesting and insightful business and general news articles, it provides a storehouse of economic and financial data on a daily, weekly, monthly, and quarterly basis. A listing of the statistical series published in the journal is as follows:

Series description	Publication schedule
Advance/decline (stocks)	Daily
American Stock Exchange composite transactions	Daily
Amex bonds	Daily
Auto sales	Monthly
Balance of payments	Quarterly
Balance of trade	Monthly
Banxquote index (deposit and CD interest rates)	Weekly
Banxquote money markets (deposit and CD interest rates)	Weekly
Bond market data bank	Daily
Bond yields (chart)	Weekly
Buying and borrowing (interest rates)	Weekly
Canadian markets (stocks)	Daily
Capacity utilization	Monthly
Cash prices (commodities)	Daily
Closed-end bond funds	Weekly
Commodities (article)	Daily
Commodity indexes	Daily
Consumer confidence	Monthly
Consumer credit	Monthly
Consumer price index	Monthly
Consumer savings rates	Weekly
Corporate dividend news	Daily
Corporate profits (Commerce Department)	Quarterly
Corporate profits (*Wall Street Journal* survey)	Quarterly
Credit markets (article)	Daily
Credit ratings	Daily
Currency trading	Daily
Digest of earnings report	Daily
Dow Jones averages (six-month charts)	Daily
Dow Jones commodity index (chart)	Weekly
Dow Jones industry groups	Daily
Durable goods orders	Monthly
Employment	Monthly
Foreign exchange rates	Daily
Foreign markets (stocks)	Daily
Futures option prices	Daily
Futures prices	Daily
GDP	Quarterly
Government agency issues	Daily
High-yield bonds	Daily
Housing starts	Monthly
Index trading (options)	Daily
Industrial production	Monthly
Insider trading spotlight	Weekly
Inventories	Monthly
Key currency cross rates	Daily
Key interest rates	Weekly

Series description	Publication schedule
Leading indicators	Monthly
Listed options quotations	Daily
Long-term options (stocks)	Daily
Manufacturers' orders	Monthly
Markets diary	Daily
Money market funds assets	Weekly
Money market mutual funds	Weekly
Money rates	Daily
Money-fund yields	Weekly
Municipal bond index	Weekly
Mutual fund quotations	Daily
Mutual fund scorecard	Daily
NASDAQ bid and asked quotations	Daily
NASDAQ national market issues	Daily
New securities issues	Daily
New York exchange bonds	Daily
NYSE composite transactions	Daily
NYSE highs/lows	Daily
Odd-lot trading	Daily
P/E ratios	Weekly
Personal income	Monthly
Producer price index	Monthly
Productivity	Quarterly
Publicly traded funds	Weekly
Retail sales	Monthly
Securities offering calendar	Weekly
Short interest (stocks)	Monthly
Short-term interest rates (chart)	Weekly
Stock market data bank	Daily
Treasury auction	Weekly
Treasury bonds, notes, and bills	Daily
Treasury yield curve	Daily
Weekly tax-exempts (bonds)	Weekly
World markets (stocks)	Daily
World value of the dollar	Daily
Yield comparisons	Daily
Yield for consumers	Daily

SOURCE: Michael Lehmann, *The Business One Irwin Guide to Using the Wall Street Journal*, 4th ed., Business One Irwin, Homewood, IL, 1993, pp. 352–354. Reprinted by permission.

The full set of the *Wall Street Journal* is available online through Dow Jones News/Retrieval and NEXIS.
Published Monday through Friday by Dow Jones and Company.

Wall Street Journal Index

This publication is an index to articles published in the *Wall Street Journal* from 1955 to the present and *Barron's National Business and Financial Weekly* from 1981 to the present. The index is divided into two segments: Corporate News and General News. Entries are organized by subject and company names, and each citation gives a short summary of the indexed article. Most libraries maintain back issues of the *Wall Street Journal* on microfiche or microfilm, and finding a particular article is generally a simple process. The *Wall Street Journal Index* is available at most libraries.
Published monthly by University Microfilms International, with quarterly updates and an annual cumulative volume.

Wilson Business Abstracts

This reference tool, available in multiple electronic formats, provides answers to business questions with abstracts from 345 business periodicals indexed in *Business Periodicals Index* (see p. 372). Searches can be done by subject, key word, company name, and SIC code.

Available electronic formats:

WILSONDISC	Updated monthly
WILSONLINE Online	Updated daily
WILSEARCH Direct Access	Updated twice weekly
WILSONTAPE	Updated monthly
WILSONWEB	Updated weekly

Indexing coverage begins with July 1982; abstracting coverage dates from June 1990. Full-text coverage begins with January 1995.

The World Almanac and Book of Facts

Robert Famighetti, editor

Although not exclusively a business publication, the *World Almanac* does have a useful economics and business section that covers a wide variety of topics, including U.S. budget receipts and outlays, national income by industry, gross domestic product, leading U.S. businesses, sales and profits of manufacturing corporations by industry group, consumer price indexes, state finance, global stock markets, personal consumption expenditures, employment statistics, and tax information.

Published annually by St. Martin's Press, New York.

FOR FURTHER INFORMATION

*See **Index to International Statistics**, p. 495*

2

ACCOUNTING AND FINANCIAL REPORTING

General

Accounting and Tax Database

This database provides indexing and abstracts to articles from more than 300 accounting, taxation, and financial management journals, newsletters, pamphlets, and proceedings. The *Accounting and Tax Database*, which won the KPMG Peat Marwick Global Information Award for "making significant contributions to the flow of business information throughout the world," also contains selected articles from more than 800 additional business journals, daily newspapers, and major news magazines, based on their relevance to the accounting and financial service industries. Available on tape or CD-ROM, or through UMI's ProQuest® product line.
Updated weekly by UMI/Data Courier.
For more information, contact University Microfilms International, 300 North Zeeb Road, Ann Arbor, MI 48106-1346.
(800) 521-0600
(800) 343-5299 (Canada)
(313) 761-4700
http://www.umi.com

The Analysis and Use of Financial Statements

Gerald I. White and Ashwinpaul C. Sondhi

This source provides a comprehensive discussion of theoretical, analytical, and practical issues involving financial statements and their preparation. Included are discussions, with illustrations, of the financial statement, inventories, long-lived assets, income taxes, retirement benefits, corporate and intercor-

porate investments, risk analysis, and valuation. Chapters conclude with actual problems and material drawn from the United States and some foreign countries.
Second edition published in 1997 by John Wiley & Sons, New York.

Encyclopedic Dictionary of Accounting and Finance

Jae K. Shim and Joel G. Siegel

This dictionary lists up-to-date technical information in more than 500 major areas of accounting and finance, including financial accounting, financial statement analysis, managerial/cost accounting, investments, and financial planning.
Published in 1990 by Prentice Hall, Englewood Cliffs, NJ.

Financial Warnings

Charles W. Mulford and Eugene E. Comiskey

The authors analyze corporate earnings and cash flows that occur in typical disasters befalling companies that suffer through major reductions in their financial conditions. This analysis helps readers identify the characteristics of those companies as a way of predicting which other ones are likely to suffer similar calamities. The authors explain how to correct, reverse, or soften the impact of large reductions in earnings.
Published in 1996 by John Wiley & Sons, New York.

The Portable MBA in Finance and Accounting

John Leslie Livingstone, editor

This guide to the basics of finance and accounting covers topics such as understanding financial statements, financial forecasting and budgeting, break-even and cost-profit-volume analyses, product pricing, evaluating acquisition targets, and managing foreign exchange risk exposure.
Published in 1997 by John Wiley & Sons, New York.

The Vest Pocket CFO

Joel G. Siegel and Jae K. Shim

This pocket-sized book offers easy-to-use solutions to many of the business problems faced by a CFO. Every major area of concern for the financial manager is covered, including financial and managerial accounting, financial analysis and planning, quantitative analysis and modeling, internal auditing and control, insurance, legal considerations, and taxation.
Published in 1992 by Prentice Hall, Englewood Cliffs, NJ.

Auditing

Miller GAAS Guide 1997: A Comprehensive Restatement of Generally Accepted Auditing Standards

Martin A. Miller and Larry P. Bailey

This guide explains all Statements on Auditing Standards (SAS), Statements on Standards for Accounting and Review Services (SSARS), and SOPs. It explores the entire audit process in detail, from preengagement planning to writing the auditor's report. It includes sections on statistical sampling techniques and procedures, internal control structure, evidence, audit risk, and related party transactions.

Published in 1996 by Harcourt Brace Jovanovich, San Diego.

Montgomery's Auditing

Vincent M. O'Reilly, Murray B. Hirsch, Philip L. Defliese, and Henry R. Jaenicke

This is a practice-tested guide for many aspects of auditing, from standards and responsibilities, risk, and engagement strategy through internal control, auditing specific cycles and accounts, and auditing reporting. Detailed guidelines cover the entire audit process and provide comprehensive auditing strategies and methods for 15 specific industries, including high technology and emerging businesses, education, construction, government, and a range of financial services.
Twelfth edition published in 1998 by John Wiley & Sons, New York.
Supplemented annually.

Financial Reporting and Disclosure

Accountants' Handbook

Martin Mellman and Steven B. Lilien
D. R. Carmichael, editor

Written by many of the nation's leading experts in all areas of accounting, *Accountants' Handbook* offers practical guidance on the full range of standards, techniques, and procedures in financial reporting, as well as fast, practice-oriented answers to accounting problems. Official pronouncements from SEC staff accounting bulletins, all FASB statements and interpretations, and technical bulletins are covered, along with detailed information on bankruptcy, estates and trusts, valuation of nonpublic companies, prospective financial statements, and benefits and compensation.
Eighth edition published in 1998 by John Wiley & Sons, New York.
Supplemented annually.

Accounting Trends and Techniques

Gerard L. Yarnall, editor

This publication provides the latest information on corporate financial statements and auditor's reports by surveying the annual reports of hundreds of industrial and merchandising corporations. It contains significant accounting presentations, and citations of FASB, APB, and SEC pronouncements. Available in both print and electronic formats.
Fifty-first edition published in 1997 by the American Institute of Certified Public Accountants.

Financial and Accounting Guide for Not-for-Profit Organizations

John J. McNally, Roger S. Bruttomesso, Richard F. Larkin, and Malvern J. Gross

A guide to the financial reporting, accounting, and control problems unique to not-for-profit organizations, this text offers advice on financial reporting, compliance auditing, and information on state charitable solicitations accounting. It provides a how-to section, with illustrations, on keeping books, submitting acceptable reports, and conducting audits of nonprofit organizations.
Published in 1998 by John Wiley & Sons, New York.
Supplemented annually.

Financial Reporting Using Computer Graphics, 1998 Cumulative Supplement

Irwin M. Jarett

This publication is a collection of practical tips and techniques for making successful financial presentations with computer graphics. A practice disk is included that presents examples of computer graphics and allows users to make changes to the sample screens and observe the impact the changes have on the graphics display file.

Published in 1998 by John Wiley & Sons, New York.
Supplemented annually.

GAAP: Interpretation and Application of Generally Accepted Accounting Principles

Patrick R. Delaney, Barry J. Epstein, James R. Adler, and Michael F. Foran

This guide for interpreting and applying generally accepted accounting principles (GAAP) presents real-world examples to illustrate accounting transactions and their presentation in financial statements. It is cross-referenced to the Financial Accounting Standards Board (FASB) current text and covers all original FASB pronouncements. The authors explain rules, terminology, concepts, and sources of GAAP affecting accounting decisions. Included are CPE examinations through which readers can earn up to 40 credits.
Published annually by John Wiley & Sons, New York.

Handbook of Governmental Accounting and Finance

Nicholas G. Apostolou and D. Larry Crumbly, editors

Comprising five parts and 41 contributed chapters, this handbook explains where the Financial Accounting Standards Board (FASB) ends and the Government Accounting Standards Board (GASB) takes over, and offers the newest GAAP methods for bringing controls up to speed with demands. Topics include dealing effectively with tighter budgets and diminishing unappropriated funds, and preparing for internal and external audits.
Second edition published in 1992 by John Wiley & Sons, New York.
Supplemented annually.

Handbook of Modern Accounting

Sydney Davidson and Roman Weil, editors

This comprehensive resource of accounting information includes topics such as financial statements, budgeting, mergers and acquisitions, cost analysis, and cash flow.
Third edition published in 1989 by Prentice Hall, Englewood Cliffs, NJ.

Miller Governmental GAAP Guide: A Comprehensive Interpretation of All Current Promulgated Governmental Generally Accepted Accounting Principles

Larry P. Bailey

This thorough restatement and analysis of all promulgated governmental accounting standards provides reporting standards for many nonprofit organizations, including hospitals, colleges, and universities.
Published annually by Harcourt Brace Jovanovich, San Diego.

National Automated Accounting Research System (NARS)

This database contains financial statements from more than 4,200 annual reports for each year on file. It covers companies traded on the New York and American stock exchanges, over-the-counter, *Fortune*-ranked, or designated as "on-margin" by the Federal Reserve. NARS also contains the complete text of a wide variety of accounting literature. For annual reports, the current five years are always available (earlier years, from 1972, are held offline); for literature, the extent of files may vary from the inception of each publication to the current period updated. Available online through LEXIS or Total On-Line Tax and Accounting Library (TOTAL). (SOURCE: *Gale Directory of Databases, Volume 1: Online Databases.*)
Updated weekly by the American Institute of Certified Public Accountants (AICPA).

Financial Statements Analysis

Financial Shenanigans: How to Detect Accounting Gimmicks and Fraud in Financial Reports

Howard Mark Schilit

This text provides tools for uncovering accounting gimmicks, to assist the reader in obtaining an accurate reading of a company's financial condition.
Published in 1993 by McGraw-Hill, New York.

How to Read a Financial Report

John A. Tracy

This nontechnical, practical guide explains the basics of the three key financial reports—the balance sheet, the income statement, and the statements of cash flows—and the relationship between them.
Fourth edition published in 1994 by John Wiley & Sons, New York.

How to Understand Financial Statements: A Nontechnical Guide for Financial Analysts, Managers, and Executives

Kenneth R. Ferris, Kirk L. Tennant, and Scott I. Jerris

This comprehensive guide provides complete instructions on how to assess the quality of a company's reported earnings, assets, and cash flow, as well as how to prepare financial statements using the most effective GAAP methods. The guide includes a ready-to-use computer disk with two programs. The first can be used to create a direct method cash-flow statement, perform ratio of cost-volume-profit analysis, and create data files. The second program allows users graphically to evaluate up to 19 financial ratios.
Published in 1992 by Prentice Hall, Englewood Cliffs, NJ.

The Vest-Pocket Guide to Business Ratios

Michael R. Tyran

This guide is a collection of more than 400 business and financial ratios.
Published in 1991 by Prentice Hall, Englewood Cliffs, NJ.

International Accounting

European Accounting Guide

David Alexander, editor

This survey of the accounting systems of 22 European nations researches and documents the financial structure of each country: Information on each includes an extensive historical background and an expert evaluation of the legal and economic environment.
Second edition published in 1995 by Harcourt Brace Jovanovich, San Diego.

International Accounting

Frederick D. S. Choi and Gerhard G. Mueller, editors

This book addresses issues, faced by multinational companies and others, caused by diverse accounting practices worldwide. Topics include the internationalization of the accounting function, financial analysis, harmonization, technical issues in accounting and auditing, financial reporting and disclosure, analysis, planning and control, and transfer pricing and taxation.
Second edition published in 1992 by Prentice Hall, Englewood Cliffs, NJ.

International Accounting Summaries: A Guide for Interpretation and Comparison

Compiled by Coopers and Lybrand International, this single-volume reference focuses on individual countries, detailing generally accepted accounting principles of more than 37 economic powers, as well as auditing requirements, financial reporting, and currency translation. It also presents the latest developments affecting the International Accounting Standards Committee and the European community. This edition includes sections on joint ventures and checklists for completing an international accounting standards disclosure or compliance statement.
Second edition published in 1993 by John Wiley & Sons, New York. Supplemented annually.

Management Accounting

The Complete Guide to Activity-Based Costing

Michael O'Guin

This step-by-step guide for implementing activity-based costing includes topics such as identifying the most- and least-profitable customers, calculating the real costs of buying versus manufacturing, and using pricing policies to boost profits.
Published in 1991 by Prentice Hall, Englewood Cliffs, NJ.

Controllership: The Work of the Managerial Accountant, 1997 Cumulative Supplement

James D. Wilson, Janice M. Roehl-Anderson, and Steven M. Bragg

This comprehensive guide to the traditional functions of the controller also shows how to evaluate short-term and strategic business plans, select the preferred financial alternative choices, and maintain a financial structure to meet business objectives. Topics include the role of the controller in international operations and investor relations, the internal audit function, and recruiting, training, motivating, and managing a professional financial staff. This edition covers computer systems and related technology.
Fifth edition published in 1997 by John Wiley & Sons, New York. Supplemented annually.

Handbook of Cost Accounting

Sidney Davidson and Roman L. Weil

The *Handbook of Cost Accounting* translates cost-accounting theory and procedures into practical examples and methods. Topics range from cost measurement to operating budgets. *Published in 1995 by McGraw-Hill, New York.*

Handbook of Financial Analysis for Corporate Managers

Vincent Muro

The *Handbook of Financial Analysis for Corporate Managers* provides scores of worksheets, checklists, and ready-to-copy spreadsheet models that make it easy to analyze, assess, and solve financial questions or problems, including identifying the most profitable product mix, discovering which cost-reduction measures will produce the greatest overall savings, and calculating break-even points.
Revised edition published in 1998 by AMACOM (American Management Association), Saranac Lake, NY.

Management Accounting Glossary

The National Association of Accountants, editor

Prepared by the 90,000-member Institute of Management Accountants (IMA), this vest-pocket-sized guide defines 816 key terms from a variety of sources, including IMS statements on management accounting, the Financial Accounting Standards Board (FASB), and Cost Accounting Standard Board (CASB).
Published in 1991 by Prentice Hall, Englewood Cliffs, NJ.

NAA Statements on Management Accounting

Compiled by the Institute of Management Accountants (formally, the National Association of Accountants), this collection of official statements provides industry-wide standards on management accounting, and represents the consensus of recognized leaders in industry, public accounting, and the academic world.
Published in 1989 by Prentice Hall, Englewood Cliffs, NJ.
Supplement published in 1991.

Relevance Lost: The Rise and Fall of Management Accounting

H. Thomas Johnson and Robert S. Kaplan

This book explores the evolution of management accounting in American business, from the early textile mills to present-day computer-automated manufacturers. The authors reveal why modern corporations must make major changes in the way they measure and manage costs.
Published in 1991 by the Harvard Business School Press, Boston.

Specialized Areas

The Accountant's Handbook of Fraud and Commercial Crime

G. Jack Bologna, Robert J. Lindquist, Anthony Walsh, and Joseph T. Wells

The *Accountant's Handbook of Fraud and Commercial Crime* shows how to recognize and deter fraud and commercial crime. It contains techniques and methods for detecting and documenting internal and external fraud and demonstrates how to set up monitoring and fraud-control mechanisms. Updates in the 1996 cumulative supplement include recent cases and developments in accounting procedures.
Published in 1993 by John Wiley & Sons, New York.
Cumulative supplement published in 1996.

Accountant's Legal Liability Prevention and Defense

George Spellmire, Wayne Baliga, and Debra Winiarski

The *Accountant's Legal Liability Prevention and Defense* shows how to safeguard against claims in audit, tax, review, compilation, and many other professional accounting engagements. Case studies illustrate common ways in which accounting firms are exposed to legal liability. The liability insurance chapter covers topics such as self-insurance and points to consider in choosing an insurance company.
Published in 1993 by Harcourt Brace Jovanovich, San Diego.

Accounting for Fixed Assets (The Wiley Institute of Management Accountants Professional Book)

Raymond H. Peterson

This comprehensive guide to the issues surrounding fixed-asset accounting includes topics such as capitalization, amortization, depreciation, taxes, and inventory. The authors examine specific accounting situations in regulated utilities, government agencies, and nonprofit organizations.
Published in 1994 by John Wiley & Sons, New York.

FAS 109: Analysis and Comments on the New Accounting for Income Taxes

James O. Stepp and Lawrence N. Petzing

This guide to the changes required by ruling 109 of the Financial Accounting Standards Board (FAS 109) includes topics such as implementation strategies, realization assessments, and business combinations.
Published in 1993 by John Wiley & Sons, New York.
Supplemented annually.

Managing the Audit Function: Corporate Audit Department Procedures Guide

Michael P. Cangemi

This manual is a collection of the techniques and procedures needed to set up and run an auditing department. Matrices developed by the author detail each component of the audit function, along with the methodology necessary for managing an audit department.
Second edition published in 1995 by John Wiley & Sons, New York.
Supplemented annually.

TRADE AND PROFESSIONAL ASSOCIATIONS

American Accounting Association

This is an academically oriented society for educators, practitioners, and students of accounting. Members receive two quarterly journals, *The Accounting Review* and *Accounting Horizons;* a newsletter, *Accounting Education News,* published six times a year; and a semiannual journal, *Issues in Accounting Education.* Members are eligible to serve on research and study committees and may utilize the services of the association's Clearing House on International Professor Exchange and Placement, continuing education workshops, and seminars.
American Accounting Association, 5717 Bessie Drive, Sarasota, FL 34233-2399.
(941) 921-7747
Fax: (941) 923-4093

American Institute of Certified Public Accountants (AICPA)

The AICPA is a national organization of certified public accountants. It creates and grades the uniform CPA Examination. The AICPA offers books, software, subscription services, practice aids, and CPA courses to its members. The AICPA's practice areas include the following: accounting and auditing, standards, tax information technology, the division for CPA firms, management consulting services, personal financial planning, business and industry, government, and accounting education.
Members receive the *Journal of Accountancy* (monthly), the *CPA Letter* (10 times a year), and, for units with fewer than 50 AICPA members, the *Practicing CPA* (monthly).
American Institute of Certified Public Accountants, 1211 Avenue of the Americas,

New York, NY 10036-8775.
(212) 596-6200
Fax: (212) 596-6213
http://www.aicpa.org

National Society of Public Accountants (NSPA)

The NSPA is an organization dedicated to representing and supporting the professional interests of independent, local, and regional accounting and tax practitioners through education opportunities, information resources, governmental representation, and a wide range of practice assistance services. Organized in 1945, it currently represents more than 20,000 accounting and tax professionals. *National Society of Public Accountants, 1010 North Fairfax Street, Alexandria, VA 22314-1547.*
(703) 549-6400
Fax: (703) 549-2984
E-mail: nsa@wizard.net
http://www.nsacct.org/

FOR FURTHER INFORMATION

*See **ABI/INFORM,** p. 370*
***Bankruptcy and Insolvency Accounting,** p. 395*
***Management Contents,** p. 376*

3

ADVERTISING

Advertising Age

This weekly trade publication, founded in 1930, covers the marketing industry and business issues that affect it. With a circulation of more than 90,000, *Advertising Age* is the largest and most popular journal in its field.
Advertising Age, 740 North Rush Street, Chicago, IL 60611.
(312) 649-5200
Fax: (312) 649-5331

Advertising Media Planning

Jack L. Sissors and Lincoln Bumba

A comprehensive introduction to media planning, *Advertising Media Planning* includes information on (1) selecting and evaluating specific advertising media, (2) basic terms and strategies, markets, and targets, (3) audience measurement techniques, and (4) response functions, media costs, and buying functions. The most recent edition adds a chapter on advertising on the Internet.
Fifth edition published in 1996 by NTC Business Books, Lincolnwood, IL.

Advertising Media Sourcebook

Peter B. Turk, Donald W. Jugenheimer, and Arnold M. Barban

Advertising Media Sourcebook contains dozens of media audience measurement sources, media cost sources, media cost estimators, and media audience reach estimators. Each reference is explained in a separate entry that includes (1) an explanation of the purpose of the source, (2) a description of how to read and understand the data, and (3) a practical application of the source to a realistic advertising media situation.
Fourth edition published in 1996 by NTC Business Books, Lincolnwood, IL.

Adweek

Adweek is a weekly trade magazine that reviews items of regional, national, and global interest for advertising agency executives. Published in six regional editions corresponding to geographical regions of the United States—New England, East, Southeast, Midwest, Southwest, and West—*Adweek* seeks to provide the context for developing and evaluating good advertising. It thus includes stories on legislative actions, creative efforts, fads, and trends. A major competitor for *Advertising Age*, *Adweek* focuses on advertising agencies and the campaigns they produce.

For the first half of 1996, *Adweek* and its two companion magazines, *Brandweek* and *Mediaweek*, had a circulation of nearly 90,000.

Broadcasting and Cable Yearbook

Formerly *Broadcasting Yearbook*, this two-volume annual directory is a comprehensive resource on the broadcasting and cable industries and includes the following information: listings of radio and television stations in the United States and Canada, with complete contact information; information on the top 38 U.S. and Canadian MSOs and their cable systems with over 20,000 subscribers; listings for advertising and marketing services for all media; and industry yellow pages.
Published annually by R. R. Bowker, New Providence, NJ.

Business Publication Rates and Data

This monthly publication contains editorial profiles, advertising rates, contract and copy regulations, mechanical requirements, issue closing dates, and circulation statements on 5,500 U.S. business, technical, and trade publications and on more than 500 international publications.
Published monthly by the Standard Rate and Data Service (SRDS).

Business-to-Business Advertising: A Marketing Management Approach

Charles Patti, Steven Hartley, and Susan Kennedy

Business-to-Business Advertising covers every step of the planning process—before, during, and after—for a business-to-business advertising campaign. It shows how to understand the behavior of business buyers and segment the market to find prospects, set advertising objectives and determine a budget, and measure the results of a campaign in terms of money, message, and media.
Published in 1991 by the NTC Publishing Group, Lincolnwood, IL.

Do-It-Yourself Advertising: How to Produce Great Ads, Brochures, Catalogs, Direct Mail, and Much More (Wiley Small Business Edition)

Fred E. Hahn and Kenneth G. Mangun

This text is a how-to guide for entrepreneurs and small businesses for writing, designing, and producing print ads, radio and television commercials, catalogs, flyers, brochures, and direct mail. The latest edition includes chapters on selecting print media, creating ads at home, and advertising on the Internet.
Second edition published in 1997 by John Wiley & Sons, New York.

Great Print Advertising: Creative Approaches, Strategies, and Tactics

Tony L. Antin

Directed at the interests and needs of product managers, this book shows how to direct the creation of effective print advertising for products. The text includes a checklist and guide for critiquing advertisements in copy and layout form. The author is a well-known designer of advertising at the *Reader's Digest.*
Published in 1993 by John Wiley & Sons, New York.

International Advertising Handbook: A User's Guide to Rules and Regulations

Barbara Sundberg Baudot

This handbook analyzes the state of advertising in industrialized countries and in the third world. It looks at laws and policies and their social, economic, and political impact on advertising.
Published in 1989 by Lexington Books, New York.

Legibility of Print

Miles A. Tinker

This book, though now old, is the definitive study on print legibility. The author, a psychologist, conducted tests on how people read, what they can read easily, and what they cannot. This is a useful reference for product managers who are making advertising decisions—and who otherwise may be led astray by art directors who too often fail to pay enough attention to the impact of typography (or lack of it) in print advertisements.
Published in 1963 by the Iowa State University Press, Ames.

Media Flight Plan III

Dennis G. Martin and Robert D. Coons

This resource teaches the basics of strategic multimedia planning, both national and spot.

It consists of a workbook and diskettes for IBM (DOS) and Apple Macintosh computer formats.
Published in 1996 by Deer Creek Publishing.

National Directory of Advertising: Print Media

This directory of more than 27,000 media sources in the United States and Canada lists all essential advertising information for magazines, journals, newspapers, newsletters, directories, and catalogs. The information for each entry includes an editorial description, ad rates, contact names, circulation, frequency, and printing information. Available in print and on diskette.
Published in 1992 by Oxbridge Communications, New York.

National Directory of Magazines: The Most Comprehensive Guide to U.S. and Canadian Magazines

Joy Goldstein, editor

This directory provides information on more than 20,000 U.S. and Canadian magazines. Listings for each publication include staff, advertising rates, circulation size, mailing list information, and production details.
Published in 1997 by Oxbridge Communications, New York.

Standard Directory of Advertisers

This two-volume directory lists more than 137,000 marketing personnel, in nearly 26,000 advertising programs. Names listed range from key senior executives to marketing managers to ad directors; entries include address, telephone number, fax number, subsidiaries and divisions, and number of employees.
Published annually by National Register Publishing, New Providence, NJ.
Periodic supplements and bulletins.

Standard Directory of Advertising Agencies

This directory of more than 9,700 advertising agencies and branch offices supplies business facts on the advertising agency business. Entries include names and titles of decision makers, actual budget figures, annual billing, and much more. The directory is available in most large libraries and can also be ordered directly from National Register Publishing, where it is available in both print and magnetic tape formats.
Published annually by National Register Publishing, New Providence, NJ.

Standard Directory of International Advertisers and Agencies

More than 2,000 companies and over 2,000 top agencies are listed in this directory covering the advertising industry in 90-plus countries. Also included is a quick reference section that answers the most commonly asked questions in international business on such topics as consulates and embassies, trade commissions and chambers of commerce, and currency and exchange rates.
Published annually by National Register Publishing, New Providence, NJ.

Strategic Media Planning: A Complete Text with Integrated Software

Kent M. Lancaster and Helen E. Katz

A book and software package, *Strategic Media Planning* allows users to manage the many sources of product, media usage, and consumer behavior data for media planning. Four programs are included on IBM-compatible and Macintosh software disks: (1) ADPLAN, for media plan development and reach/frequency analysis, (2) ADCOMP, for competitive spending analysis, (3) ADGOAL, for marketing situation analysis and goal setting, and (4) ADFLOW, for budget summaries and flowchart development.

Second edition published in 1996 by NTC Business Books, Lincolnwood, IL.

Tested Advertising Methods (Business Classics Series)

John Caples and Fred E. Hahn

This old but still valuable book is coauthored by John Caples, one of the most successful advertising copywriters and an Advertising Hall of Famer who wrote the classic "They laughed when I sat down at the piano." It provides real common sense, especially about getting the product benefits in the headline of the ad or in the beginning stages of the advertising copy.
Fifth edition published in 1997 by Prentice Hall, Englewood Cliffs, NJ.

Who's Who in Advertising, 1990–1991

This publication lists persons who have made conspicuous achievements that distinguish them from their contemporaries in advertising. It also lists incumbents in specified positions in the advertising industry. Vital statistics on each individual include specific occupation, family information, professional certification, awards, political affiliation, and address.
Published in 1990 by Marquis Who's Who, New Providence, NJ.

Writing That Works: How to Improve Your Memos, Letters, Reports, Speeches, Résumés, Plans, and Other Business Papers

Kenneth Roman and Joel Raphael

This book is a quick read that contains many useful tips about good advertising writing; it is particularly useful for anyone who approves advertisements. The authors are leading figures in the advertising industry.
Published in 1995 by HarperCollins, New York.

TRADE AND PROFESSIONAL ASSOCIATIONS

American Advertising Federation (AAF)

The goal of the AAF is to "promote a better understanding of advertising through government relations, public relations, and advertising education in order to further an effective program of advertising self-regulation." The 50,000 members receive the following publications: *AAF Annual Report to Members, AAF Washington Report,* and *American Advertising Magazine.*
American Advertising Federation, 1101 Vermont Avenue NW, Suite 500, Washington, DC 20005-0089.
(202) 898-0089
Fax: (202) 898-0159
E-mail: aaf@aaf.org
http://www.aaf.org

American Association of Advertising Agencies (AAAA)

The AAAA is the national trade association representing the advertising business with an orientation toward management. Its membership totals approximately 575 agencies, operating over 1,200 offices in the United States. Membership is conferred after an extensive examination of professional ability, financial integrity, and business ethics.
American Association of Advertising Agencies, Inc., 405 Lexington Avenue, New York, NY 10174-1801.
(212) 682-2500
Fax: (212) 682-8391
E-mail: aaaa@commercepark.com
http://www.commercepark.com/AAAA

Association of National Advertisers (ANA)

The Association of National Advertisers serves the interests of companies that advertise regionally or nationally. Membership is available only on a corporate basis. ANA pro-

vides professional programs on topics such as promotion strategy, media strategy, and television commercial production. Its publications cover the fields of advertising and marketing management, agency relations, advertising research and promotion, and merchandising and advertising issues.
Association of National Advertisers, Inc., 155 East 44th Street, New York, NY 10017.
(212) 697-5950
Fax: (212) 661-8057
Washington office: 175 K Street NW, Washington, DC 20006.
(202) 785-1525
Fax: (202) 659-3711

Magazine Publishers of America

This organization is the most important single source of information about magazines, particularly as advertising media.

Magazine Publishers of America, 575 Lexington Avenue, New York, NY 10022.
(212) 752-0055

FOR FURTHER INFORMATION

See **The Economist Pocket World in Figures,** p. 374
European Advertising, Marketing, and Media Data, p. 514
International Directory of Market Research Organizations, p. 433
Management Contents, p. 376
The New Marketing Research Systems, p. 435
PTS Marketing and Advertising Reference Service (PTS MARS), p. 435
The Survey of Buying Power, p. 436
The Survey of Media Markets, p. 436

4

BANKRUPTCY

Bankruptcy and Insolvency Accounting

Grant W. Newton and Gilbert D. Bloom

This two-volume guide offers a broad-based approach to bankruptcy and insolvency. Volume 1, *Practice and Procedure,* describes the economic, legal, accounting, and tax aspects of bankruptcy proceedings. Volume 2, *Forms and Exhibits,* illustrates the concepts and practices of Volume 1 and contains specific examples of various documents used in bankruptcy cases and out-of-court settlements. The 1997 edition highlights major changes in Sections 108 and 382 of the Bankruptcy Codes and includes information about partnership bankruptcies.
Second edition published in 1997 by John Wiley & Sons, New York.

The Bankruptcy Disclosure

This subscription publication follows all public companies in bankruptcy, default, or financial distress that have assets greater than $50 million. Information is provided on each company, its creditors, committees, securities, and plans of reorganization.
Published and updated monthly by New Generation Research, Boston.

Bankruptcy Yearbook and Almanac

Charles McHugh

This text provides comprehensive coverage of bankruptcy activity during the prior year, including U.S. court data, corporate statistics, top corporate bankruptcies, trends and topics in major corporate bankruptcies, and distressed securities markets and trading.
Fourth edition published in 1994 by New Generation Research, Boston.

Collier Consumer Bankruptcy Practice Guide

Henry J. Sommer and Lawrence P. King

Published in loose-leaf format, this three-volume set provides substantive analysis for handling a case under the bankruptcy code, keyed to the section numbers of the 1978 Code. The *Collier Bankruptcy Guide* explains liquidation, reorganization, and debt adjustment. It also discusses applicable Rules of Bankruptcy Procedure.
Revised edition published in 1997 by Matthew Bender, New York.
Periodically updated with supplements.

Collier's Handbook for Trustees and Debtors in Possession

Irving Sulmeyer, M. Rush, D. M. Lynn, M. R. Rochelle, R. J. Motern, and L. P. King (editor in chief)

This handbook is a guide for trustees in Bankruptcy Code cases and for laypeople and attorneys involved in Chapter 11 cases. Part I covers the problems incurred by a trustee in cases under Chapters 7, 11, 12, and 13 and includes forms, sample letters, checklists, and worksheets. Part II, *The Debtor in Possession Handbook,* spells out day-to-day procedures for key personnel in a Chapter 11 case.
Revised edition published in 1989 by Matthew Bender, New York.

Corporate Financial Distress and Bankruptcy: A Complete Guide to Predicting, Avoiding, and Dealing with Bankruptcy (Wiley Finance Edition)

Edward I. Altman

Edward Altman of New York University—widely regarded as one of today's leading experts on bankruptcy—examines the latest trends in this complex field, such as debtor-in-possession, lending, and prepackaged bankruptcies. He develops statistical classification techniques to assess the distress potential of companies and explores the applications of these models in a number of important practical areas. Two detailed case studies show how to do a thorough valuation analysis and suggest appropriate restructuring.
Published in 1993 by John Wiley & Sons, New York.

Saving Your Business: How to Survive Chapter 11 Bankruptcy and Successfully Reorganize Your Company

Suzanne Caplan

This book shows how to recognize the signs of a failing business and how to file for Chapter 11 bankruptcy (reorganization) rather than Chapter 7 (liquidation). It shows how to manage a company through the bankruptcy process; communicate with all parties in a bankruptcy, including secured and unse-cured creditors, customers, and employees; continue to do business with creditors; and rebuild a business after bankruptcy.
Published in 1992 by Prentice Hall, Englewood Cliffs, New Jersey.

The Small Business Bankruptcy Kit

Robert L. Davidson III

This book is directed at the interests and needs of owners of small businesses, whether sole proprietorships, partnerships, or corporations. It provides guidance to work alongside legal and tax professionals by explaining what bankruptcy is, who is eligible to file for it, and how to choose the best types of bankruptcy—Chapter 7, liquidation; Chapter 11, reorganization; Chapter 12, family farmer; and Chapter 13, wage earner. The book helps small-business owners understand the role of trustees in the bankruptcy law; how statutes, priorities, and creditor demands affect financial rights; how to secure protection against damaging actions by creditors; and how to discharge debts while retaining full control of the business. Sample forms and record-keeping worksheets are included.
Published in 1992 by John Wiley & Sons, New York.

For Further Information

*See **Predicasts' F&S Index of Corporate Change**, p. 426*

5

BENCHMARKING

Benchmarking: A Practitioner's Guide for Becoming and Staying the Best of the Best

Gerald J. Balm

This book is by the quality consultant at IBM Rochester, who facilitated the benchmarking efforts that led to the Baldrige Award. It contains a unique manufacturing case study.
Published in 1992 by the Quality and Productivity Management Association (QPMA).

Benchmarking: The Search for the Best Practices That Lead to Superior Performance

Robert C. Camp

Camp's reference—the first book on benchmarking—describes in detail the historic approach that was developed at Xerox during the 1980s, and the L. L. Bean benchmarking study.
Published in 1989 by the Quality Press/American Society for Quality Control (ASQC).

Benchmarking: A Tool for Continuous Improvement

Kathleen H. J. Leibfried and C. J. McNair

This text, a guide to the process of benchmarking, includes several interesting case studies: Avon, Janssen Pharmaceutica, and Exxon Chemical.
Published in 1992 by HarperCollins, New York.

The Benchmarking Book

Michael J. Spendolini

This basic guide to benchmarking by a retired Xerox employee focuses on developing, launching, and managing a benchmarking study.
Published in 1992 by AMACOM (American Management Association), Saranac Lake, NY.

The Benchmarking Management Guide

Gregory H. Watson et al.

This study of benchmarking by the American Productivity and Quality Center was originally published as a user's guide to benchmarking for the 130 member companies of the International Benchmarking Clearinghouse. It contains a wealth of information from surveys of the member companies (including DEC, Hewlett-Packard, IBM, Unisys, Westinghouse, and Xerox).
Published in 1993 by the Productivity Press, Cambridge, MA.

The Benchmarking Workbook: Adapting Best Practices for Performance Improvement

Gregory H. Watson

This workbook is targeted to support teams in conducting benchmarking studies. It presents a simplified process and walks the team through a case study. The book contains helpful forms and is rich in reference material.
Published in 1992 by the Productivity Press, Cambridge, MA.

INCITE

A software tool available from Quest Management Systems, INCITE offers reports on various competitive factors, which are referred to by the system as Essential Elements of Information (EEIs). EEIs can be created and maintained for a number of different market, industry, or business situations and can be accessed either through standard report formats, such as set benchmarks or competitive profiles, or through a series of specific inquiries.

Features include a reference library, which allows managers to integrate information on competitors into a single database; a search mode, which allows managers to locate specific information within the reference library through a series of key words or phrases; and an audit card, which notes the source, date of entry, and any comments for any information entered into the reference library database.

Updated as needed, approximately every 12 months, by Quest Management Systems.

Strategic Benchmarking: How to Rate Your Company's Performance Against the World's Best

Gregory H. Watson

Watson's third book on benchmarking fills a notable gap: It is aimed at the executive audience and focuses on the linkage of benchmarking to the strategic planning process. This book uses detailed case studies to illustrate how Hewlett-Packard, Ford, General Motors, and Xerox applied benchmarking concepts during the 1980s.

Published in 1993 by John Wiley & Sons, New York.

6

BUSINESS PLANS

Business Plan Workbook

Gary A. Cooper

This loose-leaf manual is a comprehensive guide to the creation of a business plan. The workbook covers plans to attract investors to a new venture, and plans to convince top management to support a particular project, product, or profit center. It provides numerous checklists and recommendations for creating an excellent business plan.
Published in 1989 by Prentice Hall, Englewood Cliffs, NJ.

Creating a Winning Business Plan: A No-Time-for-Nonsense Guide to Starting a Business and Raising Capital

Gregory I. Kravitt

A workbook format guides the reader in the development of a customized business plan to help determine and positively present the viability of a business start-up, business expansion, or business turnaround. It shows how to assess present information about management, ownership, employees, investment criteria, competitive analysis, production and operations, and government regulations.
Published in 1992 by Joraco, Inc.

The Entrepreneur's Guide to Building a Better Business Plan: A Step-By-Step Approach (Wiley Small Business Series)

Harold J. McLaughlin

The Entrepreneur's Guide combines the fundamentals of business planning with a step-by-step approach to developing a business plan. It details the necessary components for an effective business plan, including the charter and goals for products and services; market and market-share data; detailed departmental plans; and financial data. A number of sample business plans are included.
Published in 1992 by John Wiley & Sons, New York.

The Ernst & Young Business Plan Guide

Eric S. Siegel, Brian R. Ford, and Jay M. Bornstein

This comprehensive guide to planning, writing, and implementing a business plan provides a focus on the three roles of a business plan—as a tool for raising money, an aid to mapping out the future, and a measure for evaluating a company's performance. Features include a model business plan interspersed throughout the text, with a segment-by-segment critique; current examples of successful S corporations and C corporations; sections on funding and financial methods; provisions for restructuring and bankruptcy; and coverage of recent laws and regulations.
Second edition published in 1993 by John Wiley & Sons, New York.

Guide to Retail Business Planning: The Complete Handbook for Creating a Winning Plan for Any Retail Business

Warren G. Purdy

This source has been developed in conjunction with the Association of Small Business

Development Centers and represents the second installment of *Inc.*'s specific business planning series. The focus is on managers and owners of small businesses, and the book provides worksheets to guide the reader in creating a successful business plan.
Published in 1998 by Inc. Publishing.
For more information, contact Inc., 38 Commercial Wharf, Boston, MA 02110.
(617) 248-8000
Fax: (617) 248-8090

How to Really Create a Successful Business Plan

David E. Gumpert

This step-by-step process for creating a business plan shows entrepreneurial types how companies such as Ben & Jerry's, Celestial Seasonings, and Pizza Hut achieved success using their plans. Gumpert offers sage advice and tips on the writing and financing of the plan, and readers can use the questionnaires and exercises at the ends of chapters to construct their own business plans.
Third edition published in 1996 by Inc. Publishing, Boston.

How to Really Create a Successful Business Plan (Software)

This software program takes users step-by-step through the process of creating a business plan. The program asks users the questions they need to create a plan; users plug in numbers to create cash-flow statements, income statements, and balance sheets.
Program created for Inc. by Palo Alto Software.

How to Really Create a Successful Business Plan (Video)

This video uses examples and interviews with people at companies such as Ben & Jerry's and Pizza Hut for an overview of how to put together a successful business plan.
Released in 1992 by Inc. Business Resources.

The Inc. Guide to Creating a Successful Business Plan

The *Inc. Guide* takes readers step-by-step through the planning process, using excerpts from the actual business plans of companies like Celestial Seasons, Software Publishing, Ben & Jerry's, and Pizza Hut. Topics covered include explanations of the types of business plans that are right for different individuals, and how to price a product or service. Floppy disks (3.5″) are available for Windows 3.1 or later and for Macintosh. Cost is $219.00.
For more information, contact Inc. Business Resources at www.inc.com.

The Total Business Plan: How to Write, Rewrite, and Revise

Patrick D. O'Hara

This text provides a complete description of the business planning process, from concept, market planning, strategy development, research sources, and pricing concepts to writing the plan, and revising it for presentations to different target audiences. *The Total Business Plan* shows how to tailor the business plan using spreadsheet analysis, a word processor, and computer graphics.
Second edition published in 1994 by John Wiley & Sons, NY.

COMPETITOR INTELLIGENCE

Bloomberg L. P. Web site

This Web site can be accessed at the URL address www.bloomberg.com. Bloomberg specializes in providing financial news and data, collected by hundreds of reporters in news bureaus located the world over. It provides financial data, including stock quotes, market data, commodity prices, exchange rates for worldwide currencies, and news stories 24 hours a day.

Business Researcher's Handbook: The Comprehensive Guide for Research Professionals (Book One)

Leila K. Kight

This handbook shows readers how to fine-tune information requirements, organize research projects efficiently, manage investigations to get top value for time and money, and present information to management. *Published in 1983 by Washington Researchers, Washington, DC.*

Competitor Intelligence: How to Get It, How to Use It

Leonard M. Fuld

This book shows legal and ethical ways to obtain information about important aspects of the operations of competitors—including income statements and balance sheets, marketing strategy, sales force deployment, product features, and plant capacity. The author provides a methodology for intelligence gathering and gives specific advice for obtaining competitor intelligence in 50 major industries.

Published in 1987 by John Wiley & Sons, New York.

Competitor Intelligence Manual and Guide: Gathering, Analyzing, and Using Business Intelligence

Kirk W. M. Tyson

This collection presents hundreds of techniques and strategies for getting information on competitors—new-product plans, sales, costs, profits, and distribution networks. *Published in 1990 by Prentice Hall, Englewood Cliffs, NJ.*

The Complete Guide to Competitive Intelligence

Kirk W. M. Tyson

This newest edition offers hundreds of techniques and strategies for getting information on competitors—new product plans, sales, costs, profits, and distribution networks. *Published in 1998 by Kirk Tyson International.*

The Fuld Web site

Fuld & Company, located in Cambridge, Massachusetts, can be accessed at http://www.fuld.com. Launched in 1996, the "Competitive Intelligence Guide" on this site organizes a wide variety of data and provides Internet links to several hundred sources, including investment sources and information about domestic and international intelligence needs.

Hoover's

Hoover's Online service and handbooks provide information on companies, stocks, financials, and industries.

Its company information furnishes readers and subscribers with brief to in-depth profiles of over 12,000 companies, including histories, competitors, financials, and links to company Web sites.
www.hoovers.com

How Competitors Learn Your Company's Secrets (Management Solutions Series, No. 2)

Leila K. Kight, editor

This text presents the step-by-step process of preparing an entire company to resist incursions by outside information-gatherers.
Published in 1990 by Washington Researchers, Washington, DC.

How to Find Information about Companies

This three-volume work covers intelligence sources and methodologies for researching specific types of businesses. Volume 1 provides more than 9,000 sources of intelligence, including published and electronic sources; federal, state, and local regulators; and company experts. Volume 2 shows how to research specific aspects of a company, including products and services, personnel, distribution, and market share. Volume 3 shows how to research various types of companies: privately held, divisions and subsidiaries, foreign firms, service industry companies, and acquisition candidates.
Volume 1 published in 1978, updated in 1996; Volume 2 published in 1991, updated in 1996; Volume 3 published in 1992, updated in 1996.

Investext®

This database provides financial and market intelligence information. It provides the full text of more than 300,000 reports from investment banks, research firms, consulting firms, and brokerage houses. Coverage includes companies from the United States, Canada, Europe, and Japan. Also available in CD-ROM. Available online from CompuServe, Data-Star, DIALOG, Dow Jones News/Retrieval, and NEXIS.
Published and updated daily by Thompson Financial Networks.
For more information, contact Investext at 40 West 57th Street, Suite 1000, New York, NY 10019.
(212) 484-4700
(800) 662-7878 (client services)
Fax: (212) 484-4720
www.investext.com

The New Competitor Intelligence: The Complete Resource for Finding, Analyzing, and Using Information about Your Competitors

Leonard M. Fuld

This resource helps managers determine their competitors' operating costs, strategies (financial and tactical), decision-making processes, corporate structures, and production capabilities. Part I defines the key terms and discusses the ethics of searching for information about competitors. In Part II, the author details various sources, from government documents to the Yellow Pages, that the reader can use to uncover valuable information. Part III offers various "cases" and provides a tool kit for the discovery, and Part IV suggests courses of action that should follow the discovery.
Published in 1995 by John Wiley & Sons, Inc., NY.

PTSP—PROMT™

PROMT™ provides daily information and international coverage of manufacturing and service industries, technologies, business en-

vironments, and companies' products. Over 1,200 publications from around the world are consulted and translated, when necessary, into English. These sources include newsletters, government reports, investment analyses, corporate press releases, annual reports, and the like. For more information, call:
Information Access Company, 362 Lakeside Drive, Foster City, CA 94404
(415) 378-4643
(800) 321-6388
Fax (415) 378-4759

Understanding the Competition: A Practical Guide to Competitive Analysis

Kaiser Associates Inc. Staff

This guide leads readers through practical, action-oriented, and time-saving techniques for industry-, corporate-, and business-level analyses.
Published in 1984 by Washington Researchers, Washington, DC.

Washington Researchers, Ltd.

Leila Kight, president

Washington Researchers, Ltd., based in Rockville, Maryland, and established in 1974, provides custom research services, publications, and search engine references, and are experts in competitive intelligence. Through an extensive network, they are able to provide both research and reports for companies on topics from benchmarking to strategy.
Washington Researchers, Ltd., 416 Hungerford Drive, Suite 315, Rockville, MD 20850.
(301) 251-9550
Fax: (301) 251-9526
www.researchers.com

Who Knows about Industries and Markets: 1992–1993 (Briefcase Series, Book 4)

This publication lists 2,200 U.S. government experts—most of whom are in the Depart-

ment of Commerce, the Bureau of the Census, the International Trade Commission, the Department of Justice (Antitrust Division), the U.S. Customs Service, and the Congressional Budget Office—who are willing to answer questions (usually for free) about particular markets or industries. Each entry includes complete contact information.
Published in 1992 by Washington Researchers, Washington, DC.

Society of Competitor Intelligence Professionals (SCIP)

The SCIP assists members in assessing the behavior and strategies of their competitors. Membership carries with it a subscription to *Competitive Intelligence Review*. SCIP has local chapters in many cities as well as affiliates in Europe and Japan.
Society of Competitor Intelligence Professionals, 1700 Diagonal Road, Suite 520, Alexandria, VA 22314.
(703) 739-0696
Fax: 703-739-2524
E-mail: postmaster@scip.org
http://www.scip.org

FOR FURTHER INFORMATION

See **The Burwell World Directory of Information Brokers,** p. 371
Company Intelligence™, p. 422
Hoover's Handbook of American Business, p. 425
Hoover's Handbook of World Business, p. 495
INCITE, p. 398
Nelson's Directory of Investment Research, p. 420
PROMT™: Predicast's Overview of Markets and Technology, p. 377
Strategic Benchmarking: How to Rate Your Company's Performance Against the World's Best, p. 398

COMPUTERS AND INFORMATION TECHNOLOGY

Business Software Companion

Tom Badgett and Corey Sandler

This guide provides project-by-project guidance on how to use popular business software, including WordPerfect, Lotus 1-2-3, Word, DOS, DBase, Paradox, FoxPro, Quattro Pro, and Smartcom. It shows how to set up the printer, copy DOS files, format disks, set up a 1-2-3 spreadsheet, and format letters in WordPerfect.
Published in 1993 by John Wiley & Sons, New York.

Buyer's Guide to Micro Software

This database, produced by Online, Inc., is a directory of microcomputer software available for business and professionals in the United States. It provides directory, product, technical, and bibliographic information on leading software packages. Each disk includes directory information; technical specifications, including required hardware and operating systems; and an abstracted product description. Available through BRS and DIALOG.
Published and updated monthly by Online, Inc.
For more information, contact Online, Inc. at http://www.webworldinc.com/237b.htm.

Computer Database™

This database provides full-text abstracting and indexing from more than 150 journals covering every aspect of the computer, telecommunications, and electronics industries. *Computer Database* helps users find answers to questions regarding hardware, software, peripherals, robotics, neural networks, satellite communications, and videotext. It also includes product evaluations, comparisons and best buys, and profiles, complete with financial information, on computer, telecommunications, and electronics firms. Available through CompuServe, DataStar, DIALOG, Dow Jones News/Retrieval, and LEXIS/NEXIS.
Published and updated weekly by Information Access Company/Predicasts. For more information, contact Information Access Company at info@informationaccess.com.

Computer Industry Almanac

Egil Juliussen and Karen Juliussen

The *Computer Industry Almanac* is a compilation of facts, figures, and rankings covering every aspect of the computer business. It profiles more than 2,000 companies, provides a wide variety of rankings of computer companies, and looks at technology trends and industry forecasts.
Published annually by Computer Industry Almanac, Glenbrook, NY.

Datapro Directory of Microcomputer Software

This three-volume directory provides profiles of more than 18,000 applications and software systems packages. It is also available on CD-ROM (as Datapro Software Finder™) and online from DIALOG (as Datapro Software Directory).
Published and updated monthly by Datapro.

Datapro Reports

Datapro publishes a wide variety of specialized information services that analyze information technology products and services in communications, information systems, microcomputer and work group computing, office technologies, banking, retail, and manufacturing automation. These publications analyze products; provide managers with guidance in planning, designing, and managing communications, computers, and software environments; and profile vendors of information technology. Most publications are updated monthly, and international reports are available in communications, microcomputers, office technologies, and information systems.
Published by Datapro Information Services Group.
Additional information available from The Gartner Group, 600 Delran Parkway, Delran, NJ 08075.
(800) 328-2776
(609) 764-0100
Fax: (609) 764-2812
http://www.datapro@gartner.com

Datapro Software Directory

This three-volume directory provides profiles of more than 11,000 midrange and mainframe software products. It includes information on features, price, compatibility, date of introduction, and installed base of each software product. It is also available on CD-ROM (as Datapro Software Finder™) and online from DIALOG.
Published and updated monthly by Datapro.

Encyclopedia of Computer Science

Anthony Ralston and Edwin D. Reilly, editors

This single-volume reference of more than 600 articles covers the entire field of computer science: hardware, computer systems, information and data, software, mathematics of computing, theory of computing, methodologies, applications, the history of computer science, and current research in computer technology.
Third edition published in 1993 by Van Nostrand Reinhold, New York.

How to Computerize Your Small Business

Lori Xiradis-Aberle and Craig L. Aberle

Tailored for the absolute beginner, this book is a comprehensive reference for setting up a small-business computer system. It covers word processing, spreadsheet analysis, databases, software and hardware selection, and peripherals.
Revised edition published in 1995 by John Wiley & Sons, New York.

ICP Software Information Database

This database, available in print and CD-ROM formats, profiles more than 16,000 software products. The print version, *ICP Software Directories*, consists of four volumes. *The Software Directory* includes profiles of products important to management information systems and data processing management, such as resource management, data management, networking applications development, and programming. *The Cross Industry Applications Directory* is a directory of business software that includes products targeted to all industries, for example, office automation, spreadsheets, word processing, desktop publishing, accounting, and human resources. *The Industry Specific Applications Directory* of specialized software includes products targeted to markets such as insurance, banking, and manufacturing. *The Master Index* contains five separate indexes and is a road map to the foregoing three volumes. All of the information in these four volumes is available on a single CD-ROM.
Published three times per year, in January, May, and September, by ICP.

For more information, contact International Computer Programs, 823 East Westfield Boulevard, Indianapolis, IN 46220.
(317) 251-7727
Fax: (317) 251-7813
http://www.turboguide.com

Information Security: Dictionary of Concepts, Standards and Terms

Dennis Longley, Michael Shain, and William Caelli

This dictionary contains 3,500 entries on all aspects of information security.
Second edition published in 1993 by the Stockton Press, New York.

Information Sources in Information Technology

David Haynes, editor

This comprehensive guide to sources of data on information technology includes topics such as input and output technologies, data processing, magnetic media, networks, artificial intelligence, electronic mail, word processing, human-computer interactions, legislation, and copyright.
Published in 1990 by R. R. Bowker, New Providence, NJ.

PC Magazine

Each issue of this magazine contains many useful articles, surveys, product tests and advice on personal computer hardware, software, and related equipment and services.
Published monthly by Ziff-Davis Press.
http://www.zdnet.com/pcmag

Que's 1996 Computer Buyer's Guide: The Best Source for Choosing a System That's Right for You

Que's Computer Buyer's Guide provides information on IBM, Apple, and IBM-compatible PCs, as well as reviews of common peripherals

tested by various computer magazines and IT groups. The text explains software programs, printers, and modems, and provides a handy list of vendors and technical support lines.
Published in 1995 by Que Education & Training.

Software and CD-ROM Reviews on File

This subscription service offers reviews of more than 800 software programs and CD-ROMs. Each month *Software Reviews on File* provides condensations and abstracts of the actual reviews from more than 100 consumer magazines, Web sites, and other sources. It also includes software news briefs providing updates on the computer program industry, new software releases and upgrades, and best-seller lists of the most popular software sold in the various categories (e.g., database management, finance, word processing). Available in loose-leaf format through an annual subscription. Each monthly edition includes an A-to-Z cumulative index by subject (accounting, finance, management, computer graphics, education, personal finance, investments, and desktop publishing).
Updated monthly, with a cumulative index, by Facts on File.
For more information, contact Software and CD-ROM Reviews on File, 11 Penn Plaza, 15th Floor, New York, NY 10001-2006.
(212) 290-8090
(800) 363-7976
Fax: (212) 967-9051, (800) 363-7978
http://www.facts.com

The Software Encyclopedia 1997: A Guide for Personal, Professional, and Business Users

This two-volume encyclopedia offers thousands of fully annotated listings for new and established software programs. Entries are indexed two ways: by title, and by compatible system and application.
Published in 1997 by R. R. Bowker, New Providence, NJ.

Telecommunications Directory 1998: An International Guide to Electronic Transmission of Voice, Image & Data

The *Telecommunications Directory* provides detailed descriptions of more than 2,300 national and international communications systems and services, voice and data communications services, local area networks, and electronic mail services. The directory also includes information on consultants, associations, research institutes, publishers, information services, and regulatory bodies.
Ninth edition published in 1997 by Gale Research, Detroit.

TRADE AND PROFESSIONAL ASSOCIATIONS

Association for Information Technology Professionals (AITP)

The AITP, formerly the Data Processing Management Association, brings together managerial personnel, staff, educators, and individuals interested in the management of information resources and systems. Professional education programs include EDP-oriented business and management principles self-study courses and a series of videotaped management development seminars. The association conducts research projects and seminars.
Association for Information Technology Professionals, 315 South Northwest Highway, Suite 200, Park Ridge, IL 60068.
http://www.aitp.org

Information Technology Association of America (ITAA)

The ITAA is an organization composed of companies in the information technology business. The ITAA has several divisions: American Software Association; Entrepreneurs Division; Information Technology Services; Processing and Network Services; and Systems Integration. The association serves as an industry advocate and offers its 9,000 members a range of services, including assistance on computer law and a comprehensive publications program (e.g., *Membership Directory, Software and Services State Tax Report,* and *New Products and Services Guide*).
Information Technology Association of America, 1616 N. Fort Myer Drive, Suite 1300, Arlington, VA 22209-3106.
(703) 522-5055
Fax: (703) 525-2279
http://www.itaa.org

Society of Competitor Intelligence Professionals (SCIP)

The SCIP assists its over 6,000 members in assessing the behavior and strategies of their competitors. Membership carries with it a subscription to *Competitive Intelligence Review.* SCIP has local chapters in many cities as well as affiliates in Europe and Japan.
The Society of Competitor Intelligence Professionals, 1700 Diagonal Road, Suite 520, Alexandria, VA 22314.
(703) 739-0696
Fax: (703) 739-2524
E-mail: postmaster@scip.org
http://www.scip.org

FOR FURTHER INFORMATION

*See **ABI/INFORM®**, p.370*
***Information Industry Directory,** p. 376*
***The New Internet Navigator: A User's Guide to Network Exploration,** p. 376*

CONSULTING SERVICES AND CONSULTANTS

Consultants and Consulting Organizations Directory

The *Consultants and Consulting Organizations Directory* lists more than 17,000 consultants and consulting companies in the United States and Canada. Entries in this two-volume resource are arranged according to 14 broad fields, such as agriculture or marketing, and include each company's name, address, telephone number, fax number, principals, date founded, description of services, description of clients, geographic area of operation, any recent publications, and special services. The directory also includes an index that lists each consulting company by name, location, area of specialization, and personal name. In addition to the print version, the directory is available in computer diskette, online, and magnetic tape formats. Available online from HRIN.
Seventeenth edition published in 1996 by Gale Research, Detroit.

The Consultant's Proposal, Fee, and Contract Problem-Solver

Ron Tepper

This manual on conducting a consulting practice covers topics like generating leads, writing proposals, setting fees, and structuring contracts.
Published in 1993 by John Wiley & Sons, New York.

The Contract and Fee-Setting Guide for Professional Consultants

Howard L. Shenson

This step-by-step guide for conducting a consulting practice covers each stage of the consulting process, from fee setting and proposal writing to drawing up the contract and issuing the report.
Published in 1990 by John Wiley & Sons, New York.

Dangerous Company: The Consulting Powerhouses and the Businesses They Save and Ruin

James O'Shea and Charles Madigan

This investigative report unveils the best and the worst of the management consulting industry's successes and failures. The authors do not shy away from laying blame where they think it belongs, especially when it comes to corporate layoffs, reengineering, restructuring, and the like.
Published in 1997 by Times Business, New York.

The Directory of Management Consultants

James H. Kennedy, editor

This directory profiles 1,534 management consultant firms with 3,040 offices in the United States, Canada, and Mexico. Entries are indexed by services offered, industry, geography, and key principals. A description of each firm and key data on revenues and number of professionals are also included. *Revised edition published in 1997 by Kennedy Publications, Fitzwilliam, NH. Updated biennially.*

Dun's Consultants Directory

Dun's Consultants Directory identifies, locates, and classifies the top 25,000 consulting firms in nearly 200 major specialties, including agriculture, data processing, finance and accounting, health and medicine, and telecommunications. Entries are organized alphabetically, geographically, and by specialty. *Published annually by Dun's Marketing Services, Parsippany, NJ.*

Experts Contact Directory: Subject and Specialty Guide to 25,000 Academic and Government Experts

Nora Paul

The *Experts Contact Directory* is a selective compilation of contact information on 25,000 academic and government workers in the United States who have expertise in their fields. Arranged by hundreds of subject areas, the directory covers business, physical science, technology, government and public affairs, law, and many other topics. *Published in 1996 by Gale Research, Detroit.*

How to Succeed as an Independent Consultant

Herman Holtz

This guide to conducting a consulting practice includes topics such as government procurement rules, consulting as a second career, and getting the best value from the latest technology, including laptops, desktop publishing, and voice mail. It also offers advice on financial and insurance planning, IRS regulations, and consumer information. *Third edition published in 1993 by John Wiley & Sons, NY.*

FOR FURTHER INFORMATION

See **The Burwell World Directory of Information Brokers,** *p. 371*
Direct Marketing Consultants, *p. 440*
European Consultants Directory, *p. 514*
Information Industry Directory, *p. 376*
Nelson's Guide to Pension Fund Consultants, *p. 464*

COPYRIGHTS, PATENTS, AND TRADEMARKS

General

BNA's Patent, Trademark and Copyright Journal

This 20- to 40-page newsletter summarizes current case law and legislative developments in the areas of patent, trademark, and copyright law.
Published weekly by Bureau of National Affairs, Inc.
For more information, contact BNA Customer Relations, 9435 Key West Avenue, Rockville, MD 20850.
(800) 372-1033
Fax: (800) 253-0332
E-mail: icustrel@bna.com
http://www.bna.com

Daphne Hammond & Associates, Ltd.

This Washington, DC–area business can obtain, in many instances on a one-day basis, copies of patents, trademark application files and registrations, and copyright deposit material.
Daphne Hammond & Associates, Ltd., 2518 Fort Scott Drive, Arlington, VA 22202.
(703) 683-6295
Fax: (703) 415-0618

Intellectual Property: Financial Strategies for Licensing and Joint Ventures

Gordon V. Smith and Russell L. Parr

This text analyzes the business economics of licensing and joint venture strategies involving intellectual property. Topics include deriving royalty rates that are appropriate for licensing agreements, and deriving profit splits and equity ownership splits for joint ventures.
Published in 1993 by the Bureau of National Affairs, Rockville, MD.

International Treaties on Intellectual Property

Marshall A. Leaffer, editor

This volume is a collection of the full texts of the world's major agreements in all disciplines of intellectual property law—patent, trademark, copyright, and industrial design.
Second edition published in 1997 by Bureau of National Affairs, Rockville, MD.

McCarthy's Desk Encyclopedia on Intellectual Property

J. Thomas McCarthy

This comprehensive encyclopedia defines some 700 words and phrases in patent, trademark, copyright, trade secret, entertainment, and computer law. Each entry features the following: identification of the area of intellectual property law; its meaning and significance, fully annotated with cases, statutes, regulations, treaties, and bibliographic citations; and cross-references to other entries. Decisions of the U.S. Court of Appeals for the Federal Circuit that radically changed traditional rules and definitions are highlighted.
Second edition published in 1995 by the Bureau of National Affairs, Rockville, MD.

Official Gazette of the United States Patent and Trademark Office: Patents

This two-part weekly journal covers the registration of patents and trademarks. The

patent part contains all patents issued by the U.S. Patent and Trademark Office each week. The trademark part contains all applications that the Patent and Trademark Office accepts for registrations each week, as well as all registrations, registration renewals, and use affidavits it accepts each week.
Published weekly on Tuesday by the Department of Commerce, Patent and Trademark Office (U.S. Government Printing Office).

Patent, Trademark, and Copyright Laws 1997

Jeffrey M. Samuels, editor

This guide considers the most recent changes in the laws pertaining to trademarks, patents, and copyrights.
Published in 1997 by the Bureau of National Affairs, Rockville, MD.

Protecting Trade Secrets, Patents, Copyrights, and Trademarks

Robert C. Dorr

This comprehensive guide to the laws, options, and issues affecting the protection of intellectual property includes topics like federal and state laws governing patents, copyrights, and trademarks, and providing integrated protection for products or services. The 1998 cumulative supplement offers new chapters on copyrights and computer software.
Published in 1997 by John Wiley & Sons, New York.
Cumulative supplement published in 1998.

United States Patents Quarterly, Second Series

Published weekly since 1929, this case law reference source is the standard in the area of intellectual property law. It offers the full text of decisions involving patents, trademarks, copyrights, and unfair competition issues.

Weekly advance sheets give fast notification and full text of pertinent decisions from the U.S. Supreme Court, U.S. Court of Appeals for the Federal Circuit, U.S. Claims Court, U.S. District Courts, Patent and Trademark Office Board of Patent Appeals and Interferences, Patent and Trademark Office Trademark Trial and Appeals Board, U.S. Tax Court, U.S. International Trade Commission, and state courts.
Published weekly by Bureau of National Affairs, Inc.
For more information, contact Bureau of National Affairs, 9435 Key West Avenue, Rockville, MD 20850.
(800) 372-1033
Fax: (800) 253-0332
E-mail: icustre@bna.com
http://www.bna.com

World Intellectual Property Guide Books

This four-volume set covers patent, trade secret, copyright, trademark, and unfair competition law in the United States, United Kingdom, Canada, and Germany.
Published annually and updated periodically by Matthew Bender and Company, New York.

Copyrights

The Copyright Book: A Practical Guide

William S. Strong

The Copyright Book is a comprehensive guide to recent changes in U.S. copyright law, including case law on databases and compilations; copyrighting architectural designs; distributing software; "look and feel" cases; the moral rights of creators implied in the Berne convention; the implications of the Kinko's case; and new guidelines for off-air videotaping for educational use.
Fourth edition published in 1996 by the MIT Press, Cambridge, MA.

The Copyright Handbook: How to Protect and Use Written Works

Stephen Fishman

The *Copyright Handbook* provides forms and step-by-step instructions for protecting all types of written expression under U.S. and international copyright law. It contains detailed reference chapters on such major copyright-related topics as copyright infringement, fair use, works for hire, and transfers of copyright ownership.
Fourth edition published in 1997 by the Nolo Press, Berkeley, CA.

How to Copyright Software

M. J. Salone

Written expressly for software developers, this book explains copyright laws and how to enforce them; how to enforce development rights; and how to register a copyright for maximum protection. It also discusses who owns a copyright on software developed by more than one person.
Published in 1989 by the Nolo Press, Berkeley, CA.

How to Protect Your Creative Work: All You Need to Know about Copyright

David A. Weinstein

This book contains information about copyright subject matter, how copyright is acquired, the extent of copyright protection, and how to register a copyright with the U.S. Copyright Office. It contains sample agreements and registration forms.
Second edition published in 1997 by Andrews Publications, New York.

Patents

Attorneys and Agents Registered to Practice Before the United States Patent and Trademark Office, 1995

This source is a listing of patent attorneys and agents, with contact information.

Published and updated periodically by Superintendent of Documents, U.S. Government Printing Office.

CLAIMS™/U.S. Patent Abstracts, 1950+

This database contains patents listed in the general, electrical, and mechanical sections of the Official Gazette of the U.S. Patent Office and U.S. design patents. Searches can be conducted by key words, patent assignee, patent author, and application date or number. *CLAIMS™/U.S. Patent Abstract* covers the period 1950 to the present, and is available through DIALOG.
Updated weekly by IFI/Plenum Data Corporation.

Inventing and Patenting Sourcebook

Richard C. Levy

The *Inventing and Patenting Sourcebook* is a combination how-to guide and directory that takes readers step-by-step from the point of inspiration to the point of sale. The introductory essay offers advice on how to patent and trademark a product and how to select a company to approach for licensing. The book contains 35 usable forms, sample agreements, and applications for patents, trademarks, and copyrights. Each directory section provides information sources and contacts, including patent attorneys and agents, university innovation research centers, venture capital firms, and national and regional inventor organizations.
Second edition published in 1995 by Gale Research, Detroit.

The Inventor's Notebook

Fred E. Grissom, David Pressman, and Stephen Elias

The *Inventor's Notebook* is a guide to the documentation of the activities that are normally a part of successful independent inventing. Topics include conceiving, building,

testing, legally protecting, marketing, and financing an invention. Forms, instructions, references to relevant areas of patent law, and space for notes, drawings, calculations, and photographs are included.
Second Edition published in 1996 by the Nolo Press, Berkeley, CA.

PATDATA

This database includes detailed information and abstracts for all utility patents issued by the U.S. Patent and Trademark Office since 1975. The historical development of a particular patent can be traced back to 1836. Available online through BRS Information Technologies. The hourly charge is $65.00.
Updated weekly by BRS Information Technologies.
For more information, contact the U.S. Patent and Trademark Office at the Department of Commerce.
http://www.uspto.gov

Patent It Yourself

David Pressman et al., editors

A guide for inventors interested in obtaining a patent, *Patent It Yourself* explains the entire process from patent search to the actual application. Patent application forms and full instructions are included.
Sixth edition published in 1997 by the Nolo Press, Berkeley, CA.
For more information, contact Nolo Press at http:/www.nolo.com.

Patents, Copyrights and Trademarks

Frank H. Foster and Robert L. Shook

This book is a guide to protecting the rights to an invention, product, or trademark. Its coverage includes patent licensing, foreign patents, protecting computer technology and selecting a trademark.
Second edition published in 1993 by John Wiley & Sons, New York.

Trademarks

Brands and Their Companies: Consumer Products and Their Manufacturers

This two-volume set provides current information on more than 240,000 trade names, trademarks, and brand names of consumer-oriented products and their 43,000 manufacturers, importers, marketers, and/or distributors. It is available in print and in computer diskette, online, and magnetic tape formats. Available online through DIALOG as TRADE NAMES DATABASE.
Published annually by Gale Research, Detroit.

Companies and Their Brands

S. Edgar, editor

Companies and Their Brands lists 43,000 alphabetically arranged companies that manufacture, distribute, market, and import consumer-oriented products and the trade names, brands, and trademarks they hold. Each entry includes complete contact information. Text is available in print and in computer diskette, online, and magnetic tape formats. Available online through DIALOG as TRADE NAMES DATABASE.
Published annually by Gale Research, Detroit.

Compu-Mark U.S.

This national trademark-searching organization provides information about registered and unregistered names and marks in the United States and elsewhere by searching the U.S. Patent and Trademark Office records, state registration files, and information sources about unregistered marks.
Compu-Mark U.S., 1333 F Street NW, Washington, DC 20004.
(800) 421-7881.

Directory of Canadian Trademarks

This directory lists all active pending and registered trademarks filed with Consumer and

Cooperative Affairs Canada since 1867. The information includes owner name, trademark, registration, and serial number.
Published annually by Thomson & Thomson. For more information, contact Thomson & Thomson, 500 Victory Road, North Quincy, MA 02171-3145.
(800) 692-8833
(617) 490-1600
Fax: (617) 786-8273
http://www.thomson-thomson.com

Directory of U.S. Trademarks

This directory is the most comprehensive index of active trademarks filed, registered, and renewed at the U.S. Patent and Trademark Office. It includes both pending and registered trademarks and has over one million new and updated transactions. The information contained on each transaction includes the trademark, design indicator, last reported owner, registration, and serial number.
Published annually, with three cumulative updates each year, by Thomson & Thomson, North Quincy, MA.

How to Protect Your Business, Professional, and Brand Names

David A. Weinstein

This book for the businessperson provides information on how to select and protect a business name and trademark. Usable forms and sample agreements are included.
Published in 1990 by John Wiley & Sons, New York.

International Brands and Their Companies: 1995–1996

Linda Irvin and Leslie A. Norback, editors

International Brands and Their Companies contains listings of 80,000 consumer-oriented products in countries other than the United States and of the approximately 20,000 companies that make, market, or distribute them.

Lists are available in print and in computer diskette, online, and magnetic tape formats. Available online through DIALOG as TRADE NAMES DATABASE.
Fourth edition published in 1995 by Gale Research, Detroit.

International Companies and Their Brands: International Manufacturers, Importers, and Distributors, Their Addresses and Consumer Products: 1995–1996

Linda Irvin, editor

International Companies and Their Brands contains listings of 20,000 international manufacturers, exporters, and distributors of 80,000 consumer products. Lists are available in print and in computer diskette, online, and magnetic tape formats. Available online through DIALOG as TRADE NAMES DATABASE.
Fourth edition published in 1994 by Gale Research, Detroit.

International Trademark Directories

These directories provide a source of trademark information for European Community countries, Madrid Agreement countries, Switzerland, Austria, Liechtenstein, Eastern Europe, Scandinavian countries, Finland, Turkey, and others. Compilations of new filings and applications in products and classes may be selected by the user. See the Thomson & Thomson Web site (listed below) for additional directories on individual countries.
Published periodically by Thomson & Thomson.
Thomson & Thomson, 500 Victory Road, North Quincy, MA 02171-3145.
http://www.thomson-thomson.com

State Trademark and Unfair Competition Law

State Trademark and Unfair Competition Law is a state-by-state guide to the laws con-

cerning trademark registration, corporate and trade name registration, unfair business practices, false advertising, and franchising or business opportunity statutes.
Published in 1987 by Clark Boardman, New York.

Thomson & Thomson

This trademark-searching organization provides information about registered and unregistered names and marks in the United States and elsewhere by searching the U.S. Patent and Trademark Office records, state registration files, and information sources about unregistered marks.
Thomson & Thomson, 500 Victory Road, North Quincy, MA 02171-2126.
(800) 692-8833
Fax: (617) 786-8273
http://www.thomson-thomson.com

Trademark: How to Name Your Business & Product

Kate McGrath

This comprehensive do-it-yourself trademark guide designed for small businesses includes topics like conducting a trademark search, registering a trademark, and protecting and maintaining a trademark.
Second edition published in 1996 by the Nolo Press, Berkeley, CA.

Trademark Alert®
Trademark Alert® Industry Edition

This weekly publication contains information on all new trademark applications filed with the U.S. Patent and Trademark Office. Also available are industry-specific editions of *Trademark Alert* that allow users to zero in on product categories of most interest to them.
Published weekly by Thomson & Thomson, North Quincy, MA.

Trademark Service Corporation

This trademark-searching organization provides information about registered and unregistered names and marks in the United States and elsewhere by searching the U.S. Patent and Trademark Office records, state registration files, and information sources about unregistered marks.
Trademark Service Corporation, 747 Third Avenue, New York, NY 10017.
(212) 421-5730

Trademarkscan™ Online and CD-ROM

This database on trademarks and service marks provides information on all active registered trademarks and service marks and applications for registration filed at the U.S. Patent and Trademark Office, as well as in various foreign countries including Austria, Italy, Benelux (Belgium, the Netherlands, and Luxembourg), Liechtenstein, Canada, Mexico, Monaco, Spain, Denmark, Switzerland, France, Germany, Ireland, and the United Kingdom. Pending applications include both actual use and intent to use applications. The database is available in both CD-ROM and online formats, through DIALOG or Thomson & Thomson's SAEGIS™ service.
Updated periodically by Thomson & Thomson, North Quincy, MA.

World Trademark Journal

The *World Trademark Journal* provides trademark information for more than 200 countries. It lists compilations of new filings and applications in products and classes selected by the user.
Published weekly by Thomson & Thomson, North Quincy, MA.

GOVERNMENT AGENCIES

Public Libraries

Copies of patents can be obtained from U.S. Patent and Trademark Office depository libraries, located in most large cities. Many libraries keep copies of patents in a microfiche format. Many libraries provide trademark-searching services through a computer database, for a small fee.

U.S. Copyright Office

The U.S. Copyright Office registers copyrights and provides information about them.
United States Copyright Office, Register of Copyrights, Library of Congress, Washington, DC 20559-6000.
(202) 707-3000
http://lcweb.loc.gov/copyright

U.S. Patent and Trademark Office

The U.S. Patent Office grants and registers patents and trademarks. The office will also provide an index of patents, from which printed copies of patents can be ordered. Copies of patents can also be found at depository libraries located in larger cities. (In many cases, it can be very frustrating to try to get information on patents over the phone. Often it helps to contact the Patent and Trademark Office's Scientific Library. The library carries both U.S. and foreign patents, and provides limited search services.)

U.S. Patent and Trademark Office, Office of Public Affairs, Crystal Park 2, Suite 0100, Washington, DC 20231.
(703) 308-HELP
(703) 305-8341 (Public Affairs)
(800) PTO-9199
Fax: (703) 305-7786
http://www.uspto.gov

TRADE AND PROFESSIONAL ASSOCIATIONS

International Trademark Association (INTA)

Originally formed in 1878 as the United States Trademark Association, this nonprofit organization became the International Trademark Association or INTA in 1993. With some 2,000 members, it promotes trademarks as essential to commerce throughout the world. Its activities include educating business, the press, and the public to the proper use and the importance of trademarks.
International Trademark Association, 1133 Avenue of the Americas, New York, NY 10036-6710.
(212) 768-9887
Fax: (212) 768-7796
http://www.inta.org

CORPORATE AND INDUSTRIAL FINANCIAL DATA

Almanac of Business and Industrial Financial Ratios

Leo Troy

This annual volume provides comparative financial data on more than 180 fields of business and industry. It ranks small, medium, and large companies by 22 financial factors. *Published annually by Prentice Hall, New York.*

The Business One Irwin Investor's Almanac

Phyllis S. Pierce, editor

This annual publication includes, through the previous calendar year, complete Dow Jones averages with earnings, dividends, and price-earnings ratio; and records of common and preferred stocks and bonds listed on the New York Stock Exchange and the American Stock Exchange, showing the year's high and low prices, net change, volume, and dividend, and the year's most active stocks. *Published annually by Business One Irwin, Homewood, IL.*

Business Statistics of the United States 1997

Courtenay M. Slater, editor

This source provides data on numerous issues relevant to business, including employment, economic growth, the federal budget deficit, the CPI, taxes, and economic and demographic trends. Areas covered include construction, housing, oil and gas, transportation, utilities, retail and wholesale trade, government, and services.

Published in 1997 by Bernan, Lanham, MD. For more information, contact the Bernan website at http://www.bernan.com/bpbooks/busstat.html.

BusinessWeek Corporate Scoreboard

Each quarter *Business Week* presents the profit results for 900 companies in 24 industries. The results included in the "Scoreboard" include sales, profits, return on invested capital, return on common equity, price-earnings ratio, growth in common equity, growth in earnings per share, market value, and earnings per share. First-quarter results appear in a May issue, second-quarter in August, third-quarter in November, and fourth-quarter in February. *Published quarterly by Business Week.*

The BusinessWeek Global 1000

This annual July feature in a *Business Week* issue provides a country-by-country ranking of the world's 1,000 largest companies, ranked by market value (share price multiplied by latest available number of shares outstanding, translated into U.S. dollars). It also includes share price, price/book value ratio, price/earning ratio, sales, profits, and return on equity. *Published annually in a July issue of Business Week.*

The BusinessWeek 1000: America's Most Valuable Companies

This annual special issue of *Business Week* measures the value that the stock market places on 1,000 corporations and provides insight into the long-term outlook for these companies and the industries that they are a part of. The data presented include market value, sales, profits, margins, return on invested capital, return on common equity, assets, recent share price, high/low price, book value per share, price-earnings ratio, dividends, shares, outstanding earnings per share, and analysts' consensus estimates for earnings in the current year.

Published annually in an April issue of Business Week.

COMPUSTAT

The Compustat Database comprises financial (income statement, balance sheet, statement of changes in financial position), business segment, and market data on more than 7,600 U.S. and Canadian public companies. Twenty years of annual, 12 years of quarterly, 7 years of business segment, and 360 months of stock prices and dividend data are available for the above-noted companies and more than 270 industry groups, as well as selected data for more than 6,000 companies that no longer file with the SEC. The database is available online through ADP Network Services, CompuServe, Interactive Data, FactSet Data Systems, Warner Information Technologies, and Standard & Poor's Compustat Services.

Updated weekly by Standard & Poor's, New York.

Disclosure® Database

This database provides in-depth financial information on more than 12,500 companies. The information comes from reports filed with the U.S. Securities and Exchange Commission by publicly owned companies. Excerpts of 10-K and 10-Q financial reports are included, as well as 20-F financial reports and registration reports for new registrants. Available online through DIALOG, CompuServe, Dow Jones News/Retrieval, and NEXIS. Also available in CD-ROM format.

Updated weekly by Disclosure®, Inc.
For further information, contact Worldscope/Disclosure, LLC, 5161 River Road, Bethesda, MD 20816.
(800) 228-3220
Fax: (301) 215-6019
http://www.worldscope.com

Disclosure Worldscope™ Global

This database provides information on more than 9,000 companies from 40 countries. It includes general corporate information, financial statements, ratios (annual and five-year averages), and market data. Available in CD-ROM, magnetic tape, and online formats. Specific industry studies are available in a printed reference catalog. Available online through Dow Jones News/Retrieval.

Updated monthly by Disclosure®, Inc.

Dow Jones News/Retrieval

Dow Jones, the publisher of the *Wall Street Journal* and *Barron's*, has a number of databases that provide current information on market activities. They include the following:

Dow Jones Enhanced Current Quotes. Gives current quotes for common and preferred stocks and NASDAQ prices. Updated continuously throughout the day. Available online through Dow Jones News/Retrieval.

Dow Jones Futures and Index Quotes. Provides current and historical quotes for contracts traded on North American Stock Exchanges. Updated continuously throughout the day. Available online through Dow Jones News/Retrieval.

Dow Jones Real-Time Quotes. Provides real-time stock quotes from North American exchanges. Updated continuously throughout the day. Available online through Dow Jones News/Retrieval.

(SOURCE: Gale Directory of Databases, Vol. 1: Online Databases.)
All of the above published and updated by Dow Jones and Company.

Dun's Financial Record Plus

This resource provides financial data on 750,000 U.S. businesses, both public and private. The information available includes balance sheet, income statement, and 14 widely used business ratios. Coverage is for up to three years and includes company name, address, SIC code, number of employees, and D-U-N-S number. Available online through DIALOG and the Dow Jones News/Retrieval. *Updated quarterly by Dun & Bradstreet Credit Services.*

Forbes Annual Report on American Industry

This annual report from *Forbes* magazine analyzes 21 industries and looks at the results of companies within the industry according to the following criteria: profitability, growth in sales and earnings per share, sales, net income, and profit margin. *Forbes* identifies and profiles one standout performer in each industry by sorting out those with the highest profits per employee, the highest sales per employee, the best return on equity, and the lowest debt levels. Subjective criteria are also applied in selecting its standout company. *Published annually in a January issue of Forbes magazine.*

Industry Norms and Key Business Ratios

This resource contains financial norms and business ratios for more than 800 lines of business developed from over one million financial statements in the Dun & Bradstreet financial profiles of both public and private corporations. The businesses are arranged according to broad industry categories. *Published annually by Dun & Bradstreet Information Services.*

Media General Financial Services Database

This database is gathered primarily from company reports and SEC filings. It provides stock information and information from company annual and quarterly reports. Included in the database is information on more than 7,000 publicly held companies (companies listed on the New York Stock Exchange, the American Stock Exchange, and the NASDAQ over-the-counter market), 3,000 bonds, 2,300 mutual funds, and 175 industry groups and the financial markets. Available online through DIALOG and Dow Jones News/Retrieval. *Updated weekly by Media General Financial Services.*

Moody's Handbook of Common Stocks
Moody's Handbook of OTC Stocks

These two handbooks offer information on more than 2,000 companies representing 85 percent of total U.S. dollars traded. Company profiles include operating and stock performance summaries, as well as a complete business overview. *Published quarterly by Moody's Investor Services.*

Moody's Manuals

Moody's manuals are a valuable source of financial and other business information on both corporations and government institutions. There are eight manuals in this service: *Bank and Finance Manual, Industrial Manual, International Manual, Municipal and Government Manual, OTC Industrial Manual, OTC Unlisted Manual, Public Utilities Manual,* and *Transportation Manual.* The coverage of companies in the manuals includes financial data, description of business lines, corporate structure, corporate history, and corporate executives. The *Municipal and Government Manual* provides information on federal, state, and local government financing. The manuals are published annually and updated weekly or semiweekly through the New Report Service for each manual. The manuals are also available online through DIALOG as Moody's Corporate News—U.S. (corresponds to the News Re-

ports of the following manuals: *Bank and Finance, Industrial, OTC Industrial, OTC Unlisted, Public Utility,* and *Transportation*) and Moody's Corporate News International, which corresponds to the News Reports of the *International Manual.*
Published annually by Moody's Investors Service and updated weekly or semiweekly through the News Report Service for each manual.

Nelson's Directory of Investment Research

This two-volume work shows how to find research that has been done on 10,500 public companies in the United States and throughout the world. *Nelson's Directory* provides in-depth profiles of more than 400 investment research firms, including a listing of key research executives and descriptions of research services offered. There are also profiles of 10,500 publicly owned companies. The profiles include information on key executives, a five-year operations summary, and the names and phone numbers of security analysts for each company profiled.
Published annually by Nelson Publications, Port Chester, NY.

RMA Annual Statement Studies

This annual volume contains composite financial data on manufacturing, wholesaling, retailing, service, and contract businesses. It includes average balance sheet and income data for 392 different industries as well as five-year trend data for almost all of these industries. The data in the book can be used to compare an individual business's performance with the performance of the industry as a whole.
Published annually by Robert Morris Associates (The Association of Bank Loan and Credit Officers), Philadelphia.

SEC ON-LINE™

This is a full-text database of reports filed by companies with the U.S. Securities and Exchange Commission. It includes 10-Ks, 10-Qs, 20-Fs, annual reports, and proxy statements. Available online through DIALOG and LEXIS.
Updated weekly by SEC Online, Inc.

Standard & Poor's Corporation Records

This resource provides financial data and corporate descriptive information—including contact information, business summary, products and services, sales, and corporate structure—on approximately 12,000 publicly held U.S. and Canadian corporations. Also available online as Standard & Poor's Corporation Records Plus News through DIALOG and Knowledge Index. Also available on CD-ROM.
Updated biweekly by Standard & Poor's Corporation.

Standard & Poor's Industry Surveys

This resource provides a financial and business picture of 21 industries and more than 1,300 companies within these industries. Surveys are produced for the following industry groups: aerospace and air travel; autos, auto parts, and rubber; banks and financial services; chemicals; computers and office equipment; electric utilities; electronics; food and beverages; gas utilities; health care, drugs and cosmetics; insurance and investment; leisure time; media; metals, oil, and oil-field services; railroads and trucking; steel and heavy machinery; telecommunications; and textiles, apparel, and home furnishings. An annual *Basic Survey* for each industry group analyzes the operating environment and key issues faced by the industry, and provides financial data on key companies within the industry. The annual *Basic Survey* is supplemented by a monthly *Trends and Projections* newsletter; a monthly *Earnings Supplements;* and a periodic *Current Survey* providing an up-to-date analysis of issues facing the industry.

Each survey is published annually by Standard & Poor's and updated as indicated above.

Standard & Poor's Stock Reports

This loose-leaf service provides two-page reports, each of which offers a succinct profile of the activities and financial position of one of more than 4,000 companies. Reports are issued on all companies listed on the New York Stock Exchange, the American Stock Exchange, and more than 1,500 of the most active and widely held companies whose securities are traded over the counter and on regional exchanges, including Canada.

Loose-leaf service updated weekly; paper edition published quarterly by Standard & Poor's.

The Value Line Investment Survey

This weekly service reports on and evaluates approximately 1,700 stocks in 91 industries. Each stock's most recent price is reported as well as its current rankings for timeliness and safety (future price stability and the company current financial strength). A full-page report is issued on each stock about every 13 weeks. The report analyzes the company's business, looks at how its stock stands in relation to other stocks in terms of safety and probable performance over the next 12 months, and assesses the stock's future prospects. In addi-

tion to the print version, this service is available online through CompuServe as Value Line Annual Reports, Value Line DataFile, Value Line Estimates and Projection File, and Value Line Quarterly Reports.

Updated weekly by Value Line Publishing, New York.

FOR FURTHER INFORMATION

CORPORATE LISTINGS, OWNERSHIP, AND RANKINGS

America's Corporate Families

America's Corporate Families is a collection of detailed information on 11,000 U.S. ultimate parent companies and their 67,000 U.S. subsidiaries, divisions, and major branches. Listed companies have a net worth of at least $500,000, or net sales of $25 million, or 250+ employees, and a controlling interest in one or more subsidiary companies.
Published annually by Dun & Bradstreet Information Services.

America's Corporate Families and International Affiliates

America's Corporate Families and International Affiliates lists information on a total of 32,000 companies. It contains more than 1,500 U.S. ultimate parents with over 15,000 foreign subsidiaries, and nearly 3,000 foreign ultimate parents with more than 12,000 U.S. subsidiaries. To be included, a corporate family must have a U.S. family member or one or more family members elsewhere.
Published annually by Dun & Bradstreet Information Services.

Business Rankings Annual

This resource is compiled by the Brooklyn Public Library Business Library. It is a guide to published rankings and lists taken from leading business publications. The annual is arranged by subject and includes nearly 4,500 rankings, including profit, market share, sales, executive salaries, best-selling products, and advertising budgets. Each entry names a "top ten" along with the ranking criteria; the number of listings in the orig-

inal source; and the name, date, and page of the original source. Entries are indexed according to each item ranked. In addition to the print version, this resource is available on diskette and magnetic tape.
Published annually by Gale Research, Detroit.

Canadian Dun's Business Identification Service

This directory lists more than 650,000 Canadian businesses, from major corporations to rural merchants. Entries include complete contact information.
Published annually by Dun & Bradstreet Information Services.

Canadian Key Business Directory

This directory offers detailed information on more than 20,000 major businesses in Canada that each generate $20 million in sales, employ 75 individuals, have a net worth of $3.5 million, or have branches with more than 500 total employees. (All dollar figures reflect Canadian currency.) Entries are indexed alphabetically, geographically by province and city, and by line of business. Information on the executives, officers, and managers of these companies is also included.
Published annually by Dun & Bradstreet Information Services.

Company Intelligence™

This database combines company news with company directory information. More than 140,000 U.S. and 30,000 international com-

panies are included in the directory. Data include current address, ownership, and financial and marketing information. The U.S. company information is derived from *Ward's Business Directory* (see below, this chapter), and news articles are indexed by the Information Access Company. International Directories come from print directories published by Graham and Trotman of London. Available online through DIALOG.
Directory information updated annually, and news information updated daily, by Information Access Company/Predicasts.

The Corporate Directory of U.S. Public Companies

The directory lists more than 9,500 publicly traded firms, each having at least $5 million in assets. Entries are arranged alphabetically by parent company name and provide general background, stock data, and business description information.
Published annually by Gale Research, Detroit.

Directory of Corporate Affiliations

The *Directory of Corporate Affiliations* provides information on more than 117,000 of the world's leading companies, along with the names and identifications of 286,000 corporate executives.

Completely revised and updated, the five volumes of the 1997 edition provide the latest source of information on who owns whom. Only those public and private companies with at least $10 million in revenue are included. The new edition also includes the *Directory of Leading Private Companies*, formerly published as a separate entity. This is a description of 8,800 privately owned companies in the United States and their 12,200 affiliates, divisions, or subsidiaries worldwide. Available in print format, CD-ROM, tape, or online.
Published in 1997 by National Register Publishing, New Providence, NJ.
For further information, contact the publisher at http://www.reedref.com.

Directory of Multinationals

John Stopford

This two-volume directory deals exclusively with companies that control important foreign investments. It includes information on about 450 companies that account for the bulk of the world's direct foreign investment. All companies listed have at least $500 million in foreign sales. The directory lists the value of exports and foreign production of these companies.
Fourth edition published in 1993 by the Stockton Press, New York.

The Dun & Bradstreet Reference Book of American Business

This book presents business and credit information on more than 3 million large and small companies across the United States. Entries include the demography of a firm's location, how long the company has been in business, and its financial strength and overall credit appraisal. Regional and state guides are available in addition to the national edition.
Published annually by Dun & Bradstreet Information Services.

Dun's Business Identification Service

This is a collection of microfiche cards that lists nearly 10.2 million U.S. businesses. Entries cover large companies as well as companies that are either privately held or too small or too localized to be profiled elsewhere. The service is available in alphabetical or geographical sequence, and can also be purchased in Canadian and international editions. The service includes the D-U-N-S® numbers to aid in further research.
Published twice yearly by Dun & Bradstreet Information Services.

Dun's Business Rankings

This list ranks 25,000 public and private companies within 67 industries in the United

States. Companies are ranked by both sales volume and number of employees. Entries include each company's sales volume and rank; number of employees and rank; and name, address, telephone number, SIC code, and stock ticker symbol (where possible).
Published annually by Dun & Bradstreet Information Services.

Dun's Directory of Service Companies

This directory offers detailed information on 50,000 of the largest service enterprises with 50 or more employees in the following lines of business: accounting, auditing and book-keeping, advertising and public relations, amusement and recreation, architecture and engineering, consumer services, executive search, health, hospitality, management consulting, motion pictures, repair, research, social services, and law firms.
Published annually by Dun & Bradstreet Information Services.

Dun's Electronic Business Directory

This online directory provides information on approximately 9 million public and private businesses and professionals located in the United States. Each entry includes the following information: name, address, phone number, SIC code, and number of employees. Available online through DIALOG.
Updated quarterly by Dun & Bradstreet Information Services.

Dun's Regional Business Directory

This three-volume set offers information on 20,000 leading public and private regional businesses. Each edition of *Dun's Regional Business Directory* covers a single Economic Area Indicator (EAI). EAIs combine Standard Metropolitan Statistical Areas (SMSAs) with additional surrounding counties that have related economic impact. Regional coverage is currently available for 52 EAIs throughout the country.
Published annually by Dun & Bradstreet Information Services.

The Forbes 500 Annual Directory

This annual directory by *Forbes* magazine ranks the 500 largest publicly traded U.S. companies by four different criteria: sales, profits, assets, and market value. The total number of companies ranked in the 1998 directory was 779, reflecting the fact that some companies made the list by some but not all of Forbes' criteria.
Published annually in an April issue of Forbes magazine.

The Fortune Directory

This directory includes the results and rankings of *Fortune's* four annual "500" listings: the Industrial, Service, Global Industrial, and Global 500.
Published annually by Fortune magazine.

Fortune 500 Largest U.S. Industrial Corporations

This is *Fortune* magazine's annual listing of the top 500 industrial companies (ranked by sales volume and categorized by industry) in the United States. Each annual special issue also includes a "Who Did Best and Worst among the 500" section, which evaluates the list according to total return to investors, return on sales, return on assets, return on stockholders' equity, profits, change in sales, money lost, sales per employee, and sales per dollar of stockholders' equity.
Published annually in an April issue of Fortune magazine.

Fortune 500 Service Companies

This is *Fortune* magazine's annual listing of the 500 largest nonindustrial companies in the United States. The rankings of companies are within service areas. There is no overall 1–500 ranking as in the Fortune 500 Largest U.S. Industrial Companies. The special issue is widely available and can be found in nearly all libraries.

Published annually in a June issue of Fortune magazine.

Guide to Canadian Manufacturers

This is a collection of information on the top 15,000 manufacturing locations in Canada, each employing 20 or more individuals or generating $5 million or more in sales (Canadian currency). Each entry shows the company's name, address, telephone number, and four-digit SIC codes.

Published annually by Dun & Bradstreet Information Services.

Hoover's Handbook of American Business

The Web version of this source now lists more than 12,000 companies, with approximately ten more companies being added each day. The goal is to cover some 15,000 of the world's most influential and largest companies by the fall of 1998. At present, access to this source is free for basic information, but subscribers (at the current rate of $12.95 per month or $124.95 per year) have much more extensive access, including full company profiles and information on company strategy, products, services, competition, SEC documents, and ten-year historical surveys of financial data.

Published and updated by the Reference Press, Austin, TX.

For more information, contact the publisher at http://www.hoovers.com.

International Directory of Corporate Affiliations

This directory offers information on more than 57,000 companies around the world. It provides an in-depth view of non-U.S. parent companies and U.S. and worldwide holdings of international companies. The directory provides company statistics, information on key personnel, chain of command, and financial data. The directory is available in print, on disk, and online through DIALOG as CORPORATE AFFILIATIONS.

Updated semiannually by National Register Publishing (Reed Reference Publishing), New Providence, NJ.

Manufacturing USA

Arsen J. Darnay, editor

Manufacturing USA provides company profiles and rankings for about 460 top manufacturers. Organized by industry according to four-digit SIC codes, entries provide facts and tables on a number of subjects, ranging from general industry statistics to shipments and employment trends for each industry. Within each industry, profiles provide general industry statistics, indices of change, selected ratios, product share, statistical analyses by state and regions, occupations employed by various industries, up to 75 leading companies ranked by sales, and other valuable data. Entries are indexed by product, company name, occupations employed, and SIC code.

Second edition published in 1992 by Gale Research, Detroit.

Million Dollar Directory Series

This six-volume directory profiles more than 160,000 U.S. companies, 90 percent of them privately owned, each with a net worth of $750,000 or more, 250 or more employees, or $25 million in annual sales. Entries include information on headquarters location, SIC number, and company officers. The directory is also available online through DIALOG, and in other formats.

Published annually by Dun & Bradstreet Information Services.

Minority Organizations: A National Directory

This is a comprehensive source of information on approximately 9,700 minority organizations. Minority groups in the directory are defined to include African American, Hispanic, Asian, and Native American. Each entry provides contact and background information.

Fourth edition published in 1991 by Garrett Park Press, Garrett Park, MD.

National Directory of Minority-Owned Business Firms

This directory lists information on more than 40,000 minority business enterprises, arranged according to SIC business description. Entries include company address, contact name, fax number, date founded, business description, trading areas, number of employees, and sales volume.

Published annually by Business Research Services, Washington, DC.

Distributed in the United States and Canada by Gale Research, Detroit.

National Directory of Women-Owned Business Firms

This directory lists 25,000 women-owned business enterprises, arranged according to SIC business description. Each entry includes company address, contact name, fax number, date founded, business description, trading areas, number of employees, and sales volume.

Published annually by Business Research Services, Washington, DC.

Distributed in the United States and Canada by Gale Research, Detroit.

Predicasts' F & S Index of Corporate Change

This index tracks changes in ownership of U.S.-based companies, both public and private. The *Index of Corporate Change* provides information on company formations, mergers and acquisitions, joint ventures, bankruptcies, liquidations, reorganizations, foreign operations, and name and subsidiary changes. Entries identify the companies involved and the nature of the change, and each entry includes a complete source citation. The index is also available online through BRS and DIALOG as part of PTS F & S Indexes.

Published quarterly, with annual cumulative edition, by Information Access/Predicasts.

Regional Directories of Minority & Women-Owned Business Firms

This three-volume reference lists thousands of minority- and women-owned business enterprises, organized by state and SIC business description. Entries include company address, contact name, fax number, date founded, business description, trading areas, number of employees, and sales volume.

Published annually by Business Research Services, Washington, DC.

Distributed in the United States and Canada by Gale Research, Detroit.

Service Industries USA

Arsen J. Darnay, editor

Service Industries USA provides figures on more than 150 service industries and more than 4,000 leading public and private corporations and nonprofit institutions. The book is divided in two parts. Part 1 provides industry data for the United States and individual states, using various federal statistics for service industries. Each entry contains a description, general statistics, indices of change, selected ratios, statistical analyses by state and region, occupations employed, and more. Part 2 offers metro area statistics, arranged alphabetically by metropolitan area and SIC code, for more than 600 locations in the United States. Entries are indexed according to SIC code, services, metro area, company/nonprofit organization, and occupation.

Published in 1992 by Gale Research, Detroit.

Ward's Business Directory 1997

This seven-volume resource (plus supplement) is a standard feature of most public libraries. It offers current data on over 120,000 U.S. companies, more than 90 percent of which are privately held. Topics include market analyses, backgrounds, business partnerships, recruitment, and competitors. Also available on disk, magnetic tape, and other formats.
Published annually by Gale Research, Detroit.

Ward's Business Directory of U.S. Private and Public Companies

This five-volume set contains information on more than 130,000 U.S. public and private companies with sales of at least $500,000. Ward's emphasizes private companies (about 90 percent of the listings). Volumes 1 through 3 contain an alphabetical listing of the firms, including addresses, telephone numbers, sales, number of employees, and the names of up to five corporate officers. Volume 4 is a geographic state-by-state guide to the entries. Volume 5 organizes the entries according to four-digit SIC codes, and ranks each company within a given code according to its sales. In addition to the print version, the directory is available on diskette and magnetic tape.
Published annually by Gale Research, Detroit.

Who Owns Whom—North America

This one-volume reference lists North American parent companies, subsidiaries, and associates. The directory is divided into four sections: The first lists subsidiaries and associates of parent companies registered in the United States that conduct business in other parts of the world; the second lists subsidiaries and associates of parent companies registered in Canada; the third lists foreign parent companies with subsidiaries and associates in the United States and Canada; the fourth is an alphabetical index that links any family member to its ultimate parent.
Published annually by Dun & Bradstreet Information Services.

FOR FURTHER INFORMATION

See ***The BusinessWeek Global 1000,*** *p. 417*
The BusinessWeek 1000: America's Most Valuable Companies, *p. 417*
COMPUSTAT, *p. 418*
Disclosure® Database, *p. 418*
Disclosure Worldscope Global, *p. 418*
European Business Rankings, *p. 514*
F & S Index™, *p. 375*
International Directory of Company Histories, *p. 495*
Moody's International Manual and News Reports, *p. 496*
Moody's Manuals, *p. 419*
PROMT™: Predicast's Overview of Markets and Technology, *p. 377*
SEC ON-LINE™, *p. 420*
Standard & Poor's Register of Corporations, Directors, and Executives, *p. 429*
Thomas Register of American Manufacturers, *p. 532*
World Trade Centers Association World Business Directory, *p. 497*
Worldwide Branch Locations of Multinational Companies, *p. 497*

13

CORPORATE OFFICERS AND DIRECTORS

The Corporate Director

Leo Herzel and James B. Carlson

The Corporate Director supplies simple, accurate descriptions of the main legal problems directors face in the context of important strategic and business problems, such as proxy fights, mergers, acquisitions, takeovers, and bankruptcy.
Published in 1994 by McGraw-Hill,
New York.

The Corporate Finance Bluebook

The Corporate Finance Bluebook lists leading financial executives in more than 5,200 companies and 20,000 subsidiaries. Entries include sales/earnings/assets/liabilities, contact information, major suppliers, and wholly owned U.S. subsidiaries.
Published annually by National Register
Publishing, New Providence, NJ.

Corporate Yellow Book

The *Corporate Yellow Book* lists the names and titles of more than 39,000 U.S. corporate executives. Included within this list are more than 10,000 corporate board members. Entries include the officers' names, titles, addresses, telephone numbers, and a short description of each company's business, including product lines and annual revenues. Four indexes allow users to access the entries according to company or subsidiary, industry, state, or by individual's name.
Published quarterly by the Monitor
Publishing Company, New York.

International Corporate Yellow Book

This is a directory of key executives and officers within leading non-U.S. companies. Entries include the names, addresses, telephone, fax, and telex numbers of more than 30,000 executives; names, titles, and affiliations of corporate board members; descriptions of each company's business and production lines; an estimate of each company's annual revenue; and each company's main subsidiaries and affiliates. Entries are indexed by company name, industry, individual names, and U.S. subsidiaries.
Published annually by the Monitor
Publishing Company, New York.

NASDAQ Yellow Book

This is a directory of the executives running the younger high-growth companies in the United States. The *NASDAQ Yellow Book* lists the names, titles, and telephone numbers of more than 20,000 key executives in these smaller companies. Entries also include the names, titles, and affiliations of corporate board members; descriptions of each company's business and product lines; an estimate of each company's annual revenue; and addresses, telephone numbers, and fax numbers for each company as well as its main subsidiaries and affiliates (both domestic and foreign). Entries are indexed by company name, executive name, state, and industry.
Published annually by the Monitor
Publishing Company, New York.

Owners and Officers of Private Companies

This is a directory of more than 100,000 executives in over 44,000 leading private companies each having more than $5 million in sales in the United States. Each entry includes company name, address, and telephone number; key executives' names and titles; SIC codes; annual sales figures; and number of employees. Entries are indexed by company name, geographic area, and SIC code. The directory is also available on diskette and magnetic tape.
Published annually by the Taft Group.
Distributed by Gale Research, Detroit.

Reference Book of Corporate Managements

This is a four-volume set profiling the officers within 12,000 U.S. companies. Entries include condensed resumes listing each officer's business background and work history, along with name, title, year of birth, marital status, military service, and college(s) attended, with the dates of degrees earned.
Published biennially by Dun & Bradstreet Information Services.

Standard & Poor's Register of Corporations, Directors, and Executives

This three-volume set is a leading directory of company information. Volume 1, *Corporations,* provides an alphabetical listing of more than 55,000 North American (mostly U.S.) companies, including their addresses, telephone and fax numbers, subsidiaries, names and titles of key corporate officers, number of employees, and a bit of financial information such as gross sales. Volume 2, *Directors and Executives,* contains listings for about 70,000 corporate officers, partners, directors, trustees, and so on. The listings include the place and date of birth, place of residence, schools attended, and professional affiliations. Volume 3 is a series of indexes. The *S & P Register* is available in print and online versions. Customized excerpts are available on computer disk. Online versions are available from DIALOG and Mead Data Central's LEXIS and NEXIS services.
Published annually by Standard & Poor's.

Who's Who in Finance and Industry

This book provides substantive biographies of approximately 25,000 North American and international professionals in the following fields: accounting, advertising, banking and finance, communications, construction and engineering, industrial and commercial firms, insurance, investment companies, retail trade, transportation, and utilities.
Published biennially by Marquis Who's Who, New Providence, NJ.

FOR FURTHER INFORMATION

See ***Canadian Key Business Directory,*** *p. 422*
The Corporate Directory of U.S. Public Companies, *p. 423*
Directory of Corporate Affiliations, *p. 423*
Hoover's Handbook of American Business, *p. 425*
Moody's Manuals, *p. 419*
Nelson's Directory of Investment Research, *p. 420*
Ward's Business Directory of U.S. Private and Public Companies, *p. 427*
World Trade Centers Association World Business Directory, *p. 497*

14

DEMOGRAPHICS, MARKETING DATA, AND MARKETING RESEARCH

American Demographics

This business magazine is written for marketers, advertisers, and business planners. Articles generally deal with demographic trends and their implications for business.
Published monthly by American Demographics, Inc., Ithaca, NY.

Asian Americans Information Directory

Karen Backus and Julia C. Furtaw, editors

This directory lists more than 5,200 organizations, agencies, institutions, programs, services, and publications in the United States that are concerned with Asian-American life and culture. Separate sections cover 19 different Asian groups, including Chinese, Filipino, Indonesian, Japanese, Laotian, Pacific Islander, and Thai. Each entry within a nationality section provides pertinent data such as name, address, telephone number, and contact person. The directory is available in print, computer diskette, and magnetic tape formats.
Second edition published in 1994 by Gale Research, Detroit.

Atlas Software™

This software package helps businesspeople identify geographical aspects of markets (e.g., market potential by sales territory, or distribution coverage by product, or customer locations by zip code or street address) in order to optimize sales territories, target customers, and select site locations.
Published by Strategic Mapping, Inc.

Black Americans Information Directory 1992–93

Julia C. Furtaw, editor

This collection of more than 4,800 entries provides contact information on a wide range of nonprofit, private, public, educational, and governmental organizations and agencies concerned with African Americans. There are also descriptions of important sources of information, educational programs, publications, and media. The directory is available in print, computer diskette, and magnetic tape formats.
Third edition published in 1993 by Gale Research, Detroit.

The Boomer Report

This newsletter monitors the approximately 77 million members of the baby boom generation. It tracks the news stories, market studies, surveys, books, and journals that report on boomers.
Published monthly by FIND/SVP.

Brand Advantage

This two-volume collection of key consumer marketing data provides information about men and women 18 years and older. It details usage and brand-user information on nearly 3,600 consumer products in more than 300 brand categories. Volume I covers food and consumables. Volume II covers products and services. The data is organized demographically (e.g., by household income, employment status, or geographic region).
Published annually by Standard Rate and Data Service (SRDS).

Business Lists-on-Disc™

This CD-ROM database helps the user find demographic information on business, by providing data on 10 million businesses. *Business Lists-on-Disc* helps users research and analyze markets by SIC code, geography, employment size, and annual sales volume. *Updated annually by American Business Information.*

CEDDS: The Complete Economic and Demographic Data Source

This three-volume set contains economic and demographic forecasts to 2015, and historical data from 1970, for every county, state, and metropolitan area in the United States. More than 70 ranking tables are included, such as projected growth in new jobs and forecast of population increase. This reference work also includes a region-by-region analysis of the United States that identifies trends and looks at the strengths and weaknesses of the economy. Available in print, disk, and CD-ROM formats. *Published annually by Woods & Poole Economics, Inc.*

CENDATA

This online database, compiled by the U.S. Bureau of the Census, contains current and projected data on U.S. business (business establishments, employees, payroll figures) and demographic and population data from the latest census. It also includes demographic data from 200 other countries. Available online from DIALOG and CompuServe. *Updated daily by the U.S. Bureau of the Census.*

Census Catalog and Guide

This publication of the U.S. Bureau of the Census is a catalog and guide to the programs and services of the Census Bureau. It describes or lists recent products and provides a useful product overview chart. There are also separate chapters for products dealing with the following topics: agriculture; business (trade and services); construction and housing; foreign trade; geography; governments; international; manufacturing and mineral industries; population; transportation; and the Census of Population and Housing. A "Sources of Assistance" section includes the following information: a listing of the organizations (and contact information) involved in the state Data Center Program (see p. 437) and the Business/Industry Data Center Program; organizations, contact information, and services/data holdings of organizations involved in the National Clearinghouse program; participants and contact information for participants in the Federal-State Cooperative Program for Population Estimates; a listing of federal depository libraries; Bureau of the Census regional information offices; and staff and programs of the Census Bureau in Washington, DC. *Published annually by the Superintendent of Documents, U.S. Government Printing Office. Updated monthly through a free publication, the Monthly Product Announcement.*

Consumer Market Developments

This publication offers select market statistics along with eight-year projections of consumer spending and key economic indicators such as the consumer price index (CPI), housing starts and permits, unemployment, and department store sales. *Published in 1992 by Fairchild Publications, New York.*

Consumer USA

This collection profiles major U.S. consumer goods manufacturers, with complete contact information. Other features include a directory of major retailers, and a guide to official and nonofficial business information sources. *Second edition published in 1992 by Gale Research, Detroit.*

County and City Data Book: A Statistical Abstract Supplement

This extensive collection of county and city data includes entries on demographics, wages, unemployment, and workers' compensation. *Published annually by the Superintendent of Documents, U.S. Government Printing Office.*

Data Pamphlets (for an Individual County, State, or Metropolitan Statistical Area)

These pamphlets are 90-page reports containing demographic and economic data for specific geographical areas. Each pamphlet provides a forecast to 2015 and historical data from 1970. It also includes an economic analysis of the area that identifies trends and looks at strengths and weaknesses of the economy. The pamphlets are available in print and on disk. *Updated annually by Woods & Poole Economics, Washington, DC.*

Databased Marketing: The Manager's Guide to the Super Marketing Tool of the 21st Century

Herman Holtz

This comprehensive guide to the techniques involved in setting up and managing a database marketing program includes topics such as developing consumer databases, pursuing niche market groups, and selecting consultants to build marketing databases. *Published in 1992 by John Wiley & Sons, New York.*

Demographic Yearbook

The *Demographic Yearbook*, a comprehensive collection of international demographic statistics covering 220 countries or areas, includes information on population, birth rates, infant mortality, marriage, and divorce. *Published annually by the United Nations Publishing Service, New York.*

Directory of Marketing Information Companies

This directory, published by *American Demographics* magazine, lists companies providing products and services that help decision makers analyze and reach their customers. *Published annually by American Demographics, Ithaca, NY.*

Dun's Census of American Business

This directory of company statistics categorizes entries according to SIC codes and groups them according to sales volume and number of employees. The information in the *Census* can be used to establish the size of a market, identify competitors, project sales potential, determine distributor locations, and determine locations for branches, retail outlets, and service centers. *Published annually by Dun & Bradstreet Information Services.*

Findex: The Directory of Market Research Reports, Studies, and Surveys

This annual listing of more than 500 research companies and publishers that produce over 12,000 market research reports is organized alphabetically and includes the title of each report, description of contents, date of publication, number of pages, purchase price, name of publisher, and complete contact information. *Findex* is also available online through DIALOG. *Published annually, with a midyear supplement, by the Cambridge Information Group, Washington, DC.*

FIND/SVP Industry and Market Research Reports

FIND/SVP publishes industry and market research reports in many specific areas—including beverages, biotechnology, business and financial services, chemicals, computers, consumer and leisure products, demographics, drugs, electronics, energy, health care, high-technology materials, household products, metals and mining, office supplies and equipment, packaging, paper and forest products, personal care, plastics, retailing, the service industry, software, telecommunications, transportation, waste management, and water management.

The Focus Group Directory

This directory lists companies that provide focus group facilities, focus group research, and focus group moderators. The directory is organized geographically.
Published annually by the New York Chapter of the American Marketing Association.

Hispanic Americans Information Directory 1992–93

Julia C. Furtaw, editor

This directory of more than 4,800 Hispanic organizations, agencies, programs, and publications comprises 16 separate chapters and covers a wide range of topical data relating to Hispanic culture, including national, state, and local Hispanic associations; print and broadcast media, including Hispanic publishers; bilingual education programs; and federal, state, and local government agencies.
Third edition published in 1994–1995 by Gale Research, Detroit.

The Hispanic-American Almanac

Nicolas Kanellos, editor

This reference offers information on all aspects of Hispanic-American history, life, and culture in the United States, including explorers, racial diversity, education, labor and employment, and religion. The narrative text is supplemented with photographs, maps, and charts, and includes bibliographic information for further research.
Published in 1992 by Gale Research, Detroit.

The Information Catalog

This free catalog lists recent market research studies and offers dozens of market, industry, and company studies. The prices for these studies range from $15 to several thousand dollars.
Published every two months by FIND/SVP.

The Insider's Guide to Demographic Know-How: How to Find, Analyze, and Use Information about Your Customers

Diane Crispell

This book shows how to use demographic analyses to obtain useful information about the customers of a business, including their ages, marital status, earnings, and the products they want. Topics include how to conduct demographic analyses, how to avoid paying for useless information, and how to ensure the accuracy of the data. The *Insider's Guide* also provides names and telephone numbers of data specialists in the federal government.
Second edition published in 1990 by the American Demographic Press, Ithaca, NY.

International Directory of Market Research Organizations

This directory provides an alphabetical listing by country of companies doing marketing research. The information includes data, location facilities, research facilities, product expertise, expertise of international research, and contact information.
Eleventh edition published in 1993 by the Market Research Society.
Available in the United States through MacFarlane and Company, Inc.

International Directory of Marketing Research Companies

Known as the "Green Book," this directory provides information on companies that provide marketing research and advertising ser-

vices. It includes listings of 1,500 companies in the United States and 65 other countries. The companies listed provide such services as audience research, and measurement and certification of newspaper and magazine circulation.
Published annually by the New York chapter of the American Marketing Association.

The Lifestyle Market Analyst

This marketing sourcebook provides demographic and lifestyle data for the top 210 areas of dominant influence (ADIs) in the United States. It is organized by geographic location, lifestyle preferences, and consumer segments.
Published annually by Standard Rate and Data Service (SRDS).

The Lifestyle Zip Code Analyst

This marketing sourcebook looks at the demographics, economics, and lifestyles of residents associated with more than 11,000 U.S. zip codes.
Published annually by Standard Rate and Data Service (SRDS).

Market Research Handbook (Canada)

This reference work provides information for analyzing Canadian markets at the provincial, regional, and national levels. Information is provided on international trade, merchandising and services, population and labor force, income and spending, housing, motor vehicles, household facilities and equipment, and census data.
Published annually by Statistics Canada, Ottawa, Ontario.

Market Share Reporter

This collection of more than 2,000 market share entries is organized by four-digit SIC codes and indexed alphabetically. Entries are compiled from a wide variety of sources and include descriptive title of the report; data and market description; remarks on the history, scope, and other characteristics of the study; list of producers/products along with their assigned market share; and source citation (title, date, and page number of published sources). *Market Share Reporter* is available in print, online, computer diskette, and magnetic tape formats. Available online through NEXIS.
Published annually by Gale Research, Detroit.

Markets of the U.S. for Business Planners

Thomas E. Conroy, editor

This two-volume reference provides historical and current profiles of 183 urban market areas and provides the following information: business and economic profiles, projections for 1995 and 2000, market area maps, and analytical commentary.
Published in 1992 by Omnigraphics, Inc., Detroit.

Marketsearch: International Directory of Published Market Research

This publication is a directory of industrial market research from companies that have produced more than 20,000 published studies. Entries are arranged by subject area, such as agriculture, cosmetics, electrical engineering, cable television, and medical electronics. Each entry includes the country where the study was produced, the date of the study, complete contact information, and the price of the study (in the local currency).
Published annually by MacFarlane and Co., Inc.

The New Marketing Research Systems: How to Use Strategic Database Information for Better Marketing Decisions

David J. Curry

This reference book for packaged goods marketers and retailers, direct marketers, advertising agency professionals, and market researchers describes and analyzes marketing research systems based on technology that permits the collection, storage, and use of disaggregate data. Single-source, geodemographic, and micromerchandising systems are forging market data from scanners and other electronic sources into tools that solve marketing problems. The author develops critical evaluations of existing systems of new technology from the United States and Europe as well as a wide variety of databases and reports from commercial vendors including A. C. Nielsen, Information Resources, Inc., and CACI Federal.
Published in 1993 by John Wiley & Sons, New York.

The Numbers News: The Newsletter for Serious Trendwatchers

This monthly newsletter analyzes trends— such as those relating to working mothers, men and women, incomes, and consumer spending—that have an impact on marketing and business decisions.
Published monthly by The Numbers News.

The Official Guide to Household Spending: The Number One Guide to Who Spends How Much on What

Margaret Ambry

The Official Guide to Household Spending is a comprehensive collection of statistics on consumer spending and income over nine product and service categories.
Second edition published in 1993 by New Strategist Publications, Ithaca, NY.

PTS Marketing and Advertising Reference Service (PTS MARS)

This database provides users with abstracts of literature on the marketing and advertising of consumer goods and services. It provides information on market size and share, marketing strategies, consumer research, and advertising campaigns and budgets. Available online through DIALOG.
Updated every business day by Information Access/Predicasts.

The Seasons of Business: The Marketer's Guide to Consumer Behavior

Judith Waldrop

This book, written by the research editor of *American Demographics* magazine, analyzes how events such as weather patterns, agricultural cycles, and hours of daylight affect consumer behavior.
Published in 1992 by American Demographics, Ithaca, NY.

SMARTdisk™ Strategic Market Analysis: Resources and Techniques

This interactive program is designed to help users understand and predict consumer behavior. It offers an overview of trends that affect the demands for goods and services (e.g., ethnic diversity, household structure) and helps users find the data they need for decision making. It shows how to combine data from the Bureau of Labor Statistics Consumers Expenditure Survey with demographic information to make consumer demand projections.
Published in 1992 by American Demographics, Ithaca, NY.

Sourcebook of Zip Code Demographics, Census Edition

The *Sourcebook of Zip Code Demographics* profiles residential zip codes regarding popu-

lation, housing, household income, education, labor force, and other data taken from the 1990 Census Summary Tape File for 1990 Zip Codes.
Published in 1992 by CACI Marketing Systems.
Distributed by Gale Research, Detroit.

State and Metropolitan Databook

Prepared by the Bureau of the Census, U.S. Department of Commerce, this reference work provides a wide variety of information on the states and metropolitan areas of the United States. It includes statistics from the 1990 population count and the 1987 economic census data. The databook is available in print and on diskette suitable for input for leading spreadsheets, database, and mapping programs.
Fourth edition published in 1991 by the Superintendent of Documents, U.S. Government Printing Office.
For diskette information, contact the Bureau of the Census.

Statistical Record of Black America

This one-volume resource provides hundreds of current statistical facts on African Americans. Data come from a wide variety of published and unpublished statistics from private, commercial, and governmental sources. Entries are arranged in 19 broad subject chapters and cover population, business and economics, vital statistics, family, labor and employment, education, spending, crime, politics, and religion.
Second edition published in 1992 by Gale Research, Detroit.

Statistical Record of Women Worldwide

Linda Schmittroth, editor

This one-volume resource provides hundreds of current statistical facts on women worldwide. Data are culled from hundreds of published sources, including periodicals, government documents, association and corporation reports, and research centers. Entries are arranged by subject area and present statistical information in the form of charts, tables, and lists, along with complete bibliographic citations.
Second edition published in 1995 by Gale Research, Detroit.

Survey of Buying Power

This volume contains statistics based on the 1990 census. It provides at least 20 pieces of demographic and socioeconomic data for every metropolitan area, county, and major city in the United States. It also contains 26 individual metromarket ranking tables covering population, income, retail sales, household data, and a buying-power index. *The Survey of Buying Power* can be used to gauge market potential, set and measure sales quotas and performance, and allocate a media and advertising budget.
Published annually by Sales and Marketing Management magazine, New York.

The Survey of Media Markets

The Survey of Media Markets lists 13 pieces of demographic and socioeconomic data for each of the 210 Areas of Dominant Influence (ADIs) in the United States, as well as detailed breakouts showing metropolitan and nonmetropolitan coverage. It also contains five-year projections for population, income, and retail sales for metromarkets and their component counties.
Published annually by Sales and Marketing Management magazine, New York.

United Nations World Population Report

The *World Population Report* contains worldwide demographic data, with forecasts to the years 2000 and 2025.
Published annually by the United Nations Publishing Service, New York.

Ward's Sales Prospector: A Directory of Leads by State and Industry

This five-volume reference provides regional guides to nearly 134,000 privately and publicly held U.S. companies. Entries are arranged geographically. Each volume lists between 17,000 and 34,000 companies, first by state and zip code, then ranked by SIC code. Rankings typically include names of up to five key officers for each company, company type, fiscal year-end data, year established, annual sales, and number of employees. The directory is available in print, computer diskette, and magnetic tape formats.

Published annually by Gale Research, Detroit.

Women's Information Directory

Shawn Brennan, editor

The *Women's Information Directory* is a guide to approximately 6,000 organizations, agencies, institutions, programs, and publications concerned with women in the United States. Information is arranged under 20 chapters, such as national associations, women's centers, research centers, publications, and electronic databases.

Published in 1993 by Gale Research, Detroit.

The Zip Code Mapbook of Metropolitan Areas

The Zip Code Mapbook includes 320 U.S. metropolitan areas, each on an 11-by-17-inch map. Each map shows 1990 zip code boundaries, county boundaries, major highways, and location of city centers. It includes metropolitan statistical areas codes and metropolitan area summary data from the 1990 census.

Second edition published in 1992 by CACI Marketing Systems, Arlington, VA.

GOVERNMENT AGENCIES

Bureau of the Census

Part of the U.S. Department of Commerce, the Bureau of the Census collects, tabulates, and publishes a wide variety of statistical data about the people and the economy of the United States. Under the direction of Martha Farnsworth Riche, the Bureau makes available the statistical results of its censuses, surveys, and other programs through printed reports, computer tape, CD-ROM, and microfiche. It also prepares special tabulations sponsored and paid for by data users. The Bureau has 12 regional offices.

The Bureau of the Census has an online data system, CENDATA (see p. 431 for a description), available through CompuServe and DIALOG. For content information about CENDATA, contact the Data Access and Use Staff of the Data User Services Division of the Bureau of the Census at (301) 763-2074. Additional sources of Census products and services include the following:

Data Centers. The Census Bureau has a State Data Center Program available in all states and the District of Columbia, Puerto Rico, Guam, and the Virgin Islands. The Census Bureau furnishes data products, training in data access, and technical assistance to the data centers, which in turn make it available to the public. Some states also participate in the Census Bureau's Business/Industry Data Center Program, receiving economic data, assistance, and training to advance economic development and assist businesses and other users in the use of economic data. For more information, contact the National Service Program at the Bureau of the Census at (301) 763-1384.

National Clearinghouse for Census Data Services. This is a referral service of outside organizations for users needing special assistance in obtaining and using statistical data and related products prepared by the Census Bureau. The names of organizations and contact information can be obtained from the *Census Catalog and Guide* (see p. 431).

Census Bureau Training Activities. The Census Bureau conducts seminars and workshops in Washington, DC, and other cities. Contact the Training Branch, Data User Services Division, Bureau of the Census at (301) 763-1510.

Census Bureau Customer Service. This service provides general information about products and services at (301) 763-1510. The *Census Catalog and Guide* also lists Bureau subject matter specialists who may be consulted by telephone.

Telephone Contacts for Data Users. This is a free pamphlet provided by the Census Bureau. It lists the names and telephone numbers of experts in various areas, such as construction, foreign trade, transportation, and so on. *General address: The Bureau of the Census, U.S. Department of Commerce, Washington, DC 20233.*

TRADE AND PROFESSIONAL
ORGANIZATIONS

American Marketing Association (AMA)

The AMA is a professional society for marketing and market research executives, sales and promotion managers, academics, and others interested in the field of marketing. It fosters research, sponsors seminars, and conducts more than 30 annual conferences and symposia. *American Marketing Association, 250 S. Wacker Drive, Suite 200, Chicago, IL 60606. (312) 648-0536.*

FOR FURTHER INFORMATION

See *AB/INFORM®*, p. 370
American Business Climate and Economic Profiles, p. 447
American Statistics Index, p. 370
Area Wage Survey, p. 458
Bureau of Economic Analysis, p. 450
Bureau of Labor Statistics, p. 451
The Burwell World Directory of Information Brokers, p. 371
Dun's Regional Business Directory, p. 424
The Economist Pocket World in Figures, p. 374
European Advertising, Marketing, and Media Data, p. 514
Index to International Statistics, p. 495
International Marketing Data & Statistics, p. 495
Investext®, p. 402
JapanSite™: Desktop Target Marketing for Japan, p. 507
Key Indicators of County Growth 1970–2010, p. 549
PROMT™: Predicast's Overview of Markets and Technology, p. 377
Service Industries USA, p. 426
State and Local Statistics Sources, p. 550
State Statistical Abstracts, p. 550
Statistical Abstracts of the United States, p. 378
Statistics Sources, p. 378
World Factbook, p. 496

DIRECT MARKETING

Business-to-Business Direct Marketing Resource Guide

This text reveals the many resources available to help build almost any business-to-business marketing plan. It includes information on database strategies, tips on business-to-business lead generation and customer retention, and uses of state-of-the-art technology, along with a sampling of an ECHO award–winning business-to-business case study; guidelines for improving business-to-business mail delivery; and supplier indexes.
Second edition published in 1992 by McGraw-Hill, New York.

The Complete Direct Mail List Handbook: Everything You Need to Know about Lists and How to Use Them for Greater Profit

Ed Burnett

Direct mail information provided in this handbook includes the 35 major types of mailing lists, the rules for direct mail testing, the five factors that influence response, how to interpret test results, what to do about them, what it costs to "buy" a customer, and updated information on databanks, merge/purge, and computers.
Published in 1989 by Prentice Hall, Englewood Cliffs, NJ.

Database Marketing: The Ultimate Marketing Tool

Edward L. Nash

Database Marketing is a guide for developing and implementing database marketing strategies. Topics include building an in-house database; using database marketing in the packaged goods, financial services, and business-to-business areas; and tailoring strategic and creative approaches to the target market.
Published in 1993 by McGraw-Hill, New York.

Desktop Direct Marketing: How to Use Up-to-the-Minute Technologies to Find and Research New Customers

Sunny Baker and Kim Baker

Showing how to use the latest technologies to create and disseminate direct marketing material, this book includes information on software, online services, databases, and electronic advertising.
Published in 1993 by McGraw-Hill, New York.

Direct Mail List Rates and Data

This directory provides information on more than 10,000 mailing lists that reach business, consumer, and farm markets. It contains list descriptions, selections and sources, rental rates, user restrictions, and test arrangement. Available by subscription.
Published bimonthly by Standard Rate and Data Service (SRDS).

Direct Marketing

This magazine is for companies using direct mail along with other forms of media to communicate with and reach their customers.
Published monthly by Hoke Publications, Garden City, NY.

Direct Marketing Consultants

This directory lists the names of specialists who meet the diversified needs of the direct marketing business. Specialties include mergers and acquisitions, strategic planning and development, catalogs, fulfillment, database marketing, and fund-raising.
Published in 1993 by the Direct Marketing Association, New York.

The Direct Marketing Handbook

Edward L. Nash, editor in chief

The Direct Marketing Handbook is an authoritative encyclopedia of direct mail information by one of the industry's best-known practitioners.
Third edition published in 1995 by McGraw-Hill, New York.

Direct Marketing Marketplace: The Directory of the Direct Mail Industry

This directory contains entries for 19,000 direct marketing companies, executives, suppliers, prominent individuals, agencies, consultants, and media buyers involved in the direct marketing industry. The listings include company names, addresses, phone numbers, products, services, chief executives, and sales and advertising volume.
Published annually by the National Register Publishing Co. (Reed Reference Publishing), New Providence, NJ.

The Directory of Business-to-Business Catalogs

This directory lists close to 6,000 companies in 35 different product areas, from automotive to telecommunications, that sell to businesses. Available in print and CD-ROM formats.
Second edition published in 1993 by Grey House Publishing, Lakeville, CT.

Directory of Mail Order Catalogs

In this comprehensive directory containing more than 7,300 entries for mail-order companies selling consumer products throughout the United States, entries include company contact information, mailing list size, and availability. Available in print and CD-ROM formats.
Published annually by Grey House Publishing, Lakeville, CT.

DMA 1992–1993 Statistical Fact Book

This text gives direct marketers the most recent and relevant statistical support required for putting together a strategic plan and a client proposal. Information provided includes response rates, conversion rates, return on investment, allowable acquisition, costs per piece in the mail, test quantities, and rollout numbers. The *DMA Fact Book* includes more than 325 charts taken from over 100 studies and sources.
Published in 1993 by the Direct Marketing Association, New York.

The Fifth Annual Guide to Telemarketing: 1991/1992

Eugene B. Kordahl and Arnold L. Fishman

This text reports on all aspects of telemarketing for all levels of the telemarketing industry. It provides information on sales, costs, growth rates, supplier and user segmentation, salaries, organization, production, and finance, and presents profiles of 26 inbound markets, 19 telemarketing service bureaus, and 14 foreign telemarketing national profiles.
Updated in 1991 by National Telemarketing, Inc.

The Handbook of International Direct Marketing

Adam Baines, editor

This review of the world's top 40 markets for international direct mail covers key export markets in Asia, Australia, Europe, Latin America, and the Middle East. It supplies the

latest analysis of each country as a receiver and supplier of direct mail. Country-by-country guides specify DM facilities and free services, database and list services, trends in DM volumes, national consumer protection legislation, postal rates and services, and other vital information.
Published in 1992 by the European Direct Marketing Association.

Lead Generation Handbook

Bernard Goldberg

A comprehensive manual on designing and implementing lead programs to generate quality sales opportunities to motivate salespeople, this text includes 16 chapters detailing the planning, creation, execution, management, and analysis of all facets of lead generation for direct mail and telemarketing sales, seminars, trade shows, and customer programs.
Published in 1992 by Direct Marketing Publishers.

National Directory of Catalogs

This publication contains more than 7,000 entries on U.S. and Canadian catalogs, including contact information, products carried, and list rental data. Available in print and on diskette.
Published annually by Oxbridge Communications, New York.

National Directory of Mailing Lists

Containing information on more than 20,000 mailing lists, this directory includes quantity, pricing, and contact information. Available both in print and on diskette.
Published annually by Oxbridge Communications, New York.

The New Direct Marketing: How to Implement a Profit Driven Database Marketing Strategy

David Shepard Associates

This book shows how to target customers, expand the use of database marketing, and de-velop large database systems without dependence on mainframes.
Second edition published in 1993 by Business One Irwin, Homewood, IL.

NTC's Dictionary of Direct Mail and Mailing List Terminology and Techniques

Nat G. Bodian

NTC's Dictionary of Direct Mail and Mailing List Terminology and Techniques defines 1,500 key terms and concepts within the mailing list industry.
Published in 1991 by the NTC Publishing Group, Lincolnwood, IL.

Successful Direct Marketing Methods

Bob Stone

This collection of practical how-to direct marketing tips includes topics such as the scope and application of direct marketing, choosing the right media, creating and pro-ducing an effective direct marketing offer, and building and managing a direct market-ing operation.
Sixth edition published in 1997 by NTC Business Books, Lincolnwood, IL.

Successful Telemarketing

Bob Stone and John Wyman

Successful Telemarketing is a step-by-step guide to setting up and managing a telemar-keting operation. A number of case studies are presented, including AT&T, General Electric, B. F. Goodrich, and Quaker Oats.
Published in 1992 by NTC Publishing Group, Lincolnwood, IL.

Telemarketer's Guide to State Laws

Julie Crocker, editor

This compilation of all state laws affecting direct marketing today comprises a review of major telemarketing legislation, including ADMRP (automatic dialing and recorded message player), monitoring, and registration bills. A state-by-state list of the relevant telemarketing state statutes is also included. *Published annually by the Direct Marketing Association, New York.*

TRADE AND PROFESSIONAL ASSOCIATIONS

Direct Marketing Association (DMA)

Founded in 1917, the DMA is for those involved in direct marketing and those who want to know more about it. Services include Direct LINK, a direct marketing database; the DMA Library, featuring more than 500 reference books and approximately 120 trade publications; and conference and seminar presentations.
Direct Marketing Association, Inc., 11 West 42d Street, New York, NY 10036-8096. (212) 768-7277

FOR FURTHER INFORMATION

*See **Information Industry Directory,** p. 376*
***The New Marketing Research Systems,** p. 435*

16

DISTRIBUTORS AND DISTRIBUTION MANAGEMENT

American Wholesalers & Distributors Directory

Deborah M. Burek, editor

The *American Wholesalers & Distributors Directory* gives descriptive listings of more than 27,000 American wholesalers and distributors and their products. Listings cover all types of consumer products, including computers, agricultural machinery, ammunition, jewelry, camping equipment, hand tools, and grocery items. Each entry includes the company's name, address, telephone number, fax number, principal product lines, number of employees, estimated annual sales volume, principal officers, and SIC codes. In addition to entries for each individual company, the directory ranks the top 50 companies (by sales) for each four-digit SIC code. This resource is available in print, computer diskette, and magnetic tape formats.
Published annually by Gale Research, Detroit.

The Distribution Management Handbook

James A. Tompkins and Dale Harmelink, editors

The *Distribution Management Handbook* features the contributions of 30 experts in the field. Topics include distribution planning and design, warehousing methods, and quality turnarounds.
Published in 1992 by McGraw-Hill, New York.

European Wholesalers & Distributors Directory

Linda Irvin, editor

The *European Wholesalers & Distributors Directory* contains descriptive listings of about 5,000 wholesalers and distributors of finished consumer goods and industrial products in Western and Eastern Europe. Product lines covered include automobiles, electronic parts and equipment, construction materials, furniture, TV and radio, hardware, footwear, books, newspapers, and so on. Entries are arranged alphabetically by product line, then by country, and provide (when available) the company name, address, telephone, telex, cable, and fax numbers, contact name, year established, territory of distribution, annual revenue (expressed in local currency), officer names, number of employees, and products. Entries are indexed by company names, products, geographic listings, and territories served. This resource is available in print, computer diskette, and magnetic tape formats.
Published in 1992 by Gale Research, Detroit.

Guide to Distributorship Agreements

This text is a detailed guide to the process of negotiating and drafting a distributorship agreement.
Published in 1988 by ICC Publishing Corporation, New York.

Reinventing the Warehouse: World Class Distribution Logistics

Roy L. Harmon

This book looks at recent developments in warehouse management and presents warehouse designs for high-quality, low-cost customer service. The author analyzes superior operations in many areas, including retail warehousing, logistics, and service parts warehousing.

Published in 1993 by the Free Press, New York.

FOR FURTHER INFORMATION

See ***The Japanese Distribution System,*** *p. 507*

17

DIVERSITY

Affirmative Action Handbook

George W. Johnston, Peter S. Saucier, and Dawn S. Hyde, editors

This handbook is a guide to understanding and managing affirmative action. Chapters include: The Office of Federal Contract; Affirmative Action and the Supreme Court; Reverse Discrimination as an Issue; and Affirmative Action Plans for Individuals with Handicaps and Veterans.
Published in 1992 by Government Institutes, Inc., Rockville, MD.

America's Work Force Is Coming of Age: What Every Business Needs to Know to Recruit, Train, Manage, and Retain an Aging Work Force

Catherine Fyock

This book is a guide to the key issues involved in analyzing and addressing the increasingly important role of the older employee in the workplace.
Published in 1990 by Lexington Books, Lexington, MA.

Beyond Race and Gender: Unleashing the Power of Your Total Work Force by Managing Diversity

R. Roosevelt Thomas, Jr.

Beyond Race and Gender offers an action plan for dealing with the specific issues that arise in an ever more diverse workplace. It enables readers to examine the culture of their organization carefully and analyze the cultural attitudes that can sabotage a diversity program.

Published in 1992 by AMACOM Books (American Management Association), New York.

Managing a Diverse Workforce: Regaining the Competitive Edge

John P. Fernandez

Based on surveys of more than 50,000 managers, this guide to many diversity-related issues and problems includes topics such as accommodating diversity, upgrading skills, resolving conflicts, and reducing turnover.
Published in 1991 by Lexington Books, Lexington, MA.

Managing Diversity: A Complete Desk Reference and Planning Guide

Lee Gardenswartz and Anita Rowe

This guide to managing diversity in the workplace includes these topics: recruiting, training, mentoring, and promoting diverse employees to eliminate high turnover rates; building cohesive, productive, cross-cultural work teams; and using assessment tools built around a number of issues related to diversity.
Published in 1992 by Business One Irwin, Homewood, IL.

Sexual Harassment on the Job: What It Is and How to Stop It

William Petrocelli and Barbara Kate Repa

This new edition defines harassment and gives specific strategies for ending it. The

authors also discuss the "new" controversies of same-sex harassment and harassment of men ("new" in the sense that such cases are now being brought to public attention). They survey the most recent legal developments and provide current information on available resources and state-by-state procedures.
Third edition published in 1998 by the Nolo Press, Berkeley, CA.

TRADE AND PROFESSIONAL ASSOCIATIONS

The American Institute for Managing Diversity, Inc.

Affiliated with Morehouse College, the Institute holds public seminars and develops in-house programs on the issue of developing and managing a diverse workforce.
The American Institute for Managing Diversity, Inc., P. O. Box 38, 830 Westview Drive SW, Atlanta, GA 30314.
(404) 524-7316
Fax: (404) 524-0649

FOR FURTHER INFORMATION

See ***Asian Americans Information Directory,*** p. 430
Black Americans Information Directory, p. 430
Building the Competitive Workforce: Investing in Human Capital for Corporate Success, p. 489
Hispanic Americans Information Directory, p. 433
The Hispanic-American Almanac, p. 433
National Directory of Minority-Owned Business Firms, p. 426
National Directory of Women-Owned Business Firms, p. 426
Managing Workforce 2000: Gaining the Diversity Advantage, p. 491
Minority Organizations: A National Directory, p. 426
Regional Directories of Minority & Women-Owned Business Firms, p. 426
Statistical Record of Black America, p. 436
Statistical Record of Women Worldwide, p. 436
Women's Information Directory, p. 437

18

ECONOMIC DATA, TRENDS, AND PROJECTIONS: UNITED STATES

Against the Gods: The Remarkable Story of Risk

Peter L. Bernstein

In a combination of history, biography, and science, the author discusses the development of the notions of risk, risk taking, and risk management. Is investing in the stock market no more than a gamble? This book will help the reader distinguish between rational and irrational decisions, between gambling and investing, between chance and skill.
Published in 1996 by John Wiley & Sons, New York.

American Business Climate and Economic Profiles: A Concise Compilation of Facts, Rankings, Incentives, and Resource Listings for All 319 Metropolitan Statistical Areas

Priscilla Chen Geahgian, editor

This text provides facts and figures for the larger cities in the United States, arranged by more than 300 metropolitan statistical areas (MSAs) and the 50 states. The information provided includes gross state product figures, income data, labor force statistics, and state tax rates and incentives. A separate section applies 22 criteria to each MSA and state and comes up with a ranking based on such issues as education, personal and per capita income, labor, land area, population, quality of life, and sales.
Published in 1994 by Gale Research, Detroit.

BLS Electronic News Release Service

This database contains the full text of the Bureau of Labor Statistics' monthly release on consumer and producer prices, earnings, and employment; and quarterly releases on productivity, employment costs, collective bargaining, and import and export price indices. Available online from the Bureau of Labor Statistics.
Updated monthly and quarterly from the U.S. Bureau of Labor Statistics.

Business Statistics 1951–91

This research tool, prepared by the Bureau of Economic Analysis of the Department of Commerce, enables users to track business trends from 1951 through 1991. It covers production, manufacturing and labor costs, consumption of goods, and employment levels in the United States, as well as export and import statistics classified by country, continent, type of commodity, and dollar amount. Data are provided monthly for the last four years, and annual totals for prior periods. A historical appendix includes monthly data for some entries to 1963.
Published biennially by the Superintendent of Documents, U.S. Government Printing Office.

BusinessWeek Index

This regular feature of *Business Week* magazine provides a quick review of production indicators, foreign exchange, prices, leading indicators, monthly economic indicators,

monetary indicators, and money market rates.
Published weekly in Business Week magazine.

DRI Forecasts

DRI/McGraw-Hill produces and makes available online a number of time-series databases on the U.S. economy, including the following:

DRI Fixed Investment Forecast. Covers expenditures for durable equipment and construction. Updated monthly.

DRI Consumer Markets Forecast. Covers national consumer spending and discretionary income. Short-term forecasts updated monthly; long-term forecasts updated semiannually.

DRI County Forecast. Covers employment, income, and demographics for all U.S. counties. Updated semiannually.

DRI Current Economic Indicators. Provides key economic indicators for the United States, other industrialized countries, and developing countries. Updated periodically.

DRI Metropolitan Area Forecast. Contains quarterly and annual economic demographic forecasts for metropolitan statistical areas. Updated twice a year.

DRI U.S. Annual Model Forecast. Provides macroeconomic and microeconomic forecasts of the U.S. economy. Updated monthly.

(SOURCE: *Gale Directory of Databases, Vol. 1: Online Databases.*)
Available online from DRI/McGraw-Hill.

Early Economic Outlook

This fax-based information delivery system tracks key economic indexes. Each daily one-page report covers a particular topic, such as industrial production, employment, or unemployment. Every Monday the report offers an inflation outlook, and on Friday it covers economic issues dealing with Germany, Japan, the United Kingdom, or France.
Published daily by the Center for International Business Cycle Research.

ECONBASE: Time Series and Forecasts

This time-series database of macroeconomic and microeconomic data contains data arranged by month, quarter, and year. Available online from DIALOG.
Updated monthly by WEFA Group.

Economic Bulletin Board

Managed by STAT-USA, the *Economic Bulletin Board* is the world's largest source of business information sponsored by a government agency. This source covers such items as the CPI, housing starts, retail sales, national income, the GDP, trade opportunities, and reports on international marketing. Access is available online through a modem, and is based on per-minute usage and number and type of files downloaded. A free limited-access offer is extended to first-time users; call (202) 482-1986. Three modem access numbers are listed, depending on the user's modem speed: For modems below 2400 bps, call (202) 482-3870. For 9600 bps modems, call (202) 482-2584. For modems of 14.4 kbps and higher, call (202) 482-2167.
For further information, contact STAT-USA, HCHB room 4885, U.S. Department of Commerce, Washington, DC 20230.
(800) 782-8872
Fax: (202) 482-2164

Economic Indicators: How America Reads Its Financial Health

Joseph E. Plocek

Economic Indicators discusses in detail the 20 leading economic indicators, including the consumer price index (CPI), the purchasing managers' report, the merchandise trade balance, housing starts and permits, civilian unemployment report, and department store sales.
Published in 1991 by the New York Institute of Finance.

Economic Report of the President

This report is an invaluable source of information on economic conditions in the United States. In addition to the usually short report of the president, there is an extended (200+ pages) discussion of particular topics from the previous year's economy by the Council of Economic Advisors. The most useful part of the report, however, is the roughly 130-page compendium of economic data organized into ten categories: (1) national income or expenditure; (2) population, employment, wages, and productivity; (3) production and business activity; (4) prices; (5) money stock, credit, and finance; (6) government finance; (7) corporate profits and finance; (8) agriculture; (9) international statistics; and (10) national wealth.

The data are presented annually, in most cases from 1946 through the most recent year. The breadth, historical range, and topical nature (for instance, the GDP data for the fourth quarter of the year that just ended) are features that make this an invaluable reference source.
Published annually by the Superintendent of Documents, U.S. Government Printing Office.

Employment and Earnings

This monthly publication prepared by the Bureau of Labor Statistics provides data on (1) the Household Survey, the source for the breakdown of the labor force into its employed and unemployed components, and for the unemployment rate, and (2) the Establishment Survey, the source of data on employment, and hours worked by industry in the nonfarm payroll sector.
Published monthly by the Superintendent of Documents, U.S. Government Printing Office.

The Federal Reserve Bulletin

This monthly publication of the Board of Governors of the Federal Reserve System is the main source of data on money and credit in the United States. There are usually one to three articles on aspects of monetary policy and the monetary economy. In addition, the latest minutes of the Federal Open Market Committee and any regulatory changes are reported. The back of the report is given over to extensive data on money and credit conditions.
Published monthly by the Board of Governors of the Federal Reserve System.

Historical Statistics of the United States, Colonial Times to 1970, Parts I and II

These volumes are supplements to the *Statistical Abstract of the United States* and contain many of the same series constructed back through history. They comprise a specialized reference source that may be useful under certain circumstances. In many cases the reconstructed data reflect the work of noted economic historians.
Published in 1975 by the Superintendent of Documents, U.S. Government Printing Office.

The McGraw-Hill Encyclopedia of Economics

Douglas Greenwald, editor in chief

This text is a comprehensive reference on more than 300 topics in economics.
Published in 1994 by McGraw-Hill, New York.

The New Palgrave Dictionary of Money and Finance

Peter Newman, Murray Milgate, and John Eatwell, editors

This authoritative three-volume reference contains more than 1,000 essays on U.S. and international aspects of money, banking, and finance. It has overviews of the world's financial institutions and markets, analyses of innovations in financial instruments, and

explanations of economic and monetary theories. Several of the contributors are Nobel laureates in economics.
Published in 1994 by the Stockton Press, New York.

OECD Economic Surveys: United States

This publication is an annual report on the U.S. economy. It documents medium-term trends in incomes, productivity, investments, and savings, and examines the federal budget.
Published annually by the Organization for Economic Cooperation and Development (OECD).

Survey of Current Business

Compiled monthly by the U.S. Department of Commerce, Economics and Statistics Administration, Bureau of Economic Analysis, the *Survey* is the most important and comprehensive source of U.S. government–compiled economic data. Three conveniently color-coded main sections comprise the *Survey:*

The *white* pages contain three types of material. First is the "Business Situation" section, which objectively summarizes the recent economic situation as characterized in the latest economic data. Second is the presentation of the detailed *National Income and Product Account* tables, presenting the GDP data in all its forms, components, and related measures. Third are special articles and tables on regularly compiled measures such as international trade and capital flows, capital stock, and state personal income.

The *yellow* pages present economic data classified by cyclical characteristics. This section classifies some 250 economic indicators by whether they lead, coincide with, or lag behind overall economic activity.

The *blue* pages present monthly data on some 1,900 economic indicators—including personal income, industrial production, employment, and consumer prices—by whether

they lead, coincide with, or lag behind overall economic activity.
Published monthly by the Superintendent of Documents, U.S. Government Printing Office.

The U.S. Industrial Outlook

This business report prepared by the International Trade Administration of the U.S. Department of Commerce provides overviews, economic analyses, and projections (including production, employment, import competition, and prices) for more than 350 manufacturing, service, and high-tech industries that range from supercomputers to valve and pipe fittings. Industry forecasts are given for the year of publication and five years thereafter. The *U.S. Industrial Outlook* also provides profiles of international competition and international trade forecasts.
Published annually by the Superintendent of Documents, U.S. Government Printing Office.

Using Economic Indicators to Improve Investment Analysis

Evelina M. Tainer

Using Economic Indicators shows how economic indicators relate specifically to the investment strategies of individual investors, traders, and long-term institutional investors.
Published in 1993 by John Wiley & Sons, New York.

GOVERNMENT AGENCIES

Bureau of Economic Analysis (BEA)

As part of the Department of Commerce, the Bureau of Economic Analysis provides statistics on economic growth, inflation, regional development, and the United States' role in the world economy. BEA's current regional, national, and international estimates first appear as news releases, available by phone, online through the Economic Bulletin Board (see p. 000), and in printed reports. Phone information is available as follows: leading indicators, (202) 898-2450; gross domestic product, (202) 898-2451; personal income and outlays, (202) 898-2452; merchandise trade, balance of payments, and U.S. international transactions, (202) 898-2453.

BEA also issues several written reports:

BEA Reports: Gross Domestic Product. Contain a summary of national income and product account estimates, and feature GDP and corporate profits. Published monthly; available by subscription.

BEA Reports: Personal Income and Outlays. Contain a summary of national income and product account estimates, and feature personal income and outlays. Published monthly; available by subscription.

BEA Reports: Regional Reports. Provide summary estimates of state personal income (quarterly and annual) and of county and metropolitan personal income (annual). Published six times a year; available by subscription.

BEA Reports: International Reports. Provide summary estimates of merchandise, trade, balance-of-payments basis (quarterly), summary of international transactions (quarterly), capital spending of majority-owned affiliates (semiannual), and direct investment (annual). Published 13 times a year; available by subscription.

BEA Reports: Composite Index of Leading, Coincident, and Lagging Indicators. Provide summary estimates of the composite indices. Published monthly; available by subscription.

Survey of Current Business. See p. 450.

Business Statistics 1951–91. See p. 447.

All BEA Reports are available from the Superintendent of Documents, U.S. Government Printing Office. For further information, contact the Public Information Office, Bureau of Economic Analysis, Department of Commerce, Washington, DC 20230.

(202) 523-0771

The BEA also maintains a Web site with extensive statistical data: http://www.bea.doc.gov.

Bureau of Labor Statistics (BLS)

The Bureau of Labor Statistics collects, analyzes, and publishes data on employment, unemployment, prices and consumer expenditures, wages, productivity, economic growth, and employment projections. BLS data are issued in monthly, quarterly, and annual news releases and bulletins, reports, special publications, and periodicals. Data is available in print and through an electronic news service, as well as in magnetic tape, diskette, and microfiche formats.

BLS publications include the following:

Consumer Expenditure Survey. Published annually.

Consumer Price Index. Published monthly; available by subscription.

CPI Detailed Report. Provides comprehensive reports on consumer price movements and statistical tables, charts, and technical notes. Published monthly; available by subscription.

Producer Price Indexes. Published monthly; available by subscription.

Employment and Earnings. Covers employment and unemployment developments, and contains statistical tables on national, state, and area unemployment, hours, and earnings. Published monthly; available by subscription. (See description on p. 449.)

Compensation and Working Conditions. Reports on employee compensation—including wages, salaries, and benefits—and safety and health. Published monthly; available by subscription.

All BLS reports are available through the Superintendent of Documents, U.S. Government Printing Office, Office of Publications, Bureau of Labor Statistics, Department of Labor, Room 2822, 441 G Street NW, Washington, DC 20212. (202) 606-5886

The BLS also maintains a Web site with extensive statistical data: http://www.bls.gov.

The American Economics Association

This organization is a forum for educators, business executives, government administrators, journalists, lawyers, and others interested in economics and its application to present-day problems. It encourages historical and statistical research into actual conditions of industrial life and provides a nonpartisan forum for economic discussion. It sponsors the National Registry for Economists, a placement service.

American Economics Association, 204 Broadway, Suite 305, Nashville, TN 37203-2418.
(615) 322-2595

The Conference Board

The Conference Board is an organization that serves senior corporate executives. It provides a professionally managed research program in several areas, including economics. Its staff includes specialists in economic forecasting, consumer markets, public economic policy, and regional and global economic analysis. The Conference Board produces proprietary economic indicators including the "Help Wanted Index" and the "Consumer Confidence Survey."

The Conference Board, 845 Third Avenue, New York, NY 10022.
(212) 759-0900
Fax (212) 980-7014

FOR FURTHER INFORMATION

See *ABI/INFORM®,* p. 370
American Statistics Index, p. 370
The Business One Irwin Investor's Almanac, p. 417
The Irwin Guide to Using the Wall Street Journal, p. 376
CEDDS: The Complete Economic and Demographic Data Source, p. 431
County and City Data Book, p. 432
Data Pamphlets, p. 432
Economic Literature Index, p. 454
The Economist Guide to Global Economic Indicators, p. 454
Key Indicators of County Growth 1970–2010, p. 549
The Lifestyle Zip Code Analyst, p. 434
Market Movers: Understanding and Using Economic Indicators from the Big Five Economies, p. 455
OECD Economic Surveys, p. 456
State and Local Statistics Sources, p. 550
State and Metropolitan Databook, p. 550
Statistical Abstract of the United States, p. 378
Statistical Reference Index, p. 370
Statistics Sources, p. 378
Survey of Buying Power, p. 436
The Wall Street Journal, p. 379
The World Almanac and Book of Facts, p. 381

ECONOMIC DATA, TRENDS, AND PROJECTIONS: WORLDWIDE

Balance of Payments Statistics Yearbook

This two-part yearbook contains balance-of-payments statistics for most of the world, in accordance with the Balance of Payments Manual published by the International Monetary Fund (IMF). Part 1 includes both aggregate and detailed information for the world's countries. Part 2 provides tables of data on balance of payments.
Updated annually (usually in December) by the International Monetary Fund. Available by tape subscription. For further information, contact the publisher at http://imf.org.

Direction of Trade Statistics

The *Direction of Trade Statistics* provides data on exports and imports for more than 135 countries. Available in print and on magnetic tape.
Published quarterly, with an annual cumulative volume, by the International Monetary Fund, Washington, DC.

DRI Databases

DRI produces and makes available online a number of time-series databases on various countries and regions of the world economy, including the following:
DRI Asian Forecast. Provides economic forecasts for Australia, China, Hong Kong, India, Indonesia, Korea, Malaysia, Philippines, Singapore, Taiwan, and Thailand. Updated quarterly.
DRI Current Economic Indicators. Provide key economic indicators to Argentina,

Australia, Austria, Belgium, Brazil, Canada, Chile, China, Columbia, Denmark, Finland, France, Germany, Greece, Indonesia, Ireland, Israel, Italy, Japan, Korea, Mexico, Netherlands, Norway, Singapore, South Africa, Spain, Sweden, Switzerland, Taiwan, Thailand, United Kingdom, United States, and Venezuela. Updated as new data are available.
DRI Europe. Covers the macroeconomic, microeconomic, and financial indicators for Austria, Belgium, Denmark, Finland, France, Germany, Greece, Ireland, Italy, Netherlands, Norway, Portugal, Spain, Sweden, Switzerland, and the United Kingdom. Updated weekly/monthly or quarterly/annually, depending on data.
DRI European Forecast. Provides economic forecasts for Austria, Belgium, Denmark, Finland, France, Germany, Greece, Ireland, Italy, Netherlands, Norway, Portugal, Spain, Sweden, Switzerland, Turkey, and the United Kingdom. Updating varies by country and forecast.
DRI Japanese Forecast. Provides economic forecasts for the Japanese economy. Updated semiannually.
DRI Latin American Forecast. Provides economic forecasts for Argentina, Brazil, Chile, Colombia, Ecuador, Mexico, Peru, and Venezuela. Updated quarterly.
DRI World Forecast. Provides macroeconomic and microeconomic forecasts for 49 countries as well as regional forecasts. Updated from monthly to quarterly, depending on country.
(SOURCE: Gale Directory of Databases, Volume 1: Online Databases.)
Databases available online from DRI/McGraw-Hill.

Economic and Energy Indicators

The Central Intelligence Agency compiles this semimonthly resource. Coverage includes economic and energy information on the major developed countries that before the end of the Cold War were known as "noncommunist."
Published semimonthly by the National Technical Information Services.

Economic Literature Index

Offered by the American Economics Association, the *Economic Literature Index* is an index of worldwide economic literature taken from nearly 300 journals. Also available on CD-ROM and online through DIALOG.
Published and updated quarterly by the American Economics Association, Nashville, TN.

The Economist Economic and Financial Indicators

A weekly feature of the British magazine *The Economist,* this valuable source of international business information provides data and commentary on output, demand, jobs, prices, wages, commodity prices, currency, exchange rates, money and interest rates, and world stock markets.
Published weekly in The Economist (England).

The Economist Guide to Global Economic Indicators: Making Sense of Economics

The Economist Guide to Global Economic Indicators discusses and interprets all of the major economic indicators that relate to GDP and GNP; growth, trends, and cycles; population, employment, and unemployment; government revenues and expenditures; money and financial markets; and industry and commerce.
Published in 1993 by John Wiley & Sons, New York.

Government Finance Statistics Yearbook

This yearbook relating to International Monetary Fund member countries provides information on the various units of government, government accounts, the enterprises and financial institutions that governments own and control, and the national sources of data on government operations. It provides data on central government revenues, grants, expenditures, lending finance, and debt. Available in both print and magnetic tape formats.
Published annually by the International Monetary Fund, Washington, DC.

Industrial Policy in OECD Countries

This annual review analyzes recent government initiatives to promote industrial development and adjustment in Organization for Economic Cooperation and Development (OECD) countries. It also reviews trends in industry on the bases of industrial production, inputs, and performance, thus enabling users to make international comparisons.
Published annually by the Organization for Economic Cooperation and Development, Washington, DC.

IntEc CD-ROM: The Index to International Economics, Development and Finance

This bibliographic database covers articles and research papers on economic development, international trade, and monetary policy from 1981 to the present.
Published quarterly by Chadwyck Healey, Inc., with each issue cumulating the file and replacing the previous disk.

International Financial Statistics

This monthly publication is a source of statistics on all aspects of international and domestic finance. It provides, for most countries of the world, data on exchange rates, international liquidity, international banking, money and banking, interest rates, prices, production, international transactions, government accounts, and national accounts. Available in print, CD-ROM, and magnetic tape formats. *Published monthly by the International Monetary Fund, Washington, DC. An annual Yearbook issue published each September contains data spanning more than 35 years for countries covered in monthly issues.*

Labour Force Statistics

This publication is an annual statistical report on the population and labor force of the 24 member countries of the Organization for Economic Cooperation and Development (OECD).
Published annually by the Organization for Economic Cooperation and Development, Washington, DC.

Long-Term Prospects for the World Economy

This text reviews the prospects of the world's major regions, assesses the factors likely to affect the world economy, and looks at issues such as the North American Free Trade Agreement (NAFTA), European integration, and global environmental issues.
Published in 1992 by the Organization for Economic Cooperation and Development, Washington, DC.

Main Economic Indicators

This monthly publication provides statistics on Organization for Economic Cooperation and Development (OECD) countries, including recent changes in each nation's economy, statistics and indicators for GNP, industrial production, deliveries, stocks and orders, construction, wholesale and retail sales, employment, wages, prices, finance, foreign trade, and balance of payments. Available as a single copy or by subscription, in print or diskette formats. Also available online from DRI/McGraw-Hill.

Published monthly by the Organization for Economic Cooperation and Development, Washington, DC.

Market Movers: Understanding and Using Economic Indicators from the Big Five Economies

Mark Jones and Ken Ferris

Market Movers covers almost 100 of the leading economic indicators from the world's five most important economies: the United States, United Kingdom, France, Germany, and Japan.
Published in 1993 by McGraw-Hill, New York.

Monthly Statistics on Foreign Trade (Series A)

This publication provides an overall picture of trade of Organization for Economic Cooperation and Development (OECD) countries. Available by subscription in print or on diskette.
Published monthly by the Organization for Economic Cooperation and Development, Washington, DC.

OECD Economic Outlook

This is a twice-yearly survey of economic trends and prospects in Organization for Economic Cooperation and Development (OECD) countries—Australia, Austria, Belgium, Canada, Denmark, Finland, France, Germany, Greece, Ireland, Italy, Japan, Luxembourg, the Netherlands, New Zealand, Norway, Portugal, Spain, Sweden, Switzerland, Turkey, the United Kingdom, and the United States. Available in print and on diskette, as a single copy or by subscription. (The diskette contains background economic data and projections, but no analyses.)
Published semiannually by the Organization for Economic Cooperation and Development, Washington, DC.

OECD Economic Surveys

Economic surveys are done almost every year for each country belonging to the Organization for Economic Cooperation and Development (OECD). Each survey analyzes the nation's economy, provides statistical information, and makes short-term projections. A set of surveys is available by subscription.
Published annually by the Organization for Economic Cooperation and Development, Washington, DC.

The OECD STAN Database for Industrial Analysis

The Structural Analysis Industrial Database covers 46 manufacturing sectors in 12 OECD countries from 1980 to 1990.
Published in 1992 by the Organization for Economic Cooperation and Development, Washington, DC.

One Hundred Years of Economic Statistics

Thelma Liesner

This volume brings together 100 years of principal economic indicators for nine industrial nations: Australia, Canada, France, Germany, Italy, Japan, Sweden, the United Kingdom, and the United States.
Published in 1990 by Facts on File, New York.

Overseas Business Reports

Prepared by the U.S. Department of Commerce, each report offers a wide range of economic and business statistics and background information on a particular country.
Published periodically by the Superintendent of Documents, U.S. Government Printing Office.

PTS International Forecasts™

This is the online equivalent of Worldcasts (see below). Available online through DIA-LOG and Data-Star.

Updated monthly by Information Access/Predicasts.

UN Statistical Yearbook

The *UN Statistical Yearbook* contains economic and social information on 220 countries and territories. Topics include imports and exports, demographics, gross domestic product (GDP), employment, and inflation.
Published annually by the United Nations Publishing Service, New York.

World Economic and Business Review

The *World Economic and Business Review* offers analyses of the business and economic environment in more than 200 countries worldwide.
Published annually by Blackwell Publishers (England).

World Economic Outlook: A Survey of the Staff of the International Monetary Fund

The *World Economic Outlook* offers economic statistics and forecasts for the international community. Forecasts are based on considerations such as inflation, interest, debt, capital flows, and policy options available to the major economic groups.
Published semiannually by the International Monetary Fund, Washington, DC.

World Economic Survey

This annual assessment of the world economy provides an overview of important developments of the previous year and the outlook for the future. It analyzes the growth in the world economy, policy positions, international trade and payments, and international capital flows to developing countries.
Published annually by the United Nations Publishing Service, New York.

World Tables

This reference work contains a variety of business and economic statistics on 146 countries. Topics include interest and debt, private consumption, gross domestic product (GDP), and much more. *World Tables* is available in print and on computer diskette. *Published annually by The Johns Hopkins University Press, Baltimore.*

Worldcasts

This publication provides short- and long-range business and economic forecasts for products and markets outside of the United States. *Worldcasts* consists of eight volumes, four of which deal with products and four with distinct regions of the world. Available online as PTS International Forecasts™ (see above). *Published annually by Information Access/Predicasts.*

International Trade Administration (ITA)

The ITA maintains a staff of more than 350 analysts who provide free information on a wide variety of industries, such as automobiles, aerospace, confectionery products, construction, electronics, and textiles. Analysts will provide information on U.S. and international markets, current statistics, projections, trend analysis, and more. See appendixes of this text for a complete listing. *U.S. Department of Commerce, International Trade Administration, Herbert C. Hoover Building, 14th and Constitution NW, Washington, DC 20230. (202) 482-2000*

FOR FURTHER INFORMATION

See **Bureau of Economic Analysis,** *p. 450*
The Conference Board, *p. 452*
Demographic Yearbook, *p. 432.*
Economic Literature Index, *p. 454*
The Economist Pocket World in Figures, *p. 374*
F & S Index International, *p. 494*
Index to International Statistics, *p. 495*
Statistical Reference Index, *p. 370*
The Wall Street Journal, *p. 379*
Western European Economic Organizations, *p. 517*
World Factbook, *p. 496*

20

EMPLOYEE AND EXECUTIVE COMPENSATION

American Salaries and Wages Survey

The *American Salaries and Wages Survey* contains more than 38,000 salary statistics taken from more than 300 government, business, and news sources. Data on wages and jobs cover the period from January 1993 through February 1997. Entries are arranged in over 4,400 occupational classifications, and include profession, location, occupation, specialization, industry, and frequency. The source also includes comparative data rating high-, mid-, and low-salary ranges.
Published annually by Gale Research, Detroit.

AMS Office Salaries Report

The *AMS Office Salaries Report* presents salary information for 20 administrative and clerical office jobs.
Published annually by the Administrative Management Society.

Area Wage Survey

Produced by the Bureau of Labor Statistics, U.S. Department of Labor, the *Area Wage Survey* covers 70 metropolitan areas and contains information on earnings and benefits in professional, technical, clerical, office, and other occupations.
Published annually by the Superintendent of Documents, U.S. Government Printing Office.

Available Pay Survey Reports: An Annotated Bibliography

Available Pay Survey Reports is a comprehensive bibliography of compensation surveys that covers many types of jobs and organizations. Available as either a U.S. volume or an international volume.
Published in 1987 by Abbott, Langer, and Associates, Crete, IL.

Compensation

Robert E. Sibson

This text covers the planning, implementation, and management of employee compensation.
Fifth edition published in 1990 by the American Management Association, New York.

Compensation and Benefits Review

This bimonthly journal provides an in-depth look at crucial issues in the fields of compensation and benefits. Articles are written by leading academic and consulting experts.
Published bimonthly by the American Management Association, New York.

The Compensation Handbook: A State-of-the-Art Guide to Compensation Strategy and Design

Milton L. Rock and Lance A. Berger

The Compensation Handbook is a guide to the administration of compensation, from clerical pay through top-executive compensation.
Third edition published in 1991 by McGraw-Hill, New York.

CompFlash

This periodical provides a monthly update of current developments in compensation and

benefits, including, for example, tax proposals, new government regulations, innovative retirement plans, health care benefits, union demands, and executive perks.
Published monthly by the American Management Association, New York.

Employee Compensation and Benefits Alert

This reference service provides information on current developments in pay (wages, salaries, commissions, and cash bonuses), benefits (retirement plans, health care, insurance, family care, and tuition assistance), and special executive compensation plans.
Published biweekly by Warren, Gorham, & Lamont, New York.

Executive Compensation

A three-volume loose-leaf service (which includes a monthly newsletter), *Executive Compensation* reports on the latest compensation developments and issues.
Published by McGraw-Hill, New York.

Executive Compensation Answer Book

V. P. Kuraitis, Janet Ambrosi Wertman, and Bruce Overton

The *Executive Compensation Answer Book* offers concise answers to 700 essential compensation questions, including how to attract and retain top talent, how to create incentives for peak performance, and how to boost profitability.
Published in 1993 by Panel Publishers, New York.

Executive Compensation Service Reports: Reports on International Compensation

These reports cover 17 West European countries and Turkey. Individual reports list com-

pensation for 10 top management, 17 middle management, and 22 employee-level positions and make projections regarding salary, cost of living, and merit increases.
Published annually by Wyatt Data Services, Rochelle Park, NJ.

Forbes: Chief Executive Compensation Survey Issue

This annual report on executive compensation, published in a May issue of *Forbes* magazine, reports on the annual compensation of 800 chief executives. It includes information on salary and bonuses; "other" compensation, which includes payments under long-term compensation plans, thrift plan contributions, company-paid health and insurance plans, and restricted stock awards; stock gains realized from the exercise of stock options; and stock owned, which includes the value of the chief executive's stock holdings as a percentage of the firm's total market value. The report also includes information on the company's performance in terms of sales and profits.
Published annually in a May issue of Forbes.

Journal of Compensation & Benefits

The *Journal of Compensation & Benefits* covers new developments in, and offers thorough analyses of, compensation and benefit issues.
Published monthly by Warren, Gorham, & Lamont, New York.

National Survey of Professional, Administrative, Technical, and Clerical Pay

This annual survey is compiled by the Bureau of Labor Statistics.
Published annually by the Superintendent of Documents, U.S. Government Printing Office.

The New Pay: Linking Employee and Organizational Performance

Jay R. Schuster and Patricia K. Zingheim

The New Pay describes, discusses, and pleads for incentive pay for the mass of employees. *Published in 1992 by Lexington Books, New York.*

Software for Compensation Executives: A Directory of Resources

This directory provides information about 90 compensation software programs and more than 100 spreadsheets and statistical compensation programs. Published in loose-leaf format.
Updated quarterly by the American Compensation Association, Scottsdale, AZ.

Top Executive Compensation

Top Executive Compensation reports the results of an annual survey of the compensation of the five highest-paid executives in various industry and size categories.

Published annually by Conference Board, New York.

TRADE AND PROFESSIONAL ASSOCIATIONS

American Compensation Association (ACA)

The ACA is a nonprofit organization engaged in the design, implementation, and management of employee compensation and benefits programs. It offers courses in salary administration, direct compensation, benefits design and administration, executive compensation, and variable pay programs. Its publications include the *ACA Journal*, a quarterly publication, and *ACA News*, a monthly newsletter. *American Compensation Association, P.O. Box 29312, Phoenix, AZ 85038-9312.*
(602) 951-9191
Fax: (602) 483-8352

FOR FURTHER INFORMATION

*See **The Conference Board,** p. 452*

21

EMPLOYEE BENEFITS

The 401 (k) Plan Management Handbook

Jeffrey A. Miller and Larry Chambers

The 401 (k) Plan Management Handbook is a comprehensive guide to setting up and managing a 401 (k) plan, from design and compliance issues to hiring a consultant. Topics include plan-sponsor issues, investment management, participant record keeping and communications, legal compliance issues, and fiduciary responsibility under ERISA.
Published in 1991 by Probus Publishing, Chicago.

401 (k) Plans: A Comprehensive Guide

Bruce J. McNeil and Michael E. Lloyd

401 (k) Plans: A Comprehensive Guide uses a question-and-answer format to give a complete step-by-step analysis of 401 (k) plans. It discusses the benefits for both the employer and the employee, the qualification requirements, the Employee Retirement Income Security Act (ERISA) requirements, the tax consequences to all parties, and the variations of 401 (k) plans.
Published in 1993 by John Wiley & Sons, New York.

Benefits Coordinator

This reference service provides a complete analysis of the tax and legal issues affecting the full range of employer-provided benefits other than pensions. It is published as a seven-volume loose-leaf service, with up-dates and *Employee Benefits Alert Newsletter* issued every other week.
Published biweekly by Warren, Gorham & Lamont, New York.

BNA Pension Reporter

Published since 1974, the *BNA Pension Reporter* focuses on both private- and public-sector pension and employee benefits programs. Each issue reports on the latest pension developments in Washington, DC, and the states.
Published weekly by the Bureau of National Affairs, Rockville, MD.

The Complete Guide to Cost-Effective Employee Benefit Programs

Joseph G. Kozlowski and Walter Oleksy

This guide delivers a complete set of strategies and cost-control programs designed to reduce the cost of benefits while still attracting and motivating employees.
Published in 1987 by Prentice Hall, Englewood Cliffs, NJ.

Employee Benefits: Valuation, Analysis, and Strategies

Steven G. Vernon

This text provides detailed coverage of strategies and insights into understanding and communicating the value of benefits, from both the employer's and the employee's perspective.

Published in 1993 by John Wiley & Sons, New York.

Employee Benefits Cases

Published since 1981, *Employee Benefits Cases* provides the full text of precedent-setting federal and state employee benefits cases. Cases are organized three ways—topically, by point of law, and by title of case. Back volumes are available.
Published weekly by the Bureau of National Affairs, Rockville, MD.

Employee Benefits Dictionary: An Annotated Compendium of Frequently Used Terms

Virginia L. Briggs, Michael G. Kushner, and Michael J. Schinabeck

The *Employee Benefits Dictionary* defines more than 1,000 terms relating to tax-qualified and nonqualified retirement and deferred compensation arrangements; welfare benefit plans; and insurance, securities, and trust law.
Published in 1992 by the Bureau of National Affairs, Rockville, MD.

Employee Benefits Handbook

Jeffrey Mamorsky, editor

This handbook looks at the complete spectrum of benefits packages and analyzes their advantages and disadvantages, tax and legal considerations, and actuarial problems and employer costs.
Fourth edition published in 1995 by Warren, Gorham & Lamont, New York.

Employee Benefits Infosource®

This database covers literature dealing with a wide variety of topics in the computer industry field, including compensation, disability, stock option plans, stock ownership plans, flexible benefits, medical and dental insurance, pension plans, unemployment, and workers' compensation. Available online through DIALOG.
Updated monthly by the International Foundation of Employee Benefits Plans, Brookfield, WI.

Employee Benefits Infosource®: User's Guide and Thesaurus

This publication is a practical guide to using the Employee Benefits Infosource® database described in the preceding entry. It helps users save time online by targeting searches. It provides explanations of database mechanics and terminology, and listings of journal sources, journal codes, and sources included in the database.
Published in 1990 by the International Foundation of Employee Benefits Plans, Brookfield, WI.

Employee Benefits Management

This subscription service explains and reports on the tax and nontax aspects of employee benefits for employers, plan administrators, and benefits specialists. Special emphasis is placed on cost containment and data analysis.
Published twice monthly by the Commerce Clearing House, Chicago.

Employee Benefits Report

The *Employee Benefits Report* covers new developments in employee benefits and offers in-depth analyses of these and related matters.
Published monthly by Warren, Gorham & Lamont, New York.

Employee Benefits Resource Guide

This publication is a bibliography of source materials relating to employee benefits, including abstracts of books and descriptions of journals, services, and databases.
Second edition published in 1990 by the International Foundation of Employee Benefits Plans, Brookfield, WI.

Employee Benefits Software Directory

This directory contains descriptions of approximately 400 benefits-related software packages applicable to the administration of 401 (k) plans, claims filing, flexible benefits programs, COBRA compliance, benefits administration, and workers' compensation programs. *Published in loose-leaf format, with quarterly updates, by the American Compensation Association, Scottsdale, AZ.*

ERISA: A Comprehensive Guide

Martin Wald and David E. Kenty

This one-volume guide covers the Employee Retirement Income Security Act of 1974 (ERISA). Topics include health and welfare plans, severance, employee benefit plans, and pension plans.
Published in 1991 by John Wiley & Sons, New York.

ERISA: The Law and the Code

This guide to the Employee Retirement Income Security Act of 1974 (ERISA) covers such topics as the code section on retiree health accounts, premium changes in Pension Benefit Guarantee Corporation benefit plans, and excise tax changes.
Published in 1991 by the Bureau of National Affairs, Rockville, MD.

The Executive's Guide to Controlling Health Care and Liability Costs: Strategy-Based Solutions

Bruce N. Barge and John G. Carlson

This book is for senior executives who are involved in making decisions about an organization's health care, workers' compensation, and disability costs. The authors show that by making health concerns a part of an overall organizational strategy, executives can promote employee well-being, provide needed health benefits, contain costs, and ensure the organization's long-term financial stability.

Published in 1993 by John Wiley & Sons, New York.

Flexible Benefits: A How-To Guide

Richard E. Johnson

This guide is designed to help evaluate, develop, and implement a flexible benefits plan that will serve the interests of both employer and employees. It includes information on the pricing of multiple-option health plans. *Third edition published in 1988 by the International Foundation of Employee Benefits Plans, Brookfield, WI.*

Fundamentals of Flexible Compensation

Karen L. Frost, Dale L. Gifford, Christine A. Seltz, and Kenneth L. Sperling

This resource offers comprehensive coverage of flexible compensation programs: their origins and objectives, rules and regulations, current trends, designing specific program options, and structure and financing. *Second edition published in 1992 by John Wiley & Sons, New York.*

The Handbook of Employee Benefits: Design, Funding and Administration

Jerry S. Rosenbloom

This two-volume work is a comprehensive look at medical benefits, flexible benefits plans, and employee benefits communication. *Fourth edition published in 1996 by Irwin Professional Publications, Chicago.*

Health Care Handbook

Jeffrey D. Mamorsky

This text provides analysis and guidance on a broad range of issues affecting employer-provided health care, including plan design, funding and delivery, cost management, employer initiatives, legal compliance, communication, and administration.

Published and updated annually by Warren, Gorham & Lamont, New York.

Nelson's Guide to Pension Fund Consultants

This guide provides profiles of more than 350 consulting firms, with 1,800 consultants at 750 offices. Contact information is included. *Published annually by Nelson Publications, Port Chester, NY.*

Pension Claims: Rights and Obligations

Stephen R. Bruce

Pension Claims: Rights and Obligations analyzes claims involving contribution and benefits programs, accruals, vesting, fiduciary duties, discrimination, and plan termination. Leading court decisions and helpful examples are frequently incorporated into the text. *Second edition published in 1993 by the Bureau of National Affairs, Rockville, MD.*

Pensions and Other Employee Benefits: A Financial Reporting and ERISA Guide

Richard M. Steinberg, Ronald J. Murray, and Harold M. Dankner

This guide covers accounting, filing, reporting, and auditing for pensions and other postretirement employee benefits (OPEBs), health and welfare plans, employee stock option plans, and more. *Published in 1993 by John Wiley & Sons, New York.*

Retiree Health Benefits: Employer Obligations, Retiree Rights

William J. Danish

Retiree Health Benefits explores the history of benefit offerings, the "real" cost issues confronting corporations, accounting strategies for dealing with promises of lifetime benefits, legal implications, and strategies for addressing these issues from both a short- and a long-term perspective.

Published in 1993 by John Wiley & Sons, New York.

Retirement Savings Plans: Design, Regulation and Administration of Cash or Deferred Arrangements

David A. Littel, Donald C. Cardamone, and Wilhelm L. Gruszecki

Retirement Savings Plans offers clear consultant-like advice and step-by-step explanations of 401 (k) plans, simplified employee pensions (SEPs), 403 (b) tax-deferred annuities, and nonqualified plans. *Published in 1992 by John Wiley & Sons, New York.*

Trends in Pensions 1992

This reference, prepared by the Pension and Welfare Benefits Administration of the U.S. Department of Labor, provides federal government statistics on private pensions. The data come from more than 50 government publications and a wealth of previously unpublished statistics. Trends in private pensions are also described and analyzed. *Published by the Superintendent of Documents, U.S. Government Printing Office.*

Worker's Compensation Report

Worker's Compensation Report covers initiatives, trends, and controversies involving injuries and disabilities, state actions, judicial issues, legal strategies and settlements, retaliation, loss prevention, rehabilitation strategies, and medical cost containment. *Published biweekly by Bureau of National Affairs, Rockville, MD.*

TRADE AND PROFESSIONAL ASSOCIATIONS

Employee Benefits Research Institute (EBRI)

This organization develops public policy on employee benefits through research publications and educational programs. Its publications include *EBRI's Benefits Outlook* (monthly), *EBRI Issue Briefs* (monthly),

EBRI Quarterly Pension Investment Report, and *Employment Benefits Notes. Employee Benefits Research Institute, 2121 K Street NW, Washington, DC 20037.* (202) 659-0760
Fax: (202) 775-6312

International Foundation of Employee Benefits Plans

This organization conducts research on employee benefits plan management and cosponsors the Certified Employee Benefit Specialist Program in the United States and Canada. It publishes *Employee Benefits Quarterly, Employee Benefits Basics,* and *International Foundation of Employee Benefits Plans Digest* (monthly).

International Foundation of Employee Benefits Plans, 18700 West Bluemound Road, Box 69, Brookfield, WV 53008. (414) 786-6700

FOR FURTHER INFORMATION

See ***American Compensation Association,*** p. 460
Compensation and Benefits Review, p. 458
CompFlash, p. 458
The Conference Board, p. 452
Employee Compensation and Benefits Alert, p. 459
Management Contents, p. 376

22

ENVIRONMENTAL ISSUES

Canadian Environmental Directory

This national directory draws together the whole network of individuals, agencies, firms, and associates active in environment-related activities in Canada. Main alphabetical listings are organized by government, organization, and education/research establishments. The government section is divided into federal, provincial, and municipal levels and the ministries, departments, agencies, and so on, operating within these divisions.
Published annually by Gale Research, Detroit.

Costing the Earth: The Challenge for Governments, the Opportunities for Business

Francis Cairncross

Costing the Earth chronicles how industries worldwide are changing the way they produce goods to meet the growing demands of a "green" economy.
Published in 1992 by the Harvard Business School Press, Boston.

Directory of Environmental Information Sources

This environmental directory lists federal and state government resources; professional, scientific, and trade organizations; newsletters, magazines, and periodicals; and online databases.
Published in 1992 and biennially by Government Institutes, Inc., Rockville, MD.

Encyclopedia of Environmental Information Sources: A Subject Guide to about 34,000 Print and Other Sources of Information on All Aspects of the Environment

This encyclopedia of environmental information sources provides a convenient method to compile subject-specific lists for further research. Each entry offers a number of ways to locate information, such as abstracting and indexing services; bibliographies; directories, dictionaries, and encyclopedias; online databases; periodicals and newsletters; research centers and institutes; statistical sources; trade associations and professional societies; and government organizations.
Published in 1996 by Gale Research, Detroit.

Enviroline® Online

This online service provides complete bibliographic citations and custom-edited abstracts of more than 170,000 articles and reports on environmental issues. Available online through DIALOG and Orbit Search Service. Also available on magnetic tape and CD-ROM.
Published and updated monthly by R. R. Bowker, New Providence, NJ.

Environmental Abstracts

This monthly publication provides abstracts of literature dealing with environmental issues including air, water, and noise pollution; control technologies; and resource management.
Published monthly, with a cumulative volume published annually as Environmental Abstracts Annual, by R. R. Bowker, New Providence, NJ.

Environmental Industries Marketplace

Environmental Industries Marketplace contains 10,000 entries arranged alphabetically by company name. Companies listed include engineering firms, land surveyors, manufacturers, distributors, research facilities, retailers, wholesalers, transportation companies, disposal firms, and others.
Published biennially by Gale Research, Detroit.

The Environmental Law Handbook

The handbook offers current compliance information on environmental law fundamentals, enforcement and liabilities, the 1990 Clean Air Act amendments, the 1990 Oil Pollution Act, and Occupational Safety and Health Act (OSHA) penalties.
Published in 1991 by Government Institutes, Inc., Rockville, MD.

Environmental Regulatory Glossary

Thomas F. P. Sullivan, editor

This glossary records and standardizes more than 4,000 environmentally related terms, abbreviations, and acronyms.
Sixth edition published in 1993 by Government Institutes, Inc., Rockville, MD.

Environmental Reporter

This weekly subscription service reports on and provides texts of Environmental Protection Agency (EPA) regulations and enforcement activities, congressional hearings, and state government actions. Subscribers receive reference binders providing the full text of federal laws and regulations and selected state laws and regulations and court decisions.
Published and updated weekly by the Bureau of National Affairs, Rockville, MD.

Environmental Statutes

Environmental Statutes contains the complete text of all major environmental laws. Contents include the Occupational Safety and Health Act (OSHA); Resource Conservation and Recovery Act, including the Hazardous and Solid Waste Amendments of 1984; Safe Drinking Water Act; Toxic Substances Control Act; CERCLA/Superfund (SARA); Clean Water Act; National Environmental Policy Act; Pollution Prevention Act of 1990; FIFRA; and more.
Published in 1992 by Government Institutes, Inc., Rockville, MD.

Environmental Telephone Directory, 1993–1994

The *Environmental Telephone Directory* contains extensive EPA information; complete addresses and telephone numbers for all U.S. senators and U.S. representatives, with their environmental aides; full information on Senate and House committees and subcommittees and federal and executive agencies dealing with environmental issues; and detailed information on state environmental agencies.
Published in 1993 by Government Institutes, Inc., Rockville, MD.

Environmental Trends

Prepared by the Council on Environmental Quality, this text presents the dramatic changes that have taken place in land use in the United States, including human settlements, recreation sites, industry, and energy exploration. Various environmental topics covered include minerals and energy, water, climate and air quality, land resources, wetlands and wildlife, protected areas, population, transportation, and environmental risks and hazards. Statistical tables and graphs are also included, and maps, charts, and graphs are presented in full color.
Published in 1989 by the Superintendent of Documents, U.S. Government Printing Office.

EPA Headquarters Telephone Directory

This directory contains names and telephone numbers for EPA headquarters personnel in Washington, DC, as well as all ten EPA regions. A table is included for converting the Washington Interagency Telecommunications System (WITS) telephone numbers to outside commercial numbers.

Published in 1991 by the Superintendent of Documents, U.S. Government Printing Office.

Gale Environmental Sourcebook: A Guide to Organizations, Agencies, and Publications

Karen Hill and Annette Piccirelli, editors

The *Gale Environmental Sourcebook* provides descriptive information on more than 8,000 environmental organizations, information services, products, and a number of other sources. Each entry contains full contact information.

Second edition published in 1994 by Gale Research, Detroit.

The Green Consumer

John Elkington

This study analyzes how different businesses have responded to environmental concerns and looks at why many companies have not offered products consumers see as green.

Second edition published in 1990 by Penguin Books, New York.

International Environmental Law Special Report

This report is a collection of essays by noted authorities on international environmental law. Topics include international clean air issues, developments in environmental law in Eastern Europe, regulation of imports and exports, environmental regulation in Japan, environmental regulation in Mexico, and more.

Published in 1992 by Government Institutes, Inc., Rockville, MD.

Recycling Sourcebook

The *Recycling Sourcebook* provides more than 40 in-depth essays and case studies on the present state of recycling. Covering a wide range of topics, including materials technology, reduction and reuse, and programs, the essays illustrate how the challenges in the industry are being addressed by various institutions.

Published in 1992 by Gale Research, Detroit.

Resource Guide to State Environmental Management

This guide lists facts on state environmental, health, and resource departments, as well as special commissions and boards. Also included are listings of state environmental/natural resources budgets and a detailed directory of more than 75 state environmental programs. Available in electronic format as the Directory of State and Environmental Officials.

Second edition published in 1990 by the Council on State Governments, Lexington, KY.

State Environmental Law Annual Report, 1992 Edition

Written by highly regarded law firms in 41 states, this report provides a nationwide perspective on environmental law trends in each state. The report covers Alabama, Alaska, Arizona, Arkansas, California, Colorado, Connecticut, Florida, Georgia, Hawaii, Idaho, Illinois, Indiana, Kansas, Kentucky, Maine, Maryland, Massachusetts, Michigan, Minnesota, Missouri, Montana, Nevada, New Hampshire, New Jersey, New Mexico, New York, North Carolina, Ohio, Oklahoma, Oregon, Pennsylvania, Puerto Rico, Rhode Island, Texas, Utah, Virginia, Washington, West Virginia, Wisconsin, and Wyoming.

Published in 1992 by Government Institutes, Inc., Rockville, MD.

State Environmental Law Handbooks

Each handbook gives complete coverage of a state's environmental organizational structure and includes information regarding required permits and reports; hazardous and solid waste disposal; air, water, and natural resources regulation; and the relationship between federal and state regulations.
Updated as needed by Government Institutes, Inc., Rockville, MD.

Statistical Record of the Environment

Statistical Record of the Environment offers the results of more than 850 environmental studies. Topics include consumer issues, regulatory trends, financial incentives, control and management issues, production and consumption trends, and government and industry information. Each presentation provides the following: name of chart and listing organization; full text of most charts, graphs, and tables; annotations explaining foreign terms and symbols; and complete bibliographic citations.
Third edition published in 1995 by Gale Research, Detroit.

World Energy and Nuclear Directory

This directory lists energy-oriented organizations throughout the world. Alphabetically arranged within country sections, entries describe organizations involved in a wide range of energy-related scientific research, including electricity, direct energy conversion, biological energy sources, natural gas, coal technology, and other research on renewable forms of power.
Published in 1991 by Gale Research, Detroit.

World Guide to Environmental Issues and Organizations

This guide provides information on major environmental issues, from acid rain to "green politics," in leading countries. Directory information includes contact data on more than 250 environmental monitoring and pressure groups throughout the world.
Published in 1991 by Gale Research, Detroit.

GOVERNMENT AGENCIES

National Technical Information Service (NTIS)

NTIS has a large collection of environmental information, including handbooks and guides, regulations and updates, economic studies, and applied technology. For further information, request NTIS free catalog PR-868.
National Technical Information Service, 5285 Port Royal Road, Springfield, VA 22161. (703) 605-6000

U.S. Environmental Protection Agency (U.S. EPA)

The mission of the Environmental Protection Agency is to abate pollution in the areas of air, water, solid waste, pesticides, radiation, and toxic substances. The agency was created to permit coordinated and effective governmental action on behalf of the environment. Some of the key offices of the agency are the following:

Main Administration (202) 260-2090

Office of International Activities (202) 564-6613

Administration and Resources Management (202) 260-2400

Enforcement (202) 564-2440

Office of General Counsel (202) 260-8040

Office of Policy, Planning, and Evaluation (202) 260-4332

Office of the Inspector General (202) 260-3137

Solid Waste and Emergency Response (202) 260-4016

Prevention, Pesticides, and Toxic Substances (202) 260-2902
U.S. Environmental Protection Agency, 401 M Street SW, Washington, DC 20460. (202) 260-2090

Coalition for Environmentally Responsible Economics (CERES)

This project, initiated by the Social Investment Forum, establishes standards for evaluating corporate environmental performance. Signatory companies to the CERES Principles adopt basic codes of environmental performance and commit to conducting an annual self-evaluation of their progress in implementing the principles.
Coalition for Environmentally Responsible Economics, 711 Atlantic Avenue, Boston, MA 02111.
(617) 451-0927
Fax: (617) 482-6179

Council on Economic Priorities (CEP)

Established to provide ratings on and information about corporate social performance, the Council on Economic Priorities publishes *Shopping for a Better World,* a shoppers' guide to corporations. CEP's Corporate Environmental Data Clearinghouse tracks and reports on environmental performance of the Standard & Poor's 500 companies. Information on other aspects of corporate performance is available from CEP's Institutional Investor Research Service.
Council on Economic Priorities, 30 Irving Place, New York, NY 10003.
(212) 420-1133

Environmental Law Institute

This center for research and education on environmental law and policy sponsors programs in areas such as education and training, publications, and policy research and technical assistance.
Environmental Law Institute, 1616 P Street NW, Suite 200, Washington, DC 20036.
(202) 328-5150

Global Environmental Management Initiative

This organization was formed by a coalition of corporations to foster environmental excellence by businesses worldwide. Efforts include work groups, publications, and symposia focusing on issues such as total quality environmental management, stakeholder communications, and the International Chamber of Commerce Business Charter of Sustainable Development.
Global Environmental Management Initiative, 1828 L Street NW, Suite 711, Washington, DC 20036.
(202) 296-7449
Fax: (202) 296-7442

FOR FURTHER INFORMATION

See **ABI/INFORM®**, *p. 370*
The Economist Pocket World in Figures, *p. 374*
National Technical Information Service/Federal Government Electronic Bulletin Boards, *p. 482*

23

EXPORTING AND IMPORTING

Alternative Finance: Strategy and Techniques

John S. Gordon

This book identifies and describes the trade financing alternatives available to exporters and importers, how to use them, and how to locate the sources of alternative finance. *Published in 1992 by the Global Training Center, Dayton, OH.*

American Export Register

This publication provides a way to find the full range of U.S. products and services available to serve the export market. Its coverage includes more than 200,000 products and service listings; an alphabetical listing of nearly 43,000 U.S. firms; product listings in ten languages (Arabic, Chinese, French, German, Italian, Japanese, Portuguese, Russian, Spanish, and English); and a directory of import/export services (e.g., banks, cargo carriers, customs house brokers, U.S. embassies and consulates, and chambers of commerce). *Published annually by the Thomas Publishing Company, New York.*

A Basic Guide to Exporting

Prepared by the U.S. Department of Commerce, this is a comprehensive how-to guide for exporting products and services. Its coverage includes a description of what must be done before the sale (developing an export strategy, conducting market research, preparing products for export), making the sale (pricing, export regulations), and what must be done after the sale (documentation, methods of payment, financing transactions).

Published in 1992 by the Superintendent of Documents, U.S. Government Printing Office.

Bureau of the Census Foreign Trade Report: Annual U.S. Exports, Harmonized Schedule B Commodity by Country

Prepared by the Foreign Trade Division of the Bureau of the Census, this report details all U.S. exports. Available in print and on CD-ROM. *Published annually by the Superintendent of Documents, U.S. Government Printing Office.*

Bureau of the Census Foreign Trade Report: Monthly Exports and Imports—SITC Commodity by Country

This report is a comprehensive listing of U.S. exports and imports. It is available by subscription in print and on CD-ROM. *Published monthly by the Superintendent of Documents, U.S. Government Printing Office.*

Business America

This publication of the U.S. Department of Commerce is designed to help U.S. companies sell their products and services overseas. *Published biweekly by Business America Associates, Inc., 2120 Greentree Road, Pittsburgh, PA 15220-1406. (412) 833-1910*

Commerce Department's "Flash Facts" Service

If one has a touch-tone telephone and a fax machine, the Commerce Department can provide a user with instant information on exporting to a particular region or country. Simply call any of the numbers listed below and follow the instructions, and the requested information will be faxed free of charge. "Flash Facts" are available from the following Commerce Department offices:

Eastern European Business Information Center (EEBIC) (202) 482-5745

Office of Mexico (202) 482-4464

Office of the Pacific Basin (202) 482-3875 or (202) 482-3646

Business Information Service for the Newly Independent States (BISNIS) (202) 482-3145

Offices of Africa, Near East, and South Asia (202) 482-1064

For further information, call the International Trade Administration of the Department of Commerce.
(202) 377-3808

Country Marketing Plans

These international marketing plans cover 67 countries and are prepared annually by the commercial sections of the American embassies for the U.S. Foreign and Commercial Service of the Department of Commerce. The plans are available in both print and electronic formats from either the Commercial Information Management System or the National Trade Databank (see p. 475).
Published annually by the Superintendent of Documents, U.S. Government Printing Office.

Department of State Background Notes

These *Background Notes,* prepared by the Office of Public Affairs, Department of State, are a collection of short authoritative pamphlets about various countries, territories, and international organizations. Each pamphlet provides economic and trade information about a specific country, along with an overview of its people, land, history, government, political conditions, and foreign relations. The *Background Notes* are available as a set or by subscription.

Published by the Superintendent of Documents, U.S. Government Printing Office.

The Diplomat

The Diplomat is a "newsletter of international business and social etiquette" that also provides a brief background on each covered country. Available by single copy or subscription.
Published by The Diplomat.

Directory of U.S. Exporters
Directory of U.S. Importers

These guides contain business profiles of more than 23,000 active exporters and 22,000 active importers. They also contain a product index listing traded products with their harmonized commodity code numbers, customs information, listings of foreign consulates and embassies, and international banks providing foreign service.
Published annually by the Journal of Commerce, New York.

Export Administration Regulations

A complete listing of all Export Administration regulations is available. A new complete version of the regulations is issued every December. Regulations are amended on an irregular schedule, and updated information is sent only to subscribers.
Published annually by the National Technical Information Service, Springfield, VA.

Export Reference Manual

This subscription service provides the import requirements of 200 countries.
Updated weekly by the Bureau of National Affairs, Inc., Rockville, MD.

Export Sales and Marketing Manual
John R. Jagoe

This manual shows how to secure foreign markets and buyers, price and budget for ex-

port, write export contracts, ship overseas, and receive payment.
Published annually by Export USA Publications.

The Export Yellow Pages

This directory lists U.S. companies that have registered with the U.S. Department of Commerce, Office of Export Trading Company Affairs Contact Facilitation Database. To register or obtain a single copy, contact the Department of Commerce local office.
Published by the Superintendent of Documents, U.S. Government Printing Office.

The Exporter

This periodical covers the latest developments in trade and finance issues, rules, and regulations.
Published monthly by The Exporter.

Exporter's Encyclopaedia

The *Exporter's Encyclopaedia* covers more than 170 world markets and offers information on everything from import licensing and exchange regulations to documentation requirements to listings of 150 U.S.-based foreign trade zones. There is also a section with information on international risk and payment conditions for more than 100 countries.
Published annually by Dun & Bradstreet Information Services.

Exporter's Encyclopaedia Country Profile Series

A supplement to Dun & Bradstreet's *Exporter's Encyclopaedia,* the *Country Profile Series* consists of 20 individual reports—one dedicated to each of the top U.S. trading partners. Among the topics covered in each profile are import licensing regulations, customs tariff information, import taxes, preshipment procedures, documentation requirements, key con-

tacts with addresses and telephone numbers, product standards information, and business travel notes. Profiles are available for Austria, Belgium, Brazil, Canada, China, France, Germany, Hong Kong, Israel, Italy, Japan, South Korea, Mexico, The Netherlands, Saudi Arabia, Singapore, Spain, Switzerland, Taiwan, and the United Kingdom.
Published annually by Dun & Bradstreet Information Services.

Export/Import Letters of Credit and Payment Methods

John S. Gordon

This book describes in detail the letter of credit (L/C) and trade payment process. It provides an analysis of risk, details procedures, and includes helpful examples.
Published in 1997 by the Global Training Center, Dayton, OH.

Exporting: From Start to Finance

L. Fargo Wells and Karin B. Dulat

Exporting: From Start to Finance is a comprehensive guide to the intricacies of establishing an exporting operation.
Published in 1991 by Liberty Hall Press/McGraw Hill.

Exporting to Canada: Documentation and Procedures

John S. Gordon

This book describes the regulations and procedures for U.S. companies exporting to Canada. It identifies U.S. and Canadian resources and provides information on the North American Free Trade Agreement (NAFTA).
Published in 1996 by the Global Training Center, Dayton, OH.

Fast-Track Exporting

Sandra L. Renner and W. Gary Winget

Fast-Track Exporting is a step-by-step guide for small to midsize companies interested in quickly setting up an exporting operation. *Published in 1991 by AMACOM Books, New York.*

Going Global: How Europe Helps Small Firms Export

William E. Nothdurft

Going Global explores how European countries help their small and medium-size firms to successfully export their products. The Europeans have created well-integrated public and private sector export assistance programs, and this book brings together the lessons learned to help other countries develop high-yield export assistance programs. Some of the issues addressed include who should be helped with exporting, the forms of assistance most effective for reaching and serving targeted firms, where assistance should be delivered, and how export assistance should be financed.
Published in 1992 by the Brookings Institute, Washington, DC.

The Handbook of International Trade Finance

Campbell Dunford, editor

This handbook, written by 15 industry experts, delivers authoritative guidance on how to achieve and maintain business relationships in other countries in a rapidly changing global scene. It covers the fundamentals of international trade, financial and legal concerns, long-term financing, countertrade, and key contact points for establishing businesses abroad.
Published in 1991 by Woodhead Faulkner, New York.

Import Reference Manual

This subscription service analyzes all import laws and indexed texts of import statutes, regulations, and executive orders.
Updated six times a year by the Bureau of National Affairs, Inc., Rockville, MD.

"Importing From" Guides

Each unit of this series of country-specific guides covers the following areas: finding suppliers; exporting industries and products; shipping and freight transport policies; background to import/export policies; banking, finance, and foreign investments; setting up a business; travel and custom tips; and labor relations. The guides and their year of publication follow:

Importing from Brazil (1992)
Importing from China (1992)
Importing from Czechoslovakia (1992)
Importing from Hong Kong (1991)
Importing from India (1991)
Importing from Korea (1991)
Importing from Malaysia (1991)
Importing from Mauritius (1992)
Importing from Mexico (1992)
Importing from Philippines (1991)
Importing from Poland (1992)
Importing from Singapore (1992)
Importing from Taiwan (1991)
Importing from Thailand (1991)
Importing from Vietnam (1991)
Published by Probus Publishing, Chicago.

The International Trade Reporter

Published since 1974, this periodical offers timely and thorough coverage of U.S. trade policy. Regular articles cover topics such as pending legislation; congressional hearings; and proposed regulations and actions by the International Trade Commission, Commerce Department, Office of the U.S. Trade Representative, and Export/Import Bank. Available online through NEXIS.
Published weekly by the Bureau of National Affairs, Inc., Rockville, MD.

Journal of Commerce

This newspaper covers the latest domestic and foreign economic developments and provides specific coverage of export and import opportunities. Features include a daily page of export trade leads from the U.S. Depart-

ments of Agriculture and Commerce; a weekly series on conducting business in foreign countries, highlighting such information as the country's current and potential imports and exports, documentation and entry requirements, tariffs, quotas, and currency restrictions; detailed guides to ocean shipping liner services and sailing schedules; and advice for new or small exporters that examines critical aspects of successful importing, including government regulations, labeling rules, and freight and shipping insurance. Available online through DIALOG.
Published daily by the Journal of Commerce, New York.

Key Officers of Foreign Service Posts

This government directory lists names, titles, addresses, and telephone numbers of key overseas personnel.
Published three times per year by the Superintendent of Documents, U.S. Government Printing Office.

National Negotiating Styles

Hans Binnedijk, editor

This book is a study of the negotiating styles of the major trading partners of the United States, written by academics and others knowledgeable in the field.
Published in 1987 by the Center for the Study of Foreign Affairs; available through the U.S. Government Printing Office.

National Trade Databank

This source provides information on exporting (prospects, opportunities, and so forth), market research, and foreign countries. Much of the information provided in over a dozen databases has a strong U.S. bias and is written by U.S. commercial sections in various countries. Also included is information from other international agencies such as the Asian Development Bank.
Updated monthly (latest disk is September 1996).

Source: http://www.emic.demon.co.uk/cdntd&.htm.

National Trade Databank (NTBD), USA

This service, supported by the U.S. Department of Commerce, provides information on exporting and international trade. Included are reports on marketing; export opportunities; U.S. and foreign companies; and social, political, and economic conditions in foreign countries. Available on CD-ROM or at the Web site.
Updated by the U.S. Department of Commerce.
Fax: (202) 482-2164
http://www.stat-usa.gov/stat-usa.htm

The OEL Insider

This monthly newsletter of the Office of Export Licensing covers items of current or topical interest to exporters. Available by subscription.
Published monthly by the Superintendent of Documents, U.S. Government Printing Office.

Official Export Guide

This comprehensive annual contains an abbreviated Schedule B directory of U.S. goods and services, Bureau of Export Administration Regulations, market profiles, and port information.
Published annually by the North American Publishing Co., Philadelphia.

Profitable Exporting: A Complete Guide to Marketing Your Products Abroad

John S. Gordon

This excellent, useful guide to the opportunities and intricacies of exporting covers a wide variety of topics, including export readiness; identifying the most opportune markets; organizing export functions; and analyzing marketing, financial, and pricing elements. It contains an extremely helpful guide to the resources offered by the U.S. Department of Commerce. *Second edition published in 1993 by John Wiley & Sons, New York.*

The United States–European Community Trade Directory

John S. Gordon and Timothy Harper

This directory of international business and trade resources in the United States and the European Community provides a wide range of contacts (agencies, services, institutions, and private companies) useful to importers, exporters, investors, professionals, and corporate managers who want to do business in Europe. The first part covers resources available in the United States. The second section covers resources available, on a country-by-country basis, in Europe. *Published in 1993 by John Wiley & Sons, New York.*

U.S. Customs House Guide

This comprehensive reference contains an abbreviated Harmonized Tariff Schedule of the United States (known as HS or HTS), U.S. Customs regulations, port profiles, and directories. *Published annually by the North American Publishing Co., Philadelphia.*

U.S. Exports of Merchandise on CD-ROM

Compiled by the U.S. Bureau of the Census, this database gives detailed export data on a variety of products, including their value, quantity, destination, shipping weight, and country of origin. *Updated monthly by the Foreign Trade Division, U.S. Bureau of the Census.* (301) 763-7662

U.S. Imports of Merchandise on CD-ROM

Compiled by the U.S. Bureau of the Census, this database gives detailed import data on a variety of products, including their value, quantity, destination, shipping weight, and country of origin. *Updated monthly by the Foreign Trade Division, U.S. Bureau of the Census.* (301) 763-7662

World Trade

World Trade is a magazine that covers issues of general interest in international trade. *Published monthly by Taipan Press, Inc.*

GOVERNMENT AGENCIES

U.S. Department of Commerce

The International Trade Administration of the U.S. Department of Commerce provides a wide-ranging array of services to help companies do business overseas. The U.S. and Foreign Commercial Service has 47 district and 21 branch offices in the United States and 132 Overseas Commercial Sections in 68 countries outside of the United States. (A list of district overseas offices is provided in Appendix 13.) The U.S. and F.C.S. provides services geared to the marketing and information needs of the U.S. exporting and international business communities. The U.S. and F.C.S. will do the following:

1. Help pinpoint export prospects by

   a. preparing research reports performed on location in overseas markets. Contact number is (202) 482-5037.

   b. developing a customized sales survey that offers a quick assessment of how a product will sell in an overseas market. Contact number is (202) 482-3334.

   c. providing online trade leads through its Economic Bulletin Board. To subscribe, call (202) 482-3190.

d. providing a one-stop source of international trade data, the National Trade Databank (see p. 475 for more information). Contact number is (202) 482-3190.

e. checking the reputation, reliability, and financial status of prospective trading partners through World Traders Data Reports. Contact number is (202) 482-1171.

2. Help make overseas contacts

a. through its agent/distribution service, a customized overseas search for qualified agents, distributors, and representatives of U.S. firms. Contact number is (202) 482-1171.

b. by providing sales leads from international firms seeking to buy or represent U.S. products and services through the Trade Opportunities program. Contact number is (202) 482-2504.

c. by providing mailing labels and lists of prospective customers through the Export Contact List Service. Contact number is (202) 482-2504.

3. Promote products and services through

a. Commercial News USA, an international marketing magazine promoting U.S. products and services in 170 countries. Contact number is (202) 482-4918.

b. Gold Key Service, offered by Foreign Commercial Service in 47 countries. This custom-tailored service for U.S. firms planning to visit a country provides orientation briefings, market research, introductions to potential partners, and assistance in developing a sound marketing strategy. Contact number is (202) 482-0115.

c. Matchmaker Trade Delegations, an organization that matches U.S. firms with prospective agents, distributors, and other kinds of business contact overseas. Contact number is (202) 482-3119.

d. Foreign Buyer Program, which supports leading U.S. trade shows in industries with high export potential. Contact number is (202) 482-0481.

The International Trade Administration also has industry specialists with expertise and knowledge of export opportunities in a wide range of industries, from abrasives to yeast. A listing of these industry specialists appears in Appendix 12.

The International Trade Administration's country specialists will provide you with export information and opportunities from Afghanistan to Zimbabwe. A listing of country specialists appears in Appendix 11.

TRADE AND PROFESSIONAL ASSOCIATIONS

American Association of Exporters and Importers (AAEI)

The AAEI represents both exporters and importers before the executive and legislative branches of the U.S. government, as well as government regulatory agencies. It works against "self-defeating restrictions on trade no matter which industry sector is threatened." The AAEI publishes *The International Trade Alert,* special information bulletins on new or fast-breaking issues, and *International Trade Monthly.*
American Association of Exporters and Importers, 11 West 42nd Street, New York, NY 10036.
(212) 944-2230
Fax: (212) 382-2606

American Countertrade Association

The purpose of the American Countertrade Association is to promote trade and commerce between U.S. companies and their international competitors through the use of countertrade.
American Countertrade Association, 121 S. Meramec Avenue, #1102, St. Louis, MO 63105-1725.
(314) 727-5522
Fax: (314) 727-8171

FOR FURTHER INFORMATION

24

FEDERAL GOVERNMENT (U.S.)

Catalog of Federal Domestic Assistance

This comprehensive listing of all grant, loan, insurance, and other programs of government aid is available in print and through the Federal Assistance Programs Retrieval System, a nationally accessible computer system.
Published annually, with periodic supplements, by the Superintendent of Documents, U.S. Government Printing Office.
For further information, call (202) 708-5126.

CIS/INDEX to Publications of the United States Congress

This monthly publication indexes abstracts and analyzes the publications of 300 active House, Senate, and joint committees and subcommittees. These publications include committee hearings, reports, documents, and special publications. Information in the *Index* helps the user find out who supports and opposes proposals and programs; tap authoritative sources of statistics, projections, and analyses; develop proposals that conform to the plans of federal agencies; and find competitive business information. Available in print, online, and on CD-ROM (the latter under the product name of *Congressional Masterfile 2*). Available online through DIALOG.
Published monthly, with annual cumulative volume, by Congressional Information Service, Bethesda, MD.

Commerce Business Daily

Commerce Business Daily announces products and services wanted or offered by the federal government and lists bids and proposals requested by the government as well as contract awards and surplus sales. The full-text equivalent is also available online from DIALOG.
Published daily by the Superintendent of Documents, U.S. Government Printing Office.

Committees in the U.S. Congress, 1947–1992

Garrison Nelson

This two-volume work presents a comprehensive history of congressional committee membership dating back to 1947. Data include committee membership in Congress, the length of membership for each member, and leadership positions held by each member. Volume I is organized by committee, showing all members for each Congress, as well as the members' seniority. Volume II details each member's committee assignments throughout his or her career and offers brief descriptions of committee jurisdictions.
Published in 1993 by Congressional Quarterly Inc., Washington, DC.

Congressional Quarterly Weekly Report

The *Weekly Report* offers comprehensive coverage of the activities of Congress, with articles, listings of House and Senate roll call votes, the status of various appropriations, and a complete index.
Published weekly by Congressional Quarterly, Inc., Washington, DC.

Contracting with the Federal Government: A Primer for Architects and Engineers

Frank M. Alston, Margaret M. Worthington, and Louis P. Goldsman

Contracting with the Federal Government provides practical information regarding the rules and regulations that define the federal procurement process.
Revised edition published in 1992 by John Wiley & Sons, New York.

The Federal Database Finder

This publication identifies thousands of government data sources that can be accessed by computer. Sources of interest to businesspeople include, for example, news about the latest economic indicators.
Published in 1993 by Information USA, Kensington, MD.

Federal Procurement Report

This report lists all of the procurement actions of all government agencies.
Published annually by the General Services Administration, Federal Procurement Data Center.

Federal Regional Yellow Book: Who's Who in the Federal Government's Departments, Agencies, Courts, Military Installations and Service Academies Outside of Washington, DC

The *Federal Regional Yellow Book* provides addresses, titles, and telephone numbers of more than 18,000 key federal decision makers based in about 4,000 regional offices outside of Washington, DC. It includes three indexes organized by key words, locations, and names.
Published semiannually by the Monitor Publishing Company, New York.

Federal Staff Directory

The *Federal Staff Directory* contains timely information on the executive branch of the U.S. government and its 32,000 key executives. Complete contact information is provided, as are 2,600 detailed biographies.
Published annually by Staff Directories, Ltd., Alexandria, VA.

Federal Yellow Book: Who's Who in Federal Departments and Agencies

The *Federal Yellow Book* provides up-to-date listings of all changes in federal leadership and department and agency reorganizations. Complete listings include names, titles, office locations, and telephone numbers of administrators and top staff aides in the executive offices of the president and vice president; the 14 cabinet-level federal departments; more than 70 independent federal agencies; and federal information centers in 72 cities.
New editions published quarterly by the Monitor Publishing Company, New York.

Government Contracting Manual

Timothy J. Healy

This guide shows small and medium-sized businesses how to land a government contract. Topics include bidding strategies, checklists covering every step of the bidding cycle, and government agencies that bid out work.
Published in 1990 by Prentice Hall, Englewood Cliffs, NJ.

Guide to Congress

The *Guide to Congress* is a comprehensive single-volume reference to the history and intricacies of the legislative branch. Topics include the recent trend toward leadership weakness, the growth of subcommittee power, the budget process, and controversies surrounding pay and honoraria.
Published in 1991 by Congressional Quarterly, Inc., Washington, DC.

How to Find Business Intelligence in Washington

A directory of business information collected by the U.S. government, *How to Find Business Intelligence in Washington* lists thousands of sources that can provide free industry reports, marketing data, publications, and databases.
Published in 1992 by Washington Researchers, Ltd., Washington, DC.

The Insider's Guide to Winning Government Contracts

Richard L. Porterfield

The Insider's Guide is directed at small business owners and provides step-by-step instructions on selling to the government. Features include an appendix listing the products and services purchased by the government, contact information on more than 1,200 government buying offices, and interpretations of laws, regulations, and requirements involved in procuring federal contracts.
Published in 1992 by John Wiley & Sons, New York.

Internal Telephone Directories

The internal telephone directories of various federal departments are an excellent way to locate a particular person or expert within the government. These directories include the names, titles, and telephone numbers of the people who work in specific offices and divisions. The Departments of Defense, Energy, Health and Human Services, Labor, State, and Transportation all make their directories available to the public. Directories can be ordered through the Government Printing Office.

If, for some reason, the Government Printing Office is unable to provide a particular internal telephone directory, it might be a good idea to turn to the Freedom of Information Clearinghouse. Acting on the Freedom of Information Act of 1966, which requires federal agencies to make public any identifiable records when requested (with certain exceptions, such as internal personnel information or classified defense secrets), the clearinghouse may be of assistance in obtaining a particular telephone directory.
Freedom of Information Clearinghouse, P.O. Box 19367, Washington, DC 20036. (202) 833-3000

Lesko's Info-power

Matthew Lesko

Info-power is a sourcebook that contains the names of more than 30,000 sources and experts from the federal and state governments, from whom users can obtain free or low-cost advice. Sections of particular interest to businesspeople include careers and the workplace; information on people, companies, and mailing lists; economics, demographics, and statistics; patents, copyrights, and trademarks; energy; the Freedom of Information Act; and government databases and bulletin boards. Available in print or online through CompuServe.
Published in 1990 by Information USA, Kensington, MD.

Monthly Catalog of United States Government Publications

The *Monthly Catalog* provides a record and index of all federal publications received by the Government Printing Office (GPO). The bulk of the catalog is a listing of documents according to their issuing agencies. For example, all Department of Labor publications, regardless of subject, are grouped together. In addition to this grouping, the *Monthly Catalog* provides seven indexes that allow users to find a particular publication quickly by author, title, subject, title keyword, stock number (a numerical listing of GPO sales stock numbers), contract number (an alphabetical list of contract, project, and grant numbers related to technical reports), and series/report (an alphabetical list of report numbers and series statements). Cumulative indexes are compiled semiannually and annually. Although a publication or document might be included in the *Monthly Catalog*, this does not mean that it is available from the Government Printing Office (however, order forms are included in each issue). It may instead have to be ordered from the issuing agency. The *Monthly Catalog* is available at most larger libraries and is accessible through online databases, including DIALOG and BRS.

Published monthly by the Superintendent of Documents, U.S. Government Printing Office.

National Technical Information Service/Federal Government Electronic Bulletin Boards

The U.S. government has a wide variety of electronic bulletin boards that contain a store of useful information, including many files that can be downloaded to the caller's own computer. Much of this information is available without charge, as is access to the system; in some cases, however, a fee applies for downloading files. The National Technical Information Service (NTIS) number, which can be reached by modem, is (703) 321-8020.

A listing of some of the government electronic bulletin boards and their sponsors and contents follows:

3:ALIX (Library of Congress: automated library information exchange)

6:CIC-BBS (General Services Administration: Consumer Information Center)

7:CLU-IN (Environmental Protection Agency: Superfund data and information)

9:CRS:BBS (Department of Justice: Americans with Disabilities Act information)

10:Computer Security (NIST: National Computer System Laboratory Computer Security bulletin boards)

13:EBB (Department of Commerce: economic data and information)

14:ELISA System (Department of Defense: export license tracking system)

16:EPUB (Department of Energy: energy information and data)

19:FERC-CIPS BBS (Department of Energy: Federal Energy Regulatory Commission)

22:Federal BBS (Government Printing Office: fee-based Government Printing Office data)

26: Labor News (Department of Labor information and files)

27:Magawatt 1 (Department of Energy: information on energy and the Department of Energy)

40:SBA On Line (Small Business Administration information and data)

47:USCS-BBS (Customs Service: customs and exchange-rate data and information)

60:LC News Service (Library of Congress news service)

61:STIS (National Science Foundation: science and technology information system)

67: Offshore-BBS (Department of Interior: offshore oil and gas data)

68:TQM-BBS (T. Glenn: total quality management)

78:SWITCH BBS (Environmental Protection Agency and Solid Waste Management Authority: solid waste management)

82:CABB (Department of State: passport information and travel alerts)

Official Congressional Directory

This resource for identifying the components of the three branches of the federal government contains an alphabetical list of the members of Congress with their addresses, rooms, and telephone numbers; biographical sketches of members, including descriptions of congressional districts and zip codes; boards, commissions, and advisory organizations; Capitol officers and officials; committees, committee assignments, and more. The text covers all federal departments, from Agriculture to Veterans' Affairs. It also lists the foreign representatives of the diplomatic service and consular offices in the United States.

Published annually by the Superintendent of Documents, U.S. Government Printing Office.

Subject Bibliography Index

This index is a listing of more than 250 major subjects with specific bibliographies for each, representing material in over 15,000 periodicals, guides, pamphlets, and booklets. Bibliographies of interest to business researchers include accounting and auditing; banks and banking; business and business management; employment and occupations; foreign trade and tariff, government specifications and standards; insurance; labor-management relations; marketing research; occupational safety and health, personnel management, guidance, and counseling; prices, mages, and the cost of living; small business; taxes and taxation. The *Subject Bibliography Index* is available at most larger libraries and can be ordered from the Government Printing Office.
Published and updated periodically by the Superintendent of Documents, U.S. Government Printing Office.

United States Government Manual

An all-inclusive guide to the offices and agencies within the federal government, the *Government Manual* also includes information on nongovernmental organizations affiliated with the government, such as the PanAmerican Health Organization and the Smithsonian Institution. Each department within the government is broken down into its individual bureaus and offices. Key individuals within those offices are identified, along with Federal Information Centers and regional offices. The *Government Manual* can be found in most large libraries, or it can be ordered from the Government Printing Office.
Published annually by Superintendent of Documents, U.S. Government Printing Office.

U.S. House of Representatives Telephone Directory

This directory lists Washington and home district telephone numbers and office addresses of each member of the U.S. House of Representatives. It also provides contact information for each representative's staff, House committee members and staff, joint committee members and staff, House offices and staff, and general support offices as well as telephone numbers of U.S. senators and U.S. government agencies.
Published by the Superintendent of Documents, U.S. Government Printing Office.

Using Government Publications

This text shows how to access the wealth of print and electronic information available in government publications.
Revised edition published in 1993 by the Oryx Press, Phoenix, AZ.

Who Knows: A Guide to Washington Experts

This publication lists 14,000 experts in the federal government, within 13,000 areas of expertise. Each entry contains complete contact information.
Published in 1992 by Washington Researchers, Ltd., Washington, DC.

GOVERNMENT AGENCIES

Federal Information Centers

Established by the government, Federal Information Centers are clearinghouses for people who want information on the U.S. federal government. Frequently, the staff of a local information center can answer a question or find an expert who can. For information about federal agencies, programs, and services, call (800) 688-9889.
Federal Information Center, P.O. Box 600, Cumberland, MD 21501-0600.

Government Printing Office (GPO)

This organization is the primary source for printing, distribution, and sales of government documents. The GPO is responsible for the tens of thousands of magazines, pamphlets, and books published by the government each year. The Government Printing Office offers several guides to its publications, some of which are noted in this chapter. Generally, the GPO only carries current titles, and obtaining a document older than a year or two might be impossible. If this is the case, the GPO will be able to recommend a library that carries the document.

Government Printing Office Bookstores

The GPO maintains some two dozen bookstores throughout the country that stock popular government publications. A complete list of bookstores will be found in Appendix 10.

Legislation Information and Status Office (LEGIS)

In order to find a congressional transcript pertaining to a particular subject, contact LEGIS. The staff there will be able to find out if there is a specific hearing regarding any current bills in Congress. Additionally, LEGIS will perform a free keyword search on its database (printouts are 20¢ per page, and there is a $5.00 minimum charge) to determine which bills and committees have dealt with the topic at hand.

Once LEGIS has provided the information on the committees and legislation pertaining to a particular topic, obtaining a transcript is a matter of contacting the committee or congressperson and finding where transcripts are available.

Legislative Information and Status, H2 Room 968, Ford House Office Building, Washington, DC 20515.
(202) 225-1772

National Technical Information Service (NTIS)

The National Technical Information Service is the main source for the public sale of research, development, and engineering reports sponsored by the government. The NTIS also offers a selection of technical reports prepared by foreign and local governments. There are well over a million reports available, covering a wide range of topics. Of particular interest to the business community are the reports under the heading "Behavioral and Social Science," which includes topics such as administration and management, economics, human factors engineering, and personnel selection.

There are several different ways to find a specific report. Some of the more effective ones include:

NTIS Products and Services Catalog. A free catalog describes all of the print sources and computer databases of NTIS. The catalog can be ordered directly from the NTIS at (703) 487-4630; fax (703) 321-8547.

Government Reports Announcements & Index (GRA & I); Government Reports Annual Index (GRAI). Each issue of this comprehensive bibliography of NTIS documents, published biweekly, abstracts about 2,500 new titles, arranged by subject categories and subcategories. An index is included that allows access to the reports by keyword, personal author, corporate author, contract or grant number, and NTIS order or report number. Each year the 26 issues of *GRA & I* are compiled to form the *Government Reports Annual Index (GRAI)*. Both can be found at most large libraries, are accessible through online database vendors, and can be ordered directly from the NTIS.

Abstract Newsletters. These weekly newsletters contain summaries of new technical reports. There are 26 different newsletters, each devoted to a different topic, such as *Administration & Management, Business & Economics,* and *Manufacturing Technology.* All of the titles summarized in the *Abstract Newsletters* are also included in the *GRA & I.* The newsletters can be found at many libraries, although some libraries with narrow research interests might only subscribe to select titles. The newsletters can also be ordered from the NTIS, either through its

NTIS Products and Services Catalog or by contacting the NTIS order department.

NTIS Online Bibliographic Databases. NTIS sells bibliographies that result from on-line database searches. Well over 3,000 bibliographies are available. In most cases, the bibliographies each have 100 to 200 entries. Published searches can be ordered directly from the NTIS. The NTIS Online Bibliographic Database is available on CD-ROM or online through commercial vendors, including BRS and DIALOG, listed in the free NTIS catalog PR-287. The database is also available on direct lease to research and development organizations and agencies. Call (703) 487-4929 for more information.

FOR FURTHER INFORMATION

*See **American Statistics Index,** p. 370*
***Statistical Abstract of the United States,** p. 378*
***Statistical Reference Index,** p. 370*
***Who Knows about Industries and Markets,** p. 403*

25

FRANCHISING

Directory of Franchising Organizations

This directory lists the top franchises in the United States. Each entry includes a description of the franchise, contact information, and the cost of investment.
Published annually by Pilot Books, Greenport, NY.

The Encyclopedia of Franchises and Franchising

Dennis L. Foster

This encyclopedia covers every aspect of the franchise industry in an A-to-Z format.
Published in 1989 by Facts on File, New York.

Franchise Annual: Complete Handbook and Directory

The *Franchise Annual* lists approximately 5,000 franchisers in the United States, Canada, and other countries, along with discussions of the pros and cons of franchising and detailed descriptions of relevant state and federal regulations.
Published annually by the Info Press.

Franchise Bible: A Comprehensive Guide

The *Franchise Bible* covers both the franchiser's and the franchisee's sides of the franchising business. It shows how to expand a business by franchising and how to go into business for yourself by buying a franchise. It includes an offering circular; sample franchise agreements; a list of laws affecting franchise transfers, renewals, and terminations; state franchise registration and business opportunity statutes; and filing fees of franchise registration states. Available in three-ring binder or in paperback.
Published in 1991 by the Oasis Press, Grants Pass, OR.

Franchise Fraud: How to Protect Yourself Before and After You Invest

Robert L. Purvin, Jr.

This book helps potential franchisees protect themselves before entering into a contractual relationship with a franchiser. It shows how to avoid being the victim of what the author calls fraudulent practices of franchisers, such as overstating the market and promises of training and promotional support that are never fulfilled. The author shows in specific detail what to took for in a franchise and the questions to ask when entering a franchise agreement.
Published in 1994 by John Wiley & Sons, New York.

Franchise Opportunities Handbook

Prepared by the U.S. Department of Commerce, the *Franchise Opportunities Handbook* includes descriptions of U.S. franchises as well as various government assistance programs.
Published annually by the Superintendent of Documents, U.S. Government Printing Office.

The Franchise Option: How to Expand Your Business through Franchising

The Franchise Option covers such topics as test marketing, managing franchise infrastructure relationships, and nurturing and terminating franchise relationships.
Published in 1987 by the International Franchise Association, Washington, DC.

Franchising: Business Organizations

Gladys Glickman

Organized into four loose-leaf volumes, *Franchising* covers all areas of franchising, including franchise agreements; legal, business, and tax considerations; antitrust considerations; and franchise alternatives, such as distributorships, leases, branch operations, and limited partnerships.
Published and periodically updated by Matthew Bender, New York.

Franchising and Licensing: Two Ways to Build Your Business

Andrew Sherman

Franchising and Licensing is a step-by-step guide to the intricacies of franchising a business. Topics include raising capital, the development of operations manuals, the creation of a prototype, franchise agreements, franchise marketing, franchisee relationships, and so on.
Published in 1991 by AMACOM Books, New York.

The Franchising Handbook

Andrew Sherman, editor

This handbook analyzes the management, operations, marketing, financial, and legal issues peculiar to the franchising industry. Contributors to the book include many franchising professionals, and it carries the endorsement of the International Franchise Association.

Published in 1993 by AMACOM Books, New York.

The Rating Guide to Franchises

Dennis L. Foster

This guide profiles franchise opportunities in the United States and Canada. It gives a rating (from one to five stars) to each franchiser, based on six performance areas: industry experience, franchising experience, financial strength, training and services, fees and royalties, and satisfaction of franchisees. The profile also includes an overview of the franchise, franchiser services, initial investment, and fees and royalties. Contact information is also included.
Published in 1989 by Facts on File, New York.

Running a Successful Franchise

Kirk Shivell and Kent Banning

This book offers detailed, practical information on running a franchise within the constraints of a franchise agreement. Topics include transitioning from corporate life to franchise ownership, setting up and implementing management and reporting procedures, creating purchasing and inventory control policies, developing sales and marketing programs, and resolving the most common areas of conflict between franchisers and franchisees.
Published in 1992 by McGraw-Hill, New York.

Source Book of Franchise Opportunities

The *Source Book* is a listing of leading franchisers. Entries, which include complete contract information, are classified by product or service and are indexed by company name.
Published annually by Business One Irwin, Homewood, IL.

Worldwide Franchise Directory

In this listing of nearly 1,600 American, Canadian, and overseas franchisers, entries are arranged alphabetically under approximately 80 primary categories such as computer sales and service, real estate services, and tax preparation. Also included are profiles of nonfranchised chain operations with company-owned outlets. Each entry provides highlights, a general description, background sketch on the franchise, start-up and agreement information, foreign outlet contacts, training provided, financing available, number of outlets and expansion plans, equipment needed, and profile sources. The directory is available in print, computer disk, and magnetic tape formats.
Published annually by Gale Research, Detroit.

TRADE AND PROFESSIONAL ASSOCIATIONS

The American Association of Franchisees and Dealers (AAFD)

Formed in 1992, the AAFD represents the interests of franchisees and dealers. Its purpose is to help bring "fairness to franchising," and it proposes and supports federal and state legislation to develop and maintain equality in the relationship between franchiser and franchisee.
The American Association of Franchisees and Dealers, P.O. Box 81887, San Diego, CA 92138-1887.
(800) 733-9858

International Franchise Association

This association is for firms utilizing the franchise method of distribution in all industries. It holds symposia, workshops, and trade shows. Publications include *Franchise Legal Digest,* a bimonthly publication, and *Franchise Opportunities Magazine.*
International Franchise Association, 1350 New York Avenue NW, Suite 900, Washington, DC 20005.
(202) 628-8000

26

HUMAN RESOURCE MANAGEMENT, TRAINING, AND RETRAINING

The AMA Handbook for Employee Recruitment and Retention

Mary F. Cook, editor

Created under the guidance of the American Management Association, this comprehensive book combines the contributions of 14 experts to guide users in every aspect of recruiting highly qualified employees and keeping them on the job. Topics include planning, recruitment and selection programs, performance management, training, compensation, benefits, and family issues.
Published in 1992 by AMACOM Books, New York.

Americans with Disabilities Act Handbook

This is a basic resource on the Americans with Disabilities Act for people with disabilities and for businesses. It contains annotated regulations for all three titles of the act, resources for obtaining further assistance, and an appendix containing supplementary information concerning implementation. Available in loose-leaf format.
Published in 1997 by the Superintendent of Documents, U.S. Government Printing Office.

Building the Competitive Workforce: Investing in Human Capital for Corporate Success

Philip Mirvis, editor

This book, based on the Louis Harris and Associates "Laborforce 2000" survey, assesses the competitive strengths and weaknesses of the workforce of North American companies. Academic and corporate experts analyze a wide range of issues affecting workforce quality, including company policies on education and training, the aging workforce, work and family issues, and employee health benefits.
Published in 1993 by John Wiley & Sons, New York.

The Complete Do-It-Yourself Personnel Department

Mary F. Cook

This complete guide to managing a personnel department features more than 150 reproducible personnel forms, checklists and reports, model policies and programs, and ready-to-use manuals and handbooks.
Published in 1991 by Prentice Hall, Englewood Cliffs, NJ.

The Corporate Reference Guide to Work-Family Programs

Ellen Galinsky, Dana E. Friedman, and Carol A. Hernandez

This highly useful reference book on work-family issues as they relate to corporate operations looks at programs in a wide variety of industries, shows how much they cost, and indicates the ones likely to yield the greatest return on investment.
Published in 1991 by the Families and Work Institute, New York.

Disability Management: A Complete System to Reduce Costs, Increase Productivity, Meet Employee Needs, and Ensure Legal Compliance

Shiela A. Akabas, Lauren B. Gates, and Donald E. Galvin

Disability Management is an examination of how to manage disability in the workplace, save money and careers, and help companies comply with the Americans with Disabilities Act.
Published in 1992 by AMACOM Books, New York.

Employee Involvement and Total Quality Management: Practices and Results in Fortune 1000 Companies

Edward E. Lawler III, Susan Albers Mohrman, and Gerald E. Ledford, Jr.

This study presents the first systematic data to show that companies are more competitive and productive and create higher-quality services when employees are involved in decisions about their jobs and work environment.
Published in 1992 by Jossey-Bass, San Francisco.

Globalizing Management: Creating and Leading the Competitive Organization

Carole Barnett, Vladimir Pucik, and Noel Tichy, editors

This book analyzes the human talent that global businesses will need in order to compete in the next century. It looks at issues like building a globally competitive workforce, making cultural diversity a competitive advantage, building a top leadership team, and successfully implementing strategic alliances.
Published in 1992 by John Wiley & Sons, New York.

Guide to Employee Handbooks

Robert J. Nobile

This guide shows how to update, upgrade, or create an employee handbook. It provides a model handbook, handbook development guidelines, warnings about overlooked laws governing employment policies, and handbook statements.
Published annually by Warren, Gorham & Lamont, New York.

HR Alert

This biweekly news service reports on the latest developments affecting human resources management.
Published biweekly by Warren, Gorham & Lamont, New York.

HRIN Daily Developments Database

This is a full-text database of print and electronic sources of information covering a broad range of issues of interest to human resource professionals. Coverage includes topics such as benefits and training, legislation and regulation, and employee rights. Available online from HRIN: The Human Resource Information Network.
Published and updated daily by the Human Resource Information Network.

Human Resource Director's Portfolio of Personnel Forms, Records, and Reports

Axel R. Granholm

This book is a collection of 249 tested personnel forms, records, checklists, policy statements, sample letters, and reports.
Published in 1988 by Prentice Hall, Englewood Cliffs, NJ.

The Human Resource Directory

This directory contains information on 15,000 people in the human resource/personnel field.
Published in 1993 by Hunt Scanlon Publishing, Greenwich, CT.

The Human Resource Problem-Solver's Handbook

Joseph D. Levesque

This manual provides advice on supervising employees, and it surveys labor laws and the development of personnel management in the United States.
Published in 1992 by McGraw-Hill, New York.

The Human Resources Yearbook

Mary F. Cook, editor

The Human Resources Yearbook is a comprehensive directory of human resources facts, trends, laws, issues, programs, and information. Topics include statistics on labor productivity; wages and benefits; and costs of recruiting, training, and relocating.
Published in 1991 by Prentice Hall, Englewood Cliffs, NJ.

Legal Guide to Human Resources

Steven C. Kahn et al.

This publication provides practical legal guidance on recruiting, hiring, and initial placement; compensation, training, promotion, and transfer; discipline, termination, and layoff; affirmative action; retirement plans; performance appraisal; and occupational health and safety. Published as one volume in loose-leaf format.
Published in 1994 by Warren, Gosham & Lamont, New York.

Managing Workforce 2000: Gaining the Diversity Advantage

David Jamieson and Julie O'Mara

This book shows how to attract, make the best use of, and retain employees of different skills and perspectives.
Published in 1991 by Jossey-Bass, San Francisco.

Organizational Capability: Competing from the Inside Out

David Ulrich and Dale Lake

This text shows the correlation between successful people management and the bottom line. It explains the benefits to the organization of involving employees in the planning and implementation process and allowing them to see the fruits of their labor. The aim is to show how focusing organizational capability will not only meet short-term financial requirements but also build a solid foundation for the future.
Published in 1990 by John Wiley & Sons, New York.

Personnel Selection in Organizations: Frontiers of Industrial and Organizational Psychology

Neal Schmitt and Walter C. Borman, editors

This book analyzes personnel selection procedures and identifies areas in which ongoing research is needed. Coverage includes fairness in selection, computerized psychological testing, firings, layoffs, and replacement.
Published in 1993 by Jossey-Bass, San Francisco.

Work, Families, and Organizations: Frontiers of Industrial and Organizational Psychology

Sheldon Zedeck, editor

This book brings together theories and research dealing with the relationships between work and family. It looks at job stress, dual-career families, and working at home. *Published in 1992 by Jossey-Bass, San Francisco.*

The Work of Nations: Preparing Ourselves for 21st-Century Capitalism

Robert B. Reich

Reich—who served as Secretary of Labor in the Clinton administration—here provides an insightful look at the skills individuals will need in order to compete in the twenty-first century. He argues that each nation's primary assets will be composed of the insights and skills of its citizens. *Published in 1991 by Alfred A. Knopf, New York.*

TRADE AND PROFESSIONAL ASSOCIATIONS

American Society for Training and Development

This professional association is for people involved in the training and development of business, industry, education, and government employees. Publications include *National Report on Human Resources,* a monthly newsletter; *Training and Development* magazine, published monthly; *Models for HR Practices,* a four-volume series; and other books and publications. *American Society for Training and Development, 1640 King Street, Alexandria, VA 22313. (703) 683-8100*

Institute for International Human Resources

This association for executives responsible for international personnel administration acts as a clearinghouse for information on issues and concerns in international human resource management and provides a forum for networking. *Institute for International Human Resources, 606 N. Washington Street, Alexandria, VA 22314. (703) 548-3440*

GOVERNMENT AGENCIES

Equal Employment Opportunity Commission (EEOC)

The EEOC conducts investigations of job discrimination under Title VII of the Civil Rights Act of 1964, the Americans with Disabilities Act of 1992, the Equal Pay Act of 1963, and the Age Discrimination in Employment Act of 1967. *Equal Employment Opportunity Commission, 1800 L Street NW, Washington, DC 20507. (202) 663-4900 (800) USA-EEOC*

FOR FURTHER INFORMATION

See **ABI/INFORM®**, *p. 370*
Complying with ADA: A Small Business Guide to Hiring and Employing the Disabled, *p. 523*
The Conference Board, *p. 452*
EEOC Compliance Manual, *p. 523*
Employer's Guide to the Americans with Disabilities Act, *p. 524*
Management Contents, *p. 376*

27

INTERNATIONAL BUSINESS (GENERAL)

Business International

This newsletter covers developments in international management, marketing, finance, law, licensing, exporting, taxation, accounting, personnel, and planning.
Published weekly by The Economist Intelligence Unit.

Cities of the World

This four-volume collection presents up-to-date facts on more than 1,500 cities located in 140 countries. Entries include maps of capital cities and photographs depicting city life. Volumes cover (1) Africa, (2) the Western Hemisphere (excluding the United States), (3) Europe and the Mediterranean Middle East, and (4) Asia, the Pacific, and the Asiatic Middle East (plus a comprehensive index).
Fourth edition published in 1993 by Gayle Research, Detroit.

Countries of the World and Their Leaders Yearbook

Countries of the World, which provides information on 140 countries, is compiled from information gathered by the U.S. Department of State and the Central Intelligence Agency. Reports range from 4 to 20 pages and typically cover everything from politicians to geography to defense to agriculture and trade.
Published annually by Gale Research, Detroit.

Directory of Multinationals

John A. Stopford

This directory deals exclusively with companies that control important foreign invest-

ments. It includes information on hundreds of companies that account for the bulk of the world's direct foreign investment. Each of the companies included in the directory has at least $500 million in foreign sales. The directory lists the value of exports and foreign production of these companies.
Revised edition published in 1997 by Macmillan.

Doing Business in Canada

Coverage in this loose-leaf format guide includes full treatment of individual and corporate taxation, accounting procedures, contracts and agreements; the Investment Canada Act, export/import regulations, intellectual property law; banking and employment law; securities law regulation; and language legislation.
Published and updated periodically by Matthew Bender, New York.

The Economist Intelligence Unit

The Economist Intelligence Unit is part of the London-based Economist Group, which also publishes the weekly magazine *The Economist.* The EIU provides a wide range of subscription services that analyze and forecast change in the political, economic, regulatory, and business environment for 180 countries, including:

Country reports. Each report analyzes the political and economic status of a country, including the political structure, economic structure, and the 12- to 18-month outlook. Published quarterly.

Country Profiles. Each report provides an annual perspective on the long-term political and social issues affecting each country covered. Published annually.

World Outlook. A one-volume overview that forecasts the political and economic trends in more than 180 countries. Information about each country includes a comprehensive six-year series of macroeconomic indicators. Published annually.

Country Forecasts. Each report provides the political, economic, and business trends in 55 countries for the next five years. Published quarterly.

Country Risk Service. Each report assesses the solvency of 82 developing and highly indebted countries. Reports analyze growth, budget deficits, trade and current accounts, foreign financing requirements and sources, and debt service. Published quarterly.

Encyclopedia of Associations: International Organizations

This encyclopedia lists more than 11,000 international organizations, including over 5,000 national organizations of countries other than the United States. Entries are arranged in 15 general subject areas and are indexed geographically, by executive name, and by keyword. The encyclopedia is also available in the following alternative formats: computer diskette, online, magnetic tape, and CD-ROM. Available online through DIALOG.
Published annually by Gale Research, Detroit.

Europa World Yearbook

The *Europa World Yearbook* provides a comprehensive listing of facts and figures on more than 200 countries. Every country survey provides economic and demographic statistics; constitutional policies and viewpoints of prominent political parties; national press organizations, including names of principal officers and locations of foreign bureaus; and key contacts and information for trade and industry.

Published annually by Europa Publications, Ltd., London. Distributed in the United States and Canada by Gale Research, Detroit.

F & S Index International

This text provides one- or two-line summaries and an index of business and trade journal articles covering business activities in Canada, Latin America, Africa, the Middle East, Asia, and Oceania. Entries are arranged by product and industry using an SIC coding system and alphabetically by company. Also available online through BRS, DIALOG, and Data-Star as part of PTS F&S Index.
Published monthly, with quarterly and annual cumulative updates, by Information Access/Predicasts.

Financial Times

This daily newspaper, edited in the United Kingdom, is an important source of international business, financial, and economic news. Also available online through DIALOG as the Financial Times Company Abstracts (containing abstracts of articles referring to specific companies) and Financial Times Fulltext.
Published daily by Financial Times Business Information, Ltd., London.

The G. T. Guide to World Equity Markets

This guide provides information and analysis on the performance, structure, operation, and character of the world's equity markets. It covers 50 countries with a wide range of information, including market capitalization, market performance, investment climate, rights and restrictions concerning investors, taxation, and investment controls.
Seventh edition published in 1992 by Euromoney Books, Plymouth, England.

Hoover's Handbook of World Business

Alan Chai, Alta Campbell, and Patrick J. Spain, editors

A resource for information on the world's largest and most influential companies, *Hoover's Handbook* provides nearly 200 corporate profiles, including 100 European and 40 Japanese companies, along with companies from Australia, Brazil, Chile, Hong Kong, Singapore, Turkey, Venezuela, and elsewhere. The handbook also provides business and economic profiles of 67 countries and five regions. These profiles include overview and economic history; trade and business contacts, including embassies and chambers of commerce; and economic and demographic data.
Published annually by the Reference Press, Austin, TX.

Index to International Statistics (IIS)

This index is a guide to the coverage of statistical publications from the major intergovernmental organizations, including the Organization for Economic Cooperation and Development (Main Economic Indicators), International Labor Organization (Yearbook of Labor Statistics), and International Monetary Fund (International Financial Statistics). The IIS covers approximately 1,700 titles from about 100 issuing sources. Available by subscription only.
Published monthly, with annual cumulative volume, by Congressional Information Service, Inc., Bethesda, MD.

International Directory of Company Histories

This six-volume reference provides historical information on 1,250 companies with sales of $2 billion or more. Entries include information on founders, expansions, losses, labor/management actions, and other significant milestones. Corporate profiles also include company name, address, telephone and fax numbers, number of employees, sales, market value, and principal subsidiaries.
Published in 1992 by Gale Research, Detroit.

International Dun's Market Identifiers

This database contains sales, financial, marketing, and ownership information on more than 2 million Asian, African, and European companies. Information provided includes name, address, sales volume, SIC code, and number of employees. Available online through DIALOG and Dow Jones News/ Retrieval.
Updated quarterly by Dun & Bradstreet Information Service.

International Marketing Data & Statistics

This comprehensive guide to international marketing data covers more than 150 countries. Twenty-six data sections present comparative statistics and demographics for economic indicators, energy resources, consumer expenditures, and consumer prices.
Fifteenth edition published in 1992 by Euromonitor, London.
Distributed in the United States and Canada by Gale Research, Detroit.

Kompass International Guides

Kompass Guides provide company and product information for the following 45 countries: Australia, Austria, Bahrain, Belgium, Brunei, Bulgaria, Canada, China (and Hong Kong), Czech Republic, Denmark, Egypt, Finland, France, Germany, Greece, Holland, Hungary, Iceland, India, Indonesia, Ireland, Israel, Italy, Japan, Korea, Luxembourg, Malaysia, Malta, Mexico, Morocco, New Zealand, Norway, the Philippines, Poland, Portugal, Saudi Arabia, Singapore, Spain, Sweden, Switzerland, Taiwan, Tunisia, Turkey, United Arab Emirates, and the United Kingdom. The Kompass Guides for

Canada, the UK, the countries of Europe, and the countries of the Asia/Pacific region are available online through DIALOG.
Each guide is published annually by Kompass, East Grinstead, England.

Moody's International Manual and News Reports

Moody's two-volume *International Manual* is a source of financial and business information on more than 5,000 companies and institutions in 100 countries. Entries include the history and business of each company, financial information, and capital structure. The weekly news reports that accompany the manual provide ongoing coverage of the latest development in each company, such as mergers and acquisitions, joint ventures, interim earnings, and new stock and bond offerings. The International News Reports are also available through DIALOG.
Moody's International Manual is published annually, and the News Reports are published biweekly, by Dun & Bradstreet Information Services.

Principal International Businesses

This source provides facts and figures on 50,000 of the world's leading companies in 145 countries, including data on senior management, line of business, and contact information.
Published annually by Dun & Bradstreet Information Services.

Thomson Bank Directory International

This volume lists, by country, bank offices involved in international trade. The listings include head offices, branches, agencies, and representative offices located in countries other than the United States; financial figures in national currency and U.S. dollars; and complete contact information.
Revised and updated every six months by Thomson Financial Publishing, Skokie, IL.

Who's Who in International Banking

Who's Who profiles nearly 4,000 bankers from 1,000 banks around the world. Entries include education, career, civic interests, professional memberships, honors, and publications. A country-by-country banking directory is also provided.
Published in 1992 by R. R. Bowker, New Providence, NJ.

Who's Who in International Organizations

This three-volume collection provides biographical and contact information for 12,000 individuals prominent in 7,000 organizations worldwide.
Published in 1992 by R. R. Bowker, New Providence, NJ.

World Directory of Stock Exchanges

Maurice Garneau

This two-volume directory provides information on the performance of all stock exchanges of the world.
Published annually by W.I.S.E.R. Research, Montreal, Canada.

World Factbook

Compiled by the U.S. Central Intelligence Agency, this valuable reference provides demographic, economic, and geographic data on every country in the world.
Published annually by the Superintendent of Documents, U.S. Government Printing Office.

World Markets Desk Book: A Region-by-Region Survey of Global Trade Opportunities

Lawrence W. Tuller

The *Desk Book* is a region-by-region survey of 50 of the world's principal markets. Each profile covers what products and services are

needed in which countries; each country's political and economic stability; internal competition and regional stability; internal competition and regional strategy; resource cost and availability; formal and informal trade barriers; and factors influencing market entry, such as government regulations and incentives, cultural hurdles, and infrastructure development.
Published in 1992 by McGraw-Hill, New York.

World Retail Directory and Sourcebook

This book lists 3,500 addresses of retailers, information sources, libraries, conferences, and trade fairs in Western and Eastern Europe, North America, Central and South America, Africa and the Middle East, and the Far East and Oceania.
Published in 1992 by Euromonitor, London. Distributed in the United States and Canada by Gale Research, Detroit.

World Trade Centers Association World Business Directory

This four-volume publication lists more than 100,000 businesses in 190 countries interested in international trade opportunities. Businesses listed include both World Trade Centers Association (WTCA) member and nonmember companies. Typical entries include company name; address, telephone, fax, and telex numbers; business activities and products; import/export designations; revenue figures; number of employees; key officers; and corporate message. Entries are indexed alphabetically, by business activities and by product. The directory is also available on computer diskette and magnetic tape.
Published in 1992 by Gale Research, Detroit.

The World Trade System

Robert Fraser, editor

This reference presents trade profiles for every country in the world. Each profile cov-

ers principal imports and exports, trading partners, membership of regional trading associations, and political information. Users should take caution that these profiles are dated. More current and accurate information is available from the NTBD, the CIA at its Web site www.cia.gov, and other sources.
Published in 1991 by Longman Current Affairs, Harlow, England.

Worldwide Branch Locations of Multinational Companies

This volume provides contact, financial, and other information on nearly 20,000 branches, plants, and subsidiaries belonging to more than 500 multinational companies headquartered around the world.
Published in 1992 by Gale Research, Detroit.

Yearbook of International Organizations

Compiled by the Union of International Associations in Brussels, this three-volume reference contains information on more than 28,000 organizations active in over 200 countries around the world. The yearbook is available in print and on CD-ROM.
Published annually by R. R. Bowker, New Providence, NJ.

For Further Information

*See **ABI/INFORM®**, p. 370*
***America's Corporate Families and International Affiliates,** p. 422*
***Business Publication Rates and Data,** p. 391*
***The BusinessWeek Global 1000,** p. 417*
***Canadian Dun's Business Identification Service,** p. 422*
***Canadian Key Business Directory,** p. 422*
***Collaborating to Compete: Using Strategic Alliances and Acquisitions in the Global Marketplace,** p. 552*
***Company Intelligence™,** p. 422*
***Disclosure Worldscope™ Global,** p. 418*

28

INTERNATIONAL BUSINESS (ASIA AND AUSTRALIA)

1992 Korea Directory

This reference lists general traders, importers, exporters, manufacturers, agents, and banks operating in Korea.
Published in 1992 by the Korea Directory Company, Seoul.

1992 3W Register of Chinese Business

This directory provides information on over 30,000 Chinese companies, including information on ownership, assets, number of employees, sales, and products. It also contains an SIC code index, general information on Chinese provinces, international ports, and telephone city codes. Available in print or on CD-ROM and floppy disk.
Published in 1991 by 3W International Publishing.

Asia: A Directory and Sourcebook

This reference provides major sources of marketing information inside and outside Asia. It identifies all major independent and government organizations as well as providing detailed profiles of all of the major companies.
Published in 1992 by Euromonitor, London. Distributed in the United States and Canada by Gale Research, Detroit.

Asia 1991/92: Measures and Magnitude

This "Top 500" company directory for all Asian nations, excluding the People's Republic of China, contains "region at a glance" sections, complete with charts and graphs.
Published in 1991 by Asian Finance Publications, Hong Kong.

Asia and Pacific Review: The Business and Economic Report

This collection of reports on all of the countries of Asia includes key indicators, historical overviews, and recent political and economic trends.
Published in 1991 by World of Information, Saffron Walden, England.

Asian Company Handbook

This reference provides financial information on more than 1,000 companies on the stock exchanges of Hong Kong, the Republic of Korea, Taiwan, Thailand, Malaysia, and Singapore. The information includes overseas offices, export destinations, sales, stock ownership, a share price chart, and business results.
Published in 1992 by Toyo Keizai Shinposa, Tokyo.

Asian Market: Company and Industry Information Sources

This collection of information sources on Asian markets can be used to track foreign competitors, obtain market studies, track trade leads, and contact a number of experts. Entries include complete contact information.
Second edition published in 1992 by Washington Researchers, Ltd., Washington, DC.

Asia-Pacific Dun's Market Identifiers

This resource provides information on businesses in countries located within Asia as well as Australia and New Zealand. Information includes sales volume, marketing data, address, phone number, and key executives. Available online from DIALOG.
Published and updated monthly by Dun & Bradstreet Information Services.

Asia's 75,000 Largest Companies

This publication ranks the top 75,000 companies in ten countries in the Asia/Pacific region—including Hong Kong (now part of China), Japan, Malaysia, the Philippines, Taiwan, Indonesia, South Korea, Singapore, and Thailand.
Published annually by Dun & Bradstreet Information Services.

Business Asia

This newsletter provides short-term economic forecasts for Asian countries, examines business and economic trends, and analyzes major regulatory and policy developments.
Published biweekly by The Economist, London.

China Statistical Yearbook 1990

Data issued by the Chinese government cover a number of business and economic topics including population, trade, economic indicators, and production.
Published in 1991 by the State Statistical Bureau of the People's Republic of China.

Consumer Asia

These statistical and analytical surveys of Asian consumer markets concentrate on Hong Kong, Taiwan, Singapore, South Korea, Indonesia, and Malaysia and contain assessments and overviews of the region as a whole. Individual chapters concentrate on specific subjects, including energy issues, labor costs, population factors, financial markets, and demography.
Published in 1992 by Euromonitor, London. Distributed in the United States and Canada by Gale Research, Detroit.

Doing Better Business in Asia: A Handbook of Checklists and Essential Facts for Corporate Managers

This text offers managers of companies doing business in Asia a discussion of investments, joint ventures, political stability, and business planning.
Published in 1988 by Business International, New York.

Doing Business in China

William P. Streng and Allen D. Wilcox, editors

A guide to all areas of business law in the People's Republic of China, this book closely examines key issues and potential pitfalls involved in import/export transactions, technology transfers, banking and financial transactions, tax matters, and joint ventures.
First published in 1989 by Matthew Bender, New York.
Reissued in loose-leaf format and updated periodically with supplements.

Dun's Asia/Pacific Key Business Enterprises

This expanded two-volume directory lists 30,000 companies in 14 Pacific Rim countries that each have annual sales of at least $10 million (U.S. dollars) or employ 500 or more people. Profiles include company name, contact information, trading address, lines of business, import/export status, parent company name, annual sales in local currency, and number of employees.
Published annually by Dun & Bradstreet Information Services.

Far East and Australasia

Far East and Australasia offers essays on topics of concern to the region as a whole, details on international and regional organizations active there, and surveys and directories for each nation and territory.
Published in 1992 by Gale Research, Detroit.

International Business/China

This newsletter tracks issues and trends in the People's Republic of China and provides thorough corporate case studies.
Published biweekly by the Economist Intelligence Unit.

Jobson's Yearbook of Public Companies in Australia and New Zealand

This directory provides full company listings, including corporate structure, five-year financial tables, and operating results, on more than 2,000 public companies in Australia and New Zealand that are listed on either (or both) of those countries' stock exchanges.
Published annually by Dun & Bradstreet Information Services.

Key Business Directory of Australia

This two-volume set lists more than 20,000 prominent public and private businesses engaged in commercial and industrial activities in Australia. Volume I provides details on leading business enterprises, and information on marketing, sales, purchasing, and financial operations. Volume II provides information on businesses operating in the middle company size sector of Australian commerce and industry. All information is arranged alphabetically, geographically, and by line of business.
Published annually by Dun & Bradstreet Information Services.

Key Business Directory of Indonesia/Thailand

Companies listed in this directory were selected on the basis of their fulfilling one or more of the following criteria: an annual turnover in excess of Rupiah 10 billion in Indonesia, an annual turnover in excess of 150 Baht in Thailand, or employment of at least 50 people. Three sections offer alphabetical listings of 1,500 public and private companies, a breakdown of the businesses into major industries (SIC codes), and a geographical list of companies by state.
Published annually by Dun & Bradstreet Information Services.

Key Business Directory of Malaysia

This directory lists companies with annual turnovers in excess of $18 million or employing at least 50 people. Three sections offer alphabetical listings of 1,500 private and public companies, a breakdown of the businesses into major industries (SIC codes), and a geographical list of companies by state.
Published annually by Dun & Bradstreet Information Services.

Key Business Directory of Singapore

This comprehensive listing of leading businesses in Singapore is divided into three sections—alphabetical, product classification, and a "Directory of Directors," which lists the names and titles of more than 6,900 directors and executives. Entries cover company name, address, telephone and fax numbers, line of business, names of chief executives, number of employees, annual sales, import/export status, and SIC codes.
Published annually by Dun & Bradstreet Information Services.

Key Indicators of Developing Asian and Pacific Countries

This collection of statistics regarding key production output, trade, and finance of all

Asia/Pacific countries includes charts and tables.
Published in 1991 by the Economics and Resource Development Center, Asian Development Bank.

Kompass International Guides for the Asia Pacific Region

Kompass Guides provide company and product information and are available in individual editions for the following countries in the Asia/Pacific region: Australia, Brunei, India, Japan, Korea, Malaysia, the Philippines, Singapore, and Taiwan. Also available online through DIALOG as Kompass Asia/Pacific.
Published and updated annually by Kompass International.

Kothari's Industrial Directory of India

This directory provides facts and figures on nearly 2,500 joint stock companies of India and also includes general economic and business information and a statistical profile of the Indian economy.
Published in 1991 by Kothari Enterprises, Madras, India.

Major Companies of the Far East and Australasia, 1992–93

This source provides information and data on 4,500 companies of the Far East and Australasia. Volume 1 covers Southeast Asia; Volume 2, East Asia; and Volume 3, Australia and New Zealand. The coverage of each company includes its financial performance, products and services, organizational structure, and key executives.
Published in 1992 by Graham and Trotman. Distributed in the United States and Canada by Gale Research, Detroit.

Marketing to China: One Billion New Customers

Xu Bai Yi

This comprehensive guide to China's rapidly changing consumer market has appendixes that include Chinese rules and regulations governing trademarks, advertising, foreign investment, and import/export corporations.
Published in 1991 by the NTC Publishing Group, Lincolnwood, IL.

Philippine Yearbook

This government-issued body of statistical data covers all aspects of Philippine demographics, economy, and trade.
Published annually by the Republic of the Philippines, National Statistics Office, Manila.

Republic of China: A Reference Book

This well-organized reference book covers Taiwan's demographics, economy, and government organization.
Published in 1987 by the Hilit Publishing Company, Ltd.

Statistical Yearbook of the Republic of China

This collection of data, produced by the government of Taiwan, covers a number of business and economic issues, including population, the economy, trade, and production.
Published annually by Directorate-General of the Budget, Accounting, and Statistics of the Republic of China.

Who Owns Whom— Australasia and the Far East

This one-volume directory is divided into three sections: Section I lists subsidiaries and associates of parent companies registered in Australia, Hong Kong, Indonesia, Japan, Malaysia, New Zealand, Papua New Guinea, the Philippines, Singapore, South Korea, Taiwan, and Thailand. Section II lists foreign parent companies with subsidiaries and associates in the Far East and Australasia; and Section III is an alphabetical index that links any family member to the ultimate parent.

Published annually by Dun & Bradstreet Information Services.

FOR FURTHER INFORMATION

See **DRI Databases (DRI Asian Forecast),** p. 453
The Economist Intelligence Unit, p. 493
The Handbook of International Direct Marketing, p. 440
International Dun's Market Identifiers, p. 495

29

INTERNATIONAL BUSINESS (EASTERN EUROPE AND THE COMMONWEALTH OF INDEPENDENT STATES)

Consumer Eastern Europe

Information and essays on the market for consumer goods and services in Eastern European countries include chapters on demography, economic indicators, standard of living, household characteristics, advertising and media access, regional distribution, consumer expenditure, market demand, and service industries.
Published in 1992 by Euromonitor, London. Distributed in the United States and Canada by Gale Research, Detroit.

Eastern Europe and the Commonwealth of Independent States 1992

This text examines the social, political, and economic background of the region in specially commissioned introductory essays by leading experts. Separate chapters then examine different countries and include geographical profiles, chronologies, essays on recent history and the economy, statistical surveys, and various directory material.
Published in 1992 by Gale Research, Detroit.

Eastern European Business Directory

Frank X. Didik

This publication is a directory of companies—and the products and services they produce and offer—in Poland, the former Czechoslovakia (now the Czech Republic and Slovakia), Hungary, Bulgaria, Romania, the former East Germany, and the former Soviet Union. The information also includes company name and full contact information.
Published in 1993 by Gale Research, Detroit.

The East European Opportunity: The Complete Business Guide and Sourcebook

Marvin Zonis and Dwight Semler

The East European Opportunity covers economic, political, cultural, and historical issues in the former Czechoslovakia (now the Czech Republic and Slovakia), Romania, Hungary, Poland, Bulgaria, and the former Yugoslavia (now the Federal Republic of Yugoslavia, Croatia, Serbia, and Bosnia-Herzegovina). Each country is covered in a separate section that offers detailed information on the labor force, demographics, education, agriculture, geography, and industry.
Published in 1992 by John Wiley & Sons, New York.

Handbook of Reconstruction in Eastern Europe and the Soviet Union

Stephen White, editor

This handbook provides a close look at political and economic changes in the Eastern European countries of Germany, Bulgaria, Hungary, the former Czechoslovakia, the former Yugoslavia, Albania, Romania, Poland, and the former Soviet Union. Features include a detailed chronology for each country, a summary of political and economic relations, and brief biographies of key personalities.
Published in 1991 by the Longman Group, Ltd.
Distributed in the United States and in Canada by Gale Research, Detroit.

International Business/East Europe

This newsletter provides commercial intelligence on business in Central and Eastern Europe and the Commonwealth of Independent States. Its coverage includes key macroeconomic indicators, legal and tax updates, OECD trade analysis, and company case studies.
Published weekly by the Economist Intelligence Unit, London.

Major Business Organizations of Eastern Europe and the Commonwealth of Independent States

This collection of information on more than 2,000 business organizations in Albania, the Baltic republics, Bulgaria, the Commonwealth of Independent States, the former Czechoslovakia, Hungary, Poland, Romania, and the former Yugoslavia provides contact information, key officials, full descriptions, and import/export data. Ministries and chambers of commerce entries provide information on the scope of their activity and names of key officials.
Second edition published in 1992 by Graham and Trotman.
Distributed in the United States and Canada by Gale Research, Detroit.

GOVERNMENT AGENCIES

National Technical Information Service (NTIS)

In cooperation with the office of the General Counsel of the U.S. Commerce Department, the NTIS has established the Central and Eastern Europe Texts Service, which provides lists of legal and regulatory information on the countries of Eastern Europe (NTIS free catalog PR-883). NTIS also works with the Commerce Department's Eastern European Business Information Center to provide documents on doing business in Eastern Europe (NTIS free catalog PR-882).
National Technical Information Service, 5285 Port Royal Road, Springfield, VA 22161. (703) 487-4600

FOR FURTHER INFORMATION

See **Commerce Department's "Flash Facts" Service (Eastern European Business Information Center),** *p. 472*
The Economist Intelligence Unit, *p. 493*
Encyclopedia of Business Information Sources: Europe, *p. 514*
European Wholesalers & Distributors Directory, *p. 443*
F & S Index Europe, *p. 515*
Kompass International Guides, *p. 516*

INTERNATIONAL BUSINESS (JAPAN)

INTERNATIONAL BUSINESS (JAPAN)

Consumer Japan

This extensive collection of information on the Japanese consumer includes a market overview, a statistical fact file, major consumer markets, listings of major Japanese companies and retailers, and sources of more information.
Published in 1990 by Euromonitor, London. Distributed in the United States and Canada by Gale Research, Detroit.

Destination Japan: A Business Guide for the 90s

This government-produced guide for American businesses interested in exporting products to Japan provides information on export financial assistance programs, customs clearance documentation, foreign trade barriers, market information trade leads, and more. It also focuses on property protection rights, including patents, trademarks, copyrights, trade secrets, and other intellectual property rights in Japan.
Published in 1991 by the Superintendent of Documents, U.S. Government Printing Office.

Doing Business in Japan

Zentaro Kitagawa, editor

This ten-volume guide for Japanese business dealings focuses on all substantive areas, including contracts, business organizations, and regulation; employment law; securities; intellectual property; competition law; and taxation.
Published in 1980 by Matthew Bender, New York.

Now issued in loose-leaf format and updated periodically with supplements and revisions.

Industrial Groupings in Japan

This essential listing of Japanese corporations and their associated conglomerates, or *zaibatsu*, includes an analysis of the financial relationships between the two.
Published biennially by Dodwell Marketing Consultants, Tokyo.

Japan Affiliated Companies in the U.S. and Canada, 1991–1992

This directory provides data on 9,569 Japanese affiliates operating in the United States and Canada. Geographically arranged entries list company name; parent company name and the location of its headquarters in Japan; North American address; year of establishment; telephone, telex, and fax numbers; executive officers' names, type of business and product; and operating status.
Published in 1992 by the Japan External Trade Organization (JETRO).
Distributed in the United States and Canada by Gale Research, Detroit.

Japan Company Datafile

This well-organized listing of Japanese companies includes data on company background, senior personnel, sales, stockholders, and subsidiaries. Information is limited to one page per company.
Published in 1992 by Toyo Keizai Shinposha, Tokyo.

Japan Company Handbook

This two-part reference is published quarterly. The first part provides financial information on all Japanese corporations listed in the first section of the Tokyo, Osaka, and Nagoya Stock Exchanges. The second part, published three months later, does the same for the second section of those exchanges. Information on each company includes corporate names and order of listing, industry of company and its position in the industry, future prospects, income data, sales breakdown, stock price chart, company financial data, facility investment, R&D expenditure, number of employees, and principal offices.
Published quarterly, with semiannual updates, by Toyo Keizai Shinposha, Tokyo.

Japan Economic Newswire™ Plus

This full-text database is a source for a wide variety of English-language news articles covering business, financial, economic, and political developments in Japan, as reported by Kyodo News Service of Tokyo. Available online through DIALOG and NEXIS.
Updated daily by Kyodo News International.

Japan Trade Directory 1992–1993

This directory contains information on 2,900 Japanese companies that export or import products and services. Information on specific companies is organized by products or services, geographic location in Japan, and company name. Company profiles provide financial data, corporate structure, full information on trade contacts, and the company's interest in importing or exporting.
Published in 1992 by the Japan External Trade Organization (JETRO).

The Japanese Distribution System: Opportunities and Obstacles— Structure and Practices

Michael R. Czinkota and Masaaki Kotabe, editors

This guide offers information on Japan's distribution network, which has the reputation of being difficult to understand and to adapt to. Topics include retail, wholesale, and just-in-time distribution; success stories of firms operating in Japan; trade practices; industry-specific practices; and case studies of major companies.
Published in 1992 by the Probus Publishing Company, Chicago.

Japanese Overseas Investing

This listing of the overseas subsidiaries of more than 3,000 Japanese companies includes information on annual sales or production, partner firms, business results, capital, and investment ratios. Entries are arranged alphabetically by company.
Published in 1992 by Toyo Keizai Shinposha, Tokyo.

JapanSite™: Desktop Target Marketing for Japan

JapanSite seeks to evaluate site and trade areas in Japan, primarily Tokyo. It is a desktop PC application with databases, mapping files, and software, which provide access to reporting, mapping, and bar charts for more than 4,000 geographic areas in the Tokyo market. Data items include households, labor force, population, and business establishments.
Published by Demosphere International, Falls Church, VA.

Keiretsu: Inside the Hidden Japanese Conglomerates

Kenichi Miyashita and David Russell

In this text the authors examine the inner workings of the *keiretsu,* the Japanese corporate alliances, specifically Mitsubishi, Mitsui, Sumitomo, Sanwa, Fuyo, and Dai-Ichi Kangyo. It reports on how they do business and what difficulties foreign companies have in competing with them.

Published in 1993 by McGraw-Hill, New York.

Kompass Japan

This five-volume directory presents business information compiled from the database of Tokyo Shoko Research, the Japanese data and credit rating service. The information about companies includes a description of products and services, capital, number of employees, CEO, and full contact information. Company listings are divided into sections that correspond with the ten major geographic sections of Japan. The directory is also available online through DIALOG as part of Kompass Asia/Pacific.
Published annually by Kompass International.

Tokyo Business Today

This magazine publishes articles on business, industry, and finance in Japan.
Published monthly by Toyo Keizai Shinposha, Tokyo.

White Papers of Japan

This extensive and varied collection of data on Japan includes economic indicators, labor force, technology, and transportation systems.
Published annually by the Japan Institute of International Affairs.

Who's Who in Japan 1991–1992

This directory presents biographies of prominent business leaders and a listing of Japanese public and private institutions.

Published in 1991 by the Asia Press Company, Tokyo.

GOVERNMENT AGENCIES

National Technical Information Service (NTIS)

NTIS makes available major Japanese online information systems through an agreement with the Japan Information Center of Science and Technology. Call NTIS for more information.
National Technical Information Service, 5285 Fort Royal Road, Springfield, VA 22161.
(703) 487-4819

FOR FURTHER INFORMATION

See **DRI Databases (DRI Japanese Forecast)**, *p. 453*
The Economist Intelligence Unit, *p. 493*
The Handbook of International Direct Marketing, *p. 440*
Japan's High Technology: An Annotated Guide to English Language Information Sources, *p. 542*
Market Movers: Understanding and Using Economic Indicators from the Big Five Economies, *p. 455*
OECD Economic Outlook, *p. 455*
OECD Economic Surveys, *p. 456*
The OECD STAN Database for Industrial Analysis, *p. 456*

31

INTERNATIONAL BUSINESS (LATIN AMERICA)

Business International's Guide to Doing Business in Mexico

Gary Newman and Anna Szterenfeld

A collection of information on Mexican markets and opportunities, this guide discusses a number of different topics, including the Free Trade Agreement, field intelligence, unwritten rules for business success, and analyses of key Mexican industries.
Published in 1993 by McGraw-Hill, New York.

Consumer South America

This guide presents detailed data on trends in the changing markets of South American countries. Market factors for the region are divided into four chapters: (1) general market profile of the region; (2) comparative statistical profiles of the markets of each county; (3) market sizes for specific consumer products; and (4) country-by-country surveys.
Published in 1992 by Euromonitor, London. Distributed in the United States and Canada by Gale Research, Detroit.

Doing Business in Brazil

J. M. Pinheiro Neto

This overview of Brazilian business laws includes banking and investment law, commercial law, contract law, import/export regulations, patent and trademark law, and corporate law.
Published in 1979 by Matthew Bender, New York.
Reissued in loose-leaf format and updated with revisions and monthly newsletters.

Doing Business in Mexico

Joseph J. Norton

This publication covers legal aspects of trade with Mexico, including export incentives, the *Maquiladora* program, and legal aspects of importing goods into Mexico. It includes texts of U.S. and Mexican laws, treaties, and forms.
Published in 1980 by Matthew Bender, New York.
Reissued in loose-leaf format and updated with periodic supplements.

International Business— Latin America

This newsletter analyzes the economic, political, and regulatory trends in South and Central America, Mexico, and the Caribbean. Coverage includes market forecasts, key economic and business indicators, in-depth looks at corporate strategies, exchange controls, and licensing regulations.
Published weekly by the Economist Intelligence Unit.

An Introduction to Doing Business in Mexico

William E. Mooz

With a heavy emphasis on legal issues, this text surveys business and commercial law governing foreign trade particularly between the United States and Mexico.
Published in 1995 by Transnational Juris Publications, Irvington, NY.

Latin American Markets: A Guide to Company and Industry Information Sources

This market guide lists information sources for the United States and the featured countries of Argentina, Bolivia, Brazil, Chile, Colombia, Costa Rica, the Dominican Republic, Ecuador, El Salvador, Jamaica, Mexico, Panama, Peru, and Venezuela. Sources include country and regional experts, market and business research, databases and publications, government regulators, and trade promotion programs.
Published in 1992 by Washington Researchers, Ltd., Washington, DC.

Latin America's Top 25,000

This one-volume directory offers information on approximately 25,000 enterprises in more than 30 Latin American countries, including Argentina, Brazil, Chile, Mexico, Peru, and Venezuela. Business listings are arranged alphabetically, geographically, and by line of business.
Published annually by Dun & Bradstreet Information Services.

South America, Central America, and the Caribbean

This comprehensive sourcebook on the region as a whole includes detailed statistics and directories for the major countries in the Latin American and Caribbean region, including the Bahamas, Barbados, Belize, French Guiana, Guadeloupe, Martinique, Puerto Rico, and 39 others. Topics include the debt crisis, trade, drugs, and deforestation's effect on the environment.
Published in 1991 by Europa, London.
Distributed in the United States and Canada by Gale Research, Detroit.

Statistical Abstract of Latin America

This two-volume reference provides statistics for the 20 countries of Latin America. Coverage includes geography, land use, land tenure, transportation, communication, population, health, education, welfare, politics, religion, military, labor, income, and industrial production.
Published in 1991 by the Latin American Center, University of California, Los Angeles.

For Further Information

See **The Directory of Management Consultants,** *p. 408*
DRI Databases (DRI Latin American Forecast), *p. 453*
The Economist Intelligence Unit, *p. 493*
The Handbook of International Direct Marketing, *p. 440*
Kompass International Guides, *p. 495*

32

INTERNATIONAL BUSINESS (MIDDLE EAST)

Dun's Guide to Israel

This directory profiles more than 10,000 leading companies in Israel. Information on each company includes name, address, telephone and fax numbers, name of chief executive, SIC codes, number of employees, annual sales, and products exported. Text is in both English and Hebrew. Also available online through Data-Star.
Published annually by Dun & Bradstreet Information Services.

Major Companies of the Arab World 1992–1993

This text provides information on more than 6,500 major companies in 19 Arab countries, including Algeria, Egypt, Iraq, Libya, Saudi Arabia, and Syria. Company profiles are arranged by country and include complete contact information, names of directors and management staff, principal activities, number of branch offices, principal bank, financial details, principal shareholders, date of establishment, and number of employees. Profiles are indexed by name, country, and business activity within each country.

Published in 1992 by Graham & Trotman, London.
Distributed in the United States and Canada by Gale Research, Detroit.

Middle East and North Africa

This annual publication on the Middle East and North Africa offers a collection of expert, informed essays on topics of concern to the region, details on international and regional organizations, and surveys and directories for each nation and territory. Signed articles cover each country's physical and social geography, recent history, and economy. Also included is "Who's Who in the Middle East and North Africa."
Published annually by Europa, London.
Distributed in United States and Canada by Gale Research, Detroit.

FOR FURTHER INFORMATION

See **The Economist Intelligence Unit,**
   p. 493
The Handbook of International Direct Marketing, *p. 440*

33

INTERNATIONAL BUSINESS (WESTERN EUROPE)

1992 The Single Market Handbook

This comprehensive handbook on "Europe 1992" is divided into four sections and offers information and contacts for more information on subjects such as how the removal of trade barriers and new legislation will affect business, trade controls, foreign trade, transport and distribution, and media developments.
Published in 1990 by Euromonitor, London. Distributed in the United States and Canada by Gale Research, Detroit.

British Business Rankings

Britain's 5,000 largest employers are first listed in an alphabetical section showing number of employees, headquarters locations, and main SIC codes. They are then listed in rank-order within counties, by employee numbers, by sales, and within SIC groupings. Entries contain full addresses and telephone numbers.
Published annually by Dun & Bradstreet Information Services.

Consumer Europe 1997

This publication provides in-depth coverage on consumers in 24 Western European countries, such as Austria, Belgium, Denmark, Finland, France, Germany, Great Britain, the Netherlands, Norway, Poland, Spain, Sweden, and Switzerland. Entries include statistics on the production, sales, distribution, consumption, and other aspects of more than 250 consumer product categories.
Published by Gale Research, Detroit.

Directory of EC Industry Information Sources

This directory lists European Community contacts and organizations according to their industrial specialization. Coverage includes information on finding European partners, online business databases, and business and trade statistics.
Published in 1992 by the Stockton Press, New York.

Directory of European Banking and Financial Associations

Philip Moyneux

This collection of information on European banking and insurance institutions covers Austria, Belgium, Cyprus, Denmark, Finland, France, Germany, Greece, Ireland, Italy, Luxembourg, Malta, the Netherlands, Norway, Portugal, Spain, Sweden, Switzerland, Turkey, and the United Kingdom. The text identifies the main banking association that represents the relevant domestic banking industry, and offers details relating to the central bank as well as the main associations dealing in life and other types of insurance.
Published in 1990 by the St. James Press, London. Distributed in the United States and Canada by Gale Research, Detroit.

Directory of European Business

The *Directory of European Business* provides details on the top companies, organizations, government agencies, main business services, and sources of business information

in 31 countries, including Eastern Europe and the former Soviet Union. Structured by country and subdivided under profession, entries offer full company name and contact information, number of employees within the country and worldwide, activities and specialties, and parent company and subsidiaries.
Published in 1992 by Bowker-Saur, London.

Directory of European Industrial and Trade Associations

Richard Leigh, editor

Formerly titled the *Directory of European Associations, Part One,* this directory describes 6,000 industrial and trade associations. It includes national associations for all European countries (except the United Kingdom and Ireland) and regional associations of national significance. Entries contain full contact information, membership data, activities, and publications.
Published in 1991 by CBD Research, Ltd. Distributed in the United States and Canada by Gale Research, Detroit.

Doing Business in France

Issued in loose-leaf format, this practice-oriented reference provides all of the basic concepts of French business law and practice. It includes in-depth analysis of the French tax system; banking, securities, and bankruptcy procedures; practical treatment of accounting and auditing; and commerce regulations.
Published by Matthew Bender and Company, New York, and updated periodically with supplements and revisions.

Doing Business in Ireland

Patrick Ussher, Brian O'Connor, and Charles McCarthy

Issued in loose-leaf format, this text covers matters pertinent to the Irish business and legal situation, with emphasis on investment incentives, taxation, employment law, export/

import restrictions, and product liability.
Published by Matthew Bender and Company, New York, and updated periodically with supplements and revisions.

Doing Business in Spain

Fernando Pombo

Issued in loose-leaf format, this guide to the business and legal environment in the newest member of the EEC includes information on foreign investment incentives, exchange controls, taxation, labor relations, and more.
Published by Matthew Bender and Company, New York, and updated periodically with supplements and revisions.

Doing Business in the United Kingdom

Clifford Chance

Issued in loose-leaf format, this publication provides all the necessary legal background for planning business transactions and dealing with problems arising from trade and investments in the United Kingdom, including the business, private, commercial, and regulatory laws of England, Scotland, and Northern Ireland.
Published by Matthew Bender and Company, New York, and updated periodically with supplements and revisions.

Dun's Europa

This four-volume reference work provides information on more than 60,000 companies in the European Community and most of the countries from the European Free Trade Association (Austria, Finland, Norway, Sweden, Switzerland, and Turkey). Information includes executives, principal business, percent of sales that are exported, annual sales, bankers used by the company, nominal capital, issued capital, net profit or loss, and contact information.
Published in 1993 by Dun & Bradstreet International.

The Economist Atlas of the New Europe

This one-volume reference work is organized in nine sections: (1) communications and infrastructure, (2) industry and commerce, (3) finance, (4) politics, (5) international relations, (6) war and defense, (7) nature and the environment, (8) peoples and culture, and (9) Europe 2000. In each category, the atlas examines every country in terms of the effects of European political and economic unity and the nature of regionalism across the continent.
Published in 1992 by Henry Holt, New York.

The Economist Guide to the European Community: The Definitive Guide to All Aspects of the EC

Richard L. Leonard

This comprehensive text on the origins and operations of the European Community is divided into four main parts: (1) the background, (2) the institutions, (3) the EC's competencies, and (4) special problems.
Published in 1993 by Century Business, Economist Books, London.

Encyclopedia of Business Information Sources: Europe

M. Balachandran, editor

This volume lists business information sources under approximately 1,000 alphabetically arranged subjects. Within each topic category, entries are divided geographically and then by type of resource. The sources cited include a wide variety of both print and electronic references. Available in print, on disk, and on magnetic tape.
Published in 1992 by Gale Research, Detroit.

European Advertising, Marketing, and Media Data

This comprehensive collection of marketing statistics on 16 major Western European markets considers topics such as demographics, media options, and budgetary concerns.
Second edition published in 1992 by Euromonitor, London.
Distributed in the United States and Canada by Gale Research, Detroit.

European Business Rankings

Lesley Ripley Greenfield, editor

This reference collects more than 2,250 business statistics and rankings from throughout Europe. Ranking entries cover products, institutions, industries, companies, services, demographics, and economic trends for both individual countries and Europe-wide data. Each entry contains the top ten names in each list; the ranking criteria, the total number of items listed in the original rankings, and the name, date, and page of the source. Available in print, on disk, and on magnetic tape.
Published in 1992 by Gale Research International, London.

European Communities Encyclopedia and Directory

The text for this comprehensive guide to the European Community (EC) is arranged in three sections. The encyclopedia section presents in-depth descriptions of the people, events, and groups making up the EC. The directory section offers complete contact information for all major EC organizations. The essays and statistics section contains six essays covering the political, economic, and social frameworks of the Community, as well as statistical surveys covering all areas of the EC.
Published in 1991 by Europa, London.
Distributed in the United States and Canada by Gale Research, Detroit.

European Consultants Directory

Karin Koek, editor

This directory lists more than 7,500 consultants who are experts in areas such as mar-

keting, politics, health, and computer technology in 27 countries across Western and Eastern Europe. Entries are grouped by country, by broad subject terms, and then alphabetically by consulting organization. Each listing contains the name of the organization; address; telephone, telex, and fax numbers; principal executive; annual consulting revenues; and geographic areas served. The directory is available in print, on computer diskette, and on magnetic tape.
Published in 1992 by Gale Research, Detroit.

European Dun's Market Identifiers

This resource provides information on 2 million businesses in 26 European countries. Data on each company includes sales volume, marketing data, address, phone number, and key executives. Available online from DIALOG.
Published and updated quarterly by Dun & Bradstreet.

European Marketing Data and Statistics 1997

This collection of more than 100,000 statistics covers the broad marketing parameters of European business. Statistical data are presented on population, employment, production, trade, economy, living standards, consumption, market size, retailing, consumer expenditures, housing and households, health and education, culture and mass media, communications, and travel and tourism.
Published in 1997 by Euromonitor, London. Distributed in the United States and Canada by Gale Research, Detroit.

European Markets: A Guide to Company and Industry Information Sources

Each entry in this guide to more than 5,000 information sources on European business and industry offers complete contact information, including address, telephone, telex, and fax numbers, and names of specific contact people.
Fourth edition published in 1992 by Washington Researchers, Ltd., Washington, DC.

European Trends

This quarterly publication reviews issues and developments that affect the European Community. Coverage includes topics such as progress toward the integrated market, and policies affecting different sectors, the General Agreement on Trade and Tariffs (GATT), environmental policies and legislation, and recent cases before the EC Court of Justice. Available by subscription.
Published quarterly, with an annual supplement, by the Economist Intelligence Unit.

F & S Index Europe

This index of business and trade journal articles covers business activities in the European Economic Community, Western European countries outside the EEC, Eastern Europe, and the Commonwealth of Independent States. Each entry contains a two-line summary of the article cited. Entries are arranged alphabetically and by SIC code. Available in print and online through DIALOG as part of the PTS F & S Indexes.
Published monthly, with quarterly and annual compilations, by Information Access/Predicasts.

ICC International Business Research

This is a source of business intelligence on UK and European companies. It contains more than 15,000 stockbroker research reports that provide analysis and opinion on companies and industries. Available online from DIALOG.
Published and updated weekly by ICC Information Group, Ltd.

Industrial Research in the United Kingdom

This authoritative guide to more than 3,500 research and technology laboratories, centers, and associations in the United Kingdom is presented in six chapters: (1) industrial firms, (2) research associations and their consultants, (3) government departments and their laboratories, (4) universities and polytechnics, (5) trade and development associations, and (6) learned and professional societies.
Fifteenth edition published in 1993 by the Longman Group, Ltd.
Distributed in the United States and Canada by Gale Research, Detroit.

Kompass International Guides

Kompass guides provide product and company information on organizations in the following countries: Austria, Belgium, Denmark, Finland, France, Germany, Greece, Holland, Ireland, Italy, Luxembourg, Norway, Portugal, Spain, Sweden, Switzerland, and the United Kingdom. Also available online through DIALOG as Kompass Europe.
Each guide is updated annually by Kompass.

Major and Medium Companies of Europe 1992–93

This multivolume collection is arranged into three two-volume sets: Set I covers the continental European Economic Community. Set II deals with the United Kingdom. Set III covers Western Europe outside the European Economic Community. Each company entry includes (where available) contact data, principal activities, principal banks, number of employees, brand names, and trademarks.
Published in 1992 by Graham & Trotman, London.
Distributed in the United States and Canada by Gale Research, Detroit.

Major Companies of Europe

This annual three-volume collection lists more than 8,000 of Europe's leading corporations with sales in excess of $130 million. Each company entry includes (where available) contact data, principal activities, principal banks, number of employees, brand names, and trademarks. Three indexes are included: alphabetical, alphabetical by country, and alphabetical by business activity.
Published annually by Graham & Trotman, London.
Distributed in the United States and Canada by Gale Research, Detroit.

Major Financial Institutions of Europe

This directory presents more than 1,100 profiles of Europe's leading financial institutions, arranged within country chapters. Each entry provides name and address of firm; telephone, telex, and fax numbers; names of chairman and board members; principal business activities; and number of employees.
Fourth edition published in 1992 by Graham & Trotman, London.
Distributed in the United States and Canada by Gale Research, Detroit.

Medium Companies of Europe 1992–93

This three-volume directory lists 7,000 of Europe's privately owned and fast-growing medium-sized firms. Volume I covers the continental European Economic Community. Volume II deals with the United Kingdom. Volume III covers Western Europe outside the European Economic Community. Each company entry includes (where available) contact data, principal activities, principal banks, number of employees, brand names, and trademarks.
Third edition published in 1992 by Graham & Trotman, London.

Distributed in the United States and Canada by Gale Research, Detroit.

Pan-European Associations

This alphabetical guide to more than 5,000 multinational, nongovernmental associations in Europe has entries that include full contact information, subjects of interest, activities, affiliations, membership statistics, and publications.
Second edition published in 1991 by Graham & Trotman, London.
Distributed in the United States and Canada by Gale Research, Detroit.

The Price Waterhouse European Companies Handbook

The Price Waterhouse Handbook is published in three volumes: Northern Europe; Central and Southern Europe; and Eastern Europe. The information is compiled from the *Financial Times Analysis* database. Entries include company address, directors, major shareholders, and financial performance.
Published annually by Euromoney Publications PLC, London.

Trade Associations and Professional Bodies of the United Kingdom

Patricia Millard

Begun in 1962, this directory ceased publication in 1994. The most recent edition contains information on nearly 4,000 British associations. Each entry includes a complete organizational description and full contact information. Entries are indexed geographically and by subject.
Twelfth edition published in 1994 by Gale Research, Detroit.

United Kingdom Business Finance Directory 1990

Each entry in this directory of more than 1,500 British financial institutions includes a complete organizational profile and full contact information. Entries are indexed by institution, subject area, and category of service.
Published in 1990 by Graham & Trotman, London.
Distributed in the United States and Canada by Gale Research, Detroit.

The United States–European Community Trade Resources

John S. Gordon and Timothy Harper

This directory of international business and trade resources in the United States and the European Community provides a wide range of contacts (agencies, services, institutions, and private companies) useful to importers, exporters, investors, business professionals, and corporate managers who want to do business in Europe. The first part covers resources available in the United States. The second section covers resources available on a country-by-country basis in Europe.
Published in 1993 by John Wiley & Sons, New York.

Western European Economic Organizations: A Comprehensive Guide

Robert D. Fraser and Christopher Long

This is a comprehensive guide to information about economic organizations in Western Europe, such as central banks, government agencies, regulatory bodies, stock exchanges, and a wide range of political, industrial, labor, academic, and campaigning organizations. Entries include full contact information, principal officers, organizational structure, funding, aims and objectives, role in national and economic policymaking, history, affiliations, and publications.

Published in 1992 by the Longman Group, Ltd.
Distributed in the United States and Canada by Gale Research, Detroit.

Who Owns Whom— Continental Europe

This two-volume guide (Volumes 5 and 6 in the *Who Owns Whom* series) traces the structure and ownership of multinational corporate groups operating in Europe. The first volume lists parent companies in alphabetical order by company name, as well as by parent companies registered outside Europe that have continental subsidiaries and/or associates. The second offers an alphabetical listing of subsidiaries and associates and shows their parent companies.
Published annually by Dun & Bradstreet Information Services.

Who Owns Whom—United Kingdom and the Republic of Ireland

This two-volume guide (Volumes 3 and 4 in the *Who Owns Whom* series) traces the structure and ownership of multinational corporate groups operating in Britain and Ireland. The first volume lists parent companies in alphabetical order by company name. The second volume offers an alphabetical listing of subsidiaries and associates, while also showing their parent companies.

Published annually by Dun & Bradstreet Information Services.

Who's Who in European Business

Who's Who presents more than 3,000 biographies from nearly 30 countries, covering the chief executives and other leading executives of Europe's top companies. Profiles include career information, education, languages spoken, honors, and interests.
Published in 1992 by R. R. Bowker, New Providence, NJ.

For Further Information

*See **The Economist Intelligence Unit,** p. 493*
***European Accounting Guide,** p. 386*
***European Venture Capital Association (EVCA),** p. 562*
***European Venture Capital Association (EVCA) Yearbook,** p. 560*
***European Wholesalers & Distributors Directory,** p. 443*
***F & S Index Europe,** p. 515*
***The Handbook of International Direct Marketing,** p. 440*
***International Dun's Market Identifiers,** p. 495*
***OECD Economic Outlook,** p. 455*
***OECD Economic Surveys,** p. 456*
***The OECD STAN Database for Industrial Analysis,** p. 456*

34

THE JOB MARKET

Best Resumes for $75,000+ Executives

William Montag

This collection of techniques designed to get high-paying jobs includes 75 real-life resumes and cover letters for 50 mainstream positions, a listing of high-impact words and phrases from motivating resumes and cover letters, and examples of special skills, knowledge, and expertise.
Published in 1992 by John Wiley & Sons, New York.

Beyond the Uniform: A Career Transition Guide for Veterans and Federal Employees

W. Dean Lee

Beyond the Uniform is a comprehensive job-hunting and career transition guide especially designed for the military veteran entering civilian life. Topics include resumes, cover letters, interviews, networking, salary, and advice for family members.
Published in 1991 by John Wiley & Sons, New York.

The Canadian Guide to Working and Living Overseas

This guide is for both entry-level job seekers and experienced professionals. It focuses on international development work, profiling over 700 government, private-sector, non-governmental, and international organizations.
Published in 1992 by Intercultural Systems (ISSI).

Career Advisor Series

Each volume of this series offers an insider's perspective on a particular field, plus listings for hundreds of opportunities for finding entry-level positions and internships. Material in each book is divided into four parts: (1) advice from the pros, (2) job search information, (3) company listings, and (4) additional job-hunting resources. Titles include *Advertising, Book Publishing, Business and Finance, Education, Environmental Studies, Film and Video, Health Care, Magazines, Marketing and Sales, Newspapers, Performing Arts, Public Administration, Public Relations, Radio and Television,* and *Travel and Hospitality.*
Publication ceased with fifth edition (Visible Ink Press).

Career Guide to Industries

This companion to the *Occupational Outlook Handbook* (see p. 522) is prepared by the U.S. Bureau of Labor Statistics of the Department of Labor. From an industry perspective it provides information on careers in 40 diverse industries, accounting for approximately 75 percent of wage and salary jobs in the United States. It also provides information on the nature of the industry, employment, working conditions, training, advancement, and industry outlook.
Published in 1992 by the Superintendent of Documents, U.S. Government Printing Office.

CPC Annual: Who's Who in Career Planning, Placement, and Recruitment

Formerly the *College Placement Annual*, this publication lists 2,000 companies that ac-

tively recruit college graduates, as well as 2,000 college placement offices. Entries include complete contact information.
Published annually by the College Placement Council, Bethlehem, PA.

CPC National Directory

This national directory lists placement officers at corporations and university career services.
Published annually by the College Placement Council, Bethlehem, PA.

Directory of Executive Recruiters

Listings of more than 3,700 offices for over 2,000 search firms in the United States, Canada, and Mexico fill this directory. Each entry includes full contact information. Entries are indexed by management functions, industries, geography, and 5,800 individuals. Material is further arranged by method of payment (retainer or contingency), geographical area, and by alphabetical list of key principal officers of recruiting firms. Volumes since 1996 include diskette.
Published annually by Consultants News.

The Directory of Outplacement Firms

Full-page profiles of about 250 outplacement firms are presented in this directory. Each entry includes full contact information, staff size, annual revenues, fee schedules, and names of 1,100 key principals. A 100-page overview of the outplacement industry is also included.
Seventh edition published in 1993 by Kennedy Publications, Fitzwilliam, NH.

Diversity Recruitment Sourcebook

This comprehensive source for recruiters presents statistics on minority and disabled students attending U.S. colleges and universities. Includes tables and bibliographical references citing enrollment by institution in four geographic regions: Northeast, South, Midwest, and West.
Published in 1994 by the College Placement Council, Bethlehem, PA.

Electronic Job Search Revolution: Win with the New Technology That's Reshaping Today's Job Market

Joyce Lain Kennedy and Thomas J. Morrow

This book provides an overview on how to use electronic technology to conduct a job search. It offers information on computer resume databases by showing how they work, what they cost, and where they're located. It also looks at applicant tracking software, electronic recruitment ads, and computer-assisted interviewing. A companion volume by the same authors is *Electronic Resume Revolution,* which shows how to prepare a resume ready for scanning by computers.
Both books published in 1994 by John Wiley & Sons, New York.

Executive Employment Guide

This annual listing of approximately 100 employment agencies and executive search firms has entries that include complete contact information.
Published annually by the American Management Association, Saranac Lake, NY.

Executive Recruiters of North America

Christopher W. Hunt and Scott A. Scanlon, editors

This directory contains information about approximately 350 executive recruiters in North America and Mexico. It covers both generalist recruiters as well as specialists in a wide variety of industries. Each listing contains contact information and a profile of the firm.
Published in 1993 by Hunt Scanlon Publishing, Greenwich, CT.

The Hidden Job Market: A Job Seeker's Guide to America's 2,000 Little Known but Fastest-Growing High Tech Companies

The Hidden Job Market is a guide to jobs with small but fast-growing high-tech companies. Many industries are covered, including environmental, consulting, genetic engineering, energy, telecommunications, online services, and educational and training software.
Published annually by Peterson's Guides, Princeton, NJ.

Hook Up, Get Hired!: The Internet Job Search Revolution

Joyce Lain Kennedy

A follow-up to Kennedy's 1994 book, *Electronic Job Search Revolution,* this volume focuses on how computer users can surf the Net to discover job openings and find (as well as attract) potential employers. Topics include "CyberOpportunities" for small businesses, how to post and format a resume online, and how to use Internet databases to research companies and prepare for interviews.
Published in 1995 by John Wiley & Sons, New York.

The Job Bank Series

Each title in this series of 18 volumes covers a major U.S. job market. Each book focuses on a city or business region, providing company listings by industry, an assessment of the economic outlook for the area, and contact information for professional associations, chambers of commerce, and executive search and job placement agencies. Current titles in the series cover the following cities/regions: Atlanta, Boston, Chicago, Dallas/Fort Worth, Denver, Detroit, Florida, Houston, Los Angeles, Minneapolis/St. Paul, New York, Ohio, Philadelphia, Phoenix, San Francisco Bay area, Seattle, St. Louis, and Metro Washington, DC.
Each title published and updated periodically by Bob Adams, Inc., Holbrook, MA.

Job Hunter's Sourcebook: Where to Find Employment Leads and Other Job Search Resources

Michelle LeCompte, editor

Each listing within these 155 professional and occupational profiles includes full contact information and descriptions of employment leads, including sources of help-wanted ads, such as journals, newsletters, and online services; placement and job referral services of professional associations; employer directories and networking lists; handbooks and manuals; employment agencies, search firms, and job hot lines; internships; and salary surveys. The *Job Hunter's Sourcebook* is available in print, on computer disk, and on magnetic tape.
Published in 1991 by Gale Research, Detroit.

Job Seeker's Guide to Private and Public Companies

Charity Anne Dorgan and Jennifer Mast, editors

This four-volume set describes the employment opportunities available in a variety of public and private companies. Information includes company benefits, corporate affiliations, and human resources contacts. The guide is available in print, on computer diskette, and on magnetic tape.
Published in 1992 by Gale Research, Detroit.

Launching a Business Career: Tips and Secrets on Finding the Ideal First Job

Richard Fein

This comprehensive guide outlines proven job-hunting strategies. Topics include step-by-step advice on structuring a persuasive resume, mistakes to avoid, and salary negotiation.
Published in 1992 by John Wiley & Sons, New York.

National Business Employment Weekly

This is a weekly compilation of all recruitment advertising from the regional editions of the Wall Street Journal, plus editorial information and articles on job search strategies and career guidance.
Published weekly by Dow Jones & Co.

Occupational Outlook Handbook 1992–1993

This reference book is produced by the U.S. Bureau of Labor Statistics, a division of the Department of Labor. It describes about 250 occupations in detail, covering 107 million jobs. The following information is provided for each occupation listed: the nature of the work; working conditions; how many jobs the occupation provided in 1990; training, qualifications needed, and opportunities for advancement; job outlook and factors that will affect employment through the year 2005; how much people in this occupation generally earn; and sources of additional information.
Published in 1992 by the Superintendent of Documents, U.S. Government Printing Office.

Peterson's Hidden Job Market 1998: 2,000 High-Growth Companies That Are Hiring at Four Times the National Average

This guide is designed for job seekers in a variety of fields and with various areas of expertise. It includes detailed company listings.
Seventh edition published in 1997 by Peterson's Guides, Princeton, NJ.

Peterson's Job Opportunities for Engineering, Science, and Computer Graduates

Each guide in this series profiles companies hiring both entry-level people and experienced professionals. Complete contact information for each company is provided.
Published annually by Peterson's Guides, Princeton, NJ.

Professional Careers Sourcebook, Second Edition

This sourcebook includes profiles of 110 professional careers. Each profile has information on general career guides, professional associations, standards and certification agencies, directories of educational programs, handbooks related to the profession, and professional periodicals.
Published in 1991 by Gale Research, Detroit.

Researching Your Way to a Good Job

Karmen Crowther

This comprehensive guide to doing research as an integral part of the job hunt includes topics such as investigating a company's background, products and services, current financial situation, and management style; incorporating advance knowledge into a persuasive resume and cover letter; and the various types of informational material available.
Published in 1993 by John Wiley & Sons, New York.

What Color Is Your Parachute?

Richard N. Bolles

A career self-help guide, this best-seller provides a systematic approach to finding a job or a career that is right for each person, as well as advice on how to handle the process psychologically.
Revised edition published in 1992 by Ten Speed Press, Berkeley, CA.

Worldwide Guide: The Only Guide to Global Job Opportunities

The *Worldwide Guide* profiles approximately 250 international companies hiring people at all levels, from entry-level to experienced professionals. Profiles contain background information about each company and provides complete contact information.
Published annually by Peterson's Guides, Princeton, NJ.

35

LABOR AND EMPLOYMENT LAW

Affirmative Action Compliance Manual for Federal Contractors

This monthly loose-leaf service provides summaries of the latest court rulings, regulatory activity, and congressional actions dealing with affirmative action. The service also includes a comprehensive reference manual containing actual internal policy instructions used by the Office of Federal Contract Compliance Programs.
Published and updated monthly by the Bureau of National Affairs, Inc., Rockville, MD.

BNA Employee Relations Weekly

A weekly service that offers complete coverage and broad perspective on every aspect of employee relations, *BNA Employee Relations* covers topics such as substance abuse testing, employee privacy rights, child care and elder care benefits, early retirement, health care cost containment, and pay equity.
Published weekly by the Bureau of National Affairs, Inc., Rockville, MD.

Complying with the ADA: A Small Business Guide to Hiring and Employing the Disabled

Jeffrey G. Allen

This text is a comprehensive guide for owners and managers of small businesses to the Americans with Disabilities Act. It covers recruitment, interviewing, testing, compensation, training, and other issues involved in hiring the disabled and offers guidelines for accessibility under the concept of reasonable accommodation.

Published in 1993 by John Wiley & Sons, New York.

Drafting and Revising Employment Contracts

Kurt H. Decker and H. Thomas Felix

This employer's guide to the legal aspects of employment contracts covers all of the general legal principles for forming, drafting, and implementing employment contracts. Employment contracts clauses are examined in both general and specialized terms. The book contains actual sample clauses involving compensation, restrictive covenants, alternate dispute resolution mechanisms, and legal issues that arise over employee termination, as well as complete contract examples involving various occupations, professions, and employers.
Published in 1991 by John Wiley & Sons, New York.
Supplement issued in 1992.

EEOC Compliance Manual

This loose-leaf service offers advance notice of possible regulatory changes, key Equal Employment Opportunity Commission (EEOC) activities, and new employment testing guidelines. EEOC notices are distributed as soon as they are issued, covering such topics as age discrimination, equal pay processing procedures, and issuing notices of right to sue.
Published and updated periodically by the Bureau of National Affairs, Inc., Rockville, MD.

The Employee Handbook: A Complete Ready-to-Use Model with Sample Policies and Procedures

Richard T. Egbert

This comprehensive guide to the creation or revision of an employee handbook comes with ready-to-use policies and procedures that can be tailored to specific needs or situations.
Published in 1990 by Prentice Hall, Englewood Cliffs, NJ.

Employer's Guide to the Americans with Disabilities Act

James G. Frierson

A comprehensive guide to the Americans with Disabilities Act (ADA), this book clarifies the changes needed to comply with the act, defines controversial terms such as *disabled* and *qualified,* and outlines policies that both accommodate employees and avoid liability.
Published in 1992 by John Wiley & Sons, New York.

Employment Guide

This loose-leaf service covers a wide range of company policy issues, including hiring, retirement, safety and health, wages and salaries, dealing with unions, employee benefits, rules and discipline, and employment laws and regulations. Model forms and checklists and ready-to-use policies are included.
Published, and updated regularly, with a biweekly news service, by the Bureau of National Affairs, Inc., Rockville, MD.

Employment Law Deskbook

This comprehensive loose-leaf reference covers every stage of the employer/employee relationship, from the initial employment application through termination or resignation. Features include practical charts, checklists,

tables, and sample forms. A state-by-state summary of key employment-related statutes is included.
Published, and updated annually, by Matthew Bender, New York.

Fair Employment Practices

Issued weekly since 1969, this loose-leaf guide to equal employment opportunity laws, policies, programs, and rules covers federal and state laws and regulations (full text), regulated actions, court decisions (full text), Equal Employment Opportunity Commission rulings (full text), record keeping and reporting, and company and union practices.
Published weekly by the Bureau of National Affairs, Inc., Rockville, MD.

A Handbook for Grievance Arbitration

Arnold M. Zack

This comprehensive guide prepares arbitrators and representatives of unions and management for grievance arbitration. The text is arranged chronologically, beginning with advice on avoiding arbitration, progressing to arrangements for the hearing, then covering the hearing itself, and concluding with the decision.
Published in 1992 by Lexington Books, Lexington, MA.

Individual Employment Rights

This loose-leaf service offers the full text of major decisions from around the country involving employment rights issues outside the traditional labor-management relations context. Topics include invasion of privacy; wrongful discharge; lie-detector testing; defamation; AIDS, drug, and alcohol testing; employment at will; and performance appraisal.
Published biweekly by the Bureau of National Affairs, Inc., Rockville, MD.

Labor Arbitration Reports

This loose-leaf service covers the latest awards and settlements in every type of labor dispute, including rulings by arbitrators, boards, and fact-finding bodies; arbitrator's interpretations of contract terms; and practices and procedures. Issues covered include drug and alcohol testing, absenteeism, sexual harassment, discipline and discharge, seniority, pay, benefits, and overtime.
Published weekly by Bureau of National Affairs, Inc., Rockville, MD.

Labor Law

Theodore W. Kheel

This 11-volume publication is a loose-leaf guide to all aspects of management relations. Topics include the Taft-Hartley Act, Labor-Management Reporting and Disclosure Act, rights of individual employees, union representation of employees, economic coercion by management and labor, federal wage and hour laws, discrimination, sexual harassment, Railway Labor Act, and the Employee Retirement Income Security Act (ERISA). *Labor Law* also includes the monthly *Labor and Employment Law Newsletter*, prepared by the New York law firm of Kaye, Scholer, Fierman, Hays & Handler.
Published, and updated quarterly, by Matthew Bender, New York.

Labor Law Developments

Carol Holgren, editor

This is a compilation of papers presented at the Southwestern Legal Foundation Labor Law Institute by outstanding practitioners, labor law professors, and NLRB members.
Published annually by Matthew Bender, New York.

Labor Law Reports

This 16-volume loose-leaf reference set covers the latest legal developments in management-labor relations. Topics include labor relations, employment practices, wages and hours, and state labor laws.
Published, and updated weekly, by the Commerce Clearing House, Chicago.

The Law of the Workplace: Rights of Employers and Employees

James Hunt

This text is a basic resource on state and federal labor statutes, rules, and regulations, and the agencies that administer and enforce them. The book explains laws governing work eligibility, plant closings, bankruptcy, medical insurance, maternity leave, and affirmative action programs. Main chapters also address hiring and firing, workplace privacy, collective bargaining, and pensions.
Second edition published in 1988 by Bureau of National Affairs, Inc., Rockville, MD.

Managing ADA: The Complete Compliance Guide

Robert A. Naeve and Art Cowan

A how-to-comply guide to the 1990 Americans with Disabilities Act, *Managing ADA* includes the full text of the act, lists resources, and offers checklists, flowcharts, analysis, and interpretation of the legislation. It discusses types of employers and facilities affected; employment, accommodation, and public service requirements; and how to adjust employment policies and procedures to comply.
Published in 1992 by John Wiley & Sons, New York.

Primer on Equal Employment Opportunity

Nancy Sedmak and Michael D. Levin-Epstein

An introduction to federal fair-employment practices, the *Primer* covers sexual harassment, affirmative action, and discrimination based on age, gender, national origin, and religion. Materials on the Immigration Reform and Control Act, the Americans with Disabilities Act, the Age Discrimination in Employment Act, as well as legislation enacted in response to the Supreme Court's decision on pensions are also included.

Fifth edition published in 1991 by Bureau of National Affairs, Inc., Rockville, MD.

Primer on Individual Employee Rights

Alfred G. Feliu

This guide to the expanding field of employee rights covers legislation, contract rights, hiring procedures, employees' rights to information, employee testing, lifestyle and privacy issues, negligence claims, and public policy issues.

Published in 1992 by Bureau of National Affairs, Inc., Rockville, MD.

Primer of Labor Relations

John J. Kenny and Linda G. Kahn

A survey of federal labor regulation and policy, this volume explains the three major statutes: the Wagner Act (National Labor Relations Act), the Taft-Hartley Act (Labor-Management Relations Act), and the Landrum-Griffin Act, as well as other important laws as they have been interpreted by courts and the National Labor Relations Board.

Twenty-fourth edition published in 1989 by Bureau of National Affairs, Inc., Rockville, MD.

Primer on Occupational Safety and Health

Fred Blosser

This is a comprehensive, nontechnical introduction to occupational safety and health laws, overseen by the Occupational Safety and Health Administration (OSHA). It includes topics such as federal and state requirements of OSHA, performance and specification standards, the standard-setting process, standards enforcement, the rights and responsibilities of employees and employers under OSHA, record-keeping requirements, and antidiscrimination provisions.

Published in 1992 by Bureau of National Affairs, Inc., Rockville, MD.

Primer on Wage and Hour Laws

Joseph E. Kalet

This collection provides concise discussions of basic federal wage and hour requirements. It highlights the 1989 amendments to the Fair Labor Standards Act and reviews such issues as compensatory time eligibility, retaliations, "regular" versus collectively bargained rates of pay, "willful" violations, statutes of limitations, record keeping, enforcement, damages, and penalties.

Second edition published in 1990 by Bureau of National Affairs, Inc., Rockville, MD.

Primer on Workers' Compensation

Jeffrey V. Nackley

A comprehensive outline of the laws governing job-related injuries, accidents, and diseases, this book addresses topics such as work-related stress, partial disability, federal preemption, settlements, and rehabilitation. It also includes a state-by-state summary of laws, scheduled injuries, and workers' compensation agencies.

Second edition published in 1989 by Bureau of National Affairs, Inc., Rockville, MD.

Sexual Harassment in Employment Law

Barbara Lindemann and David D. Kadue

This book offers an insightful study of laws governing claims charging sexual harassment in the workplace. Topics include specific details from court cases, theories of sexual harassment including *quid pro quo*, hostile environment, and harassment by supervisors, coworkers, and nonemployees.

Published in 1992 by Bureau of National Affairs, Inc., Rockville, MD.

Stay Out of Court: The Manager's Guide to Preventing Employee Lawsuits

Rita Risser

This comprehensive guide to employment law is designed to give managers the tools to prevent employee lawsuits. The text addresses potential trouble areas in employee relations, including discrimination, harassment, wrongful termination, drug testing, and references. Specific coverage is given to dismissing employees without being sued, preventing sexual harassment, illegal questions to avoid in interviews, writing disciplinary warnings, and counseling troubled employees.
Published in 1993 by Prentice Hall, New York.

U.S. Labor and Employment Laws

Ruth Clarke West, editor

This one-volume reference contains all of the constitutional provisions and major federal laws governing employment in both the private and public sector. Topics include federal sector labor relations, constitutional provisions, antitrust, labor-management relations, fair employment practices, veterans' employment and training, wage-hour laws, and alien employment.
Published in 1991 by Bureau of National Affairs, Inc., Rockville, MD.

Your Rights at Work

Darien A. McWhirter

A guide to employment law, *Your Rights at Work* covers developments such as the 1991 Civil Rights Bill, the new definition of sexual harassment, new laws on age and handicap discrimination, and numerous changes in the law on privacy in the workplace, including the Polygraph Protection Act. Also included are state-by-state checklists showing how different states interpret employee rights and obligations.

Published in 1992 by John Wiley & Sons, New York.

Your Rights in the Workplace

Dan Lacey

A comprehensive guide to employee workplace rights, this book includes topics such as illegal firing and layoffs, wages and overtime, maternity and parental leave, unemployment and disability insurance, workers' compensation, job safety, and discrimination based on sex, race, and age.
Published in 1991 by the Nolo Press, Berkeley, CA.

GOVERNMENT AGENCIES

Equal Employment Opportunity Commission (EEOC)

The EEOC acts on charges of job discrimination filed under Title VII of the Civil Rights Act of 1964, which prohibits discrimination by employers based on race, color, religion, sex, or national origin; the Americans with Disabilities Act of 1990; the Equal Pay Act of 1963; and the Age Discrimination in Employment Act of 1967.
Equal Employment Opportunity Commission, 1801 L Street NW, Washington, DC 20507.
(202) 663-4900

National Labor Relations Board (NLRB)

The NLRB is charged with preventing and remedying unfair labor practices by employers and labor organizations, and for conducting secret-ballot elections in union representation elections.
National Labor Relations Board, 1717 Pennsylvania Avenue NW, Washington, DC 20570.
(202) 254-8064

U.S. Department of Labor

The Department of Labor is a rich source of information on the latest developments in labor law and relations. Key offices within the department include the Employment and Training Administration; Bureau of Labor Management Relations and Cooperative Programs; Pension and Welfare Benefits Administration; Bureau of Labor Statistics (which publishes a helpful telephone directory that lists the bureau's experts and their areas of expertise); Office of Productivity and Technology; Occupational Safety and Health Administration (OSHA); Assistant Secretary for Veterans' Employment Training; and the Women's Bureau.

Department of Labor, 200 Constitution Avenue NW, Washington, DC 20210.
Main number: (202) 523-6666
Public affairs: (202) 523-7316
Note: In addition to these federal agencies, most states have a state labor department and a state human rights commission that also enforce labor and employment laws and provide a wealth of free information.

FOR FURTHER INFORMATION

See **Guide to Employee Handbooks,**
   p. 490

36

MANAGING A COMPANY

Bass and Stogdhill's Handbook of Leadership: Theory Research, and Managerial Application

Bernard M. Bass and Ralph M. Stogdhill

This text is a comprehensive and authoritative presentation of the theories and models of leadership in organizations.
Second edition published in 1990 by the Free Press, New York.

The Change Masters: Innovation and Entrepreneurship in the American Corporation

Rosabeth Moss Kanter

Kanter's book is an influential and extremely interesting analysis of how individuals can gauge change in their organizations. The author suggests ten reasons why innovation and entrepreneurship are stifled, and proposes a theory of change that will allow creativity to flourish.
Second edition published in 1983 by Simon & Schuster, New York.

Corporate Culture and Performance

John P. Kotter and James L. Heskett

Using extensive case studies from companies such as Hewlett-Packard, Xerox, and Nissan, the authors of this text analyze how the culture of an organization influences its economic performance.
Published in 1992 by the Free Press, New York.

Influence without Authority

Allan R. Cohen and David L. Bradford

The authors employ many interesting and useful case studies to show how to influence people at work over whom you have no authority. This is a highly useful book at a time when many companies are trying to do away with rigid hierarchical structures.
Published in 1989 by John Wiley & Sons, New York.

Intelligent Enterprise: A Knowledge and Service Based Paradigm for Industry

James Brian Quinn

This book is an analysis of how technology revolutionizes a company's strategy and services. The author shows that companies will derive competitive advantage from knowledge of a few highly developed core service skills.
Published in 1992 by The Free Press, New York.

Managing across Borders: The Transnational Solution

Christopher Bartlett and Sumantra Ghoshal

This book shows how to manage companies in today's global business environment, including how to develop organizational structures, administrative processes, and management perspectives.
Published in 1989 by the Harvard Business School Press, Boston.

Managing for Excellence: The Guide to Developing High Performance in Contemporary Organizations

David L. Bradford and Allan R. Cohen

Written for middle managers, this book provides the useful concept of the *manager as developer.* The authors show how managers can foster the growth and development of their subordinates.
Published in 1984 by John Wiley & Sons, New York.

Managing with Power: Politics and Influence in Organizations

Jeffrey Pfeffer

Pfeffer, a professor at the Stanford Business School, shows that effective use of power is an important aspect of effective leadership. He presents an insightful analysis of power and politics at the organizational level.
Published in 1992 by the Harvard Business School Press, Boston.

The Portable MBA in Management

Allan R. Cohen, editor

This book covers a broad array of important management topics, including building a vision, creating teams, power and influence, organizational change, strategic negotiating, and managing diversity. Each chapter is written by a leading person in the field.
Published in 1993 by John Wiley & Sons, New York

TRADE AND PROFESSIONAL ASSOCIATIONS

American Management Association (AMA)

The AMA membership includes managers in industry, commerce, government, and nonprofit organizations, as well as university teachers of management. Its purpose is to increase knowledge and skills in management areas. The association maintains an extensive library and conducts the Management Information Service, which provides films, cassettes, tapes, and records covering all areas of management studies and expertise. Publications include *Management Review,* a monthly magazine specializing in management trends and techniques, and *Compensation and Benefits Review,* a bimonthly journal.
American Management Association, 135 West 50th Street, New York, NY 10020-1201. (212) 586-8100

FOR FURTHER INFORMATION

See **Building the Competitive Workforce: Investing in Human Capital for Corporate Success,** p. 489
The Conference Board, p. 452
Globalizing Management: Creating and Leading the Competitive Organization, p. 490
Managing Workforce 2000: Gaining the Diversity Advantage, p. 491
Organizational Capability: Competing from the Inside Out, p. 491
Strategic Benchmarking: How to Rate Your Company's Performance Against the World's Best, p. 398

37

MANUFACTURING AND QUALITY

The Baldrige Quality System: The Do-It-Yourself Way to Transform Your Business

Stephen George

This book explains how to use the Malcolm Baldrige National Quality Award to manage quality within an organization by employing the Baldrige criteria to measure and evaluate standards.
Published in 1992 by John Wiley & Sons, New York.

Corporate Quality Universities: Lessons Learned From Programs That Produce Results

Jeanne C. Meister

This detailed study assesses quality training programs, such as Motorola University, that return employees to the corporate classroom for lessons in quality and continuous improvement.
Published in 1993 by Business One Irwin, Homewood, IL.

Delivering Quality Service: Balancing Customer Perceptions and Expectations

Valarie A. Zeithaml, A. Parasuraman, and Leonard L. Barry

This book provides a model on service quality that shows how to balance a customer's perception of the value of a service with the customer's need for that service.
Published in 1990 by the Free Press, New York.

The Deming Management Method

Mary Walton

The principles of W. Edwards Deming are explained and applied in this book. The author analyzes Deming's "14 Points for Managers" and "Deadly Diseases of Management."
Published in 1988 by the Putnam Publishing Group.

Juran on Quality by Design: The New Steps for Planning Quality into Goods and Services

J. M. Juran

This comprehensive guide to planning, setting, and reaching quality goals employs three case examples that encompass the three major sectors of the economy—service, manufacturing, and support. The text offers a practical plan for companies to achieve strategic, market-driven goals by following a structured approach to planning quality.
Published in 1992 by the Free Press, New York.

Out of the Crisis

W. Edwards Deming

W. Edwards Deming is America's quality guru, and this book presents his philosophy on how the style of American management must be transformed in order for the country to regain its competitive edge.
Published in 1986 by the Massachusetts Institute of Technology—Center Advanced Engineering Study, Cambridge.

Reinventing the Factory: Productivity Breakthroughs in Manufacturing Today

Roy L. Harmon and Leroy D. Peterson

Focusing on the concepts that are reinforcing manufacturing, this text looks at the focused factory—the reorganization of existing plants into multiple, smaller "factories within a factory." A follow-up book, *Reinventing the Factory II: Managing the World Class Factory*, discusses how cross-training, new-generation account systems, and the empowerment of subplant methods can lead to fail-safe product and process quality.
Published in 1990 by the Free Press, New York.

Thomas Register of American Manufacturers

This comprehensive (26-volume) guide to the products, services, catalogs, trademarks, and shipping services of American manufacturing companies enables users to locate the companies supplying products and services; shows how to get catalogs, capabilities brochures, and detailed shipping information; and provides profiles of more than 150,000 U.S. companies, including trademarks, brand names, and names and addresses of owners. The guide is also available online through DIALOG as Thomas Register Online.
Published annually by Thomas International, Inc.

Total Quality Control

Armand V. Feigenbaum

A comprehensive, authoritative handbook on using quality to achieve excellence with an organization, *Total Quality Control* focuses on this element as a primary function of general management. The impact of total quality control on such areas as product design, manufacturing, sales, and distribution is also examined.

Published in 1991 by McGraw-Hill, New York.

GOVERNMENT AGENCIES

National Technical Information Service (NTIS)

NTIS and the Federal Quality Institute have established a central clearinghouse for total quality management, and offer both a free brochure (Publication number PR-894) and a free bibliography (Publication number PR-868).
National Technical Information Service, 5285 Port Royal Road, Springfield, VA 22161.
(703) 487-4650

TRADE AND PROFESSIONAL ORGANIZATIONS

American Society for Quality Control (ASQC)

ASQC is a large and diverse professional organization, with more than 200 local chapters, 19 divisions, and 7 technical committees. Membership includes subscriptions to *Quality in Progress*, a monthly magazine, and *On Q*, a newsletter.
American Society for Quality Control, P.O. Box 3066, Milwaukee, WI 53201-3066.
(800) 248-1946
(414) 272-8575
Fax: (414) 272-1734

National Association of Manufacturers (NAM)

This association channels the views of manufacturers on public policy to the White House, federal agencies, and the U.S. Congress. NAM provides telephone assistance for members with questions about specific issues and concerns relating to their field. Publications include *America's Workforce in the 1990's: Trends Affecting Manufacturers; 1998 Association Council Directory*, which lists more than 150 manufacturing trade associations; and others.

National Association of Manufacturers (Washington Headquarters), 1331 Pennsylvania Avenue NW, Suite 1500, North Lobby, Washington, DC 20004-1703. (202) 637-3000

FOR FURTHER INFORMATION

See **Guide to Canadian Manufacturers,** p. 425

Manufacturing USA, p. 425

National Technical Information Service/Federal Government Electronic Bulletin Boards, p. 482

Statistical Abstract of the United States, p. 378

38

MERGERS AND ACQUISITIONS

Acquisitions, Mergers, Sales, Buyouts, and Takeovers

Charles A. Scharf, Edward E. Shea, and George C. Beck

This comprehensive guide provides detailed and practical information on leveraged buyouts, financial valuation methods, technology licensing, government rules, and joint ventures.
Fourth edition published in 1995 by Prentice Hall, Englewood Cliffs, NJ.

The Acquisitions Yearbook

Edward E. Shea

The previous year's developments in the field of mergers and acquisitions are reviewed extensively in this yearbook. Topics include financial valuation methods, government regulations, and joint ventures.
Published annually by Prentice Hall, Englewood Cliffs, NJ.

The Art of M & A: A Merger/ Acquisition/Buyout Guide

Stanley Foster Reed and Alexandra Reed Lajoux

This all-encompassing guide covers issues and developments in the field of mergers and acquisitions, such as strategic alliances; international issues involving opportunities in (the former) Eastern Bloc countries; and turnarounds, bankruptcies, and restructuring.
Published in 1994 by Business One Irwin, Homewood, IL.

Business Organizations: Corporate Acquisitions and Mergers

Byron E. Fox and Eleanor M. Fox

Issued in loose-leaf format, this four-volume guide studies the antitrust, corporate securities, and financial aspects of mergers and acquisitions.
Published and updated periodically with supplements and revisions by Matthew Bender and Company, New York.

Buyouts Newsletter

This newsletter reports on current developments in the field of mergers and acquisitions. Coverage includes developments in fund formations, leveraged acquisitions, and all types of special situations.
Published biweekly by Securities Data Company Publishing, New York.

Directory of Buyout Financing Sources

This directory presents information on hundreds of sources of equity, mezzanine and debt financing for leveraged buyouts, leveraged acquisitions, recapitalizations, restructuring, and other transactions. Entries for each firm cover its investment or lending criteria, key contacts, preferred deal sizes and types, and services offered.
Published annually by Securities Data Company Publishing, New York.

Directory of M & A Intermediaries

Each entry in this collection of in-depth profiles of more than 500 investment banks,

business brokers, and other deal makers includes information on services offered, fees charged, geographic/industry focus, and preferred transaction size.
Published annually by Securities Data Company Publishing, New York.

M & A Filings Database

This database contains detailed abstracts of every original and amended mergers and acquisitions document released by the Securities and Exchange Commission since early 1985. Users are provided with an array of M & A transaction information on publicly traded companies, including company name, SIC code, ticker symbol, CUSIP number, and other vital information. Available online through WESTLAW and DIALOG.
Published and updated daily by Charles E. Simon Company.

Managing Acquisitions: Creating Value through Corporate Renewal

Philippe C. Haspeslagh and David B. Jemison

This book provides managers with a different perspective on the mergers and acquisitions process. In the opinion of the authors, the traditional view of corporate acquisitions looks only at preacquisition strategic fit and addresses only the potential for creation. The authors maintain that real value is created after the acquisition through managerial actions, not financial engineering.
Published in 1991 by the Free Press, New York.

Mergers & Acquisitions

Ernst & Young

A complete back-to-the-basics guide, this book shows readers how to go about structuring, financing, and integrating a merger or acquisition. Topics include restructuring financially troubled companies, niche acquisitions, international mergers and cross-border

alliances, and partial buy-ins.
Second edition published in 1992 by John Wiley & Sons, New York.

Mergers & Acquisitions: Managing the Transaction

Joseph C. Krallinger

A step-by-step resource for the buyer or seller, this book provides information on everything from how to first approach making a merger to closing and postclosing issues. Detailed appendixes cover legal paperwork and purchase investigation work.
Published in 1997 by McGraw-Hill, New York.

Mergers and Acquisitions Manual

Simon Partner

This step-by-step guide to mergers and acquisitions incorporates ready-to-use forms, contracts, letters, and documents that can be used when buying, selling, or defending a company.
Published in 1991 by Prentice Hall, Englewood Cliffs, NJ.

Mergers and Acquisitions Sourcebook

This yearly guide covers all M & A activity of the previous 12 months.
Published annually by the Quality Services Company, Santa Barbara, CA.

Mergers & Corporate Policy

This newsletter reports on the most recent developments in the M & A field. Coverage includes developing deals and acquisition strategies; conditions in the junk bond and distressed credit markets; trends in commercial bank lending; legal and legislative developments; and full details on proposed, completed, and withdrawn mergers, acquisitions, and divestitures.
Published weekly by Securities Data Company Publishing, New York.

The Merger Yearbook

This yearbook lists M & A deals that were announced, completed, or withdrawn in the previous year, including corporate acquisitions, mergers, divestitures, and leveraged buyouts. Complete information on every transaction in every major industry sector includes facts on parent companies, prior owners, prices, and types of payment. The yearbook is organized by Standard Industry Classification (SIC).

Published annually by Securities Data Company Publishing, New York.

FOR FURTHER INFORMATION

See ***Corporate Finance Sourcebook,***
p. 560
Predicasts' F&S Index of Corporate Change, *p. 426*

39

NEW-PRODUCT DEVELOPMENT

Compressing the Product Development Cycle

Bernard N. Slade

This guide to developing and implementing a faster new-product development process analyzes the principal reasons for America's long development cycles, explores the factors that drive the product cycle, and proposes practical steps to shorten the product's path to market.
Published in 1992 by AMACOM, Saranac Lake, NY.

How to Bring a Product to Market for Less Than $5,000

Don Debelak

Topics in this step-by-step guide to getting a product to market for the smallest possible investment include setting up a product flow-chart, predetermining manufacturing costs, and reducing expenses.
Published in 1991 by John Wiley & Sons, New York.

New Product Development: Managing and Forecasting for Strategic Success

Robert J. Thomas

Analyzing the strategic nature of new-product development, this book shows both how to manage the process and how to use forecasting tools to achieve company targets. It provides in-depth material on forecasting market opportunity, estimating sales and

profits, entering markets, and tracking a new product's launch. Spreadsheet models are also provided.
Published in 1993 by John Wiley & Sons, New York.

New Product Development Checklists

George Gruenwald

This collection of proven, ready-to-use checklists for developing new products from mission to market allows managers to assign responsibilities, review and evaluate progress, and make go/no-go decisions.
Published in 1991 by NTC Publishing Group, Lincolnwood, IL.

New Product Development Planner

Jeannemarie Caris-McManus

A loose-leaf guide to the development, testing, and commercialization of new products, this workbook provides a reference point for companies and individuals passing through the various stages of new-product development.
Published in 1991 by AMACOM, Saranac Lake, NY.

Profiting from Innovation

William G. Howard, Jr., and Bruce R. Guile

This nuts-and-bolts handbook demonstrates how managing technical resources and innovations is the key to business success. Topics

include using project teams for commercialization, managing quality, integrating systems, and knowing when to quit.
Published in 1991 by the Free Press, New York.

PTS New Product Announcements Plus®

This online database provides the full text of news releases by organizations in both manufacturing and service industries. The news releases provide information on new-product introduction, new technologies, licenses, and joint ventures. Available online from Datastar and DIALOG.
Updated weekly by Information Access Company/Predicasts.

Revolutionizing New Product Development

Steven C. Wheelright and Kim B. Clark

This book on product development shows how leading companies use cutting-edge principles to bring high-quality products to market faster than the competition. The companies used as examples include Honda, Compaq, Applied Materials, Sony, and The Limited. The authors demonstrate how these companies used innovative practices such as design for manufacturability, quality function deployment, computer-aided design, and computer-aided manufacturability.
Published in 1992 by the Free Press, New York.

For Further Information

See ***A Directory of Strategic Management Software Tools,*** p. 553
PROMT:™ Predicast's Overview of Markets and Technology, p. 377

40

REAL ESTATE

The Arnold Encyclopedia of Real Estate

Alvin L. Arnold

This authoritative work provides definitions and explanations of terms and expressions used in the practice of real estate, including legal and banking terms as they relate to real estate.
Second edition published in 1993 by John Wiley & Sons, New York.

Commercial Real Estate Leases: Preparation and Negotiation/Forms: 1997 Cumulative Supplement

Mark A. Senn

This two-volume set is for real estate professionals needing information and guidance on how to structure sound, workable leases for commercial office space, shipping centers, or single-tenant properties. The first volume is a legal analysis of the lease, and the second volume consists of forms that have been used successfully in thousands of leases.
Published in 1997 by John Wiley & Sons, New York.

Directory of Foreign Investment in the U.S.: Real Estate and Businesses, 1996

This directory lists more than 11,000 real estate properties and businesses that are wholly or partly owned (at least 10 percent) by foreign investors. Entries are arranged in two sections. Section I—Real Estate—is arranged alphabetically by city within each of the United States and provides details on for-

eign real estate investments. Each entry includes the foreign owner's name and country; property name, address, and telephone number; property description; purchase date and price; and seller. Section II—Businesses—lists foreign-owned manufacturing, service, retail, wholesale, and import/export firms in the United States.
Published in 1995 by Gale Research, Detroit.

Finance, Insurance & Real Estate USA

Arsen J. Darnay, editor

This publication is a collection of statistical profiles and listings of leading companies involved in the finance, insurance, and real estate industries, including mortgage bankers and brokers; foreign trade and international banks; savings and loan institutions; securities and commodities brokers and services; insurance carriers, agents, and brokers; and real estate firms. Each entry offers detailed profiles that include statistics on selected assets and liabilities, inputs/outputs, revenues, occupations, employment, and state and regional data.
Fourth edition published in 1990 by Gale Research, Detroit.

Foreign Investment in United States Real Estate

Jeremy D. Smith

This comprehensive guide covers every aspect of foreign real estate investment activity in the United States, including the legal, fi-

nancial, and tax aspects of acquiring property. Topics include protecting against U.S. tax liability, exchanging risk losses, and the impact of U.S. immigration law on real estate transactions.
Published in 1992 by Wiley Law Publications.

Limited Partnerships: How to Profit in the Secondary Market

Richard Wallack and Brent R. Donaldson

The secondary trading of real estate limited partnership interests is an underdeveloped market that is growing. This book provides one of the best explanations available on how this market works—and how to make money in it.
Published in 1992 by Dearborn Trade, Chicago.

Managing and Leasing Residential Properties

Paul D. Lapides

This book presents the basic tools necessary for successful residential management. It includes guidance for setting policies, procedures for implementing them, and forms.
Published in 1992 and supplemented annually by Wiley Law Publications.

The McGraw-Hill Real Estate Handbook

Robert Irwin, editor in chief

This encyclopedia of real estate covers residential, commercial, office, and industrial properties and row land. It looks at current finance, investment, and tax issues; the best financing methods; property management; and computerized investment analysis.
Second edition published in 1993 by McGraw-Hill, New York.

Modern Real Estate Practice Series

Each volume of this book series covers the real estate practices of a different state. Topics range from real estate law to financing to fair housing. States covered in the series include Alabama, Arizona, Connecticut, Idaho, Illinois, Maryland, Massachusetts, Minnesota, New Hampshire, New York, Pennsylvania, Ohio, Virginia, and Wisconsin.
Titles are published and updated periodically by Dearborn Trade, Chicago.

Negotiating Real Estate Transactions, 1997 Cumulative Supplement

Mark A. Senn, editor

This hands-on guide covers all kinds of real estate contracts, financial arrangements, letters, agreements, and leases. Included is comprehensive material on contracts for purchase and sale, construction, real estate finance, opinion letters, and environmental issues in real estate transactions.
Published in 1997 and supplemented annually by John Wiley & Sons, New York.

The Real Estate Directory of Major Investors, Developers, and Brokers

Major real estate companies (those with portfolios of $1 million and over) are profiled in this comprehensive guide of more than 4,100 firms and 7,600 executives.
Published in 1992 by the National Register—Reed Reference Publishing, New Providence, NJ.

Real Estate Limited Partnerships

Theodore S. Lynn, Harry F. Goldberg, and Michael Hirshfield

This book provides an overview of the organization, structure, and ongoing operating con-

sequences of private real estate limited partnerships. Topics such as passive loss limitation, at-risk rules, and bankrupt partnerships are addressed.
Published in 1991 by John Wiley & Sons, New York.

Structuring Real Estate Joint Ventures

Robert Bell

This guide to structuring and managing real estate joint ventures includes topics such as the Uniform Partnership Act; financial instruments such as participating mortgages and leases; and international investment.
Published in 1991 by John Wiley & Sons, New York.

Uniform Standards of Professional Appraisal Practice: Applying the Standards

Dennis S. Tosh and William B. Rayburn

This book provides coverage of the Appraisal Foundation's standards, including appraising, reporting, and reviewing personal property and business valuation.
Fourth edition published in 1997 by Dearborn Trade, Chicago.

TRADE AND PROFESSIONAL ASSOCIATION

National Association of Realtors (NAR)

The NAR is a federation of 50 state associations and 1,848 local real estate boards. It promotes education, high professional standards, and modern techniques in specialized real estate work, such as brokerage, appraisal, property management, and land development. It also conducts research programs and maintains a library relating to real estate topics.
National Association of Realtors, 430 N Michigan Avenue, Chicago, IL 60611-4087. (312) 329-8200

FOR FURTHER INFORMATION

*See **ABI/INFORM®**, p. 370*

41

RESEARCH AND DEVELOPMENT

Directory of American Research and Technology

This annual directory lists more than 11,000 U.S. and Canadian corporate facilities active in commercially applicable basic or applied research. Entries include key personnel, complete contact information, staff size, and research activities. The directory is available in print, online (through ORBIT Search Service), on CD-ROM, and on magnetic tape. *Published annually by R. R. Bowker, New Providence, NJ.*

Government Research Directory

Jacqueline K. Barrett, editor

More than 3,700 research facilities and programs of the U.S. government are listed in this directory, including research facilities operated by the federal government, contractor-operated facilities, user-operated facilities supported by the federal government, government-supported cooperative research programs, government agencies and bureaus that are research organizations, and administrative offices and similar units. Each entry includes the following contact information: name, address, telephone, and fax number; description of the center's history and current status; information on research activities and programs; and details on publications, seminars, and libraries. The directory is available in print, on computer diskette, online (through DIALOG as part of the Research Centers and Services Directory), and on magnetic tape. *Tenth edition published in 1997 by Gale Research, Detroit. New editions published biennially.*

International Research Centers Directory 1998

This directory lists 7,200 government, university, independent, nonprofit, and commercial research centers in more than 145 countries. Each entry includes full contact information, research activities, and publications. The directory is available in print, online (through DIALOG as part of the Research Centers and Services Directory), and on magnetic tape. *Tenth edition published in 1997 by Gale Research, Detroit. New editions published biennially.*

Japan's High Technology: An Annotated Guide to English Language Information Sources

Dawn E. Talbot

More than 500 directories are identified in this book, along with online databases, abstracting and indexing tools, newsletters, and translation guides that provide information on Japanese high technology. *Published in 1991 by the Oryx Press, Phoenix.*

NTIS Online Bibliographic Database (National Technical Information Service)

Providing information on government-sponsored research and development, this multidisciplinary database has coverage that includes administration and management, business and economics, energy, health planning, library and informational science, and

transportation. Available in CD-ROM and online from DIALOG.
Updated biweekly by the National Technical Information Service, Department of Commerce.

R&D Ratios and Budgets

This research service is designed for professional managers seeking information on the R&D budgeting practices of major corporations. The service is available through FIND/SVP.
Published annually by Schonfeld & Associates.

Research Centers Directory

Listing more than 12,000 nonprofit research and development companies in the United States and Canada, this two-volume directory groups entries into five broad categories. Each entry includes the name of the parent institution, full contact information, the year it was established, number of staff, research activities, and publications. The directory is available in print form, on magnetic tape, or online through DIALOG as part of the Research Centers and Services Directory.
Twenty-third edition published in 1997 by Gale Research, Detroit.

Research Services Directory

Annette Piccirelli, editor

This directory lists more than 4,000 for-profit research and development companies in the United States and Canada. Each entry includes complete contact information, company description, principal, clients, rates, memberships, description of services, equipment, databases, patents, licenses, and publications. The directory is available in print, on magnetic tape, or online through DIALOG as part of the Research Centers and Services Directory.

Twenty-third edition published in 1995 by Gale Research, Detroit.
New editions published every three years.

Third Generation R&D

Phillip A. Roussel, Kamal N. Saad, and Tamara J. Erickson

Third Generation R&D outlines a pragmatic method for linking R&D to long-term business planning. Topics include integrating technology and research capabilities with overall management strategy, breaking organizational barriers that isolate R&D, fostering a spirit of partnership between R&D and other units, and creating managed portfolios of R&D projects that match corporate goals.
Published in 1991 by the Harvard Business School Press, Boston.

The U.S. Sourcebook of R&D Spenders

This directory gives information on publicly owned corporations that spend on R&D. The data for each corporation includes its corporate name, address, telephone number, projected R&D budget for the calendar year, annual R&D growth, projected sales for the calendar year, sales growth rate, and R&D-to-sales ratio. The directory is available online through FIND/SVP.
Published annually by Schonfeld and Associates, Lincolnshire, IL.

FOR FURTHER INFORMATION

See ***Industrial Research in the United Kingdom,*** *p. 516*
National Technical Information Service/Federal Government Electronic Bulletin Boards, *p. 482*
PROMT:™ Predicast's Overview of Markets and Technology, *p. 377*

42

SMALL BUSINESS AND ENTREPRENEURSHIP

Allen Fishman Business Financing Kit

This collection of tools and techniques for obtaining financing for expanding an established business, funding an acquisition, or starting a new business includes ready-to-use applications, letters, checklists, and business plans.
Published in 1990 by Prentice Hall, Englewood Cliffs, NJ.

Business Plans to Manage Day-to-Day Operations: Real Life Results for Small Business Owners and Operators

Christopher R. Malburg

This guide shows step-by-step how to develop a business plan, then how to use it as a blueprint for conducting the day-to-day operations of a small business. Topics include setting goals, building teams, delegating responsibilities, and motivation. A computer disk that offers the latest tools for business charting and forecasting is included.
Published in 1993 by John Wiley & Sons, New York.

Choosing a Business Form: To Incorporate or Not to Incorporate

Richard P. Mandell

This easy-to-understand overview of a complex topic is a chapter in the book *The Portable MBA in Finance and Accounting* (edited by John Leslie Livingstone). It examines whether a business should be organized as a sole proprietorship, partnership, corporation, or some other legal form. The pluses and minuses of each form, the exposure of

the owners of the business to personal liability, and the impact of the business form on income taxes paid are examined.
Published in 1992 by John Wiley & Sons, New York.

The Complete Guide to Money and Your Business

Robert E. Butler and Donald Rappaport

This comprehensive guide to small-business finance and financial management considers topics like getting, using, managing, and keeping money; preparing and using balance sheets and income statements; and minimizing tax liabilities.
Published in 1987 by Prentice Hall, Englewood Cliffs, NJ.

The Complete Handbook for the Entrepreneur

Gary Brunner, Joel Ewan, and Henry Custer

This comprehensive handbook addresses the 120 topics most entrepreneurs need to consider while starting or operating a business. Topics include sales forecasting, using a corporation as a tax shelter, and conducting market research.
Published in 1989 by Prentice Hall, Englewood Cliffs, NJ.

The Complete Information Bank for Entrepreneurs and Small Business Managers

This book provides an annotated bibliography to sources of interest to managers of

small businesses and to entrepreneurs. Included are listings for government agencies that provide free information, as well as books on management, networking systems, information technology, management associations, and financing arrangements.
Published in 1988 by the American Management Association, Saranac Lake, NY.

The Entrepreneur and Small Business Problem Solver: An Encyclopedic Reference and Guide

William A. Cohen

This comprehensive reference covers all aspects of starting and managing a business, including legal aspects, sources of capital, developing a business plan, buying a business, protecting ideas, leasing and buying equipment, record keeping, financial management, and marketing and advertising.
Second edition published in 1990 by John Wiley & Sons, New York.

External Assistance for Start-Ups and Small Businesses

Elizabeth J. Gatewood and Keiron E. Hylton

This chapter of *The Portable MBA in Entrepreneurship* (see p. 547) is an informative and useful overview of the wealth of information and resources available from nonprofit organizations and federal, state, and local government. It contains a guide to myriad Small Business Administration programs, such as SBA Development Centers, Service Corps of Retired Executives, small-business institutes, financial assistance programs, procurement assistance, and export assistance.
Published in 1994 by John Wiley & Sons, New York.

Free Help from Uncle Sam to Start Your Own Business (or Expand the One You Have)

William Alarid and Gustav Berle

This practical book covers a wide variety of topics useful to people in small business,

such as selling to the federal government, obtaining governmental financial assistance, receiving help from the government in international trade, and providing help for women, minorities, and the disadvantaged.
Third edition published in 1992 by the Puma Press, Santa Monica, CA.

Going Public

Paul Joubert

This chapter in *The Portable MBA in Finance and Accounting* (edited by John Leslie Livingstone) is a practical guide to the pluses and minuses of taking a company public. It looks at the factors involved in managing an initial public offering (IPO) of stock.
Published in 1992 by John Wiley & Sons, New York.

Guerrilla Financing: Alternative Techniques to Finance Any Small Business

Bruce Brechman and Jay Conrad-Levinson

This book looks at nontraditional ways to get money to finance a small business, such as receivable financing, equipment financing, real estate financing, government financing, and bank financing. The authors also cover traditional venture capital and informal venture capital.
Published in 1991 by Houghton Mifflin, Boston.

How to Buy a Business: Entrepreneurship through Acquisition

Richard A. Joseph, Anna A. Nekoranel, and Carl H. Steffans

This book shows how the active small business marketplace works. The text covers a wide range of topics, including finding and evaluating acquisition candidates; financing, negotiating, and structuring the deal; understanding legal and tax implications; and determining current and future value.
Published in 1992 by Dearborn Trade, Chicago.

How to Buy or Sell the Closely Held Corporation

Lawrence C. Silton

This source suggests strategies and practical aids to buying or selling a closely held company, including valuing a business, negotiating price and terms, guaranteeing payment, and minimizing taxes.
Published in 1987 by Prentice Hall, Englewood Cliffs, NJ.

How to Form Your Own Corporation without a Lawyer for under $75

Ted Nicholas

This book shows how to save legal fees by using a simple set of instructions to incorporate without using a lawyer. It includes forms such as a certificate of incorporation and other useful material.
Published in 1992 by Dearborn Trade, Chicago.

How to Form Your Own Nonprofit Corporation

Anthony Mancuso

Written for arts groups, educators, social service agencies, medical programs, environmentalists, and anyone who wants to start a nonprofit organization, this book explains all the legal formalities involved in creating and operating a tax-exempt nonprofit corporation. Features include detailed information on differences between all 50 states; ready-to-use forms for articles, bylaws, and minutes; and complete instructions for obtaining federal 501(c)(3) tax exemption and for qualifying for public charity status with the Internal Revenue Service.
Published in 1990 by the Nolo Press, Berkeley, CA.

Inc: The Magazine for Growing Companies

This general-interest business magazine is geared toward entrepreneurs and small-business owners. Coverage includes tips and advice on starting and running a small business, profiles of leading entrepreneurs, and rankings of successful entrepreneurial companies.
Published monthly by the Goldhirsh Group, Inc.

The Legal Guide for Starting & Running a Small Business

Fred S. Steingold

This comprehensive guide to the legal issues involved in establishing and running a small business includes advice on whether to form a sole proprietorship, partnership, or corporation; buying a franchise or existing business; negotiating a lease; hiring and firing employees; working with independent contractors; and resolving business disputes.
Published in 1992 by the Nolo Press, Berkeley.

Money Sources for Small Business: How You Can Find Private, State, Federal, and Corporate Financing

William Alarid

This book shows how to obtain business financing from federal and state governments, venture-capital clubs, small-business investment companies, and computerized matching services.
Published in 1991 by the Puma Press, Santa Monica, CA.

The New Venture Handbook

Ronald E. Merrill and Henry D. Sedgwick

This complete guide to setting up and running an entrepreneurial business covers topics such as developing a business concept, conducting market surveys, team building, buying an existing business or franchise, and day-to-day managing.
Published in 1992 by AMACOM, Saranac Lake, NY.

The Partnership Book: How to Write a Partnership Agreement

Dennis Clifford and Ralph Warner

This step-by-step guide to drafting and writing a partnership agreement has sample clauses covering all key issues—from each partner's initial contribution to what happens if one partner leaves.
Published in 1991 by the Nolo Press, Berkeley.

The Portable MBA in Entrepreneurship

William Bygrave, editor

This book presents an overview of the most important topics and issues involved in starting, managing, and growing a business. Coverage includes entry strategies for starting a business, marketing for start-up businesses, developing a business plan, equity financing, debt and other forms of financing, external assistance for start-ups, legal and tax issues, protecting intellectual property, harvesting a business, and the economics of entrepreneurship.
Published in 1994 by John Wiley & Sons, New York.

Purchase and Sale of Small Businesses: Tax and Legal Aspects

Marc J. Lane

This publication contains more than 100 complete forms commonly used in the purchase or sale of a business.
Second edition published in 1991 by John Wiley & Sons, New York.

The Small Business Incorporation Kit

Robert L. Davidson III

This reference deals with everything from what *incorporation* means, to the pros and cons of do-it-yourself incorporation, to the actual running of the corporation.
Published in 1992 by John Wiley & Sons, New York.

Small Business Sourcebook

Carol A. Schwartz, editor

Volume I of this two-volume directory provides a small-business profile for each of 224 different small businesses, including a variety of retail, service, and manufacturing operations. The second volume includes general small-business information. These resources cover federal and state government agencies, venture-capital firms, incubators, and other sources of information and assistance.
Fifth edition published in 1992 by Gale Research, Detroit.

Starting and Operating a Small Business in [Name of State]

Loose-leaf packets are available under this title for each of the 50 states and the District of Columbia. Each packet is divided into 11 chapters. Chapters 1 through 10 cover federal laws, regulations, and tax codes that affect small businesses. These chapters are the same in each of the 51 packets. Chapter 11 in each packet deals with the particular conditions of an individual state and includes forms, checklists, and a directory of state information sources and assistance offices.
Published annually by Oasis Press/PSI Research.

The States and Small Business: A Directory of Programs and Activities

This directory is designed to help potential and existing business owners who are seeking management, financial, or procurement information and assistance at the state level. It contains a complete list of small-business development centers and subcenters and a directory of names, addresses, and telephone numbers of the SBA's ten regional advocates.
Published in 1989 by the Superintendent of Documents, U.S. Government Printing Office.

Taking Money Out of Your Corporation: Perfectly Legal Ways to Maximize Your Income

M. John Storey

This book discusses 30 techniques, ranging from compensating family members to barter to retirement planning, that are designed to maximize the personal assets of business owners.
Published in 1993 by John Wiley & Sons, New York.

GOVERNMENT AGENCIES

Small Business Administration (SBA)

The SBA offers a wide variety of programs and activities to help entrepreneurs and small businesses (usually defined as organizations with $5 million or less in yearly sales). The SBA is headquartered in Washington, DC, and has 108 field offices (see Appendix 9) for addresses and phone numbers). SBA headquarters has a toll-free (800) 827-5722 "answer desk" that provides an automated guide to information and services available through the SBA. Following are some SBA activities and the telephone numbers of their headquarters:

Financial assistance	202-205-6490
Disaster assistance	202-205-6734
Surety bonds	202-205-6540
Minority small-business development	202-205-6540
Women's business ownership	202-205-6673
Innovation, research, and technology	202-205-6450
International trade	202-205-6720
Small-business development centers	202-205-6766

Small Business Administration, 409 Third Street NW, Washington, DC 20416.
(800) 827-5722

TRADE AND PROFESSIONAL ASSOCIATIONS

American Women's Economic Development Corporation (AWED)

AWED offers programs designed specifically for women business owners and women contemplating business ownership, including expert individual counseling, training programs conducted by experienced businesspeople, networking sessions, and peer group support for any stage of business development. Services include counseling, offered at the New York office or by telephone, and the AWED hot line to answer urgent questions. AWED also offers membership in American Women in Enterprise, which includes a subscription to *Women in Enterprise* newsletter, access to a business advice hot line, and discounts on many executive services.
American Women's Economic Development Corporation and American Women in Enterprise, 641 Lexington Avenue, Ninth Floor, New York, NY 10022.
(800) 222-2933
(212) 692-9100

The MIT Enterprise Forum

This organization provides advice, support, and educational services to innovative and technology-based companies. Case presentations that address the needs of start-up as well as more established companies are conducted at meetings held twice a month.
MIT Enterprise Forum of Cambridge, Inc., Massachusetts Institute of Technology, Room W59-220, 201 Vassar Street, Cambridge, MA 02139.
(617) 253-8240
Fax: (617) 258-7264

FOR FURTHER INFORMATION

See ***National Technical Information Service/Federal Government Electronic Bulletin Boards,*** *p. 482*
The Small Business Bankruptcy Kit, *p. 396*

43

STATE AND LOCAL GOVERNMENT

The Book of the States

This publication provides comparative data on issues such as state constitutions, elections, and federal-state relations, as well as reports on problems and major issues in state finances; government reorganization, management, productivity, and efficiency; and state offices.
Published in 1992 by the Council of State Governments, Lexington, KY.

Economic Development in the States

This three-volume series includes the following titles:
Volume 1: State Business Incentives and Economic Growth: Are They Effective? A Review of the Literature. This text looks at the effect of business incentives on state economic growth. A comprehensive bibliography on state business incentives is included.
Volume 2: The Changing Arena: State Strategic Economic Development. This features new approaches to economic development in a changing economic environment. Comments from corporate executives are included.
Volume 3: The States and Business Incentives: An Inventory of Tax and Financial Incentive Programs. This volume describes what states have done by means of tax and financial programs to create, expand, and recruit business and industry.
All three volumes published in 1989 by the Council of State Governments, Lexington, KY.

Key Indicators of County Growth 1970–2010

This directory provides an overview of economic data and demographic trends of the economies in counties of the United States. It provides historical and projected data for key indicators including population, personal income, total employment, and earnings per job. Available in print and on data disks.
Published in 1992 by NPA Data Services, Washington, DC.

Moody's Municipal and Government Manual and News Reports

This loose-leaf resource offers information on 15,000 municipalities and more than 1,100 federal, state, and local government and regulatory agencies. Entries cover states, counties, cities, towns, villages, taxing districts, and school districts, and contain complete bond descriptions, Moody's ratings, and key statistics and financials. Twice-weekly news reports provide ongoing coverage of important changes and developments with regard to the states, municipalities, or government agencies.
Published annually by Moody's Investors Service (Dun & Bradstreet).
News report updates published twice weekly.

Municipal Yellow Book: Who's Who in the Leading City and County Governments and Local Authorities

This sourcebook provides names, titles, addresses, and telephone numbers of people in-

volved in the shaping and administration of policy and the writing and enforcement of regulations for city, county, and local governments. Also included are listings of all departments, agencies, subdivisions, and branches of municipal governments.
Published semiannually by Monitor Publishing Company, New York.

National Survey of State Laws

Richard A. Leiter, editor

This survey considers differences and similarities between current state laws that apply to a range of relevant business topics in all 50 states and the District of Columbia. Each law listed is treated as a separate chapter, which begins with a general description of the law, followed by state-by-state summaries that compare specific aspects of these laws.
Published in 1992 by Gale Research, Detroit.

State Administrative Officials Classified by Function

This directory groups its listings of high-ranking state administrators by function rather than title. Names, addresses, and telephone numbers of officials are provided in 147 topical areas, including such categories as child support enforcement, geographic information systems, and recycling.
Published biennially by the Council of State Governments, Lexington, KY.

State and Local Statistics Sources

M. Balachandran and S. Balachandran, editors

This collection of 40,000 citations to state and local statistics, arranged in 54 state and territorial chapters, covers more than 50 subjects, including agriculture, banks and banking, communications, foreign trade, insurance, salaries and wages, and other issues.
Second edition published in 1993 by Gale Research, Detroit.

State and Metropolitan Databook

This reference work, prepared by the Bureau of the Census of the U.S. Department of Commerce, provides a wide variety of information on the states and metropolitan areas of the United States. It includes statistics from the 1990 population count and 1987 economic census data. The information is available in print, and on diskette suitable for leading spreadsheet, database, and mapping programs.
Fourth edition published in 1991 by the Superintendent of Documents, U.S. Government Printing Office.
For diskette information, contact the Bureau of the Census at (301) 763-4100.

State Elective Officials and the Legislatures

Arranged alphabetically by state, this directory lists key executive branch officials and supreme court justices, and provides the names, addresses, party affiliations, and districts of state legislators.
Published biennially by the Council of State Governments, Lexington, KY.

State Legislative Leadership, Committees and Staff

This directory is divided into two sections: *Legislative Organization*, which offers state-by-state listings of legislative leadership committee and research agency contacts; and *Legislative Directory*, which lists leadership contacts by function for all states. The volume also provides names, addresses, and telephone numbers.
Published biennially by the Council of State Governments, Lexington, KY.

State Statistical Abstracts

Most states publish statistical abstracts containing data similar to that found in *The Statistical Abstract of the United States*. See Appendix 14, "Guide to State Statistical Abstracts."

State Yellow Book: A Directory of the Executive, Legislative and Judicial Branches of the 50 State Governments

Organized by branch of government, this directory lists more than 35,000 leaders in the executive and legislative branches of state governments. Also included are profiles all 50 states, the District of Columbia, and the insular U.S. territories, which provide information on demographics, history, and geography; fiscal, economic, and educational data; listings of military installations; and sources for obtaining public records. County information is also provided, including county names, seats, and zip codes.

Published quarterly by Monitor Publishing Company, New York.

FOR FURTHER INFORMATION

See *American Business Climate and Economic Profiles,* p. 447

Business Dateline®, p. 371
County and City Data Book: A Statistical Abstract Supplement, p. 432
Data Pamphlets (for an individual County, State, or Metropolitan Statistical Area), p. 432
The Dun & Bradstreet Reference Book of American Business, p. 423
Lesko's Info-power, p. 481
Resource Guide to State Environmental Management, p. 468
State Environmental Law Annual Report, p. 468
State Environmental Law Handbooks, p. 469
State Tax Reports, p. 556
State Trademark and Unfair Competition Law, p. 414
The States and Small Business: A Directory of Programs and Activities, p. 547
Statistical Abstract of the United States, p. 378
Telemarketer's Guide to State Laws, p. 441

44

STRATEGIC PLANNING AND JOINT VENTURES

The Art of the Long View: Planning for the Future in an Uncertain World

Peter Schwartz

This provocative and gracefully written book describes how to use a "scenario" approach to chart a company's future. The scenarios are stories that help people to visualize and chart different kinds of futures in an uncertain world.
Published in 1991 by Doubleday, New York.

Business Alliances Guide: The Hidden Competitive Weapon

Robert Porter Lynch

A comprehensive guide to planning, negotiating, and managing strategic partnerships, this source provides counsel on topics such as deciding among various types of alliances, finding the best partner, avoiding the six most costly mistakes involved in alliances, and measuring risks and rewards.
Published in 1993 by John Wiley & Sons, New York.

Collaborating to Compete: Using Strategic Alliances and Acquisitions in the Global Marketplace

Joel Bleeke and David Ernst, editors

This text explores the increasingly effective expansion methods of cross-border alliances and acquisitions. Topics include discussions on the usefulness of cross-border alliances for one's own business, the difficulties of breaking into foreign markets and dealing with the European Community, and how to

formulate decision-making techniques for structuring and managing global collaborations.
Published in 1993 by John Wiley & Sons, New York.

Competitive Advantage: Creating and Sustaining Superior Performance

Michael E. Porter

A sequel to *Competitive Strategy* (see below), this book shows managers how to evaluate the competitive position of the individual firm. A professor at Harvard Business School, Porter provides a framework of value chain analysis to look at the underlying activities of an organization.
Published in 1985 by the Free Press, New York.

Competitive Advantage of Nations

Michael E. Porter

This study is based on thorough analyses of some 100 service and manufacturing industries in ten countries. Porter theorizes on why some nations are able to compete more effectively than others in international markets.
Published in 1998 by the Free Press, New York.

Competitive Strategy: Techniques for Analyzing Industries and Competitors

Michael E. Porter

Many consider this book, by Harvard Business School's Professor Porter, to be the most

influential book on business strategy in recent decades. It focuses on the need to understand industry structure and the behavior of competitors within that structure.
Published in 1980 by the Free Press, New York.

A Directory of Strategic Management Software Tools

Planning Review magazine publishes an annual guide to software products of interest to managers and strategic planning professionals. The directory provides the name of each product; describes its functions; notes its compatibility with DOS, Windows, UNIX, ASCII, and so on; and provides supplier information. Software tools for the following areas are covered: relational spreadsheets, specialty planning tools, proprietary shareholder value models, decision support models, data analysis, project management, competitive intelligence tools, new-product introduction tools, tools for developing visual representations and models of a business, and spreadsheet add-in products.
Published annually in the July/August issue of Planning Review.

Growing Your Business Internationally: How to Form Profitable Overseas Partnerships, Alliances, and Joint Ventures

Marvin V. Bedward and Mark V. Anderson

This step-by-step guide to business expansion in international markets covers topics such as finding the right partner, negotiating the partnership, managing the relationship, and forming partnerships and alliances in Asia and Europe.
Published in 1992 by Probus Publishing, Chicago.

PIMS™ Competitive Strategy Database

This source provides financial and marketing data on strategic business units of 2,700 companies in several hundred worldwide indus-

tries. Information includes income statements, balance sheets, market share, and degree of product differentiation and quality. Available online through the Strategic Planning Institute.
Published and updated periodically by The Strategic Planning Institute, Cambridge, MA.

Real-Time Strategy: Improvising Team-Based Planning for a Fast Changing World

Lee Tom Perry, Randall G. Scott, and W. Norman Smallwood

This text is an in-depth look at how self-directed teams formulate and implement operational-level strategies in real time. The book can be useful for managers wanting to keep up to date with the evolution from top-down strategic planning to involving a much wider array of managers and business professionals in strategy development and implementation.
Published in 1993 by John Wiley & Sons, New York.

Strategic Planning: What Every Manager Must Know

George A. Steiner

This comprehensive guide to strategic planning includes topics such as organizing a planning system, acquiring and using information, identifying opportunities, developing objectives, and translating strategic plans into current decisions.
Published in 1979 by the Free Press, New York.

Strategic Planning for the Entrepreneurial Business

This self-study course offered by the American Management Association (AMA) covers a wide variety of subjects, including identifying business opportunities, expanding market share, entering new markets, and strengthening competitive position.

Published by the American Management Association, New York.

Strategic Planning Workbook

*Joseph C. Krallinger and
Karsten C. Hellebust*

This book unites theory and practice and provides a system for strategic planning. It shows how to evaluate the performance of a business critically and looks at current methods for using debt financing, cash flow, and working capital in budgeting and developing a strategic plan.
Second edition published in 1993 by John Wiley & Sons, New York.

Strategy: Seeking and Securing Competitive Advantage

*Cynthia A. Montgomery and
Michael E. Porter, editors*

This text presents seminal articles from the *Harvard Business Review*.
Twelfth edition published in 1991 by the Harvard Business School Press, Boston.

TRADE AND PROFESSIONAL ASSOCIATIONS

The Planning Forum

This international business organization is dedicated to advancing the understanding and practice of strategic management as the integrating force for improving organizational performance and achieving global competitiveness. This mission is accomplished through a variety of knowledge-based services: the annual International Strategic Management Conference, the Research & Education Foundation; *Planning Review,* a bimonthly peer-reviewed business journal; and *Network,* a monthly executive briefing.
*The Planning Forum, 5500 College Corner Pike, P.O. Box 70, Oxford, OH 45056-0070.
(513) 523-4185
Fax: (513) 523-7599*

FOR FURTHER INFORMATION

See **CEDDS: The Complete Economic and Demographic Data Source,** p. 431
Markets of the U.S. for Business Planners, p. 434
Predicasts' F & S Index of Corporate Change, p. 426

45

TAXES

Bender's Federal Tax Service

This service organizes tax information into different topical areas. Coverage includes individuals, corporations, partnerships, estate and gift taxes, business expenses, tax accounting, compensation, procedures, and administration. Available in print and CD-ROM.
Published in loose-leaf format, with monthly updates, by Matthew Bender, New York.

Bender's Master Federal Tax Handbook

This publication is an abridgment of *Bender's Federal Tax Service* (see preceding entry).
Published annually by Matthew Bender, New York.

Daily Tax Report

This subscription service provides reports each business day on tax information, policy, and court decisions.
Published every business day by the Bureau of National Affairs, Inc., Rockville, MD.

The Ernst & Young Tax Guide

This source presents information that taxpayers need each year to comply with income tax filing requirements. The guide includes *IRS Publication 17, Your Federal Income Tax,* along with comprehensive commentary, usable tax return forms, and hundreds of tips and explanations.
Published annually by John Wiley & Sons, New York.

The Federal Tax Directory

The Federal Tax Directory is an online service containing a comprehensive list of names, addresses, and telephone numbers for 17,000 tax officials in Congress, the courts, executive agencies, and states. The directory also includes the same information on tax-related organizations, corporate tax managers, international tax specialists, and tax journalists. Available online through LEXIS.
Published and updated monthly by Tax Analysts.

Federal Tax Guidebook

Alan Prigal

This guidebook explains the basic rules of income, estate, and gift taxes. Its coverage includes income and deductions, business transactions, corporate distributions, fiduciary income tax, and pension and profit-sharing plans.
Published in loose-leaf format, with semiannual updates, by Matthew Bender, New York.

International Tax Summaries: A Guide for Planning and Decisions

This guide to the tax systems of more than 100 countries in North America, South America, Europe, Asia, Africa, and the South Pacific includes information on corporate and individual taxes; nonresident tax liabilities; capital gains; available grants and incentives; controls; restrictions; and fines.
Published annually by John Wiley & Sons, New York.

S Corporation Tax Guide

Robert Jamison

This guide to the complex rules of S corporation taxation devotes special attention to tax-planning and tax-saving strategies. Topics include eligibility requirements, filing a subchapter S election, selecting the S corporation's tax year, income measurement and reporting distributions to shareholders, passive activity rules and limits, and changing from a C corporation to an S corporation.
Published annually by Harcourt Brace Jovanovich Miller, San Diego.

Small Business Tax Planner

This two-volume loose-leaf reference contains dozens of how-to tax-planning essays that are organized by subject and tailored for the small-business tax planner. A detailed topic index lists specific areas of interest, such as choosing whether to use a C corporation, an S corporation, or a partnership; reducing the cost of maintaining a qualified plan; deducting the legal expenses of a small business; planning buy-sell agreements; and more.
Published, with monthly updates, by Research Institute of America Tax Publishing Division, Valhalla, NY.

State Tax Reports

This subscription service provides specialized issues covering the state and local tax levies of each state.
Monthly reporting (twice monthly for California and New York) by Commerce Clearing House, Inc.

The Tax Adviser

This periodical reports on tax developments and presents suggestions that show how to save money in tax planning and compliance. *The Tax Adviser* reports and comments on IRS rulings and proposed regulations, court decisions, and legislation.

Published monthly by the American Institute of Certified Public Accountants, New York.

Tax Notes Today (TNT)

A comprehensive daily tax information service, this source contains both current news and full-text tax documents. In addition to standard tax documents from Congress, the IRS, and the courts, *Tax Notes Today* publishes U.S. Treasury tax correspondence, congressional testimony, and government reports. The file is updated each business day of the year, and tax documents generally appear online in full text within 24 hours of their release. Most documents are prefaced by detailed analytical summaries and are classified by Code section. This service is also available online through LEXIS and DIALOG.
Published, and updated daily, by Tax Analysts.

Tax Practice Series

This tax subscription service covers a wide variety of tax issues including alternative minimum tax, C corporations, compensation planning, compliance computation of tax liability, deductions, estate and gift taxation, exempt organizations, foreign taxation, gross income, IRS practice and procedure, partnerships, private foundations, S corporations, tax accounting, tax credits, and taxation of trusts.
Published, with weekly supplements, by the Bureau of National Affairs, Inc., Rockville, MD.

Your Federal Tax Advisor

This authoritative guide features complete A-to-Z explanations of newly enacted tax laws; an in-depth look at new tax changes, including tax breaks, revenue codes, rulings, regulations, and court decisions; practical solutions to the most common tax questions; and tax reduction strategies.
Published annually by Prentice Hall, Englewood Cliffs, NJ.

TRADE AND PROFESSIONAL ASSOCIATIONS

National Tax Association (NTA)

The NTA membership includes government and corporate tax officials, accountants, consultants, economists, attorneys, educators, and others interested in the field of taxation. Its purposes are to promote scientific, non-political study of taxation and to encourage better understanding of the common interests of national, state, and local governments in matters of taxation and public finance.

National Tax Association-Tax Institute Of America, 5310 E. Main Street, Suite 104, Columbus, OH 43213.
(614) 864-1221

FOR FURTHER INFORMATION

See **Accounting and Tax Database,** *p. 382*
The Business One Irwin Investor's Almanac, *p. 417*
FAS 109: Analysis and Comments on the New Accounting for Income Taxes, *p. 388*

TRAVEL AND RELOCATION

Craighead's International Business, Travel, and Relocation Guide to 71 Countries

Formerly *International Business Travel and Relocation*, this guide offers information about the economies, customs, communications, tours, attractions, and other aspects of 71 countries around the world. Individual country profiles are divided into five sections and include maps, statistics, restrictions, currency, culture, transportation, and health. *Sixth edition published in 1992 by Gale Research, Detroit.*

The Ernst & Young Almanac of U.S. Business Cities: A Guide to America's 66 Leading Business Centers

Prepared by Ernst & Young, this almanac provides detailed information about the business environment of 66 major American cities, including industry trends, business incentives, labor costs and availability, real estate costs, workforce educational levels, and socioeconomic data. *Published in 1992 by John Wiley & Sons, New York.*

International Herald-Tribune Guide to Business Travel: Asia

Robert K. McCabe

This business travel guide presents detailed information on transportation, business practices, currency, hotels, restaurants, and nightlife in 16 cities in Asia, including Tokyo, Hong Kong, Beijing, and Singapore. *Published in 1988 by NTC Publishing Group, Lincolnwood, IL.*

International Herald-Tribune Guide to Business Travel: Europe

Allan Tillier and Roger Beardwood

For each of 27 cities in Europe, this guide offers advice on how to conduct business and provides information on hotels, restaurants, transportation, nightlife, and attractions. Detailed maps highlight hotel locations. *Published in 1992 by NTC Publishing Group, Lincolnwood, IL.*

Worldwide Travel Information Contact Book

Burkhard Herbote, editor

This country-by-country guide offers more than 25,000 information sources for business travelers. Entries contain full contact information for national and international ministries, departments, and boards of tourism; hotel, travel, and transportation associations; travel agencies/tour operators; mapping agencies; national railways, park authorities, and departments of wildlife; mountain and ski clubs; tourist newspapers and magazines; chambers of commerce; and embassies. *Second edition published in 1992 by Gale Research, Detroit.*

For Further Information

See **Cities of the World,** p. 493
**National Technical Information
  Service/Federal Government
Electronic Bulletin Boards,** p. 482

VALUING A BUSINESS

Handbook of Business Valuation

*Thomas L. West and
Jeffrey D. Jones, editors*

A comprehensive guide to business valuation approaches and methods, this book examines subjects such as business and real estate appraisals, valuation methods, special-purpose methods, financial statements, appraisal reports, and the use and abuse of expert witnesses. A series of worksheets helps users record asset values, calculate cash flow, and compute value.
*Published in 1992 by John Wiley & Sons,
New York.*

Valuation: Measuring and Managing the Value of a Company

*Tom Copeland, Tim Koller,
and Jack Murrin*

McKinsey and Company consultants Copeland, Koller, and Murrin help readers esti-
mate the value of alternative corporate and business strategies and the value of specific programs within these strategies; assess major transactions such as mergers, acquisitions, divestitures, recapitalization, and share repurchases; and review and target the performance of business operations.
*Published in 1990 by John Wiley & Sons,
New York.*

Valuing Small Business and Professional Practices

Shannon Pratt

An authoritative step-by-step guide to business valuation, this source includes cash value analysis, valuing minority interests, and court decisions affecting the valuation of specific types of professional practices.
*Second edition published in 1993 by
Business One Irwin, Homewood, IL.*

VENTURE CAPITAL/SOURCES OF CAPITAL

Buyouts Directory of LBO Financing Sources

More than 600 companies and organizations that provide acquisition financing are listed in this directory, which features complete contact information including geographic and industry considerations, type of information required, loan/investment size range, and turnaround time.
Published biennially by Securities Data Company Publishing.

Corporate Finance Sourcebook

This directory lists and provides contact information for more than 20,000 key financial experts in 3,600 organizations providing corporate growth capital. A mergers and acquisition section, covering public offerings of the past three years and mergers and acquisitions over $100 million, is also included.
Published in 1997 by National Register Publishing, New Providence, NJ.

The Ernst & Young Guide to Raising Capital

Created by Ernst & Young, this is a guide to raising capital to foster business growth, develop new products, and expand into new markets. It provides information on a wide variety of strategies to help business owners and entrepreneurs meet their goals, including joint ventures, public issues, management buyouts, franchising, Employee Stock Ownership Plans, and cross-border alliances.
Published in 1994 by John Wiley & Sons, New York.

European Venture Capital Association (EVCA) Yearbook

This yearly volume presents the results of the annual European venture-capital survey of the following countries: Austria, Belgium, Denmark, Finland, France, Germany, Greece, Hungary, Iceland, the Republic of Ireland, Italy, the Netherlands, Norway, Portugal, Spain, Sweden, Switzerland, and the United Kingdom. It also includes a directory of all EVCA members, with full addresses, details, contact names, and an outline of each member's investments criteria.
Published annually by the European Venture Capital Association, Zavertem, Belgium.

IVCI Directory of Domestic and International Venture Groups

More than 145 venture groups in the United States and overseas are listed in this directory, which includes complete contact information on each.
Published annually by the International Venture Capital Institute, Stamford, CT.

Pratt's Guide to Venture Capital Sources

Daniel Bokser, editor

A comprehensive worldwide guide to the venture-capital industry, this resource book provides investment, operating, and management data on nearly 800 venture-capital firms. It offers current information on competitors, industry sectors, and leading venture-capital sources in the United States and Canada, and around the world. Each firm's

listing includes its name, address, telephone number, fax number, geographic/industry investment preferences, management roster, capital under management, recent investments, compensation method, project preferences, and type of financing.
Twenty-second edition published in 1998 by Venture Economics.

SBA Loans: A Step-by-Step Guide

Patrick D. O'Hara

This guide provides clarification of the Small Business Administration (SBA) guaranteed loan program, gives tips on how to apply for part of the $6 billion in loans given out or secured annually, and shows how to improve your chance of qualifying for a loan. Instruction on how to write out a business plan and fill out all required forms for a loan is also included.
Third edition published in 1998 by John Wiley & Sons, New York.

Technology Capital Network, Inc.

This not-for-profit confidential network provides high-net-worth individuals with a mechanism for examining opportunities to invest in entrepreneurial ventures. TCN also serves professional venture-capital funds and corporate investors. TCN provides entrepreneurs with a cost-effective process for reaching wealthy individuals and others interested in investing in early-stage or high-growth private companies.
MIT Enterprise Forum of Cambridge, Technology Capital Network, Inc.

Venture Capital: Where to Find It

This directory of the members of the National Association of Small Business Investment Companies includes complete contact information.
Published annually by the National Association of Small Business Investment Companies, Alexandria, VA.

Venture Capital at the Crossroads

William D. Bygrave and Jeffry A. Timmons

This book examines the role of the venture-capital industry in the creation of new businesses. Original research is provided on the dimensions of the industry, and how risk-taking and the time perspectives of its practitioners are changing.
Published in 1992 by the Harvard Business School Press, Boston.

Venture Capital Directory

More than 400 companies that offer funding for small and minority-owned businesses are listed in this book, which includes complete contact information for each.
Published annually by the Forum Publishing Company, Centerport, NY.

Venture Capital Journal

This newsletter covers the full spectrum of activities that involve or interest venture capitalists, their limited partners, and growing businesses. Features include accurate, timely data on disbursements, fund-raising totals, capital commitments, and venture-backed initial public offerings (IPOs); the "Venture Capital 100" index of aftermarket performance of leading venture-backed companies; and new techniques to improve or expand in the venture capital and private equity marketplace.
Published monthly by Securities Data Company Publishing, New York.

The Venture Capital Review

This magazine reports on issues of special relevance to the European venture capital industry.
Published quarterly by the European Venture Capital Association, Zavertem, Belgium.

European Venture Capital Association (EVCA)

The EVCA has 290 members from 22 countries. It promotes the development of venture capital in Europe through lobbying activities with the European Commission and through networking among EVCA members. The organization encourages the transnational syndication of venture-capital investments within Europe. The EVCA also runs a number of training programs. The monthly *Newsline* is published for members.
European Venture Capital Association,
Kieberpark-Minervastraat 6, Box 6, B-1930,
Zavertem, Belgium.
32 2 720 60 10
Fax: 32 2 725 30 66

National Venture Capital Association (NVCA)

The NVCA has a membership of more than 200 professional venture-capital organizations. The association fosters a broader understanding of the importance of venture capital to the vitality of the U.S. economy and seeks to stimulate the free flow of capital to young companies.
National Venture Capital Association, 1655
North Fort Meyer Drive, Suite 700,
Arlington, VA 22209.
(202) 528-4370
Fax: (703) 525-8841

FOR FURTHER INFORMATION

*See **The Business One Irwin Investor's**
Almanac, p. 417*

DIRECTORY OF PUBLISHERS, VENDORS, AND DATABASE PROVIDERS

Abbott, Langer, and Associates
548 First Street
Crete, IL 60417
(708) 672-4200

ABILL Communications
355 Park Avenue South
New York, NY 10010
(212) 592-6200

Bob Adams, Inc.
260 Center Street
Holbrook, MA 02343
(781) 767-8100
Fax (781) 767-0994

Addison Wesley Longman Ltd.
Edinburgh Gate
Harlow, Essex M2O 2JE
ENGLAND
44 (1279) 623623
Fax 44 (1279) 431059

Advertising Age
740 North Rush Street
Chicago, IL 60611
(312) 649-5200
Fax (312) 649-5331

Adweek
1515 Broadway, 12th Floor
New York, NY 10036
(212) 536-6527
Fax (212) 536-5353

AMACOM
See American Management Association

American Business Information
5711 S. 86th Circle
P.O. Box 27347
Omaha, NE 68127
(402) 593-4565
Fax (402) 331-6681

American Compensation Association
14040 N. Northsight Boulevard
Scottsdale, AZ 85260-3601
(602) 951-9191
Fax (602) 483-8352

American Demographics, Inc.
P.O. Box 68
Ithaca, NY 14851
(607) 273-6343
(800) 828-1133

American Economics Association
2014 Broadway, Suite 305
Nashville, TN 37203
(615) 322-2595

American Institute of Certified Public
   Accountants (AICPA)
1221 Avenue of the Americas
New York, NY 10036
(212) 596-6200

American Management Association
1601 Broadway
New York, NY 10019
(212) 586-8100

American Management Association
Extension Division
P.O. Box 1026
Saranac Lake, NY 12983
(518) 891-5510

American Marketing Association
250 S. Wacker Drive, Suite 200
Chicago, IL 60606
(312) 648-0536

Andrews Publications
175 Stafford Avenue
Building 4, Suite 140
Wayne, PA 19087
(800) 345-1101
Fax (610) 225-0501

Asia Press Co. Ltd.
Dowa Building 4F
2122 Ginza 7-Chome
Chiyoda-ku
Tokyo 104
JAPAN

Asian Finance Publications, Ltd.
3/F Hollywood Center
233 Hollywood Road
HONG KONG

Aspen Publishers Inc.
1185 Sixth Avenue, 37th Floor
New York, NY 10036
(212) 597-0200
Fax (212) 597-0338

ASQC Quality Press (American Society for
  Quality Control)
611 E. Wisconsin Avenue
Milwaukee, WI 53202
(414) 272-8575

Matthew Bender & Company, Inc.
2 Park Avenue, 7th Floor
New York, NY 10016-5602
(212) 448-2000

R. R. Bowker (Reed Reference Publishing)
121 Chanlon Road
New Providence, NJ 07974
(800) 521-8110

Brookings Institution
1775 Massachusetts Avenue, NW
Washington, DC 20036
(202) 797-6258
Fax (202) 797-6004

Bureau of National Affairs
9435 Key West Avenue
Rockville, MD 20850
(800) 372-1033
Fax (800) 253-0332
E-mail icustrel@bna.com
http://www.bna.com

Burwell Enterprises
3724 FM 1960 West, Suite 214
Houston, TX 77068
(281) 537-9051
Fax (281) 537-8332
http://www.burwellinc.com

Business America Associates, Inc.
2120 Greentree Road
Pittsburgh, PA 15220-1406
(412) 833-1910

Business One Irwin
1818 Ridge Road
Homewood, IL 60430
(708) 798-4477
(800) 634-3961

Business Week
1221 Avenue of the Americas
39th Floor
New York, NY 10020
(212) 512-2511

CACI Marketing Systems
1100 N. Glebe Road
Arlington, VA 22201
(800) 243-6272

Cambridge Information Group
7200 Wisconsin Avenue
Bethesda, MD 20814
(301) 961-6750

Center for the Study of Foreign Affairs
Foreign Services Institute
U.S. Department of State
2201 C Street, NW
Washington, DC 20520
(202) 647-4000

Chadwyck Healy, Inc.
1101 King Street, Suite 380
Alexandria, VA 22314
(703) 683-4890
Fax (703) 683-7589

and

The Quaram, Barnwell Road
Cambridge CB5 8SW
ENGLAND
(0223) 215 512

Clark Boardman Callaghan & Co.
375 Hudson Street
New York, NY 10014-3658
(212) 929-7500

College Placement Council
62 Highland Avenue
Bethlehem, PA 18017
(610) 868-1421
(800) 544-5272

Commerce Clearing House, Inc.
4025 W. Peterson Avenue
Chicago, IL 60646
(773) 866-6000
(800) 248-3248

CompuServe Incorporated
5000 Arlington Centre Blvd.
Columbus, OH 43220-5439
(614) 457-8600

Computer Industry Almanac
P.O. Box 600
Glenbrook, NV 89413
(702) 749-5053
(702) 749-5864

Conference Board Inc.
845 Third Avenue, 3rd Floor
New York, NY 10022-6679
(212) 759-0900
Fax (212) 980-7014

Congressional Information Service
4520 East-West Highway, Suite 800
Bethesda, MD 20814-3389
(301) 654-1550
(800) 638-8380
Fax (301) 654-4033

Congressional Quarterly, Inc.
1414 22nd Street, NW
Washington, DC 20037
(202) 887-6279
(800) 432-2250

Council of State Governments
2760 Research Park Drive
Lexington, KY 40511-8410
(606) 244-8000

Datapro Information Services
(See the Gartner Group Advisory Products)

Data-Star
2440 West El Camino Real
Mountain View, CA 94040
(800) 221-7754

and

Laupenstrasse
18 A, CH-3008
Bern
SWITZERLAND

Dearborn Trade
155 N. Wacker Drive
Chicago, IL 60606
(800) 621-9621

Demosphere International, Inc.
2735 Hartland Road
Falls Church, VA 22043
(703) 560-0440

The DIALOG Corp.
2440 West El Camino Real
Mountain View, CA 94040
(800) 334-2564

Diamond, Inc.
1-4-2 Kasumingaseki
Chiyoda-ku, Tokyo 100
JAPAN
(03) 35046381
Fax (03) 35046397

Direct Marketing Publications
c/o Direct Marketing Association, Inc.
1120 Avenue of the Americas
New York, NY 10036-8096
(212) 768-7277

Disclosure®, Inc.
5161 River Road
Bethesda, MD 20816
(301) 951-1300

Dodwell Marketing Consultants
C.P.O. Box 297
Tokyo, 100-91
JAPAN

Doubleday
1540 Broadway
New York, NY 10036
(212) 354-6500
Fax (212) 302-7985

Dow Jones and Company, Inc.
P.O. Box 300
Princeton, NJ 08543-0300
(609) 520-4000

Dow Jones and Company, Inc.
National Business Employment Weekly
P.O. Box 435
Chicopee, MA 01021
(800) 562-4868

DRI/McGraw-Hill
Data Products Division
24 Hartwell Avenue
Lexington, MA 02173
(781) 863-5100

Dun & Bradstreet Information Services
3 Sylvan Way
Parsippany, NJ 07054
(973) 605-6000
(800) 526-0651
Fax (973) 605-6911
Moody's Investor Service
(800) 342-5647

Dun & Bradstreet United Kingdom
Holmers Farm Way
High Wycombe
Bucks HP 12 4 UL
ENGLAND
(0494) 422 000
Fax (0494) 422 260

Economics and Resource Development
    Center
Asian Development Bank
P.O. Box 789
1099 Manila
PHILIPPINES

The Economist Books
Axe and Bottle Court
70 Newcomen Court
London SE1 1YT
ENGLAND

Entrepreneur Group, Inc.
2392 Morse Avenue
Irvine, CA 92614
(714) 261-2325
Fax (714) 755-4211

Euromoney Books
Plymouth Distributors Limited
Estover Plymouth PL6 7PZ
ENGLAND
Fax 44 (752) 695 668

Euromoney Publications PLC
Nestor House, Playhouse Yard
London EC4V 5EX
ENGLAND

Euromonitor PLC
87-88 Turnmill Street
London EC1M 5QU
ENGLAND
(071) 2518024
Fax (071) 6083149

Europa Publications Inc.
18 Belford Square
London WCI 3JN
ENGLAND
(071) 5808236

European Direct Marketing Association
34 rue de Gouvernement
Provisoire
13-100 Brussels
BELGIUM
2 217 63 09

European Venture Capital Association
Kieberpark-Minervastraat 6
Box 6, B-1930
Zavertem
BELGIUM
32 2 720 60 10
Fax 32 2 725 30 66

Facts on File
11 Penn Plaza, 15th Floor
New York, NY 10001
(800) 443-8323
Fax (212) 213-4578

Fairchild Publications Inc.
7 West 34th Street
New York, NY 10001-8100
(212) 630-4210

Families & Work Institute
330 Seventh Avenue
New York, NY 10001
(212) 465-2044
Fax (212) 465-8637

The Financial Times Business Information,
    Ltd.
50-64 Broadway
London, SW1 0DB

ENGLAND
(071) 7992002
Fax (071) 7992259

FIND/SVP
625 Avenue of the Americas, 6th Floor
New York, NY 10011
(212) 645-4500
(800) 346-3787

Forbes, Inc.
60 Fifth Avenue
New York, NY 10011
(212) 620-2200
Fax (212) 620-2417

Forum Publishing Co.
383 East Main Street
Centerport, NY 11721
(516) 754-5000

The Foundation Center
79 Fifth Avenue
New York, NY 10003
(212) 620-4230
(800) 424-9836

Four Commerce Park Square
23240 Chagrin Boulevard
Beachwood, OH 44122
(216) 292-8288
Fax (216) 464-7609

The Free Press
1230 Avenue of the Americas
New York, NY 10020
(800) 323-7445

Gale Research, Inc.
645 Griswold Street
835 Penobscot Building
Detroit, MI 48226
(313) 961-2242
(800) 877-4253
Fax (313) 961-6083

Garrett Park Press
4604 Waverly Avenue
Garrett Park, MD 20896
(301) 946-2553

Gartner Group Advisory Products
600 Delran Parkway
Delran, NJ 08075
(800) 328-2776
(609) 764-0100
Fax (609) 764-2812
http://www.datapro@gartner.com

General Services Administration
Federal Procurement Data Center
Washington, DC 20407
(202) 401-1529
Fax (202) 401-1546

Globetech Publishing
8 Cannon Road
Wilton, CT 06897
(203) 762-3432

Goldhirsh Group, Inc.
477 Madison Avenue
New York, NY 10022
(212) 326-2600

Government Institutes Inc.
Four Research Place
Suite 200
Rockville, MD 20850
(301) 921-2300
Fax (301) 921-0373

Government Printing Office
732 North Capitol & H Street NW
Washington, DC 20401
(202) 512-0000

Grey House Publishing Inc.
Pocket Knife Square
Lakeville, CT 06039
(860) 435-0868
(800) 562-2139
Fax (860) 435-0867

Daphne Hammond & Associates, Ltd.
2518 Fort Scott Drive
Arlington, VA 22202
(703) 683-6295
Fax (703) 415-0618

Harcourt Brace & Co.
6277 Sea Harbor Drive
Orlando, FL 32887
(407) 345-2000

Harcourt Brace & Company
525 B Street, Suite 1900
San Diego, CA 92101
(619) 231-6616
Fax (619) 699-6320

HarperCollins Publishers
10 East 53rd Street
New York, NY 10022
(212) 207-2000
(800) 242-7737

Harvard Business School Press
Division of Harvard Business School
    Publishing
60 Harvard Way
Boston, MA 02163
(617) 495-6700
(800) 988-0886
Fax (617) 496-1029

Hilit Publishing Co., Ltd.
11F-7, No. 79, Hsin-Tai 5th Rd.
Sec. 1, Shih-Ji Town
Taipei County
TAIWAN
886-2-26984565
Fax 886-2-26984980

Hoke Publications, Inc.
224 Seventh Street
Garden City, NY 11530-9823
(516) 746-6700

Henry Holt & Co., Inc.
115 West 18th Street
New York, NY 10011
(212) 886-9200
(800) 488-5233
Fax (212) 633-0748

Houghton Mifflin Co.
222 Berkeley Street
Boston, MA 02116
(617) 351-5000
(800) 225-3362

Hoovers, Inc.
1033 La Posada Drive, Suite 250
Austin, TX 78752
(512) 374-4500
Fax (512) 374-4501

Human Resource Network
6045 North Scottsdale Rd., Suite 108
Scottsdale, AZ 85250
(602) 948-1991
Fax (602) 948-1667

Hunt Scanlon Publishing
1 East Putnam Street
Greenwich, CT 06830
(203) 629-3629

ICC Publishing Inc.
156 Fifth Avenue
Suite 308
New York, NY 10010
(212) 206-1150
Fax (212) 633-6025

IFI/Plenum Data Corp.
3202 Kirkwood Highway, Suite 203
Wilmington, DE 19808
(302) 998-0478
(800) 331-4955
Fax (302) 998-0733

Inc. Business Products
Department 4413
P.O. Box 1365
Wilkes-Barre, PA 18703-1365
(800) 524-1013

Inc. Publishing
38 Commercial Wharf
Boston, MA 02110
(617) 248-8000
Fax (617) 248-8090

Information Access Company
362 Lakeside Drive
Foster City, CA 94404
(800) 321-6388
(650) 378-5200
Fax (650) 378-5368
http://www.informationaccess.com

Information USA, Inc.
(800) 955-7693

International Computer Programs
823 East Westfield Boulevard
Indianapolis, IN 46220
(317) 251-7727
Fax (317) 251-7813
http://www.turboguide.com

International Foundation of Employee
    Benefits Plans
Box 69
Brookfield, WI 53008
(414) 786-6700
Fax (414) 786-8670

International Franchise Association
1350 New York Avenue NW
Suite 900
Washington, DC 20005
(202) 628-8000

International Monetary Fund, Publication
    Services
700 19th Street NW
Suite 10-540
Washington, DC 20431
(202) 623-7430

International Venture Capital Institute, Inc.
P.O. Box 1333
Stamford, CT 06904
(203) 323-3143

Iowa State University Press
2121 South State Avenue
Ames, IA 10010
(515) 292-0140
(800) 862-6657
Fax (515) 292-3348

The Johns Hopkins University Press
Division of The Johns Hopkins University
2715 North Charles Street
Baltimore, MD 21218-4319
(410) 516-6900
(800) 537-5487
Fax (410) 516-6968

Jossey-Bass Inc. Publishers
350 Sansome Street
San Francisco, CA 94104
(415) 433-1767

Journal of Commerce
2 World Trade Center
New York, NY 10048
(212) 837-7000

Kennedy Publications
Division of Kennedy Information LLC
Kennedy Place
Route 12 S
Fitzwilliam, NH 03447
(800) 531-0007
Fax (601) 585-9555

Alfred A. Knopf, Inc.
Subsidiary of Random House, Inc.
201 East 50th Street
New York, NY 10022
(212) 751-2600
(800) 638-6460
Fax (212) 572-2593

The Korea Directory Company
371-3 Kum-Ho
4th Sung-Dong-Ku
Seoul 133-094
KOREA
82 (2) 292-5295
Fax 82 (2) 296-2969

Kyodo News International, Inc.
50 Rockefeller Plaza, Suite 815
New York, NY 10020
(212) 397-3723
(800) 536-3510
Fax (212) 397-3721

Leadership Directories
104 Fifth Avenue
2nd Floor
New York, NY 10011
(212) 627-4140
Fax (212) 645-0931

Lexis-Nexis
9443 Springboro Pike
Miamisburg, OH 45401
(800) 227-4908

Macmillan Inc.
55 Railroad Avenue
Greenwich, CT 06830
(203) 862-7500
Fax (203) 862-7712

Marquis Who's Who
A Division of Reed Elsevier Inc.
121 Chanlon Road
New Providence, NJ 07974
(908) 464-6800
Fax (908) 464-3553

Massachusetts Institute of Technology
  Libraries
Document Services, MIT Libraries
160 Memorial Drive
Building 14, Room 0551
Cambridge, MA 02139-4307
(617) 253-5667
Fax (617) 253-1690

McGraw-Hill, Inc.
1221 Avenue of the Americas
New York, NY 10020
(212) 512-2000

Media General Financial Services
318 East Cary Street
Richmond, VA 23219
(804) 649-6549

The MIT Press
5 Cambridge Center
Cambridge, MA 02142
(617) 253-5646
(800) 356-0343

Monitor Publishing Co.
104 Fifth Avenue, Second Floor
New York, NY 10011
(212) 627-4140
Fax (212) 645-0931

Robert Morris Associates
One Liberty Place
1650 Market Street
Suite 2300
Philadelphia, PA 19103-7398
(215) 446-4000
Fax (215) 446-4101

National Policy Association (NPA)
1424 16th Street NW
Suite 700
Washington, DC 20036
(202) 265-7685
Fax (202) 797-5516

National Register Publishing
A Division of Reed Elsevier Inc.
121 Chanlon Road
New Providence, NJ 07974
(800) 521-8110

National Technical Information Service
5285 Port Royal Road
Springfield, VA 22161
(703) 487-4600

National Textbook Company (NTC)
A Division of NTC Publishing Group
4255 West Touhy Avenue
Lincolnwood, IL 60646
(847) 679-5500
(800) 323-4900
Fax (847) 679-2494

Nelson Information
Subsidiary of K III Communications
    Corporation
One Gateway Plaza
Box 591
Port Chester, NY 10573
(914) 937-8400
(800) 333-6357
Fax (914) 937-8483

New Generations Research, Inc.
225 Friend Street
Boston, MA 02114
(617) 573-9550

New Strategist Publications
P.O. Box 242
Ithaca, NY 14851
(607) 273-0913

New York Law Publishing Company
345 Park Avenue South
New York, NY 10010
(800) 888-8300

The New York Times Company
229 West 43rd Street
New York, NY 10036-3959
(212) 556-1573
Fax (212) 556-6862

Nolo Press
950 Parker Street
Berkeley, CA 94710
(800) 992-6656
Fax (510) 548-5902

North American Publishing Co.
401 North Broad Street
Philadelphia, PA 19108
(215) 238-5300
Fax (215) 238-5457

Oasis Press/Hellgate Press
Imprint of PSI Research
300 North Valley Drive
Grants Pass, OR 97526
(541) 479-9464
(800) 228-2275
Fax (541) 476-1479

Omnigraphics, Inc.
Penobscot Building
Detroit, MI 48226
(313) 961-1340
(800) 234-1340
Fax (313) 961-1383

Online, Inc.
462 Danbury Road
Wilton, CT 06897
(203) 761-1466
Fax (203) 761-1444
http://www.webworldinc.com/237b.htm

Questel.ORBIT, Inc.
8000 Westpark Dr.
McLean, VA 22102
(800) 456-7248
Fax (703) 893-4632

Organization for Economic Cooperation
    and Development
OECD Washington
2001 L Street NW
Suite 650
Washington, DC 20036-4922
(202) 785-6323
(800) 456-6323
Fax (202) 785-0350

The Oryx Press
P.O. Box 33889
Phoenix, AZ 85067-3889
(602) 265-2651
(800) 279-6799
Fax (602) 265-6250

Oxbridge Communications, Inc.
150 Fifth Avenue
New York, NY 10011
(212) 741-0231
(800) 955-0231
Fax (212) 633-2938

Peterson's
Division of Thompson Information Inc.
Box 2123
Princeton, NJ 08543-2123
(609) 243-9111
(800) 338-3282
Fax (609) 243-9150

Pilot Books
Subsidiary of Ungerleider & Co., Inc.
127 Sterling Avenue
Greenport, NY 11944
(516) 477-1094
Fax (516) 477-0978

Prentice Hall
15 Columbus Circle
New York, NY 10023
(212) 373-8000

Productivity Press, Inc.
541 NE 20 Avenue
Portland, OR 97232
(503) 235-0600
(800) 394-6868
Fax (800) 394-6286

Quality Press
Division of American Society for Quality
    (ASQ)
611 E. Wisconsin Avenue
Milwaukee, WI 53203
(414) 272-8575
(800) 248-1946
Fax (414) 272-1734

Quality Services Co.
5920 Overpass Road
Santa Barbara, CA 93111-2048
(805) 964-7841
Fax (805) 964-1073

Reed Elsevier, Inc.
121 Chanlon Road
New Providence, NJ 07974
(800) 521-8110
Fax (908) 665-6688

Reed Information Services, Ltd.
Windsor Court
East Grinstead
West Sussex RH 19 1XD
ENGLAND
(0342) 326 972
Fax (0342) 317 241

Republic of the Philippines
National Statistics Office
Ramon Magsaysay Blvd.
Sta. Mesa
P.O. Box 779
Manila
PHILIPPINES 1008
632-713-7074
Fax 632-713-7073

Research Institute of America Group
117 East Stevens Avenue
Valhalla, NY 10595-1264
(800) 431-9025

Sales and Marketing Magazine
355 Park Avenue South
New York, NY 10017
(212) 592-6708

Schonfeld & Associates
One Sherwood Drive
Lincolnshire, IL 60069
(847) 948-8080
(800) 205-0030
Fax (847) 948-8096

Securities Data Company Publishing
(SDC)
40 West 57th Street
11th Floor
New York, NY 10019
(212) 765-5311

Simon & Schuster
1230 Avenue of the Americas
New York, NY 10020
(212) 698-7000
(800) 223-2348
Fax (212) 698-7007

Special Libraries Association
1700 18th Street NW
Washington, DC 20009
(202) 234-4700
Fax (202) 265-9317

SRDS (Standard Rate and Data Service)
1700 W. Higgins Rd.
Des Plaines, IL 60018
(847) 375-5000
(800) 851-7737
Fax (847) 375-5001

Staff Directories, Ltd.
815 Slaters Lane
Alexandria, VA 22314
(703) 739-0900

Standard & Poor's
25 Broadway
New York, NY 10004-1064
(212) 208-8000
(800) 852-1641
Fax (212) 412-0241

Statistics Canada
Statistical Reference Center
Lobby of R. H. Coats Building
Holland Avenue
Tunney's Pasture
Ottawa, Ontario K1A 0T6
CANADA
(613) 951-8116
Fax (613) 951-0581

Stock Exchange of Singapore, Ltd.
20 Cecio St.
Singapore 049705
REPUBLIC OF SINGAPORE
535-3788
Fax 535-0775

Stockton Press
Division of Grove's Dictionaries Inc.
345 Park Avenue South
New York, NY 10010
(212) 689-9200
(800) 221-2123
Fax (212) 689-9711

The Strategic Planning Institute
1030 Massachusetts Avenue
Cambridge, MA 02138
(617) 491-9200
Fax (617) 491-1634

Tax Analysts
6830 North Fairfax Avenue
Arlington, VA 22213
(800) 955-2444
Fax (703) 533-4444

Ten Speed Press
Box 7123
Berkeley, CA 94707
(510) 559-1600
(800) 841-2665
Fax (510) 524-1052

Thomas Publishing Co., Inc.
5 Penn Plaza
New York, NY 10001
(212) 695-0500

Thomson & Thomson
500 Victory Road
North Quincy, MA 02171-3145
(800) 692-8833
(617) 490-1600
Fax (617) 786-8273
http://www.thomson-thomson.com

Thomson Financial Networks
Division of The Thomson Corporation
4709 Golf Road
6th Floor
Skokie, IL 60076-1253
(847) 676-9600
(800) 321-3373
Fax (847) 933-8101

Transnational Juris Publications
One Bridge Street
Irvington-on-Hudson, NY 10533
(914) 591-4288
Fax (914) 591-2688

UMI/Data Courier
P.O. Box 1346
Ann Arbor, MI 48106-1346
(502) 583-4111
(800) 521-0600
Fax (502) 589-5572
http://www.umi.com

United Nations Bookstore
United Nations
Room GA-32, Lower Level
New York, NY 10017
(212) 963-7680
(800) 553-3210

United States Bureau of the Census
Washington, DC 20233
(301) 457-4608

  Census Customer Services
  Federal Building 3
  4700 Silver Hill Rd.

Suitland, MD 20746
(301) 457-4100 order
(301) 457-4714 general information
Fax (301) 457-3842

Census Public Information Office
(301) 457-3030
Fax (301) 457-3670

Census CD-ROM
(301) 457-4100

United States Copyright Office
Register of Copyrights
Library of Congress
Washington, DC 20559
(202) 707-3000
Fax (202) 707-6859

United States Government Printing Office
Superintendent of Documents
732 N. Capitol
Washington, DC 20401
(202) 512-0000

University of California Press
2120 Berkeley Way
Berkeley, CA 94720
(510) 642-4247
(800) 822-6657
Fax (510) 643-7127

University Microfilms International (UMI)
Box 1346
Ann Arbor, MI 48106-1346
(313) 761-4700
(800) 521-0600
Fax (313) 665-5022

Value Line Publishing
220 E. 42nd St.
New York, NY 10017-5891
(212) 907-1500
Fax (212) 907-1925

Van Nostrand Reinhold
Division of International Thomson
  Publishing
115 Fifth Avenue
New York, NY 10003
(212) 254-3232

Warren, Gorham & Lamont
Subsidiary of Research Institute of America
    Inc.
395 Hudson Street
New York, NY 10014
(212) 971-5000
(800) 922-0606

Washington Researchers Ltd.
Box 19005
Washington, DC 20036-9005
(202) 333-3533
Fax (202) 625-0656

John Wiley & Sons, Inc.
605 Third Avenue
10th Floor
New York, NY 10158
(212) 850-6000
(800) 225-5945

H. W. Wilson Company
950 University Avenue
Bronx, NY 10452
(718) 588-8400
(800) 367-6770
Fax (800) 590-1617
E-mail custserv@hwwilson.com
http://www.hwwilson.com

Woods & Poole Economics, Inc.
1794 Columbia Road NW, Suite 4

Washington, DC 20009-2808
(202) 332-7111
(800) 786-1915
Fax (202) 332-6466

World Almanac Books
Subsidiary of K-III Reference Corporation
One International Boulevard
Suite 444
Mahwah, NJ 07495
(201) 529-6860
Fax (201) 529-6901

The World Bank
Publications Department
1818 H Street, NW
Washington, DC 20006
(202) 477-1234

Wyatt Data Services
218 Route 17 North
Rochelle Park, NJ 07662
(201) 843-1177

Ziff-Davis Press
Division of Macmillan Computer
    Publishing
5903 Christie Avenue
Emeryville, CA 94608
(510) 601-2000
(800) 428-5331
Fax (510) 601-2099

Appendixes

APPENDIX 1

INTERNATIONAL TIME ZONES
Standard Time in 100 Major Cities around the World
When It Is 12 Noon in New York City

City	Time
Alexandria, Egypt	7:00 P.M.
Amsterdam, Netherlands*	6:00 P.M.
Anchorage, Alaska	7:00 P.M.
Asunción, Paraguay	1:00 P.M.
Athens, Greece	7:00 P.M.
Auckland, New Zealand	5:00 P.M. (next day)
Baghdad, Iraq	8:00 P.M.
Bangkok, Thailand	12:00 midnight
Beijing, China	1:00 A.M. (next day)
Belgrade, Yugoslavia	6:00 P.M.
Berlin, Germany	6:00 P.M.
Bogotá, Colombia	12:00 noon
Bombay, India	10:30 P.M.
Boston, Massachusetts	12:00 noon
Brussels, Belgium*	6:00 P.M.
Bucharest, Romania	7:00 P.M.
Budapest, Hungary	6:00 P.M.
Buenos Aires, Argentina*	2:00 P.M.
Cairo, Egypt	7:00 P.M.
Calcutta, India	10:30 P.M.
Cape Town, Republic of South Africa	7:00 P.M.
Caracas, Venezuela	1:00 P.M.
Casablanca, Morocco*	6:00 P.M.
Chicago, Illinois	11:00 A.M.
Colombo, Sri Lanka (Ceylon)	10:30 P.M.
Copenhagen, Denmark	6:00 P.M.
Delhi, India	10:30 P.M.
Denver, Colorado	10:00 A.M.
Detroit, Michigan	12:00 noon
Dublin, Ireland	5:00 P.M.
Geneva, Switzerland	6:00 P.M.
Glasgow, Scotland	5:00 P.M.
Halifax, Nova Scotia	1:00 P.M.
Havana, Cuba	12:00 noon
Helsinki, Finland	7:00 P.M.
Ho Chi Minh City (Saigon), Vietnam	1:00 A.M. (next day)
Hong Kong, China	1:00 A.M. (next day)
Honolulu, Hawaii	7:00 A.M.
Houston, Texas	11:00 A.M.
Istanbul, Turkey	7:00 P.M.
Jakarta, Indonesia	12:00 midnight
Jerusalem, Israel	7:00 P.M.
Johannesburg, Republic of South Africa	7:00 P.M.
Juneau, Alaska	9:00 A.M.
Karachi, Pakistan	10:00 P.M.
Kuala Lumpur, Malaysia	12:30 A.M. (next day)

City	Time
La Paz, Bolivia	1:00 P.M.
Lima, Peru	12:00 noon
Lisbon, Portugal*	6:00 P.M.
London, England	5:00 P.M.
Los Angeles, California	9:00 A.M.
Madrid, Spain*	6:00 P.M.
Manila, Philippines	1:00 A.M.
Melbourne, Australia	3:00 A.M.
Mexico City, Mexico	11:00 A.M.
Miami, Florida	12:00 noon
Montevideo, Uruguay	2:00 P.M.
Montreal, Quebec	12:00 noon
Moscow, Russia*	8:00 P.M.
Nairobi, Kenya	8:00 P.M.
Nome, Alaska	6:00 A.M.
Oslo, Norway	6:00 P.M.
Ottawa, Ontario	12:00 noon
Panama City, Panama	12:00 noon
Paris, France*	6:00 P.M.
Perth, Australia	1:00 A.M. (next day)
Philadelphia, Pennsylvania	12:00 noon
Prague, Czech Republic	6:00 P.M.
Quito, Ecuador	12:00 noon
Rangoon, Burma	11:30 P.M.
Regina, Saskatchewan	10:00 A.M.
Reykjavík, Iceland	4:00 P.M.
Rio de Janeiro, Brazil	2:00 P.M.
Rome, Italy	6:00 P.M.
Saint John's, Newfoundland	1:30 P.M.
Saint Louis, Missouri	11:00 A.M.
Saint Petersburg, Russia	8:00 P.M.
Salt Lake City, Utah	10:00 A.M.
San Francisco, California	9:00 A.M.
San Juan, Puerto Rico	1:00 P.M.
Santiago, Chile	1:00 P.M.
São Paulo, Brazil	2:00 P.M.
Seattle, Washington	9:00 A.M.
Shanghai, China	1:00 A.M. (next day)
Singapore	12:30 A.M. (next day)
Sofia, Bulgaria	7:00 P.M.
Stockholm, Sweden	6:00 P.M.
Sydney, Australia	3:00 A.M. (next day)
Tehran, Iran	8:30 P.M.
Tel Aviv, Israel	7:00 P.M.
Tokyo, Japan	2:00 A.M. (next day)
Toronto, Ontario	12:00 noon
Vancouver, British Columbia	9:00 A.M.
Vienna, Austria	6:00 P.M.
Vladivostok, Russia*	3:00 A.M. (next day)
Warsaw, Poland	6:00 P.M.
Washington, D.C.	12:00 noon
Wellington, New Zealand	5:00 A.M. (next day)
Winnipeg, Manitoba	11:00 A.M.
Zürich, Switzerland	6:00 P.M.

* Time is one hour in advance of the standard meridian.

APPENDIX 2

WEIGHTS AND MEASUREMENTS CONVERSIONS
Approximate Conversion Measures
Source: Statistical Abstract of the United States.

Abbreviation	When you know conventional	Multiply by	To find metric	Abbreviation
in	inch	2.54	centimeter	cm
ft	foot	30.48	centimeter	cm
yd	yard	0.91	meter	m
mi	mile	1.61	kilometer	km
in^2	square inch	6.45	square centimeter	cm^2
ft^2	square foot	0.09	square meter	m^2
yd^2	square yard	0.84	square meter	m^2

APPENDIX 3

THE 100 BEST COMPANIES TO WORK FOR IN AMERICA

Source: Robert Levering, Milton Moskowitz, and Maura Griffin Solovar, *Fortune* magazine, January 12, 1998, pp. 84–95, http://pathfinder.com/fortune/1998/980112/lis.html. Reprinted by permission.

Acipco
Acxiom
Adobe Systems
A. G. Edwards
Alagasco
AlliedSignal
American Management Systems
Amgen
Analog Devices
Apogee
Baldor Electric
Baptist Health Systems
BE&K
Beaumont (Wm.) Hospital
Bright Horizons
Bureau of National Affairs
Cisco Systems
CMP Media
Compaq Computer
Corning
Deere
Deloitte & Touche
Donnelley
Eddie Bauer
Erie Insurance
Fannie Mae
Federal Express
Fel-Pro
First Tennessee Bank
Four Seasons Hotels
Fuller (H.B.)
General Mills
Gillette
Glaxo Wellcome

Goldman Sachs
Grainger (W.W.)
Granite Rock
Great Plains Software
Hallmark Cards
Harley-Davidson
Herman Miller
Hewlett-Packard
Honda of America Mfg.
Intel
Interface
Johnson & Johnson
Johnson (S.C.) Wax
Kingston Technology
Lands' End
L.L. Bean
Life Technologies
Los Angeles Dodgers
Lowe's Companies
Lucas Digital
Marriott International
Mary Kay Cosmetics
Mattel
MBNA
McCormick
Medtronic
Merck
Merrill Lynch
Microsoft
Minnesota Mining and Manufacturing
Moog
Morgan (J. P.)
Morrison & Foerster

Motorola
Nordstrom
Odetics
Ohio National Financial
Patagonia
PeopleSoft
Procter & Gamble
Publix Super Markets
Quad/Graphics
REI
Rosenbluth Intl.
SAS Institute
Security Benefit
Shell Oil
Smucker (J. M.)
Southwest Airlines
St. Paul Companies
Starbucks
Steelcase
Sun Microsystems
Synovus Financial
TDIndustries
Tennant
Texas Instruments
Timberland
UNUM
USAA
Valassis Communications
Wegmans Food Markets
Whole Foods Market
W. L. Gore
Worthington Industries
Xerox

APPENDIX 4

THE FORTUNE 100
The Largest U.S. Corporations

Source: Fortune magazine, April 27, 1998, pp. F1–F3. Reprinted by permission.

Rank 1997	Rank 1996	Company	Location	Revenues $ million	Revenues % of change from 1996
1	1	General Motors	Detroit, MI	178,174	5.8
2	2	Ford Motor	Dearborn, MI	153,627	4.5
3	3	Exxon	Irving, TX	122,379*	2.5
4	4	Wal-Mart Stores	Bentonville, AR	119,299	12.4
5	5	General Electric	Fairfield, CT	90,840	14.7
6	6	Intl. Business Machines	Armonk, NY	78,508	3.4
7	9	Chrysler	Auburn Hills, MI	61,147	−0.4
8	8	Mobil	Fairfax, VA	59,978*	−17.0
9	10	Philip Morris	New York, NY	56,114*	2.9
10	7	AT&T	New York, NY	53,261	−28.5
11	36	Boeing	Seattle, WA	45,800	101.9
12	11	Texaco	White Plains, NY	45,187*	1.4
13	12	State Farm Insurance Cos.	Bloomington, IL	43,957	2.8
14	16	Hewlett-Packard	Palo Alto, CA	42,895	11.7
15	14	E. I. du Pont de Nemours	Wilmington, DE	41,304*	4.1
16	17	Sears Roebuck	Hoffman Estates, IL	41,296	8.0
17	40	Travelers Group	New York, NY	37,609	76.2
18	13	Prudential Ins. Co. of America	Newark, NJ	37,073	N/A
19	15	Chevron	San Francisco, CA	36,376*	−6.0
20	18	Procter & Gamble	Cincinnati, OH	35,764	1.4
21	20	Citicorp	New York, NY	34,697	6.4
22	19	Amoco	Chicago, IL	32,836*	0.3
23	22	Kmart	Troy, MI	32,183	2.4
24	30	Merrill Lynch	New York, NY	31,731	26.9
25	33	J.C. Penney	Plano, TX	30,546	29.2
26	23	American International Group	New York, NY	30,520	8.2
27	25	Chase Manhattan Corp.	New York, NY	30,381	10.8
28	99	Bell Atlantic	New York, NY	30,194	130.8
29	24	Motorola	Schaumburg, IL	29,794	6.5
30	N/A	TIAA-CREF	New York, NY	29,348	18.5
31	21	PepsiCo	Purchase, NY	29,292†	−7.4
32	26	Lockheed Martin	Bethesda, MD	28,069	4.4
33	29	Fannie Mae	Washington, DC	27,777	10.9
34	27	Dayton Hudson	Minneapolis, MN	27,757	9.4
35	162	Morgan Stanley Dean Witter Discover	New York, NY	27,132	200.5
36	28	Kroger	Cincinnati, OH	26,567	5.5
37	N/A	Lucent Technologies	Murray Hill, NJ	26,360	N/A
38	43	Intel	Santa Clara, CA	25,070	20.3
39	32	Allstate	Northbrook, IL	24,949	2.7
40	85	SBC Communications	San Antonio, TX	24,856	78.8
41	34	United Technologies	Hartford, CT	24,713	5.1
42	60	Compaq Computer	Houston, TX	24,584	35.8
43	35	Metropolitan Life Insurance	New York, NY	24,374	4.9
44	50	Home Depot	Atlanta, GA	24,156	23.6
45	31	ConAgra	Omaha, NE	24,002	−3.3
46	48	Merck	Whitehouse Station, NJ	23,637	19.2

Rank				Revenues	
1997	1996	Company	Location	$ million	% of change from 1996
47	38	BankAmerica Corp.	San Francisco, CA	23,585	6.9
48	41	GTE	Stamford, CT	23,260	9.0
49	39	Johnson & Johnson	New Brunswick, NJ	22,629	4.7
50	65	Safeway	Pleasanton, CA	22,484	30.2
51	55	Walt Disney	Burbank, CA	22,473	19.9
52	37	United Parcel Service	Atlanta, GA	22,458	0.4
53	49	Costco	Issaquah, WA	21,874	11.8
54	62	NationsBank Corp.	Charlotte, NC	21,734	24.1
55	42	USX	Pittsburgh, PA	21,057*	−0.1
56	53	BellSouth	Atlanta, GA	20,561	8.0
57	94	Enron	Houston, TX	20,273	52.5
58	44	International Paper	Purchase, NY	20,096	−0.2
59	54	CIGNA	Philadelphia, PA	20,038	5.7
60	45	Dow Chemical	Midland, MI	20,018	−0.2
61	57	Sara Lee	Chicago, IL	19,734	6.0
62	59	MCI Communications	Washington, DC	19,653	6.3
63	46	Loews	New York, NY	19,648*	−1.6
64	52	Atlantic Richfield	Los Angeles, CA	19,272*	0.5
65	56	American Stores	Salt Lake City, UT	19,139	2.5
66	68	Caterpillar	Peoria, IL	18,925	14.5
67	63	New York Life Insurance	New York, NY	18,899	8.9
68	58	Coca-Cola	Atlanta, GA	18,868	1.7
69	47	Columbia/HCA Healthcare	Nashville, TN	18,819	−5.5
70	61	AMR	Fort Worth, TX	18,570	4.6
71	67	Aetna	Hartford, CT	18,540	11.0
72	51	Xerox	Stamford, CT	18,166	−6.9
73	64	American Express	New York, NY	17,760	2.8
74	73	J. P. Morgan & Co.	New York, NY	17,701	11.6
75	71	UAL	Elk Grove Tnshp., IL	17,378	6.2
76	66	RJR Nabisco Holdings	New York, NY	17,057*	−0.0
77	80	Lehman Brothers Holdings	New York, NY	16,883	18.4
78	76	Bristol-Myers Squibb	New York, NY	16,701	10.9
79	113	Ingram Micro	Santa Ana, CA	16,582	37.9
80	70	Supervalu	Eden Prairie, MN	16,552	0.4
81	300	Duke Energy	Charlotte, NC	16,309	242.8
82	77	Ameritech	Chicago, IL	15,998	7.2
83	75	Federated Department Stores	Cincinnati, OH	15,668	2.9
84	74	Phillips Petroleum	Bartlesville, OK	15,424*	−2.4
85	153	PG&E Corp.	San Francisco, CA	15,400	60.2
86	69	Fleming	Oklahoma City, OK	15,373	−6.8
87	102	US West	Englewood, CO	15,352	18.9
88	N/A	Electronic Data Systems	Plano, TX	15,236	5.5
89	81	Minnesota Mining & Mfg.	St. Paul, MN	15,070	5.9
90	82	Sprint	Westwood, KS	14,874	4.5
91	72	Eastman Kodak	Rochester, NY	14,713	−9.4
92	89	Albertson's	Boise, ID	14,690	6.6
93	84	AlliedSignal	Morristown, NJ	14,472	3.6
94	92	Sysco	Houston, TX	14,455	7.9
95	110	Federal Home Loan Mortgage	McLean, VA	14,399	18.8
96	114	First Union Corp.	Charlotte, NC	14,329	19.6
97	123	Fluor	Irvine, CA	14,299	29.8
98	83	American Home Products	Madison, NJ	14,196	0.8
99	93	Archer Daniels Midland	Decatur, IL	13,853	4.0
100	108	Raytheon	Lexington, MA	13,674	10.9

* Excise taxes have been deducted.
† Includes revenues of discontinued operations of at least 10 percent.

APPENDIX 5

THE WORLD'S LARGEST CORPORATIONS

Source: Fortune magazine, August 4, 1997. Reprinted by permission.

Rank 1996	Rank 1995	Company	Location	$ million	% change from 1995
1	4	General Motors	U.S.	168,369.0	(0.3)
2	7	Ford Motor	U.S.	146,991.0	7.2
3	2	Mitsui	Japan	144,942.8	—
4	1	Mitsubishi	Japan	140,203.7	—
5	3	Itochu	Japan	135,542.1	—
6	10	Royal Dutch/Shell Group	Brit./Neth.	128,174.5	16.7
7	6	Marubeni	Japan	124,026.9	—
8	9	Exxon	U.S.	119,434.0	8.6
9	5	Sumitomo	Japan	119,281.3	—
10	8	Toyota Motor	Japan	108,702.0	(2.1)
11	12	Wal-Mart Stores	U.S.	106,147.0	12.0
12	20	General Electric	U.S.	79,179.0	13.1
13	11	Nissho Iwai	Japan	78,921.2	—
14	15	Nippon Telegraph & Telephone	Japan	78,320.7	(4.4)
15	18	International Business Machines	U.S.	75,947.0	5.6
16	13	Hitachi	Japan	75,669.0	(10.1)
17	16	AT&T	U.S.	74,525.0	(6.4)
18	14	Nippon Life Insurance	Japan	72,575.0	(12.8)
19	22	Mobil	U.S.	72,267.0	8.3
20	17	Daimler-Benz	Germany	71,589.3	(0.9)
21	27	British Petroleum	Britain	69,851.9	22.6
22	19	Matsushita Electric Industrial	Japan	68,147.5	(3.2)
23	24	Volkswagen	Germany	66,527.5	8.2
24	34	Daewoo	South Korea	65,160.2	27.2
25	25	Siemens	Germany	63,704.7	5.0
26	30	Chrysler	U.S.	61,397.0	15.4
27	23	Nissan Motor	Japan	59,118.2	(5.5)
28	44	Allianz	Germany	56,577.2	1.9
29	29	U.S. Postal Service	U.S.	56,402.0	3.9
30	31	Philip Morris	U.S.	54,553.0	2.7
31	38	Unilever	Brit./Neth.	52,067.4	4.7
32	41	Fiat	Italy	50,509.0	10.0
33	40	Sony	Japan	50,277.9	5.7
34	26	Dai-Ichi Mutual Life Insurance	Japan	49,144.7	(15.3)
35	50	IRI	Italy	49,055.7	17.1
36	39	Nestlé	Switzerland	48,932.5	2.4
37	32	Toshiba	Japan	48,415.8	(8.7)
38	46	Honda Motor	Japan	46,994.5	6.7
39	47	Elf Aquitaine	France	46,818.0	7.6
40	21	Tomen	Japan	46,506.3	—
41	75	Bank Of Tokyo-Mitsubishi	Japan	46,451.0	42.0
42	42	VEBA Group	Germany	45,246.2	(2.2)
43	33	Tokyo Electric Power	Japan	44,735.0	(14.6)
44	61	Texaco	U.S.	44,561.0	21.1
45	36	Sumitomo Life Insurance	Japan	44,063.3	(13.1)
46	118	Sunkyong	South Korea	44,031.0	—
47	45	NEC	Japan	43,932.7	(3.6)

Rank		Company	Location	$ million	% change from 1995
1996	1995				
48	48	Électricité de France	France	43,658.7	0.3
49	52	State Farm Insurance Companies	U.S.	42,781.2	4.8
50	43	Deutsche Telekom	Germany	41,910.7	(9.2)
51	53	Philips Electronics	Netherlands	41,036.5	2.2
52	49	Union des Assurances de Paris	France	40,736.7	(3.0)
53	51	Prudential Insurance Company of America	U.S.	40,175.0	(2.8)
54	54	Fujitsu	Japan	39,982.3	2.6
55	58	E. I. du Pont de Nemours	U.S.	39,689.0	5.5
56	55	Deutsche Bank	Germany	39,413.0	4.2
57	59	RWE Group	Germany	39,289.2	5.5
58	64	ENI	Italy	38,843.5	5.5
59	81	Chevron	U.S.	38,691.0	20.6
60	84	Hewlett-Packard	U.S.	38,420.0	21.9
61	66	Sears, Roebuck	U.S.	38,236.0	8.7
62	28	Metro Holding	Switzerland	36,567.7	(21.5)
63	60	Renault	France	35,979.1	(2.5)
64	72	ING Group	Netherlands	35,912.5	8.0
65	71	Procter & Gamble	U.S.	35,284.0	5.5
66	79	BMW (Bayerische Motor Werke)	Germany	34,727.9	7.9
67	77	Crédit Agricole	France	34,619.6	5.9
68	70	ABB Asea Brown Boveri	Switzerland	34,574.0	2.5
69	35	Nichimen	Japan	34,545.1	—
70	101	Total	France	34,513.0	26.8
71	67	Samsung	South Korea	34,286.5	(2.2)
72	74	Peugeot	France	33,914.7	2.5
73	107	PDVSA	Venezuela	33,855.0	30.0
74	63	Hoechst	Germany	33,838.8	(7.1)
75	57	Meiji Life Insurance	Japan	33,175.4	(12.8)
76	65	Mitsubishi Electric	Japan	33,072.6	(9.1)
77	100	Amoco	U.S.	32,726.0	18.3
78	106	AXA	France	32,681.4	24.9
79	82	Citicorp	U.S.	32,605.0	2.9
80	62	Mitsubishi Motors	Japan	32,601.2	(11.0)
81	76	CIE Générale des Eaux	France	32,428.8	(0.7)
82	78	BASF	Germany	32,409.6	0.5
83	87	Bayer	Germany	32,298.0	3.8
84	86	GAN	France	32,259.5	3.3
85	80	Alcatel Alsthom Group	France	31,683.8	(1.5)
86	89	PepsiCo	U.S.	31,645.0	4.0
87	69	Kmart	U.S.	31,437.0	(9.3)
88	37	Kanematsu	Japan	30,868.8	—
89	115	Zurich Insurance	Switzerland	30,760.5	22.3
90	111	Ssangyong	South Korea	30,530.8	20.2
91	95	Carrefour	France	30,277.1	4.5
92	56	Industrial Bank of Japan	Japan	30,208.0	(21.0)
93	119	Assicurazioni Generali	Italy	29,618.5	22.6
94	92	France Télécom	France	29,564.5	(1.6)
95	314	Novartis	Switzerland	29,310.2	127.3
96	104	HSBC Holdings	Britain	28,859.9	8.2
97	140	PEMEX (Petróleos Mexicanos)	Mexico	28,429.5	27.3
98	73	Daiei	Japan	28,281.2	(14.7)
99	94	VIAG	Germany	28,207.7	(3.6)
100	109	American International Group	U.S.	28,205.3	9.0

APPENDIX 6

AMERICA'S MOST ADMIRED COMPANIES
Source: Edward A. Robinson, *Fortune* magazine, March 3, 1997, p. 70. Reprinted by permission.

1. Coca-Cola 8.87
2. Mirage Resorts 8.44
3. Merck 8.34
4. UPS 8.31
5. Microsoft 8.29
6. Johnson & Johnson 8.27
7. Intel 8.27
8. Pfizer 8.23
9. Procter & Gamble 8.18
10. Berkshire Hathaway 8.18
11. 3M 8.14
12. Hewlett-Packard 8.06
13. Corning 8.03
14. Home Depot 7.99
15. Levi Strauss Associates 7.97
16. Walt Disney 7.97
17. McDonald's 7.95
18. General Electric 7.92
19. Gillette 7.91
20. Boeing 7.89
21. Enron 7.89
22. Rubbermaid 7.81
23. Herman Miller 7.78
24. Cardinal Health 7.66
25. Goodyear Tire & Rubber 7.64
26. USAA 7.62
27. Motorola 7.61
28. American Intl. Group 7.5829.
29. J. P. Morgan 7.57
31. Omnicom Group 7.56
32. M. A. Hanna 7.52
33. Interpublic Group 7.50
34. American Brands 7.49
35. Kimberly-Clark 7.49
36. DuPont 7.48
37. Oracle 7.46
38. Merrill Lynch 7.46
39. Fed. Natl. Mortgage Assn. 7.45
40. Mobil 7.45
41. Norfolk Southern 7.44
42. Albertson's 7.41
43. Caterpillar 7.41
44. Exxon 7.40
45. Southwest Airlines 7.39
46. Coca-Cola Enterprises 7.38
47. Alcoa 7.38
48. Leggett & Platt 7.37
49. Anheuser-Busch 7.36
50. Deere 7.35
51. Emerson Electric 7.35

52. Xerox 7.35
53. Manpower 7.34
54. General Re 7.32
55. Sun Microsystems 7.32
56. Citicorp 7.31
57. Walgreen 7.30
58. Fed. Home Loan Mtg. Assn. 7.30
59. Freeport-McMoRan 7.30
60. Williams 7.27
61. Chubb 7.26
62. Abbott Laboratories 7.24
63. Wal-Mart Stores 7.24
64. Marriott International 7.24
65. Morgan Stanley Group 7.23
66. Liz Claiborne 7.23
67. Southern 7.22
68. Freeport-McMoRan C&G 7.22
69. Sysco 7.21
70. Fluor 7.20
71. Eli Lilly 7.19
72. Northwestern Mut. Life 7.18
73. Campbell Soup 7.18
74. Lockheed Martin 7.17
75. Armstrong World Ind. 7.17
76. CUC International 7.17
77. Eastman Kodak 7.16
78. Federal Express 7.16
79. Chrysler 7.15
80. Compaq Computer 7.15
81. FPL Group 7.14
82. General Mills 7.14
83. Sara Lee 7.13
84. Dow Chemical 7.12
85. Columbia/HCA Healthcare 7.11
86. PanEnergy 7.10
87. Tyco International 7.10
88. HON Industries 7.10
89. Publix Super Markets 7.10
90. Nucor 7.09
91. State Farm Group 7.08
92. Amoco 7.07
93. United HealthCare 7.07
94. Olsten 7.06
95. Nordstrom 7.06
96. Dow Jones 7.06
97. Washington Mutual 7.06
98. ConAgra 7.06
99. Unifi 7.05
100. Sears Roebuck 7.05
101. Schering-Plough 7.05

102. IBM 7.04
103. Springs Industries 7.03
104. Monsanto 7.03
105. Estée Lauder 7.01
106. Nestlé 6.99
107. Gannett 6.98
108. Tribune 6.97
109. Premark International 6.96
110. Shaw Industries 6.96
111. Golden West Financial 6.96
112. Household International 6.95
113. PepsiCo 6.95
114. Union Pacific 6.95
115. Safeway 6.95
116. AMR 6.94
117. Alco Standard 6.94
118. Hilton Hotels 6.94
119. AlliedSignal 6.94
120. Charles Schwab 6.93
121. Circus Circus Enterprises 6.92
122. American Home Products 6.92
123. Illinois Tool Works 6.92
124. United Technologies 6.91
125. Allstate 6.90
126. CPC International 6.89
127. McKesson 6.89
128. Clorox 6.89
129. CSX 6.88
130. Honeywell 6.88
131. Chevron 6.87
132. Brunswick 6.87
133. SBC Communications 6.86
134. Burlington Northern Santa Fe 6.85
135. Ryder System 6.85
136. BankAmerica 6.85
137. VF 6.84
138. H. J. Heinz 6.84
139. Bristol-Myers Squibb 6.83
140. A. Schulman 6.83
141. Colgate-Palmolive 6.82
142. New York Life Insurance 6.80
143. Cyprus Amax Minerals 6.80
144. Russell 6.79
145. Genuine Parts 6.79
146. Textron 6.78

147. Philip Morris 6.76
148. Marsh & McLennan 6.76
149. Sonat 6.76
150. Cooper Tire & Rubber 6.76
151. Texas Instruments 6.75
152. NationsBank 6.74
153. PacifiCare Health Systems 6.74
154. Unilever 6.74
155. American Express 6.74
156. Banc One 6.73
157. Arrow Electronics 6.73
158. Vulcan Materials 6.72
159. Mitchell Energy & Devel. 6.71
160. Intl. Flavors & Fragrances 6.71
161. Travelers Group 6.70
162. Dell Computer 6.70
163. NGC 6.70
164. Host Marriott 6.69
165. KN Energy 6.67
166. Phelps Dodge 6.67
167. First Data 6.67
168. ADVO 6.67
169. American Honda Motor 6.66
170. Computer Associates Intl. 6.66
171. Turner Broadcasting 6.66
172. Dean Witter Discover 6.66
173. May Department Stores 6.63
174. Brinker International 6.62
175. Parker Hannifin 6.61
176. Kroger 6.60
177. Ingersoll-Rand 6.60
178. Automatic Data Proc. 6.60
179. Circuit City Stores 6.60
180. ITT Hartford Group 6.60
181. UAL 6.58
182. Office Depot 6.58
183. J.C. Penney 6.56
184. Bergen Brunswig 6.54
185. Knight-Ridder 6.54
186. Harrah's Entertainment 6.54
187. Toys "R" Us 6.54
188. Johnson Controls 6.53
189. BP America 6.53
190. Ford Motor 6.52
191. Texaco 6.52
192. Kimball International 6.52
193. Chase Manhattan 6.52
194. American Electric Power 6.50
195. Wendy's International 6.49
196. Weyerhaeuser 6.48
197. WestPoint Stevens 6.48
198. PPG Industries 6.48

199. Mead 6.47
200. Arco 6.47
201. New York Times 6.45
202. Rockwell International 6.45
203. International Paper 6.45
204. Thermo Electron 6.45
205. Halliburton 6.45
206. American Greetings 6.45
207. Lowe's 6.44
208. Principal Mutual Life Ins. 6.44
209. Dover 6.44
210. Seagate Technology 6.43
211. Union Camp 6.42
212. Black & Decker 6.42
213. TRW 6.42
214. First Union 6.42
215. Cummins Engine 6.41
216. Dana 6.41
217. Tejas Gas 6.41
218. AK Steel Holding 6.41
219. Northwest Airlines 6.41
220. Jacobs Engineering Group 6.41
221. Foster Wheeler 6.41
222. Pacific Gas & Electric 6.40
223. Student Loan Mtkg. Assn. 6.40
224. Polaris Industries 6.40
225. Edison International 6.40
226. Daimler-Benz NA 6.39
227. Siemens 6.39
228. McDonnell Douglas 6.38
229. Centex 6.38
230. Reynolds Metals 6.38
231. Reader's Digest Assn. 6.38
232. Stanley Works 6.38
233. Texas Utilities 6.37
234. Pulte 6.37
235. Warner-Lambert 6.36
236. R. R. Donnelley & Sons 6.36
237. TIAA 6.35
238. Tenneco 6.35
239. BellSouth 6.35
240. Computer Sciences 6.33
241. Bayer 6.32
242. Dayton Hudson 6.32
243. U.S. Healthcare 6.32
244. Equitable 6.32
245. Oryx Energy 6.31
246. Owens-Corning 6.31
247. Supervalu 6.30
248. ITT 6.29
249. Cone Mills 6.29
250. Sprint 6.29
251. Avon Products 6.28
252. Phillips Petroleum 6.28
253. Alumax 6.25

254. American Stores 6.25
255. Bear Stearns 6.25
256. A. G. Edwards & Sons 6.24
257. Roadway Express 6.23
258. Ameritech 6.22
259. Raytheon 6.21
260. General Dynamics 6.20
261. CREF 6.20
262. Bridgestone/Firestone 6.19
263. Kelly Services 6.18
264. McGraw-Hill 6.18
265. Becton Dickinson 6.18
266. Standard Fed. Bancorp 6.18
267. Union Carbide 6.17
268. MCI Communications 6.17
269. Newell 6.17
270. First Chicago NBD 6.16
271. Entergy 6.16
272. Asarco 6.15
273. B. F. Goodrich 6.15
274. RJR Nabisco Holdings 6.15
275. Coleman Holdings 6.14
276. Adolph Coors 6.14
277. ITT Industries 6.13
278. The Limited 6.13
279. Furniture Brands Intl. 6.13
280. Burlington Industries 6.13
281. Winn-Dixie Stores 6.12
282. Sundstrand 6.11
283. Mark IV Industries 6.10
284. Loews 6.10
285. US Freightways 6.09
286. Delta Air Lines 6.09
287. Bell Atlantic 6.09
288. Peter Kiewit Sons' 6.09
289. Landstar System 6.09
290. Viacom 6.08
291. Mohawk Industries 6.08
292. Liberty Mutual Ins. Group 6.08
293. American Standard 6.07
294. Hoechst Celanese 6.07
295. Pitney Bowes 6.05
296. BASF 6.05
297. Federated Dept. Stores 6.05
298. Raychem 6.05
299. Baxter International 6.00
300. Case 6.00
301. Northrop Grumman 5.98
302. Bankers Trust N.Y. 5.97
303. CDI 5.97
304. Crown Cork & Seal 5.97
305. J. B. Hunt Transport Svcs. 5.96
306. Food Lion 5.96
307. Volt Information Sciences 5.95
308. Pharmacia & Upjohn 5.94

309. Canon U.S.A. 5.94
310. Dresser Industries 5.93
311. Price/Costco 5.92
312. Charter One Financial 5.90
313. Conrail 5.88
314. Metropolitan Life Ins. 5.88
315. Comdisco 5.88
316. Dillard Department Stores 5.86
317. Continental Airlines 5.86
318. IBP 5.85
319. Times Mirror 5.85
320. Air Express International 5.84
321. Equitable Resources 5.84
322. Collins & Aikman 5.83
323. American General 5.83
324. Aramark 5.82
325. Tenet Healthcare 5.81
326. Whirlpool 5.81
327. EG&G 5.81
328. Time Warner 5.80
329. Masco 5.79
330. General Motors 5.76
331. Fleetwood Enterprises 5.76
332. H. F. Ahmanson 5.75
333. Owens-Illinois 5.75
334. Dun & Bradstreet 5.74
335. Fleet Financial Group 5.72
336. U.S. Industries 5.70
337. Airborne Freight 5.69
338. Nationwide Ins. Enterprise 5.69
339. Helene Curtis Industries 5.69
340. CIGNA 5.68
341. USG 5.68
342. Pittston 5.67
343. Bausch & Lomb 5.67
344. Polaroid 5.66
345. Public Svc. Entpr. Group 5.65
346. NorAm Energy 5.64
347. Georgia-Pacific 5.64
348. GTE 5.64

349. Mascotech 5.63
350. Alaska Air Group 5.63
351. AT&T 5.61
352. Great Western Financial 5.57
353. Consolidated Freightways 5.55
354. Warnaco Group 5.55
355. WellPoint Health Netwks. 5.54
356. Novell 5.54
357. Alberto-Culver 5.53
358. USX 5.51
359. Ball 5.49
360. Bally Entertainment 5.49
361. Enserch 5.49
362. UST 5.47
363. Ruby Tuesday 5.47
364. Fleming 5.47
365. Con Edison of N.Y. 5.44
366. Turner Corp. 5.43
367. Tandy 5.42
368. LTV 5.36
369. Unicom 5.35
370. Melville 5.33
371. Salomon 5.31
372. US West 5.31
373. Fred Meyer 5.31
374. Schuller 5.28
375. Aetna Life & Casualty 5.26
376. Champion International 5.23
377. Inland Steel Industries 5.22
378. Brown-Forman 5.21
379. Caliber System 5.21
380. Triarc 5.20
381. Health Systems Intl. 5.18
382. J. E. Seagram 5.15
383. W. R. Grace 5.12
384. Occidental Petroleum 5.11
385. Archer Daniels Midland 5.11
386. Digital Equipment 5.11
387. Foamex International 5.11
388. PaineWebber Group 5.10
389. Humana 5.09

390. Fieldcrest Cannon 5.06
391. Dial 5.04
392. Westinghouse Electric 5.03
393. Universal 5.02
394. Kellwood 5.01
395. FHP International 4.99
396. Maxxam 4.95
397. Outboard Marine 4.94
398. Southland 4.92
399. James River of Va. 4.91
400. NYNEX 4.88
401. Apple Computer 4.87
402. Prudential Ins. Cos. of Amer. 4.84
403. Unisys 4.80
404. Dimon 4.78
405. A&P 4.77
406. Boise Cascade 4.77
407. Lehman Brothers Holdings 4.74
408. Merisel 4.73
409. America West Airlines 4.73
410. Woolworth 4.72
411. Bethlehem Steel 4.67
412. Shoney's 4.67
413. Fruit of the Loom 4.63
414. Glendale Federal Bank 4.60
415. Yellow 4.59
416. Foodmaker 4.58
417. Southern Pacific Rail 4.58
418. Whitman 4.55
419. Stone Container 4.49
420. Family Restaurants 4.47
421. Arkansas Best 4.46
422. Cal Fed Bancorp 4.44
423. Amerco 4.44
424. Beverly Enterprises 4.31
425. USAir Group 4.13
426. Flagstar 4.07
427. Morrison Knudsen 4.05
428. Canandaigua Wine 4.03
429. Kmart 3.82
430. Standard Commercial 3.76
431. TWA 3.42

APPENDIX 7

INC. 500: The 1997 Ranking of the Fastest-Growing Private Companies in America

Reprinted with permission of *Inc.* magazine, Goldhirsh Group, Inc., 38 Commercial Wharf, Boston, MA 02110. *The 1997 Ranking of the Fastest-Growing Private Companies in America,* Inc. 500, 1997. (http://www.inc.com) Reproduced by permission of the publisher via Copyright Clearance Center, Inc.

Rank ('97)	Company/Location	Business Description	Sales Growth 1992–96 (% increase)	1996 Sales ($000)	1992 Sales ($000)	Profit Range* '96	Profit Range* '92	No. of Employees '96	No. of Employees '92	Date Founded
1	Optiva Bellevue, WA	Sells hygiene devices & mfrs. sonic toothbrushes	31,507	$ 72,695	$ 230	F	C	338	25	1988
2	Duke & Co. New York, NY	Provides investment banking, private placement, & IPO svcs.	17,576	40,831	231	B	F	363	51	1979
3	Natural Gas Transmission Services Dallas, TX	Markets & trades natural gas & electricity	13,315	154,943	1,155	D	D	20	3	1992
4	Scrip Plus Fresno, CA	Provides funding resources	13,189	116,412	876	F	C	90	3	1991
5	Accord Human Resources Oklahoma City, OK	Provides employee leasing svcs.	8,454	50,128	586	F	F	40	8	1992
6	New World Technologies Ashland, MA	Manufactures computer-based solutions	8,341	27,266	323	E	E	78	5	1991
7	TH Properties Franconia, PA	Develops residential property	8,176	20,277	269	C	D	25	0	1992
8	Commercial Financial Services Tulsa, OK	Restructures, collects, & resolves bank & FDIC loans	7,858	344,745	4,332	A	A	1,266	45	1986
9	International Profit Associates Buffalo Grove, IL	Provides mgmt. consulting svcs. for small to midsize cos.	7,198	33,934	465	C	F	576	82	1991
10	PhotoDisc Seattle, WA	Publishes digital stock photography online & on CD-ROM	7,195	28,231	387	C	F	157	4	1991
11	Transecon Broomfield, CO	Distributes metaphysical & environmental prods.	7,144	14,487	200	D	D	86	2	1989
12	Paradigm Health Concord, CA	Provides specialty managed care svcs.	7,058	39,080	546	D	F	130	20	1991
13	Nantucket Allserve Cambridge, MA	Develops, sells, & markets Nantucket Nectars juice prods.	6,363	24,493	379	D	F	85	6	1990
14	PC Club Industry, CA	Sells & svcs. computers	6,347	32,816	509	D	D	105	10	1991
15	Evolutionary Technologies International Austin, TX	Provides software tools for data conversion & migration	6,089	17,205	278	D	F	148	30	1991

* Profit range: A—16% or more; B—11% to 15%; C—6% to 10%; D—1% to 5%; E—Break-even; F—Loss.

Rank ('97)	Company/Location	Business Description	Sales Growth 1992–96 (% increase)	1996 Sales ($000)	1992 Sales ($000)	Profit Range* '96	'92	No. of Employees '96	'92	Date Founded
16	Hoveround Sarasota, FL	Manufactures & distr. power mobility devices	5,567	$ 15,698	$ 277	A	F	64	11	1992
17	Staffing Edge Des Moines, IA	Provides temporary staffing svcs.	5,501	14,786	264	C	F	105	4	1992
18	Agro Power Development East Brunswick, NJ	Develops, produces, & markets produce	5,445	11,090	200	C	F	284	4	1989
19	Tyan Computer Milpitas, CA	Develops, mfrs., & sells systs. boards	5,318	19,124	353	C	F	34	7	1989
20	Unifi Communications Lowell, MA	Provides messaging networks & fax-delivery svcs.	5,209	25,218	475	F	F	653	45	1990
21	NetScout Systems Chelmsford, MA	Manufactures network instrumentation & mgmt. software	4,796	30,648	626	A	D	114	17	1984
22	Mainline Information Systems Tallahassee, FL	Provides technological prods. & svcs.	4,766	18,879	388	D	D	65	8	1989
23	Gearon & Co. Atlanta, GA	Provides consulting svcs. for telecom. industry	4,660	22,324	469	A	A	175	7	1991
24	United Services Associates Birmingham, AL	Provides custodial svcs.	4,564	13,340	286	D	E	344	235	1971
25	PixelVision Acton, MA	Manufactures flat-panel monitors & electronics	4,472	18,198	398	F	C	65	5	1991
26	Hospitality Systems Boca Raton, FL	Manufactures touch-screen point-of-sale systs. for restaurants & hotels	4,427	9,100	201	F	F	100	6	1992
27	Automatic Answer San Juan Capistrano, CA	Provides voice processing svcs.	4,367	10,275	230	E	F	42	4	1988
28	Rigid Structures Houston, TX	Manufactures preengineered metal buildings	4,333	15,914	359	D	A	85	2	1990
29	RPM Consulting Columbia, MD	Provides internetworking & network mgmt. consulting svcs.	4,198	8,639	201	A	A	98	6	1992
30	Triton Systems Long Beach, MS	Manufactures ATM machines	4,190	40,968	955	A	F	91	13	1979
31	Cybertech International Oak Brook, IL	Provides software consulting svcs., systs. integration, & prods.	3,994	10,111	247	C	D	124	2	1990
32	Aerobotics Industries Euless, TX	Provides engineering, manufacturing, tooling, & prototyping svcs.	3,872	12,990	327	A	F	100	12	1989
33	Advanced Information Systems Group Longwood, FL	Provides systs. integration svcs.	3,869	16,035	404	D	D	41	7	1991
34	Westt, Inc. Menlo Park, CA	Provides electromechanical technology consulting svcs.	3,851	9,799	248	C	F	51	7	1989

Rank ('97)	Company/Location	Business Description	Sales Growth 1992–96 (% increase)	1996 Sales ($000)	1992 Sales ($000)	Profit Range* '96	Profit Range* '92	No. of Employees '96	No. of Employees '92	Date Founded
35	DSET Bridgewater, NJ	Distributes software engineering tools	3,839	$ 13,117	$ 333	B	A	90	6	1989
36	Greenpages Kittery, ME	Resells computers	3,712	48,609	1,275	E	F	99	15	1992
37	HR Alternatives Kingsport, TN	Provides temporary staffing svcs.	3,614	8,357	225	C	E	22	2	1992
38	SBA Boca Raton, FL	Provides site development svcs. for wireless telecom. industry	3,569	60,276	1,643	D	B	365	11	1989
39	Compunnel Software Group Iselin, NJ	Offers software development & consulting svcs.	3,363	8,693	251	D	E	125	27	1989
40	Mabis Healthcare Lake Forest, IL	Distributes wholesale medical prods.	3,349	13,039	378	D	F	22	7	1992
41	Insync Systems Milpitas, CA	Manufactures gas-control systs. for semiconductor equip.	3,161	90,370	2,771	F	D	300	24	1989
42	Wyncom Lexington, KY	Provides educational & professional development svcs.	3,154	41,548	1,277	D	A	100	12	1986
43	VSI Group Columbia, MD	Provides staffing & contract-labor svcs.	3,129	9,590	297	B	F	550	180	1990
44	High Technology Solutions San Diego, CA	Provides systs. integration svcs.	3,115	23,695	737	D	C	278	20	1990
45	UP Herndon, VA	Creates interactive learning systs.	3,103	6,502	203	C	F	51	3	1992
46	Houston Associates Silver Spring, MD	Provides communications, telecom., & systs. engineering svcs.	3,082	22,371	703	D	F	250	12	1982
47	Empower Trainers & Consultants Overland Park, KS	Provides computer consulting & training svcs.	3,060	6,541	207	F	D	85	6	1990
48	Foreside Co. Gorham, ME	Distributes home prods.	3,018	11,007	353	C	F	131	2	1990
49	Adrian Industrial Constructors Mont Belvieu, TX	Provides construction & fabrication svcs. for petrochemical industry	2,888	6,275	210	F	E	100	6	1992
50	Nature's Choice Lyndhurst, NJ	Provides vegetative waste composting svcs.	2,804	6,301	217	D	D	45	2	1991
51	Unitel McLean, VA	Provides telemarketing svcs.	2,795	7,962	275	C	A	550	9	1991
52	Bay State Computers Lanham, MD	Offers computer-related information mgmt. svcs. & sells hardware	2,784	18,657	647	D	D	30	3	1988
53	City Federal Funding & Mortgage College Park, MD	Provides mortgage banking svcs.	2,783	12,050	418	B	B	124	12	1992
54	Support Net Indianapolis, IN	Provides computer distr. svcs.	2,782	140,245	4,866	C	D	141	32	1982
55	Transaction Information Systems New York, NY	Provides software & consulting svcs.	2,766	32,526	1,135	C	C	280	24	1992

Rank ('97)	Company/Location	Business Description	Sales Growth 1992–96 (% increase)	1996 Sales ($000)	1992 Sales ($000)	Profit Range* '96	Profit Range* '92	No. of Employees '96	No. of Employees '92	Date Founded
56	Technical Solution Troy, MI	Provides computer hardware, software, & systs. integration svcs.	2,697	$ 11,075	$ 396	D	D	17	2	1992
57	Revere Group Northbrook, IL	Provides business & technology consulting svcs.	2,696	18,423	659	B	C	195	28	1991
58	Berkshire Computer Products Hopkinton, MA	Provides systs. integration svcs.	2,644	29,414	1,072	D	D	27	5	1988
59	Republic Group Anaheim, CA	Leases & finances equip.	2,611	5,584	206	A	D	81	3	1992
60	Hartex Property Group Dallas, TX	Acquires & manages multifamily residential real estate	2,572	28,649	1,072	A	A	135	6	1991
61	SQL Financials Atlanta, GA	Provides finan. svcs.	2,540	13,200	500	F	F	180	10	1991
62	Dynamic Data Solutions Minneapolis, MN	Provides computer consulting & training & software development svcs.	2,525	13,336	508	A	A	150	4	1987
63	Financial Independence Network Boscobel, WI	Publishes & direct markets finan. information prods.	2,502	23,469	902	B	F	79	2	1987
64	Sytel Bethesda, MD	Provides information systs. svcs.	2,488	29,456	1,138	D	B	250	26	1987
65	Force 3 Crofton, MD	Sells computers to government	2,481	72,019	2,790	D	F	72	5	1991
66	MediaTel San Francisco, CA	Provides electronic document delivery svcs.	2,474	14,567	566	D	F	64	3	1989
67	Crystal Group Hiawatha, IA	Manufactures industrial rack-mount personal computers	2,451	10,483	411	A	A	31	4	1991
68	RMR Industries Watertown, SD	Manufactures store fixtures, panelized walls, & interior millwork	2,427	12,233	484	D	F	106	23	1992
69	CAP Ventures Norwell, MA	Offers consulting svcs. for electronic imaging industry	2,398	6,071	243	D	D	38	6	1991
70	Hi Tech Consultants Southfield, MI	Provides computer consulting & contract programming svcs.	2,392	6,305	253	B	D	110	20	1990
71	SCI (Spearman Construction) Bossier City, LA	Designs & builds food-industry projects	2,372	16,757	678	D	F	30	3	1992
72	Optical Technology Group Bethesda, MD	Provides software development svcs.	2,365	8,479	344	A	A	50	10	1992
73	Protocol Interface San Rafael, CA	Provides internetworking training svcs.	2,346	10,543	431	A	A	100	5	1992
74	Solutions Consulting Canonsburg, PA	Provides systs. integration consulting svcs.	2,343	15,735	644	A	A	52	3	1990

Rank ('97)	Company/Location	Business Description	Sales Growth 1992–96 (% increase)	1996 Sales ($000)	1992 Sales ($000)	Profit Range* '96	'92	No. of Employees '96	'92	Date Founded
75	Capricorn Systems Atlanta, GA	Provides computer software consulting	2,324	$ 19,049	$ 786	D	C	275	27	1991
76	Serviceware Oakmont, PA	Sells prepackaged knowledge bases	2,276	5,037	212	F	D	80	2	1991
77	Equipe Technologies Sunnyvale, CA	Manufactures robots used in pro- duction of computer chips	2,228	34,988	1,503	A	A	100	12	1990
78	Dentrix Dental Systems American Fork, UT	Develops clinical & practical mgmt. systs.	2,222	10,355	446	A	F	76	16	1985
79	Universal Fabric Structures Quakertown, PA	Manufactures portable fabric structures	2,184	16,902	740	D	F	30	2	1992
80	i Market, Inc. Waltham, MA	Develops & distr. target-marketing software	2,136	11,963	535	F	F	65	12	1991
81	Caelum Research Silver Spring, MD	Provides informa- tion technology & applied-science svcs.	2,128	11,361	510	D	F	110	12	1987
82	Select Comfort Minneapolis, MN	Manufactures & markets air sleep systs.	2,121	98,699	4,444	F	F	751	0	1987
83	Global Management Systems Bethesda, MD	Provides integration systs. consulting svcs.	2,103	17,334	787	A	A	149	7	1988
84	MedicaLogic Beaverton, OR	Develops & distr. electronic medical record software	2,096	9,664	440	F	F	143	4	1985
85	PC Ware Long Island City, NY	Sells computers	2,086	24,238	1,109	D	F	22	10	1990
86	Progressive System Technologies Austin, TX	Supplies automa- tion & contamina- tion control equip.	2,081	16,704	766	E	D	112	7	1991
87	Microsysts. Technology Tampa, FL	Manufactures data- entry automation solutions	2,055	5,775	268	A	F	28	5	1989
88	Laser Pros International Oregon, WI	Sells & svcs. laser printers	2,051	6,734	313	A	A	55	4	1990
89	R.J. Gordon & Co. Los Angeles, CA	Provides business consulting svcs. for merchants & banks	2,026	30,701	1,444	A	A	104	38	1987
90	Sabinsa Piscataway, NJ	Manufactures & distr. electronic devices	2,015	14,697	695	C	C	30	0	1983
91	Market Scan Information Systems Westlake Village, CA	Leases software to automobile industry	1,977	5,213	251	A	D	30	3	1988
92	New England Computer Resources Providence, RI	Integrates micro- computer technolo- gies for institutions	1,955	7,254	353	A	A	15	4	1991
93	Cabot Marsh Bethlehem, PA	Offers health care consulting svcs.	1,947	5,321	260	C	F	74	3	1991
94	Mitchell Gold Taylorsville, NC	Manufactures furni- ture	1,938	11,250	552	D	D	103	7	1989
95	KRA Silver Spring, MD	Provides policy evaluation & re- search svcs. to government	1,923	16,791	830	C	D	250	65	1981

Rank ('97)	Company/Location	Business Description	Sales Growth 1992–96 (% increase)	1996 Sales ($000)	1992 Sales ($000)	Profit Range* '96	Profit Range* '92	No. of Employees '96	No. of Employees '92	Date Founded
96	M-Cubed Information Systems Rockville, MD	Provides systs. integration svcs.	1,919	$ 4,907	$ 243	F	F	50	5	1985
97	International Software Solutions Herndon, VA	Provides software consulting & systs. administration svcs.	1,917	4,963	246	C	B	75	8	1992
98	CableLink Salt Lake City, UT	Sells computer cables	1,917	4,115	204	C	E	22	5	1992
99	Amicus Legal Staffing Nashville, TN	Provides legal staffing	1,910	4,845	241	B	F	35	2	1991
100	CSI Digital Seattle, WA	Provides systs. integration mgmt. svcs.	1,909	23,520	1,171	F	D	55	15	1991
101	Network Personnel Wilmington, DE	Provides executive recruitment & temporary staffing svcs.	1,900	11,700	585	F	F	44	10	1990
102	WorkRite Ergonomics Novato, CA	Manufactures ergonomic furniture & accessories	1,892	5,359	269	B	D	40	4	1991
103	KSM Associates Yardley, PA	Provides information technology consulting & software development	1,875	4,028	204	A	C	45	2	1990
104	SR Hoeft Direct St. Louis, MO	Provides direct-response acquisitions & loyalty programs	1,810	8,498	445	B	F	29	3	1991
105	DB Design Group Milpitas, CA	Manufactures semiconductor test equip.	1,794	4,090	216	D	C	36	2	1989
106	DMS Direct Marketing Services Scottsdale, AZ	Provides telecom. svcs.	1,773	15,733	840	D	D	1,000	100	1991
107	National Safety Alliance Nashville, TN	Provides substance-abuse testing programs for workplace	1,773	7,210	385	D	F	65	12	1988
108	Balboa Capital Irvine, CA	Provides high-tech equip. leasing & financing	1,747	50,833	2,752	D	C	108	25	1988
109	Paranet Houston, TX	Provides mgmt. & computer network support svcs.	1,746	66,225	3,587	B	B	818	50	1990
110	Supercircuits Leander, TX	Sells microcameras & equip.	1,736	6,004	327	B	A	6	2	1989
111	CritiCom Lanham, MD	Provides turnkey videoconferencing & telecom. svcs.	1,723	7,239	397	D	D	23	9	1990
112	Ford, Cicoletti & Co. San Jose, CA	Provides finan. systs. svcs.	1,699	3,760	209	C	B	33	2	1991
113	Cirque Salt Lake City, UT	Manufactures GlidePoint prods.	1,691	11,586	647	D	D	67	6	1991
114	ID Technology Fort Worth, TX	Provides labeling, coding, & marketing svcs.	1,682	6,273	352	D	F	35	3	1989
115	Celtic Leasing Irvine, CA	Leases general business equip.	1,677	39,140	2,203	D	D	19	3	1991
116	Excell Data Bellevue, WA	Provides computer consulting, software development, & network svcs.	1,674	24,164	1,362	D	F	320	35	1991

Rank ('97)	Company/Location	Business Description	Sales Growth 1992–96 (% increase)	1996 Sales ($000)	1992 Sales ($000)	Profit Range* '96	'92	No. of Employees '96	'92	Date Founded
117	TeleKey Atlanta, GA	Sells prepaid calling cards	1,668	$ 3,871	$ 219	F	F	18	3	1991
118	Oxford Associates Bethesda, MD	Measures & improves sales & marketing performance	1,657	5,992	341	A	A	40	4	1991
119	Concentrix Rochester, NY	Provides communications svcs.	1,643	6,520	374	F	F	70	8	1991
120	R&D Data Productions Princeton, NJ	Resells computers & accessories	1,613	6,183	361	D	B	6	1	1991
121	Space Electronics San Diego, CA	Designs, mfrs., & sells microelectronic components for space flight	1,607	10,598	621	A	F	75	7	1992
122	InstallShield Schamburg, IL	Creates & distr. software development tools	1,599	10,229	602	F	F	93	7	1987
123	Jones Business Systems Houston, TX	Provides systs. integration/distribution svcs.	1,589	26,181	1,550	D	F	120	20	1991
124	TCI Press Seekonk, MA	Provides commercial printing svcs.	1,588	8,591	509	B	C	50	9	1989
125	EnviroMetrics Software New Castle, DE	Provides environmental software solutions	1,586	4,164	247	C	D	35	3	1992
126	Computer Sales & Service Columbia, SC	Sells & svcs. computers for corporate accounts	1,585	6,454	383	D	F	23	4	1992
127	International Postal Consultants Savage, MD	Provides international mailing & shipping svcs.	1,577	11,803	704	A	C	36	6	1991
128	Unitek Fremont, CA	Provides computer consulting svcs.	1,568	4,154	249	B	A	48	4	1992
129	Century Personnel Overland Park, KS	Provides permanent & temporary employment svcs.	1,557	12,978	783	B	E	67	10	1974
130	CJ's Casino Emporium Las Vegas, NV	Sells slot machines & other gaming-related equip.	1,554	8,734	528	D	C	25	3	1990
131	Misty Mate Tempe, AZ	Manufactures & distr. outdoor cooling mist systs.	1,549	3,545	215	D	F	40	3	1989
132	Zachary Software Clearwater, FL	Markets software development tools	1,534	5,639	345	F	F	26	6	1991
133	Good Catalog Portland, OR	Sells mail-order prods.	1,531	20,516	1,258	D	F	77	15	1992
134	Western New York Contract Staffing Services Williamsville, NY	Provides professional staffing svcs.	1,528	8,871	545	D	F	500	50	1992
135	Indusa Technical Wheaton, IL	Provides software consulting svcs.	1,527	10,102	621	A	E	100	8	1989
136	Spencer Reed Group Overland Park, KS	Provides executive search & specialty staffing svcs.	1,520	15,566	961	C	C	202	30	1990
137	CompuWorks Pittsfield, MA	Provides computer networking, training, & support	1,517	3,251	201	C	B	38	3	1987
138	Synygy Bala Cynwyd, PA	Provides mgmt. consulting & information svcs.	1,496	3,480	218	D	C	25	4	1991

Rank ('97)	Company/Location	Business Description	Sales Growth 1992–96 (% increase)	1996 Sales ($000)	1992 Sales ($000)	Profit Range* '96	'92	No. of Employees '96	'92	Date Founded
139	New Wave Technologies Gaithersburg, MD	Distributes document imaging & mass storage solutions	1,496	$ 13,473	$ 844	D	F	22	3	1992
140	Bristol Technology Ridgefield, CT	Develops cross-platform applications	1,479	8,085	512	A	D	50	6	1991
141	EMG Hunt Valley, MD	Provides real estate due-diligence engineering svcs.	1,476	15,599	990	C	D	165	16	1986
142	Aeronex San Diego, CA	Manufactures high-purity fluid-delivery systs.	1,459	4,678	300	D	D	40	4	1990
143	Raymond Karsan Associates Wayne, PA	Provides human resources svcs.	1,450	27,882	1,799	C	C	178	30	1986
144	Staff Administrators Denver, CO	Provides employment svcs.	1,449	77,976	5,035	F	F	3,397	210	1991
145	Encore Orthopedics Austin, TX	Provides rapid prototyping svcs.	1,443	17,621	1,142	C	F	80	25	1992
146	P2 Holdings San Leandro, CA	Designs, mfrs., & distr. orthopedic implants	1,442	18,803	1,219	F	B	220	20	1989
147	Management Decisions Norcross, GA	Provides employment svcs. for computer industry	1,430	9,560	625	C	F	133	2	1981
148	Millennium Computer Rochester, NY	Develops imaging, graphics, & client/server software	1,428	8,051	527	A	D	60	4	1985
149	G. A. Sullivan St. Louis, MO	Provides software development svcs.	1,410	5,285	350	D	F	76	6	1982
150	McNeil Technologies Springfield, VA	Provides mgmt. support svcs.	1,408	3,800	252	F	F	64	20	1985
151	Metasys Charlotte, NC	Manufactures transportation mgmt. software	1,404	6,619	440	D	C	115	3	1991
152	Command Technologies Warrenton, VA	Provides systs. engineering svcs.	1,400	11,384	759	D	F	147	36	1988
153	Maintech Philadelphia, PA	Distributes & mfrs. automation equip.	1,398	6,950	464	A	A	13	1	1988
154	GoldMine Software Pacific Palisades, CA	Sells contract-mgmt. software	1,387	11,968	805	A	D	80	12	1989
155	Protek Electronics Sarasota, FL	Manufactures contracts & designs electronics	1,371	9,119	620	D	E	134	14	1987
156	Advanced Solutions International Alexandria, VA	Develops & markets business software	1,367	4,561	311	D	D	55	7	1991
157	ClariNet Communications San Jose, CA	Provides Internet news svcs.	1,366	3,914	267	D	B	37	3	1989
158	DAP Mueller & Associates Visalia, CA	Provides temporary staffing svcs.	1,356	5,999	412	E	B	19	3	1991
159	Security Leasing Paartners St. Louis, MO	Provides finan. svcs. for life safety equip. dealers	1,355	3,551	244	A	B	12	4	1990

Rank ('97)	Company/Location	Business Description	Sales Growth 1992–96 (% increase)	1996 Sales ($000)	1992 Sales ($000)	Profit Range* '96	'92	No. of Employees '96	'92	Date Founded
160	Software Information Systems Lexington, KY	Provides computer software consulting svcs.	1,353	$ 7,438	$ 512	D	D	24	9	1982
161	Heartland Mortgage/ Home Finance Naperville, IL	Provides mortgage brokerage svcs.	1,346	10,396	719	B	B	275	12	1987
162	JJ Wild Canton, MA	Provides consulting & networking svcs., hardware, & peripheral systs.	1,343	22,234	1,541	D	F	48	6	1956
163	Association Communications Seattle, WA	Provides long-distance & data communications svcs.	1,342	6,415	445	C	B	15	3	1989
164	Rumarson Technologies Kenilworth, NJ	Sells computer hardware Sells & svcs.	1,341	10,676	741	A	E	55	5	1992
165	Remtech Services Newport News, VA	computer systs.	1,340	8,194	569	D	E	152	14	1988
166	TriNet Employer Group San Leandro, CA	Provides professional svcs. for employers	1,339	119,994	8,336	F	F	60	6	1988
167	Garg Data International Newport Beach, CA	Provides computer integration svcs.	1,335	16,273	1,134	C	C	250	7	1991
168	International Data Response Chicago, IL	Provides outsourced telemarketing svcs.	1,335	66,651	4,645	F	C	2,500	600	1986
169	National Integration Services Rochester, NY	Manufactures custom touch-screen displays	1,320	9,375	660	D	C	30	4	1992
170	FormMaker Software Atlanta, GA	Provides multi-platform document-automation software & svcs.	1,307	20,458	1,454	F	F	239	34	1983
171	Austin Innovations Austin, TX	Develops & markets technology-based prods.	1,292	8,685	624	D	E	50	5	1990
172	Designer Checks Anniston, AL	Manufactures personal & business checks	1,271	34,602	2,523	D	F	450	50	1992
173	Linkage Lexington, MA	Provides consulting svcs. for organizational development	1,268	11,385	832	A	C	58	7	1988
174	Wheat International Commercial Reston, VA	Provides telecom. & information technology svcs.	1,268	6,154	450	B	A	51	5	1989
175	Case & Associates General Contractors Houston, TX	Provides general contracting svcs. specializing in hotel construction	1,261	20,474	1,504	D	D	60	4	1988
176	McClain Group Richmond, VA	Provides general mgmt. & information technology consulting svcs.	1,258	3,666	270	A	A	16	3	1992
177	Platinum Communications Warren, NJ	Distributes new & refurbished telecom./data equip.	1,258	5,824	429	D	A	17	2	1992

Rank ('97)	Company/Location	Business Description	Sales Growth 1992–96 (% increase)	1996 Sales ($000)	1992 Sales ($000)	Profit Range* '96	'92	No. of Employees '96	'92	Date Founded
178	Quest Consulting Oak Brook, IL	Provides Oracle consulting svcs.	1,253	$ 3,274	$ 242	D	B	11	1	1991
179	Nexgen SI Irvine, CA	Provides network transition svcs.	1,246	15,719	1,168	C	D	223	20	1990
180	Chase Plastic Services Clarkston, MI	Distributes thermo-plastics	1,235	16,840	1,261	D	D	25	3	1992
181	Manhattan Associates Atlanta, GA	Supplies ware-house mgmt. systs. for retail & grocery suppliers	1,229	13,702	1,031	A	E	83	11	1990
182	Neverdahl-Loft & Associates Lincoln, NE	Provides software support for insur-ance cos.	1,226	5,515	416	C	F	63	7	1990
183	Black Cat Computer Wholesale Amherst, NY	Distributes com-puter components & custom-built computer systs.	1,222	5,487	15	C	D	16	1	1992
184	Microplastics St. Charles, IL	Manufactures cus-tom injection-molding prods.	1,215	6,906	525	D	C	76	4	1989
185	National Network Services Denver, CO	Designs, installs, & svcs. data, voice, & video networks	1,215	7,009	533	A	B	69	9	1989
186	Systems Solutions Group San Francisco, CA	Provides systs. de-velopment svcs.	1,201	4,683	360	A	A	41	4	1990
187	Paige's Security Services Marina, CA	Provides private security guard svcs.	1,198	17,307	1,333	C	C	570	200	1987
188	Signal Fairfax, VA	Provides informa-tion, engineering, mgmt., & multi-media svcs.	1,196	54,472	4,202	B	D	700	58	1987
189	Stellart Materials Northville, MI	Manufactures refractories & concrete	1,195	2,836	219	E	F	18	8	1990
190	BLW King of Prussia, PA	Provides sales, in-stallation, & service of electronic secu-rity prods.	1,189	3,983	309	B	D	38	5	1986
191	Ultimate Software Group Ft. Lauderdale, FL	Develops human resources mgmt. software	1,188	6,621	514	E	E	240	40	1990
192	Superior Electronics Group Sarasota, FL	Manufactures test-ing equip. & soft-ware for cable TV & telephone cos.	1,188	33,174	2,576	D	D	315	12	1977
193	Core Technology Group Los Gatos, CA	Provides informa-tion systs. consult-ing	1,185	20,892	1,626	D	D	70	15	1985
194	Dine-a-Mate Binghamton, NY	Provides dining, travel, & recreation coupon programs	1,184	13,249	1,032	C	C	121	29	1974
195	Success Develop-ment International Jacksonville, FL	Produces real es-tate & finan. train-ing prods. & conferences	1,182	7,347	573	C	A	42	5	1989

Rank ('97)	Company/Location	Business Description	Sales Growth 1992–96 (% increase)	1996 Sales ($000)	1992 Sales ($000)	Profit Range* '96	'92	No. of Employees '96	'92	Date Founded
196	Radio Spirits Schaumburg, IL	Produces & distr. cassettes of old-time radio shows	1,180	$ 4,339	$ 339	C	B	12	3	1989
197	Leslie Contracting Fayetteville, GA	Provides general contracting svcs.	1,176	43,318	3,395	C	E	125	15	1990
198	Floppy Copy Salt Lake City, UT	Packages computer software	1,169	11,697	922	B	D	28	8	1988
199	Transaction Billing Resources Hazlet, NJ	Provides bank & credit card authorization & collection svcs.	1,168	3,436	271	A	F	8	4	1985
200	Productive Data Systems Englewood, CO	Provides information resource svcs.	1,163	33,235	2,632	C	E	500	60	1986
201	Moeller Design & Development Seattle, WA	Manufactures prototypes	1,158	3,672	292	A	B	25	5	1989
202	Electronic Systems of Richmond Richmond, VA	Provides systs. integration svcs. & Internet solutions	1,148	21,496	1,722	C	C	17	10	1983
203	Schwartz Communications Waltham, MA	Offers high-tech public relations svcs.	1,145	6,100	490	A	E	81	4	1990
204	Campbell Software Chicago, IL	Provides work-force-mgmt. software	1,144	11,854	953	F	F	106	8	1989
205	Cellular Warehouse Dublin, CA	Sells cellular, paging, home security, & satellite TV svcs.	1,143	16,066	1,293	D	F	104	10	1990
206	Majestic Systems Integration Brentwood, TN	Provides computer consulting svcs.	1,142	2,547	205	D	E	33	5	1992
207	Fawcette Technical Publications Palo Alto, CA	Provides information on Windows & Internet tools	1,140	15,900	1,282	F	F	50	4	1990
208	Consumer Health Network Piscataway, NJ	Provides managed health care svcs.	1,137	7,892	638	A	F	65	10	1988
209	Global Services Tulsa, OK	Provides computer hardware, software, & network svcs.	1,136	3,337	270	F	C	40	1	1992
210	FNX, Ltd. Wayne, PA	Develops, mfrs., & sells risk mgmt. software	1,134	11,266	913	B	D	103	14	1992
211	Adams Golf Plano, TX	Designs & mfrs. golf clubs	1,127	3,522	287	B	F	50	4	1987
212	Animatics Santa Clara, CA	Designs & mfrs. motion-control devices	1,124	2,546	208	B	F	18	3	1987
213	Indiana Custom Trucks Lagrange, IN	Manufactures custom sleepers for semi trucks	1,124	5,030	411	D	F	77	15	1990
214	ARIS Seattle, WA	Provides technical training & project consulting	1,121	26,898	2,203	C	B	246	20	1990
215	Innovative Telecom Nashua, NH	Provides telecom. svcs.	1,118	12,026	987	F	F	140	11	1989

Rank ('97)	Company/Location	Business Description	Sales Growth 1992–96 (% increase)	1996 Sales ($000)	1992 Sales ($000)	Profit Range* '96	Profit Range* '92	No. of Employees '96	No. of Employees '92	Date Founded
216	New Horizons Computer Learning Center Beaverton, OR	Provides computer application & technical support training	1,118	$ 4,702	$ 386	B	F	60	9	1980
217	Excel Hyannis, MA	Manufactures programmable switches for telecom.	1,114	62,049	5,111	B	C	211	20	1988
218	College & University Computers Williamsburg, VA	Manufactures & sells personal computers	1,110	4,781	395	C	D	15	2	1990
219	Imagetec Buffalo Grove, IL	Provides office prods. sales & svcs.	1,110	8,396	694	B	F	65	10	1992
220	CSSI—Computer Support Services Irving, TX	Provides computer outsourcing svcs.	1,109	9,574	792	C	D	185	12	1988
221	IntellAgent Control Dallas, TX	Develops software for groupware, Internet, & corporate intranets	1,105	5,002	415	F	F	78	4	1991
222	EET Knoxville, TN	Provides environmental, health, safety, & technology svcs.	1,101	4,601	383	D	B	63	4	1990
223	Sensors Unlimited Princeton, NJ	Provides compound semiconductor technology svcs.	1,098	3,343	279	F	F	22	2	1991
224	Trillium Digital Systems Los Angeles, CA	Develops & markets portable integrated communications software	1,097	11,499	961	A	F	58	14	1988
225	Pegnato & Pegnato Roof Management Marina del Rey, CA	Provides facility repair & maintenance svcs.	1,087	6,124	516	F	A	80	8	1992
226	Actium Conshohocken, PA	Provides client/server integration svcs.	1,086	49,192	4,146	C	D	316	58	1987
227	PB Albuquerque, NM	Provides computer networking svcs.	1,084	7,579	640	D	F	30	4	1988
228	Eclipse Marketing Provo, UT	Sells residential pest control	1,083	5,535	468	A	A	73	6	1991
229	Wynne Systems Long Beach, CA	Sells software to rental-service industries	1,082	4,883	413	D	C	24	5	1991
230	Class Travel International Redondo Beach, CA	Coordinates international events & related travel svcs.	1,081	3,178	269	F	F	25	4	1990
231	Modernica Los Angeles, CA	Manufactures, designs, & sells furniture	1,080	2,950	250	D	D	15	0	1990
232	Physicians Formulary International Phoenix, AZ	Sells pharmaceutical & medical prods. wholesale	1,077	7,142	607	C	A	16	3	1990
233	Design Toscano Arlington Heights, IL	Sells historical European reproductions for homes & gardens	1,076	11,034	938	D	E	45	5	1989

Rank ('97)	Company/Location	Business Description	Sales Growth 1992–96 (% increase)	1996 Sales ($000)	1992 Sales ($000)	Profit Range* '96	'92	No. of Employees '96	'92	Date Founded
234	**Imagecom** Arlington Heights, IL	Provides systs. integration svcs.	1,075	$ 4,454	$ 379	B	C	16	4	1990
235	**Sullivan Advertising** Cincinnati, OH	Provides direct-response advertising svcs.	1,071	6,641	567	D	D	17	5	1988
236	**Quality Research** Huntsville, AL	Develops high-tech information & weapons systs.	1,065	11,200	961	D	D	129	14	1988
237	**Accent Systems** Nicholasville, KY	Provides systs. integration svcs.	1,063	7,697	662	C	C	26	8	1988
238	**Command Software Systems** Jupiter, FL	Develops & publishes security & antivirus software	1,062	8,625	742	F	F	87	8	1984
239	**Staffing Services of Michigan** Clinton Township, MI	Provides temporary staffing svcs.	1,062	4,286	369	D	F	24	6	1992
240	**Computer Free America** Springfield, OH	Manufactures computers & provides Internet telecom. svcs.	1,060	5,045	435	D	D	42	3	1991
241	**Hall Kinion & Associates** San Jose, CA	Provides high-tech staffing svcs.	1,060	50,571	4,361	D	F	235	20	1990
242	**Share Group** West Somerville, MA	Provides telemarketing svcs.	1,051	16,061	1,495	D	A	336	78	1986
243	**Vantage Technology** Effingham, IL	Rents medical lasers to hospitals	1,050	2,703	235	B	D	19	5	1990
244	**Coastal Telephone** Houston, TX	Provides long-distance service	1,049	43,262	3,766	D	F	140	22	1986
245	**UniDirect** Scotts Valley, CA	Distributes & markets UNIX & World Wide Web software	1,047	28,166	2,455	D	E	85	2	1991
246	**Lenny & Vinny's** Tampa, FL	Owns & manages chains of pizzerias & bakeries	1,044	3,971	347	F	F	80	6	1991
247	**Miller Audio/Video** Rossville, GA	Provides audio- & videotape duplication svcs.	1,044	3,227	282	D	D	38	4	1984
248	**Syncro Development** Langhorne, PA	Provides PC software development svcs.	1,042	5,891	516	A	C	46	7	1990
249	**BDS Business Center** Glastonbury, CT	Develops software applications	1,040	8,343	732	A	E	80	18	1985
250	**Chesapeake Center** Springfield, VA	Provides health care svcs.	1,035	10,682	941	D	D	251	25	1978
251	**Bregman & Company** Bethesda, MD	Provides environmental consulting	1,033	2,980	263	B	D	46	5	1984
252	**Cecchetti Sebastiani Cellar** Sonoma, CA	Produces & sells wine	1,030	2,679	237	D	F	1	1	1985
253	**Kali's SportNaturals** Berkeley, CA	Produces, markets, & distr. Clif Bar	1,006	10,939	989	C	D	26	3	1986
254	**Friends Assisting Seniors & Families** West Palm Beach, FL	Provides svcs. for elderly	1,002	2,756	248	A	A	14	3	1989
255	**AMC Computer** New York, NY	Provides systs. integration, network design, & turnkey projects	1,000	34,939	3,176	B	B	88	9	1984

Rank ('97)	Company/Location	Business Description	Sales Growth 1992–96 (% increase)	1996 Sales ($000)	1992 Sales ($000)	Profit Range* '96	'92	No. of Employees '96	'92	Date Founded
256	**Applied PC Systems** West Springfield, MA	Offers systs. integration, application development, & training svcs.	1,000	$ 3,497	$ 318	A	F	35	11	1989
257	**Database Marketing** Santa Ana, CA	Provides direct mail advertising svcs.	999	4,836	440	B	F	27	5	1992
258	**PulseCard** Overland Park, KS	Provides credit card financing svcs. for health care	998	3,853	351	F	F	26	4	1988
259	**Kramer Lead Marketing Group** Dallas, TX	Provides lists & direct mail svcs.	996	2,203	201	D	F	8	2	1985
260	**Alpha Employment** Franklin Park, IL	Provides temporary employment svcs. for manufacturing industry	987	3,043	280	C	F	618	57	1962
261	**Hi Per Sports** Colorado Springs, CO	Supplies off-road motorcycle accessories	986	2,422	223	C	F	11	3	1991
262	**AEM** San Diego, CA	Manufactures electronic components, materials, & equip.	985	4,751	438	B	D	82	5	1986
263	**American Fluid Technologies** Hopkins, MN	Distributes reverse-osmosis-related prods. & svcs.	982	2,738	253	D	E	13	38	1991
264	**Chip Express** Santa Clara, CA	Manufactures ASIC semiconductors	979	28,631	2,654	D	F	135	2	1989
265	**Central Pharmacy Services** Atlanta, GA	Distributes nuclear medicine to health care facilities	975	17,955	1,670	F	E	185	12	1986
266	**Qualix Group** San Mateo, CA	Develops software solutions	975	16,535	1,538	C	F	80	30	1990
267	**Mendez** Grand Junction, CO	Provides general contracting svcs.	972	15,114	1,410	C	D	60	15	1982
268	**Enviro-Check** Orlando, FL	Provides water conservation & submetering svcs.	972	3,558	332	F	C	30	14	1991
269	**Capitol Hill Software** Lanham, MD	Develops, markets, & supports PC-based software for public affairs	971	2,227	208	A	B	22	4	1988
270	**Integrated Information Systems** Tempe, AZ	Provides Internet & client/server software & systs. integration svcs.	968	2,200	206	E	F	46	6	1989
271	**Laser Tek Industries** Richmond, IL	Remfrs. laser, fax, & printer cartridges	967	11,135	1,044	D	D	102	15	1991
272	**Technology Advancements** Playa del Rey, CA	Provides aerospace engineering svcs.	963	4,953	466	D	D	70	10	1989
273	**Telegroup** Fairfield, IA	Provides domestic & international long-distance svcs.	962	213,208	20,070	E	D	346	55	1989
274	**Choice Solutions** Colleyville, TX	Provides systs. integration svcs.	957	10,690	1,011	D	F	40	15	1991
275	**Betek Manufacturing** San Jose, CA	Offers turnkey electronic manufacturing svcs.	953	17,806	1,675	A	A	75	21	1985

Rank ('97)	Company/Location	Business Description	Sales Growth 1992–96 (% increase)	1996 Sales ($000)	1992 Sales ($000)	Profit Range*		No. of Employees		Date Founded
						'96	'92	'96	'92	
276	E Source Boulder, CO	Provides energy efficiency & information svcs.	952	$ 3,525	$ 335	C	F	24	6	1992
277	Movies & Games 4 Sale Irving, TX	Distributes used videocassettes & video games	951	23,948	2,279	A	F	69	21	1988
278	SouthStar Steel Charlotte, NC	Imports & distr. stainless-steel bars	949	69,400	6,616	F	D	60	6	1991
279	RJE International Irvine, CA	Distributes underwater navigation prods.	948	2,683	256	D	E	6	1	1990
280	International Data Products Gaithersburg, MD	Provides PCs, notebooks, & software to government	945	87,776	8,398	E	D	154	33	1984
281	Peacock Alley Dallas, TX	Manufactures luxury bed & bath linens	943	9,546	915	D	C	45	15	1973
282	JWA Security Services Sacramento, CA	Provides security guard, investigation, & alarm svcs.	943	10,053	964	D	D	525	107	1981
283	Corridor Group Overland Park, KS	Provides health care consulting svcs.	940	4,265	410	A	A	15	3	1989
284	Riester Phoenix, AZ	Provides advertising & public relations svcs.	940	9,587	922	D	D	28	10	1989
285	Intrinsix Westborough, MA	Provides electrical engineering consulting svcs. & designs circuits	939	10,267	988	D	E	83	14	1985
286	Merit Distributing Bothell, WA	Manufactures PCs & provides network svcs.	934	21,551	2,085	D	D	42	7	1992
287	Quick Solutions Columbus, OH	Provides computer consulting svcs.	934	7,090	686	C	C	95	20	1991
288	Concepts In Communications Pittsburgh, PA	Provides telecom. & tracking systs. for health care industry	933	3,006	291	B	F	22	4	1991
289	Advanced Mobile Solutions Moraga, CA	Designs & mfrs. cellular phone accessories	926	69,087	6,733	A	A	55	16	1985
290	Create-a-Check Salt Lake City, UT	Manufactures & sells check-writing software & supplies	924	2,663	260	E	F	29	17	1991
291	CNC Sales & Applications North Royalton, OH	Sells & svcs. machining centers	920	15,327	1,502	D	D	39	15	1983
292	Research Triangle Consultants Cary, NC	Sells electronic commerce software & provides consulting svcs.	918	2,057	202	D	D	20	3	1991
293	Omicron Systems Philadelphia, PA	Distributes computer equip. & software	916	3,669	361	D	F	4	1	1989
294	Taj Technologies Minneapolis, MN	Provides custom software development	914	3,834	378	D	D	55	6	1987
295	Univenture Columbus, OH	Manufactures compact disc packaging & storage prods.	912	17,212	1,700	C	D	111	23	1988

Rank ('97)	Company/Location	Business Description	Sales Growth 1992–96 (% increase)	1996 Sales ($000)	1992 Sales ($000)	Profit Range* '96	'92	No. of Employees '96	'92	Date Founded
296	Dreyfuss Hunt Boston, MA	Publishes health & finan. mgmt. newsletters	912	$ 2,905	$ 287	B	A	7	1	1987
297	E-Tek Dynamics San Jose, CA	Manufactures fiber-optic & communication devices & components	910	40,915	4,051	A	C	339	46	1983
298	Quality Imaging Products Levine, CA	Remfrs. cartridges for laser printers & copiers	910	2,060	204	A	A	37	4	1990
299	Magic Solutions Paramus, NJ	Provides help-desk software technology	909	29,289	2,902	E	E	235	2	1988
300	Parrot Ice Drink Products of America Houston, TX	Manufactures fruit beverages & dispensers	908	15,579	1,545	A	B	60	13	1986
301	Intelecon Services Dallas, TX	Provides audio-visual event staging, production, & equip. sales & svcs.	907	8,042	799	D	A	72	6	1991
302	Camber Huntsville, AL	Builds flight simulators & provides engineering svcs.	904	53,649	5,345	D	D	431	56	1985
303	Boxlight Poulsbo, WA	Distributes presentation & projection equip.	902	42,270	4,218	D	D	85	9	1985
304	Linksys Group Irvine, CA	Provides networking solutions	901	21,529	2,151	A	A	30	8	1988
305	PC Wholesale San Antonio, TX	Sells personal computers	897	11,952	1,199	D	D	35	6	1991
306	Eichrom Industries Darien, IL	Manufactures chemicals that remove metals from liquids	894	5,238	527	F	F	26	6	1990
307	Advanced Modular Power Systems Ann Arbor, MI	Manufactures electrical power systs.	892	2,787	281	D	D	30	6	1990
308	Preferred Technology San Francisco, CA	Provides stock execution svcs.	892	21,121	2,130	C	A	110	30	1982
309	NCI Information Systems McLean, VA	Provides telecommunication & information technology svcs.	891	52,303	5,278	D	C	788	69	1986
310	Microbar Sunnyvale, CA	Manufactures cabinets for chemical mgmt.	891	17,762	1,793	C	F	112	14	1991
311	Hoover's Austin, TX	Creates & publishes company information online & in print	888	3,960	401	F	F	60	9	1990
312	Sophisticated Systems Columbus, OH	Provides computer consulting & resells hardware & software	887	21,049	1,221	D	D	57	2	1990
313	Precision Bilt Spokane, WA	Provides commercial & industrial contracting svcs	886	4,871	494	D	C	10	1	1981
314	Goldhil Home Media Thousand Oaks, CA	Provides videotape production & distribution svcs.	881	6,609	674	C	F	13	4	1991

Rank ('97)	Company/Location	Business Description	Sales Growth 1992–96 (% increase)	1996 Sales ($000)	1992 Sales ($000)	Profit Range* '96	'92	No. of Employees '96	'92	Date Founded
315	Marketvision/Gateway Cincinnati, OH	Provides market research svcs.	880	$ 2,255	$ 230	C	F	32	11	1992
316	Independent Capital Management, Inc. Irvine, CA	Provides finan. svcs.	877	4,193	429	D	D	86	10	1988
317	Accelerated Technology Mobile, AL	Develops & mfrs. operating systs. software	877	2,871	294	C	F	36	6	1990
318	Armstrong Data Services Vienna, VA	Offers professional, engineering, & technical svcs.	874	21,508	2,209	D	F	385	51	1970
319	K.E.Y. Resources San Francisco, CA	Provides staffing svcs.	873	11,399	1,171	D	D	42	18	1992
320	Business Response Creve Coeur, MO	Provides telephone & computer svcs.	871	9,589	988	D	D	230	12	1986
321	Oneida Sales & Services Buffalo, NY	Manufactures & sells concrete & fencing prods.	867	7,085	733	D	E	40	5	1984
322	SolutionsIQ Bellevue, WA	Provides business software prods. & svcs.	866	16,848	1,744	D	F	186	31	1979
323	Subsystem Technologies Rosslyn, VA	Provides systs. integration svcs.	866	5,069	525	D	D	50	5	1986
324	Network Plus Quincy, MA	Provides long-distance telephone svcs.	864	75,135	7,794	D	D	250	30	990
325	Albany Molecular Research Albany, NY	Provides pharmaceutical research & manufacturing svcs.	863	6,261	650	A	A	66	9	1991
326	Realogic Cleveland, OH	Provides advanced technology & systs. integration consulting	863	14,840	1,541	D	D	155	30	1987
327	Excel Management Systems Columbus, OH	Provides computer consulting svcs.	862	11,236	1,168	D	D	80	15	1989
328	Statprobe Ann Arbor, MI	Provides health care research svcs.	861	8,883	924	E	C	191	21	1988
329	AccuData America Cape Coral, FL	Distributes marketing databases	861	6,120	637	C	F	65	8	1990
330	Executive Staffing Services of Columbia Columbia, SC	Provides temporary employment svcs.	858	1,974	206	D	D	9	2	1991
331	Dippin' Dots Paducah, KY	Manufactures novelty ice cream prods.	857	11,702	1,223	C	C	65	30	1987
332	Arizona Gazebos Phoenix, AZ	Manufactures & sells gazebos	854	2,348	246	C	B	30	7	1989
333	Power Source Distributors Burns, TN	Manufactures & distr. health food supplements	854	4,428	464	A	C	25	5	1988
334	Locus Direct Marketing Group Redlands, CA	Provides direct mail & database marketing svcs.	851	7,009	737	D	F	23	4	1990
335	Forn Services Downers Grove, IL	Imports & designs clothing	850	2,300	242	D	F	10	3	1989

Rank ('97)	Company/Location	Business Description	Sales Growth 1992–96 (% increase)	1996 Sales ($000)	1992 Sales ($000)	Profit Range* '96	'92	No. of Employees '96	'92	Date Founded
336	Premier Technologies Long Lake, MN	Manufactures high-tech digital announcement devices	849	$ 5,923	$ 624	A	C	43	6	1991
337	Island Automated Medical Services Saint Petersburg, FL	Provides medical billing svcs.	848	5,537	584	D	D	60	3	1992
338	Somero Enterprises Jaffrey, NH	Manufactures & markets construc-tion equip.	844	20,492	2,171	C	F	75	18	1986
339	Ensemble Dallas, TX	Provides computer consulting svcs.	843	4,103	435	C	B	51	5	1991
340	Fugazy Executive Travel Boston, MA	Provides corporate travel mgmt. svcs.	840	27,918	2,970	D	D	225	50	1973
341	Donjr Concrete Construction Lewisville, TX	Provides concrete construction svcs.	833	25,739	2,760	D	D	236	13	1985
342	Miramar Systems Santa Barbara, CA	Manufactures PCs	830	5,403	581	A	F	27	6	1990
343	Polybutylene Specialties Spring, TX	Provides general contracting svcs.	826	7,356	794	D	D	100	2	1989
344	ECI Conference Call Services Wayne, NJ	Provides worldwide audio teleconfer-encing	826	8,457	913	D	D	84	16	1991
345	Spinecare Brooklyn, NY	Provides health care svcs.	824	1,858	201	A	A	20	0	1987
346	Lloyd Lamont Design Herndon, VA	Provides architec-tural design svcs.	822	10,830	1,174	D	F	112	6	1986
347	Tier Technologies Walnut Creek, CA	Provides applica-tion development svcs. for Fortune 500 cos.	808	16,102	1,774	C	D	124	19	1991
348	Hi-Tech Electronic Sign Clearwater, FL	Sells LED displays for advertising & communications cos.	807	5,633	621	D	F	92	10	1984
349	Let's Talk Cellular of America Miami, FL	Sells cellular phones, communi-cations equip., & accessories	801	13,593	1,508	E	F	215	0	1989
350	Citipost New York, NY	Operates overnight delivery svcs.	798	8,067	898	D	C	192	24	1991
351	YMLA Los Angeles, CA	Manufactures men's clothing	791	12,926	1,451	D	D	60	6	1991
352	Staffworks Milwaukee, WI	Provides staffing svcs.	787	11,119	1,254	D	A	40	6	1992
353	Advanced Practical Thinking Training Des Moines, IA	Conducts training sessions & sells training-related materials	785	3,000	339	B	C	5	1	1991
354	BindView Develop-ment Houston, TX	Develops network systs. mgmt. soft-ware	780	11,002	1,250	A	A	79	10	1990
355	American Leather Dallas, TX	Manufactures custom leather-upholstered furni-ture	767	9,554	1,102	D	F	110	18	1990

Rank ('97)	Company/Location	Business Description	Sales Growth 1992–96 (% increase)	1996 Sales ($000)	1992 Sales ($000)	Profit Range* '96	Profit Range* '92	No. of Employees '96	No. of Employees '92	Date Founded
356	Computer Parts Unlimited Moorpark, CA	Resells computer parts & equip.	767	$ 11,728	$ 1,353	C	C	75	8	1991
357	Universal Systems & Technology Fairfax, VA	Provides information technology & simulation svcs.	766	21,560	2,489	D	B	150	20	1988
358	Tech Prose Walnut Creek, CA	Provides technical-writing svcs.	766	4,166	481	C	C	12	2	1988
359	Delta Corporate Services Parsippany, NJ	Provides information technology consulting svcs.	766	16,482	1,904	D	E	185	50	1991
360	S3LTD Virginia Beach, VA	Provides contracting svcs. for government	765	10,385	1,200	E	F	350	45	1985
361	Red & Blue Auto Rental San Diego, CA	Provides car rental svcs.	763	2,270	263	D	C	18	3	1986
362	Quality Data Systems Bloomington, MN	Provides information technology consulting svcs.	759	3,178	370	C	A	48	8	1991
363	Integram Fairfax, VA	Provides business-to-customer communication svcs.	757	6,170	720	B	F	20	7	1992
364	United Audio Visuals Muskego, WI	Rents audio & visual equip.	756	1,865	218	D	A	10	1	1990
365	Nanonics Phoenix, AZ	Sells nanominiature electronic connectors	755	3,353	392	B	F	37	10	1988
366	Syncro Vac Elgin, TX	Manufactures high-vacuum components	753	27,022	3,169	B	F	140	30	1982
367	RSI Hollywood, FL	Provides employee background screening svcs.	751	5,353	629	D	F	93	14	1988
368	Bottomline Technologies Portsmouth, NH	Develops & sells disbursement software & training svcs.	750	18,067	2,125	C	D	185	40	1989
369	New Concepts Santa Clara, CA	Repairs internal subassemblies for notebook computers	750	2,482	292	A	C	30	5	1991
370	Matrix Resources Atlanta, GA	Provides information systs. placement svcs.	749	60,098	7,078	B	C	500	100	1983
371	Teams Tempe, AZ	Provides assessment svcs. for businesses	748	3,442	406	A	F	45	10	1978
372	Ultimate Software Consultants Lombard, IL	Provides software consulting svcs.	747	9,741	1,150	C	E	87	12	1988
373	DPS Fresno, CA	Designs, mfrs., & sells alarm & control systs. for phone cos.	745	4,747	562	A	D	32	19	1986
374	GI Apparel Farmingdale, NJ	Manufactures & sells imprinted sportswear	743	11,683	1,386	C	D	159	25	1989
375	FGM Herndon, VA	Develops computer software & integrates computer systs	741	6,113	727	D	D	64	14	1987

Rank ('97)	Company/Location	Business Description	Sales Growth 1992–96 (% increase)	1996 Sales ($000)	1992 Sales ($000)	Profit Range* '96	'92	No. of Employees '96	'92	Date Founded
376	Professional Exhibits & Graphics Sunnyvale, CA	Manufactures trade-show graphics	741	$ 6,607	$ 786	D	E	40	14	1992
377	LaserCare Los Angeles, CA	Manufactures laser printers & supplies	739	1,845	220	D	D	24	10	1986
378	Interface Data Systems Phoenix, AZ	Manufactures electronic control devices	738	6,747	805	D	F	122	35	1991
379	Atlantic Realty Companies Vienna, VA	Provides real estate development, planning, & consulting svcs.	735	3,440	412	A	A	21	2	1992
380	Communications Products Indianapolis, IN	Provides network/telecom. integration systs.	730	16,118	1,942	F	D	87	13	1983
381	Barber Martin & Associates Richmond, VA	Provides advertising, marketing, & public relations svcs.	730	38,169	4,601	D	D	51	22	1988
382	General Shelters of Texas, S.B. Center, TX	Develops building structures & cooling systs.	729	8,559	1,032	D	F	119	6	1990
383	Rochester Software Associates Rochester, NY	Manufactures digital document production software	726	4,008	485	A	A	16	4	1986
384	Austin Tanner Garrett Tallahassee, FL	Provides computerized voice & fax svcs.	725	5,331	646	A	B	36	4	1987
385	Envirotech Services Enid, OK	Provides civil engineering & environmental consulting svcs.	724	1,780	216	C	F	27	1	1992
386	Alphatech Arlington, VA	Provides computer consulting svcs.	723	5,318	646	C	C	71	7	1989
387	Atlantic Search Group Cary, NC	Provides technical consulting for pharmaceutical & other industries	720	6,531	796	D	C	100	25	1986
388	Custom Transportation Service Braintree, MA	Provides transportation & limousine svcs.	719	4,292	524	C	E	142	18	1988
389	Delta Group Albuquerque, NM	Manufactures cables, wire harnesses, & electromechanical assemblies	711	5,606	691	D	F	70	18	1987
390	CD Smith Drug St. Joseph, MO	Provides wholesale pharmaceutical distribution svcs.	710	301,523	37,221	D	F	140	50	1886
391	Davis Co. Marlborough, MA	Provides temporary employee & mgmt. svcs.	709	30,940	3,824	D	D	52	8	1988
392	Computer Aided Service Los Altos, CA	Provides software & diagnostic equip. for automotive svcs.	708	15,046	1,861	F	F	75	50	1989
393	Hoff & Associates Ann Arbor, MI	Provides product design & engineering svcs.	708	2,732	338	D	B	24	4	1991
394	World Wide Technology St. Louis, MO	Provides systs. integration svcs.	706	81,582	10,119	D	D	92	24	1990

Rank ('97)	Company/Location	Business Description	Sales Growth 1992–96 (% increase)	1996 Sales ($000)	1992 Sales ($000)	Profit Range* '96	Profit Range* '92	No. of Employees '96	No. of Employees '92	Date Founded
395	Ex Officio Seattle, WA	Designs, imports, & distr. adventure-travel apparel	703	$ 6,937	$ 864	E	F	24	6	1986
396	Dazel Austin, TX	Manufactures mgmt. software	701	8,828	1,102	F	A	96	12	1991
397	ACS Systems & Engineering Virginia Beach, VA	Provides systs. integration, installation, & engineering design svcs.	694	8,228	1,036	C	D	130	2	1990
398	Radiant Systems Raleigh, NC	Manufactures heating equip. for engines	694	6,590	830	D	F	58	6	1989
399	Hamlin, Power & Reaves Springfield, IL	Provides automotive marketing & training svcs. & sells used cars	693	30,362	3,827	D	D	90	20	1989
400	Warm Springs Machining Waynesboro, PA	Manufactures & distr. hydraulic dump prods.	692	7,619	962	C	E	80	20	1989
401	National Computer Resource Wichita, KS	Sells new & used computer equip. & peripherals	691	8,024	1,014	D	D	51	10	1991
402	Logical Solution Lenexa, KS	Sells computers	691	10,239	1,294	D	D	22	3	1991
403	Triggiano Enterprises Phoenix, AZ	Manufactures construction-paper prods.	691	9,281	1,173	C	D	29	4	1991
404	NIE International Phoenix, AZ	Distributes computer systs. & parts	690	25,243	3,196	D	D	75	15	1990
405	Solid Concepts Valencia, CA	Provides rapid-prototyping & manufacturing svcs.	690	4,154	526	A	A	63	3	1991
406	Born Information Services Group Wayzata, MN	Provides information systs. consulting svcs.	686	35,604	4,528	C	D	426	99	1990
407	Continuus Software Irvine, CA	Provides client/server change & configuration mgmt.	686	16,099	2,049	F	F	125	33	1987
408	Analytical Graphics King of Prussia, PA	Provides software & satellite analysis tools for aerospace industry	685	6,962	887	E	D	66	10	1989
409	InfiNet Systems Turlock, CA	Provides systs. & network integration svcs.	684	2,978	380	D	A	18	3	1992
410	Micro Interactive New York, NY	Develops interactive multimedia software	683	3,310	423	B	B	40	9	1990
411	Jaffe Associates Washington, DC	Provides marketing, mgmt., & communication svcs.	682	3,510	449	F	C	25	6	1978
412	DPR Construction Redwood City, CA	Provides general construction contracting svcs.	681	619,557	79,294	D	D	925	125	1990
413	Triad Data New York, NY	Provides technology consulting svcs.	680	35,392	4,537	B	D	450	65	1985

Rank ('97)	Company/Location	Business Description	Sales Growth 1992–96 (% increase)	1996 Sales ($000)	1992 Sales ($000)	Profit Range* '96	'92	No. of Employees '96	'92	Date Founded
414	Infotech Enterprise Alexandria, VA	Provides software development & geographic information systs. svcs.	680	$ 2,059	$ 264	C	C	24	4	1990
415	Landmark Financial Services Dallas, TX	Provides residential mortgage svcs.	678	6,689	603	D	A	80	10	1988
416	Sun Time Enterprises Clearwater, FL	Manufactures licensed sports watches	678	7,783	1,001	B	A	50	5	1991
417	Key Environmental Services Cedarburg, WI	Provides environmental & geotechnical engineering & consulting svcs.	678	2,317	298	A	F	30	5	1992
418	Madison Research Huntsville, AL	Provides engineering & information technology svcs.	677	9,701	1,249	D	E	167	22	1986
419	Concrete Technology Largo, FL	Manufactures decorative concrete coatings	676	4,780	616	B	F	14	4	1992
420	Monitronics International Dallas, TX	Provides residential & commercial security svcs.	675	6,033	778	F	F	75	21	1988
421	M Squared San Francisco, CA	Provides interim mgmt. svcs.	675	7,011	905	D	F	25	3	1987
422	Midwest Datacomm Downers Grove, IL	Provides svcs. for local area networks & voice & data cabling	673	4,048	524	D	F	24	8	1990
423	Massachusetts Bay Brewing Boston, MA	Brews & distr. malt beverages	671	11,369	1,475	D	E	62	12	1986
424	Rich, Florin/Solutions Marlborough, MA	Provides compensation consulting svcs.	688	2,579	336	A	A	12	3	1992
425	OC Arlington, VA	Provides engineering & training svcs.	666	25,659	3,349	D	C	254	90	1987
426	Paradysz Matera & Co. New York, NY	Provides direct marketing svcs.	666	9,006	1,176	A	D	85	18	1990
427	Sharpe Capital New York, NY	Provides securities svcs.	663	12,366	1,620	D	F	85	11	1986
428	Stevens Professional Staffing New York, NY	Provides temporary staffing svcs.	662	2,638	346	E	E	3	1	1992
429	Interlink Communication Systems Clearwater, FL	Provides computer network integration svcs.	661	18,470	2,428	C	C	28	5	1990
430	Micro Modeling Associates New York, NY	Provides computer consulting svcs.	657	15,636	2,066	A	A	134	22	1989
431	Cost Management Systems Vienna, VA	Provides information systs. & consulting svcs.	652	12,834	1,707	D	D	150	29	1986
432	Granite Properties Dallas, TX	Provides commercial real estate investment svcs.	650	36,896	4,919	A	A	70	2	1991

Rank ('97)	Company/Location	Business Description	Sales Growth 1992–96 (% increase)	1996 Sales ($000)	1992 Sales ($000)	Profit Range* '96	'92	No. of Employees '96	'92	Date Founded
433	New Media Cleveland, OH	Provides information technology systs.	650	$ 8,660	$ 1,155	B	A	129	24	1988
434	Key Temporaries Atlanta, GA	Provides temporary employment svcs.	649	6,300	841	C	B	30	9	1988
435	Ringmasters Ogden, UT	Designs & distr. corporate, public safety, & religious prods.	648	2,288	306	A	D	22	2	1987
436	J. J. Grace Van Nuys, CA	Provides newspaper advertising outsourcing & graphic design svcs.	645	2,792	375	E	E	36	5	1987
437	Triad Technology Group Portland, OR	Provides staffing & recruiting svcs. for information technology firms	643	2,005	270	D	F	29	2	1992
438	ChemPro Spartanburg, SC	Manufactures & markets consumer & industrial cleaners	641	9,624	1,299	B	F	27	7	1990
439	Logistics Management Memphis, TN	Repairs & refurbishes electronic equip.	641	22,427	3,028	D	F	412	47	1989
440	Pinnacle Group Athens, AL	Designs, develops, & implements software & information solutions	638	24,120	3,270	B	C	228	15	1989
441	Indoff St. Louis, MO	Distributes & supplies storage equip. & furniture	637	50,889	6,902	D	F	200	30	1971
442	Emerald Resources North Syracuse, NY	Provides medical distr. svcs. for nursing homes & hospitals	637	3,222	437	D	D	12	6	1990
443	Construction Coordinators Needham, MA	Designs & constructs commercial projects	637	4,605	625	D	D	25	6	1991
444	United States Information Systems Nyack, NY	Provides telecom. svcs.	635	13,294	1,809	A	B	101	15	1988
445	DeBari Associates New York, NY	Provides litigation support & document-imaging svcs.	635	2,087	284	C	A	12	1	1987
446	Systems Integration Solutions San Francisco, CA	Provides consulting, information technology, & contracting svcs.	634	29,156	3,973	C	D	300	40	1990
447	BGB South San Francisco, CA	Manufactures trade-show exhibits	632	2,312	316	A	A	34	3	1991
448	NetPro Computing Scottsdale, AZ	Develops, publishes, & markets network utility software	629	7,009	961	D	F	52	9	1991
449	RapidPak Appleton, WI	Manufactures food packaging equip.	628	3,747	515	C	F	15	14	1989
450	Plitt Co. Chicago, IL	Distributes wholesale seafood prods.	627	10,765	1,480	D	D	46	7	1916
451	CIBT McLean, VA	Provides travel & visa svcs.	627	9,746	1,340	D	F	88	27	1989

Rank ('97)	Company/Location	Business Description	Sales Growth 1992–96 (% increase)	1996 Sales ($000)	1992 Sales ($000)	Profit Range*		No. of Employees		Date Founded
						'96	'92	'96	'92	
452	Dataworks Denver, CO	Publishes mgmt. logbooks for hospitality industry	627	$ 3,401	$ 468	A	C	74	16	1989
453	Bertech Industries Torrance, CA	Distributes electronic tools & supplies	625	3,190	440	D	C	18	1	1983
454	Maslow Media Group Arlington, VA	Provides staffing svcs. for video & film industry	625	4,174	576	A	A	7	3	1989
455	Eclipse Consulting Noblesville, IN	Provides computer consulting svcs.	620	2,649	368	D	A	39	6	1991
456	Russ Thomas Construction Cincinnati, OH	Provides commercial construction svcs.	617	14,446	2,014	C	D	215	20	1989
457	GeoAccess Overland Park, KS	Provides software & consulting svcs. for managed health care industry	616	9,708	1,356	A	A	82	11	1990
458	Noble-Met Salem, VA	Manufactures metal microtubing	614	8,084	1,132	A	A	55	9	1989
459	Bell Oaks Atlanta, GA	Offers executive search svcs.	613	2,568	360	C	F	34	4	1970
460	CAP Engineering Consultants Coral Gables, FL	Provides engineering consulting svcs.	612	5,744	807	B	A	90	14	1989
461	Maxim Computer Systems Fremont, CA	Sells & svcs. high-performance enterprise LANs	612	7,785	1,094	D	D	25	14	1988
462	Environmental & Occupational Risk Management San Jose, CA	Provides environmental safety consulting & engineering svcs.	610	6,594	929	D	A	69	20	1990
463	Liberty Bidco Investment Farmington Hills, MI	Invests in small businesses through debt or equity position	608	2,944	416	A	F	5	3	1988
464	Triumph Technologies Burlington, MA	Provides computer network integration & engineering svcs.	607	15,196	2,149	D	C	32	7	1988
465	Staffing Consultants Chicago, IL	Provides temporary staffing svcs.	605	11,594	1,644	D	F	42	21	1989
466	Architectural Specialties Trading Pensacola, FL	Manufactures commercial architectural woodwork	604	5,032	715	A	F	61	23	1990
467	Recore Arlington, TX	Supplies wholesale automotive parts	602	5,557	792	A	A	28	3	1991
468	Embedded Support Tools Canton, MA	Develops & mfrs. embedded systs. development tools	601	8,276	1,181	A	D	40	8	1989
469	Metro Technologies Manassas, VA	Sells computer & data communications equip.	601	17,757	2,534	C	A	68	3	1990
470	Party Land Plymouth Meeting, PA	Franchises retail party supply stores	598	2,986	428	D	F	130	6	1986
471	Retail Systems International Chula Vista, CA	Manufactures bar-code equip.	597	2,706	388	D	D	19	5	1991
472	Enterprise Networking Systems Redwood City, CA	Provides systs. integration svcs.	597	31,767	4,560	D	D	66	19	1989

Rank ('97)	Company/Location	Business Description	Sales Growth 1992–96 (% increase)	1996 Sales ($000)	1992 Sales ($000)	Profit Range* '96	'92	No. of Employees '96	'92	Date Founded
473	ShapsGroup Los Altos, CA	Provides accounts-payable recovery svcs.	595	$ 2,676	$ 385	D	E	7	1	1991
474	Policy Studies Denver, CO	Provides mgmt. consulting & information technology svcs.	595	20,594	2,963	D	E	414	49	1984
475	Aspen Temporary Services Takoma Park, MD	Provides temporary help svcs.	595	7,448	1,072	D	D	280	75	1988
476	ABCOW Services San Diego, CA	Provides temporary employment svcs.	594	3,450	497	D	F	12	3	1989
477	Babbidge Facilities Construction New Haven, CT	Offers general contracting & mgmt. svcs.	589	2,475	359	D	D	6	2	1992
478	Entact Irving, TX	Provides environmental consulting & remediation svcs.	588	13,093	1,902	B	F	85	15	1991
479	Optical Laser Huntington Beach, CA	Distributes optical technology	586	19,797	2,885	E	F	35	6	1988
480	Ascher Group Roseland, NJ	Provides staffing svcs.	584	3,840	561	D	F	9	5	1981
481	Freeman Associates Wellesley, MA	Provides media marketing svcs. for print, online, & trade-show planning	584	2,557	374	A	A	30	4	1986
482	Novtek San Jose, CA	Manufactures test equip. for flash-memory prods.	582	9,056	1,327	A	D	32	10	1986
483	Power Devices Laguna Hills, CA	Sells thermal mgmt. materials	579	2,765	407	D	F	34	8	1984
484	Dove Data Products Florence, SC	Manufactures & recycles computer printer supplies	577	3,061	452	E	F	37	10	1991
485	ABC Technologies Beaverton, OR	Develops software & svcs. for activity-based mgmt.	576	10,134	1,499	C	F	84	20	1989
486	Magellan's International Travel Santa Barbara, CA	Publishes mail-order catalogs	576	4,847	717	D	F	45	15	1989
487	Planned Systems International Columbia, MD	Provides systs. integration svcs.	576	9,356	1,385	D	D	165	8	1988
488	Computer Networks Pleasanton, CA	Provides systs. integration svcs.	574	4,304	639	D	D	13	1	1991
489	Lancast Nashua, NH	Develops & mfrs. data communications equip.	574	15,060	2,236	D	C	64	12	1981
490	Boulder Heuristics Boulder, CO	Develops high-tech software & provides consulting svcs.	573	6,096	906	C	C	46	9	1988
491	Valcom Middleton, WI	Provides PC technology solutions	573	42,859	6,371	D	F	97	31	1984
492	TeleMark Portland, OR	Provides telemarketing svcs.	571	29,480	4,396	E	C	1,400	422	1987
493	Working Assets Funding Service San Francisco, CA	Provides donation-linked long-distance telephone svcs.	569	104,418	15,611	C	F	87	32	1985

Rank ('97)	Company/Location	Business Description	Sales Growth 1992–96 (% increase)	1996 Sales ($000)	1992 Sales ($000)	Profit Range* '96	'92	No. of Employees '96	'92	Date Founded
494	**American Incorporators Registered Agents** Wilmington, DE	Provides incorporating svcs.	568	$ 1,789	$ 268	B	A	6	3	1979
495	**Harrington Group** Orlando, FL	Develops & sells software for quality-assurance industry	567	1,508	226	E	F	20	3	1991
496	**System One Technical** Tampa, FL	Provides solutions for information technology & telecom. cos.	563	46,237	6,971	E	D	189	25	1987
497	**HCI Technologies** Reston, VA	Provides telecom. & information systs. consulting svcs.	563	9,567	1,443	E	B	115	21	1985
498	**Original American Scones** Oak Park, IL	Manufactures fresh & frozen baked goods	563	10,534	1,590	E	C	175	41	1986
499	**Empire Graphics** New York, NY	Provides commercial printing svcs.	562	4,947	747	A	A	51	2	1991
500	**Telogy Networks** Germantown, MD	Manufactures software-based telecom. systs. & prods	559	10,807	1,639	F	F	128	18	1989

APPENDIX 8

AVERAGE ANNUAL PAY, BY STATE: 1994 AND 1995

Source: Statistical Abstract of the United States 1997, Table 669 (from U.S. Bureau of Labor Statistics, USDL News 96-393). Figures given are for workers covered by state unemployment insurance laws and for federal civilian workers covered by unemployment compensation, approximately 97 percent of wage and salary civilian employment in 1995. Table excludes most agricultural workers on small farms, all armed forces, elected officials in most states, railroad employees, most domestic workers, most student workers at school, employees of certain nonprofit organizations, and most self-employed individuals. Pay includes bonuses, cash value of meals and lodging, and tips and other gratuities.

State	Average Annual Pay		Percent Change, 1994–1995*
	1994	1995*	
United States	$26,939	$27,845	3.4
Alabama	23,616	24,396	3.3
Alaska	32,657	32,685	0.1
Arizona	24,276	25,324	4.3
Arkansas	20,898	21,590	3.3
California	29,878	30,716	2.8
Colorado	26,155	27,122	3.7
Connecticut	33,811	35,127	3.9
Delaware	27,952	29,120	4.2
District of Columbia	40,919	42,453	3.7
Florida	23,918	24,710	3.3
Georgia	25,313	26,303	3.9
Hawaii	26,746	26,977	0.9
Idaho	21,938	22,839	4.1
Illinois	29,107	30,099	3.4
Indiana	24,908	25,571	2.7
Iowa	22,189	22,875	3.1
Kansas	22,907	23,709	3.5
Kentucky	22,747	23,490	3.3
Louisiana	23,178	23,894	3.1
Maine	22,389	23,117	3.3
Maryland	28,416	29,133	2.5
Massachusetts	31,024	32,353	4.3
Michigan	29,541	30,543	3.4
Minnesota	26,422	27,383	3.6
Mississippi	20,382	21,120	3.6
Missouri	24,628	25,669	4.2
Montana	20,218	20,516	1.5
Nebraska	21,500	22,368	4.0
Nevada	25,700	26,647	3.7
New Hampshire	25,555	26,602	4.1
New Jersey	33,439	34,534	3.3
New Mexico	22,351	22,960	2.7
New York	33,439	34,938	4.5
North Carolina	23,460	24,402	4.0
North Dakota	19,893	20,492	3.0
Ohio	26,134	26,867	2.8
Oklahoma	22,293	22,671	1.7
Oregon	24,780	25,833	4.2
Pennsylvania	26,950	27,904	3.5
Rhode Island	25,454	26,375	3.6

State	Average Annual Pay		Percent Change, 1994–1995*
	1994	1995*	
South Carolina	22,477	23,292	3.6
South Dakota	19,255	19,931	3.5
Tennessee	24,106	25,046	3.9
Texas	25,959	26,900	3.6
Utah	22,811	23,626	3.6
Vermont	22,964	23,583	2.7
Virginia	26,035	26,894	3.3
Washington	26,362	27,453	4.1
West Virginia	22,959	23,489	2.3
Wisconsin	24,324	25,099	3.2
Wyoming	22,054	22,351	1.3

* Preliminary.

APPENDIX 9

SMALL BUSINESS ADMINISTRATION FIELD OFFICES
Source: http://www.sba.gov/cgi-bin/replace/states/me

Office	Address	Telephone
Region I		
Augusta, ME (DO)	40 Western Ave., 04330	(207) 622-8378
Boston, MA (RO)	10 Causeway St., 02222-1093	(617) 565-8415
Boston, MA (DO)	10 Causeway St., 02222-1093	(617) 565-5590
Concord, NH (DO)	143 N. Main St., 03301	(603) 225-1400
Hartford, CT (DO)	330 Main St., 06106	(203) 240-4700
Montpelier, VT (DO)	87 State St., 05602	(802) 828-4422
Providence, RI (DO)	380 Westminister Mall, 02903	(401) 528-4562
Springfield, MA (BO)	Ste. 140, 1441 Main St., 01103	(413) 785-0268
Region II		
Buffalo, NY (DO)	111 West Huron St., 14202	(716) 551-4301
Elmira, NY (BO)	333 East Water St., 14901	(607) 734-8130
Hato Rey, PR (DO)	252 Ponce de León Ave., 00918	(809) 766-5572
Melville, NY (BO)	35 Pinelawn Rd., 11747	(516) 454-0750
New York, NY (RO)	26 Federal Plaza, 10278	(212) 264-1450
New York, NY (DO)	26 Federal Plaza, 10278	(212) 264-2454
Newark, NJ (DO)	Two Gateway Ctr., 4th Fl., 07102	(201) 645-2434
Rochester, NY (BO)	100 State St., 14614	(716) 263-6700
St. Croix, VI (POD)	3013 Golden Rock, 00820	(809) 778-5380
St. Thomas, VI (POD)	3800 Crown Bay, 00802	(809) 774-8530
Syracuse, NY (DO)	100 S. Clinton St., 13260	(315) 448-0423
Region III		
Baltimore, MD (DO)	10 S. Howard St., 21201-2525	(410) 962-4392
Charleston, WV (BO)	550 Eagan St., 25301	(304) 347-5220
Clarksburg, WV (DO)	168 W. Main St., 26301	(304) 623-5631
Harrisburg, PA (BO)	100 Chestnut St., 17101	(717) 782-3840
King of Prussia, PA (RO)	475 Allendale Rd., 19406	(610) 962-3700
King of Prussia, PA (DO)	475 Allendale Rd., 19406	(610) 962-3800
Pittsburgh, PA (DO)	960 Penn Ave., 15222	(412) 644-2780
Richmond, VA (DO)	1504 Santa Rosa Rd., Dale Bldg., Ste. 200, 23229	(804) 771-2400
Washington, DC (DO)	1110 Vermont Ave. NW, 20005	(202) 606-4000
Wilkes-Barre, PA	20 N. Pennsylvania Ave., 18701-3589	(717) 826-6497
Wilmington, DE (BO)	824 N. Market St., 19801-3011	(302) 573-6294
Region IV		
Atlanta, GA (RO)	1720 Peachtree Rd. NW, 30309-2482	(404) 347-4999
Atlanta, GA (DO)	1720 Peachtree Rd. NW, 30309	(404) 347-4749
Birmingham, AL (DO)	2121 8th Ave. N, 35203-2398	(205) 731-1344
Charlotte, NC (DO)	200 N. College St., 28202-2137	(704) 344-6563
Columbia, SC (DO)	1835 Assembly St., 29201	(803) 765-5377
Coral Gables, FL (DO)	1320 S. Dixie Hgwy., 33146-2911	(305) 536-5521
Gulfport, MS (BO)	Ste. 203, 1 Government Plaza, 39501-7758	(601) 863-4449
Jackson, MS (DO)	101 W. Capitol St., 39201	(601) 965-4378
Jacksonville, FL (DO)	7825 Baymeadows Way, 32256-7504	(904) 443-1900
Louisville, KY (DO)	600 Dr. M. L. King Jr Pl., 40202	(502) 582-5971
Nashville, TN (DO)	50 Vantage Way, 37228-1500	(615) 736-5881

Office	Address	Telephone
Region V		
Chicago, IL (RO)	500 W. Madison St., 60661-2511	(312) 353-5000
Chicago, IL (DO)	500 W. Madison St., 60661-2511	(312) 353-4528
Cincinnati, OH (BO)	525 Vine St., 45202	(513) 684-2814
Cleveland, OH (DO)	1111 Superior Ave., 44114-2507	(216) 522-4180
Columbus, OH (DO)	2 Nationwide Plaza, 43215-2592	(614) 469-6860
Detroit, MI (DO)	477 Michigan Ave., 48226	(313) 226-6075
Indianapolis, IN (DO)	429 N. Pennsylvania, 46204-1873	(317) 226-7272
Madison, WI (DO)	212 E. Washington Ave., 53703	(608) 264-5261
Marquette, MI (BO)	501 South Front St., 49855	(906) 225-1108
Milwaukee, WI (BO)	310 W. Wisconsin Ave., 53203	(414) 297-3941
Minneapolis, MN (DO)	100 N. 6th St., 55403-1563	(612) 370-2324
Springfield, IL (BO)	511 W. Capitol Ave., 62704	(217) 492-4416
Region VI		
Albuquerque, NM (DO)	625 Silver Ave. SW, 87102	(505) 766-1870
Corpus Christi, TX (BO)	606 North Carancahua, 78476	(512) 888-3331
Dallas/Ft. Worth, TX (RO)	4300 Amon Carter Blvd., 76155	(817) 885-6581
Dallas/Ft. Worth, TX (DO)	4300 Amon Carter Blvd., 76155	(817) 885-6500
El Paso, TX (DO)	10737 Gateway West, 79935	(915) 540-5676
Harlingen, TX (DO)	222 East Van Buren St., 78550	(210) 427-8533
Houston, TX (DO)	9301 Southwest Freeway, 77074-1591	(713) 773-6500
Little Rock, AR (DO)	2120 Riverfront Dr., 72202	(501) 324-5278
Lubbock, TX (DO)	1611 Tenth St., 79401-2693	(806) 743-7462
New Orleans, LA (DO)	365 Canal St., 70130	(504) 589-6685
Oklahoma City, OK (DO)	Ste. 670, 200 N.W. 5th St., 73102	(405) 231-5521
San Antonio, TX (DO)	727 E. Durango, 78206	(210) 472-5900
Region VII		
Cedar Rapids, IA (DO)	215 4th Avenue Rd. SE, 52401-1806	(319) 362-6405
Des Moines, IA (DO)	210 Walnut St., 50309	(515) 284-4422
Kansas City, MO (RO)	Ste. 307, 323 W. 8th St., 64105-1500	(816) 374-6380
Kansas City, MO (DO)	Ste. 501, 323 W. 8th St., 64105-1500	(816) 374-6708
Omaha, NE (DO)	11145 Mill Valley Rd., 68154	(402) 221-4691
Springfield, MO (BO)	620 S. Glenstone St., 65802-3200	(417) 864-7670
St. Louis, MO (DO)	815 Olive St., 63101	(314) 539-6600
Wichita, KS (DO)	100 East English St., 67202	(316) 269-6616
Region VIII		
Casper, WY (DO)	100 East B St., 82602	(307) 261-5761
Denver, CO (RO)	721 19th St., 80202	(303) 844-0500
Denver, CO (DO)	721 19th St., 80201	(303) 844-3984
Fargo, ND (DO)	657 2nd Ave. N, 58108	(701) 239-5131
Helena, MT (DO)	301 South Park, 59626	(406) 441-1081
Salt Lake City, UT (DO)	125 South State St., 84138	(801) 524-5800
Sioux Falls, SD (DO)	101 South Main Ave., 57102	(605) 330-4231
Region IX		
Mongmong, GU (BO)	Ste. 302, 400 Route 8, 96927	(671) 472-7277
Fresno, CA (DO)	2719 N. Air Fresno Dr., 93727-1547	(209) 487-5791
Glendale, CA (DO)	330 N. Brand Blvd., 91203-2304	(818) 552-3210
Honolulu, HI (DO)	300 Ala Moana Blvd., 96850-4981	(808) 541-2990
Las Vegas, NV (DO)	301 East Stewart St., 89125-2527	(702) 388-6611
Phoenix, AZ (DO)	2828 N. Central Ave., 85004-1025	(602) 640-2316
Sacramento, CA (DO)	Ste. 215, 660 J St., 95814-2413	(916) 498-6410
San Diego, CA (DO)	550 W. C St., 92101	(619) 557-7252

Office	Address	Telephone
Region IX (*cont.*)		
San Francisco, CA (RO)	Ste. 2200, 455 Market St., 94105	(415) 744-2118
San Francisco, CA (DO)	455 Market St., 6th Fl., 94105-2445	(415) 744-6820
Santa Ana, CA (DO)	200 W. Santa Ana Blvd #700, 92701	(714) 550-7420
Region X		
Anchorage, AK (DO)	222 West 8th Ave., 99513-7559	(907) 271-4022
Boise, ID (DO)	1020 Main St., 93702-5745	(208) 334-1696
Portland, OR (DO)	222 S.W. Columbia St., 97201-6695	(503) 326-2682
Seattle, WA (RO)	Ste. 1805, 1200 6th Ave., 98101-1128	(206) 553-5676
Seattle, WA (DO)	Ste. 1700, 1200 6th Ave., 98101-1128	(206) 553-7310
Spokane, WA (DO)	West 601 First Ave., 99204-0317	(509) 353-2800

RO = regional office   DO = district office
BO = branch office   POD = post of duty

APPENDIX 10

U.S. GOVERNMENT PRINTING OFFICE BOOKSTORES

Source: http://www.access.gpo.gov/su_docs/sale/abkst001.html, document name: printing.off.

City	Address	Telephone
Washington, DC, area:		
Main Bookstore	710 N. Capitol St. NW	202-512-0132
McPherson Square	1510 H St. NW	202-653-5075
Warehouse Sales Outlet	8660 Cherry Lane, Laurel, Md.	301-953-7974
Atlanta, GA	Ste. 120, 999 Peachtree St. NE	404-347-1900
Birmingham, AL	2021 Third Ave. N	205-731-1056
Boston, MA	Rm. 169, 10 Causeway St.	617-720-4180
Chicago, IL	Ste. 124, 401 South State St.	312-353-5133
Cleveland, OH	Rm. 1653, 1240 E. 9th St.	216-522-4922
Columbus, OH	Rm. 207, 200 N. High St.	614-469-6956
Dallas, TX	Rm. IC50, 1100 Commerce St.	214-767-0076
Denver, CO	Rm. 117, 1961 Stout St.	303-844-3964
Detroit, MI	Ste. 160, 477 Michigan Ave.	313-226-7816
Houston, TX	Ste. 120, 801 Travis St.	713-228-1187
Jacksonville, FL	Ste. 100, 100 West Bay St.	904-353-0569
Kansas City, MO	120 Bannister Mall, 5600 E. Bannister Rd.	816-765-2256
Los Angeles, CA	C-Level, ARCO Plaza, 505 South Flower St.	213-239-9844
Milwaukee, WI	Ste. 150, 310 W. Wisconsin Ave.	414-297-1304
New York, NY	Rm. 2-120, 26 Federal Plaza	212-264-3825
Philadelphia, PA	100 North 17th St.	215-636-1900
Pittsburgh, PA	Rm. 118, 1000 Liberty Ave.	412-644-2721
Portland, OR	1305 S.W. First Ave.	503-221-6217
Pueblo, CO	201 West 8th St.	719-544-3142
San Francisco, CA	Rm. 141-S, 303 2nd St.	415-512-2770
Seattle, WA	Rm. 194, 915 Second Ave.	206-553-4270

APPENDIX 11

EXPORT ASSISTANCE CENTER DIRECTORY
U.S. Department of Commerce, International Trade Administration, U.S. and Foreign Commercial Service

District/Address	Telephone
Anchorage, AK (3601 C St., Ste. 700, 99503)	(907) 271-6237
Ann Arbor, MI (425 S. Main St., Ste. 103, 48104)	(313) 741-2430
Atlanta, GA (285 Peachtree Center Ave. NE, Ste. 200, 30303-1229)	(404) 657-1900
Austin, TX (1700 Congress, 2nd Fl., 78701, P.O. Box 12728, 78711)	(512) 916-5939
Baltimore, MD (World Trade Center, Ste. 2432, 401 E. Pratt St., 21202)	(410) 962-4539
Birmingham, AL (950 22nd St. N, Rm. 707, 35203)	(205) 731-1331
Boise, ID (700 W. State St., 2nd Fl., 83720)	(208) 334-3857
Boston, MA (164 Northern Avenue World Trade Center, Ste. 307, 02210)	(617) 424-5990
Buffalo, NY (111 W. Huron St., Rm. 1304, 14202)	(716) 551-4191
Charleston, SC (P.O. Box 975, 29402; 81 Mary St., 29403)	(803) 727-4051
Charleston, WV (405 Capitol St., Ste. 807, 25301)	(304) 347-5123
Charlotte, NC (521 E. Morehead St., Ste. 435, Charlotte, 28202)	(704) 333-4886
Chicago, IL (55 W. Monroe St., Ste. 2440, 60603)	(312) 353-8045
Cincinnati, OH (36 E. 7th St., Ste. 2650, 45202)	(513) 684-2944
Clearwater, FL (1130 Cleveland St., 34615)	(813) 461-0011
Cleveland, OH (600 Superior Ave. E., Ste. 700, 44114)	(216) 522-4750
Columbia, SC (1835 Assembly St., Ste. 172, 29201)	(803) 765-5345
Columbus, OH (37 N. High St., 4th Fl., 43215)	(614) 365-9510
Dallas, TX (P.O. Box 420069, 75342-0069, 2050 N. Stemmons Fwy., Ste. 170, 75207)	(214) 767-0542
Delaware: Served by the Philadelphia, Pa., U.S. Export Assistance Center	(215) 597-6101
Denver, CO (1625 Broadway, Ste. 680, 80202)	(303) 844-6622
Des Moines, IA (210 Walnut St., Rm. 817, 50309)	(515) 284-4222
Detroit, MI (211 W. Fort St., Ste. 2220, 48226)	(313) 226-3650
Eugene, OR (1445 Willamette St., Ste. 13, 97401-4003)	(541) 465-6575
Fort Worth, TX (711 Houston St., 76102)	(817) 212-2673
Fresno, CA (390-B Fir Ave., Clovis, 93611)	(209) 325-1619
Grand Rapids, MI (301 W. Fulton St., Ste. 718-S, 49504)	(616) 458-3564
Greensboro, NC (400 W. Market St., Ste. 400, 27401)	(910) 333-5345
Greenville, SC (Park Central Office Park, Bldg. 1, Ste. 109, 555 N. Pleasantburg Dr., 29607)	(864) 271-1976
Harlem, NY (163 W. 125th St., Ste. 904, New York, NY 10027)	(212) 860-6200
Harrisburg, PA (One Commerce Square, 417 Walnut St., 3rd Fl., 17101)	(717) 232-0051
Highland Park, IL (610 Central Ave., Ste. 150, 60035)	(847) 681-8010
Honolulu, HI (P.O. Box 50026—300 Ala Moana Blvd., Rm. 4106, 96850)	(808) 541-1782
Houston, TX (500 Dallas, Ste. 1160, 77002)	(713) 718-3062
Indianapolis, IN (11405 N. Pennsylvania St., Ste. 106, Carmel, 46032)	(317) 582-2300
Inland Empire, CA (2940 Inland Empire Blvd., Ste. 121, Ontario, 91764)	(909) 466-4134
Kansas City, MO (601 E. 12th St., Rm. 635, 64106)	(816) 426-3141
Knoxville, TN (301 E. Church Ave., 37915)	(423) 545-4637
Little Rock, AR (425 W. Capitol Ave., Ste. 700, 72201)	(501) 324-5794
Long Beach, CA (One World Trade Center, Ste. 1670, 90831)	(562) 980-4550
Long Island, NY (1550 Franklin Ave., Rm. 207, Mineola, 11501)	(516) 739-1765
Los Angeles (Downtown), CA (350 S. Figueroa St., Ste. 172, 90071)	(213) 894-8784
Los Angeles (West), CA (1150 Olympic Blvd., Ste. 975, 90064)	(310) 235-7104
Louisville, KY (601 W. Broadway, Rm. 634B, 40202)	(502) 582-5066
Marlborough, MA (100 Granger Blvd., Unit 102, 01752)	(508) 624-6000

District/Address	Telephone
Memphis, TN (22 N. Front St., Ste. 200, 38103)	(901) 544-4137
Miami, FL (P.O. Box 590570, 33159; 5600 N.W. 36th St., Ste. 617, 33166)	(305) 526-7425
Middletown, CT (213 Court St., Ste. 903, 06457-3346)	(860) 638-6950
Milwaukee, WI (517 E. Wisconsin Ave., Rm. 596, 53202)	(414) 297-3473
Minneapolis, MN (110 S. 4th St., Rm. 108, 55401)	(612) 348-1638
Montana: Served by the Boise, Idaho, Export Assistance Center	(208) 334-3857
Monterey, CA (411 Pacific St., Ste. 200, 93940)	(408) 641-9850
Montpelier, VT (National Life Building, Drawer 20, 05620-0501)	(802) 828-4508
Nashville, TN (Parkway Towers, Ste. 114, 404 James Robertson Pkwy., 37219)	(615) 736-5161
New Orleans, LA (365 Canal St., Ste. 2150, New Orleans, 70130)	(504) 589-6546
New York, NY (6 World Trade Center, Rm. 635, 10048)	(212) 466-5222
Newark, NJ (One Gateway Center, 9th Fl., 07102)	(201) 645-4682
North Dakota: Served by the Minneapolis, Minn. Export Assistance Center	(612) 348-1638
Novato, CA (330 Ignacio Blvd., Ste. 102, 94949)	(415) 883-1966
Oakland, CA (530 Water St., Ste. 740, 94607)	(510) 273-7350
Oklahoma City, OK (301 N.W. 63rd St., Ste. 330, 73116)	(405) 231-5302
Omaha, NE (11135 "O" Street, 68137)	(402) 221-3664
Orange County, CA (3300 Irvine Ave., Ste. 305, Newport Beach, 92660)	(714) 660-1688
Orlando, FL (200 E. Robinson St., Ste. 1270, 32801)	(407) 648-6235
Oxnard, CA (300 Esplanade Dr., Ste. 2090, 93030)	(805) 981-8150
Philadelphia, PA (615 Chestnut St., Ste. 1501, 19106)	(215) 597-6101
Phoenix, AZ (2901 N. Central Ave., Ste. 970, 85012)	(602) 640-2513
Pittsburgh, PA (2002 Federal Bldg., 1000 Liberty Ave., 15222)	(412) 395-5050
Pontiac, MI (Oakland Pointe Office Bldg., 250 Elizabeth Lake Rd., 48341)	(248) 975-9600
Portland, ME (511 Congress St., 04101)	(207) 541-7400
Portland, OR (One World Trade Center, Ste. 242, 121 S.W. Salmon St., 97204)	(503) 326-3001
Portsmouth, NH (17 New Hampshire Ave., 03801-2838)	(603) 334-6074
Providence, RI (One West Exchange St., 02903)	(401) 528-5104
Raymond, MS (704 E. Main St., Raymond, 39164)	(601) 857-0126
Reno, NV (1755 E. Plumb Lane, Ste. 152, 89502)	(702) 784-5203
Richmond, VA (704 E. Franklin St., Ste. 550, 23219)	(804) 771-2246
Rochester, NY (111 W. Huron St., Rm. 1304, 14604)	(716) 263-6480
Rockford, IL (P.O. Box 1747, 61103)	(815) 987-8123
Sacramento, CA (917 7th St., 2nd Fl., 95814)	(916) 498-5155
Salt Lake City, UT (324 S. State St., Ste. 221, 84111)	(801) 524-5116
San Antonio, TX (1222 N. Main, Ste. 450, 78212)	(210) 228-9878
San Diego, CA (6363 Greenwich Dr., Ste. 230, 92122)	(619) 557-5395
San Francisco, CA (250 Montgomery St., 14th Fl., 94104)	(415) 705-2300
San Francisco/World Trade Center, CA (345 California St., 7th Fl., 94104)	(415) 705-1053
San Jose, CA (101 Park Center Plaza, Ste. 1001, 95113)	(408) 271-7300
San Juan, PR (525 F. D. Roosevelt Ave., Ste. 905, 00918)	(787) 766-5555
Santa Clara, CA (5201 Great America Pkwy., #456, 95054)	(408) 970-4610
Santa Fe, NM (P.O. Box 20003, 87504-5003)	(505) 827-0350
Savannah, GA (6001 Chatham Center Dr., Ste. 100, 31405)	(912) 652-4204
Scranton, PA (One Montage Mountain Rd., Ste. B, Moosic, 18507)	(717) 969-2530
Seattle, WA (2001 6th Ave., Ste. 650, 98121)	(206) 553-5615
Shreveport, LA (5210 Hollywood Ave.—Annex Shreveport, 71109)	(318) 676-3064
Siouxland, SD (Augustana College, 2001 S. Summit Ave., Rm. SS-29A, Sioux Falls, 57197)	(605) 330-4264
Somerset, KY (2292 S. Highway 27, Ste. 320, 42501)	(606) 677-6160
Spokane, WA (1020 W. Riverside, 99201)	(509) 353-2625
St. Louis, MO (8182 Maryland Ave., Ste. 303, 63105)	(314) 425-3302
Tallahassee, FL (The Capitol, Ste. 2001, 32399-0001)	(904) 488-6469
Toledo, OH (300 Madison Ave., 43604)	(419) 241-0683
Trenton, NJ (3131 Princeton Pike, Bldg. #6, Ste. 100, 08648)	(609) 989-2100
Tulsa, OK (700 N. Greenwood Ave., Ste. 1400, 74106)	(918) 581-7650

District/Address	Telephone
Westchester, NY (707 West Chester Ave., White Plains, 10604)	(914) 682-6218
Wheaton, IL (201 East Loop Rd., 60187)	(312) 353-4332
Wheeling, WV (1310 Market St., 2nd Fl., 26003)	(304) 233-7472
Wichita, KS (151 N. Volutsia, 67214)	(316) 269-6160
Wyoming: Served by the Denver, Colo., U.S. Export Assistance Center	(303) 844-6622

Web site addresses for the Commercial Service State Homepages are http://www.ita.doc.gov/uscs/**.

** is the two-letter state abbreviation or mail code.

APPENDIX 12

INDUSTRIAL SECTOR OFFICERS OF THE INTERNATIONAL TRADE ADMINISTRATION OF THE U.S. DEPARTMENT OF COMMERCE
(As of June 17, 1997)

Industry	Contact	Phone (202) 482
Abrasive products	Presbury, Graylin	5158
Accounting	Chittum, J. Marc	0345
Adhesives/sealants	Prat, Raimundo	0810
Advanced materials	Brosler, Lauren	4431
Advertising	Harsh, Bruce	4582
Aerospace, Office of	Bath, Sally H.	1229
Aerospace—space market support	Wells, Kim	2232
Aerospace—space programs	Farner, Kim	2232
Aerospace (trade promotion)	Largay, Tony	6236
Aerospace financing issues	Montgomery, Jon	6234
Aerospace industry analysis	Elliott, Frederick	1233
Aerospace industry data	Green, Ronald	3068
Aerospace information and analysis	Green, Ronald	3068
Aerospace market development	Largay, Tony	6236
Aerospace market promotion	Largay, Tony	6236
Aerospace marketing support	Pederson, Heather	6239
Aerospace trade policy	Elliott, Frederick	1233
Agricultural chemicals	Kelly, Michael	0811
Agricultural machinery	Wiening, Mary	4708
Air, gas compressors	Heimowitz, Leonard	0558
Air, gas compressors (trade promotion)	Zanetakos, George	0552
Air couriers	Alford, Eugene	5071
Air pollution control equipment	Fredell, Eric	0343
Air traffic control equipment	Ballard, Shannon	3786
Air transport services	Alford, Eugene	5071
Air-conditioning equipment	Shaw, Eugene	3494
Aircraft and aircraft engines (market support)	Pederson, Heather	6239
Aircraft auxiliary equipment	Pederson, Heather	6239
Aircraft parts (market support)	Ballard, Shannon	3786
Airlines	Alford, Eugene	5071
Airport (major projects)	Thompson, Michael	5126
Airport equipment	Ballard, Shannon	3786
Alcoholic beverages	Hodgen, Donald A.	3346
Aluminum	Cammarota, David	5157
Aluminum oxide	Presbury, Graylin	5158
Analytical instrument	Litman, George	3411
Analytical and scientific instruments (trade promotion)	Manzolillo, Franc	2991
Apparel	Tucker, Joanne	4058
Apparel (trade promotion)	Molnar, Ferenc	5153
Artificial intelligence	Diaz, Mike	0397
Asbestos/cement products	Pitcher, Charles B.	0385
Audiovisual services	Siegmund, John E.	4781
Auto industry (trade promotion)	White, John C.	0671
Auto industry affairs	Misisco, Henry	0554
Auto parts and suppliers	Reck, Robert O.	1418
Aviation services	Alford, Eugene	5071
Avionics marketing	Pederson, Heather	6239

Industry	Contact	Phone (202) 482
Bakery products	Hodgen, Donald A.	3346
Ball bearings	Reise, Richard	3489
Banking services	Shuman, John	3050
Basic paper and board manufacturing	Stanley, Gary	0376
Bauxite, alumina	Cammarota, David	5157
Beer	Hodgen, Donald A.	3346
Belting and hose	Prat, Raimundo	0810
Beryllium	Males, Barbara	0606
Beverages	Hodgen, Donald A.	3346
Bicycles	Vanderwolf, John	0348
Biomass energy equipment	Garden, Les	0556
Biotechnology	Arakaki, Emily	0130
Boats, pleasure	Vanderwolf, John	0348
Books	Lofquist, William S.	0379
Breakfast cereal	Hodgen, Donald A.	3346
Bridges (major projects)	Thompson, Michael	5126
Broadcasting equipment	Jenci, Krysten	2952
Brooms and brushes	Harris, John M.	1178
Building materials and construction	Pitcher, Charles B.	0385
Business equipment (trade promotion)	Fogg, Judy A.	4936
Business forms	Bratland, Rose Marie	0380
CAD/CAM/CAE software	Swann, Vera A.	0396
Canned food products	Hodgen, Donald A.	3346
Carbon black	Prat, Raimundo	0810
Cellular radio telephone equipment	Paddock, Richard	5235
Cement	Pitcher, Charles B.	0385
Cement plants (major projects)	Haraguchi, Wallace	4877
Chemical industries machinery (Trade Promotion)	Shaw, Eugene	3494
Chemical plants (major projects)	Haraguchi, Wallace	4877
Chemicals and allied products	Kelly, Michael J.	0128
Chinaware	Bratland, Rose Marie	0380
Chromium	Presbury, Graylin	5158
Civil aircraft agreement	Elliott, Frederick	1233
Civil aviation policy	Alford, Eugene	5071
Coal exports		1466
Cobalt	Presbury, Graylin	5158
Columbium	Presbury, Graylin	5158
Commercial lighting fixtures	Vandermuhll, Tony	2390
Commercial printing	Lofquist, William S.	0379
Commercial/industrial refrigeration equipment	Shaw, Eugene	3494
Commercialization of space (market)	Wells, Kim	2232
Computer, large scale	Ebenfeld, Wayne	1987
Computer and DP services	Tallarico, Jennifer	5820
Computer consulting	Tallarico, Jennifer	5820
Computer software	Hijikata, Heidi	0571
Computers, personal/portables	Woods, R. Clay	3013
Computers, systems (hardware)	Miles, Timothy	2990
Computers, workstations	Woods, R. Clay	3013
Computers (trade promotion)	Fogg, Judy A.	4936
Confectionery products	Hodgen, Donald A.	3346
Construction machinery, large off-road	Heimowitz, Leonard	0552
Construction services	Haraguchi, Wallace	4877
Construction statistics	MacAuley, Patrick	0132
Consumer electronics	Daly, Laureen	3360
Consumer goods		0338

Industry	Contact	Phone (202) 482
Conveyors/conveying equipment	Wiening, Mary	4708
Containers and packaging		0132
Copper	Males, Barbara	0606
Cosmetics (overseas trade-show recruitment)	Kimmel, Edward	3640
Countertrade services	Mitchell, Paula	4471
	Verzariu, Pompiliu	4434
cutlery	Bratland, Rose Marie	0380
Dairy products	Hodgen, Donald A.	3346
Data processing services	Tallarico, Jennifer	5820
Database services	Tallarico, Jennifer	5820
Dental equipment (devices and supplies)	Priestley, Duaine	2410
Dental Equipment (trade promotion)	Keen, George	2010
Desalination (major projects)	Holroyd, William	6168
Desalination/water reuse	Wheeler, Frederica	3509
Diamond industrial	Presbury, Graylin	5158
Direct marketing	Harsh, Bruce	4582
Disk storage	Valverde, Daniel	0573
Distilled spirits	Hodgen, Donald A.	3346
Dolls	Freilich, Jonathan	5783
Drugs	Hurt, William	0128
Durable consumer goods	Ellis, Kevin	1176
Education services/manpower training (trade promotion)	Chittum, J. Marc	0345
Electric industrial apparatus	Fouque, Julie	2390
Electrical power plants (major projects)	Collier, Andrew	0680
Electrical test and measuring	Andrews, Michael	2795
Electricity	Collier, Andrew	0680
Electricity/power generation/transmission and distribution equipment (trade promotion)	Collier, Andrew	0680
Electronic components	Ruffin, Marleen	0570
Electronic components (director)	Donnelly, Margaret	5466
Electronic database services	Tallarico, Jennifer	5820
Electronics (printed circuit boards)	Mussehl-Aziz, Jodee	3360
Electro-optical instruments (trade promotion)	Manzolillo, Franc	2991
Elevators, moving stairways	Wiening, Mary	4708
Employment services (trade promotion)	Chittum, J. Marc	0345
Energy		1466
Energy, renewable	Garden, Les	0556
Energy, renewable (technical and equipment)	Garden, Les	0556
Engineering/construction services	Smith, Jay	4642
Entertainment industries	Siegmund, John E.	4781
Entertainment services	Candilis, Wray O.	0339
Environmental technologies	(Main Number)	5225
Equipment, used	Bodson, John	0681
Explosives	Kelly, Michael	0811
Export trading companies	Busby, W. Dawn	5131
Fabricated metal construction materials	Williams, Franklin	0132
Farm machinery	Wiening, Mary	4708
Fasteners (industrial)	Reise, Richard	3489
Fats and oils	Hodgen, Donald A.	3346
Fencing (metal)	Williams, Franklin	0132
Ferroalloys products	Presbury, Graylin	5158
Ferrous scrap	Bell, Charles	0608
Fertilizers	Kelly, Michael	0811

Industry	Contact	Phone (202) 482
Fiber optics	Sandall, Stuart	2006
Filters/purifying equipment	Fredell, Eric	0343
Financial services	Muir, S. Cassin	0349
Fisheries	National Marine Fisheries Service	2379
Flexible manufacturing systems	Pilaroscia, Megan	0609
Flour	Hodgen, Donald A.	3346
Flowers	Hodgen, Donald A.	3346
Food processing/packaging machinery (trade promotion)	Shaw, Eugene	3494
Food products machinery	Shaw, Eugene	3494
Food retailing	Hodgen, Donald A.	3346
Footwear	Byron, James E.	4034
Forest products	Stanley, Gary	0376
Forest products, building materials	Kristensen, Chris	0384
Forestry/woodworking equipment (trade promotion)	Abrahams, Edward	0312
Forgings, semifinished steel	Bell, Charles	0608
Fossil fuels		1466
Foundry industry	Bell, Charles	0608
Frozen foods products	Hodgen, Donald A.	3346
Fruits	Hodgen, Donald A.	3346
Fur goods	Byron, James E.	4034
Furniture	Freilich, Jonathan	5783
Gallium	Cammarota, David	5157
Games and children's vehicles	Freilich, Jonathan	5783
Gaskets/gasketing materials	Reise, Richard	3489
General aviation aircraft	Alford, Eugene	5071
General industrial machine	Robinson, Raymond	0610
Generator sets/turbines (major projects)	Collier, Andrew	0680
Germanium	Cammarota, David	5157
Glass, flat	Williams, Franklin	0132
Glassware (household)	Bratland, Rose Marie	0380
Gloves (work)	Byron, James E.	4034
Giftware (trade promotion)	Simon, Les	0341
Grain mill products	Hodgen, Donald A.	3346
Greeting cards	Bratland, Rose Marie	0380
Grocery retailing	Hodgen, Donald A.	3346
Handbags	Byron, James E.	4034
Handsaws, saw blades	Abrahams, Edward	0312
Hand/edge saws	Abrahams, Edward	0312
Hard-surfaced floor coverings	Williams, Franklin	0132
Hardware (export promotion)	Kimmel, Edward	3640
Hazardous waste	Jonkers, Loretta	0564
Health care services	Francis, Simon	2697
Heating equipment, furnaces	Manger, John	2732
Helicopters	Green, Ronald	3068
High-tech trade, U.S. competitiveness	Hatter, Victoria L.	3895
Hoists, overhead cranes	Wiening, Mary	4708
Home video	Candilis, Wray O.	0339
Hose and belting	Prat, Raimundo	0128
Hotel and restaurant equipment	Kimmel, Edward	3640
Household appliances	Harris, John M.	1178
Household appliances (trade promotion)	Simon, Les	0341
Household furniture	Freilich, Jonathan	5783
Housewares (export promotion)	Simon, Les	0341

Industry	Contact	Phone (202) 482
Housing (manufactured)	Pitcher, Charles B.	0385
Housing construction	Pitcher, Charles B.	0385
Hydropower, plants (major projects)	Collier, Andrew	0680
Industrial chemicals	Hurt, William	0128
Industrial controls	Bodson, John	0681
Industrial drives/gears	Reise, Richard	3489
Industrial equipment (trade promotion)	Shaw, Eugene	3494
Industrial gases	Kostalas, Antonios	2390
Industrial organic chemicals	Hurt, William	0128
Industrial robots	Pilaroscia, Megan	0609
Industrial trucks	Wiening, Mary	4708
Information industries	Tallarico, Jennifer	5820
Information services	Candilis, Wray O.	0339
Infrastructure (main number)	Smith, Jay	4642
Infrastructure/water	Holroyd, William	6168
Inorganic chemicals	Kamenicky, Vincent	0812
Inorganic pigments	Kamenicky, Vincent	0812
Insulation	MacAuley, Patrick	0132
Insurance	Muir, S. Cassin	0349
Intellectual property rights (services)	Siegmund, John E.	4781
Investment management	Muir, S. Cassin	0349
Iron	Bell, Charles	0608
Irrigation (major projects)	Smith, Jay	4642
Irrigation equipment	Wiening, Mary	4708
Jams and jellies	Hodgen, Donald A.	3346
Jewelry	Harris, John M.	1178
Jewelry (trade promotion)	Capone, Ludene	2087
Jute products	Corey, Maria	4058
Kitchen cabinets	Willis, Suzanne	0577
Laboratory instruments	Litman, George	3411
Laboratory instruments (trade promotion)	Manzolillo, Franc	2991
Lasers/electro-optics (trade promotion)	Manzolillo, Franc	2991
Lawn and garden equipment	Vanderwolf, John	0348
Lead products	Larrabee, David	0607
Leasing: equipment, vehicles, services	Uzzelle, Elnora	0351
Leather apparel	Byron, James E.	4034
Leather products	Byron, James E.	4034
Leather tanning	Byron, James E.	4034
Legal services	Chittum, J. Marc	0345
Liquefied natural gas plants (major projects)	Haraguchi, Wallace	4877
Local area networks		0572
Logs, wood		0375
Luggage	Byron, James E.	4034
Lumber		0377
Machine tool accessories	Pilaroscia, Megan	0609
Magazines	Bratland, Rose Marie	0380
Magnesium	Cammarota, David	5157
Major projects	Smith, Jay	4642
Management consulting	Chittum, J. Marc	0345
Management and research services (trade promotion)	Chittum, J. Marc	0345
Manifold business forms	Bratland, Rose Marie	0380

Industry	Contact	Phone (202) 482
Man-made fiber	Tucker, Joanne	4058
Margarine	Hodgen, Donald A.	3346
Marine insurance	Johnson, C. William	5012
Marine port/shipbuilding equipment (trade promotion)	Capone, Ludene	2087
Marine port/shipbuilding (major projects)	Thompson, Michael	5126
Marine recreational equipment (trade promotion)	Capone, Ludene	2087
Maritime shipping	Johnson, C. William	5012
Materials, advanced	Cammarota, David	5157
Materials handling machinery (trade promotion)	Wiening, Mary	4708
Meat products	Hodgen, Donald A.	3346
Mechanical power transmission equipment	Reise, Richard	3489
Medical instruments	Kader, Victoria	4073
Medical instruments and equipment (trade promotion)	Keen, George B.	2010
Medical services	Francis, Simon	2697
Mercury	Larrabee, David	0607
Metal building products	Williams, Franklin	0132
Metal powders	Cammarota, David	5157
Metal-cutting machine tools	Pilaroscia, Megan	0609
Metal-forming machine tools	Pilaroscia, Megan	0609
Metals, secondary	Bell, Charles	0608
Metalworking	Mearman, John	0315
Metalworking equipment	Pilaroscia, Megan	0609
Millwork	Stanley, Gary	0377
Mineral-based construction materials (clay, concrete, gypsum, asphalt, stone)	Pitcher, Charles B.	0385
Mining machinery	Heimowitz, Leonard	0552
Mining machinery (trade promotion)	Zanetakos, George	0558
Mobile homes		0132
Molybdenum	Cammarota, David	5157
Monorails (trade promotion)	Wiening, Mary	4708
Motion pictures	Siegmund, John E.	4781
Motor vehicles	Warner, Albert T.	0669
Motorcycles	Vanderwolf, John	0348
Motors, electric	Mearman, John	0315
Multichip modules	Priestley, Duaine	2410
Music (prerecorded)	Siegmund, John E.	4781
Musical instruments (trade promotion)	Harris, John M.	1178
Mutual funds	Muir, S. Cassin	0349
Natural gas		1889
Newspapers	Bratland, Rose Marie	0380
Nonalcoholic beverages	Hodgen, Donald A.	3346
Non-current-carrying wiring devices	Bodson, John	0681
Nondurable goods	Simon, Les	0341
Nonferrous foundries	Cammarota, David	5157
Nonferrous metals	Larrabee, David	0607
Nonmetallic minerals	Shaw, Robert	5124
Nonresidential construction	MacAuley, Patrick	0132
Nuclear power plants (major projects)	Collier, Andrew	0680
Nuclear power plants/machinery	Collier, Andrew	0680
Numerical controls for machine tools	Pilaroscia, Megan	0609
Nuts, edible	Hodgen, Donald A.	3346
Nuts, bolts, washers	Reise, Richard	3489
Ocean shipping	Johnson, C. William	5012
Oil and gas (fuels only)	Rasmussen, John	1889

Industry	Contact	Phone (202) 482
Oil field machinery	Rasmussen, John	1889
Oil shale (major projects)	Haraguchi, Wallace	4877
Operations and maintenance	Chittum, J. Marc	0345
Organic chemicals	Hurt, William	0128
Outdoor lighting fixtures	Bodson, John	0681
Outdoor power equipment (trade promotion)	Simon, Les	0341
Overseas export promotion	Kimmel, Edward	3640
Packaging and containers	Bodson, John	0681
Packaging machinery	Shaw, Eugene	3494
Paints/coatings	Prat, Raimundo	0810
Paper		0375
Paper and board packaging		0375
Paper industries machinery	Abrahams, Edward	0312
Pasta	Hodgen, Donald A.	3346
Paving materials (asphalt and concrete)	Pitcher, Charles B.	0385
Pectin	Hodgen, Donald A.	3346
Periodicals	Bratland, Rose Marie	0380
Pet food	Hodgen, Donald A.	3346
Pet products	Kimmel, Edward	3640
Petrochemicals	Hurt, William	0128
Petrochemicals, cyclic crudes	Hurt, William	0128
Petrochemicals plants (major projects)	Haraguchi, Wallace	4877
Petroleum, crude and refined products	Rasmussen, John	1889
Pharmaceuticals	Hurt, William	0128
Pipelines (major projects)	Haraguchi, Wallace	4877
Photographic equipment and supplies	Watson, Joyce	0574
Plastic construction products (most)	Williams, Franklin	0132
Plastic materials/resins	Prat, Raimundo	0810
Plastic products	Prat, Raimundo	0810
Plastic products machinery	Shaw, Eugene	3494
Plumbing fixtures and fittings	Pitcher, Charles B.	0385
Plywood/panel products	Stanley, Gary	0377
Pollution control equipment	Jonkers, Loretta	0564
Porcelain electrical supplies	Burroughs, Helen	4931
Ports	Thompson, Michael	5126
Potato chips	Hodgen, Donald A.	3346
Poultry products	Hodgen, Donald A.	3346
Power hand tools	Abrahams, Edward	0312
Power generation (major projects)	Collier, Andrew	0680
Precious metal jewelry	Harris, John M.	1178
Prefabricated buildings (metal)	Williams, Franklin	0132
Prefabricated buildings (wood)	Williams, Franklin	0132
Prepared meats	Hodgen, Donald A.	3346
Pretzels	Hodgen, Donald A.	3346
Primary commodities	Siesseger, Fred	5124
Printed circuit boards	Judee, Mussehl	0429
Printing and publishing	Lofquist, William S.	0379
Printing trade services	Bratland, Rose Marie	0380
Printing trades machinery/equipment	Robinson, Raymond	0610
Process control instruments	Litman, George	3411
Process control instruments (trade promotion)	Manzolillo, Franc	2991
Professional services	Candilis, Wray O.	0339
Pulp and paper machinery (trade promotion)	Abrahams, Edward	0312
Pulp and paper mills (construction and major projects)	Haraguchi, Wallace	4877
Pumps, pumping equipment	Manger, John	2732
Pumps, valves, compressors (trade promotion)	Zanetakos, George	0552

Industry	Contact	Phone (202) 482
Radio and TV broadcasting	Siegmund, John E.	4781
Radio and TV communications equipment	Gossack, Linda	4523
Railroad equipment (trade promotion)	Heimowitz, Leonard	0558
Recorded music	Siegmund, John E.	4781
Recreational equipment	Vanderwolf, John	0348
Refractory products	Cammarota, David	5157
Refrigeration equipment (industrial only)	Pitcher, Charles B.	0385
Renewable energy equipment	Garden, Les	0556
Residential lighting fixtures	Bodson, John	0681
Retail trade	Schavey, Aaron	4117
Rice milling	Hodgen, Donald A.	3346
Roads, railroads, mass transportation	Thompson, Michael	5126
Robots/factory automation	Pilaroscia, Megan	0609
Roller bearings	Reise, Richard	3489
Rolling mill machinery	Abrahams, Edward	0312
Roofing, asphalt	Pitcher, Charles B.	0385
Rubber	Prat, Raimundo	0810
Rubber, natural and synthetic	Prat, Raimundo	0128
Rubber products	Prat, Raimundo	0810
Saddlery and harness products	Byron, James E.	4034
Safety and security equipment (trade promotion)	Daly, Laureen	3360
Satellites, communications	Jenci, Krysten	2952
Satellites and space vehicles (marketing)	Farner, Kim	2232
Science and electronics (trade promotion)	Maroni, Bart	4125
Scientific instruments (trade promotion)	Manzolillo, Franc	2991
Scientific measurement/control equipment	Litman, George	3411
Screw machine products	Reise, Richard	3489
Screws, washers	Reise, Richard	3489
Security management services	Chittum, J. Marc	0345
Security/safety equipment (trade promotion)	Daly, Laureen	3360
Semiconductor manufacturing equipment	Andrews, Michael	2795
Semiconductors	Roark, Robin	3090
Semiconductors, Japan	Daly, Laureen	3360
Services database development	Tallarico, Jennifer	5820
Shingles (wood)	Stanley, Gary	0377
Shipbuilding (projects)	Thompson, Michael	5126
Shipping	Johnson, C. William	5012
Shoes	Byron, James E.	4034
Silverware	Harris, John M.	1178
Sisal products	Manger, John	2732
Small arms, ammunition	Vanderwolf, John	0348
Small business	Sjoberg, Millie	4792
Snack food	Hodgen, Donald A.	3346
Soaps, detergents, cleaners	Hurt, William	0128
Software	Hijikata, Heidi	0571
Software (trade promotion)	Fogg, Judy A.	4936
Solar cells/photovoltaic devices	Garden, Les	0556
Solar equipment, ocean/biomass/geothermal	Garden, Les	0556
Soy products	Hodgen, Donald A.	3346
Space commercialization (equipment)	Wells, Kim	2232
Space policy development	Wells, Kim	2232
Space services	Plock, Ernest	5620
Special industry machinery	Shaw, Eugene	3494
Speed changers	Reise, Richard	3489
Sporting and athletic goods	Vanderwolf, John	0348
Sporting goods (trade promotion)	Capone, Ludene	2087
Steel industry	Bell, Charles	0608
Steel markets	Bell, Charles	0608

Industry	Contact	Phone (202) 482
Storage batteries	Larrabee, David	0607
Sugar products	Hodgen, Donald A.	3346
Supercomputers	Ebenfeld, Wayne	1987
Switching	Leuck, Jason	4202
Tea	Hodgen, Donald A.	3346
Technology affairs	Shykind, Edwin B.	4694
Telecommunications	Jenci, Krysten	2952
Telecommunications (cellular technology)	Paddock, Richard	5235
Telecommunications (major projects)	Paddock, Richard	5235
Telecommunications (network equipment)	Paddock, Richard	5235
Telecommunications (trade promotion)	Kemper, Alexis	1512
Telecommunications (wireless)	Gossack, Linda	4523
Telecommunications, terminal equipment	Cadwell, Nathaniel	0399
Telecommunications services	Tallarico, Jennifer	5820
Teletext services	Tallarico, Jennifer	5820
Textile machinery	Manger, John	2732
Textiles	Tucker, Joanne	4058
Textiles (trade promotion)	Molnar, Ferenc	5153
Timber products (tropical)	Willis, Suzanne	0577
Tin products	Manger, John	2732
Tires	Prat, Raimundo	0128
Tools/dies/jigs/fixtures	Pilaroscia, Megan	0609
Tourism services	Johnson, Scott	0140
Toys and games	Freilich, Jonathan	5783
Transborder data flows	Tallarico, Jennifer	5820
Transformers	Fouque, Julie	2390
Transportation industries	Johnson, C. William	5012
Transportation services (trade promotion)	Johnson, C. William	5012
Travel services	Johnson, Scott	0140
Tropical commodities	Willis, Suzanne	0577
Trucking services	Wolfe, Claudia	5086
Trucks, trailers, buses (trade promotion)	White, John C.	0671
Tungsten products	Manger, John	2732
Turbines, steam	Mearman, John	0315
Uranium	Collier, Andrew	0680
Used, reconditioned equipment (trade promotion)	Bodson, John	0681
Value-added tTelecommunications services	Tallarico, Jennifer	5820
Valves, pipe fittings (except brass)	Reise, Richard	3489
Vegetables	Hodgen, Donald A.	3346
Video services	Siegmund, John E.	4781
Videotex services	Tallarico, Jennifer	5820
	Siegmund, John E.	4781
Wallets, billfolds, flat goods	Byron, James E.	4034
Wastepaper		0375
Watches	Harris, John M.	1178
Water and sewage treatment plants (major projects)	Smith, Jay	4642
Water resource equipment	Carpenter, Denise	1500
Water supply and distribution	Carpenter, Denise	1500
Welding/cutting apparatus	Abrahams, Edward	0312
Windmill components	Garden, Les	0556
Wine	Hodgen, Donald A.	3346
Wire cloth, industrial	Reise, Richard	3489
Wire and wire products	Bell, Charles	0608
Yarns (trade promotion)	Molnar, Ferenc	5153
Yeast	Hodgen, Donald A.	3346

APPENDIX 13

THE COMMERCIAL SERVICE OF THE U.S. DEPARTMENT OF COMMERCE
Commercial Service Posts Abroad
Source: http://www.ita.doc.gov/uscs/intfld.html (last update: December 1, 1997).

ALGERIA *Algiers*
Post: American Embassy
Telephone: 011-213-2-60-39-73
Fax: 011-213-2-69-39-79
Workweek: Saturday–Wednesday
Street address: 4 Chemin Cheich Bachir Brahimi
Mailing address: U.S. Dept. of State (Algiers), Washington, DC 20521-6030

ARGENTINA *Buenos Aires*
Post: American Embassy
Telephone: 011-54-1-777-4533, X2226
Fax: 011-54-1-777-0673
Street address: 4300 Colombia 1425
Mailing address: Unit 4334, APO AA 34034

ARMENIA *Yerevan*
Post: American Embassy
Telephone: 011-3742-151-144
Fax: 011-3742-151-138
Street address: 18 Gen Bagramian
Mailing address: U.S. Dept. of State (Yerevan), Washington, DC 20521-7020

AUSTRALIA *Sydney*
Post: American Consulate General
Telephone: 011-61-2-9373-9200
Fax: 011-61-2-9221-0573
Street address: Hyde Park Tower—36th Fl., Park and Elizabeth Sts.
Mailing address: Unit 11024, APO AP 96554-0002
E-mail address: OSydney@doc.gov

Brisbane
Post: American Consulate
Telephone: 011-61-7-831-3330
Fax: 011-61-7-832-6247
Street address: 383 Wickham Terrace
Mailing address: Unit 11018, APO AP 96553-0002

Melbourne
Post: American Consulate General
Telephone: 011-61-3-9526-5925
Fax: 011-61-3-9510-4660
Street address: 553 St. Kilda Rd.
Mailing address: Unit 11011, APO AP 96551-0002
E-mail address: OMelbour@doc.gov

Perth
Post: American Consulate General
Telephone: 011-61-9-231-9410
Fax: 011-61-9-231-9444
Street address: 16 St. George's Terrace, 13th Fl.
Mailing address: Unit 11021, APO AP 96553-0002

AUSTRIA *Vienna*
Post: American Embassy
Telephone: 011-43-1-313-39-2296
Fax: 011-43-1-310-6917
Street address: Boltzmanngasse 16, A-1091

AZERBAIJAN *Baku*
Post: American Embassy
Telephone: 011-9-9412-98-03-35
Fax: 011-9-9412-96-04-69
Street address: Azadliq Prospetati 83
Mailing address: U.S. Dept. of State (Baku), Washington, DC 20521-7050

BELARUS *Minsk*
Post: American Embassy
Telephone: 011-375-172-31-50-00
Fax: 011-375-172-34-78-53
Street address: Starivilenskaya 346-220002
Mailing address: U.S. Dept. of State (Minsk), Washington, DC 20521-7010

BELGIUM *Brussels*
Post: American Embassy
Telephone: 011-32-2-508-2425
Fax: 011-32-2-512-6653
Street address: 27 Boulevard du Regent
Mailing address: PSC 82, Box 002, APO AE 09724-1015

Brussels
Post: U.S. Mission to the European Community
Telephone: 011-32-2-513-2746
Fax: 011-32-2-513-1228
Street address: 40 Blvd. du Regent, B-1000
Mailing address: PSC 82, Box 002, APO AE 09724

BOSNIA *Sarajevo*
Post: American Embassy
Telephone: 011-387-71-445-700
Fax: 011-387-71-659-722
Street address: 43 ul. Dure, Dakovica
Mailing address: U.S. Dept. of State (Sarajevo), Washington, DC 20521-7030

BRAZIL *São Paulo*
Post: American Consulate General
Telephone: 011-55-11-853-2811
Fax: 011-55-11-853-2744
Street address: Rua Estados Unidos 1812
Mailing address: APO AA 34030-0002

Belém
Post: American Consular Agency
Telephone: 011-55-91-223-0800
Fax: 011-55-91-223-0413
Mailing address: APO AA 34030

Belo Horizonte
Post: American Consular Agency
Telephone: 011-55-31-213-1571
Fax: 011-55-31-213-1575
Mailing address: APO AA 34030-3505
Street address: Minas Trade Center Rua Timbiras, 1200, 7th Fl.

Brasília
Post: American Embassy
Telephone: 011-55-61-321-7272
Fax: 011-55-61-225-3981
Street address: Avenida das Nocoes, Lote 3
Mailing address: Unit 3500, APO AA 34030

Rio de Janeiro
Post: American Consulate General
Telephone: 011-55-21-292-7117
Fax: 011-55-21-240-9738
Street address: Avenida Presidente Wilson, 147 Castelo
Mailing address: APO AA 34030

BULGARIA *Sofia*
Post: American Embassy
Telephone: 011-359-2-980-5241
Fax: 011-359-2-980-68-50
Street address: 1 Saborna St.
Mailing address: Unit 1335, APO AE 09213-1335

CANADA *Ottawa*
Post: American Embassy
Telephone: 1-613-238-5335
Fax: 1-613-238-5999
Street address: World Exchange Plaza, 45 O'Connor, Ste. 1140, Postal Code K1P-1A4
Mailing address: P.O. Box 5000, Ogdensburg, NY 13669-0430

Calgary
Post: American Consulate General
Telephone: 1-403-266-8962
Fax: 1-403-266-6630
Street address: 615 MacLeod Trail S.E., Rm. 1050
Mailing address: c/o AmEmbassy Ottawa, P.O. Box 5000, Ogdensburg, NY 13669

Halifax
Post: American Consulate General
Telephone: 1-902-429-2480
Fax: 1-902-429-7690
Street address: Ste. 910, Cogswell Tower, Scotia Square, Halifax, NS B3J 3K1
Mailing address: c/o AmEmbassy Ottawa, P.O. Box 5000, Ogdensburg, NY 13669

Montreal
Post: American Consulate General
Telephone: 1-514-398-9695
Fax: 1-514-398-0711
Street address: 455 Rene Levesque Blvd., 19th Fl., Montreal, Qc H2Z-1Z2
Mailing address: P.O. Box 847, Champlain, NY 12919-0847

Toronto
Post: American Consulate General
Telephone: 1-416-595-1700
Fax: 1-416-595-0051
Street address: 360 University Ave., Ste. 602, Toronto, ON M5G-1S4
Mailing address: P.O. Box 135, Lewiston, NY 14092

Vancouver
Post: American Consulate General
Telephone: 1-604-685-4311
Fax: 1-604-687-6095
Street address: 1095 W. Pender St., 20th Fl., Vancouver, BC V6E-2M6
Mailing address: P.O. Box 5002, Point Roberts, WA 98281-5002

CHILE *Santiago*
Post: American Embassy
Telephone: 011-56-2-330-3310
Fax: 011-56-2-330-3172
Street address: Andres Bello 2800, Los Condes
Mailing address: Unit 4111, APO AA 34033

CHINA *Beijing*
Post: American Embassy
Telephone: 011-86-10-6532-6924
Fax: 011-86-10-6532-3297
Street address: Xiu Shui Bei Jie 3
Mailing address: PSC 461, Box 50, FPO AP 96521-0002
E-mail address: OBeijing@doc.gov

Chengdu
Post: American Consulate General
Telephone: 011-86-28-558-9642
Fax: 011-86-28-558-9221
Street address: No. 1 S. Shamian St., Shamian Island
Mailing address: PSC 461, Box 100, FPO AP 96521-0002
E-mail address: uscscd@public.cd.sc.cn

Guangzhou
Post: American Consulate General
Telephone: 011-86-20-8667-4011
Fax: 011-86-20-8666-6409
Street address: China Hotel 14/F Liu Hua Rd.
Mailing address: PSC 461, Box 100, FPO AP 96521-0002
E-mail address: OGuangzh@doc.gov

Shanghai
Post: American Consulate General
Telephone: 011-86-21-6279-7630
Fax: 011-86-21-6279-7639
Street address: 1469 Huai Hai Middle Rd.
Mailing address: PSC 461, Box 200, FPO AP 96521-0002
E-mail address: OShangha@doc.gov

Shanghai
Post: U.S. Commercial Center
Telephone: 011-86-21-6279-7640
Fax: 011-86-21-6279-7639
Street address: Shanghai Centre Ste. 631, East Tower 1376 Nanjing Xi Lu
E-mail address: AChang1@doc.gov

Shenyang
Post: American Consulate General
Telephone: 011-86-21-6279-7640
Fax: 011-86-21-6279-7649
Street address: 40 Lane 4, Section 5 Sanjing St., Heping District
Mailing address: PSC 461, Box 45, FPO AP 96521-0002

COLOMBIA *Bogotá*
Post: American Embassy
Telephone: 011-57-1-315-2126, X2684
Fax: 011-57-1-315-2171
Street address: Calle 22 D bis No. 47-51, Santa Fe de Bogotá
Mailing address: Unit 5120, APO AA 34038

COSTA RICA *San José*
Post: American Embassy
Telephone: 011-506-220-2454/3939
Fax: 011-506-231-4783
Street address: Embajada de los Estados Unidos, Frente al Centro, Commercial del Oeste, Unit 2508, Pavas, San Jose, Costa Rica
Mailing address: APO AA 34020

CÔTE D'IVOIRE *Abidjan*
Post: American Embassy
Telephone: 011-225-21-4616
Fax: 011-225-22-2437
Street address: 0 I.B.P. 1712
Mailing address: U.S. Dept. of State (Abidjan), Washington DC 20521-2010

CROATIA *Zagreb*
Post: American Embassy
Telephone: 011-359-2-980-5241
Fax: 011-359-2-981-8977
Street address: Andrije Hebranga 2
Mailing address: Unit 345, APO AE 09213-1345

CZECH REPUBLIC *Prague*
Post: American Embassy
Telephone: 011-422-2421-9844
Fax: 011-422-2421-9965
Street address: Hybernska 7a 117 16 Praha 1
Mailing address: U.S. Dept. of State (Prague), Washington, DC 20521-5630

DENMARK *Copenhagen*
Post: American Embassy
Telephone: 011-45-3142-3144
Fax: 011-45-3142-0175
Street address: Dag Hammarskjölds Alle 24
Mailing address: APO AE 09176

DOMINICAN REPUBLIC *Santo Domingo*
Post: American Embassy
Telephone: 1-809-221-2171
Fax: 1-809-688-4838
Street address: Corner of Calle Cesar Nicolas Penson & Calle Leopoldo Navarro
Mailing address: Unit 5515, APO AA 34041-0008

ECUADOR *Quito*
Post: American Embassy
Telephone: 011-593-2-561-404
Fax: 011-593-2-504-550
Street address: Avenida 12 de Octubre y Avenida Patria
Mailing address: Unit 5334, APO AA 34039-3420

Guayaquil
Post: American Consulate General
Telephone: 011-593-4-323-570
Fax: 011-593-4-325-286
Street address: 9 de Octubre y Garcia Moreno
Mailing address: APO AA 34039

EGYPT *Cairo*
Post: American Embassy
Telephone: 011-20-2-357-2340
Fax: 011-20-2-355-8368
Workweek: Sunday–Thursday

Street address: 3 Lazougi St., Garden City, Cairo
Mailing address: Unit 64900, Box 11, APO AE
09839-4900

Alexandria
Post: American Consulate General
Telephone: 011-20-3-482-5607
Fax: 011-20-3-482-9199
Street address: 3 El Faranna St.
Mailing address: Unit 64900, Box 24, FPO AE
09839-4900

FINLAND *Helsinki*
Post: American Embassy
Telephone: 011-358-9-171-931
Fax: 011-358-9-635-332
Street address: Itainen Puistotie 14ASF
Mailing address: APO AE 09723

FRANCE *Paris*
Post: American Embassy
Telephone: 011-33-1-4312-2370
Fax: 011-33-1-4312-2172
Street address: 2 Avenue Gabriel
Mailing address: APO AE 09777

Paris
Post: US Mission to the OECD
Telephone: 011-33-1-4524-7437
Fax: 011-33-1-4524-7410
Street address: 19 Rue de Franqueville, 75016
Paris
Mailing address: APO AE 09777

Bordeaux
Post: American Consulate General
Telephone: 011-33-56-526595
Fax: 011-33-56-51-60-42
Street address: 22 Cours du Marechal Foch
Mailing address: c/o American Embassy Paris,
APO AE 09777

Lyon
Post: American Consulate General
Telephone: 011-33-472-407-220
Fax: 011-33-478-391-409
Street address: 7 Quai General Sarrail
Mailing address: c/o American Embassy Paris,
APO AE 09777

Marseille
Post: American Consulate General
Telephone: 011-33-491-549-200
Fax: 011-33-491-550-947
Street address: 12 Boulevard Paul Peytral
Mailing address: c/o American Embassy Paris,
APO AE 09777

Nice
Post: U.S. Commercial Office
Telephone: 011-33-93-88-89-55

Fax: 011-33-93-87-07-38
Street address: 31 Rue du Marechal Joffre
Mailing address: c/o American Embassy Paris,
APO AE 09777

Strasbourg
Post: American Consulate General
Telephone: 011-33-88-35-31-04
Fax: 011-33-88-24-06-95
Street address: 15 Avenue d'Alsace
Mailing address: c/o American Embassy Paris,
Unit 21551, APO AE 09777

GEORGIA *Tbilisi*
Post: American Embassy
Telephone: 011-995-32-989-967
Fax: 011-995-32-933-759
Street address: 25 Atoneli
Mailing address: U.S. Dept. of State (Tbilisi),
Washington, DC 20521-7060

GERMANY *Bonn*
Post: American Embassy
Telephone: 011-49-228-339-2895
Fax: 011-49-228-334-649
Street address: Deichmanns Ave 29
Mailing address: Unit 21701, Box 53170, Bonn,
APO AE 09080 PSC 117

Berlin
Post: American Embassy Office
Telephone: 011-49-30-238-5174
Fax: 011-49-30-238-6290
Street address: Neustaedtische Kirchstrasse 4-5
10117 Berlin
Mailing address: Unit 10117, APO AE 09235-
5500

Düsseldorf
Post: U.S. Commercial Office
Telephone: 011-49-211-431-744
Fax: 011-49-211-431-431
Street address: Emmanual Lutz Str. 1B
Mailing address: Unit 21701, Box 30, APO AE
09080

Frankfurt
Post: American Consulate General
Telephone: 011-49-69-956-79-013
Fax: 011-49-69-561-114
Street address: Platenstrasse 1, 60320
Frankfurt/Main
Mailing address: PSC 115, APO AE 09213-0115

Hamburg
Post: American Consulate General
Telephone: 011-49-40-4117-1304
Fax: 011-49-40-410-6598
Street address: Alsterufer 27/28, 20354
Mailing address: U.S. Dept. of State (Hamburg),
Washington, DC 20521-5180

Leipzig
Post: American Consulate General
Telephone: 011-49-341-213-8421
Fax: 011-49-341-213-8441
Street address: Wilhelm-Seyfferth-Strasse 4, 04107 Leipzig
Mailing address: PSC 120, Box 1000, APO AE 09265

Munich
Post: American Consulate General
Telephone: 011-49-89-2888-748
Fax: 011-49-89-285-261
Street address: Koeniginstrasse 5
Mailing address: APO AE 09178

GREECE *Athens*
Post: American Embassy
Telephone: 011-30-1-729-4302
Fax: 011-30-1-721-8660
Street address: 91 Vasilissia Sophias Blvd.
Mailing address: PSC 108, APO AE 09482

GUATEMALA *Guatemala*
Post: American Embassy
Telephone: 011-502-3-31-1541 X259
Fax: 011-502-3-31-7373
Street address: 7-01 Avenida de la Reforma, Zona 10
Mailing address: Unit 3306, APO AA 34024

HONDURAS *Tegucigalpa*
Post: American Embassy
Telephone: 011-504-36-9230/38-5114
Fax: 011-504-38-2888
Street address: Avenido La Paz
Mailing address: APO AA 34022

HONG KONG *Hong Kong*
Post: American Consulate General
Telephone: 011-85-22-521-1467
Fax: 011-85-22-845-9800
Street address: 26 Garden Rd., 17th Fl.
Mailing address: PSC 464, Box 30, FPO AP 96522-0002
E-mail address: OHongKon@doc.gov

HUNGARY *Budapest*
Post: American Embassy
Telephone: 011-36-1-302-6100
Fax: 011-36-1-302-0089 or 0091
Street address: V. Szabadsag Ter 7
Mailing address: U.S. Dept. of State (Budapest), Washington, DC 20521-5270

INDIA *New Delhi*
Post: American Embassy
Telephone: 011-91-11-611-3033
Fax: 011-91-11-419-0025

Street address: Shanti Path, Chanakyapuri 110021
Mailing address: U.S. Dept. of State (New Delhi), Washington, DC 20521-9000

Bangalore
Post: Commercial Office, US&FCS
Telephone: 011-91-80-558-1452
Fax: 011-91-80-558-3630
Street address: W-202, 2d Fl., West Wing, Sunrise Chambers 22 Ulsoor Rd., Bangalore 560 042
Mailing address: Same
Note: Cable to AmConGen, who will pass to Bangalore

Calcutta
Post: American Consulate General
Telephone: 011-91-33-242-1074
Fax: 011-91-33-242-2335
Street address: 5/1 Ho Chi Minh Sarani, Calcutta 700071
Mailing address: U.S. Dept. of State (Calcutta), Washington, DC 20521-6250

Chennai
Post: American Consulate General
Telephone: 011-91-44-827-7542
Fax: 011-91-44-827-0240
Street address: 220 Mount Rd., Chennai 600006
Mailing address: U.S. Dept. of State (Chennai), Washington, DC 20521-6260

Mumbai
Post: American Consulate General (formerly Bombay)
Telephone: 011-91-22-265-2511
Fax: 011-91-22-262-3851/3850
Street address: 4, New Marine Lines, Mumbai 400020
Mailing address: U.S. Dept. of State (Bombay), Washington, DC 20521-6240

INDONESIA *Jakarta*
Post: American Embassy
Telephone: 011-62-21-344-2211
Fax: 011-62-21-385-1632
Street address: Medan Merdeka Selatan 5
Mailing address: Box 1, APO AP 96520
E-mail address: OJakarta@doc.gov

Jakarta
Post: U.S. Commercial Center
Telephone: 011-62-21-526-2850
Fax: 011-62-21-526-2855
Street address: World Trade Center Wisma, Metropolital II, 3d Fl., Jalan Jenral Sudiman 29-31, Jakarta 12920
E-mail address: OJakart1@doc.gov

Surabaya
Post: American Consulate General
Telephone: 011-62-31-561923/5676880
Fax: 011-62-31-5677748/5674492
Street address: Jalan Raya Dr., Sutomo 33,
 Box 18131
Mailing address: APO AP 96520
E-mail address: OSurabay@doc.gov

IRAQ *Baghdad*
Post: American Embassy
Telephone: 011-964-1-719-6138
Fax: 011-964-1-718-9297
Workweek: Sunday–Thursday
Street address: Opp. For. Ministry Club (Masbah
 Quarter)
Mailing address: U.S. Dept. of State (Baghdad),
 Washington DC 20521-6060

IRELAND *Dublin*
Post: American Embassy
Telephone: 011-353-1-667-4755
Fax: 011-353-1-667-4754
Street address: 42 Elgin Rd., Ballsbridge
Mailing address: U.S. Dept. of State (Dublin),
 Washington, DC 20521-5290

ISRAEL *Tel Aviv*
Post: American Embassy
Telephone: 011-972-3-519-7327
Fax: 011-972-3-510-7215
Street address: 71 Rehov, Tel Aviv 63432
Mailing address: PSC 98, Box 100, APO AE 09830

ITALY *Rome*
Post: American Embassy
Telephone: 011-39-6-46741
Fax: 011-4674-2113
Street address: Via Veneto 119/A
Mailing address: PSC 59, APO AE 09624

Florence
Post: American Consulate General
Telephone: 011-39-55-211-676
Fax: 011-39-55-283-780
Street address: Lungarno Amerigo Vespucci 38
Mailing address: APO AE 09624

Genoa
Post: American Consulate General
Telephone: 011-39-10-247-1412
Fax: 011-39-10-290-027
Street address: Banca d'Americae d'Italia
 Building Piazza Portello
Mailing address: PSC 59, Box G, APO AE 09624

Milan
Post: American Consulate General
Telephone: 011-39-2-6592-260

Fax: 011-39-2-6592-561
Street address: Via Principe Amerdeo 2/10,
 20121 Miliano
Mailing address: PSC 59, Box M, APO AE 09624

Naples
Post: American Consulate General
Telephone: 011-39-81-761-1592
Fax: 011-39-81-761-1869
Street address: Piazza della Repubblica
Mailing address: PSC 810, Box 18, FPO AE
 09619-0002

JAMAICA *Kingston*
Post: American Embassy
Telephone: 1-876-926-8115
Fax: 1-809-920-2580
Street address: Jamaica Mutual Life Center, 2
 Oxford Rd., 3d Fl., Kingston 5
Mailing address: U.S. Dept. of State (Kingston),
 Washington DC 20521-3210

JAPAN *Tokyo*
Post: American Embassy
Telephone: 011-81-3-3224-5060
Fax: 011-81-3-3589-4235
Street address: 1-10-5 Akasaka 1-chome
 Minato-ku (107)
Mailing address: Unit 45004, Box 204, APO AP
 96337-5004
E-mail address: OTokyo@doc.gov

Tokyo
Post: U.S. Trade Center
Telephone: 011-81-3-3987-2441
Fax: 011-81-3-3987-2447
Street address: 7th Fl., World Import Mart 1-3
 Higoshi Ikebukuro 3-chome Toshima-ku,
 Tokyo 170
Mailing address: Unit 45004, Box 258, APO AP
 96337-0001
E-mail address: OTokyo1@doc.gov

Fukuoka
Post: American Consulate
Telephone: 011-81-92-751-9331
Fax: 011-81-92-713-9222
Street address: 5-26 Ohori 2-chome Chuo-ku
 Fukuoka-810
Mailing address: Box 10, FPO AP 98766

Nagoya
Post: American Consulate
Telephone: 011-81-52-203-4277
Fax: 011-81-52-201-4612
Street address: 10-33 Nishiki 3-chome Naka-ku,
 Nagoya 460, Japan
Mailing address: c/o AmEmbassy Tokyo Unit
 45004, Box 280, APO AP 96337-0001
E-mail address: ONagoya@doc.gov

Osaka-Kobe
Post: American Consulate General
Telephone: 011-81-6-315-5957
Fax: 011-81-6-315-5963
Street address: 11-5, Nishitnma 2-crome Kita-Ku Osaka (530)
Mailing address: Unit 45004, Box 239, APO AP 96337-0002
E-mail address: OOsakaKo@doc.gov

Sapporo
Post: American Consulate
Telephone: 011-81-11-641-1115
Fax: 011-81-11-643-1283
Street address: Kita 1-Jo Nishi 28-chome Chuoku Sapporo 064
Mailing address: APO AP 96337-0003

KAZAKHSTAN *Almaty*
Post: American Embassy
Telephone: 011-7-3275-81-15-77
Fax: 011-7-3275-81-15-76
Street address: 99/97 Furmanova St. Almaty, 480012
Mailing address: U.S. Dept. of State (Almaty), Washington, DC 20521-7030

KENYA *Nairobi*
Post: American Embassy
Telephone: 011-254-2-212-354
Fax: 011-254-2-216-648
Street address: Moi/Haile Selassie Ave.
Mailing address: P.O. Box 30137, Unit 64100, APO AE 09831

KOREA *Seoul*
Post: American Embassy
Telephone: 011-82-2-397-4535
Fax: 011-82-2-739-1628
Street address: 82 Sejong-Ro Chongro-Ku
Mailing address: Unit 15550, APO AP 96205-0001
E-mail address: OSeoul@doc.gov

KUWAIT *Kuwait*
Post: American Embassy
Telephone: 011-965-539-6362/5307
Fax: 011-965-538-0281
Workweek: Saturday–Wednesday
Street address: Al Masjeed Al Aqsa St., Plot 14, Block 14, Bayan Plan 3602
Mailing address: Unit 6900, Box 10, APO AE 09880-9000

MACEDONIA *Skopje*
Post: American Embassy
Telephone: 011-389-91-116-180
Fax: 011-389-91-117-103
Street address: Bul Linden BB, 9100 Skopje

Mailing address: U.S. Dept. of State (Skopje), Washington, DC 20521-7120

MALAYSIA *Kuala Lumpur*
Post: American Embassy
Telephone: 011-603-457-2724
Fax: 011-603-242-1866
Street address: 376 Jalan Tun Razak
Mailing address: APO AP 96535-5000

MEXICO *Mexico*
Post: American Embassy
Telephone: 011-52-5-209-9100
Fax: 011-52-5-207-8837
Street address: Paseo de la Reforma 305, Colonia Cuauhtemoc, 06500 Mexico, D.F. Mexico
Mailing address: P.O. Box 3087, Laredo, TX 78044-3087

Mexico
Post: U.S. Trade Center
Telephone: 011-52-5-591-0155
Fax: 011-52-5-566-1115
Street address: Liverpool 31, Co. Juarez, 06600 Mexico, D.F. Mexico
Mailing address: P.O. Box 3087, Laredo, TX 78044-3087

Guadalajara
Post: American Consulate General
Telephone: 011-52-3-825-2700, X371/52-3-827-0258
Fax: 011-52-3-826-3576
Street address: Jal. Progreso 175
Mailing address: P.O. Box 3088, Laredo, TX 78044-3098

Monterrey
Post: American Consulate General
Telephone: 011-52-83-45-2120
Fax: 011-52-83-45-5172/343-4440
Street address: N.L. Avenida Constitucion 411 Poniente
Mailing address: P.O. Box 3098, Laredo, TX 78044-3098

MOROCCO *Casablanca*
Post: American Consulate General
Telephone: 011-212-2-26-45-50
Fax: 011-212-2-22-02-59
Street address: 8 Blvd. Moulay Youssef
Mailing address: PSC 74, Box 24, APO AE 09718

Rabat
Post: American Embassy
Telephone: 011-212-7-622-65
Fax: 011-212-7-656-61

Street address: 2 Ave. de Marrakech
Mailing address: PSC 74, Box 003, APO AE 09718

NETHERLANDS *The Hague*
Post: American Embassy
Telephone: 011-31-70-310-9417
Fax: 011-31-70-363-2985
Street address: Lange Voorhout 102
Mailing address: PSC 71, Box 1000, APO AE 09715

Amsterdam
Post: American Consulate General
Telephone: 011-31-20-575-5351
Fax: 011-31-20-575-5350
Street address: Museumplein 19
Mailing address: Box 1000, APO AE 09715

NEW ZEALAND *Auckland*
Post: American Consulate General
Telephone: 011-649-303-2038
Fax: 011-649-302-3156
Street address: 4th Fl., Yorkshire General Bldg., Shortland and O'Connell Sts.
Mailing address: PSC 467, Box 99, FPO AP 96531-1099
E-mail address: OAucklan@doc.gov

Wellington
Post: American Embassy
Telephone: 011-644-472-2068
Fax: 011-644-471-2380
Street address: 29 Fitzherbert Terr., Thorndon
Mailing address: PSC 467, Box 1, FPO AP 96531-1001

NIGERIA *Lagos*
Post: American Embassy
Telephone: 011-234-1-261-0078, X383
Fax: 011-234-1-261-9856
Street address: 2 Eleke Crescent, Victoria Island
Mailing address: U.S. Dept. of State (Lagos), Washington DC 20521-8300

NORWAY *Oslo*
Post: American Embassy
Telephone: 011-47-22-44-8550
Fax: 011-47-22-55-8803
Street address: Drammensveien 18
Mailing address: PSC 69, Box 1000, APO AE 09707

PAKISTAN *Islamabad*
Post: American Embassy
Telephone: 011-92-51-826-161
Fax: 011-92-51-823-981
Workweek: Sunday–Thursday
Street address: Diplomatic Enclave, Ramna 5

Mailing address: P.O. Box 1048, Unit 6220, APO AE 09812-2200

Lahore
Post: American Consulate General
Telephone: 011-92-42-636-5530
Fax: 011-92-42-636-5177
Workweek: Sunday–Thursday
Street address: 50 Shahrah-E-Bin Badees
Mailing address: Unit 62216, APO AE 09812-2216

PANAMA *Panama*
Post: American Embassy
Telephone: 011-507-227-1777
Fax: 011-507-227-1713
Street address: Avenida Balboa y Calle 38, Apartado 6959
Mailing address: Unit 0945, APO AA 34002

PERU *Lima*
Post: American Embassy
Telephone: 011-51-1-434-3040
Fax: 011-51-1-434-3041
Street address: Avenida la Encalada Cuadro 17, Lima 33
Mailing address: Unit 3780, APO AA 34031

PHILIPPINES *Manila*
Post: American Embassy
Telephone: 011-632-890-9362
Fax: 011-632-895-3028
Street address: 395 Senator Gil Puyat Ave., Extension Makati
Mailing address: APO AP 96440
E-mail address: OManila@doc.gov

POLAND *Warsaw*
Post: American Embassy
Telephone: 011-48-2-628-3041
Fax: 011-48-2-628-8298
Street address: Aleje Ujazdowskle 29/31
Mailing address: c/o AmConGen (WAW), Unit 1340, APO AE 09213-1340

Warsaw
Post: U.S. Trade Center
Telephone: 011-48-2-621-4515
Fax: 011-48-2-621-6327
Street address: Aleje Jerozolimski 56C IKEA Bldg., 2d Fl., 00-803 Warsaw

PORTUGAL *Lisbon*
Post: American Embassy
Telephone: 011-351-1-727-5086
Fax: 011-351-1-726-8914
Street address: Avenida das Forcas Armadas
Mailing address: PSC 83, Box FCS, APO AE 09726

Oporto
Post: American Business Center
Telephone: 011-351-2-606-3094
Fax: 011-351-2-600-2737
Street address: Apartado No. 88 Rua Julio Dinis 826, 3d Fl.
Mailing address: c/o AmEmbassy Lisbon, APO AE 09726

ROMANIA *Bucharest*
Post: American Embassy
Telephone: 011-40-1-210-4042
Fax: 011-40-1-210-0690
Street address: Strada Tudor Arghezi 7-9
Mailing address: The Commercial Service U.S. Embassy (Bucharest-5260), c/o U.S. Department of State, Washington, DC 20521-5260

RUSSIA *Moscow*
Post: American Embassy
Telephone: 011-7-502-224-1105
Fax: 011-7-402-224-1106
Street address: Novinsky Bulvar 19/23
Mailing address: APO AE 09721

St. Petersburg
Post: American Consulate General
Telephone: 011-7-812-850-1902
Fax: 011-7-812-850-1903
Street address: Furshatskaya 15
Mailing address: Box L, APO AE 09723

Vladivostok
Post: American Consulate General
Telephone: 011-7-4232-268-458
Fax: 011-7-4232-268-445
Street address: Ulitsa Mordovtseva 12
Mailing address: APO AE 09721

SAUDI ARABIA *Riyadh*
Post: American Embassy
Telephone: 011-966-1-488-3800
Fax: 011-966-1-488-3237
Workweek: Saturday–Wednesday
Street address: Collector Rd. M, Diplomatic Quarter
Mailing address: Unit 61307, APO AE 09803-1307

Dhahran
Post: American Consulate General
Telephone: 011-966-3-891-3200
Fax: 011-966-3-891-8332
Workweek: Saturday–Wednesday
Street address: Between Aramco Headquarters and Dhahran International Airport, P.O. Box 81, Dhahran Airport, 31932
Mailing address: Unit 66803, APO AE 09858-6803

Jidda
Post: American Consulate General
Telephone: 011-966-2-667-0040
Fax: 011-966-2-665-8106
Workweek: Saturday–Wednesday
Street address: Palestine Rd. Ruwais, P.O. Box 149
Mailing address: Unit 62112, APO AE 09811-2112

SINGAPORE *Singapore*
Post: American Embassy
Telephone: 011-65-476-9037
Fax: 011-65-476-9080
Street address: 1 Columbo Ct. # 05-16
Mailing address: FPO AP 96534-0001
E-mail address: OSingapo@doc.gov

SLOVAK REPUBLIC *Bratislava*
Post: American Embassy
Telephone: 011-421-7-533-0861
Fax: 011-421-7-335-096
Street address: Hviezdoslavovo Namestie 4 81102 Bratislava
Mailing address: U.S. Dept. of State (Bratislava), Washington, DC 20521-5840

Bratislava
Post: American Business Center
Telephone: 011-421-7-361-079
Fax: 011-421-7-361-085
Street address: Grosslingova 35 81109 Bratislava

SOUTH AFRICA *Johannesburg*
Post: American Consulate General
Telephone: 011-27-11-442-3571
Fax: 011-27-11-442-3770
Street address: 1 Commercial Service Office, 15 Chaplin Rd., Illovo 2196
Mailing address (Pouch): U.S. Dept. of State (Johannesburg), Washington, DC 20521-2500
Mailing address (Int'l): P.O. Box 2155, Johannesburg 2000, South Africa

Cape Town
Post: American Consulate General
Telephone: 011-27-21-214-269
Fax: 011-27-21-254-151
Street address: Broadway Industries Center, Herrengracht, Foreshore
Mailing address: U.S. Dept. of State (Cape Town), Washington DC 20521-2480

SPAIN *Madrid*
Post: American Embassy
Telephone: 011-34-1-577-4000
Fax: 011-34-1-577-2301
Street address: Serrano 75
Mailing address: PSC 61, Box 0021, APO AE 09642

Barcelona
Post: American Consulate General
Telephone: 011-34-3-280-2227
Fax: 011-34-3-205-7705
Street address: Paseo Leina Elisenda, 23 08034 Barcelona, Spain
Mailing address: PSC 61, Box 0005, APO AE 09642

SWEDEN *Stockholm*
Post: American Embassy
Telephone: 011-46-8-783-5346
Fax: 011-46-8-660-9181
Street address: Strandvagen 101
Mailing address: U.S. Dept. of State (Stockholm), Washington DC 20521-5750

SWITZERLAND *Bern*
Post: American Embassy
Telephone: 011-41-31-357-7270
Fax: 011-41-31-357-7336
Street address: Jubilaeumstrasse 93
Mailing address: U.S. Dept. of State (Bern), Washington DC 20521-5110

Geneva
Post: U.S. Mission to the GATT
Telephone: 011-41-22-749-5281
Fax: 011-41-22-749-4885
Street address: Botanic Building 1-3 Avenue de la Paix
Mailing address: U.S. Dept. of State (Geneva), Washington, DC 20521-5130

Zürich
Post: American Consulate General
Telephone: 011-41-1-552-070
Fax: 011-41-1-382-2655
Street address: Zolliikerstrasse 141
Mailing address: U.S. Dept. of State (Zurich), Washington DC 20521-5130

TAIWAN *Taipei*
Post: American Institute in Taiwan
Telephone: 011-886-2-720-1550
Fax: 011-886-2-757-7162
Street address: 600 Min Chuan East Rd., Taipei
Mailing address: American Institute in Taiwan, Commercial Unit, Dept. of State (Taipei), Washington DC 20521
E-mail address: OTaipei@doc.gov

Kao-hsiung
Post: American Institute in Taiwan
Location: Kao-hsiung Office
Telephone: 011-886-7-224-0154
Fax: 011-886-7-223-8237
Street address: 3d Fl., #2 Chung Cheng 3d Road, Kaohsiung

Mailing address: American Institute in Taiwan, Commercial Unit, Dept. of State (Kao-hsiung), Washington DC 20521
E-mail address: OKaohsiu@doc.gov

THAILAND *Bangkok*
Post: American Embassy
Telephone: 011-662-255-4365
Fax: 011-662-255-2915
Street address: Diethelm 93/1 Wireless Rd., Towers Bldg.
Mailing address: APO AP 96546
E-mail address: OBangkok@doc.gov

TURKEY *Ankara*
Post: American Embassy
Telephone: 011-90-312-467-0949
Fax: 011-90-312-467-1366
Street address: 110 Ataturk Blvd.
Mailing address: PSC 93, Box 5000, APO AE 09823

Istanbul
Post: American Consulate General
Telephone: 011-90-1-251-1651
Fax: 011-90-1-252-2417
Street address: 104-108 Mesrutiyet Caddesi, Tepebasi
Mailing address: PSC 97, Box 0002, APO AE 09827-0002

İzmir
Post: American Consulate General
Telephone: 011-90-232-421-3643
Fax: 011-90-232-463-5040
Street address: 92 Ataturk Caddesi (3d Fl.)
Mailing address: PSC 88, Box 5000, APO AE 09821

TURKMENISTAN *Ashkabad*
Post: American Embassy
Telephone: 011-9-7-3632-35-00-45
Fax: 011-9-7-3632-51-13-05
Street address: 9 Pushkin St.
Mailing address: U.S. Dept. of State (Ashkabad), Washington, DC 20521-7070

UKRAINE *Kiev*
Post: American Embassy
Telephone: 011-380-44-417-2669
Fax: 011-380-44-417-1419
Street address: 10 Yuria Kotsyubinskono
Mailing address: U.S. Dept. of State (Kiev), Washington DC 20521-5850

UNITED ARAB EMIRATES *Dubai*
Post: American Consulate General
Telephone: 011-971-4-313-584
Fax: 011-971-4-313-121

Workweek: Saturday–Wednesday
Street address: Dubai International Trade Center, 21st Fl.
Mailing address: U.S. Dept. of State (Dubai), Washington DC 20521-6020

Abu Dhabi
Post: American Embassy
Telephone: 011-971-2-273-666
Fax: 011-971-2-271-377
Workweek: Saturday–Wednesday
Street address: 8th Fl., Blue Tower Bldg., Shaikh Khalifa Bin Zayed St.
Mailing address: U.S. Dept. of State (Abu Dhabi), Washington DC 20521-6010

UNITED KINGDOM *London*
Post: American Embassy
Telephone: 011-44-71-408-8019
Fax: 011-44-71-408-8020
Street address: 24-31 Grosvenor Square
Mailing address: PSC 801, Box 40, FPO AE 09498-4040

UZBEKISTAN *Tashkent*
Post: American Embassy
Telephone: 011-7-3712-771-407
Fax: 011-7-3712-776-953
Street address: 82 Chelanzanskaya
Mailing address: U.S. Dept. of State (Tashkent), Washington, DC 20521-7110

VENEZUELA *Caracas*
Post: American Embassy
Telephone: 011-58-2-977-2792
Fax: 011-58-2-977-2177
Street address: Calle F con Calle Suapure Colinas de Valle Arriba Codigo Postal 1060
Mailing address: Unit 4958, APO AA 34037

VIETNAM *Hanoi*
Post: Commercial Service
Telephone: 011-844-824-2422
Fax: 011-844-824-2421
Street address: U.S. Commercial Center, 31 Hai Ba Trung, 4th Fl.
E-mail address: 10313.3220@compuserve.com

APPENDIX 14

GUIDE TO STATE STATISTICAL ABSTRACTS
Source: Statistical Abstract of the United States 1997.

This bibliography includes the most recent statistical abstracts for states published since 1986 plus those issued in late 1997 or early 1998. For some states, a near equivalent has been listed in substitution for, or in addition to, a statistical abstract. All sources contain statistical tables on a variety of subjects for the state as a whole, its component parts, or both. The page counts given for publications are approximate. Internet sites also contain statistical data and were accessed in early September 1997.

Alabama

University of Alabama, Center for Business and Economic Research, Box 870221, Tuscaloosa 35487, (205) 348-6191.
Internet site: http://www.cba.ua.edu/cber/
Economic Abstract of Alabama. 1997. 488 pp.

Alaska

Department of Commerce and Economic Development, Division of Trade & Development, P.O. Box 110804, Juneau 99811-0804, (907) 465-2017.
Internet site:
http://www.state.ak.us/local/akpages/COMMERCE/tdpub/htm
The Alaska Economy Performance Report. 1996.

Arizona

University of Arizona, Economic and Business Research, College of Business and Public Administration, McClelland Hall 204, Tucson Arizona 85721-0001, (520) 621-2155, fax (520) 621-2150.
Internet site:
http://www.bpa.arizona.edu/newpage
Arizona Statistical Abstract: A 1993 Data Handbook. 616 pp.
Arizona Economic Indicators. 52 pp. Biennial.
Arizona's Economy. 20 pp. Quarterly newsletter and data.

Arkansas

University of Arkansas at Little Rock, Institute for Economic Advancement, Economic Research, 2801 South University, Little Rock 72204, (501) 569-8550.
Arkansas State and County Economic Data. 16 pp. Revised annually.

University of Arkansas at Little Rock, Institute for Economic Advancement, Census State Data Center, Little Rock 72204, (501) 569-8530.
Arkansas Statistical Abstract, 1996. 688 pp. Revised biennially.

California

Department of Finance, 915 L St., 8th Fl., Sacramento 95814, (916) 322-2263.
Internet site: http://www.dof.ca.gov/
California Statistical Abstract, 1996.

Pacific Data Resources, P.O. Box 1922, Santa Barbara, CA 93116-1922, (800) 422-2546.
California Almanac, 6th ed. 275 pp. Biennial.

Colorado

University of Colorado, Business Research Division, Campus Box 420, Boulder 80309, (303) 492-8227.
Internet site: http://www.colorado.edu/libraries/govpubs/online/htm
Statistical Abstract of Colorado, 1987. 600 pp. Latest and last edition.

Connecticut

Connecticut Department of Economic & Community Development, 505 Hudson St., Hartford 06106, (800) 392-2122.
Internet site: http://www.state.ct.us/ecd/
Connecticut Market Data. 1995. 140 pp. (Diskette also available.)
Connecticut Town Profiles, 1996–97. 340 pp.

Delaware

Delaware Economic Development Office, P.O. Box 1401, 99 Kings Highway, Dover 19903, (302) 739-4271.
Internet site: http://www.state.de.us/govern/agencies/dedo/index.htm
Delaware Statistical Overview, 1996.

University of Delaware, Bureau of Economic Research, College of Business and Economics, Newark 19716-2730, (302) 831-8401.
Delaware Economic Report 1994–95. 200 pp. Last edition. Bureau of Economic Research no longer exists.

District of Columbia

Office of Planning, Data Management Division, Presidential Bldg., Ste. 500, 415 12th St. NW, Washington, DC 20004, (202) 727-6533.
1990 Census, Population and Housing for the District of Columbia. 72 pp.
1990 Census: Social, Economic and Housing. 44 pp. for each of nine volumes.
Socio-Economic Indicators by Census Tract. 221 pp.
Socio-Economic Indicators of Change by Census Tract, 1980–1990. 146 pp.

Office of Policy and Evaluation, Executive Office of the Mayor, 1 Judiciary Square, Ste. 1000, 441 4th St. NW, Washington, DC 20001, (202) 727-6979
Indices—A Statistical Index to DC Services, Dec. 1994–96. 331 pp.

Florida

University of Florida, Bureau of Economic and Business Research, Box 117145, Gainesville 32611-7145, (352) 392-0171.
Internet site: http://www.cba.ufl.edu/bebr/
Florida Statistical Abstract, 1996. 30th ed. 800 pp. Also available on diskette.
Florida County Perspectives, 1996. One profile for each county. Annual.
Florida County Rankings, 1996.
Florida and the Nation, 1997.

Georgia

University of Georgia, Selig Center for Economic Growth, Terry College of Business, Athens 30602-6269, (706) 542-4085.
Internet site: http://www.selig.uga.edu/

University of Georgia, College of Agricultural and Environmental Sciences, Cooperative Extension Service, Athens 30602-4356, (706) 542-8938, fax (706) 542-8934.
Internet site: http://www.uga.edu/caes/
The Georgia County Guide. 1997. 16th ed. 200 pp. Annual.

Office of Planning and Budget, 254 Washington St. SW, Atlanta 30334-8501, (404) 656-0911.
Georgia Descriptions in Data. 1990–1991. 249 pp. No longer being published.

Hawaii

Hawaii State Department of Business, and Economic Development & Tourism, Research and Economic Analysis Division, Statistics Branch, P.O. Box 2359, Honolulu 96804. Inquiries (808) 586-2481; copies 808-586-2424.
Internet site: http://www.hawaii.gov/dbedt
The State of Hawaii Data Book 1996: A Statistical Abstract. 29th ed. 649 pp.

Idaho

Department of Commerce, 700 West State St., Boise 83720-0093, (208) 334-2470.
Internet site: http://www.idoc.state.id.us
County Profiles of Idaho, 1996.
Idaho Community Profiles, 1997.
Idaho Facts, 1997.
Idaho Facts Data Book, 1995.
Profile of Rural Idaho 1993.

University of Idaho, Center for Business Development and Research, Moscow 83844-3229, (208) 885-6611.
Idaho Statistical Abstract. 4th ed. 1996.

Illinois

University of Illinois, Bureau of Economic and Business Research, 428 Commerce West, 1206 S. 6th St., Champaign 61820, (217) 333-2332.
Illinois Statistical Abstract. 1996. 875 pages.

Indiana

Indiana University, Indiana Business Research Center, School of Business, 801 W. Michigan BS4015 Indianapolis 46202-5151, (317) 274-2204.
Internet site: http://www.iupui.edu/it/ibrc/
Indiana Factbook, 1994–95. 413 pages.

Iowa

Public Interest Institute, c/o Iowa Wesleyan College, 600 N. Jackson St., Mount Pleasant 52641, (319) 385-3462
1996 Statistical Profile of Iowa.

Kansas

University of Kansas, Institute for Public Policy and Business Research, 607 Blake Hall, Lawrence 66045-2960 (785) 864-3701.
Internet site: http://www.ukans.edu/cwis/units/IPPBR/IPPBRmain.html
Kansas Statistical Abstract, 1996. 35th ed. 1997.

Kentucky

Kentucky Cabinet for Economic Development, Division of Research, 500 Mero St., Capital Plaza Tower, Frankfort 40601, (502) 564-4886.
Internet site: http://www.state.ky.us/edc/cabmain.htm
Kentucky Deskbook of Economic Statistics. 33d ed. 1997.

Louisiana

University of New Orleans, Division of Business and Economic Research, New Orleans 70148, (504) 286-6248.
Internet site: http://leap.nlu.edu/STAAB.HTM
Statistical Abstract of Louisiana. 9th ed. 1994.

Maine

Maine Department of Economic and Community Development, State House Station 59, Augusta 04333, (207) 287-2656.

Maine: A Statistical Summary. Updated periodically.

Maryland

Regional Economic Studies Institute, Towson University, Towson 21252-7097, (410) 830-3778.

Maryland Statistical Abstract. 1995–1996. 349 pp.

Massachusetts

Massachusetts Institute for Social and Economic Research, Box 37515, University of Massachusetts at Amherst 01003-7515, (413) 545-3460, fax 413-545-3686.

Internet site: http://www.umass.edu/miser/

Population Estimates for Massachusetts Cities and Towns. 1995.

Projection of the Population, Mass., Cities and Towns, Years 1990–2010.

Minnesota

Department of Trade and Economic Development, Business and Community Development Division, 500 Metro Square Bldg., St. Paul 55101, (612) 296-8283.

Compare Minnesota: An Economic and Statistical Factbook, 1994–95. 165 pp.

Economic Report to the Governor: State of Minnesota, 1992. 148 pp.

Office of State Demographer, Minnesota Planning, 300 Centennial Bldg., St. Paul 55155, (612) 296-2557.

Minnesota Population and Household Estimates, 1996. Available diskette in Lotus, dBase, or ASCII format.

Minnesota Population Projections, 1990.

Mississippi

Mississippi State University, College of Business and Industry, Division of Research, Mississippi State 39762, (601) 325-3817.

Mississippi Statistical Abstract. 1996. 554 pp.

Missouri

University of Missouri, Business and Public Administration Research Center, Columbia 65211, (573) 882-4805.

Internet site: http://tiger.bpa.missouri.edu/research/centers/bparc/

Statistical Abstract for Missouri, 1995. 256 pp. Biennial.

Montana

Montana Department of Commerce, Census and Economic Information Center, 1424 9th Ave., Helena 59620, (406) 444-2896.

Internet site: http://commerce.mt.gov/celc/index.htm

Statistical Reports from the Montana County Database. Separate county and state reports; available by subject section as well as complete reports by county and state, updated periodically.

Nebraska

Department of Economic Development, Division of Research, Box 94666, Lincoln 68509, (402) 471-3784.

Internet site: http://www.ded.state.ne.us/

Nebraska Statistical Handbook. 1995–1996. 300 pp. Available only on Internet.

Nevada

Department of Administration, Budget and Planning Division, Capitol Complex, Carson City 89710, (702) 687-4065.

Nevada Statistical Abstract. 1996. 225 pp. Biennial.

New Hampshire

Office of State Planning, 2½ Beacon St., Concord 03301-4497, (603) 271-2155.

Current Estimates and Trends in New Hampshire's Housing Supply. Update: 1996. 32 pp.

1996 Population Estimates for New Hampshire Cities and Towns.

New Hampshire Population Projections for Counties by Age & Sex, Apr. 1997, 2000–2020.

New Jersey

New Jersey State Data Center, NJ Department of Labor, CN 388, Trenton 08625-0388, (609) 984-2595.

Internet site: http://www.state.nj.us/labor/lra/njsdc.html

New Jersey Source Book, 1993. 156 pp.

New Mexico

University of New Mexico, Bureau of Business and Economic Research, 1919 Lomas NE, Albuquerque 87131-6021, (505) 277-6626, fax (505) 277-2773.

Internet site: http://www.unm.edu/bber/

County Profiles. 1997. 72 pp.

Community Profiles for Selected New Mexico cities.

Population Projections for the State of New Mexico, 1997.

New York

Nelson A. Rockefeller Institute of Government, 411 State St., Albany 12203-1003, (518) 443-5522.

New York State Statistical Yearbook, 1996. 21st ed. 582 pp.

North Carolina

Office of Governor Office of State Planning, 116 W. Jones St., Raleigh 27603-8003, (919) 733-4131.

Internet site:
http://www.ospl.state.nc.us/Demographer
*Statistical Abstract of North Carolina Counties,
1991.* 6th ed. No longer being published.

North Dakota

University of North Dakota, Box 8369, Bureau of
Business and Economic Research, Grand
Forks 58202, (701) 777-2637.
The Statistical Abstract of North Dakota. 1988.
700 pp.

North Dakota Department of Economic
Development & Finance, 1833 E. Bismark
Expressway, Bismark 58504-6708, (701) 328-
5300.
*State of North Dakota Economic, Demographic,
Public Services, and Fiscal Condition.*
September 1995. 155 pp.

Ohio

Department of Development, Office of Strategic
Research, P.O. Box 1001, Columbus 43216-
1001, (614) 466-2115.
Internet site: http://www.odod.ohio.gov/
Research products and services. Updated
continuously.

The Ohio State University, School of Public Policy
and Management, 1775 College Rd.,
Columbus 43210-1399, (614) 292-7731.
Benchmark Ohio, 1993. 300 pp. Biennial.

Oklahoma

University of Oklahoma, Center for Economic and
Management Research, 307 W. Brooks St.,
Rm. 4, Norman 73019, (405) 325-2931.
Internet site: http://www.nt.cba.ou.edu/
Statistical Abstract of Oklahoma, 1996. 441 pp.
Annual.

Oregon

Secretary of State, P.O. Box 3370, Rm. 136, State
Capitol, Salem 97310, (503) 986-2234.
Internet site: http://sosinet.sos.state.or.us/
Oregon Blue Book. 1997–1998. 476 pp. $14.
Biennial.

Pennsylvania

Pennsylvania State Data Center, Institute of State
and Regional Affairs, Penn State Harrisburg,
777 W. Harrisburg Pike, Middletown 17057-
4898, (717) 948-6336.
Internet site: http://
howard.hbg.psu.edu/psdc/psdchome1.1.html
Pennsylvania Statistical Abstract, 1996. 301 pp.

Rhode Island

Rhode Island Economic Development Corporation,
1 W. Exchange St., Providence 02903, (401)
277-2601, fax (401) 277-2102.
Internet site: http://www.riedc.com/
*Rhode Island 1990 Census of Population and
Housing Summary.* May 1994.
The Rhode Island Economy. May 1997.

South Carolina

Budget and Control Board, Office of Research and
Statistical Services, R. C. Dennis Bldg., Rm.
425, Columbia 29201, (803) 734-3781.
Internet site: http://www.state.sc.us/drss/
South Carolina Statistical Abstract: 1997. 440 pp.

South Dakota

University of South Dakota, State Data Center,
Vermillion 57069, (605) 677-5287.
Selected Social and Economic Characteristics.
550 pp.
1997 South Dakota Community Abstracts. 400 pp.

Tennessee

University of Tennessee, Center for Business and
Economic Research, Knoxville 37996-4170,
(615) 974-5441.
Internet site: http://cber.bus.utk.edu/
Tennessee Statistical Abstract, 1996–97. 16th ed.
807 pp. Biennial.

Texas

Dallas Morning News, Communications Center,
P.O. Box 655237, Dallas 75265-5237, (214)
977-8261.
Texas Almanac, 1998–99. 672 pp.

University of Texas, Bureau of Business Research,
Austin 78713, (512) 471-5180.
Texas Fact Book, 1989. 6th ed. 250 pp. No longer
published.

Utah

University of Utah, Bureau of Economic and
Business Research, 401 Kendall D. Garff
Building, Salt Lake City 84112, (801) 581-6333.
Internet site:
http://www.business.utah.edu/BEBR/
Statistical Abstract of Utah. 1996. Triennial.

Utah Foundation, 10 West 100 South, Ste. 323,
Salt Lake City 84101-1544, (801) 364-1837.
Statistical Review of Government in Utah. 1997.

Vermont

Labor Market Information, Department of
Employment and Training, 5 Green Mountain
Dr., P.O. Box 488, Montpelier 05601-0488,
(802) 828-4202.

Internet site: http://www.det.state.vt.us/
Demographic and Economic Profiles. Annual.
Regional county reports also available.

Virginia

University of Virginia, Weldon Cooper Center for
Public Service, 918 Emmet St., North Ste. 300,
Charlottesville 22903-4832, (804) 982-5585.
Internet site:
http://128.143.238.20/cpspubs/default.html
Virginia Statistical Abstract, 1996–97. 950 pp.
Biennial.

Washington

Washington State Office of Financial
Management, Forecasting Division, P.O. Box
43113, Olympia 98504-3113, (360) 902-0599.
Internet site: http://www.wa.gov/ofm/
Washington State Data Book, 1995. 300 pp.
Population Trends for Washington State. 48 pages.
Annual.

West Virginia

West Virginia University, College of Business and
Economics, Bureau of Business and Economic
Research, P.O. Box 6025, Morgantown 26506-
6026, (304) 293-7835.

Internet site: http://www.wvu.edu/colbe/research/
bureau/home.htm
West Virginia Statistical Abstract. 1995. 400 pp.
Biennial.
County Data Profiles. 50 pp. Annual.
Census Data Profiles. 30 pp.
West Virginia Economic Outlook. 50 pp. Annual.

West Virginia Research League, Inc., 405 Capitol
St., Ste. 414, Charleston 25301-1721, (304)
346-9451.
Economic Indicators. 1995. 215 pp.
The 1996 Statistical Handbook. 94 pp.

Wisconsin

Wisconsin Legislative Reference Bureau, P.O. Box
2037, Madison 53701-2037, (608) 266-7098.
1997–1998 Wisconsin Blue Book. 950 pp.
Biennial.

Wyoming

Department of Administration and Information,
Division of Economic Analysis, 327 E. Emerson
Bldg., Cheyenne 82002-0060, (307) 777-7504.
Internet site: http://www.state.wy.us.ai.ai.html
The Equality State Almanac 1996. 120 pp.
Socioeconomic Statistics of Puerto Rico. 1992.

APPENDIX 15

GUIDE TO FOREIGN STATISTICAL ABSTRACTS

This bibliography presents recent statistical abstracts for Mexico, Russia, and member nations of the Organization for Economic Cooperation and Development. All sources contain statistical tables on a variety of subjects for the individual countries. Many of the following publications provide text in English as well as in the national language(s). For further information on these publications, contact the named statistical agency that is responsible for editing the publication.

Australia
Australian Bureau of Statistics, Canberra.
Yearbook Australia. 1997. 767 pp. Annual. (In English.)

Austria
Österreichisches Statistisches Zentralamt, P.O. Box 9000, A-1033 Vienna.
Statistisches Jahrbuch for die Republik Österreich. 1996. 612 pp. Annual. (In German.)

Belgium
Institut National de Statistique, 44 rue de Louvain, 1000 Brussels.
Annuaire statistique de la Belgique. 1994. 822 pp. Annual. (In French and Dutch.)

Canada
Statistics Canada, Ottawa, Ontario KIA OT6.
Canada Yearbook: A review of economic, social and political developments in Canada. 1997. 515 pp. Irregular. (In English and French.)

Croatia
Republika Hrvatska, Republicki Zavod Za Statistiku.
Statistiku Ijetopis. 1995. 644 pp. (In English and Serbo-Croatian.)

Czech Republic
Czech Statistical Office, Sokolovska 142, 186 04 Praha 8.
Statisticka Rocenka Ceske Republiky. 1996. 707 pp. (In English and Czech.)

Denmark
Danmarks Statistik, Postboks 2550 Sejrogade 11 DK 2100, Copenhagen.
Statistical Yearbook. 1995. 559 pp. Annual. (In Danish with English translations of table headings.)

Finland
Central Statistical Office of Finland, Box 504 SF-00101 Helsinki.
Statistical Yearbook of Finland. 1996. 661 pp. Annual. (In English, Finnish, and Swedish.)

France
Institut National de la Statistique et des Etudes Economiques, Paris 18, Blvd. Adolphe Pinard, 75675 Paris (Cedex 14).
Annuaire Statistique de la France. 1997. 1002 pp. Annual. (In French.)

Germany
Statistische Bundesamt, Postfach 5528, 6200 Wiesbaden.
Statistisches Jahrbuch für die Bundesrepublik Deutschland. 1996. 755 pp. Annual. (In German.)
Statistisches Jahrbuch für das Ausland. 1996. 399 pp.

Greece
National Statistical Office, 14-16 Lycourgou St., 101-66 Athens.
Concise Statistical Yearbook 1995. 254 pp. (In English.)
Statistical Yearbook of Greece. 1994–1995. 528 pp, plus 7 pages of diagrams. Annual. (In English and Greek.)

Iceland
Hagstofa Islands/Statistical Bureau, Hverfisgata 8-10, Reykjavík.
Statistical Abstract of Iceland. 1994. 303 pp. Irregular. (In English and Icelandic.)

Ireland
Central Statistics Office, Earisfort Terrace, Dublin 2.
Statistical Abstract. 1996. 411 pp. Annual. (In English.)

Italy
ISTAT (Istituto Centrale di Statistica), Via Cesare Balbo 16, 00100 Rome.
Annuario Statistico Italiano. 1996 679 pp. Annual. (In Italian.)

Japan
Statistics Bureau, Management & Coordination Agency, 19-1 Wakamatsucho, Shinjuku Tokyo 162.

Japan Statistical Yearbook. 1997 914 pp. Annual.
(In English and Japanese.)

Luxembourg

STATEC (Service Central de la Statistique et des
Etudes), P.O. Box 304, L-2013, Luxembourg.
Annuaire Statistique. 1996. Annual. (In French.)

Mexico

Instituto Nacional de Estadistica Geografia e
Informatica, Avda. Insurgentes Sur No. 795-PH
Col. Napoles, Del. Benito Juarez 03810
Mexico, D.F.
*Anuario estadistico de los Estados Unidos
Mexicanos.* 1993. 610 pp. Annual. Also on disc.
(In Spanish.)
Agenda Estadistica 1994. 186 pp.

Netherlands

Centraal Bureau voor de Statistiek. 428 Prinses
Beatrixlaan, P.O. Box 959, 2270 AZ Voorburg.
Statistisch Yearbook 1996. 599 pp. (In Dutch.)

New Zealand

Department of Statistics, Wellington.
New Zealand Official Yearbook. 1996. 592 pp.
Annual. (In English.)

Norway

Central Bureau of Statistics, Skippergate 15, P.B.
8131 Dep. N-Oslo 1.
Statistical Yearbook. 1996. 445 pp. Annual. (In
English and Norwegian.)

Portugal

INE (Instituto Nacional de Estatistica), Avenida
Antonio Jose de Almeida, P-1078 Lisbon
Codex.
Anuario Estatistico: de Portugal. 1995. 339 pp. (In
Portuguese.)

Russia

State Committee of Statistics of Russia, Moscow.
Russian Federation in the Year 1993. Statistical
yearbook. 1993. 383 pp. (In Russian.)

Slovakia

Statistical Office of the Slovak Republic, Mileticova
3, 824 67 Bratislava.
Statisticka Rocenka Slovensak 1996. 681 pp.
(In English and Slovak.)

Slovenia

Statistical Office of the Republic of Slovenia,
Vozarski Pot 12, 61000 Ljubljana.
Statisticni Letopis Republike Slovenije 1996. 619
pp. (In Slovenian.)

Spain

INE (Instituto Nacional de Estadistica), Paseo de
la Castellana, 183, Madrid 16.
Anuario Estadistico de Espana. 1995. 878 pp.
Annual. (In Spanish.)
Anuario Estadistico. 1988. (Edicion Manual.) 976 pp.

Sweden

Statistics Sweden, S-11581 Stockholm.
Statistical Yearbook of Sweden. 1997. 566 pp.
Annual. (In English and Swedish.)

Switzerland

Bundesamt for Statistik, Hallwylstrasse 15, CH-
3003, Bern.
Statistisches Jahrbuch der Schweiz. 1997. 464 pp.
Annual. (In French and German.)

Turkey

State Institute of Statistics, Prime Ministry, 114
Necatibey Caddesi, Bakanliklar, Yenisehir,
Ankara.
Statistical Yearbook of Turkey. 1996. 690 pp. (In
English and Turkish.)
Turkey in Statistics 1994. 150 pp. (In English and
Turkish.)

United Kingdom

Central Statistical Office, Great George St.,
London SW1P 3AQ.
Annual Abstract of Statistics. 1991. 349 pp.
Annual. (In English.)

APPENDIX 16

DIRECTORY OF USEFUL WEB SITES AND PHONE NUMBERS OF U.S. GOVERNMENT AGENCIES

Office	URL	Telephone Number
Bureau of International Labor Affairs (ILAB)	http://www.dol.gov/dol/ilab/	(202) 219-6373
Bureau of Labor Statistics (BLS)	http://stats.bls.gov/dolbls.htm	(202) 606-5900
Commodity Futures Trading Commission	http://www.cftc.gov/cftc/	(202) 418-5080
Employment Standards Administration (ESA) (U.S. Dept. of Labor)	http://www.dol.gov/dol/esa/	(202) 219-8743
Employment and Training Administration (ETA) (U.S. Dept. of Labor)	http://www.doleta.gov/	(202) 219-6871
Environmental Protection Agency (EPA)	http://www.epa.gov/	202-260-2090
Export-Import Bank of the United States	http://www.exim.gov/	(202) 565-EXIM (3946)
Federal Communications Commission (FCC)	http://www.fcc.gov/	(202) 418-0200
Federal Deposit Insurance Corporation (FDIC)	http://www.fdic.gov/	(800) 934-3342 (Consumers Affairs Hot Line)
Federal Information Center*	http://www.gsa.gov/et/ fic-firs/fichome.htm	(800) 688-9889
Federal Trade Commission (FTC)	http://www.ftc.gov/	(202) 326-2222
Government Printing Office (GPO)	http://www.access.gpo.gov/	(202) 512-0132
Library of Congress	http://www.loc.gov/	(202) 707-5000
National Archives and Records Administration	http://www.nara.gov/	(202) 501-5400
National Labor Relations Board	http://www.nlrb.gov/	(202) 273-1991 (Director of Information)
Occupational Safety and Health Administration (OSHA)	http://www.osha.gov/index.html	(202) 219-8148
Office of Management and Budget (OMB)	http://www.whitehouse.gov/ WH/EOP/OMB/html/ ombhome.html	(202) 395-7250
Pension and Welfare Benefits Administration (PWBA)	http://www.dol.gov/dol/pwba/	(202) 219-8921
Pension Benefit Guaranty Corporation	http://www.pbgc.gov/	(202) 326-4000
Securities & Exchange Commission (SEC)	http://www.sec.gov/	(202) 942-7040
Small Business Administration (SBA)	http://www.sbaonline.sba.gov/	(800) 8ASK-SBA
Social Security Administration	http://www.ssa.gov/	(800) 772-1213
THOMAS: Legislative Information on the Internet	http://thomas.loc.gov/	n/a
U.S. Department of Agriculture	http://www.usda.gov/	(202) 720-2791
U.S. Department of Commerce	http://www.doc.gov/	(202) 482-2000
U.S. Department of Education	http://www.ed.gov/	(800) 872-5327
U.S. Department of Energy	http://www.doe.gov/	(202) 208-0200
U.S. Department of Health and Human Services	http://www.os.dhhs.gov/	(202) 619-0257
U.S. Department of Housing and Urban Development (HUD)	http://www.hud.gov/	(202) 708-1422
U.S. Department of the Interior	http://www.doi.gov/	(202) 208-3100
U.S. Department of Justice	http://www.usdoj.gov/	(202) 514-2000
U.S. Department of Labor	http://www.dol.gov/	(202) 219-8211
U.S. Department of Transportation	http://www.dot.gov/	(202) 366-4000

* The Federal Information Center no longer has individual phone numbers for different states or areas.

Office	URL	Telephone Number
U.S. Department of Veterans Affairs	http://www.va.gov/	(800) 827-1000
U.S. House of Representatives	http://www.house.gov/	(202) 225-3121
U.S. Senate	http://www.senate.gov/	(202) 224-3121
U.S. State Department	http://www.state.gov/	(202) 647-4000
Veterans' Employment and Training Service (VETS)	http://www.dol.gov/dol/vets/	(202) 219-8611
White House	http://www.whitehouse.gov/ WH/Welcome.html	(202) 456-1414
Women's Bureau (WB) (U.S. Dept. of Labor)	http://www.dol.gov/dol/wb/	(202) 219-6652

APPENDIX 17

INTERNATIONAL DIALING CODES

This table lists Country Codes and International Direct Dialing (IDD) prefixes.

Country Code

The country code should be used when dialing *to* that particular country *from* another country. In some cases you will also need to dial a city or area code.

IDD Prefix

The IDD prefix is the access code that you dial to make a call *from* that country *to* another country. This is followed by the country code for the country you are calling (see above). The IDD situation in many countries has been changing regularly.

Source: AT&T International Dialing Guide; Microsoft TechNet Knowledge Base; personal reports. http://kropla.com/dialcode.htm—updated 16 January 1998. Copyright © 1996–1998 Steve Kropla. All rights reserved.

Country	Country Code	IDD Prefix	Country	Country Code	IDD Prefix
Afghanistan	93	00	Burkina Faso	226	00
Albania	355	00	Burma (Myanmar)	95	0
Algeria	213	00	Burundi	257	90
American Samoa	684	00	Cambodia	855	00
Andorra	376	00	Cameroon	237	00
Angola	244	00	Canada	1	011
Anguilla	264*	011	Cape Verde Islands	238	0
Antarctica	672		Cayman Islands	345*	011
Antigua	268*	011	Central African Republic	236	19
Argentina	54	00	Chad	235	15
Armenia	374	8~10	Chatham Island		
Aruba	297	00	(New Zealand)	64	00
Ascension Island	247	01	Chile	56	00
Australia	61	0011	China (PRC)	86	00
Austria	43	00	Christmas Island	672	00
Azerbaijan	994	8~10	Cocos-Keeling Islands	61	0011
Bahamas	242	001*	Colombia	57	90
Bahrain	973	0	Comoros	269	10
Bangladesh	880	00	Congo	242	00
Barbados	246*	011	Cook Islands	682	00
Barbuda	268*	011	Costa Rica	506	00
Belarus	375	8~10	Croatia	385	00
Belgium	32	00	Cuba	53	119
Belize	501	00	Cuba (Guantánamo Bay)	5399	00
Benin	229	00	Cyprus	357	00
Bermuda	441*	011	Czech Republic	420	00
Bhutan	975	00	Denmark	45	00
Bolivia	591	00	Diego Garcia	246	00
Bosnia and			Djibouti	253	00
Herzegovina	387	00	Dominica	767*	011
Botswana	267	00	Dominican Republic	809*	011
Brazil	55	00	Easter Island	56	00
British Virgin Islands	284*	011	Ecuador	593	00
Brunei	673	00	Egypt	20	00
Bulgaria	359	00	El Salvador	503	0

Country	Country Code	IDD Prefix	Country	Country Code	IDD Prefix
Equatorial Guinea	240	00	Kuwait	965	00
Eritrea	291	00	Kyrgyz Republic	7	8~10
Estonia	372	8~00	Laos	856	14
Ethiopia	251	00	Latvia	371	00
Faeroe Islands	298	009	Lebanon	961	00
Falkland Islands	500	0	Lesotho	266	00
Fiji Islands	679	05	Liberia	231	00
Finland	358	00, 990, 994, 999	Libya	218	00
			Liechtenstein	41	00
France	33	00	Lithuania	370	8~00
French Antilles	596	00	Luxembourg	352	00
French Guiana	594	00	Macao 85300		
French Polynesia	689	00	Macedonia		
Gabon	241	00	(former Yugoslav Rep.)	389	00
Gambia	220	00	Madagascar	261	16
Georgia	995	8~10	Malawi	265	101
Germany	49	00	Malaysia	60	00
Ghana	233	00	Maldives	960	00
Gibraltar	350	00	Mali Republic	223	00
Greece	30	00	Malta	356	00
Greenland	299	009	Marshall Islands	692	00
Grenada	473*	011	Martinique	596	00
Guadeloupe	590	00	Mauritania	222	00
Guam	671	011	Mauritius	230	00
Guantánamo Bay	5399	00	Mayotte Island	269	10
Guatemala	502	00	Mexico	52	98 (or 95†)
Guinea (PRP)	224	00	Micronesia	691	011
Guinea-Bissau	245	00	Midway Island	808	00
Guyana	592	001	Moldova	373	8~10
Haiti	509	00	Monaco	377	00
Honduras	504	00	Mongolia	976	00
Hong Kong	852	001	Montserrat	664*	011
Hungary	36	00	Morocco	212	00~
Iceland	354	00	Mozambique	258	00
India	91	00	Myanmar	95	0
Indonesia	62	001	Namibia	264	09
Iran	98	00	Nauru	674	115
Iraq	964	00	Nepal	977	00
Ireland	353	00	Netherlands	31	00
Israel	972		Netherlands Antilles	599	00
(Bezeq LTD)		00	Nevis	869	011
(Golden Lines)		012	New Caledonia	687	00
(Barak LTD)		013	New Zealand	64	00
(Bezeq LTD)		014	Nicaragua	505	00
Italy	39	00	Niger	227	00
Ivory Coast			Nigeria	234	009
(Côte d'Ivoire)	225	00	Niue	683	00
Jamaica	876*	011	Norfolk Island	672	00
Japan	81	001	North Korea	850	00
Jordan	962	00	Norway	47	00
Kazakhstan	7	8~10	Oman	968	00
Kenya	254	00	Pakistan	92	00
Kiribati	686	00	Palau	680	00
Korea (North)	850	00	Panama	507	0
Korea (South)	82	001	Papua New Guinea	675	05

Country	Country Code	IDD Prefix	Country	Country Code	IDD Prefix
Paraguay	595	00	Sweden	46	009
Peru	51	00	Switzerland	41	00
Philippines	63	00	Syria	963	00
Poland	48	0~0	Taiwan	886	002
Portugal	351	00	Tajikistan	7	8~10
Puerto Rico	787	1*	Tanzania	255	00
Qatar	974	0	Thailand	66	001
Réunion Island	262	00	Tinian Island	670	011
Romania	40	00	Togo	228	00
Rota Island	670	011	Tokelau	690	00
Russia	7	8~10	Tonga Islands	676	00
Rwanda	250	00	Trinidad and Tobago	868*	011
St. Helena	290	01	Tunisia	216	00
St. Kitts-Nevis	869	011*	Turkey	90	00
St. Lucia	758	011*	Turkmenistan	993	8~10
St.-Pierre and Miquelon	508	00	Turks and Caicos Islands	649*	011
St. Vincent and the			Tuvalu	688	00
Grenadines	809*	011	Uganda	256	00
Saipan Island	670	011	Ukraine	380	8~10
San Marino	378	00	United Arab Emirates	971	00
São Tomé and Príncipe	239	00	United Kingdom	44	00
Saudi Arabia	966	00	United States of America	1	011
Senegal	221	00	U.S. Virgin Islands	1	011
Serbia	381	00	Uruguay	598	00
Seychelles Islands	248	00	Uzbekistan	7	8~10
Sierra Leone	232	00	Vanuatu	678	00
Singapore	65	001	Vatican City	379	00
Slovak Republic	421	00	Venezuela	58	00
Slovenia	386	00	Vietnam	84	00
Solomon Islands	677	00	Wake Island	808	00
Somalia	252	19	Wallis and Futuna Islands	681	19~
South Africa	27	09 or 091	Western Samoa	685	0
South Korea	82	001	Yemen	967	00
Spain	34	07~	Yugoslavia	381	99
Sri Lanka	94	00	Zaire	243	00
Sudan	249	00	Zambia	260	00
Suriname	597	00	Zimbabwe	263	110
Swaziland	268	00			

* From United States and Canada: Dial 1 + code + phone number.
  From other countries: Dial IDD + 1 + code + phone number.
† Use 95 to dial United States/Canada/Caribbean; country code not needed.
~ Await a second tone at this stage.

APPENDIX 18

FEDERAL RESERVE BANKS
http://woodrow.mpls.frb.fed.us/info/sys/banks.html

Boston	Cleveland	Chicago	Kansas City
New York	Richmond	St. Louis	Dallas
Philadelphia	Atlanta	Minneapolis	San Francisco

Federal Reserve Banks

Board of Governors of the Federal Reserve
    System
20th & Constitution Ave. NW
Washington, DC 20551
(202) 452-3000

The Federal Reserve System's 12 district offices
are:

First District—BOSTON
600 Atlantic Ave.
Boston, MA 02106
(617) 973-3000

Second District—NEW YORK
33 Liberty St.
New York, NY 10045
(212) 720-5000

Third District—PHILADELPHIA
Ten Independence Mall
Philadelphia, PA 19106
(215) 574-6000

Fourth District—CLEVELAND
1455 E. Sixth St.
Cleveland, OH 44114
(216) 579-2000

Fifth District—RICHMOND
701 E. Byrd St.
Richmond, VA 23219
(804) 697-8000

Sixth District—ATLANTA
104 Marietta St. NW
Atlanta, GA 30303-2713
(404) 521-8500

Seventh District—CHICAGO
230 S. LaSalle St.
Chicago, IL 60604
(312) 322-5322

Eighth District—ST. LOUIS
411 Locust St.
St. Louis, MO 63102
(314) 444-8444

Ninth District—MINNEAPOLIS
250 Marquette Ave.
Minneapolis, MN 55480
(612) 340-2345

Tenth District—KANSAS CITY
925 Grand Ave.
Kansas City, MO 64198
(816) 881-2000

Eleventh District—DALLAS
2200 N. Pearl St.
Dallas, TX 75201
(214) 922-6000

Twelfth District—SAN FRANCISCO
101 Market St.
San Francisco, CA 94105
(415) 974-2000

REFERENCES

Ahern, Dave, and Greg Stohr. 1997. *Chattanooga Times,* 20 March, C6.

Allen, Jeffrey G. 1993. *Complying with the ADA: A small business guide to hiring and employing the disabled.* New York: John Wiley & Sons, Inc.

Allimadi, Milton G. 1993. High-tech scanner system smoothes chemical inventory. *Journal of Commerce,* 15 January, 7A.

AMEX fact book. 1997. New York: American Stock Exchange, Inc.

Atrix International declares one-for-four reverse split. 1997. *Business Wire,* 10 December.

Atwood, Brett. 1997. Ticketmaster, Microsoft in legal lawsuit concerns links between Web sites. *Billboard,* 10 May.

Belden, Tom. 1977. Computer figures crucial to making aircraft—CATIA brings designs together. *The Seattle Times,* 11 February, D1.

Berry, Mike. 1998. Ask, and teachers, students, parents speak up. *Orlando Sentinel,* 15 March, K3.

Blume, Marshall E. 1975. Betas and their regression tendencies. *Journal of Finance* (June): 785–796.

Bohl, Don L. 1997. Case study: Saturn Corp.—a different kind of pay. *Compensation & Benefits Review* 29 (20 November).

Boone, Louis E., and David L. Kurtz. 1995. *Contemporary marketing plus.* 8th ed. Fort Worth: Dryden Press.

Boston Consulting Group. 1970. *Perspective on experience.* Boston: Boston Consulting Group.

Brealey, Richard A., and Stewart C. Myers. 1991. *Principles of corporate finance.* 4th ed. New York: McGraw-Hill.

Brennan, Catherine M. 1997. Fired Westinghouse researcher loses discrimination suit appeal. *Daily Record,* 28 March, 26.

Brigham, Eugene F., and Louis C. Gapenski. 1994. *Financial management.* 7th ed. Fort Worth: Dryden Press.

Brown, Warren. 1997. The caddy they ducked. *The Washington Post,* 11 September, E1.

Buckley, Monica. 1997. Landmark verdict spotlights computer keyboard injuries. *U.S. Business Litigation* 2, no. 10 (May): 1.

Burns, Greg. 1997. Futures industry to ease entry. *Chicago Tribune,* 6 August, Business section, 1.

Bush, Robert P. 1995. Up close and personal, marketing research and technology. *Business Perspectives* 8 (22 March): 1.

Capell, Kerry. 1996. Going for the green in the pink sheets. *Business Week,* 19 August, 82.

Case, John. 1996. Corporate culture. *Inc.,* November, 42–53.

Chandler, Alfred D., Jr. 1977. *The visible hand: The managerial revolution in American business.* Cambridge: Harvard University Press.

Chapman, Jacquelyn F., and Judith A. McFarland. 1995. Diversity of the customer base: A business necessity. *Journal of Education for Business* 71 (1 October): 17.

CKS Group, Inc. announces fourth quarter fiscal 1997 results. 1997. *Business Wire,* 17 December.

Clatworthy, Mike, Mike Jones, and Howard Mellett. 1997. The accounting policies of British Gas and the water companies—a conundrum. *Management Accounting* (London) 75, no. 5 (May): 36–38.

Collier, Andrew. 1997. MGM looking for a $1.3 bil loan. *The Hollywood Reporter,* 17 September.

Cost reduction could become as easy as ABD. 1995. *Management Today,* August, 10.

Dalglish, Brenda. 1997. Tee-Comm slides into receivership. *Financial Post* (Toronto), 23 May, 1.

Davis, Bruce. 1997. Goodyear weighs SR [synthetic rubber] projects. *Rubber and Plastics,* 27 January, 5.

De Marrais, Kevin G. 1996. Last gasp for vended cigarettes? Legislative assault may doom machines. *The Record,* 23 August, B1.

Deal, Terrence E., and Allan A. Kennedy. 1982. *Corporate cultures: The rites and rituals of corporate life.* Reading, Mass.: Addison-Wesley.

Dime says bond sale will reduce earnings. 1996. *Bloomberg News,* 24 December, B6.

Dretka, Gary. 1997. Intrigue ads a picture of adventurous selling. *Chicago Tribune,* 4 July, 1.

Dumaine, Brian. 1994. Managing: The trouble with teams. *Fortune,* 5 September, 86–92.

Eaton, Leslie. 1997. Stock trades: A better deal for investors isn't simple. *The New York Times,* 25 April, C1, C6.

Energy Information Administration. 1995. Projections: EIA, Office of Integrated Analysis and Forecasting, DESTINY International Energy Forecast Software.

Enter McBoeing—a giant firm gets defensive. 1996. *The Sacramento Bee,* 29 December, FO3.

Fama, Eugene F., and Kenneth R. French. 1992. The cross-section of expected stock returns. *Journal of Finance* 47, no. 2 (June): 427–465.

Farrelly, Paul, and Marie Woolf. 1997. African gold rush from cape to city. *The Observer,* 8 June, Business, 8.

Fasig, Lisa Biank. 1997. Retailers home in on house brands: Stores cultivate own labels to complement, compete with major national names. *The Cincinnati Enquirer,* 27 July, 11.

Ferris, Craig T. 1997. WPPSS may change its old name to get away from some old memories. *Bond Buyer,* 10 December, 6.

Ferris, Gerald R., Sherman D. Rosen, and Darold T. Barnum, eds. 1995. *Handbook of human resource management.* Cambridge, Mass.: Blackwell Publishers.

Fess, Philip E., and Carl S. Warren. 1993. *Accounting principles.* 17th ed. Cincinnati: South-Western Publishing Co.

Financial executives using ABCs for strategic decision making. 1997. *Business Wire,* 20 March.

Fine, Howard. 1997. Companies take ADA compliance in stride. *Orange County Business Journal,* 24 February, 1.

Fisher, Anne, with Jeremy Kahn. 1997. The world's most admired companies. *Fortune,* 27 October, 220.

Fitch, Malcolm, and Duff McDonald. 1997. Money rates the 15 most widely held stocks. *Money,* 1 November, 104.

Flaherty, Edward. n.d. The Federal Reserve System in detail: Its organization and powers. Unpublished paper. Web site: http://garnet.acns.fsu.edu/~eflahert/power.html.

Fletcher, Meg. 1997. NIOSH: OSHA: Companies not waiting for ergonomic standards. *Business Insurance,* 27 January, 3.

Foskett, Ken. 1996. New senator faces obstacles getting around Capitol. Cox News Service, 14 November.

Frook, John Evan. 1997. Testing new waters on the Web—car auction house to wed systems integrator in new venture. *InternetWeek,* 29 September.

Gaare, Mark. 1997. Fresh chickens from killer eggs. *Electronic Buyer News,* 5 May, 68.

Garmisa, Steven P. 1996. Corporate restructuring plans hit a snag. *Chicago Daily Law Bulletin,* 6 December, 5.

Gibson, William. 1984.20*Neuromancer.* New York: Ace Books.

Gifford, Dun, Jr. 1997. Brand management: Moving beyond loyalty. *Harvard Business Review* (March-April): 9–10.

Goldbogen, Jessica. 1997. Mail bonding: How stores are connecting with new residents. HFN (Home Furnishing Network), 9 June, 51.

Goodrich, Lawrence J. 1997. Seeing red digits after 2002. *Christian Science Monitor,* 8 May, 1.

Government Accounting Office Report. 1997. No. 08-29-1997. Federal Document Clearing House.

Greenberg, Herb. 1997. Talking about payments to AOL and ill-logical inventories. *San Francisco Chronicle,* 18 July, C1.

Hamel, Gary, and C. K. Prahalad. 1994. *Competing for the future.* Boston: Harvard Business School Press.

Hammer, Michael, and James Champy. 1993. *Reengineering the corporation: A manifesto for business revolution.* New York: HarperCollins.

Hardwicke, John W., and Robert W. Emerson. 1997. *Business law.* 2d ed. Hauppauge, N.Y.: Barron's Educational Series, Inc.

Hedden, Carole. 1997. From launch to relaunch: The secret to product longevity lies in using the right strategy for each stage of the life cycle. *Marketing Tools* 4 (September): 52.

Hellmich, Nanci. 1996. Consumers sink teeth into olestra chips. *USA Today,* 30 September, 6D.

Hiebeler, Robert, Thomas B. Kelly, and Charles Ketteman. 1998. *Best practices: Building your business with customer-focused solutions.* New York: Simon & Schuster.

Honore, Carl. 1997. Europe's next step; clouded dreams; folks wary of plan to tighten continental bond. *Houston Chronicle,* 1 June, 1.

Hoogvelt, Ankie, and Anthony G. Puxty. 1987. *Multinational enterprise: An encyclopedic dictionary of concepts and terms.* London: Macmillan.

Howes, Daniel. 1997. GM's $1 billion buys rights to Olympic tie-in: Deal is "unprecedented in its range and scope," top spokesman says. *The Detroit News,* 29 July, B1.

Humphrey-Hawkins Report. 1997. Federal Reserve Board Web site: http://www.bog.frb.fed.us/boarddocs/hh/9707section1.htm.

Jensen, M. C., ed. 1972. *Studies in the theory of capital markets.* New York: Praeger.

Johnson, Gregory S. 1997. Just-in-time makes Big 3 vulnerable to Ssrikes. *Journal of Commerce,* 30 April, 1B.

Johnsson, Henry J., P. McHugh, A. Pendlebury, and W. Wheeler. 1993. *Business process reengineering.* New York: John Wiley & Sons, Inc.

Josephson, Paul. 1997. Saving Russia's scientists. *Christian Science Monitor,* 24 January, 19.

Kanell, Michael E. 1996. Pager makers have got customers' number. *The Atlanta Journal and Constitution,* 14 July, D8.

Kaplan, Fred. 1997. Man against machine: Guile versus gigabytes. *Boston Globe,* 6 May, A1, A10.

Kaplan, Robert S., and David P. Norton. 1996. *The balanced scorecard: Translating strategy into action.* Boston: Harvard Business School Press.

Kapoor, Jack R., Les R. Dlabay, and Robert J. Hughes. 1996. *Personal finance.* 4th ed. Chicago: Irwin.

Keenan, Tim. 1995. Young lions roar: A. O. Smith Barrie team practices cutting-edge management. *Ward's Auto World,* May, 73.

Kerwin, Kathleen, and Bill Vlasic. 1998. Autos. *Business Week,* 12 January, 102.

Klott, Gary L. 1987. *The New York Times complete guide to personal investing.* New York: Times Books.

Kotler, Philip. 1994. *Marketing management: Analysis, planning, implementation, and control.* 8th ed. Englewood Cliffs, N.J.: Prentice Hall.

Kotler, Philip, and Gary Armstrong. 1994. *Principles of marketing.* 6th ed. Englewood Cliffs, N.J.: Prentice Hall.

Kotler, Philip, and Gary Armstrong. 1996. *Principles of marketing.* 7th ed. Englewood Cliffs, N.J.: Prentice Hall.

Kovatch, Karen. 1997. SafeGuard wants to backup the retail software game. *Pittsburgh Business Times & Journal,* 14 July, 4.

Krishnakuma, B. 1997. Storage battery acceleration in demand. *Business Line,* 25 May, 15.

Kristof, Kathy M. 1994. Small fry takes on Wal-Mart. *Newsday,* 10 June, A65.

Kubik, Maraline. 1997. Robotics increase productivity, quality, total employees at GM's fab plant. *Business Journal of the Five-County Region* (Youngstown, Ohio) 13, no. 16 (April): 31.

LeRoy, Michael H., and James M. Schultz. 1995. The legal context of human resource management: Conflict, confusion, cost, and role-conversion. In *Handbook of human resource management,* edited by Gerald R. Ferris, Sherman D. Rosen, and Darold T. Barnum. Cambridge, Mass.: Blackwell Publishers.

Levin, Gary. 1997. Ad vets have no regrets in hedging bets on nets. *Variety,* 20–26 October, 31.

Levy, Robert A. 1971. On the short-term stationarity of beta coefficients. *Financial Analysts Journal* (November-December): 55–62.

LI business spotlight/generics are the speciality/drug maker expands with liquid niche. 1996. *Newsday,* 20 October, F11.

Lieberman, David. 1996. The squeeze goes on—computer and communications OEMs see an accelerating rush to market for new products that will nevertheless have a shorter useful life out in the real world. *OEM Magazine,* 1 September, 13.

Linter, John. 1965. The valuation of risk assets and the selection of risky investments in stock portfolios and capital budgets. *Review of Economics and Statistics* 47: 13–37.

Longworth, R. C. 1996. Corporate giants dwarf many nations. *Chicago Tribune,* 11 October, 1.

Lundegaard, Karen M. 1996. A chance to be your own boss, sort of. *Baltimore Business Journal,* 8 November, 27.

Machacek, John. 1997. RIT getting $2 million toward "remanufacturing" technology. Gannett News Service, 24 September.

Maclean, Natalie. 1997. Competitive advantage vital element C. *Calgary Herald,* 15 February, E4.

Madore, James T. 1997. The face of retail/James Zimmerman, new honcho for Macy's, Bloomies and all of Federated, wants to make them special again. *Newsday,* 28 April, C12.

Maharry, Mike. 1997. Boeing tries to build 'em faster; ideas from workers at Frederickson plant turn into time-saving ways to make plane parts. *News Tribune,* 7 September, G1.

Mandelker, Jeannie, and Anne Ashby Gilbert. 1997. Crush rivals by launching great products. *Your Company,* 1 October, 54.

Mandell, Mel. 1995. Offshore savings. *World Trade* 8, no. 3 (April): 26–32.

Mazda to introduce merit-based personnel system. 1997. Jiri Press Ticker Service, 25 March.

McCann's relationship marketing unit lands in Europe. 1997. *Advertising Age,* February.

McGovern, Cynthia. 1997. Boards of directors score starring roles. *Financial Post* (Toronto), 3 May, A-12.

MCI delivers advanced technology and services to rural America. 1997. PR Newswire Association, Inc., 20 March.

McMorris, Frances A. 1977. Age-bias suits may become harder to prove. *The Wall Street Journal,* 20 February, B1.

McNeil, Laura J. 1996. Unsuspecting lease encounters: Internal auditors must be alert to the inherent risks in leasing programs. *Internal Auditor* 53 (1 August): 48.

McQuaid, John. 1997. Breaux battling consumer index bias. *The Times-Picayune* (New Orleans), 17 February, A1.

Milazzo, Don. 1997. Consignment shop gives old software new life. *Birmingham* (Alabama) *Business Journal,* 26 May, 11.

Millman, Nancy, and Genevieve Buck. 1997. A chain devours its own: Oversaturation, McDonald's and others find, has its limits. *Chicago Tribune,* 2 March, 1.

Modigliani, Franco, and Merton H. Miller. 1958. The cost of capital, corporation finance, and the theory of investment. *American Economic Review* 48 (June): 261–297.

Moore, Jonathan, and Pete Engardio. 1998. Can giant become a big wheel? *Business Week,* 26 January, 86.

Mortished, Carl, ed. 1996. Arjo Wiggins. *The Times* (London), 6 September, C176.

Motamedi, Beatrice. 1991. Levi's new strategy—shrink to fit jeans giant's sales soar despite cutbacks in personnel and PR. *San Francisco Chronicle,* 28 March, C1.

Mukhina, Tatyana. 1997. Capital flight via Latvian banks. *Moscow News,* 3 July.

Natarajan, Arun. 1997. Intel's ConnectedPC site showcases products. *Business Wire,* 24 September, 7.

Negroponte, Nicholas. 1995. *Being digital.* New York: Alfred A. Knopf.

Netscape: Industry partners to bring Netscape client software to millions of Enterprise customers. 1997. M2 Presswire, 21 August.

Northeast Polk to lose Orlando TV stations. 1996. *Ledger* (Lakeland, Florida), 16 December, D1.

Omnicom to purchase Fleishman-Hillard and create world's largest public relations group. 1997. *Business Wire,* 9 April.

Ossorio, Sonia. 1994. Anatomy of a mailing list. Gannett News Service, 30 March.

Over 30 companies invest in Najin-Sonbong economic zone. 1996. *BBC Summary of World Broadcasts, Part 3 Asia-Pacific; North and South Korea,* 27 February.

Panic, Mica. 1995. The Bretton Woods system: Concept and practice. In *Managing the global economy,* edited by Jonathan Michie and John Grieve Smith. Oxford: Oxford University Press.

Pate, Kelly. 1995. Ameritech, Cellular One spar about voice quality on the air. *Radio Comm. Report,* 30 January, 20.

Peters, Thomas J., and Robert Waterman. 1982. *In search of excellence: Lessons from America's best-run companies.* New York: Warner Books.

Peters, Tom. 1994. Heed these six key ideas to transform your business. *The Baltimore Sun,* 12 September, 10C.

Picton, John. 1997. Firm helps keep tabs on storage. *Toronto Star,* 21 July, E3.

Pitfalls and potential of franchising. 1996. *Financial Times,* 9 December, 8.

Planning, organizing, and managing benchmarking: A user's guide. 1992. Houston: APQC.

Plunkett, Marguerite M. 1997. Wachovia buys Boca's 1st United Bancorp. *The Palm Beach Post,* 8 August, 1A.

Pollock, Dennis. 1996. It's hard work, for starter. *The Fresno Bee,* 6 September, C1.

Porter, Michael E. 1980. *Competitive strategy: Techniques for analyzing industries and competitors.* New York: Free Press.

————. 1985. *Competitive advantage: Creating and sustaining superior performance.* New York: Free Press.

Presner, L. 1991. *The international business dictionary and reference.* New York: John Wiley & Sons, Inc.

Quist, Janet. 1995. ADEA bill wins House approval without dissent. *Nation's Cities Weekly,* 3 April, 1.

Rand, Ben. 1996. Companies rush to tailor products, services to over-50 customers. Gannett News Service, 30 May, S10.

Rao, Sujata. 1997. Diamond deal a gem for De Beers. *Moscow Times,* 23 July, no. 1255, n.p.

Rapaport, Richard. 1997. PR finds a cool new tool. *Forbes ASAP,* 13 October, 100.

Remanufactured Jeeps get green light from federal agency. 1995. *The Atlanta Journal and Constitution,* 29 December, S4.

Reyes, Carmina E. 1996. SEC proposes rules on loan agreements. *Business Daily,* 19 August.

Robbins, Stephen P. 1994. *Management.* 4th ed. Englewood Cliffs, N.J.: Prentice Hall.

Roberts, James A., and Lawrence B. Chonko. 1996. Pay satisfaction and sales force turnover: The impact of different facets of pay on pay satisfaction and its implications for sales force Management. *Journal of Managerial Issues* 8 (22 June): 154.

Roll, Richard. 1977. A critique of the asset pricing theory's tests. *Journal of Financial Economics* 4 (March): 129–176.

Romell, Rick. 1996. Two-day own a business expo to cater to budding entrepreneurs. *Journal Sentinel* (Milwaukee), 18 October, Business section, 7.

Ross, Stephen A. 1976. The arbitrage theory of capital asset pricing. *Journal of Economic Theory,* December, 341–360.

Roth, Martin S. 1995. Effects of global market conditions on brand image customization and brand performance. *Journal of Advertising* 24 (1 December): 55.

Roy, Elizabeth. 1997. N.Y. limits its localities' investments more than most states do, report says. *Bond Buyer,* 6 May, 23.

Rubinstein, Ed. 1997. The power retailers: Wal-Mart. *Discount Store News,* 3 March, 66.

Rudd, Vivienne. 1997. The vision thing (point of purchase industry). *Soap, Perfumery, & Cosmetics* 70 (1 April): 39.

Seneviratne, Kalinga. 1997. South Pacific: Scams may affect offshore banking potential. International Press Service English News Wire, 25 March.

Senge, Peter. 1994. *The fifth discipline: The art and practice of the learning organization.* New York: Currency/Doubleday.

Sharpe, William F. 1964. Capital asset prices: A theory of market equilibrium under conditions of risk. *Journal of Finance* (September): 425–442.

Shecter, Barbara. 1997. Molson turns up heat in beer wars. *Financial Post* (Toronto), 26 April, 43.

Sherefkin, Robert. 1997. GM undecided about American axle sale. *Crain's Detroit Business,* 16 June, 3.

Shirland, L. 1993. *Statistical quality control.* New York: John Wiley & Sons, Inc.

Sickinger, Ted. 1997. Sprint finds satisfaction in Stones. *The Kansas City Star,* 15 August, B1.

Smith, Jerd. 1997. Phone "Safety net" unveiled, telcom upstarts won't need to build their own monitoring operations. *Rocky Mountain News,* 1 October, 7B.

SOP takes adverse view of stat reports. 1996. *The Insurance Regulator,* 8 January, 2.

Steinhauer, Jennifer. 1997. Squeezing into the jeans market. *The New York Times,* 14 March, 1, 15.

Stern, Aimee L. 1997. Management: You can keep your staff on the competitive track if you . . . inspire your team with a mission statement. *Your Company,* 1 August, 36.

Stewart, Janet Kidd. 1996. McDonald's signs deal with Disney. *Chicago Sun-Times,* 24 May, 43.

Sturgeon, Jeff. 1997. Seminar refutes studies. *Roanoke Times & World News,* 21 May, A5.

Swoboda, Frank. 1996. Bridging a cultural divide: Mitsubishi's Illinois plant becomes test lab for managing diversity. *The Washington Post,* 1 December, H1.

Tagliabue, John. 1997. Buona notte, guten tag: Europe's new workdays. *The New York Times,* 12 November, D1, 6.

Taylor, Frederick Winslow. 1911. *The principles of scientific management.* New York: Harper and Brothers.

Taylor, Sam G., and Steven F. Bolander. 1995. A framework for flow manufacturing scheduling systems. *Industrial Management* 37, no. 6 (November 21): 1–ff.

Tiernan, Becky. 1997. Opening doors: Hiring of disabled increases but many barriers still exist. *Tulsa World,* 2 March, E1.

Todd, Susan. 1997. Harley-Davidson hasn't lost its luster among analysts. *The Morning Call* (Allentown, Pa.), 27 July, D3.

Toronto Sun. 1996. 13 November, News section, T2.

Toth, S. E. 1993. How we slashed response time. *Management Review* 82, no. 2 (February): 51–54.

Tuller, Lawrence W. 1992. *McGraw-Hill handbook of global trade and investment financing.* New York: McGraw-Hill.

Turban, Efraim, James Wetherbe, and Ephraim R. McLean. 1995. *Information technology for management: Improving quality and productivity.* New York: John Wiley & Sons, Inc.

UNICEF to unveil cartoons for children's rights campaign. 1997. M2 Presswire, 17 December.

U.S. Bureau of the Census. 1995. *Statistical abstract of the United States.* Washington, D.C.

U.S. Department of Justice. 1997. Civil Rights Division. *Myths and facts about the Americans with Disabilities Act.* Publication #3105. ADA Information Line, (800) 514-0301.

U.S. Senate. 1997. Committee on the Environment and Public Works. Testimony on March 18, 1997, by Chee Mee Hu, vice president and assistant director, and Charles E. Emrich, assistant vice president, Moody's Investment Service. Washington, D.C.: GPO.

Varadan, M. S. S. 1997. Identifying and developing core competencies. *The Hindu,* 6 August, 27.

Wessels, Walter J. 1993. *Economics.* 2d ed. Hauppauge, N.Y.: Barron's Educational Series, Inc.

Weston, Randy. 1996. Monsanto takes SAP R/3 module for test drive. *Computerworld,* 9 December, 77.

When the mask cracks: Wide-ranging reform of the way business and finance is carried out is changing the face of Japan, says William Dawkins. 1997. *Financial Times* (London), 28 May, 19.

Why we kick the tires. 1997. *Brandweek,* 29 September.

Wiener, Norbert. 1954. *The human use of human beings: Cybernetics and society.* Boston: Avon Books.

Williamson, Richard. 1997. Small airlines form trade group. *Rocky Mountain News,* 25 February, 2B.

Wilson, James M. 1996. Henry Ford: A just-in-time pioneer. *Production & Inventory Management Journal* 37, no. 2 (second quarter): 26–31.

Wilson, Riley. 1997. Phillips takeover thwarted. *Tulsa World,* 7 February, A3.

Witchel, Arnie. 1997. Finding what motivates people. *Electronic Media,* 27 January, 38.

Wong, Alex. 1997. Playing the name game: More companies changing monikers. *Record,* 11 July, B1.

Woods, Bob. 1996. Dell to double U.S. manufacturing capability. *Newsbytes,* 2 October.

Zimmerman, Liza B. 1997. Study: Dairy can be cash cow for supermarkets; Dairy Management Inc. study. *Supermarket News,* 29 September, 36.

INDEX